CASE:
Computer-Aided
Software Engineering

CASE:
Computer-Aided
Software Engineering

T. G. Lewis

Oregon State University

VNR **VAN NOSTRAND REINHOLD**
_____ New York

Printed in the United States of America

Van Nostrand Reinhold
115 Fifth Avenue
New York, New York 10003

Chapman and Hall
2-6 Boundary Row
London, SE1 8HN, England

Thomas Nelson Australia
102 Dodds Street
South Melbourne 3205
Victoria, Australia

Nelson Canada
1120 Birchmount Road
Scarborough, Ontario M1K 5G4, Canada

16 15 14 13 12 11 10 9 8 7 6 5 4 3 2 1

Trademark acknowledgements: Anatool is a trademark of Advanced Logical Software, Inc.; FullPaint is a trademark of Ann Arbor Softworks, Inc.; Image Grabber is a trademark of Sabastian Software; ResEdit, Macintosh XL, Macintosh II, LaserWriter, and RMaker are trademarks of Apple Computer Corp.; MacWrite, MacPaint, and MacDraw are registered trademarks of Claris Corp.; MicroPlanner+ is a trademark of Micro Planning International; PowerTools is a trademark of ICONIX Software Engineering; Ready, Set, Go! is a trademark of Letraset USA; SuperPaint is a trademark of Silicon Beach Software, Inc.; THINK Pascal is a trademark of Symantec, Inc.; ThunderScan is a trademark of Thunderware, Inc.

Library of Congress Cataloging-in-Publication Data

Lewis, T. G. (Theodore Gyle), 1941–
    CASE: computer-aided software engineering / T.G. Lewis
        p. cm.
    Includes index.
    ISBN 0-442-00361-7
    1. Computer-aided software engineering.   I. Title.
QA76.758.L49   1991
005.1—dc20

Contents

Preface

This book is intended mainly for practitioners who manage, design, code, test, and market modern software products. In addition, this book can serve as the text for a first course on software engineering in either an undergraduate or graduate program at most American universities. The material is suitable for a two-quarter sequence or a one-semester course. Lectures should be accompanied by small programming tasks and a course project — the Development Project — assigned early in the course so students can work on the project in parallel with the lectures. The course is highly pragmatic, and informal, and introduces many software tools to the software development process — hence the CASE designation.

The goals of this book are:

- To explain software engineering from a practical point of view, with an emphasis on CASE tools.
- To give a historical perspective of the development of software engineering.
- To cover both technical and human issues of software engineering, because it is still largely a human-driven activity.
- To relate software development techniques, tools, projects, and team structures to the kind of group environment in which software engineers must work and succeed. Specific recommendations for organizing software development teams are provided to guide developers through a successful project.
- To illustrate the concepts of software engineering through the consistent and pervasive use of a "real" example. The example is CoCoPro, a commercially available cost estimation tool based on the CoCoMo model.

The nature of software development is surveyed in the first chapter. The following three chapters prepare the reader to develop a successful software product. Chapter two surveys the field of lifecycle cost estimating and describes CoCoPro, the development project used throughout the text as an illustration of the ideas. Chapter three discusses the organization of teams to clarify the roles of each participant and to show how typical software development teams are organized. Chapter four covers general design issues the good designer must be aware of, and chapter five begins the journey through the development project. These first five chapters should be mastered before the development project is attempted.

The early stages of the software development lifecycle are explained in chapters six, and seven. The development project is defined in these chapters and the outline of an application is provided as a high-level design. Here is where front-end CASE tools, which enter directly into the production of a running program, will be applied.

Chapters eight and nine give details of code production. We introduce the notion of a *cliche* in programming and use this concept to introduce details of the Macintosh. While very specific and detailed, this approach shows what a practicing programmer does during coding. Chapter nine is devoted exclusively to implementation and includes more specific examples. Readers are frequently "protected" from such details in a formal course on software engineering, but the approach taken here gives readers a glimpse into the real world of software development, on a real machine.

Chapters ten and eleven cover both the practical and semiformal approaches to software verification and validation. Chapter ten shows how to do unit and system integration testing. Chapter eleven describes more mathematical means of verifying software components.

Chapter twelve generalizes the information previously supplied by attempting to quantify "complexity." While highly controversial, complexity metrics are beginning to be used in the form of automated CASE tools. Chapter thirteen shows how several complexity metrics can aid in software maintenance.

Chapter fourteen introduces the notion of rapid prototyping and shows how to produce running applications using certain radically productive CASE tools that are not yet widely accepted. Rapid prototyping violates the waterfall model of software development, and where it applies, improves programmer productivity by a factor of 100!

If this book is used in a classroom setting, development teams should be assigned by the instructor. Team size should not exceed five or six students each, with three as the ideal. Team members follow the methodology described in the text and develop a commercial quality software product, complete with documentation and user manual. The development project should be limited to 5,000 to 8,000 lines of source code and should perform some useful function. CoCoPro, an implementation of CoCoMo (Cost Construction Model), is used as the sample development project.

The text recommends the use of the Apple Macintosh™ computer as both the design and development machine. The development project is implemented on a Macintosh, for Macintosh computers, in full compliance with Macintosh user interface rules and guidelines. Therefore, a considerable amount of time and effort is devoted to study of this machine and its software.

Why the Macintosh? The Macintosh system is itself an example of good software design. Its user interface is the result of years of scientific study. Direct manipulation with the mouse radically alters the programmer's experience and forces changes in the principles of both design and coding style. The toolbox is one of the best examples of reusable software, and the parameterized use of toolbox routines through the "resource" file is innovative, yet consistent with maintainable software design.

We use the Macintosh Pascal language as our implementation language because there are several state-of-the-art implementations of it (including object-oriented versions), and because it has been extended to incorporate modularity, one of the most beneficial features of modern programming languages. Separately compiled modules are called *units* in Macintosh Pascal, and are similar to the Modula II concept of modules, and the Ada™ concept of packages. However, most students of computer science are familiar with Pascal and should not have to learn a new language to apply the principles described in this book.

We also use a number of commercially available and homegrown CASE tools. These are the main focus of the book, which makes this text different from many others. The graphical interface of the Macintosh has stimulated development of a number of innovative and powerful tools for programmers. These tools are described in some detail, but the best exposure is to use them in one of the labs that accompany each lecture portion of the course. Classroom software should be made available for check-out from a lab consultant. Several copies are recommended for each class of twenty students.

The author has made several of these CASE tools available to the reader. To obtain these tools, contact the author, directly. These programs are intended to be used as pedagogical devices and are made available as is. The author is not responsible for correctness or completeness.

To obtain the programs, the author may be contacted by mail at the following address: Ted Lewis, Department of Computer Science, Oregon State University, Corvallis, OR 97331-3902; or, by Email: lewis@cs.orst.edu.

Acknowledgments

I would like to thank my students for the feedback they provided over the past five years while I was developing this course. Special thanks go to the exceptional students who produced high-quality software projects that are used in this book to illustrate many ideas: MacMan by Abdullah Al-Dhelaan; CoCoPro by Sherry Yang, Kirt Winter, Bob Singh, Abdennour Moussoui, and Ab Van Etten; OSU by Jim Armstrong, Fred Handloser III, Sharada Bose, Sherry Yang, Shyang-Wen Chia, Mu Hong Lim, Jagannath Raghu, Muhammed Al-Mulhem, and Haesung Kim; GrabBag by Jorge Sanchez; Style by Al Lake; UniTool by Tom Sturtevant, Mu-hong Lim, and Anil Kumar Yadav; and Vigram by Chia-Chi Hsieh and Kritawan Kruatrachue. Sherry Yang was directly involved in a number of these tools, and worked diligently to produce many of the figures and examples used in the pages to follow.

1

What Is Software Engineering?

PREVIEW

In this introductory chapter we survey the evolution of software engineering from troubled practice to emerging discipline. The lessons learned during the 1960s and 1970s were applied during the 1980s and led to a new approach called Computer-Aided Software Engineering, or CASE.

CASE tools incorporate what software engineers know about both the artifacts and the processes of software engineering. The artifacts — the program listings, documentation, data, and resource files — are only the most obvious components of software engineering. The process — the procedures, rules-of-thumb, and interaction among team members — is much more difficult to quantify. Yet both artifact and process are evolving toward automated means of producing, maintaining, and distributing software products.

We survey what is known about artifacts — application programs, for example — and what has been discovered about process — design, testing, inspection technology, and early defect removal, for example — to come up with recommendations for the practicing programmer. These recommendations will be followed as the book unfolds.

THE AGE OF SOFTWARE ENGINEERING

If computers are the steam engines of the postindustrial revolution, then computer software is the steam. Software is that invisible, almost ethereal quantity that goes into every industrial control system, business information system, video game, communication network, and transportation system, as well as thousands of other systems that we depend on daily. Unlike the steam of the industrial revolution, the intellectual steam of software consists of both artifact and process.

Software as artifact is literature in a tangible form: program listings, diagrams, and various kinds of documentation. More rigorously, **software** *is the sum total of computer programs, procedures, rules, and associated documentation and data pertaining to the operation of a computer system*[1]. We will be principally concerned with the manufacture and

---

GROWTH OF SOFTWARE ENGINEERING[2]

Pre-1969. Software development is out of control because of cost overruns and failures, especially in operating systems development. The term *software engineering* was coined as the theme of the NATO-sponsored meetings in 1968 and 1969.

1969-1971. First principles were established through research into good programming practices. Advantages of top-down design, stepwise refinement, and modularity were recognized. New programming languages including Pascal; new group techniques including Chief Programmer Teams introduced.

1972-1973. Structured programming and notions of programming style emerge. GOTO controversy subsides. Awareness of total software lifecycle grows and management and development aids are proposed.

1974-1975. Reliability and quality assurance concerns give rise to systematic testing procedures, notions of formal program correctness, models of fault tolerance and total system reliability. Early analysis of actual allocation of software development effort and expense appears.

1976-1977. Requirements, specification, and design. Renewed attention on early development phases prior to coding. Abstraction and modular decomposition as design techniques; structure charts, metacode as design representations. Increasing efforts to integrate and validate successive development phases of the software lifecycle.

1978-1980. Dispersion, assimilation. Increased use of automated software development tools; development of software engineering courses. First principles of 1969-1971 era begin to find widespread use in software industry.

1980-1989. Rise of CASE and the software engineering workstation. Automated tools corresponding to each phase of the software lifecycle begin to appear on stand-alone workstations.

1990-beyond. Application of expert systems techniques to software engineering. Combination of software engineering workstation, expert systems, and automated techniques for software development to find widespread use in the software engineering industry.

delivery of both programs and documentation to a user of the system in the form of a **software product:** *a product designated for delivery to a user*[1]. We will also call the software product an application, which consists of the deliverables of a software product, but does not include test cases, internal documentation, and miscellaneous software tools used to develop an application.

Software as process is difficult to define in rigorous terms because contemporary software developers build software systems without a complete understanding of the "physics" of software development. This has not discouraged the practicing software developer any more than the lack of a theoretical understanding of Newtonian mechanics discouraged the builders of ancient civilizations. Rather than wait for a theory to explain the dynamic nature of software development, practitioners have collected a group of techniques that seem to work, and have adopted *a systematic approach to the development, operation, maintenance, and retirement of software*[1] called **software engineering.**

Software engineering, more than anything else, is the practical side of software as process. It is deeply concerned with the **software development process** — *the process by which user needs are translated into software requirements, software requirements are transformed into design, the design is implemented in code, and the code is tested, documented, and certified for operational use*[1].

The gradual growth of software engineering is evidence of the struggle to understand software as both artifact and process involving machines, humans, and ideas. Growth has been slow because of the intellectual difficulty of formulating "laws" of software development and because of the extreme high degree of craftsmanship required to build

---

SOCIETY AND SOFTWARE

The software industry plays a major role in the computer industry and in the competitiveness of nations. As a vivid example of the concern over software, FORTUNE Magazine (How To Break The Software Logjam, September 25, 1989, pp. 100–112) published an alarming article on the "software crisis" in America. Here are some statistics on cost and complexity of popular software systems:

Product	Lines of Code	Effort (man-yr)	Cost ($million)
Lotus 1-2-3 version 3.0	400K	263	22
Space Shuttle	25.6M	22,096	1,200
1989 Lincoln Continental	83.5K	35	1.8
CitiBank Teller Machine	780K	150	13.2
IBM Checkout Scanner	90K	58	3

What is the solution to the high cost of software? Both technical and social complexities govern the production of software.

tools for software developers. It is clear, however, that such laws and tools are beginning to emerge in the form of theories and **automated tools** — *software tools that aid in the synthesis, analysis, modeling, or documentation of software*[1]. In the early 1980s these programs became known as CASE (Computer-Aided Software Engineering) tools. Hence the theme of this book: CASE tools in the form of simulators, analytic aids, design representations, documentation aids, and program generators provide the framework for the systematic study of software development.

We approach the study of software engineering through an understanding of artifact and process. First we examine the artifacts of software development, and then we look at the process itself. What is the nature of an application, and what are the factors that influence the process of software development?

THE NATURE OF AN APPLICATION

Applications differ from one another, but a typical application consists of source statements for doing the following:

- *Model Calculations:* Perform the calculations or operations intended by the application, e.g. payroll, stress, simulation, graphical, or database calculations.
- *User Inputs:* Interact with the user in order to capture the user's inputs. This may involve simple or complex interactions such as checking the input data for errors (bounds checking), and inserting the data into the program's data structures.
- *User Outputs:* Format and print or display the results of calculations, e.g. report writing.
- *Control:* Exert control in the form of comparisons, looping, and branching to carry out the logic of the program.
- *Help-Message Processing:* If the user requests help, display the appropriate help message and respond to user inquiry.
- *Error Processing:* In the event of an error during input, output, calculations, communications, etc. respond by displaying an error message, and then recover from the error.
- *Moving Data:* Move data from one data structure to another or from a database to the program's internal data structures. Sorting, searching, and formatting are data moving operations used to prepare the data for further processing.
- *Data Declaration:* Declare all data structures used by the application. For example, in Pascal **const**, **type**, and **var** statements are used to declare all data structures.
- *Comments:* Provide clear, precise, and informative comments.

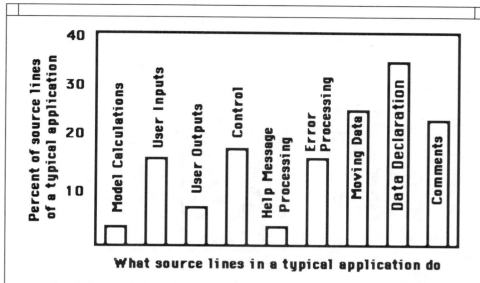

A typical application contains a very small percentage of statements devoted to the model calculations — a surprising observation given that this is the main purpose of the application. Notice that most of the program source statements involve data handling such as input/output, moving, and declaring data objects.

A glance at the list above might suggest an approach to developing an application: design and implement each of the parts, and then put them together into a single program. Unfortunately, because of the complexity implied in the terms of "design," "implement," and "put together" as we have used them here, software development is not so simple. **Complexity** — *the degree of complication of a system or system component*[1] — is determined by such factors as the number and intricacy of interfaces, the number and intricacy of branches, the degree of statement nesting, the types of data structures, and many other poorly understood characteristics of an application. These features of an application are missing from our list and are difficult to quantify. Hence, building an application is more than piecing together parts as the list above might suggest.

The complexity of software as artifact is responsible for "programmer productivity" difficulties. To understand the human side of programmer productivity, we need to understand what a programmer does when building an application. The activities of typical programmers in a typical project consist of the following:

- **Reading** about the system they are building and the tools and techniques they are going to use.

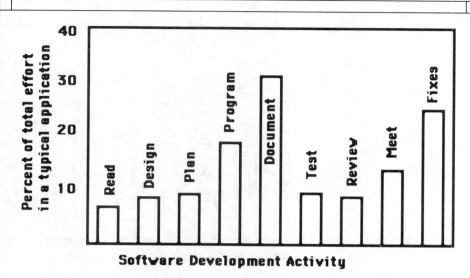

A typical software development project uses a programmer's talents in a variety of ways. Note, however, that actual programming takes up less than 20% of a typical programmer's effort. Documentation and fixing defects consume much more time than actual programming.

- **Designing** *is the process of defining the overall structure of the application, its components, modules, interfaces, and data structures, and then documenting the design*[1]. Design is not the same as programming, nor is it the same as program design. The design of an application involves the selection of data structures, algorithms, specification of information flows, as well as detailed program design.

- **Planning** *is describing an approach to be taken, the tasks to be performed, and the time schedules to be met*. Typically, a *WBS* (Work Breakdown Structure) is included in a plan that tells what is to be done, who is to do it, and when it is to be completed.

- **Programming** includes implementation of appropriate algorithms and data structures, commenting, and desk checking routines for correctness.

- **Producing documentation** — *any written or pictorial information describing, defining, specifying, reporting, or certifying activities, requirements, procedures, or results associated with programs, user manuals, and design, test, and modification documents*.

- **Testing** *is the process of exercising or evaluating a system component by manual or automated means to verify that it satisfies requirements or to identify differences between expected and actual results*[1]. Testing is not to be confused with debugging or defect removal. See Fixing for a description of defect removal.

- **Reviewing**: Several review steps are carried out at various stages of the project. A *design review* is done immediately following the design stage to check on the correctness, completeness, consistency, and clarity of the design. Similarly, a *code review* is carried out to assure the quality of the coding.
- **Meeting** to discuss designs, plans, code, and documentation, and to carry out reviews.
- **Fixing** defects discovered during reviews, tests, and trial runs of the application (typically by *alpha testers* — in-house users of the application, or *beta testers* — monitored users of the application).

These activities go far beyond the simple activity of coding algorithms in some programming language. Furthermore, it is not obvious how the activities of a typical programmer match the parts of a typical program. If we could match the two, it would be much easier to develop a theory of software construction based on the artifacts produced by the process instead of on the intangibles of human activities such as "reading," "designing," and "programming." To complicate matters even more, programmers do not typically work alone — they work in teams. How might we associate the effort of a team of programmers with the parts of a typical program?

Unfortunately, there is no theory of software development which can reliably predict the amount of programmer effort needed to produce a certain program part. For example, no theory exists for estimating how many control statements can be produced by a programmer in an hour, or the number of error messages needed by a certain application, or the number of data declarations derived by a certain design methodology. Unlike manufacturing processes, the software development process is a poorly understood intellectual process with few measures of productivity, progress, or quality.

THE NATURE OF SOFTWARE ENGINEERING

In the 1970s a number of alarming observations were made about the difficulty of producing large-scale applications. For example, it was noted that the cost of producing applications was growing at a high rate and that many projects were failing or resulting in unreliable products. The aggregate of these observations became known as the software crisis. Some of the characteristics of the software crisis were:

- *Maintenance Problems:* **Maintenance** — *the modification of a software product after delivery to correct defects, improve performance, or adapt it to a changed environment*[1] — became a major cost factor in the software business.
- *Large-Program Cost:* Large programs cost far more per line of source code than do small programs. As the size of an application grows, the productivity of programmers, as measured in lines of source code per unit of time, decreases.
- *Programmer Productivity:* Individual human variances are extreme among programmers. The variance ranged up to a factor of 28 in one study. This means there was really no reliable way to predict the time, cost, or quality result of a software project.

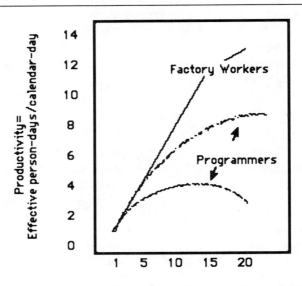

N= Number of interacting people

PROGRAMMER PRODUCTIVITY

The Industrial Revolution achieved great increases in productivity by putting many workers on an assembly line. This practice breaks down totally in a postindustrial information society.

The graph above shows how programmer productivity drops off as the number of interacting individuals increases. Even the best programmer team fails to compare with the typical factory worker in terms of productivity. The reason of course is that the assembly line worker is able to work relatively independently. The nature of an assembly line is serial activity, whereas the nature of a software development project is parallel activity with a lot of interaction among the parts.

Unfortunately, it is not possible to increase productivity, nor to hurry a software development project by simply adding programmers. This observation has become widely acknowledged in the software development business and is often called *Brooks' Law*[3].

- *Programming Language Invariance:* Programmer productivity is invariant with respect to the high-level language used. That is, the rate at which a programmer produces lines of code is not altered by the language used to express each line of code. Instead, the complexity of the application impacts productivity more than does the programming language. In the 1960s and 1970s, operating systems were considered more complex than business applications, for example, so the productivity of business applications programmers was falsely perceived to be several times greater than that of operating systems programmers. Since complexity is difficult to quantify, however, the productivity of programmers is difficult or impossible to quantify. (High-level languages are quantifiably better in this respect than assembler-level languages, however.)

- *Defect Removal Costs:* Defect removal costs are a major factor in programming. While design, coding, and testing are all related, the testing and correcting of programs was found to consume an unexpectedly large share of overall effort. This observation in the mid–1970s prompted practitioners to emphasize the importance of quality control in software development, and led to the next observation.

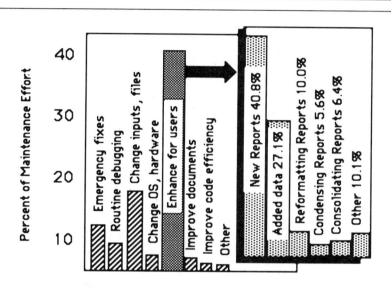

Kind of Software Maintenance Activity

WHAT IS MAINTENANCE?

Most programmers do maintenance work: the number of practicing programmers modifying and adapting old systems to new requirements continually increases. But what exactly is a maintenance activity?

The charts above show the typical breakdown of maintenance activity for a typical system[4]. The interesting thing here is that the bulk of the work involves enhancements to existing code. Of these enhancements, over forty percent of the work is in generating new reports from the existing database.

These data show why in the 1990s there will occur a shift toward application generators, or 4GL systems — 4th Generation Languages — to do many applications. The savings in enhancement effort will repay the investment in tools, training, and machine time many times over each year.

The second observation is one we will constantly come back to: the development programmer should design and implement code that is easy to enhance, modify, and understand. The cost of developing maintainable code is high, but it saves money in the long run.

- *Early Defect Removal:* Early defect removal leads to gains in productivity. In fact, the earlier a defect is uncovered in the process of software development, the greater is the positive impact on cost and productivity.

Several studies have shown that maintenance was a big problem in the 1970s, and indications are that the problem is even greater now[6]. In the 1980s the number of maintenance programmers grew from 50% to 70% of the programming work force. That software engineering is a complex activity is quite evident in software maintenance. The complexities of maintenance were listed by Lientz in 1980 and still prevail[6]:

- *Poor Documentation:* The poor quality of documentation was cited as the number one cause of maintenance difficulty.
- *Enhancements:* The constant demand of users for enhancements and extensions to the product fuels greater demand for maintenance work.
- *Time Constraints:* Maintenance takes time, and schedules typically put pressure on programmers to complete modifications quickly. Also, time pressure may be responsible for low-quality results which exacerbate the maintenance problem.

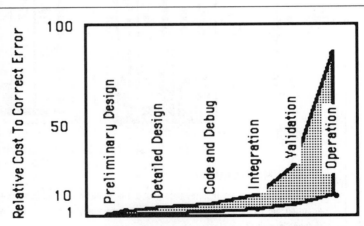

RELATIVE COST OF FIXING ERRORS

Boehm[5] has shown by a number of different collections of data that the relative cost of defect removal increases as the software development project evolves toward its conclusion. The costs are nearly zero during the preliminary design phase, increase at each intermediate phase, and become rather imposing after the software product is released and put into operation. The interval between best and worst case in the chart above represents a 95% confidence interval for the projects sampled by Boehm.

The damage caused by "buggy" software may be much greater if the unreliable product damages the company reputation. Rumors about a word processor that crashes and destroys the accumulated work of a writer can stop sales of the software overnight. It is also possible that the software developer is legally responsible for failures of a product developed and sold to the public. A defective program can be as dangerous as a defective automobile, bridge, building, or other human-made artifact.

As a consequence, it has become common practice for software development companies to adopt a defensive approach to polishing their software products. In-house testing — called *alpha testing* — is done by programmers and internal users. Typically, alpha testing is done in stages along with the evolution of the project so that early feedback can be obtained by the programmers.

A small collection of trusted users of the product called *beta testers* are invited to use the product before it is made available to the public. A *beta test copy* of the program is given to pioneering users with the understanding that they will report bugs, inconveniencies, or performance problems with the product. If the concept of early defect removal is practiced, the beta testing is completed in a few months. However, a product that spends a long time in beta testing is likely to become *vaporware* — software that never reaches the marketplace.

Two important points should be made here. First, new application software must be designed with a bias toward *maintainability*, and second, CASE tools can have a major impact on reducing both the time and effort needed to make modifications to existing application software. The first point will prompt us to focus on a software design philosophy called "accommodating change" and the second point stresses the importance of CASE in the development process. We will come back to both of these points many times throughout this book.

Effect of Size of Program and Size of Team

Studies of the effect of program size on programmer productivity occupied many researchers throughout the 1970s. This "law of large programs" will reappear in the following chapter when cost estimating models are discussed. What happens, however, is easily understood once we consider the communication problems typical of teams as well as the complexity of the programs the teams are trying to create.

Suppose the size of a program is measured in LOC (Lines Of Code). Furthermore, assume a single programmer can implement the program in E months of concentrated effort. A simple measure of programmer productivity, PP, is given by,

$PP = LOC/E$ (lines of code per month)

Now assume N programmers are employed to implement the same size program. As the number of communicating parts increases to N, the number of communication "interactions" increases to $N(N - 1)/2$, see (Figure 1-1). Thus, the effort that goes into communicating increases more rapidly than the linear increase in work that can be done.

N = 3, Interactions = 3

N = 5, Interactions = 10

FIGURE 1-1. Number of interactions versus number of parts

Communication Effort $= \mu N^2$

where μ is a constant representing the amount of effort per interaction, and we have simplified $N(N - 1)$ to N^2. See the figure relating the number of communicating parts to the number of interactions.

With N programmers, the total effort rises to $E + \mu N^2$ because of the need to communicate. If the work is evenly spread over all N programmers, group programmer productivity becomes:

$(GroupPP = LOC/(E + \mu N^2)$

Finally, comparing the single programmer productivity rate with the group programmer rate shows a decrease in productivity as N increases.

$(GroupPP/PP = E/(E + \mu N^2)$

This simplified model is inadequate to explain all of the effects of size on programming teams, but it does show how increasing the number of programmers can have a negative impact on overall progress. This observation has become known as Brooks' law of diminishing returns: "adding programmers to a late programming project, makes the project completion date even later," Brooks[3].

Effect of High-Level Languages

A **high-level language**, or **higher order language** *is a programming language that usually includes features such as nested expressions, user-defined data types, and parameter passing not normally found in lower order languages, that does not reflect the structure*

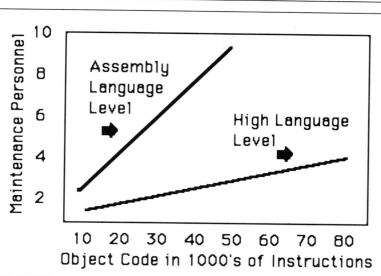

LANGUAGE EFFECT ON MAINTENANCE

Assembly Language programs may be more efficient when they run, but they are much more costly to maintain. Since the maintenance effort continues to grow in proportion to the total software effort, it is important to consider the costs of maintenance as well as development, runtime efficiency, and so forth.

In the graph above it is clear that the effect of language level on enhancement and maintenance costs is dramatic[4]. Perhaps the best way to achieve speed and low maintenance costs is to develop strictly in a high-level language, then when the program is working correctly, tune it by measuring the performance of a typical run. These measurements can then be used to find the bottlenecks to performance in the high-level source code. If speed is a major concern, then the bottleneck code can be rewritten as tight assembly-language coded routines.

of any one computer or class of computers, and that can be used to write machine-independent source programs; a single, higher order language statement may represent multiple machine operations[1]. Such languages are often called HOLs and include the well-known high-level languages Pascal, FORTRAN, and COBOL.

The overall effect of high-level language selection on programmer productivity is minimized by the small effect that coding has on the software development project. It is more important to use modern structured programming style than it is to use a particular programming language, according to observations made on several large programming projects. These stylistic guides include accepted practices such as single-entry-single-exit coding constructs, modularity, clean interface definitions, simplicity in selection of both algorithm and data structures, and common sense in naming variables, documentation, and so forth. While development productivity may be invariant with respect to language, maintenance effort can be negatively impacted by both language level and **robustness** — *the extent to which software can continue to operate correctly despite the introduction of invalid inputs*[1] — of the language. For example, the strong type-checking of Pascal and Ada programming languages can greatly improve the maintenance picture by catching interface and typing errors during compilation.

Effect of Early Defect Removal

One of the most difficult tasks of software development is the detection and removal of a **defect** (also *bug, fault, error*) — *a discrepancy between a computed, observed, or measured value or condition and the true, specified, or theoretically correct value or condition*[1]. A defect or bug results in software containing a fault, e.g. omission or misinterpretation of user requirements, incorrect translation or omission of a design specification, or a coding error. Software defects arise from human action or inaction and not from wear and tear on the software.

Early defect removal and the idea of early defect detection played a major role in shaping the modern software engineering process. Here is where software as process becomes as important as software as artifact. The software process is simply to inspect the software artifact at every stage along the production line to locate and remove defects as soon as possible.

When first applied this technique seemed to work well at every phase of development, but it was soon discovered that test inspections are counterproductive. Subsequently, inspections have been restricted to the design, coding, and system integration stages of development. This means a team of inspectors would:

- Inspect and critique the design immediately after it is completed and before it is committed to coding.
- Inspect and critique the source code program immediately after it has been written and before it is executed by computer. Rework the source code if necessary until it complies with coding standards.
- See that individual program modules are tested by each programmer. Each programmer is responsible for locating and removing defects in individual modules.
- Inspect and critique the completed application and its test results. The integrated modules within the application are subjected to a number of predesignated tests, which verify that the complete system satisfies the original requirements.

These steps are overly simplified as we will soon realize, but they lay the groundwork for a more sophisticated plan. Collectively called *walk-throughs*, they are the major contributors to software quality. The inspection and walk-through are formal processes defined as follows:

Walk-through — *a review process in which a designer or programmer leads one or more members of the development team through a segment of design or code that he or she has written while other members ask questions and make comments about technique, style, possible errors, violation of development standards, and other problems*[1].

Inspection — *a formal evaluation technique in which software requirements, design, or code are examined in detail by a person or group other than the author to detect faults, violations of development standards, and other problems*[1].

The walk-through and corresponding inspection process are currently the most effective means of **software quality assurance** — *actions that provide adequate confidence that the product conforms to established requirements*[1]. The way to guarantee quality is to guarantee that the software product performs according to customer requirements at every stage in the development process.

Importance of Early Defect Removal

The importance of defect removal at the earliest stages cannot be overstated. The consequences of late error detection and defect removal complicate the tasks of testing, documenting, and managing the development project. Early defect removal reduces effort because it reduces various forms of complexity:

- *Testing:* Testing becomes more complex and costly as the project matures because as defects accumulate they interact to produce more complex problems. A design error may be compounded by a coding error. Correcting the design error may prevent the coding error from ever occurring. Leaving both until later increases the difficulty of identifying the source of the errors. Furthermore, as the system evolves and it gets larger, it becomes more difficult to modify. Clearly it is best to make corrections when the system is small and manageable.

- *Documentation:* Documentation must be updated to reflect the changes made in the system. If a defect is discovered after ten thousand copies of the user's manual have been printed, then every copy must be recalled and changed. If hundreds or thousands of users have been trained to use the software, then a modification in the software may require costly retraining.

- *Managing:* Communication of problems and changes involves many people and procedures. The development team may have lost some of the original development members or the team may even have disbanded. Earlier tests will have to be repeated to verify that modifications to correct one error do not introduce new errors in other parts of the system.

A corollary to the rule of early defect removal was observed in the 1970s: most errors in large software systems occur in the early stages of development — requirements analysis, planning, and design. The actual impact of coding on overall error rates was lower than software engineers expected[4]. This observation had a dramatic impact on software engineering. It caused a greater awareness of the importance of rigorous analysis of what the users wanted from the system as well as the creation of a whole new category of software engineering tools — the forerunners of the CASE tools that are the subject of this book.

THE LIMITS OF SOFTWARE ENGINEERING PRODUCTIVITY

As we have seen, software products are complex systems developed by people working together in teams. The dynamics of groups of humans working on complex systems is poorly understood and yet large, complex, and costly systems are constructed and put into use. We have also seen that software engineering is the process of controlling complexity, restricting the interaction of individuals in order to cope with loss of productivity that is a consequence of having too many interacting parts, and above all else, constantly inspecting the evolving product to guarantee quality.

The question naturally arises, What are the limits to productivity? If we know the limiting factors to productivity, then perhaps the limits can be pushed back, or circumvented. Perhaps automated tools could be used to alleviate the bottlenecks in the development process. In any case, knowing the limitations will help software engineers make correct estimates of the schedules, costs, and quality of software products.

The limits to software engineering productivity are:

- *Complexity:* We have encountered the notion of complexity before, and it will continue to reappear throughout this book. There are many kinds of complexity: psychological, mathematical, systematic, and so forth. Perceived complexity of a software system is a rather vague idea in software engineering, but it can usually be defined indirectly through a number of program attributes that measure the structure and relationships among components of a program — the *program architecture*[1]. A complex program architecture is one containing many interfaces, code that is difficult to read, data structures that are difficult to understand, and components that are difficult to modify.

- *Size:* Size is used as a measure of complexity because a large program is inherently more difficult to understand and modify than a small program. The effects of size are so renowned in software engineering that the phrase *programming-in-the-large* has been coined to indicate the step up in difficulty experienced by software engineers when developing large programs as opposed to small, algorithmic, well-defined programs.

- *Communication:* Human interaction is a variable of great importance in software engineering because software development is a cooperative activity. Large gains in productivity made in assembly line industries have not occurred in the software industry because adding people to the software "production line" does not increase productivity. Instead, individual productivity diminishes because of the increased need to communicate.

- *Time:* Programmers are always being asked, How long will it take? This question is one of the most difficult to answer because time and effort are not easily traded off in software engineering. Doubling effort does not cut time in half. In fact, the difficulty of completing a software project bears no linear relationship to the time required. A project that is easily completed in six months may be nearly impossible to complete in five months, even with added people. The trade-off between time, effort, and quality of product is poorly understood at best.

- *Visibility of Software:* We might characterize software as an invisible artifact. The intangible nature of human thought, the elusiveness of principles of computing, and the lack of a widely accepted method of developing software have all contributed to the invisibility of software. Physicists, biologists, and electrical engineers have well-established theories and clearly defined terms. Software engineers are unable to agree on the interpretation of such basic terms as *program, software,* and *software system.* At least, the definitions provided are not useful for building models of either the process or the resulting artifacts.

The consequences of these factors are limitations on what can be produced by teams of software engineers given finite amounts of time, money, and talent. These limitations begin to operate in greater force as the size, duration, or complexity of the resulting program grows. Jones[7,8,9] divides development projects into classes according to the size of the resulting programs. He then measures the effect of program size on the cost and quality of the project. His analysis is interesting because it suggests techniques that work, and other techniques that do not work, when applied to software engineering (as it was practiced in the 1970s).

Programming-in-the-Small

Programming-in-the-small is a single-programmer activity. Much of the simplicity of programming in this style is derived from the fact that a team of programmers is *not* needed to achieve the desired result. When the time or size of project dictates added personnel, the project departs from the realm of classic programming-in-the-small. Programming-in-the-large involves complexities that often defeat techniques that work well for a single programmer.

Small programs have less than 2K lines of code. These programs are easy to develop and the only complexity that enters into the project is the possibility of misunderstandings between programmer and user. The techniques that work best are:

- *Top-down, structured coding:* The programmer creates both the design and the code using techniques of **stepwise refinement**, *a methodology in which data definitions and processing steps are defined broadly at first and then with increasing detail*[1].

- *Logic and code inspections:* The logic and code of the program are inspected by another programmer during both a design and code walk-through.

- *Tools:* Interactive editing, compiling, and debugging tools are used along with a high-level language. The use of a high-level language has a dramatic impact on the time taken to write and debug the program.

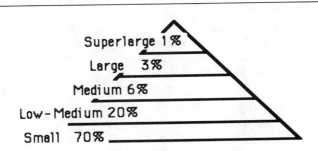

The Hypothetical Mix of Program Size Ranges

LIMITS OF PRODUCTIVITY

The pyramid represents a hypothetical mix of programs arranged by size. Very few superlarge programs have been developed compared to the number of small programs. One reason is that large and superlarge programs are very difficult and costly to develop. Cost is high because programmer productivity decreases as the size of the project increases.

As the size of program being developed increases, the ability of individual programmers to cope with program size diminishes, as shown by the table below[9,10]. Productivity rates are measured in lines of assembler language code per person-month, PM. The LOC (lines of code) measurement excludes comment lines and roughly equals the number of statements in a program.

Program Size	Productivity Range	Median LOC/PM
Superlarge (>512K)	36 – 250	72
Large (64–512K)	63 – 500	166
Medium (16–64K)	125 – 1000	250
Low-medium (2–16K)	200 – 1250	400
Small (<2K)	333 – 2000	667

The LOC measure can be misleading because it does not always relate to the amount of effort that goes into a program. For example, when structured programming was introduced in the early 1970s, the LOC measure of productivity indicated a *decrease* in individual productivity when structured programming was used. This surprising result caused concern until it was realized that structured programs are shorter than equivalent unstructured programs. Thus the same functionality was implemented in fewer lines of error-free code.

The limits of programmer productivity mean that automated CASE tools will be needed for superlarge programming projects. Such tools must be able to amplify human productivity by automating such tasks as design, testing, and code writing.

Programming-in-the-Large

Low-medium (2K to 16K lines of code) and medium (16K to 64K) programs are done by teams of programmers. This places even greater importance on walk-throughs, in which members of the team inspect each other's designs and code. Also, at the upper reaches of this class, controlling complexity of size and visibility are the most important factors in defining success. In addition to the methods used by individual programmers as described before, techniques that work for larger programs are:

- *Planning Mechanisms:* A formal plan of action, sometimes called the *WBS* (work breakdown structure[4]) is needed. The WBS usually contains both the program architecture as a hierarchy chart showing modules and their connection to one another, and a corresponding hierarchy chart showing activities. The activities are assigned to programmers along with estimated completion dates and estimates of cost. The principal purpose of the WBS is to establish a plan, control costs, and monitor deadlines.

- *Documented Specifications:* While the WBS assigns responsibility for specific tasks, the specifications describe what is to be done. More formally, a **specification** *is a document that prescribes in a complete, precise, verifiable manner, the requirements, design, behavior, or other characteristics of a system or system component*[1]. Alternately, a specification document concisely states a set of requirements to be satisfied by the product.

- *Team Structure:* A formal team structure with a leader and associated responsibilities is needed. For example, a Chief Programmer Team consisting of a chief programmer, backup programmer, secretary/librarian, and additional programmers and specialists as needed, employs procedures to enhance group communication and methods to optimize the use of each member's skills (design, debugging, coding, tool-making are examples of skills which might be optimized)[1].

- *Formal Test Cases:* A formal mechanism must be established to create test data, manage the verification of quality through application of the test data, and enforce the rule of early defect removal. A **test case**[1] *is a specific set of test data and associated procedures developed for a particular objective, such as to exercise a particular program path or to verify compliance with a specific requirement.* These test cases are applied according to a test plan which is part of the specification.

Clearly, this class of programs introduces "overhead" in the form of paper work and "bureaucracy," but as the complexity and size increases, the need for additional control also grows. Added effort is needed to control complexity, and it is this added effort that contributes to decreased programmer productivity, as measured by lines of code produced in a given period of time.

As a generalization, complexity arises because of the increase in the number of program components and functions to be performed. The logic of individual program components may be trivial, but the way in which the components interact can be quite difficult to grasp. This means that testing must be formalized.

Formal testing is a time-consuming process that includes review of specifications, logic, and data structures, inspection of module design and module code, and several tests:

a *unit test* of each module by itself

a *function test* of collections of modules

a *component test* of major subcomponents

a *system integration test* of the entire system.

(A **module** as used here is *a program unit that is discrete and identifiable with respect to loading, compiling, and combining with other units*[1].)

For larger programs, tools for aiding both manager and programmer to plan, control, and inspect become more important than tools for producing the artifact itself. This observation is key to understanding the software engineering process.

Programming-at-the-Limits

When programs become large (64K to 512K) and superlarge (over 512K) they become almost intractable in a number of ways. In fact, some software developers believe that employing automated techniques that manipulate reusable components is the only way to develop superlarge programs. **Reusability** — *the extent to which a module can be used in multiple applications*[1] — is simply a method of building large systems from prefabricated, tested, high-quality parts. Reusability avoids the problems of constructing software by not constructing software at all, but instead by borrowing proven parts from other systems.

Jones[7] is skeptical of the usefulness of basic programming-in-the-small techniques even as a partial solution to the daunting task of programming-at-the-limits:

"One of the chief concerns with large systems, and even more so with superlarge, is the theoretical observation that top-down design may be difficult, and top-down development perhaps impossible, due to the excessive difficulty of isolating a true 'top.'"

The challenge facing software developers of large systems is easily illustrated. The specifications of a large system might easily fill a book of 300 pages. At the rate of 25 pages per day, a single programmer will take 12 days just to read the specifications! This is not the full extent of the effort required, however, because each member of the team must read the specifications to prepare for the design review. If the team consists of ten programmers, then a total effort of 120 days (or over one-third of a person-year) is required to simply hold a design inspection. When the review is held, the entire document is checked page by page, which will take 6 days if we assume an inspection rate of 50 pages per day. This process introduces an intangible complexity in every large system, yet it must be completed in order to detect and remove defects as early as possible.

A small program may take two weeks for a single programmer to complete, thus yielding a programmer productivity rate of 667 lines of code per person-month. A medium program may consume 250–300 person-months of effort, resulting in productivity rates in the range of 125–1,000 lines of code per person-month. But a superlarge program can easily take 1,000 person-years of effort, and yield only 36–250 lines of code per person-month. In addition, a superlarge program will consume thousands of hours of computer time, produce tons of paper documentation, and require an enormous support staff.

EVOLVING COMPLEX SYSTEMS

The age of the computer has now been joined by the age of software engineering. This new field of study is still in the process of evolving into a discipline complete with principles and theories. Nonetheless, many aspects of software engineering are not understood or only partially understood. We know that software engineering deals with both artifact and process. A study of artifacts such as programs and their documentation gives a partial picture of software engineering. For a complete picture, we must also study the process, including both human and machine aspects.

A central theme of software engineering is one of coping with various kinds of complexity — complexity of size, overwhelming detail, intricacy of communication among programmers, time limitations, and the invisibility of software.

FIVE LAWS OF PROGRAM EVOLUTION

1. Continuing Change

A program that is used and that, as an implementation of its specification, reflects some other reality, undergoes continuing change or becomes progressively less useful. The change or decay process continues until it is judged more cost effective to replace the program with a recreated version.

2. Increasing Complexity

As an evolving program is continuously changed, its complexity, reflecting deteriorating structure, increases unless work is done to maintain it or reduce it.

3. The Fundamental Law (of program evolution)

Program evolution is subject to dynamics that render the programming process, and hence measures of global project and system attributes, self-regulating, with statistically determinable trends and invariances.

4. Conservation of Organization Stability (invariant work rated)

The global activity rate in a project supporting an evolving program is statistically invariant.

5. Conservation of Familiarity (perceived complexity)

The release content (changes, additions, deletions) of the successive releases of an evolving program is statistically invariant.

M. M. Lehman, "On Understanding Laws, Evolution, and Conservation in the Large-Program Lifecycle," Journal of Systems and Software, vol. 1, #3. pp. 213–221, Reprinted by permission from Elsevier Science Publishing, New York, NY.

Complexity can be either reduced or managed by careful construction of the artifacts — the programs and documentation — and by the application of process-amplifying tools, also known as CASE tools.

CASE tools are designed to assist human programmers cope with the complexity of the processes and the artifacts of software engineering. For example, a simple text editor is an invaluable CASE tool for managing the text of a document or program. A graphic editor might be used as a CASE tool to document the design of a large software system. CASE tools are essential for programming-in-the-large.

Programming consists of human activities, and even though CASE tools can reduce much of the labor of programming, the most dramatic improvements in programmer productivity come from improvements in the social processes surrounding a software development project. Quality control inspections that result in early defect removal, for example, contribute significantly to reductions in time and cost, and indirectly lead to increased programmer productivity.

BOEHM'S TOP TEN

1. Finding and fixing a software problem after delivery of the product is 100 times more expensive than defect removal during requirements and early design phases.

2. Nominal software development schedules can be compressed up to 25% (by adding people, money, etc.), but no more.

3. Maintenance costs twice what development costs.

4. Development and maintenance costs are primarily a function of the size, e.g. the number of source lines of code, in the product.

5. Variations in humans account for the greatest variations in productivity.

6. The ratio of software to hardware costs has gone from 15:85 in 1955 to 85:15 in 1985 and continues to grow in favor of software as the dominant cost.

7. Only about 15% of the development effort is in coding.

8. Application products cost three times as much per instruction as individual programs; system software products costs nine times as much.

9. Walk-throughs catch 60% of the errors.

10. Many software processes obey a Pareto distribution:

- 20% of the modules contribute to 80% of the cost.
- 20% of the modules contain 80% of the errors.
- 20% of the errors consume 80% of the repair budget.
- 20% of the modules take 80% of the execution time.
- 20% of the tools are used 80% of the time.

Boehm, B. "Industrial Software Metrics Top 10 List," IEEE Software, 4,5 (Sept.1987), 84–85.

We have learned that software maintenance is a big problem and continues to grow as more software comes into existence. It is no longer practical to emphasize development time and effort at the expense of maintenance. Rather, the trend now is to develop software that is easy to maintain, enhance, and modify. This in turn requires even greater emphasis on clear, concise, well-documented designs and programs. A maintainable program consists of source code *and* documentation of its design, construction, testing, and variant versions.

We have also learned that as a system grows, controls in the form of planning, managing, and coordination also grow in importance. Large program size causes programmer productivity to plunge. There currently appear to be only two approaches for reversing the productivity plunge. First, programmers can reuse existing designs and programs. Second, programmers can create automated CASE tools for generating error-free designs and code. Perhaps a combination of these two approaches is the answer. In any case, the challenge for software engineers of the 1990s is to find ways to increase programmer productivity and software quality, and at the same time reduce both the time and the effort needed to build an application.

Terms and Concepts

alpha test
application
automated tools
beta test
CASE
chief programmer team
code review
complexity
component test
control
defect
defect removal
design
design review
documentation
fault
function test
high-level language
higher order language
inspection
maintenance
model calculations
module

plan
program architecture
programmer productivity
programming-in-the-large
programming-in-the-small
reusability
robustness
software
software crisis
software development process
software engineering
software product
software quality assurance
specification
step-wise refinement
system integration test
test case
test plan
testing
unit test
walk-through
WBS

DISCUSSION QUESTIONS

1. Some software engineers claim that a special kind of psychology governs the behavior of programmers, and hence the process of software development. Make a list of rules and principles of "software psychology." Examples: "The last 20% of a project takes 80% of the effort to complete"; or "The maximum number of levels of nesting in a program must not exceed seven, because the number seven is a known limit to human concentration."

2. Give several reasons why the field of software engineering should not be called "software science" instead. What is the difference between a scientific discipline and an engineering discipline?

3. What is an artifact, and what is a process? Why is the study of software engineering divided into the study of both artifacts and processes? What purpose does such a division serve?

4. Give several examples of automated tools for producing software. What is the meaning of CASE? Give examples of CASE tools.

5. Software engineers often talk of "difficult" or "complex" systems. What do they mean? What is a good definition of a difficult or complex system? Is there a difference between programs that are difficult to understand and programs that are difficult to write or design?

6. There is a distinct difference between program design and program coding. Make a list of the activities required for designing, and then make a list of activities required for coding.

7. Programmer productivity is measured in LOC — lines of code — or in KDSI — thousands of delivered source instructions. Give several reasons why these measures of productivity might be misleading.

8. What is the difference between alpha testing and beta testing? What is the difference between unit testing and system testing? List some other kinds of testing.

9. Why is maintenance a growing problem in software engineering? What are some things that a development programmer can do to ease the burden of the maintenance programmer?

10. Is there an optimal size of a programmer team? If the overhead due to team communication increases as the square of team size, N, and the effort per team member decreases inversely proportional to N, then what is the best value of N? (Hint: there are a number of ways this problem can be analyzed, all of which may be reasonable under certain assumptions. Justify your own analysis of the effect of team size on productivity.)

11. High-level languages have long been thought to improve productivity during development, but the language invariance observation seems to suggest just the opposite. In terms of single statements, the time and effort required for a programmer to write a single line of FORTRAN, for example, is about the same as the time taken to write a single line of Assembly Language. Recall, however, that a single line of a high-level language compiles into the equivalent of five to eight assembly language statements. Rephrase the language invariance observation to include this "mechanical advantage" after compilation.

12. Early defect removal is known to save development costs, but what does early defect removal itself cost to perform? Testing is expensive, and it is not always certain when the end of a testing phase has been reached. How can we determine when all bugs have been removed? If the cost of additional debugging is linear with time, and the cost of keeping a product off the market grows with the delay in product release time, what is the best time to stop testing and start selling? (Hint: this is a debatable discussion question with a multitude of answers.)

13. A walk-through is a meeting where either a design or source code document is discussed. If you are a programmer preparing for a walk-through of your source code, what things would you bring to the meeting? What topics would you expect to be covered? How would you present your program to the group?

14. What is meant by the phrases "invisibility of software," "programming-in-the-large," and "program architecture"? Explain each term and tell why they are important to software engineers.

15. Software engineers frequently discuss modularity, modular decomposition, and modular structured programming. According to the definition given in the chapter, a module is a separately compiled program unit, yet languages like ISO Standard Pascal do not support separate compilation. What does this say about the usefulness of those languages for modular programming? Why is modularity important? What are the modules in languages like FORTRAN, COBOL, C, Pascal, and Ada?

16. What is reusability? Why is it important? Give examples of reusable programs or program parts. Give suggestions for increasing the reusability of existing programs or program designs.

17. What is top-down design and why is it considered good? Why is it thought to be inadequate for large program development projects?

18. Rewrite the Laws of Program Evolution in your own words. What do they mean to a development programmer? designer? maintenance programmer? user?

REFERENCES AND FURTHER READING

1. Institute of Electrical and Electronics Engineers, Inc. 1983. *Glossary of Software Engineering Terminology, ANSI/IEEE Std 729–1983*. New York: IEEE.

2. Wasserman, A.I., and L. A. Belady. 1978. "Software Engineering: The Turning Point." *IEEE Computer* 11, no. 9 (September): 31.

3. Brooks, F.P. Jr. 1974. "The Mythical Man-Month." Datamation 20, no. 12 (December): 44–52.

4. Boehm, B. W. 1981. *Software Engineering Economics*. Englewood Cliffs, NJ: Prentice-Hall.

5. Boehm, B. W. 1976. "Software Engineering." *IEEE Trans. Computers*, December: 1226–1241.

6. Lientz, B. P., and E. B. Swanson, 1980. *Software Maintenance Management*, 214, Reading, Mass: Addison-Wesley.

7. Jones, T. C. 1977. "Program Quality and Programmer Productivity." *IBM Tech. Report TR02.764* January: 80, San Jose, Ca: Santa Teresa Labs.

8. _____ . 1981. *Programming Productivity: Issues for the Eighties*. New York: IEEE Computer Society.

9. _____ . 1979. "The Limits of Programming Productivity." *Proceedings of Joint SHARE/GUIDE/IBM Application Development Symposium* (October) 77–82.

10. Lehman, M. M. n.d. "On Understanding Laws, Evolution, and Conservation in the Large-Program Lifecycle." *Journal of Systems & Software 1*, no. 3: 213–221.

2

Models of the Software Lifecycle

PREVIEW

In this chapter we develop the concept of a software lifecycle power function and show that various power functions exist. These functions are then applied to the problem of estimating how much effort, time, and money are needed to construct a software system.

We study four models in detail: the early model by Brooks which spans development phases of the lifecycle; the Norden-Rayleigh-Putnam model which spans the entire lifecycle; the CoCoMo model proposed by Boehm which uses detailed factors called cost drivers to estimate the development effort and time, and the function point method, which makes estimates based on design information only. A CASE tool called CoCoPro is used to compute CoCoMo estimates, store past results, and calibrate Boehm's three project models; and a tool called UniTool combines CoCoPro with the function point method to yield a complete estimating system.

CoCoPro and UniTool provide a basis for estimating the development time, effort, and cost, given the modular design of a software system as inputs.

WHAT IS THE SOFTWARE LIFECYCLE?

A **software lifecycle** *is the period beginning when a software product is conceived and ending when the product is no longer available for use*[1]. Study of the software lifecycle is useful for several reasons. First, knowledge of the software lifecycle tells us something about the process of software engineering. From a model of how a software product is designed, put together, and sold, we can discover how to improve programmer productivity, estimate how much time will be needed to accomplish each task, and estimate how much the overall project will cost. Second, we can learn how to improve the quality of the software product as well as how to control software development projects. For example, a software development team can identify bottlenecks in previous projects and eliminate them in subsequent projects. Finally, identification of the steps or phases of a software lifecycle point the way toward the creation of automated CASE tools for improving both product quality and time to market. Automation of all phases in the software lifecycle is a major goal of software engineers. What then are the activities within the software lifecycle, and how do they interact?

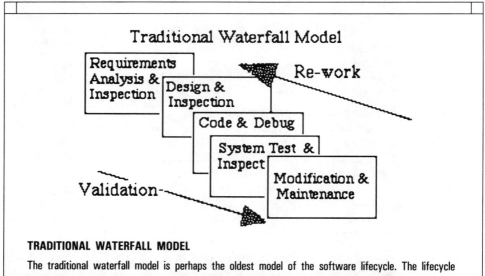

TRADITIONAL WATERFALL MODEL

The traditional waterfall model is perhaps the oldest model of the software lifecycle. The lifecycle is divided into sequential steps or phases. First, requirements are determined and inspected for customer approval, the system is designed and another inspection performed to guarantee quality through early defect removal; then the system is coded and tested first in parts and then as a whole before final acceptance. The last phase continues until the system is taken out of use.

In reality, few programs follow the waterfall model from start to finish. Instead, the phases overlap and are often repeated. An error may be discovered during coding that leads to a change in the design, for example. In fact, some software engineers claim that this model is of theoretical interest only, and is never actually used. Nonetheless, the waterfall model provides a framework, albeit an arbitrary one, for studying the lifecycle.

Unfortunately, the software lifecycle is poorly understood, and a concise, accurate mathematical representation of the lifecycle has not been discovered. This is understandable given the complexity of most software products and the fact that software development is inherently a human activity. We learned in the previous chapter that programmer productivity

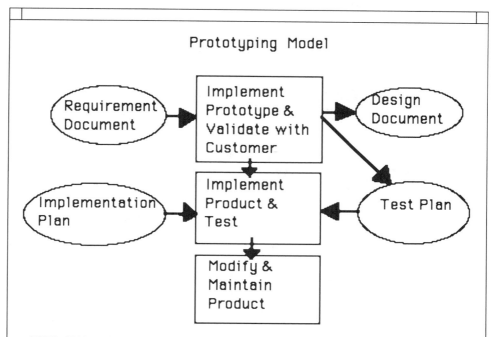

Prototyping Model

RAPID PROTOTYPING MODEL

An alternative to the waterfall model, the rapid prototyping model, appeared in the 1970s. This model combines many of the phases typically carried out as separate steps — requirements, design, and implementation — into a single phase called *rapid prototyping*. A prototype is a partially or fully operational model or mock-up of the final product.

The customer interacts vigorously with the developer during prototyping so that the requirements evolve with the system. This helps the customer define what is wanted and helps the developer understand what the customer wants. This information is documented and retained for use later on when the prototype is transformed into the real system.

The real system is a fully operational version with improved performance, maintainability, and quality vis-à-vis the prototype. It has full error recovery and full operational capability. The real system may be programmed from parts of the prototype, from a program generator, or manually from scratch. Prototyping strategies are still evolving and will most likely change during the next few years.

varies widely among programmers. Hence, it is unlikely that an accurate model of programmer productivity can be developed with our present knowledge. Yet workable lifecycle models exist and are used on a routine basis by developers and their managers. These models have one thing in common: they define a collection of distinct phases of activity and the interactions among these activities.

Many models of the software lifecycle have been proposed but no model has gained widespread acceptance among software engineers. The **waterfall model** *consists of a set of discrete activities occurring in a given order during the development and use of the software product*. The sequentially ordered activities described by the waterfall model are easy to understand, but the model is criticized as overly simplistic. As this model is one of the oldest and most widely known, however, it will be referred to frequently throughout this book.

Estimating the Cost of the Software Lifecycle

In general, a software lifecycle is broken down into phases. Each phase represents a portion of the overall effort needed to complete the cycle. The total effort within each of these phases, however, may exceed 100% due to overlaps and unexpected additional effort. For example, the phases of a typical large-scale software lifecycle shown in Figure 2-1 total 120%. How are we to interpret the extra 20% of effort? In the breakdown below, we see that 10% went into project management, and another 10% into an unexpected "development extension" which was required to complete the product.

The models developed in this chapter will be idealized. That is, we will assume perfect estimates of effort so that the total will be 100%, and we will ignore imperfections such as the effects of human variances, the unpredictable effects of hiring and firing of personnel, and so forth. Nonetheless, the models often take into consideration factors that are difficult to estimate, such as programmer productivity and software complexity and reliability.

Functional specifications	**20%**
Design and code	**15%**
Test and validation	**20%**
Development extension	**10%**
Program modifications	**25%**
Program maintenance	**20%**
Project management	**10%**
Total	*120%*

FIGURE 2-1. Lifecycle phase as a percentage of total effort

One of the most important benefits derived from a software lifecycle model is the ability to obtain cost and time estimates. Software engineers are frequently asked, How long will it take, and what will it cost, to develop this program? In order to answer such questions, we must quantify what we mean by "cost," "effort," and "time."

Let a lifecycle begin at some arbitrary point in time, say $t = 0$, and continue in time indefinitely. Furthermore, let the total effort of a software lifecycle, K, be the sum total of effort used to complete a lifecycle. Effort is measured in units of person-years, MY, or person-months, MM, and the rate of expenditure of effort is measured in person-years/year, MY/YR. (In the early years of software engineering, the profession was dominated by men, so the measure of effort was man-years or man-months, hence the designation MY or MM. Modern software engineers are both men and women, but we have retained the old-fashioned designation.)

Rarely does a software lifecycle consume effort at a constant rate. Instead effort starts at zero, builds up over time, reaches a peak, and declines to zero again. Thus, the rate of expenditure dy/dt is a function of time which we must integrate from $t = 0$ to some time, t_f in order to estimate the total person-years of effort. We call the rate

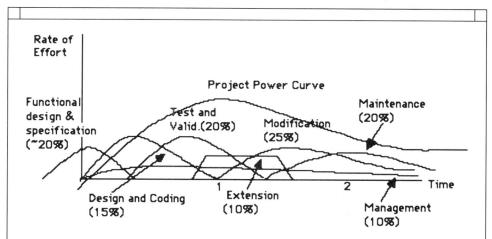

THE POWER CURVE

The power curve is the sum of the rate of expenditure of effort for each of the separate phases: functional design and specification, design and coding, test and validation, project extension, modification, maintenance, and management. Effort is measured in person-months or person-years, and the rate of expenditure of effort is measured in units of person-months per month, or person-years per year. Time is measured in normalized units by dividing the elapsed time by the development time. Thus at point 1, elapsed time equals development time.

The areas under each curve represent the amount of effort expended for each of the seven phases. For example, the area under the design and coding curve is 15%, which means 15% of the total effort went into design and coding. The area under the project curve represents the total effort spent on the entire project.

of effort expenditure the *power function*. For example, since the development phase runs from $t = 0$ to $t = t_d$, the development effort can be computed by integrating the power function dy/dt from $t = 0$ to $t = t_d$ to obtain the effort "used up" by development.

The power function dy/dt is the key to obtaining a valid model of software lifecycle time and cost. Several proposals have been tested on data collected from actual projects. While able to yield only rough estimates of the actual costs, these power functions have led to insights that in turn have contributed to valuable tools for estimating software development projects. We examine only a few of the most promising models.

BROOKS' LAW OF LARGE PROGRAMS

One of the earliest models of the power function was first proposed by Brooks[2]. This model concentrates on the activities most familiar to programmers: design and coding, test and validation, and extension. Extension is a corrective phase that compensates for time overrun. An extension is added to the project if the development time is incorrectly estimated and more time is needed to complete the development phase. These three phases are collectively known as the development phase of the lifecycle. Thus, Brooks' model covers only a part of the complete software lifecycle.

Brooks observed that effort increased more than linearly with an increase in the size of the program (where size is equal to number of lines of source code). This led Brooks to formulate a law of large programs based on the number of lines of source code, S_s, used to implement the code. The law of large programs relates complexity to the amount of effort required to produce a large program; see Figure 2-2.

$$K_d = mS_s^{3/2}$$

where

K_d = programming effort in person-months or person-years
m = application constant
S_s = size of the program in LOC (lines of machine language code).

According to the formula, when $S_s = 1$, m equals the effort to develop one line of code. But this is an oversimplification of the model, because m incorporates application complexity factors such as the nature of the application, the amount of time allocated to complete the project, the kinds of tools used, and so forth. For example, the value of m for a business application is vastly different than for an operating system project. The application constant, m, depends on the productivity of individual programmers, and more importantly, on the complexity of the application.

Brooks observed that the effort *increased* whenever additional power was applied to speed up a failing software development project. We can analyze this effect by revisiting the calculations made in chapter one. If the development team consists of N interacting programmers, then we must also account for the effort that goes into coordinating N interacting team members.

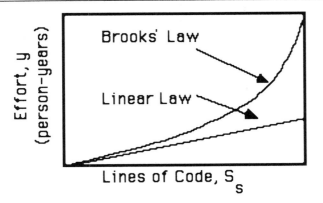

FIGURE 2-2. Brooks' law is nonlinear

Suppose we call the interaction among the N programmers the *communication effort*, K_c. A modified law of large programs can now include this effort:

$$K_d(N) = mS_s^{3/2} + K_c[N(N-1)/2].$$

In this version of Brooks' model, the total number of interactions between all members of the team of N programmers is $N(N-1)/2$, and each of these interactions is assumed to consume K_c person-months of effort. Accordingly, the development effort $K_d(N)$ is a function of N — the amount of effort expended by N interacting programmers. The team must expend both coding and communication effort to produce S_s lines of source code.

When $N = 1$, the extended formula reduces to the law of large programs:

$$K_d(1) = mS_s^{3/2}.$$

This formula assumes equal programmer ability, thus m and K_c are constant for all programmers.

Now, assume a division of labor where each individual programmer is responsible for developing S_j lines of code. Thus the total number of lines of code, S_s, equals the sum of the lines of code produced by each of the N individual programmers (assuming no "overhead" due to interfacing the separate parts):

$$S_s = S_1 + S_2 + \dots + S_N.$$

This "divide and conquer" approach is intended to reduce the overall effort by applying programmers in parallel. If S_j lines of code are assigned to each programmer, then it may be possible to lower the single programmer effort $K_d(1)$ by solving N less ambitious subproblems instead of one large problem. That is, we may be able to beat the law of large programs.

Each programmer must expend K_{dj} person-months of effort in developing S_j lines of code. Thus

$$K_{dj} = mS_j^{3/2}; j = 1, \dots, n.$$

With this in mind, it is possible to optimize the total effort $K_d(N)$ by careful allocation of S_j to each of the programmers. This is done by minimizing the cost function:

$$\text{Cost} = K_d(N) + \lambda \left[S_s - \sum_{j=1}^{N} S_j \right];$$

where

$$K_d(N) = m\left(\sum_{j=1}^{N} S_j^{3/2} \right) + E_c[N(N-1)/2]$$

λ = an optimization constant, determined during minimization.

The resulting allocation of lines of code to programmer j is not surprising given that m and K_c are equal for all programmers:

$$S_j = S_s/N; \ j = 1, \dots, N.$$

This value is substituted into the equation for total development effort to obtain the optimal team effort $K_d^*(N)$ for N programmers:

$$K_d^*(N) = K_d(1)/\sqrt{N} + K_c[N(N-1)/2]$$

Notice the diminishing returns from increasing the number of interacting programmers assigned to a software development project. Since $\sqrt{N}$ increases only moderately with increasing values of N, the advantage of subdivision rapidly diminishes. Replacing N with $10N$ yields only a three fold improvement in the first term of the equation for $K_d^*(N)$ while contributing a fifty fold increase in effort due to the second term.

The disappointing result for $K_d^*(N)$ shows what can happen to a late software project. If additional programmers are added to a failing project, the effort required may increase because the number of interacting parts increases (N is greater). This in turn may move the project upward along the effort curve, therefore increasing the effort

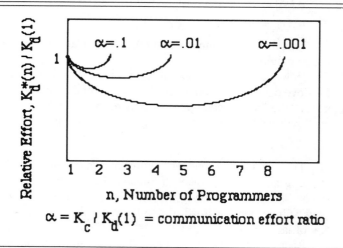

FIGURE 2-3. Optimal project size depends on the ratio of communication to productive work

needed. The best value of N that reduces overall effort the greatest amount will depend on K_c. If communication losses are small, then N can be greater than if communication losses are large. Typically, programmer teams are kept small because of the high cost of communication; see Figure 2-3.

Brooks' model of programmer productivity explains why large programming projects suffer from lower programmer productivity, but it does not tell us how to estimate the length of time required to develop S_s lines of code, nor does it tell us how to estimate the total cost. However, Brooks' idea that software projects might be modeled as a costly and time-consuming endeavor gave impetus to development of many other, more extensive models of the lifecycle.

THE NORDEN-RAYLEIGH MODEL

Lord Rayleigh (1842–1919) explained why the sunset is orange and the summer sky is blue. He also gave us the Rayleigh curve which was used by Norden to explain the behavior of research-and-development lifecycles[3]. First, we derive the general formula, which describes the Rayleigh curves of Figure 2-4, and then we use the formula to model the software lifecycle.

A Rayleigh wave is a surface disturbance caused by two forces: 1) a rising edge and 2) a decaying edge. Ocean swells and earthquakes are examples of Rayleigh waves because they travel across the surface of the earth, and they exhibit a rising edge (the "swell"), and a decaying edge (the trough following the crest of the wave). The shape of such waves depends on the relative amounts of rising and decaying forces present. Suppose we model the rising force as a function of time, $r(t)$, and the decaying force as another function of time, $d(t)$. Furthermore, suppose we postulate a "wave equation" by assuming that the time rate of change in the swell is proportional to both $r(t)$ and $d(t)$:

$$dw/dt = r(t)\,d(t),$$

where we have assumed a constant of proportionality of unity, and dw/dt means the first derivative of $w(t)$ with respect to time.

Norden[3] claimed that Rayleigh waves are analogous to the organizational phenomenon experienced by research-and-development workers. In Norden's view, $r(t)$ is the rising skill or learning curve experienced by the workers, and $d(t)$ is the decaying amount of work to be carried out at time t. Work, $w(t)$, is assumed to total to unity, so that

$$0 \le w(t) \le 1$$

We can obtain the actual effort in terms of person-hours by multiplying w by some scale factor. For example, if a total of K person-hours is needed to complete 100% of the project, then at any time in the project, $Kw(t)$ person-hours will have been expended up to time t. For simplicity, we derive an expression for $w(t)$ and then multiply by K to translate into person-hours of effort.

A number of functions might be assumed for $r(t)$ and $d(t)$, but Norden suggested these simple functions:

$$r(t) = 2at,$$

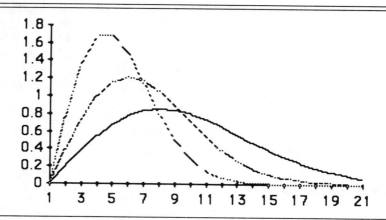

FIGURE 2-4. Rayleigh curve

where

  a = constant which determines the shape of the curve,
  t = elapsed time from start of the project
  2 = a convenient constant.

For $d(t)$, Norden assumed that rate of effort decays directly proportional to the amount of work remaining to be done. Hence,

$$d(t) = [1 - w(t)].$$

This yields the general wave equation,

$$dw(t)/dt = 2at[1 - w(t)]$$

which can be solved to obtain,

$$w(t) = 1 - e^{-at^2},$$

where we have assumed time runs from zero to infinity. The total effort, then, is

$$Kw(t) = K[1 - e^{-at^2}].$$

The assumptions made by Putnam have held up rather well under study by a number of other researchers[5], but for an alternate model based on the assumptions:

$$r(t) = w(t), \, d(t) = [1 - w(t)]$$

leading to a differential equation of the form

$$dw(t)/dt = w[1 - w(t)], \text{ see Parr}[13].$$

DIFFERENTIAL EQUATIONS: SPECIAL EDITION

In order to derive the solution to Norden's version of the Rayleigh wave equation, you must solve a differential equation of the form,

$$\{D + p(t)\}\ y(t) = q(t)$$

where D is the differential operator, t is time, and y is the function to be found.

The general solution to equations of this form are found by discovering an "integrating function" that makes the equation a "perfect" differential. In this case the integrating function $I(t)$ is easy:

$$I(t) = e^{u(t)}, \text{ where } u(t) = \text{anti-derivative of } p(t)$$

Then, the solution is given by:

$$y(t) = [\textstyle\int_0^t I(\S)\ q(\S)\ d\S]/I(t)$$

In addition, when $p(t) = q(t)$ as is the case with the Rayleigh equation,

$$y(t) = 1 - e^{u(0) - u(t)}$$

For example, when $p(t) = q(t) = 2a$,

$$y(t) = 1 - e^{-2at}$$

When $p(t) = q(t) = 2at$,

$$y(t) = 1 - e^{-at^2}$$

PUTNAM'S SLIM MODEL

How can the Norden model be applied to the software lifecycle? To answer this question, we must find connections between "effort" and lines of code (LOC); general time and software development time; and the notion of complexity discussed earlier. In this section we show how these connections are made.

The Norden-Rayleigh model was studied extensively by Putnam, who used the model to explain the lifecycles of several large-scale data-processing projects for the U.S. military. The following analysis and values were obtained from these lifecycles and may *not* apply to new situations. For a critical evaluation of this and other models, see the article by Moranda[6].

According to Norden, the Rayleigh wave equation models any research-and-development lifecycle as follows:

$$w(t) = K[1 - e^{-at^2}]$$

where

$w(t)$ = the fraction of the total work achieved at time t, $0 \leq w \leq K$.

t = time: the project starts at $t = 0$ and ends at infinity or some finite time, t_f.

K = the total applied effort expended throughout the lifecycle, measured in person-hours, person-months, or person-years, MY.

a = determines the shape of the curve and is called the *intensity* of the project.

dw/dt = the first derivative of $w(t)$, and is called the power curve because it describes the rate of expenditure of effort.

Putnam[14] applied Norden's analysis to several military software projects and arrived at the following observations, which are a combination of mathematical derivation and empirical study:

First, the point in time when the power curve peaks, t_{max}, is related to the intensity as follows:

$$a = 1/(2t^2_{max}).$$

EXAMPLE OF COST ESTIMATING WITH PUTNAM'S MODEL

These ideas are illustrated in the following example. Suppose a microcomputer system is to be developed in two years. The project manager determines that this project is of moderate complexity, $C = 15$. We want to know in advance what the expended effort will be and how much it will cost to develop the software from $t = 0$ to $t_d = 2$ years.

(a) What is the expected effort, K? $C = 15 = K/t_d^3$, therefore $K = (15)(8) = 120$ person-years.

(b) We compute the costs of both development and total effort, assuming $U = 25,000/MY$. What are the relative costs, $TOTAL and $DEV?

$TOTAL = $U(K) = (25,000)(120) = $3M$ $DEV = (0.40) ($TOTAL) = (0.40)(3M) = $1.2M$

(c) What is the expected size, S_s? Assume old technology, $T = 4980$.

$S_s = (4980)(120^{1/3})(2^{4/3}) = 61,851$ lines

(d) Assume two bytes per line of code: What is the size of memory required?

$(2)(61,851) = 128$ kilobytes

We can see from the example that the sizing equation relates the total effort to the finished product size. It means that given a technology and a fixed length of time, a fixed number of lines of source code can be produced. The amount of code does not vary with language or personality of programmers. Such an assumption may not be true in individual cases, but Putnam's results appear to be *accurate in the large*.

For large projects, Putnam observed that the development time $t_d = t_{max}$. That is, the power curve peaks at the point in time when the software is delivered. Thus, t_d is a pivot point in the project.

t_d = the time spent on developing the code, certifying it, and releasing it. This does not include modification, maintenance, nor management. Extension time is not reflected in the time estimate, t_d.

K_d = the effort applied to develop the application, but not to maintain or modify the code nor to manage the project.

A most intriguing observation made by Putman is the placement of development time at the peak of the power curve; see Figure 2-5. Placement of t_d suggests that t/t_d equals 1.0 at the maximum point of the software lifecycle. This point is reached by the combined efforts of all phases, thus the expenditure of effort is at its most furious intensity just at the moment development is completed!

However, $t_d \neq t_{max}$ for small projects in general. Instead, t_{max} occurs somewhere between the start time and t_d. For projects ranging between 18,000 and 70,000 LOC, it is recommended that $t_d \approx 2t_{max}$. We assume a large project for the remainder of the discussion, and use $a = 1/(2t^2_d)$. Thus, K_d equals the effort expended to develop the software in t_d months.

Then, the power equation becomes:

$$dw/dt = Dte^{-t^2/2t_d^2}, \text{ where } D = K/t^2_d.$$

Putnam calls D the "difficulty" of the software development project and attaches great significance to this relation. In fact, empirical data led Putnam to postulate an indirect relationship between difficulty and programmer productivity P as:

P = constant $D^{-2/3}$, where P = total number of source lines/total number of person-months = S_s/K.

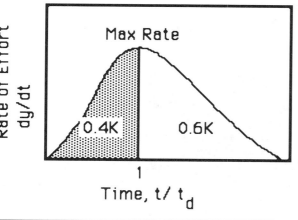

Putnam's adaptation of Rayleigh's curve assumes that the development time peaks at the point where $dw(t)/dt$ is a maximum. That is, the solution to the equation:

$$d^2w(t)/dt^2 = 0 = 2ae^{-at^2}[1 - 2at^2]$$

From this we can compute the relation:

$$a = 1/(2t^2_{max}) = 1/(2t^2_d)$$

We can also compute the area under the curve at this point, as $e^{-1/2} = 0.4$, approximately.

FIGURE 2-5. The peak is reached at $t/td = 1$

Thus, the total number of source lines S_s is proportional to P times K:

$$S_s = \text{constant } PK = \text{constant } D^{-2/3}K = \text{constant } (K^{1/3}t^{4/3}{}_d)$$

Finally, the constant in the size equation is T, the state of technology.

T = the state of technology. A few of the items that affect technology are: unstructured versus structured programming, batch versus interactive development systems, and automated versus manual test methods.

The Software Size Equation

Putnam's model is the first to relate the effort and time to the LOC that can be produced.

$$S_s = T(K\, t_d^4)^{1/3}$$

where S_s is the number of lines of source code in a piece of software developed in time t_d by total effort K, using a level of technology given by the constant T.

Putnam evaluated several large-scale software projects *after* completion. Curve-fitting techniques were used to estimate T for two different environments:

T = 4980. The environment consisted of a batch development computer system, unstructured coding methods, "fuzzy" design requirements, and restricted access to the test machine.

T = 10040. The environment consisted of an on-line interactive development system, structured coding methods, well-defined requirements, and unrestricted access to the test machine.

The size equation is nonlinear in total effort, K, and development time, t_d. As it turns out, these two parameters can be traded off, one for the other. The trade-off is nonlinear, however, due to the nonlinear nature of the sizing equation. Trading time and effort leads to the conservation law proposed by Putnam.

Software Project Complexity

Putnam classified the military software he studied noting the similarity among lifecycle curves. By ranking projects according to a complexity function given by dividing difficulty by development time,

$$C = D/t_d$$

he found that software projects could be grouped along "complexity planes" defined by $C = 8$, 15, and 27; see Figure 2-6.

Putnam's quantitative measures are especially interesting because of their relevance to development time. Here, Putnam claims that a project is made more complex by decreasing the development time. An alternate interpretation of this relationship is that there is a minimum development time t_d, given a fixed complexity and a fixed level of effort, K.

C	Type of Project Studied
8	new systems
15	modified systems
27	major revisions

Putnam found that whenever "new" systems projects were plotted on the same graph with "modified" and "highly revised" systems projects, they coincided with complexity values 8, 15, and 27, respectively.

FIGURE 2-6. Putnam's levels of complexity

The ranking of types of projects further suggests a "difficulty gradient" related to the problem of understanding a program. The more complex a program is, the more difficult it is to modify. Hence, the complexity quantity may provide a way to begin an analysis of software lifecycle costs.

Time-Effort Conservation Law

In the size equation

$$S_s = T(Kt_d^4)^{1/3}$$

the number of lines of code is fixed by the middle term, (Kt_d^4). In fact, exchanging effort for development time leads to the same productivity. This observation yields the conservation law:

$$Kt_d^4 = \text{constant}$$

Putnam's time-effort conservation law states that effort and time can be exchanged, but the product of effort and the fourth power of time remains constant. Notice how much more important time is than effort in this law.

We can use the conservation law above to study the effects of a compressed development time schedule. Suppose the microcomputer project from the example on page 38 is compressed by 25%. Now,

$$t_d = 1.5 \text{ YR.}$$

Effort was previously computed to be 120 MY, and time was 2 YR, so the constant in the time-effort conservation law can be computed directly:

$$(120)(2)^4 = 1920 \text{ (before compression).}$$

Using 1920, but substituting the shortened development time of 1.5 years into the conservation law, yields a revised estimate of the total effort:

$$K = (1920)(1.5^4) = 376.4 \text{ MY (after time compression).}$$

Thus the result of a 25% acceleration in the development schedule is devastating to the cost of the software.

$TOTAL = $9.4 M
$DEV   = $3.8 M

In this example, accelerating the development schedule by 25% triples the cost of the project. Correspondingly we would expect a cost reduction if more development time were allowed. Clearly time costs money.

The Norden-Rayleigh-Putnam model provides a macroscale handle on a very important part of the software lifecycle: the size and cost. Given the following parameters:

T = state of technology
K = total effort
t_d = development time

we can compute various quantities of enormous value using Putnam's formulas. These formulas yield a first-order estimate of the effort, cost, and size of a software life cycle. The reader should be warned that the values of T, D, and C may be subject to change within an application area, among different programmers, and over a period of time. Each project manager should determine these parameters from careful evaluation and/or time-motion studies.

THE BOEHM CONSTRUCTIVE COST MODEL

The previous models of lifecycle costs were developed from an examination of the underlying phenomenon. These models assume that "laws" of software engineering exist and the task of the software engineer is to discover these laws. Boehm[7] developed an empirical model based on observation instead of attempting to discover the underlying principles. The *CoCoMo* (**CO**nstructive **CO**st **MO**del) system is based on a database of observed quantities called **drivers** — *factors which influence the development time and applied effort.*

There are three levels of CoCoMo — Basic, Intermediate, and Extended. We will describe the first two levels, and use the intermediate level model to estimate the effort, time, and cost to develop a small project.

CoCoMo describes the development phase beginning after the software requirements have been approved and ending when the product is released for sale. The maintenance, modification, and other phases are not included, but they can be estimated separately by applying CoCoMo with a different selection of drivers. CoCoMo covers management time and effort during development and documentation time and effort, and assumes good management practices. CoCoMo estimates do not consider user training, installation of the finished product, or conversion to the new product.

A CoCoMo person-month consists of 152 hours of working time. This is a working estimate that includes holidays, vacations, and sick leave. Conversion units for CoCoMo measures of person-months, MM, are given below:

1 MM = 152 person-hours
1 MM = 19 person-days
1 MM = 1/12 of a person-year

The interesting feature of CoCoMo is that it considers a wide variety of factors in software development. These factors are entered into the CoCoMo model as cost drivers. Intermediate CoCoMo uses an estimate of the number of lines of delivered code in KDSI (thousand lines of delivered instructions), and fifteen cost drivers to compute both effort, MM, and development time, TDEV:

Product Factors:
RELY = required software reliability (how forgiving is the program?)
DATA = size of the database (is the database large and unwieldy?)
CPLX = product complexity (is this a complex system?)

Computer Factors:
TIME = execution time constraints (Must the program be fast?)
STOR = main storage constraints (Do you have enough main memory?)
VIRT = machine stability (How reliable is the computer?)
TURN = computer turnaround time (How responsive is the computer?)

Personnel Factors:
ACAP = programmer analyst capability (Experienced designer?)
AEXP = programmer familiarity with the application
PCAP = programmer capability (Experienced programmer?)
VEXP = machine familiarity and experience
LEXP = programming language experience (Do programmers know the language?)

Project Factors:
MODP = modern programming practices (Structured programming?)
TOOL = use of software tools (CASE tools?)
SCED = development schedule (Tight or relaxed?)

Each of these factors is estimated by the software engineer. The estimate is converted into a number and used as a multiplier to adjust the effort and time estimates. The base effort and time estimates are obtained from one of three modes, the choice depending on the kind of product being developed.

The Three CoCoMo Modes

CoCoMo is calibrated to fit observed projects, but unfortunately real projects vary greatly in their scope, complexity, and duration. We have already seen how programmer productivity varies with product size. Similarly, CoCoMo estimates must be adjusted according to the **development mode** — *the level of difficulty of a program.*

Organic Mode

This mode of development is characterized by a relatively small software development team working on a well-understood application in a highly familiar, in-house environment. This mode of development enjoys small communication overhead, stable hardware, well-known algorithms, and the programmer productivity usually associated with small programs (less than 50 KDSI).

The model equations for intermediate CoCoMo organic mode cost estimating are:

$$K_d = MM = 3.2(KDSI)^{1.05};$$
$$t_d = TDEV = 2.5(MM)^{0.38}.$$

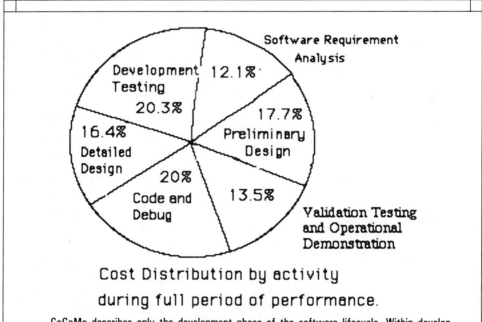

Cost Distribution by activity during full period of performance.

CoCoMo describes only the development phase of the software lifecycle. Within development, the fraction of effort and thus cost is divided into parts as shown above, however, these percentages may vary from one project to another as we have seen earlier. Therefore, the development time may vary from one project to another. CoCoMo adapts to this variation in two ways: 1) by changing the mode of the model, and 2) by altering the cost driver weighting factors as discussed.

Source: R. W. Wolverton, "The Cost of Developing Large-Scale Software", IEEE TRANSACTIONS ON COMPUTERS, June 1974), pp. 282–303, Reprinted by permission of IEEE, Inc., New York, NY.

Semidetached Mode

This mode falls in between the "easy" level of organic mode projects, and the "difficult" level of the embedded mode projects. These projects are characterized by more complex problems and more rigorous demands for communication, time, and size. Typical products at this level of difficulty consist of 300 KDSI, and typical algorithms are more complex than those found in organic mode products.

The model equations for intermediate CoCoMo semidetached mode cost estimating are:

$$K_d = MM = 3.0(KDSI)^{1.12};$$
$$t_d = TDEV = 2.5(MM)^{0.35}$$

Embedded Mode

This mode is characterized by demanding time constraints, interactions between hardware and software, customer and developer, and volatility in requirements (constant change). Typical products exhibit a high degree of interaction, often including difficult timing considerations such as found in real-time transaction processing software, or concurrent processing applications, e.g. an operating system.

The model equations for intermediate CoCoMo embedded mode cost estimating are:

$$K_d = MM = 2.8(KDSI)^{1.20};$$
$$t_d = TDEV = 2.5(MM)^{0.32}$$

Given estimates of the program size, *KDSI*, we can compute *MM* and *TDEV* using the equations above. Then, personnel costs, the average programmer productivity, PP; average personnel staffing, FSP (full-time staff person); and peak FSP, can be determined from the following relations:

$$Cost = \$U\ (MM);\ dollars$$

where

$$\$U\ = \$COST/person\text{-}month$$
$$PP\ = 1000\ (KDSI/MM);\ statements\ per\ person\text{-}month$$
$$FSP = MM/TDEV;\ full\text{-}time\ staff\ persons$$
$$Peak\ FSP = MM\ (2/TDEV)\ e^{-0.5};\ approximately[4]$$
$$= 1.21\ (MM/TDEV);$$
$$= 1.21\ FSP$$

The peak FSP is computed by approximating the Rayleigh power function for the development phases covered by CoCoMo only. This shifts the peak applied effort to time point *TDEV*/2 from the start of development. In other words, we get a different maximum point along the time axis because only part of the entire lifecycle is modeled by CoCoMo.

Consider this short example. Suppose a project of 32 KDSI is to be estimated using the organic mode formulas. Substitution of 32 into the equations yields a Basic CoCoMo estimate as follows (the formulas are slightly different for Basic CoCoMo, so do not be confused by the slightly different coeficients in the formulas):

Effort, MM = $2.4(32)^{1.05}$ = 91 person-months

Time, $TDEV$ = $2.5(91)^{0.38}$ = 14 months

Productivity, PP = 1000(32/91) = 352 statements/person-months

Average staffing, FSP = 91/14 = 6.5 persons

Peak FSP = 1.21 FSP = 7.9 persons

These estimates can be used to allocate people to various tasks throughout the project development lifecycle or to simply explain why projects are time-consuming and expensive. For example, if we assume programmers cost $3,000 per month, then the cost of developing 32 KDSI is given by the simple cost formula:

COST = 3,000(91) = $273,000

This example shows how to use the basic formulas in CoCoMo estimating, but the example ignores the fine tuning made possible by using the intermediate CoCoMo cost drivers. The computational labor increases, however, and so we rely on a CASE tool called CoCoPro to do the work for us. CoCoPro is a computer program for computing the intermediate CoCoMo estimates.

Distribution of Effort

Boehm[7] gives sample phase distributions which can be used to further break down the costs of development. You can use these distributions to allocate the overall effort to sub-phases as shown in Table 2-1.

TABLE 2-1. Distribution of effort recommended by Boehm[7]

	Product Size			
Phase	Small (2 KDSI)	Intermediate (8 KDSI)	Medium (32 KDSI)	Large (128 KDSI)
Effort:				
Planning	6%	6%	6%	6%
Design	16%	16%	16%	16%
Coding	68%	65%	62%	59%
Testing	16%	19%	22%	25%
Time:				
Planning	10%	11%	12%	13%
Design	19%	19%	19%	19%
Coding	63%	59%	55%	51%
Testing	18%	22%	26%	30%

These numbers were collected from sixty-three projects studied by Boehm. The projects ranged from organic to embedded, business, scientific, and systems programs, micro to maxi computer systems, and programming languages such as FORTRAN, COBOL, Jovial, Pascal, and assembly language. Even so, the percentages given by Boehm may not fit your particular environment, project, or programming tools. Therefore, it is best to collect your own database of percentages and cost data. Once a database is created, CoCoMo estimates can become a reliable basis for making decisions about effort, time, and cost.

COCOPRO: A CASE TOOL FOR DEVELOPMENT COST ESTIMATING

CoCoPro implements Intermediate CoCoMo as discussed in the previous sections of this chapter. In addition, CoCoPro provides database storage for projects that have been completed in the past. This database can be used to calibrate the intermediate CoCoMo models to a new set of projects. The calibration computes new coefficients for MM and TDEV based on past history. In this way, CoCoPro provides a way to tailor cost estimates to new situations and new team organizations.

The pull-down menus define what CoCoPro can do: the Project menu controls storage of project estimation reports. To create a new report, select New; to open an existing report select Open. Similarly, reports can be saved and printed. Suppose we create a report for a student project consisting of 6.5 KDSI using the organic mode equations.

First, select the New item from menu Project and enter the name of the project: Sample Project, see Figure 2-7. Next, select the Organic mode from the CoCoMo menu, then choose Calculate. The equations for intermediate CoCoMo will automatically be used to compute estimates, see Figure 2-8.

Enter the name of the component, number of lines of code, and select the cost drivers in the data capture dialog shown in Figure 2-9. We have assumed a small project and novice expertise in the example. Cost driver values are ranked as VLow, up to XtraHi. A numerical value corresponds to each of these ranks. The numerical values can be observed, but when using CoCoPro it is not necessary to know what they mean.

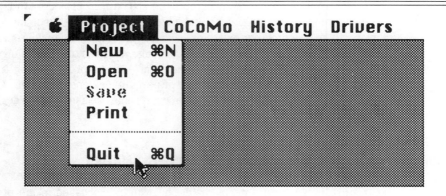

FIGURE 2-7. Starting CoCoPro

The cost driver rankings are somewhat vague and subject to human interpretation. Boehm[7] gives tables that explain each driver — for example, CPLX rankings indicate the complexity of the product under development. The table from Boehm is reproduced as an example in Table 2-2.

After the input data is captured, a dialog appears containing the results, as shown in Figure 2-10.

MM   = 9.04 person-months
TDEV   = 5.77 months
FSP   = 1.57 people
Peak FSP = 1.90 people

This project is suitable for two programmers working for 3 – 4 months. The distribution of effort and time suggests that if the project is preplanned, a team of three people can easily complete the design and coding phases within a three-or four-month period.

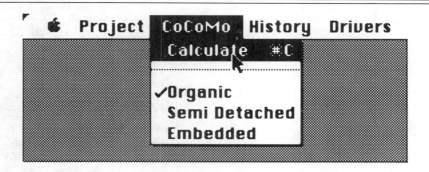

FIGURE 2-8. Calculation of organic mode estimates

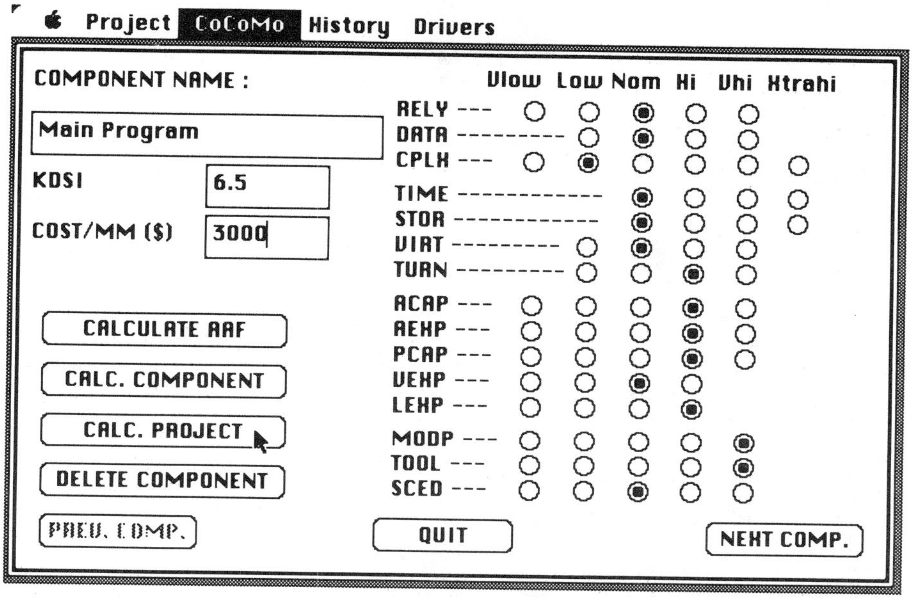

FIGURE 2-9. Select drivers by settling Vlow, Low, Nom, Iti, Vlto, or Xtrahi

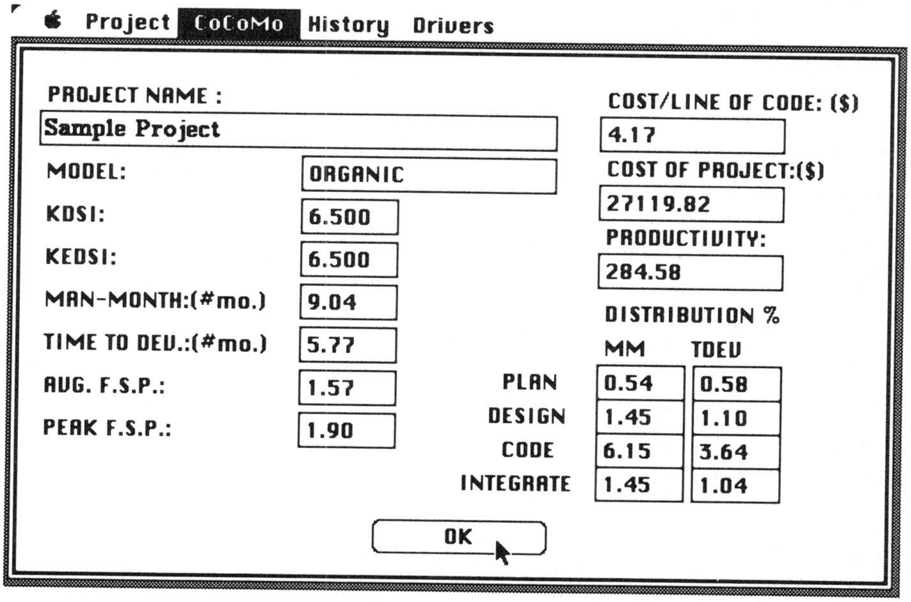

FIGURE 2-10. Estimates computed from data in figure 2-9

TABLE 2-2. Complexity rating, CPLX, versus type of module

Rating	Control Operations	Computational Operations	Device-dependent Operations	Management Operations
Very low	Straightline code with a few non-nested SP* operators: DOs, CASEs, IFTHENELSEs, simple predicates.	Evaluation of simple expressions: e.g., $A = B + C * (D - E)$.	Simple read, write statements with simple formats.	Simple arrays; main memory.
Low	Straightforward nesting of SP operators. Mostly simple predicates.	Evaluation of moderate-level expressions, e.g., $D = SQRT(B**2 - 4*A*C)$.	No cognizance needed of particular processor or I/O device characteristics. I/O done at GET/PUT level. No cognizance of overlap.	Single file subsetting with no data structure changes, no edits, no intermediate files.
Nominal	Mostly simple nesting. Some inter-module control. Decision tables.	Use of standard math and statistical routines. Basic matrix/vector operations.	I/O processing includes device selection, status checking, and error processing.	Multi-file input and single file output. Simple structural changes, simple edits.
High	Highly nested SP operators with many compound predicates. Queue and stack control. Considerable inter-module control.	Basic numerical analysis: multivariate interpolation, ordinary differential equations. Basic truncation, roundoff concerns.	Operations at physical I/O level (physical storage address translations; seeks, reads, etc.). Optimized I/O overlap.	Special purpose subroutines activated by data stream contents. Complex data restructuring at record level.
Very high	Reentrant and recursive coding. Fixed-priority interrupt handling.	Difficult but structured N.A.: near-singular matrix equations, partial differential equations.	Routines for interrupt diagnosis, servicing, masking. Communication line handling.	A generalized, parameter-driven file structuring routine. File building, command processing, search optimization.
Extra high	Multiple resource scheduling with dynamically changing priorities. Microcode-level control.	Difficult and unstructured N.A.: highly accurate analysis of noisy, stochastic data.	Device timing-dependent coding, micro-programmed operations.	Highly coupled, dynamic relational structures. Natural language data management.

SP = Structured programming

Source: Barry W. Boehm, SOFTWARE ENGINEERING ECONOMICS, ©1981, p. 122. Reprinted by permission of Prentice-Hall, Inc., Englewood Cliffs, New Jersey.

CoCoPro Reports

The report file contains cost estimates for each of the components in the project (in this example, there is only one component), and a cost estimate for the entire project (all components combined). In addition, the file shows the numerical values of the cost drivers used and other useful information, see Figure 2-11.

A Sample Report from CoCoPro

Component Name: Main Program
KDSI: 6.50
KEDSI: 6.50
MM: 9.04
Cost Per MM: 3000.00
TDEV: 5.77
Design Percent: 100.00
Code Percent: 100.00
Integration_Percent: 100.00
Average FSP: 1.57
Peak FSP: 1.90
Component Cost: 27119.82
Productivity: 719.03
Cost Per Instruction: 4.17

RELY	NOM	1.00
DATA	NOM	1.00
CPLX	LOW	0.85
TIME	NOM	1.00
STOR	NOM	1.00
VIRT	NOM	1.00
TURN	HI	1.07
ACAP	HI	0.86
AEXP	HI	0.91
PCAP	HI	0.86
VEXP	NOM	1.00
LEXP	HI	0.95
MODP	VHI	0.82
TOOL	VHI	0.83
SCED	NOM	1.00

Project Name: Sample Project
Model: Organic

KDSI: 6.50
KEDSI: 6.50
MM: 9.04
TDEV: 5.77
Total Cost: 27119.82
Average FSP: 1.57
Peak FSP: 1.90
Productivity: 284.58
Cost Per Instruction: 4.17

Distribution:

	MM	TDEV
Plan	0.54	0.58
Design	1.45	1.10
Code	6.15	3.64
Integrate	1.45	1.04

FIGURE 2-11. A CoCoPro file in the form of a report

In addition, CoCoPro can use previous project data to calibrate the standard models provided by Boehm. This is done by fitting the organic, semidetached, and embedded formulas to new observations using least-squares curve fitting techniques. Only those past projects selected by the user are included in the calibration.

CoCoPro History Files

After each project is completed it is entered into the database by selecting Provide Actuals under the History menu. Data is entered much as before, along with cost driver rankings and actual numerical values for MM and TDEV, see Figure 2-12.

Past projects are saved in CoCoPro so the mathematical model can be modified by calibration, see Figure 2-12. Calibration is done by fitting a new curve through the data points provided by actual projects. A least-squares curve is fit to selected actuals by computing the coefficients å, β, å', and β':

$$\text{MM} = \text{å} \ (KDSI)^{\beta}; \text{ and TDEV} = \text{å}'(MM)^{\beta'}$$

Actuals are entered in the same manner as estimates except the user must provide the actual effort and time values. The cost drivers for an actual project are also entered so that the calibration can include all factors.

Calibration is necessary to tune the CoCoPro tool to the characteristics of the team, corporation, or technology used by programmers. If cost estimates are consistently low, this probably indicates the need for calibration.

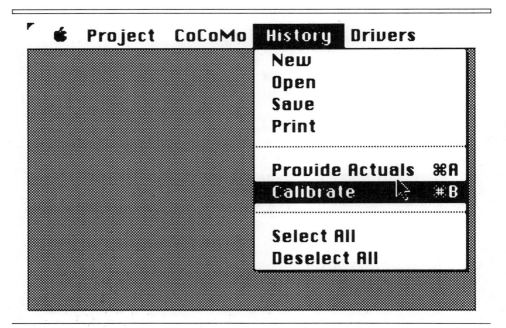

FIGURE 2-12. CoCoPro keeps a history file of past projects

CoCoPro uses default values for the various cost driver multipliers, see the sample report file output. These can be changed by the user, but beware: they have been carefully estimated by Boehm, and are not linear functions of "difficulty," "complexity," or other qualities of software projects. They are, rather, empirically determined values.

FUNCTION POINT ESTIMATING

A major drawback of all models studied thus far is the need to know, in advance, the size, effort, or time required to complete one or more phases of the software lifecycle. In practice, it is difficult to accurately predict the size of a project, the total effort it will require, or the time it will take. Perhaps it would be better to estimate the size, effort, and time from an estimate of the number of functions the software is to perform. This idea was developed by Albrecht[8] and is called the *function point method*.

Function point estimating is done by counting the functions to be performed by the software, adjusting the counts according to "complexity," and making the estimate from the sum of weighted function points. The counts are obtained from the design by totalling:

- Number of external inputs, IN
- Number of external outputs, OUT
- Number of logical internal files, FILES
- Number of interface files, INT
- Number of external inquiries, INQ

These numbers are entered into the FP Worksheet as shown in Figure 2-13. The total FP is tallied and then adjusted according to the processing complexity, PC, which is obtained by ranking each of the "complexity factors" shown in the PC Worksheet of Figure 2-14.

FP Worksheet

Count	Simple	Average	Complex	Total
IN	_____ ×3 = _____	_____ × 4 = _____	_____ × 6 = _____	_____
OUT	_____ ×4 = _____	_____ × 5 = _____	_____ × 7 = _____	_____
FILES	_____ ×7 = _____	_____ ×10 = _____	_____ ×15 = _____	_____
INT	_____ ×5 = _____	_____ × 7 = _____	_____ ×10 = _____	_____
INQ	_____ ×3 = _____	_____ × 4 = _____	_____ × 6 = _____	_____

Total FP = _____

FIGURE 2-13. Worksheet for collecting total FP

PC Worksheet

Data communications = _____   Online up-date = _____
Distributed functions = _____   Complex processing = _____
Performance = _____   Reusability = _____
Heavily used configuration = _____   Installation ease = _____
Transaction rate = _____   Operational ease = _____
On-line data entry = _____   Multiple sites = _____
End-user efficiency = _____   Facilitate change = _____

Enter the following value: Total PC = _____

0 = not present, or no influence   1 = insignificant influence
2 = moderate influence   3 = average influence
4 = significant influence   5 = strong influence, throughout

PCA = 0.65 + (0.01 × PC)   FPA = FP × PCA = _____

FIGURE 2-14. Worksheet for collecting processing complexity

The adjusted function point count, FPA, is used to estimate effort, time, and size through regression formulas that must be developed for each software development environment. In fact, Albrecht calibrated 22 projects over a five-year period (1974–1978), and found that DMS/VS took an average of 25 SLOC per function point, PL/I took 65 SLOC/FP, and COBOL averaged 100 SLOC/FP. Specifically, least-squares estimators were proposed as follows:

$$SLOC = 66\ FP \qquad \text{Simplified Overall Model}$$
$$SLOC = 118.7\ FP - 6,490 \qquad \text{COBOL}$$
$$SLOC = 73.1\ FP - 4,600 \qquad \text{PL/I}$$

Similarly, effort measured in work-hours, WH, can be estimated:

$$WH = 54\ FP - 13,390 \qquad \text{Overall}$$
$$WH = 0.3793\ SLOC - 2,913 \qquad \text{COBOL}$$
$$WH = 0.6713\ SLOC - 13,137 \qquad \text{PL/I}$$

Notice the great difference in productivity depending on the language and system used. DMS/VS is a very high-level (4GL) language, and PL/I and COBOL are traditional third-generation languages. This is the first time we have encountered a model which places such heavy emphasis on implementation language.

Behrens[9] reports confirmation of the function point approach by applying it to 24 development projects in 1980 and 1981 (more recent technology was used). His results support the contention that project size, development environment, and programming language are determinants of programmer productivity. Interestingly, Behrens' data does not support some of the CoCoMo factors such as programmer experience. Perhaps the strongest influence on productivity is on-line interactive development systems. This claim is certainly supported by the vastly increased productivity enjoyed by workstation programmers.

UniTool: An Application of Function Points

UniTool is an extension to CoCoPro which provides a "front end" for collecting estimates of system design complexity and SLOC. UniTool is used principally to automate the process of estimating KDSI for CoCoPro, but it also provides scheduling information which can be used to partition the work into a WBS (Work Breakdown Structure) chart.

UniTool uses the modular design of a software system to estimate the SLOC. For example, a simple system is shown in Figure 2-15, containing two modules. Module Main is a main program with only one procedure attached. Module Used contains three functions/procedures. The arcs between modules indicates a call relationship; Module Main calls two of the procedures in Module Used. Each module encapsulates data and function, thus the design given by the programmer is an Object-Oriented Design.

A programmer draws the design using the tools shown: a selection (arrow), box (object), arc (call), and operation (procedure/function) tool is all that is needed. Thus, Module Main and Module Used are drawn by selecting the Object Icon from the tool palette, as shown in Figure 2-15. The two call arcs are drawn by selecting the drawing tool and clicking on the source and destination objects. As many operations as desired are placed in each object with the operation tool.

Information regarding function points for each object is entered through dialogs as shown in Figure 2-16. These dialogs are obtained by double-clicking on the desired object or operation. This information is used along with the following formulas to estimate SLOC:

$$\text{SLOC} = (K)(FP_d)$$

$$FP_d = C_{\text{object}} \sum FP_{\text{operation}} + \text{Base}_{\text{object}};\ \text{Summation over all operations in the object}$$

$$FP_{\text{operation}} = \#\text{Parameters} * C_{\text{operation}} + \text{Base}_{\text{operation}}$$

where

SLOC	= Source Lines of Code
FP	= Function Point
C_{object}	= Complexity of objects: simple = 1, average = 2, or complex = 3 in UniTool
$C_{\text{operation}}$	= Complexity of operations: simple = 1, average = 2, complex = 3 in UniTool
$\text{Base}_{\text{object}}$	= Base value for all objects: 1 in UniTool
$\text{Base}_{\text{operation}}$	= Base value for all operations: 0 in UniTool
#Parameters	= Number of parameters in the procedure/function of an operation

The SLOC obtained from these estimates are scaled to KDSI and passed on to CoCoPro for estimation of the development time and effort.

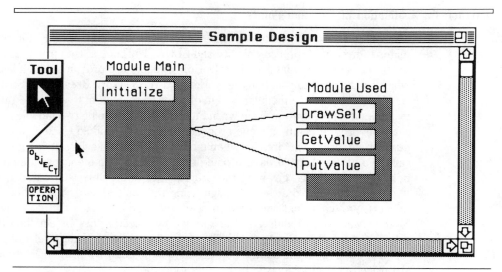

FIGURE 2-15. A UniTool design

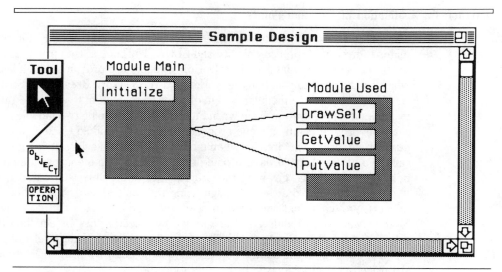

FIGURE 2-16. Entering function point information into UniTool

VALIDITY OF COST ESTIMATES

How well do these cost estimation models work in practice? The intermediate CoCoMo model was shown by Boehm to be modestly accurate — within 20% of the actuals 68% of the time[7]. However, Boehm advises against using CoCoMo estimates alone or without careful study of what the computed numbers mean. Furthermore, Boehm recommends several different models be used to compute and compare cost estimates. If comparisons reveal large differences, then the estimates should be carried out again. After each iteration, change the inputs and make adjustments to account for the differences obtained from each model.

Cost estimates can be altered during the project when more accurate information is made available. Alterations during the project are usually necessary anyway, because:

- Input values are (inaccurate) estimates themselves, and as the project unfolds, better estimates can be obtained;
- The models are only approximations; as we learn their weaknesses we can compensate for them;
- Some projects are unique and do not fit the models very well;
- Projects are subject to changes — shortened time, more or less people, changes in requirements for the finished application;
- The models are calibrated on projects which may not be very representative of your project.

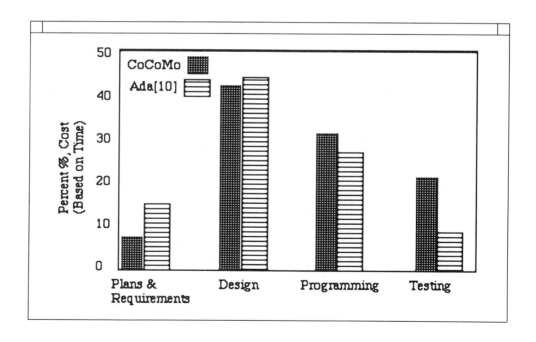

The biggest problem with CoCoMo estimating is accurate approximation of the cost driver values and their application. The KDSI estimate is especially difficult to obtain prior to design and coding. UniTool is an attempt to remove this problem, but UniTool is itself an estimating tool, and there are no guarantees that SLOC estimates from UniTool will be accurate.

The remaining fifteen drivers in the intermediate CoCoMo model are equally difficult to "guess" prior to full understanding of the project. The Norden-Rayleigh model requires estimates of two of the three parameters (development time, total effort, and lines of code) in order to compute the remaining parameter.

Kemerer[11] studied four different cost estimating models including CoCoMo and Putnam's SLIM model to determine which model was best at predicting time and effort estimates for business data processing applications. All the models tested were judged to need more research and development before they could be deemed reliable. Kemerer found generally that Putnam's SLIM consistently overestimated effort — probably because it was calibrated for complex real-time military projects, which are thought to be more difficult than business data-processing applications.

CoCoMo, Kemerer concluded, also overestimated effort for the same reason: the default calibration of CoCoMo is geared to difficult military projects. In addition, the study found that basic CoCoMo performed as well as the intermediate and detailed CoCoMo models. We might conclude either that the cost drivers add nothing to the estimates or that they are difficult to use.

Rubin[12] and Boehm[3] provide additional comparisons of cost estimation models. Rubin's ongoing evaluation, and observation that estimates can vary as high as 8 to 1 calls for caution when using any tool. In particular, Rubin reports results in Table 2-3 for an estimate of a project with the following characteristics:

SLOC = 60,000 of COBOL (no reusable components)
On-line development environment
Two Functions
Nine Inputs
Thirty Outputs
Five Databases (Files)
Seven Inquiries
High reliability
Demanding performance (response)
Average processing logic
Cpu and storage constraints are considered tight
Program modules are:
   10 error checking
    8 data compacting
   10 mathematical
    3 logic control
    1 data formatting
   21 reporting and printing
    9 screen display
    3 sorting

TABLE 2-3. **Results of the study by Rubin[12]**

Estimate	JS-2	SLIM	GECOMO	ESTIMACS	PCOC	SPQR/10
Effort	940 PM	200 PM	363 PM	17,100 PHRS	345 PM	437 PM
Duration	31 M	17 M	23 M	16 M	23 M	28 M
Peak Staff	43	17	22	15	24	16

Results obtained from six cost estimation tools are shown in Table 2-3. Effort is measured in PM (Person-Months), and PHRS (Person-Hours). Duration is measured in M (Months), and peak staff requirements in number of people. Development time seems to be the most consistent across the different tools, yet these estimates vary by as much as 2 to 1.

SLIM is based on the Norden model; GECOMO is based on CoCoMo; ESTIMACS is based on function points; and the remaining models are similar to CoCoMo in that they use various mathematical functions to compute estimates from SLOC.

These results point to the importance of calibrating the models to the working environment of the programming team. Business data-processing projects are different from real-time military projects. The cost models must be calibrated for one or the other, and cannot be reliably used for both kinds of projects. CoCoMo has been criticized for being inaccurate, principally because poor selection of the cost driver rankings can vary the estimates by up to a factor of 40. However, the ability to calibrate the models against a list of actual project values makes this CASE tool the best possible method of obtaining reasonably accurate estimates.

CoCoMo makes no pretense about its ability to model what actually goes on in a software development project. Instead, CoCoMo is based on observed data — not theories about the software development process. The observations are fed back into the tool to make improved estimates. It would be a mistake to attempt to explain the process part of software engineering through CoCoMo; instead, CoCoMo should be used to give an expert software engineer information for the purpose of making intelligent decisions.

Terms and Concepts

actuals
communication effort
development mode
drivers
duration
effort
function point
KDSI
MM

peak FSP
power curve
productivity
rapid prototyping
software lifecycle
state of technology
TDEV
waterfall model

DISCUSSION QUESTIONS

1. Show that K is the area under the Norden-Rayleigh power curve by taking the limit of y as time goes to infinity.

2. Suppose $\$U$ = \$30,000 and K = 100. What is the development cost of a software project if the Norden-Rayleigh-Putnam model is used?

3. Plot the curve of S_S versus difficulty, D. Plot S_S versus complexity, C. What can you say about code productivity as a function of difficulty or complexity?

4. Suppose a software project is estimated to require 50,000 lines of source code to complete. Also, the project is thought to be extremely complex, C = 27. What will be the total effort if the project develops the 50,000 lines of code in three years? Suppose the project succeeds — what level of technology, T, was observed? Now perform a similar calculation using intermediate CoCoMo Organic mode — assume all but the CPLX cost driver is nominal.

5. Given a level of technology, T = 10,000, and a development time t_d = 2 years, how much effort is needed to develop 28,000 lines of code? Using $KDSI$ = 28, compute the effort needed using basic CoCoMo Organic mode calculations. How do the two results compare?

6. In question 5, what happens to K when t_d is changed to 1.75? 1.5? Draw a graph of K versus t_d.

7. Use Brooks' model and application constant $m = 2 \times 10^{-7}$ to estimate the number of lines of source code that a single programmer can produce in one year. How many lines of code can a single programmer produce in one year according to the Putnam equations? According to CoCoMo equations? What does this tell you about the validity of these models for extremely small projects?

8. Use the Brooks, Norden-Rayleigh-Putnam, and CoCoMo models to estimate the time to develop a computer program for one of your programming classes. What assumptions did you make for each model? How did the estimates compare?

9. In Brooks' modified model, suppose $K_d(1)$ = 10, and K_c = 0.05. Given these parameters, what is the best sized team?

10. Discuss or solve the optimization problem for finding the minimum effort equation for Brooks' model equations when m varies from programmer to programmer. Let each application constant be denoted by m_i for i = 1, 2, ... , n. Can you compute the best sizes S_j now?

11. Discuss how programmer productivity might vary between two teams developing the same application program if one team develops the application in an assembler language, and the other team develops in a high-level language.

12. Use CoCoMo to compute the time and effort to develop a program of size 64 KDSI. Assume the same cost drivers in each case, but compare the results obtained for each of the modes: Organic, Semidetached, and Embedded. What do these results tell you about the productivity of programmers in each category of "difficulty"?

REFERENCES AND FURTHER READING

1. Institute of Electrical and Electronics Engineers, Inc. 1983. *ANSI/IEEE Standard Glossary of Software Engineering Terminology, Std 729–1983*. New York: Institute of Electrical and Electronics Engineers, Inc.

2. Brooks, F. P. 1975. *The Mythical Man-Month*. Reading, MA: Addison-Wesley.

3. Norden, P. 1970. "Using Tools For Project Management." *Management of Production*; ed. M.K. Starr. Baltimore, MD: Penguin Books.

4. Boehm, B. W. 1975. "The High Cost of Software," In *Practical Strategies for Developing Large Software Systems*; ed. E. Horowitz, 3–14. Reading, MA: Addison-Wesley.

5. Weiner-Ehrlich, W. K., J. R. Hamrick, and V. F. Rupolo. 1984. "Modeling Software Behavior in Terms of a Formal Life Cycle Curve: Implications for Software Maintenance." *IEEE Transactions on Software Engineering* SE-10, no. 4 (July): 376–383.

6. Moranda, P. B. 1978. "Software Quality Technology: (Sad) Status of; (Unapproached) Limits to; (Manifold) Alternatives to." *Computer Magazine* 11, (November): 72–78.

7. Boehm, B. W. 1981. *Software Engineering Economics*, Englewood Cliffs, NJ: Prentice-Hall.

8. Albrecht, A. J., and J. E. Gaffney. 1983. "Software Function, Source Lines of Code, and Development Effort Prediction: A Software Science Validation." *IEEE Transactions Software Engineering* SE-9, no. 6 (November): 639–648.

9. Behrens, C. A. "Measuring the Productivity of Computer Systems Development Activities with Function Points." *IEEE Transactions Software Engineering* SE-9, no. 6 (November): 648–652.

10. Baskette, J. 1987. "Lifecycle Analysis of an Ada Project." *IEEE Software* 4, no. 1 (January): 40–54.

11. Kemerer, C. F. 1987. "An Empirical Validation of Software Cost Estimation Models." *Communications of the ACM* 30, no. 5 (May): 416–429.

12. Rubin, H. A. 1987. "A Comparison of Software Cost Estimation Tools." *System Development* 7, no. 5 (May).

13. Boehm, B. W. 1984. "Software Engineering Economics." *IEEE Transactions on Software Engineering* SE-10, no. 1 (January): 4–21.

14. Putnam, L. H. 1978. "A General Empirical Solution to the Macrosoftware Sizing and Estimating Problem." *IEEE Transactions Software Engineering* SE-4, no. 4 (July): 345–361.

3

The Project

PREVIEW

The project is the message — success depends on how well the project is organized, focused, managed, defined, estimated, anticipated, and staffed. Every project begins with planning documents. In this chapter we describe two planning documents: the SCM Plan and the SQA Plan. They describe the objectives of the project, the level of quality expected, and how that level of quality can be assured.

Next, we look at the people who are going to do the work. Team structure is important because we know programmer productivity is largely affected by communication among team members. We define the responsibilities of each member of a software development team and give guidelines for productive participation.

Finally, we examine how to decompose the time estimates given by CoCoPro, activities given by the SCM Plan, and structure of the team into a responsibility matrix and a schedule of activities. A CPM diagram summarizes what is to be done, by whom, and when it must be completed. The CPM diagram is used to track advances or bottlenecks throughout the development phase.

THE PROJECT PLAN

The software development project consists of plans, people, machines, social structures, and relationships too numerous to fully describe here. Instead, we describe the nature and content of a miniature version of a real-world project which we'll call the Development Project. This project, however, has most of the components and complexities typically associated with a larger commercial project. Thus it provides an excellent learning opportunity. The principal components of the Development Project are the Plan, the Team, and the CASE tools used to manage it.

Like all well-organized projects, our project begins with a **project plan** — *a management document describing the approach that will be taken for the project. The plan typically describes the goal of the project, the resources it will require, the methods that will be used, the configuration management and quality assurance procedures that will be followed, the schedules, the project organization, and so on*[1].

Two new terms are introduced in the definition of Project Plan. The first is **configuration management** — *(1) the process of identifying and defining the configuration items in a system, controlling the release and change of these items throughout the system lifecycle, recording and reporting the status of configuration items and change requests, and verifying the completeness and correctness of configuration items, (2) a discipline applying technical and administrative direction and surveillance to (a) identify and document the functional and physical characteristics of a configuration item, (b) control changes to those characteristics, and (c) record and report change processing and implementation status*[1].

THE (SOMETIMES HUMOROUS) LAWS OF PROJECT PLANNING

Many books have been written on how to manage large and complex projects, but the field of project management remains elusive. These rules are perhaps as accurate and fitting as any we know:

- Projects progress quickly until they reach 90% complete, then they remain 90% complete forever.
- The first 90% of a project takes 90% of the effort; the last 10% of the project takes 90% of the effort.
- Murphy's Law: If something can go wrong, it will.
- The trapdoors to failure outnumber the shortcuts to success. — *L. B. Johnson*
- For every complex problem, there is a solution — that won't work. — *H. L. Mencken*
- No problem is so formidable that you can't just walk away from it. — *C. Schulz*
- Whenever anyone says "theoretically," they really mean "not really." — *David Parnas*

This lengthy definition of configuration management might be simply stated as the process of controlling complexity and change in a project. The "things" being controlled and changed are called **configuration items** — *(1) a collection of hardware or software elements treated as a unit for the purpose of configuration management, (2) an aggregation of hardware/software, or any of its discrete portions that satisfies an end-use function and is designated for configuration management*[1]. Configuration items vary widely in size, complexity, and type. They may be any artifact of the project, for example, aircraft, program listings, or test data.

The overriding goals of configuration management are the goals of software engineering: to assure completion of the project on time, on budget, and at a level of quality sufficient to satisfy customer requirements. **Quality** — *the totality of features and characteristics of a product that bears on its ability to satisfy customer needs* — is the dominant factor in software development projects[1]. Therefore, emphasis is placed on **quality assurance** — *a planned and systematic pattern of all actions necessary to provide adequate confidence that the product conforms to technical requirements* — in software development configuration management[1].

Quality control and orderly progression of the project are both guaranteed by stepping through the project. At each step a **baseline** — *a specification or product that has been formally reviewed and agreed upon, that thereafter serves as the basis for further development, and that can be changed only through a formal change control procedure* — is established before the next step is allowed to begin[1]. Baselines usually correspond with major events such as design or code walk-throughs.

We will follow the IEEE Standard for Software Configuration Management Plans[1] in the following documentation. The plan describes a project that will be carried out in the remainder of this book. The product to be produced is CoCoPro, the CoCoMo CASE tool used in the previous chapter. The goal of the project is to produce a commercial quality software product that will run on an Apple Computer Corporation Macintosh™ computer.

The Development Project Plan

The following reporting format has been adapted from the IEEE Standard for Software Configuration Management Plans. It gives an overview of the Development Project and how it is to be achieved. This plan will henceforth be referred to as the SCM (Software Configuration Management) plan.

1. Introduction
This section provides an overview of the SCM Plan for the Development Project to be carried out in concert with this book.
(a) Purpose of the Plan
This plan establishes the ground rules for conducting a project in software engineering. The SCM plan is to be used as a guide during the design, implementation, and testing of the Development Project and should be consulted by the development team whenever questions or conflicts arise.

(b) Scope of the SCM Plan

The SCM Plan is meant to produce a commercial quality CASE tool for computing software development cost estimates using the intermediate CoCoMo model described in chapter two. This product, called CoCoPro, will be able to retain actual data on previously completed projects and will be able to use this data to calibrate the intermediate cost models of Boehm to derive more accurate cost estimations.

The SCM Plan also calls for complete documentation throughout the development phase: requirements analysis, design, interface, source code, test cases, test data, and sample run documentation. In addition, a complete user manual will be produced, along with working examples of the completed product. Programmers will be expected to keep a daily log of their activities and the problems they encounter, as well as time and effort logs that can be collected by the project leader, so that numerical values can be established for the length of time and amount of effort that went into each component of the project. All documents must be available on diskette and kept current to within two days. These diskettes must be available upon request during any period.

The CoCoPro software will be fully designed, documented, and implemented on the Apple Macintosh™ computer. Furthermore, time schedules and responsibilities will be monitored on a weekly basis to assure progress. Specific activities, assignments, and work breakdowns will be developed in later sections of this chapter.

(c) Definitions and Acronyms

CoCoMo and CoCoPro are to be used as described in the previous chapter. Also, various cost driver acronyms will be used according to the definitions given by Boehm[2]. SCM means Software Configuration Management. All other terms conform to the IEEE Glossary of Software Engineering Terminology[3].

(d) References

See chapter two for additional references.

2. Management

This section of the SCM describes the organization and responsibilities of the software development team members.

(a) Briefly, the project will be managed by a designated Lead Programmer, as described in the next section. Typically, programmers will be divided into several teams, each team having one Lead Programmer, one Test and Documentation Programmer, and one or more Associate Programmers. Technical management is provided by the Lead Programmer.

An organizational chart for each team will be posted by the Lead Programmer. This chart is to be used by team members for reporting results, problems, successes, and information useful to other team members.

(b) SCM Responsibilities and Interface Control
Each team will conduct frequent meetings for the purpose of communicating interface information, changes, and updates to the state of the project. Walk-throughs will be conducted after the requirements document has been written, after the design documentation has been prepared, and after the initital coding has been completed. At each stage, either approval or re-work will be decided before continuing on to the next stage.

The form of requirements, design, and program documentation, as well as details such as interface specification, will be described in later chapters. These documents will be produced by all members of the team, but they will be maintained by the Test and Documentation Programmer. Copies of the current version must be obtained from the Test and Documentation Programmer.

(c) Policies and Procedures
Naming conventions, tools, and other issues that arise during development will be decided by the Lead Programmer of each team. These include but are not limited to:

> Architecture of the software system
> Program modules and their names
> Version designation numbers and what they mean
> Format of specifications, manuals, and other forms of documentation
> Changes in requirements and/or functionality
> Changes in the user interface
> Amount and level of testing
> Quality standards and quality metrics

The project will be based on both the performance of the resulting program and the quality of its implementation. All artifacts will be inspected: design, coding, testing, quality of logs, quality of interpersonal communication with other members of the team, and documentation.

3. SCM Activities
This section identifies the activities to be performed by the team and its management in order to assure quality of the product.

(a) Configuration Identification
Identify the baselines and correlate them to the steps or phases of the lifecycle. For example, a *functional baseline* is a specification of what functions are to be delivered to the customer. In this case, the functions are defined by the CoCoMo intermediate model:

> Compute MM and TDEV given KDSI and the 15 cost drivers of the CoCoMo model
>
> Collect and maintain a database of actuals
>
> Calibrate the model from the actuals

Print reports

Also compute associated values such as productivity, peak FSP, and so on, as defined in chapters one and two

As another example, a design baseline is established by accepting the design made by the team and approved by the customer. Similarly, a *code baseline* is established by accepting the first version of the source code prior to integration testing.

(b) Configuration Control

During the various phases of the project all change documents will be given to the Lead Programmer, who will check them and then pass them on to the Test and Documentation Programmer, who in turn will incorporate them into the "most current version" of the project. The Test and Documentation Programmer is responsible for keeping backup copies, current versions, and maintaining version control at all times. All other members of the team must obtain "current version" copies of the program and documentation from the Test and Documentation Programmer.

Interface and implementation changes are to be submitted to the Lead Programmer only. After approval, the Lead Programmer will give the change to the Test and Documentation Programmer, who will incorporate the change into the current version. The new versions will then be passed on to other members of the team in a controlled and orderly fashion (complete with version numbers, etc.).

(c) Configuration Status Accounting

All programmers will report their progress in a weekly (or more frequent) meeting of the team. The report will identify:

What subsystem is being worked on

The status of the job at the end of the previous meeting

What has been done since the last meeting

Any problems that have arisen

Goals to be reached before the next meeting

Whether the work is going according to schedule

The Lead Programmer will report the status of the team to the customer. If problems are reported, the customer will work with the Lead Programmer to come up with solutions. All changes in the specifications must be acceptable to the customer.

The customer will not attend team meetings, but the Lead Programmer will be expected to maintain a log of meetings identifying:

When the meeting was held and who attended

What was discussed, emphasizing progress and delays

What problems were encountered and what solutions were proposed

What goals were agreed upon for the next meeting

Miscellaneous comments

4. Tools, Techniques, and Methodologies

Most of these will be described throughout the remainder of the book, but here are a few examples:

The standard Macintosh™ user interface will be followed at all times.

The (reusable) toolbox routines will be used as much as possible.

Libraries of (reusable) routines will be used as much as possible.

Low-level toolbox and library routines will be avoided whenever higher level routines are available — for example, the low-level file I/O routines will be avoided.

Designs must be traceable, that is, a maintenance programmer must be able to trace the evolution of the project from requirement, to design, to coding, and ultimately to the end product by reading the various documents produced by the team.

Coding standards must be followed without exception.

Design consistency must be followed. An object-oriented design philosophy will be advocated and will be described later in more detail.

CASE tools will be used: CoCoPro to estimate the time and effort needed to achieve success, Micro Planner Plus™ to design and control the project, PRISM FreeFlow™ to specify system requirements and functionality, Structure Charts and PDL (Program Design Language) to specify software architecture, an object-oriented design rule to specify separately compiled modules, Think Pascal™ Programming Environment for implementation and unit testing, and various other methods to test, document, and polish the final product.

In addition, a variety of tools specifically designed for the Macintosh™ will be used to aid in development. For example, graphic editors will be used to design the user interface objects such as menus, dialogs, and windows. The output files produced by such editors will be processed by a resource compiler, Rmaker, prior to combining the application code with the user interface resources.

The SCM Plan is our starting point for beginning the Development Project. It forms a planning baseline from which other (updated) baselines can be obtained.

The Quality Assurance Plan

Recall the importance of early defect removal and the concept of defect detection during requirements specification and design. The SQA (Software Quality Assurance) plan provides a method for achieving early defect detection and removal.

1. Purpose

This SQA Plan is for achieving a commercial quality version of CoCoMo called CoCoPro, that includes both executable application software and associated documentation. In other words, the resulting CoCoPro software must be free of errors and robust enough to be used by someone other than the developers. It must recover from all errors and compute correct estimates based on the CoCoMo intermediate mode equations. It must be easy and straightforward to use, performing its calculations quickly. The software must run on all models of the Macintosh™ personal computer, and must be free of all model machine dependencies.

2. Reference Documents
   Consult the SCM Plan for additional references.

3. Management
   The SQA Plan is to be carried out by all members of the software development team. Each Associate Programmer will thoroughly debug and test all modules he or she writes; all modules will be tested a second time by the Test and Documentation Programmer prior to incorporation into the "current version"; design and code walk-throughs will be carried out by the Lead Programmer in the presence of the customer; system integration will be performed by the entire team.

4. Documentation
   Three test documents will be created:
   (a) SRS (Software Requirements Specification) lists the functional and performance requirements of the product.
   (b) SDD (Software Design Description) lists the major components of the system architecture and the interfaces among the components.
   (c) SVVP (Software Verification and Validation Plan) is a checklist to verify that the functions and performance specification of the SRS have been met, that the SDD specification has been implemented in code, and that the code executes correctly.

5. Standards, Practices, and Conventions
   The team leader will publish a list of standards and practices to be followed during design, implementation, and testing.

6. Reviews
   The team leader will conduct one or more of the following reviews:
   (a) SRR (Software Requirements Review): A check of the completeness and adequacy of the functions to be implemented.
   (b) PDR (Program Design Review): A check of the technical adequacy of the system architecture.
   (c) CDR (Critical Design Review): A check of the adequacy and completeness of the modular design.
   (d) SVVR (Software Verification and Validation Review): A check of the SVVP list.
   (e) A Functional Audit prior to release of the product to make sure it works.

(f) A Physical Audit to make sure all elements such as code and documentation, are present.

Test Data and Test Results will be documented and retained as part of the programmer's documentation (on the Documentation disk). Each programmer will keep a log of unit testing and results.

Test cases and test adequacy will be determined by the Test and Documentation Programmer following guidelines and techniques described in this book.

7. Problem Reporting

All problems will be logged in a daily log maintained by each team member. These problems will be discussed by the team at each meeting. Solutions to problems will be logged.

Changes to interfaces, implementations, and documentation will be coordinated by the Test and Documentation Programmer as described in the SCM Plan.

8. Tools and Techniques

Consistency among all documents produced by CASE tools will be maintained at all times. The data dictionary created by design will be consistent (same names, types, constants, etc.) with the source code. This consistency permits any programmer to trace the design, code, and test phases.

The Think Pascal Debugging tools will be turned on at all times, except when the final version of the product is generated (using the "Build and Save..." command). The final version of CoCoPro must run as a stand-alone application.

9. Controls

Code and documentation control will be performed by the Test and Documentation Programmer as described in the SCM Plan.

This completes the SQA Plan for the Development Project. Again, this plan gives a test baseline that can be modified and improved as the project evolves.

In summary, the following checklist should be consulted when developing quality control checks. The product or its documentation should be:

Unambiguous
Complete
Verifiable
Consistent
Modifiable
Traceable
Usable

We will refer to these quality attributes again when evaluating various ways to specify both the design and implementation of software products.

These two documents will be constantly consulted, questioned, and sometimes modified as the team progresses from start to finish.

TEAM STRUCTURE

Software engineers rarely work alone. They nearly always work in a group called a *development team*. There are many ways to organize a development team, but we are mainly concerned with the organizational structure of a novice team, one that will be implementing a small or medium-size project for the first time. This team structure is similar to a typical real-world team except for the team size, the duration of the project, and the task of recording progress and lessons learned throughout the project.

Chief Programmer Team

The **Chief Programmer Team**, which we mentioned in chapter one, is *a software development group consisting of a chief programmer, a backup programmer, a secretary/librarian, and additional programmers and specialists as needed. The team employs support procedures designed to enhance group communication and to make optimum use of each member's skills*[1]. The CPT is good for large teams that expect turnover to occur during the project. This usually means less-experienced programmers join the team before the work is completed. Hence, senior programmers must assist junior programmers.

The **Chief Programmer** is *a senior-level programmer whose responsibilities include producing key portions of the software, coordinating the activities of the other team members, and providing overall technical expertise of the software being developed*[1]. The Chief Programmer is so critically important to the success of the project that a *backup programmer* is employed to aid the Chief Programmer and to step into the Chief Programmer's position when needed.

ON TEAM STRUCTURE

A variety of team structures have been proposed by software engineers. A democratic structure establishes communication links between all members of the team. A lead programmer communicates equally with all other programmers and the responsibility for overall quality of the project is more or less distributed over all members.

The obvious disadvantage of this structure is the $N(N-1)/2$ growth in communication links as the size, N, of the team grows. This can cause loss of productivity as we saw earlier.

The Chief Programmer team structure was advocated in the early 1970s as a remedy for poor-quality software. It is modeled after the hierarchical structure of a corporation or military organization. This cuts down on communication overhead by reducing the number of communication links in the team.

The Chief Programmer is responsible for the overall quality and timeliness of the work. The other members of the team are dedicated to helping the Chief Programmer succeed.

The Development Project will most likely be done by a team of novice programmers who are experimenting with various approaches to team programming. Therefore the CPT must be modified to accommodate the pedagogical nature of the project. Instead of the CPT structure, we advocate a development programmer team structure.

Development Programmer Team

This team structure is designed to help students implement a small project and to teach the importance of teamwork, application structuring, and programming-in-the-large. This team consists of three or more people assigned to specific duties and organized as follows:

Lead Programmer

Writes glue code
Designs data structures and selects algorithms
Creates and maintains application global data structures
Creates and maintains application resource files
Writes main processing modules
Chairs meetings and keeps log of time and effort of team
Creates and maintains chart of activities and completion dates
Performs quality control checks and the final application test
Conducts walk-throughs
Assigns programmers to tasks as needed

Test and Documentation Programmer

Prepares test cases
Performs unit and system tests
Maintains most-recent version of all modules in application
Maintains design and system architecture documentation
Maintains (computerized) interface specifications for all modules
Collects and catalogs documentation from associates
Creates user manual
Creates glossary of terms (user and programmer terms)
Keeps (computerized) minutes of meetings
Keeps time and activity log for own activities for Lead Programmer
Participates in walk-throughs

Associate Programmer

Writes structure charts for own modules
Writes detail design diagrams for own routines
Writes source code, .DOC, and other files for own code
Performs unit testing and submits results to Test Programmer
Submits updates to interfaces and routines to Lead Programmer
Submits changes to resource files to Lead Programmer
Keeps log of time and effort spent and submits to Lead Programmer
Participates in walk-throughs

A typical team consists of a lead programmer, test and documentation programmer, and two or three associate programmers. A team of this size can produce an application of 5–10K lines of source code in 10 weeks if they are good, well-organized programmers.

Logs are kept as a record of time and effort spent on each activity in the project. This data becomes very important and useful for estimating future project times and effort, and for identifying problem areas. For example, if a particular team has difficulty with file access, it will show up in several programmer logs. This information can be used to improve team performance through training or informal discussions.

The log in Figure 3-1 shows many instances of communication with other members of the team. Statements like, "...worked with...," and "met with..." suggest a lot of interaction. At least four other members were consulted during the three-month span.

CoCoMo Project Time Log for Jones

date	hours	task
1/12	3	structure charts & diagrams
1/13	1	menus & events
1/18	2	worked on globals
1/27	1	updating discs
2/2	2	preliminary coding
2/4	4	plum diagrams (detail design)
2/5	2	documenting & miscellaneous glue code
2/6	1	entering times in log
2/7	4	glue code and testing menu
2/8	2	met with Sue, worked on dialogs
2/9	2	met with Jan to help with code
2/10	3	met with Karl, worked on code
2/11	2	met with John, calculations
2/14	4	testing & debugging
2/16	4	coding & testing
2/20	3	met with Jan & Karl, file reading
2/21	3	worked with Karl
2/24	5	debugging/gluecode
2/25	4	updating time log & debugging
2/26	3	coding & working with Karl, file accessing problems
2/27	3	working with Sue on Interfacing Dialogs
2/28	4	preparing materials for presentation
3/1	2	coding DoHistory and preparing materials for presentation
3/2	6	integrating and testing
3/3	5	integrating and testing
3/4	3	making copies of code and charts for class
3/5	6	coding and testing on file accessing
3/6	4	integrating read/write to files
3/7	3	coding error checking and debugging
3/9	6	history file accessing. Worked with Karl
3/10	6	correcting errors in History file reading
3/11	10	History calculations/worked with John and printed files
3/12	10	printing files, updating logs, integrating and testing

FIGURE 3-1. Sample programmer log book

THE PSYCHOLOGY OF DEVELOPMENT TEAMS

The main purpose of the Development Project is to provide experience with programming-in-the-large and to teach how to work as team members. This goal is difficult to achieve when the members of the team do not know each other, lack "real-world" motivations, and are more interested in software than they are in psychology. Nonetheless, team interaction is critical to the success of the project. This theme recurs time and again in software engineering. Therefore, it is productive to examine team dynamics in some detail.

We first look at the logs of two teams that developed the same CoCoPro CASE tool proposed here as the Development Project. Each team maintained a log as required by the SCM Plan. As we shall see, one log was written by a successful team, while the other describes the activities of an unsuccessful team.

A Team That Works

The *team log* is a record of what happened during the development period. It is important to analyze team logs to discover why some programming projects succeed while others fail. For example, here is an excerpt from a team log showing normal progress:

Minutes of CoCoMo Project Team #1

January 12 Set appropriate dates on work schedule breakdown. Design to be essentially complete by January 26.

Discussed the meaning of the Drivers menu, and the meaning of the New item in the File menu.

January 14 Discussed the "provide history actuals" dialog and other user interface issues. Terminology of KDSI and EDSI debated. Changed File menu to Project menu to more accurately reflect the meaning of the commands in it. Also changed the Drivers menu by removing all references to abbreviation of drivers and lumping those commands under a Change Driver Values item. One dialog to be used to allow these changes.

Adopted some coding standards. Prefixes of all exported data or procedures to be the first three letters of the unit in uppercase followed by an underscore.

All identifiers to be lowercase with underscore separators between logical separations or words. Constants to be in all uppercase letters.

January 19 Discussed whether or not to allow multiple components in a project. Adopted the idea of placing each component in a separate section in the report file, along with a summary for the whole project.

Looked at the history records and how they should be formatted.

Examined the call hierarchy of the units and adopted some general rules.

January 21 Reviewed global declarations and constants. Adopted the idea of linked lists being used to hold the data in memory, but left exact details of implementation to Bob in CoCoMo_RAM.

Decided to allow the user to calculate the results of a component and see these displayed in a window. Also decided that we would let the user see the results of the calculation of a project in a separate dialog.

January 26 Changed right menu and split the Change Driver Attributes item into four components (Product, Personnel, Computer, and Project instead of just Driver) to reflect forced structure of the underlying dialog. These had to be adjusted due to the limits of the Macintosh dialog manager.

February 2 Discussed history files and how the user would enter new data into a history file and how the form of these should be done. Deferred decision until next meeting to study the problem in more detail.

February 4 Examined changes to History menu, and decided to make the entire menu system more homogeneous. Files will be handled with New, Open, and Save (or Save as...) commands in the Project, History, and Drivers menus.

Set the date of the first integration of components as being February 6 at 2:30 p.m. Intend to at least get all dialogs working through the menu system, and perhaps write report files.

February 6 Pushed back date of integration of project to February 9. Problems will undoubtedly be found, especially with code that uses another's code.

February 9 Integration begins! With some hitches early because of changes in interfaces, the menu comes up and dialogs for data entry are showing up as planned. Hitches in how button numbers are handled caused some problems that could not be immediately solved.

February 11 Second integration meeting. Made excellent progress with more items working.

February 11–March 2 Continued meetings for integration. Polishing of code. Last minute glitch after building project. T/Doc programmer will check initialization routines to see if that is the problem.

This record of team activity reveals some important characteristics of the successful team. Examining the log shows this team to be communicative, pragmatic, purposeful, flexible, and able to deal with complexity.

- *Communication* The team members were communicative, holding many short meetings that focused on specific problems.
- *Pragmatism* Problems were identified and decisions made to solve them, but if a quick decision was not possible, the decision was deferred until the problem could be thought out.
- *Purpose* The team established goals and identified action items to be set into motion.
- *Flexibility* Changes in the design were made when it was realized that the design was inadequate or awkward. Similarly, due dates were changed when it was realized that they were unrealistic.
- *Complexity* Complex or difficult areas were identified and isolated so extra effort could be applied.

Thus, the successful team is one that can communicate, be pragmatic when decisions cannot be easily made, establish and achieve goals, remain flexible throughout the project, and conquer complex issues that arise unexpectedly.

A Team That Fails

The team log and all other documentation must be kept up to date at all times. This helps to identify failures early on and to initiate corrective actions. A log from an unsuccessful project readily shows what can go wrong. This log has many indicators of disaster.

Minutes of CoCoMo Project Team #2

January 9 We set regular meeting times twice weekly: on Wednesdays at 2000 and Sundays at 1700. We next discussed what the purpose of each file in our system is. Next meeting will be Sunday at 1700.

January 11 Bob typed up a brief explanation of what each file is for and what they all contain. A discussion followed to make sure everyone understood the details about each file. We need to decide on a data structure and then start writing code. Next meeting is Monday at 2000.

January 14 Three of the members did not show up. For the next meeting everyone needs to have ideas on what kind of data structure will be good for this project so we can discuss them and come up with a final version. Next meeting will be Sunday.

January 18 Outline of user's manual submitted by Sue. Not much discussion. Finally, we started to define what each associate programmer is responsible for and needs to accomplish. Further refinement and detail is left up to the individual. Everyone needs to come to the next meeting prepared and with interfaces.

January 21 We decided that file handling and file access were different but hard to totally separate, so those two associates will work closely together. They will write routines to get the contents of a file and put them into RAM.

There were a few problems with the data structure. Mainly that it wasn't general enough. The problems were taken care of and the corrected version can be seen in the file, DATA_STRUCT.doc. We defined what units are and discussed what each associate needs to know from the other associates. This includes what is imported, what is exported, and what is hidden.

January 28 Each associate presented the interface they came up with. We discussed each interface and refined them so they can all interact smoothly. This took a lot of time and discussion to get everyone to agree on the format and on what exactly (in terms of specific procedures) is required from each associate.

February 2 New idea came up. Put all the drivers from the Driver Menu into one dialog under one item, Change Driver Values, instead of 16 different items. The 15 cost drivers will each have radio buttons and when one of these is clicked, a data entry dialog box will appear below this dialog and the value can be modified or entered at that moment. Discussed further details of implementation. Next meeting will be Wednesday.

February 4 We thought about changing the history records to be doubly linked lists. RAM routines will get a handle to the data structure and pass that to the routines that need them. Everyone needs to work on coding this weekend and get as far as possible. We will work out all problems on Monday and see if the code fits together into one project. We will see how close we come.

February 9 So what exactly does File Access do? Some more constants need to be added to the globals. In order for anything to be added, one must make sure that no side effects will also be added. Use as parameters in the interface if at all possible so this is avoided. The new constants include: previous, next, select, done, ok, and cancel. Other dialog items will be local constants to the dialog unit.

February 16 At this meeting we mostly argued and discussed changes being made and what each associate needs to get done. We need to work on making sure the code that is written in each unit is written in such a way that it least affects the other units if changes must be made, i.e. when providing information for other units just fill a data structure or variable. Unit1 can get that information in any way it wants. Unit2 does not need to know anything about Unit1 except the name of the structure containing the information asked for. Our main problem at this time is COMMUNICATION.

February 18 No one showed up except Bob and Becky. We discussed the exact changes needed for the driver menu, i.e. there will be only three options, Driver Modify, Driver Select, and Driver Save. There was another slight error in the globals. STR255_TYPE was defined by us and it needs to be just STR255 so it will work in all the toolbox routines.

February 23 We got together on Saturday and Sunday and put it all together. It is almost working and just needs to be debugged and cleaned up and made user friendly.

February 26 Our project is working. Now what we must do is concentrate on making it beautiful and user friendly. We need to work on documentation and structure charts and plum diagrams. Deadline is March 3. Our deadline is our next meeting, Sunday at 2000. At that time we will meet for our own walk-through and testing.

March 1 We met to go over what has been done and what is left to do. The rest of the night and Monday we must finish everything for the alpha tests.

March 4 (After the Due Date) Should we pass records or handles in our final version? Final decision needs to be made tonight. OK, we will go with records. But our application is such that it should be easy to switch if one desires. It also should be easy to switch from RAM-based files to disk-based files if that is desired. We talked about all the error alerts we need. So far we have next to none. We need them for errors such as: Divide by zero, Wrong mode, File not open, Cost values are different than the current cost values in the report file. At least two history records need to be selected. Some of these might be able to be taken care of by simply disabling the menu item. We'll let Bob take care of that. We also need to set the dirty bit. Who? Main! We need to check for CoCoMo.Driver existence and make sure it's locked. If it's not, we must lock it so it can't be written to, only read from.

This team produced a barely working application that was unreliable and difficult to use. Why? An interpretation of the log tells why, and suggests how this team might improve its performance in future projects:

- *Communication* The team members were reluctant to meet, revealing a lack of commitment to the project. This uncommitted attitude is also clear in the team's lack of preparation and lack of action items. The major action item resulting from many of the meetings was simply a time for the next meeting. Unless members of the team are committed to the successful completion of the project, it is doomed to failure.

- *Pragmatism* Team members seemed uncertain about what to do. Decisions were postponed and difficult issues lingered on from one meeting to the next. Lingering decisions and action items need to be resolved at each meeting. Problems were rarely solved, therefore little progress was made.

- *Purpose* Either the design was not understood or it was not followed. Many discussions focused on the purpose of the application and how it was to operate. Early defect removal was impossible because members were not sure what the requirements and specifications were. As a result, many changes were mulled over throughout the project, which wasted time and prevented progress. Design walk-throughs and an emphasis on design documentation would have prevented this problem.

- *Flexibility* Desperation began to set in as the project neared its due date. This was evident in the compulsion to code. The team members turned their attention to coding before they were sure about the design. This came back to haunt them later when the program did not perform as expected and was not robust. Instead the team should have held off on coding until they were confident about their understanding of the task, even if it meant missing deadlines.

- *Complexity* Complex issues of interface specification, file formats, and error handling were never resolved. The complexity of the system therefore escalates and finally overwhelms the team. They were busy patching code when the due date arrived. Testing and documentation were put off until the end, but then time ran out and these two very important tasks never got done.

The team should have invested effort in conquering the complexity of the application early on. This means defining as soon as possible modules, interfaces, and sequential tasks. While such activity might appear to be wasteful because it does not produce lines of code, it would have served them well in the long run.

Team Dynamics

Classroom groups like the two teams described above have been studied by psychologists in order to understand how they arrive at solutions to problems, how they respond to peer leaders, and how their performance can be improved. The results of these classroom studies can be used by other groups to improve their chances of successfully solving group problems.

The Development Project has all of the traditional problems of communication, coordination, work, and interpersonal interaction that psychologists call *group dynamics*. Tuckman[3] found a pattern of development common to all groups as they struggle to solve a problem together. The pattern defines four phases which we have expressed in terms of software development:

1. Task Definition Phase. This is the period of time when team members define their tasks and set limitations on what they can do in the short time available. The project is broken into modules, and one or more module is assigned to each programmer. If a module is thought to be too large or complex, the team scales the module down to a manageable size. For example, the CoCoPro database might be run out of the main memory instead of from a disk file. This simplified version of the application can be done in a shorter period of time.

2. Emotional-Reactive Phase. During this period, team members react emotionally to their assigned tasks. This usually creates a problem because one or more members do not like the task assigned to them and resist carrying out the work. For example, a team member might feel unfairly burdened with the most difficult or time-consuming part of the project. This resentment is expressed as an unwillingness to complete the work.

3. Emotional-Proactive Phase. Following the emotional-reactive phase, feelings, opinions, and dislike for the tasks are openly discussed. The resentful, overworked person expresses concern and resentment to the others. It is important that these conflicts be resolved by the team before continuing. If the conflict persists, some members of the team will not remain committed, and the project will most likely fail.

4. Solution Phase. This is the period of time when productive work is accomplished. Plans can be made, and tasks performed. The team will remain in this phase as long as conflicts are resolved through an open exchange of feelings, information, and other concerns.

Most teams tend to alternate in a cyclical fashion between emphasizing work activities and social-emotional activities. In fact, most programmers will spend nearly half of their time on social-emotional concerns, without which the project would probably fail. The reasons so much time is dedicated to social-emotional concerns have been identified by Gibbs[4]. The phases given by Tuckman must be accompanied by:

1. Formation of trust: gaining of confidence in self and in the group.

2. Concentration as a group on the work to be done.

3. Achievement: success on small tasks leading to success on larger tasks.

4. Independence to do their own work for all of the group members.

These are important factors to be considered by the Lead Programmer because it is the Lead Programmer's job to motivate and assist the others. The Lead Programmer must foster trust, work, recognition for achievement, and participation in the design and coding of the product. He or she must also be able to move the team through the four phases of group development quickly, and with a minimum of "bloodshed." How is this done?

French[5] has studied the dynamics of leaders and suggests five qualities of power that can enhance leadership:

1. Expert Power: The leader is an outstanding or expert programmer.

2. Referent Power: Others admire or respect the leader.

3. Legitimate Power: The Lead Programmer was chosen by a respected supervisor.

4. Reward Power: The Lead Programmer can reward the other programmers through favoritism, money, or other incentives.

5. Coercive Power: The Lead Programmer can punish the other programmers with threats, intimidation, or other negative factors.

These sources of power are ordered from best to worst in terms of effectiveness. A democratic leader uses expertise and referent power to lead; an autocratic leader uses the other three sources of power to lead. The democratic leader will not only be able to lead the Development Team to success, but will risk less retaliation than the autocratic leader after the project is over!

What does it take to be a democratic leader? Here are some suggestions for the Lead Programmer:

- Be a source of ideas for getting things done.
- Suggest where to find information if you do not know how to do something.
- Suggest ways to present results to others.
- Offer help or advice voluntarily.
- Be open to group opinion and consensus decision-making.
- Distribute group functions — delegate authority. Let different people design, code, test, document, and furthermore, let them make suggestions for how best to do their tasks.
- Encourage independence. Make and guard interface specifications, but once defined, allow each programmer to go off and design his or her own modules, algorithms, and data structures.
- Stimulate open communication. Openly discuss progress or lack of it with all members of the team. If a problem exists, discuss it openly and get group suggestions on how to solve the problem. This applies to technical as well as other problems such as inadequate time, poor coding, errors, lack of understanding of the problem, and so on.

- Be well prepared and well organized. Come to meetings with a clear idea of what is to be achieved, and do not waste time.

Finally, here are some things to avoid doing:

- Hold on tightly to authority.
- Limit other team members' influence on the project.
- Compete with other powerful members of the team — instead, win them over to your point of view or recruit their support.

The Development Programmer Team is a learning lab. It will be perhaps the first large programming project that some members of the team have worked on. Accordingly, mistakes are going to be made and lessons learned. These mistakes need not be fatal to the project if all team members understand the dynamics of groups.

PROJECT STRUCTURE

The structure of a software development project can be examined from several vantage points. The software lifecycle vantage point suggests a sequence of phases as in the waterfall model. Each phase is divided into activities, and each activity is assigned to one or more person to be carried out in a prescribed period of time. The activities are usually organized in a hierarchical structure — one activity leading to others — until the entire project is completed.

A second view of the structure of a project focuses attention on the product itself. The project conforms to the parts of the program being constructed. The program can be organized as a hierarchy of components, thus this approach can also be organized in a hierarchical structure — one component of the product being completed before another — until the entire program is finished.

Both views of the project structure serve to identify what tasks are to be performed. These tasks are obtained by breaking down the components of the project one at a time into activities to be done. This breakdown is often called the WBS — work breakdown structure — of the project. We will discuss two methods of WBS documentation: the Product WBS and the Activity WBS.

Once a WBS document is produced, it is used to create a *responsibility matrix*, outlining tasks and identifying the people who will perform them. The responsibility matrix is a familiar document to most managers. It often includes due dates, slippages, and so forth, and is updated as the project unfolds to accommodate changes in schedule and availability of people.

Finally, large projects must be controlled throughout the lifecycle, so scheduling and tracking tools are used to monitor progress, avoid pitfalls, and eliminate bottlenecks. A CASE tool called Micro Planner Plus™ from Micro Planning Software Ltd. will be used to schedule the tasks defined by the WBS document. Micro Planner is a project management tool based on CPM (Critical Path Method) well known to managers in other disciplines.

The Work Breakdown Structure

We want to derive the responsibility matrix for the Development Project by decomposing it into two kinds of WBS's: the Product WBS and the Activity WBS. These two documents are usually derived after the preliminary planning and requirements analysis phases have been carried out. Requirements analysis is not discussed until the next chapter, but for the time let us assume that this has been done. The WBS documents of Figure 3-2 show hierarchical structure of the CoCoPro project from two vantage points: product and activities.

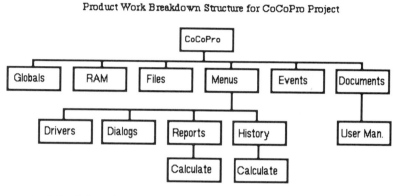

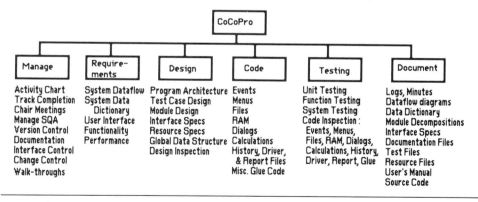

FIGURE 3-2. Product and activity WBS for CoCoPro

These documents can be used to derive the responsibility matrix as shown in Figure 3-3. In an actual matrix, individual names appear in place of Lead, T&D (Test and Document Programmer), A1, and A2 (Associate Programmers 1 and 2). The CoCoPro system can be constructed by four programmers:

Responsibility Matrix

Task	Lead	D&T	A1	A2
Responsibility Matrix	✓			
Completion dates	✓			
Chair team meetings	✓			
System-level design	✓			
Dataflow design	✓			
Data dictionary	✓			
System Architecture design	✓			
System Test	✓	✓		
Test cases		✓		
Test data		✓		
Manage SQA		✓		
Design Inspection	✓	✓	✓	✓
Collect logs, minutes, documents		✓		
Version control		✓		
Documentation		✓		
Source code		✓		
Interfaces		✓		
Meeting minutes		✓		
User's manual		✓		
Writes logs	✓	✓	✓	✓
Modules (Design & test)	✓		✓	✓
Globals	✓			
Events	✓			
Menus	✓			
Glue Code	✓			
Resources	✓		✓	✓
Files, RAM, History, Report, Driver			✓	
Dialogs, Calculations				✓
Misc. routines			✓	✓
Code Inspection	✓	✓	✓	✓
Unit tests	✓	✓	✓	✓
Functional		✓	✓	✓
Interface Modification		✓	✓	✓
Acceptance	✓			

FIGURE 3-3. Responsibility matrix for development terms

Scheduling and Tracking the Project

The WBS documents tell what to do, but they do not tell when to do each task. In fact, it is not clear from the WBS whether or not the project can be completed on schedule. We can use the estimates from CoCoPro along with the WBS list to schedule and track the progress of all activities. The project management technique called CPM — Critical Path Method — is used to locate and correct bottlenecks in our schedule. Micro Planner Plus™ incorporates CPM as well as tracking techniques to automate this kind of project management.

A Micro Planner Plus™ model begins with a simplified version of the Activity WBS. First, recall the effort and time estimates given by CoCoPro for 6.5 KDSI and the distribution shown in Figure 3-4:

MM   = 9.06
TDEV   = 5.77 months
FSP   = 1.57
Peak FSP = 1.90

These estimates suggest a two-person project lasting 5.77 months. How much can this project be compressed if we use four people? Recall Putnam's effort-time law, where K_d = FSP = 1.57, and t_d = TDEV = 5.77 months:

$$\text{Constant} = K_d \, t_d^4 = (1.57)(5.77^4) = 1{,}740.2$$

Maximum FSP = 4, so to get the average FSP we must divide by 1.21 (this comes from the CoCoMo equations for peak FSP). Hence, replacing K_d with 4.0/1.21 = 3.31, and substituting into the effort-time law,

$$1{,}740.2 = (3.31) \, t_d^4$$

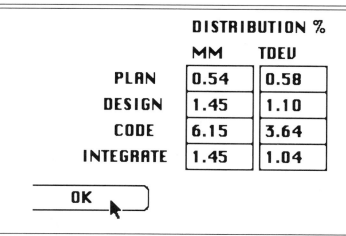

FIGURE 3-4. CoCoPro distribution of effect

yields the new TDEV of 4.8 months. The compression of time in exchange for effort is given by the multipliers

Time: Multiply by 4.8/5.77 = 0.83
Effort: Multiply by 3.31/1.57 = 2.1

This gives new distributions of effort and time, as in Table 3-1.

These numbers can be converted into weeks and days by assuming a 5-day week. Multiply by 19 to obtain the CoCoMo equivalent of days in a month, and then divide by 5, as in Table 3-2.

Now, decompose the activities one step further to arrive at an initial schedule of activities. The project includes documentation as well as planning, designing, coding, and integration. Further breakdown into these steps gives a good picture of what goes on in a small development project.

Planning time

(1,4) breaks down into Requirements Analysis: 1,2 and Test Cases: 0,2.

Design

(3,2) breaks down into Design: 2,0 and User's Manual: 1,2.

Code

(11,2) breaks down into Module Coding & Unit Testing: 8,3; Test Driver Coding: 1,3; Code Acceptance: 0,2 and Code Documentation: 0,4.

Integrate

(3,1) breaks down into System Test: 3,0 and System Acceptance: 0,1.

These estimates along with the project model shown as a CPM diagram is analyzed by Micro Planner Plus™ in the next section. Is this a workable schedule? Where are the bottlenecks? Are there enough resources (people) at the right time in the schedule?

TABLE 3-1. New effort and time distributions

Plan	1.13	.48
Design	3.05	.91
Code	12.92	3.02
Integrate	3.05	.86

TABLE 3-2. Conversion into weeks and days

Phase/Activity	Effort (People-Weeks)	Time (weeks, days)
Plan	1.13	1,4
Design	3.05	3,2
Code	12.92	11,2
Integrate	3.05	3,1

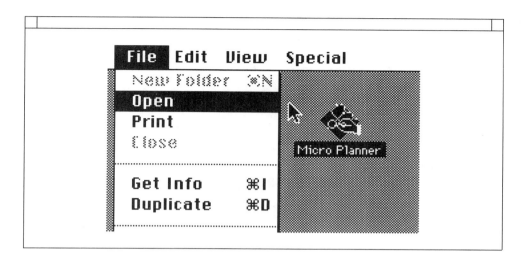

Planning with MicroPlanner Plus

To get a better idea of the details of the CoCoPro project, we use an automated tool called MicroPlanner Plus™. CPM is a method of project management in which the critical path is identified, and then all activities on the critical path are carefully managed so that the project can be completed on time. Slippage in any activity along the critical path will result in slippage of the entire project.

CPM tools like MicroPlanner Plus take a diagram containing labelled nodes and arcs as inputs and produce a variety of reports as outputs. A CPM diagram for a small software project is shown in Figure 3-5.

CPM Chart of Programming Project Activities

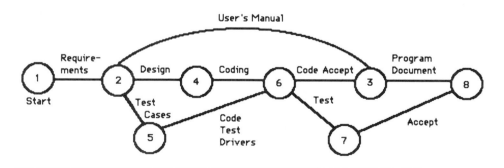

FIGURE 3-5. CPM diagram of a small project

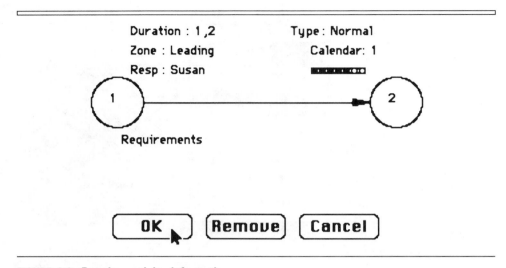

FIGURE 3-6. Entering activity information

The nodes of the diagram represent events — points in time marking the beginning or ending of an activity. The arcs represent activities — tasks to be performed in order to complete the project. The structure of the diagram indicates the order of activities. If one activity is to be finished before a second activity can begin, then the first activity is shown as an arc pointing to the beginning event of the second activity. Similarly, events and activities can take place at the same time, as shown by parallel arcs and nodes in the diagram.

The events and activities are labelled with useful information. For example, in Figure 3-6 an activity is labelled with estimates of how many weeks and days are required, the person assigned responsibility for the activity, and the "zone" or sub-project title. A zone is simply a name for a group of activities that must be done — such as Documentation, Coding, or Leading the project. Zones consume resources in the form of worker effort.

Each activity is assigned a resource (one of the previously defined zones) along with a relative start and finish time, see Figure 3-9. The start time is equal to the number of weeks and days into the activity when the resource is applied. Thus, a start time of 0 indicates that the resource is applied at the beginning of the activity. A finish time of 1,2 indicates that the resource is removed after 1 week and 2 days into the activity schedule.

A quantity of 0.75 means that only three-quarters of the resource are used by the activity. This probably means that the Leader is assigned to two or more activities and so must divide time between them. In this example, the Lead Programmer is assigned 75% of her time to Requirements Analysis; see Figure 3-8(a).

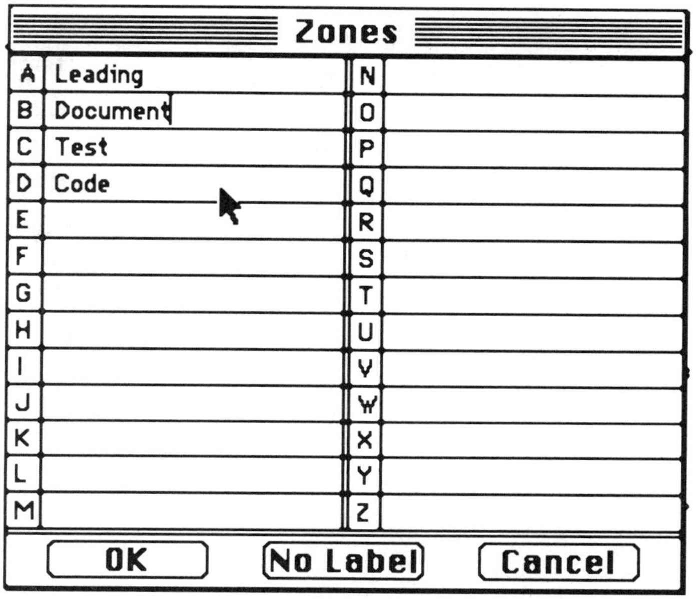

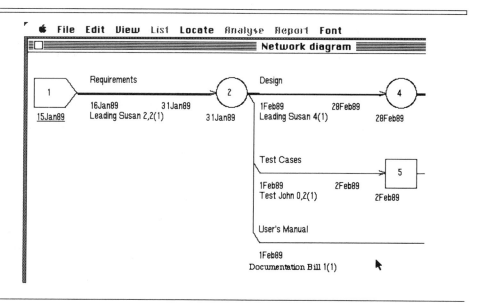

FIGURE 3-7. Creating zones

FIGURE 3-8a. Early stages of CoCoPro as a CPM diagram

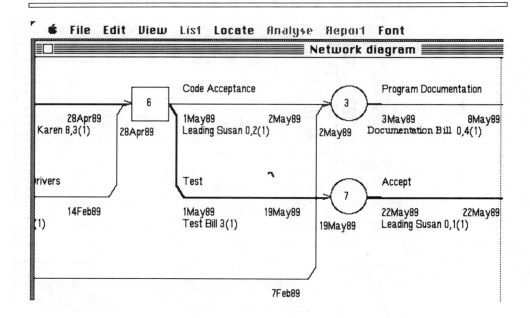

FIGURE 3-8b. Later stages of CoCoPro as a CPM diagram

It is possible that a resource becomes overloaded. The Histogram feature of Micro Planner Plus™ shows the loading on any one of the resources, see Figure 3-10. For example, the Test and Document Programmer will be overloaded near the end of the project.

No.	Resource	Start	Finish	Quantity	L
1	Leader	0	1,2	0.75	Total
2					
3					
4					
5					

Resource Usage

Activity [1] ━━ [2]   Cost : 16

FIGURE 3-9. Assigning resources

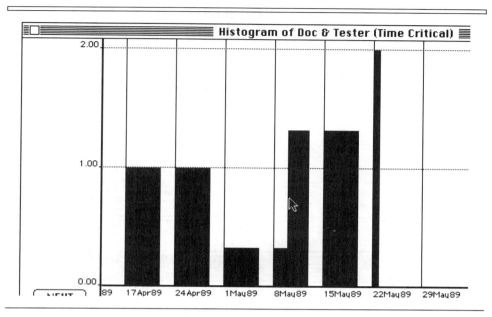

FIGURE 3-10. Resource overloading shown by Histogram display

After entering the events, activities, and the estimates of time and resources needed to complete each activity, we can produce various reports. These reports are updated as the project progresses, thus tracking the project. One of the most useful reports is the **Gantt Chart** — *a barchart showing when each activity begins and ends*, see Figure 3-11. The Gantt Chart and CPM charts both show the critical path through the diagram. The longest path is called critical, because the project cannot be completed in less time than it takes to go through the critical path.

The activities in the Gantt Chart are stretched over time. Each bar is divided into days and shaded according to its status. A dark bar means that the activity lies on the critical path; a gray bar means the activity is done in a certain time interval, but it does not lie on the critical path; and the outlined bars mean the resource is idle, indicating a slack period. Periods of slack time are candidates for management. If resources are spread over more than one activity, slack resources can be assigned to activities on the critical path to expedite completion of the project.

The Micro Planner Plus™ reports show starting and ending dates of all activities, give histograms of resource utilization, and tell where the bottlenecks (critical path activities) exist in the plan. For example, the Development Project Plan Report in Table 3-3 tells when to start each activity, and when each event (milestone) must occur.

TABLE 3-3. Development project plan report

Activity	Time Period
Requirements	16 Jan – 24 Jan
User Manual	25 Jan – 31 Jan
Design	25 Jan – 8 Feb
Code Test Drivers	27 Jan – 8 Feb
Code	8 Feb – 7 Apr
Code Accept	10 Apr – 11 Apr
Test	10 Apr – 28 Apr
Program Documentation	12 Apr – 17 Apr
Accept	1 May

FIGURE 3-11a. Gantt Chart of CoCoPro. Black indicates the critical path

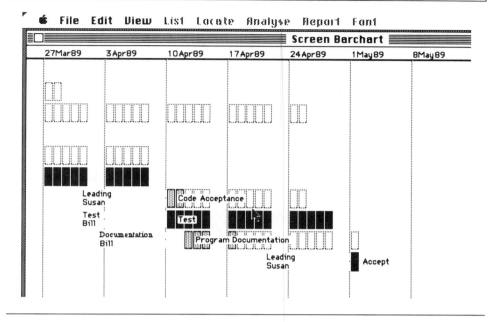

FIGURE 3-11b. Gantt Chart continued

STRUCTURE AND PURPOSE

Projects are complex systems in their own right: they consist of many interacting parts and relationships. In addition, much uncertainty surrounds the activities of a project. We cannot be certain, for example, exactly how long each activity will take, nor how many people are needed at any point in time. Software projects are even more uncertain because of our lack of understanding of the software development process.

The uncertainty of large, complex, software projects means we must apply all of the tools and techniques available to control the orderly progress toward completion. This includes planning carefully, making realistic estimates, and exercising tight control over resources. The wise project leader must establish milestones and guide the team toward achievement of the milestones on time and on budget.

The Development Team has additional complexities of its own. Novices, for example, are inexperienced at making estimates, and are not always sure of their ability to complete tasks within schedule. In addition, first-time team leaders face difficulties in leading their peers because of motivational forces. Careful recording of activities in logs, however, can be a rewarding and educational experience for all team members.

A well-defined team structure replaces uncertainty with concrete directions for what team members are to do and when they are expected to complete each activity. The product structure and the SQA Plan dictate what is expected of the final product.

The project has a strong purpose beginning with the SCM Plan and extending into the early phases of software development. The plan contains several steps:

- Complete the SCM Plan. This defines the goal of the project for all team members.
- Complete the SQA Plan. This establishes the quality objectives for all team members.
- Create an Activity WBS, and if possible a preliminary Product WBS. This provides details for the team.
- Decompose the Activity WBS into activities to be scheduled. This paves the way for using CPM tools.
- Use estimates from CoCoPro, for example, to arrive at time and effort estimates for the activities.
- Draw a CPM diagram using a CPM tool such as Micro Planner Plus™.
- Analyze the schedule; print various reports.
- Analyze the reports. Is the project realistic? Can it be done sooner? What are the bottlenecks?
- Use and refine the CPM schedule. Iterate while performing the activities defined by the CPM diagram.
- Keep logs so that the next project can be estimated more accurately based on the current project.

While we have not followed a complete project through its lifecycle, it is clear that each project must be monitored as it is completed. As new information about completion times and expended effort is obtained, we can update the information stored in Micro Planner Plus™ and produce new estimates or reveal new bottlenecks before it is too late to do anything about delays or overloads. The usefulness of such CASE tools becomes more apparent as they are used.

Terms and Concepts

activities	functional baseline
backup programmer	Gantt chart
baseline	group dynamics
CDR	overload
chief programmer	PDR
chief programmer team	pedagogical programmer team
code baseline	project plan
configuration item	quality
configuration management	quality assurance
CPM	resource
CPT	responsibility matrix
development team	SCM Plan
events	SDD

slack   team log
SQA Plan   WBS
SRS   zone
SVVP

DISCUSSION QUESTIONS

1. What is the purpose of the formal SCM Plan and SQA Plan? What are they used for, and how do they fit into the overall development process?

2. Does the sample Student Project CPM diagram give time estimates that match with the CoCoPro estimates? Explain differences between the two estimates. Compare average FSP obtained from the two methods.

3. Use CoCoPro and Micro Planner Plus™ to obtain a schedule of activities for a student project that consists of 10,000 lines of code. Assume the same list of activities as shown. Also assume the same CoCoPro cost drivers as used here.

4. Suppose the CoCoPro estimates of average and peak FSP recommend that a project use three and five people, respectively. Now, suppose your team consists of eight people. What do you do with this size of team?

5. Convert the following time estimates into weeks and days for use in Micro Planner Plus™:

1.55 months
0.75 months
1.33 years
13 days

6. Develop a schedule and resource allocation for the following CPM diagram. Identify the critical path and determine starting and ending dates for each activity. Assume the project starts on 16 January 1989.

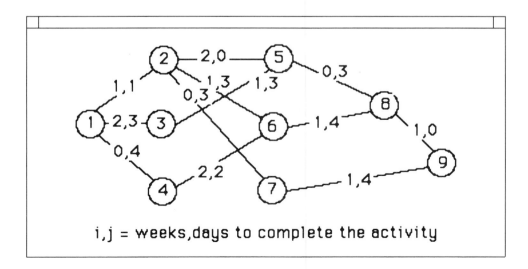

i,j = weeks,days to complete the activity

REFERENCES AND FURTHER READING

1. Institute of Electrical and Electronics Engineers, Inc. 1984. *Software Engineering Standards.* New York: Institute of Electrical and Electronics Engineers, Inc.

2. Boehm, B. W. 1981. *Software Engineering Economics.* Englewood Cliffs, NJ: Prentice-Hall.

3. Tuckman, B. W. 1965. "Developmental Sequence in Small Groups." *Psychological Bulletin* 63: 384–399.

4. Gibb, J. 1964. "Climate for Trust Formation," In *T-Group Theory and Laboratory Method*; eds. L. Bradford, J. Gibb, and K. Benne, 279–309. New York: John-Wiley and Sons.

5. French, J. Jr., and R. Raven. 1959. "The Bases of Social Power," In *Studies in Social Power*; ed. D. Cartwright. Ann Arbor, MI: Institute for Social Research.

4

The Elements of Design

PREVIEW

Every good design starts inside the head of a good designer, so good designers must possess insight into what makes a good software product. In this chapter we enumerate many of the attributes of good software product design. These attributes are usually obvious to the experienced programmer, but what is not so obvious is how a good designer trades one set of attributes for another in just the right places. Several examples illustrate the art of trading one desirable attribute for another more desirable attribute, and reveal in small measure how a designer decides among many alternatives.

One of the most important design considerations is the user interface. We use the novel specification language of the Macintosh system to define all windows, menus, icons, and dialogs in the application. This approach departs from traditional methods of specifying a software product, but modern software designers are highly aware of the need for a clean user interface. Thus, a thorough user interface specification constitutes the first step toward product design, which subsequently leads into the highly important requirements analysis step of the traditional waterfall lifecycle model.

WHAT THE DESIGNER MUST KNOW

Designing software is much more than learning a collection of rules, developing skill at programming, and knowing how to use a CASE tool. The software designer must know something about the application, understand and appreciate the many trade-offs involved in making a computer do what is desired in a fast, compact, and efficient manner, and be constantly aware of the need for human interface considerations. A product that simply works without failure is not sufficient — the product must satisfy many other needs as well. What are these needs and how do they affect the overall design? These are some of the issues addressed by the software designer.

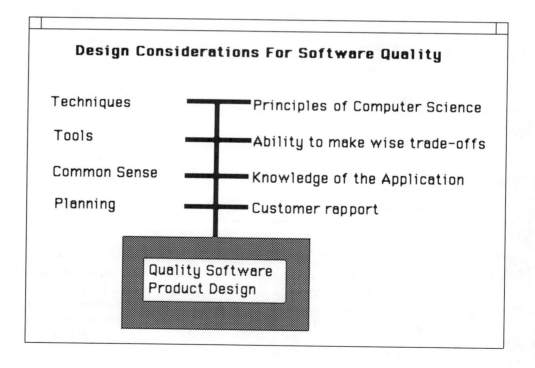

The goals of most successful software products depend on the intended user, but we can generally assume that all users want a system that is easy to use, fast, compact, maintainable, and properly packaged so that the system works well with other systems. These goals often conflict with one another. For example, speed may be exchanged for compactness, or vice versa. A small program may sacrifice error recovery for compactness, or an easy-to-use program may sacrifice speed. A good designer knows how to balance each of these features to achieve a product that is considered "good" by users.

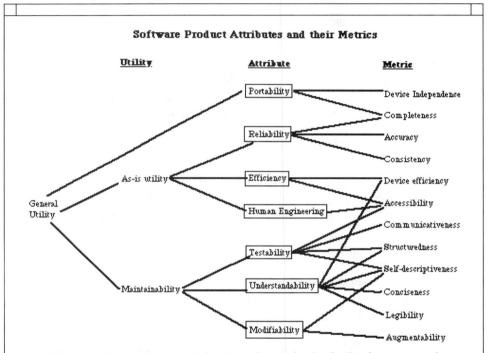

Software Product Attributes and their Metrics

There have been many proposals for the attributes of a "perfect" software proposal. The classification above is one of the most often cited breakdowns which shows not only many important attributes of software quality, but also how they relate to one another. As you can see, one group of attributes is more important to the designer while the other group is perhaps of more interest to the user. Portability is equally important to user and developer. While this classification identifies metrics for each attribute, few numerical measures for these attributes have ever been suggested by practicing software engineers.

Source: Boehm, B. W., Brown, J. R., Kaspar, H., Lipow, M., MacLeod, G. L., and Merritt, M. J. (1978). "Characteristics of Software Quality," Elsevier North-Holland, New York, NY. 10017.

We can get good software product design by following practices learned from great designers. Studies have shown that the best designers produce structures that are faster, smaller, simpler, and produced with less effort[1]. What are good practices of great designers? To answer this question we look at the following attributes of quality software products:

Ease of use
Speed and responsiveness
Size and compactness
Maintainability
Packaging

Ease of Use

Programs that are difficult to learn how to use or difficult to operate are short-lived because people simply do not have time to learn complex procedures, read large and complex manuals, or attend long and boring training lectures. Additionally, complex or difficult programs encourage errors, cause fatigue, and generally are wasteful of human resources.

What constitutes an "easy" program? How can a software designer build easy-to-use software? We strive for the following:

Simple to operate.   User-interface is obvious.
Simple to learn.   Underlying concepts are well-known and understood.
Consistent.   System does what the user expects: no surprises.

GRAPHIC USER INTERFACES

One of the most profound achievements of the 1980s was the acceptance of graphic user interfaces. A *graphic interface* is a user interface that uses graphic images in place of text to communicate with the user of a program.

The earliest graphic user interfaces were developed at XEROX PARC by Alan Kay (icons and windows), Douglas Englebart (the mouse) and others in the 1960s and 1970s. This early work culminated in the design of SMALLTALK and several systems that embodied the object-oriented design of SMALLTALK. However, graphic interfaces did not become widely recognized or used until they were implemented as part of the Apple Macintosh™ and SUN Workstation system software.

Modern graphic interfaces follow several ad hoc standards: the Macintosh™ "look and feel" standard enforced by Apple Computer corporation; the widely adopted X-Windows followed by developers of UNIX-based systems; and the MS-Windows standard advocated for use on IBM PC computers and compatibles.

While all somewhat different, the widely used graphic interfaces more or less stem from the "desktop" metaphor, which suggests that the screen of a computer is a simulated desktop complete with file folders, sheets of paper, and various "objects" resembling real objects commonly found on a real desktop.

Convenient. System does all it can for the user, without causing misunderstanding.
Efficient. System minimizes the user's effort.
Robust. System informs user of error conditions, and recovers from all errors.

These are desirable attributes, but what do they mean? A program is both simple to operate and easy to learn, for example, if it is based on some well-known and easy to understand *paradigm* — an example or model. The desktop metaphor of the Macintosh is a popular paradigm used in this book. The electronic spreadsheet was one of the first paradigms or models used to reduce the time to learn how to use a computer program.

Current software technology relies heavily on visual metaphors — graphic paradigms, if you will — to convey a simple, obvious model of some well-known and easily understood entity.

Graphic metaphors are not in themselves sufficient to ease the task of learning and operating a software product. The operations and *objects* in the metaphor must be consistent, efficient, and convenient as well. Operations such as opening a file, printing a report, calculating a balance, or moving a paragraph must be easy to perform and unambiguous. Objects such as files, reports, formulas, and paragraphs must be manipulated in some consistent, efficient, and convenient way.

By consistent, we mean that the program contains no surprises for the user. One way to avoid surprises is to use consistent images of the objects being manipulated. For example, menus always appear at the top of the Macintosh screen and contain commands that can be performed by the program. The user can depend on the command being available if the menu item is highlighted when selected. There are no surprises because there are no exceptions to this rule.

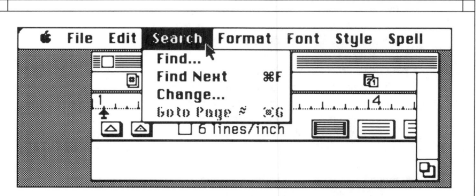

A *modeless dialog* allows the user to manipulate other desktop objects such as the menu as shown above. A modeless dialog is shown in the background, beneath the pulled down menu. On the contrary, a *modal dialog* as shown below, forces the user to deal with the dialog before anything else can be selected.

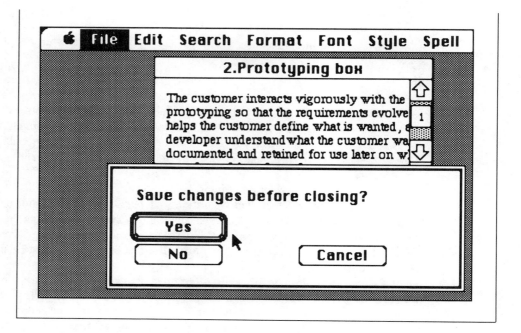

A second method of achieving consistency is to enforce *modeless* operation. A user interface is said to be **modeless** *if the meaning of a command is independent of the state of the program.* In other words, a certain command has an expected effect on the program regardless of when the command is performed. For example, a modeless ERASE command removes a selected paragraph in a word processor application and also removes a file as expected when the file icon is selected later in the same program. Selecting the ERASE command when nothing is selected has, as expected, no effect. In this example, the ERASE command has one meaning: remove or delete the selected object. The command is independent of the program's state — paragraph-selected is one state, file-selected is a different state. Regardless of the state of the application program, the operation does what the user expects.

Easy-to-use also suggests convenience. For example, a mouse-controlled cursor can be used to select a page of text from a document within a word processor application. Suppose the document being processed is several hundred pages long. Using the mouse to select all of the text would be inconvenient. Rather, the word processor software should allow the user to SELECT-ALL text in one command. While all text can be selected by dragging the mouse across hundreds of pages, it is far more convenient for the user to select a single command.

A second illustration of convenience is more subtle. Consider an application program designed to work with data produced by other programs. For example, a page layout program might accept graphic documents produced by a graphics design program as well as text produced by various word processors. The page layout application can do this in two ways, one more convenient than the other. The graphics and text can be imported into the page layout application by cutting the graphics or text from one application to the desktop clipboard and then pasting the clipboard information into the page layout document. This method takes two steps and usually means exiting one program to enter another. While this approach is certainly workable, it is very inconvenient for the user. Instead, a more convenient way to achieve the desired result is to provide a command that automatically reads and translates documents from one format to another. The second approach is more difficult for the designer and programmer of the page layout application to do, but it is much more convenient for the user than the first approach.

The last example is also an illustration of efficiency. A good program saves the user's energy rather than simply augmenting a difficult or time-consuming processing step. The most pronounced impact of efficiency in design is in the automation of long sequences of operations. Suppose a certain application permits the user to perform a series of operations, one immediately following another. These operations can be done one at a time, or if the application minimizes the user's effort, a single operation should be made available that does all of the operations in the series automatically.

Examples of efficiency-increasing designs are: batch commands in an operating system, whereby a group of commands are stored in a batch file to be carried out by the operating system as a unit; keyboard macros, whereby a stream of application commands are collected together and assigned to a single command key and performed as a batch whenever the command key is pressed; and "short-cut" command sequences, whereby a mouse double-click, or a command key is substituted for a menu item so that an experienced operator can use the keyboard in place of a pull-down menu command.

 Warning: take corrective action

 Option: the application wants you to decide

 Error: an error occurred -- command ignored

Error messages are reported in special windows called alert dialogs. Each dialog contains an icon showing the severity of the alert. Warnings tell the user of impending doom, options ask for more information, and error alerts tell what went wrong.

In all cases, a good alert is one that tells the user in simple language what the problem is, and, if possible, how to correct it.

Finally, we strive for **robustness** — *the extent to which an application can continue to operate correctly despite the introduction of invalid inputs*. Applications that crash and leave unrecoverable results are unacceptable to the user. Robustness can be achieved in a variety of ways, some more acceptable than others. For example, an application program can prevent errors from occurring by limiting the flexibility and power of the application, but this may be an undesirable approach because it limits the usefulness of the application. On the other hand, a poorly designed application can inadvertently allow the user to get painted into a corner.

The user interface typically distinguishes between alerts, error messages, and bombs. An **alert** *is a warning message that tells the user what the consequences might be if the operation is carried out*. Alerts are used to prevent the user from making self-destructive selections, and should be issued whenever the user is about to perform an irreversible operation. For example, a global search-and-replace operation such as changing all "-ing" endings to "-ed" endings in a word processor document is irreversible, so an alert is displayed which gives the user a chance to back out of the operation or continue with full awareness of the consequences.

An **error message** *informs the user that an error has occurred*. While an alert warns of an impending condition, an error message tells the user that an error has already occurred. Often, the user is given a chance to correct the error and continue, but sometimes the error is not recoverable. When an error is so severe that the application is terminated, the error is called a *bomb*. Fatal errors must be made impossible, or else the application must be able to gracefully terminate by saving enough information for the user to recover later on.

Error numbers are totally useless and should be avoided in the design of the application. Error messages must be clear and specific. For example, the message, "File not found" is of little use, but the message, "File Payroll.text could not be opened because it is locked" can be used to remedy the error.

Robustness (or the lack of it) is one of the main contributors to software quality. A robust program must be able to avoid or recover from:

- Bad or invalid inputs such as text in place of numbers
- Errors in calculations such as dividing by 0
- File I/O — closed, missing, already open, locked, disk failure, end-of-file marker reached
- Memory problems — insufficient memory, pointer reference error, array overrun, indexing error
- Timing problems, race conditions in real-time concurrent systems or shared database systems
- Improper usage, such as opening a file twice or saving over existing file

Speed and Responsiveness

Many capable applications have been commercial failures due to sluggish performance. Performance is especially important in real-time applications, but even in ordinary productivity

---

REAL-TIME APPLICATIONS

Speed and responsiveness are perhaps the most important attributes of a real-time system — a system that responds fast enough to "keep up" with changes in its inputs. Real-time systems often control life-threatening processes such as the operation of transit systems, power plants, and the like. Responding to an emergency in a power plant after the plant has "melted down," is not acceptable performance for real-time software.

High-speed software is difficult to implement because of the temptation to sacrifice maintainability, modularity, and standard coding practices for the sake of speed. However, there is a rule among system developers that says to "make work, first, then make it fast." What this means is that a properly designed and implemented software system should be tuned up for speed only after it has been constructed in accordance with principles of good design.

---

applications such as word processing, spreadsheet applications, and database management software, speed is important. The careful designer tries to design software that runs fast and yields snappy responses to user commands.

As we saw with ease of use, speed and responsiveness may be in conflict with other desirable attributes. For example, many applications written for personal computers bypass the operating system to directly access the screen. This is done to obtain responsiveness, but the resulting application is difficult to maintain and usually cannot be run on compatible hardware.

It is often a mistake to strive for the fastest algorithm, most efficient storage structure, and tightest code possible simply to achieve the greatest amount of speed. Speed often sacrifices robustness; compactness often sacrifices responsiveness; and tight code often sacrifices maintainability. The mark of a good design is how carefully these trade-offs are managed.

Speed and responsiveness are two different attributes of software. To see the difference consider the following example. A certain compiler translates source code into machine code by reading the entire source code into memory, analyzing the source code, and then writing the binary object code to a disk file. This is called a batch compiler because the source program is translated all at once. Speed is achieved in this compiler by reading the entire source code into memory prior to translation. If a file is too large for the memory of a particular computer, the batch compiler will not work. Alternately, an incremental compiler reads a piece of the source code from the disk file, translates it, and reports errors as they are encountered. The correct, completely translated source code statements are written to an output binary file as obtained, so a file of any size can be processed. The incremental compiler is more responsive because it reports errors as soon as they are encountered, and it allows the incorrect statements to be corrected immediately. Therefore the incremental compiler is "faster" (more responsive) than the batch compiler.

Benchmark Results for Five Compilers
Size of Code vs. Execution Speed

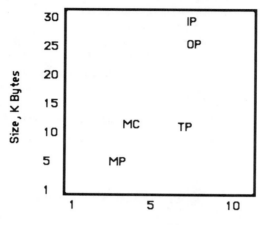

Speed, seconds

MP = Marshal Pascal, MC = Microsoft C
TP = Turbo Pascal, OP = Oregon Pascal-2
IP = IBM Pascal

Source: Dr. Dobb's Journal of Software Tools, #127, May 1987, p. 56

MEASURING COMPILER PERFORMANCE

The quality of code produced by a compiler can be measured in terms of execution speed and memory size. The speed and size of five popular compilers for personal computers is shown relative to four benchmark programs. The results show major performance differences, but the trend toward compactness and speed is evident. Compilers that produce compact code also produce fast code.

This data does not tell the entire story, however, because we have not shown times for compiling, robustness of the compiler, or other attributes such as ease of use. Such benchmarks are useful, but should be carefully considered alongside of other factors.

Sieve finds prime numbers, I/O does disk file input and output, and Gauss-Seidel inverts a matrix of real numbers.

	Sieve	I/O	Gauss-Seidel	Average
Marshal Pascal	4.8s, 2.4K	1.8s, 5.1K	4.9s, 11.5K	3.8s, 6.3K
Microsoft C 4.0	5.8s, 6.5K	1.9s, 8.9K	6.0s, 23.6K	4.6s, 13K
Turbo Pascal	14.2s, 11.5K	2.2s, 12.5K	4.7s, 13.5K	7.0s, 12.5K
Oregon Pascal-2	7.2s, 11.7K	2.5s, 22K	11.8s, 37.6K	7.3s, 28.7K
IBM Pascal	11.7s, 27K	2.5s, 24.5K	7.6s, 34.6K	7.3s, 28.7K

s = seconds   K = 1024 bytes

SPEED VS. RESPONSE VS. POWER IN THE DATABASE WORLD

	Sort	Index	Index Lookup	Search(no-index)	Report
Relational					
(not programmable)					
R:Base 4000	31.5s	66s	1.8s	240s	45s
PowerBase	118s	140s	2s	NA	564s
PC-File/R	65s	20s	6s	2.5s	540s
Query Language					
(programmable)					
dBase III+	14.2s	10.7s	0.1s	3.7s	488s
Informix-SQL	40s	2.5s	0.1s	2.5s	120s
R:Base 5000	12.9s	31.2s	3.5s	5.7s	681s

Source: PC Magazine, vol. 5, no. 12, (June 24, 1986), pp. 116, 186)

Developers of database management application software have difficult choices to make among factors such as speed, response, power, and ease of use. Their software is often misunderstood by users who lump together all database management software into one category. In the comparison shown here, two categories are considered: programmable and nonprogrammable relational database systems running on personal computers. The programmable systems are more difficult to use, but also more powerful — an immediate trade-off which distinguishes many software products.

The data were collected from a benchmark application that used three files: one contained only 5 records, and the other two contained 500 records including both alphabetical and numerical fields. A report was generated which had to access all files, format the output and perform a minor calculation. Therefore, this application measures response and speed of processing. All times are measured in seconds, and were run on an IBM PC/XT with a 10MB disk drive.

The lookup and search operations were measured to compare response times, the sort and report operations to compare speeds. The database systems varied highly in both categories and for both attributes. It is not clear that one is always traded off for another; we can, however, make several observations. R:Base 5000 is the best sorter of the lot, but it does poorly on lookups, so we might conclude that this product has traded responsiveness for speed. The slowness of its report generator, however, is probably due to other factors, such as its sophistication and ease of use. The nonprogrammable products are generally slower and less responsive than the programmable products. The nonprogrammable products are also easier to understand, set up, and use, hence we might conclude that these products have traded power for ease of use. Such generalizations are difficult to support, but clearly this example illustrates that there are several ways of looking at application software performance.

Though the incremental compiler is more responsive than the batch compiler in this example, when no errors occur in the source code the batch compiler completes the translation *before* the incremental compiler. One application is fast in the sense of raw processing speed, while the other application is fast in the sense of user interaction. We say the batch compiler is *fast*, and the incremental compiler is *responsive*.

Speed and responsiveness are different facets of performance. Both kinds of performance involve trade-offs, as in the comparison between the batch and incremental compilers. This extreme comparison holds a lesson for software designers that may be more universal than it seems at first.

At one extreme we strive for raw performance in the form of batch speed, while at the other extreme we strive for performance as measured by responsiveness. A database management system which can update a relation very quickly is thought to be responsive, but if the same database management system takes all night to create a backup copy of the same relation, it is considered slow. Software designers often strike a balance between batch and interactive performance by amortizing, or spreading out, performance over the user's session time, the length of time the user actually uses the application.

We can illustrate *performance amortization* with a simple example. Consider a word processor that incorporates a spelling checker and a document formatter. The idea is to overlap keystrokes with other operations to amortize performance over the user's session time. While the computer is waiting for the user to strike the next key, the application does two other operations in the background: 1) the text in the document is examined one word at a time and a list of misspelled words is created, and 2) the previously entered text is formatted and written to a print file in preparation for a print command.

Both of these background activities pay off handsomely when the user requests a list of misspelled words or when the document is printed. This is a gamble, of course, because the user may edit the document, thus changing the words and format. If this occurs, the previous work may have to be discarded. On the other hand, if the user does not change the previously entered text, spell-checking and printing of the document are done quickly, giving the appearance of speed.

This example shows how an application can be designed to give the user an illusion of speed, when in fact the time taken to do a given operation is amortized over the session time. This example also suggests that speed and response are again trade-offs to be carefully made — the background processing idea escalates the complexity and decreases the maintainability of the application.

Size and Compactness

Earlier we defined the size of an application as the number of source lines of code. Here, we are interested only in *size* as measured by the amount of memory — RAM and disk memory — required by the application. RAM space may be affected not only by the size of the source code but also by the size of internal data structures, resources, and file buffers. Disk memory can be a major factor in the design of an application as well because such simple operations as sorting can greatly increase the amount of disk space required.

Compactness is different from *smallness*. An application is considered compact if it is tightly coded, uses little extra memory space, or uses algorithms that conserve time and/or space. Again, these attributes may compete with other attributes such as maintainability and speed.

We have already seen several instances where the size of an application is sacrificed for speed, convenience, or robustness. While it is desirable to keep an application as small as possible, it may be that a judicious exchange of size for speed is warranted.

The most important size and compactness constraint is that the application be able to fit into the memory of the computer for which the application is intended. If most users own computers with 2MB RAM and the application requires 4MB, the application will be a failure in the marketplace. Similarly, if the application with all of its support files and resources takes more space than is available on a distribution diskette, then the application cannot be sold: a miscalculation leading to commercial failure.

Finally, size requirements are often difficult to know in advance. The data structures of a certain application may grow during program execution. If the application exceeds the amount of memory available it will terminate (hopefully, with grace). For example, to achieve maximum speed many word processors work on documents contained wholly in RAM. When a large document is constructed, the word processor may run out of memory. In this case, it is very important that the program be as compact as possible so that large documents will have as much room in RAM as possible.

Maintainability

While we have discussed the importance of maintainability elsewhere, we will reiterate several important points. The maintainability of an application is more important to the developer than the user. This means the designer must carefully balance the obvious goals of speed, compactness, and ease of use against the following:

Understandability. The degree to which a program's source code can be comprehended.

Modifiability. The degree to which a program can be changed and enhanced.

Modularity. The degree of modularity as measured by the number of modules and the interface among modules.

Documentation. The degree of self-descriptiveness or self-documentedness of an application.

Portability. The ease of converting an application to run on a machine, operating system, or model of computer other than the system it was designed to run on.

Standard Code. The source code has followed a carefully defined standard for code quality.

The first three attributes — understandability, modifiability, and modularity — are all related to the structural design of an application. Here is where the designer has a major impact on the maintainability of an application. In fact, the impact is so critically important that many CASE tools have been developed to enforce various forms of structure, such as *procedural, control, data,* and *I/O.*

Procedural.   Functional decomposition and interface control.
Control.   Single-entry, single-exit (SESE) source code.
Data.   Abstraction away from representation, toward "objects."
I/O.   Abstraction away from devices, toward "objects."

The last two forms advocate the use of objects in the design. *Object-oriented design* is a particular kind of design methodology which we will examine later. Briefly, it is a method that attempts to suppress details at a certain level of the application by encapsulating storage structures and devices in modules called *objects*. These modules are different from the modules obtained by functional decomposition because the objects encapsulate both function and "state" information. For the time being, think of the "state" of an object as the value of its storage elements.

Data abstraction separates the data from the control portion of the program by encapsulating the storage elements and all allowable operations on the storage elements as modules. These modules communicate with the remaining parts of the system by procedure calls. For example, a list is abstracted and separated from the remaining parts of an application by encapsulating the list data structure and all operations — GET-ELEMENT, PUT-ELEMENT, ADD-ELEMENT, and so on, in a separately compiled module called the *abstract data type*. Whenever an element of the list is needed, the GET-ELEMENT procedure is called, and whenever an element is updated, the PUT-ELEMENT operation is called. It is impossible to access an element of a list without calling one of the operations defined for the list.

Device abstraction separates the I/O devices from the remaining parts of the application by treating all devices as if they are data abstractions. Thus, the keyboard, screen, disk, and communication device port are converted into data objects. Since all objects consist of state and function, the abstracted device is used by calling access procedures defined on the device abstraction. The impact of this decision on portability, maintainability, and understandability is quite obvious. These ideas will be developed in later chapters, but for now the key ingredient of data and I/O abstraction is the concept of *encapsulation* of both data and the operations allowed to be performed on the data.

Some of the CASE tools developed to enforce and track these desirable forms of structure are:

Structure Charts.   Hierarchical, graphical description of functions and their interfaces

Cross Reference Dictionaries.   Origin, flow, and reference to all names and values in a system

Control Reference Dictionaries.   Definitions and relationships among all functions and modules

Test Case Banks.   Collections of all test cases and test data used to verify the application

As before, these attributes must be carefully traded against other attributes when designing an application. For example, decomposing an application's functions into procedures can be carried to an extreme. Too many functions are difficult to manage, but too few make changes difficult to achieve. While a small procedure is easier to understand than a large one, the proliferation of procedures may be just as difficult to comprehend.

Packaging

A final consideration often overlooked by the novice designer is *packaging*. Packaging plays an important role in determining the success of the product. Simply put, packaging has to do with how well the product works within the hardware and software environments for which it is intended. A good package is one that works on a variety of hardware configurations and matches up well with software products made by other developers. Here are a few of the many considerations in designing a good package:

Compatibility Perhaps the most important packaging consideration is hardware and software compatibility. The product must fit in with existing hardware and software systems. For example, a graphics application must be able to work with a variety of graphics devices — (e.g. mouse, tablet, light pen, plotter, scanner). Furthermore, a good graphics package must be able to read and convert paint, draw, and design files created by other programs. It is not sufficient for a new product to stand alone. Instead, it must enhance the user's existing software base. A new word processor must be able to work with files created by other applications, such as spreadsheets, graphics, and database files.

Device flexibility A good package works with a variety of printers, monitors, disk drives, scanners, and other input/output devices. In addition, the package must be able to adapt to additional devices as they become available. For example, a software product should work equally well with both impact and laser printers, floppy and hard disks, color and black-and-white monitors, and various kinds of keyboards.

Default settings A good package can be configured to work with a variety of systems. The defaults should be automatic, or else adjustable by the user. For example, a graphics program should be able to automatically adjust to color versus black-and-white screens, different sized screens, and different aspect ratios. If it is necessary to require the user to set parameters which describe the hardware configuration, the settings should be made once only, and automatically retrieved each time the program is started.

Installation A good package is easy to install. If a special installation procedure is necessary, it should be as automatic as possible. If this is not the case, installation should be self-instructive. If the user is required to read the manual to install the software, packaging is a failure. For example, installation of a software product onto a hard disk should be as simple as copying the product from the distribution disk to the user's hard disk. Unfortunately, many copy protection techniques prevent this simplified approach. Instead, an install program must be run. The install program should be simple, direct, and unobtrusive. One way to streamline installation is to make it automatic upon start-up of the machine.

Documentation A major part of the package is the user's documentation. This document should be arranged for two kinds of readers, the novice who is anxious to get started and the expert who refers to the manual as a reference document. The novice needs to know the obvious — how to start the program, how to do the most straightforward and simple operations, and how to quit. The expert needs a quick reference to the deeper aspects of operation.

The need for dual novice and expert references puts an unusual strain on technical writers of software documentation. If the manual is too simplistic, it will discourage the expert, but if it is too complex it will discourage beginners. Rather than attempt to do both in a single manual, it is best to produce two manuals — one for the novice and a second one for the expert user. These two manuals can be bound together or separately, but the intended reader should be clearly indicated in each case.

The novice manual should consist of a simple example of using the product, definition of terms, and miscellaneous items such as installation and configuration. The expert manual should be organized along functional lines with easy-to-reference commands and a full index, and should be divided into topics that parallel the operation of the product. For example, the expert manual might contain chapters on entering data, updating files, and producing printed reports.

The software should be designed so that the manual is needed only infrequently. Users dislike reading manuals, and more than one software product has failed because it could not be comprehended without reading a book. However, in the rare cases where the manual is called upon, the information must be easy to find, easy to understand, and it must solve the user's problem.

One way to minimize the need for a manual is to incorporate on-line help documentation in the software itself. This approach has both advantages and disadvantages. Clearly, the advantage is ease of use for the user, but the disadvantage is that the size and sometimes the speed of the product are affected. An on-line help facility may consume as much memory as the rest of the application.

A few miscellaneous points:

- Little things are very important to successful designs.
- Copy protection must be unobtrusive.
- The user interface must be seamless, making smooth transitions.
- Sexist, racist, and other offensive statements must be abolished.
- The best software extends what the user already does in a smooth, effortless way. This may be an elusive goal, but it is nonetheless extremely important for success.

These are all laudable goals, but how do we achieve them? In the next section we will review the principles of user interface design and show that a good software design begins with a good user interface. If we can define the product as a sequence of user interactions, and these interactions promote the goals of good design, then we have taken the first step toward designing a successful software product.

DESIGN TRADE-OFF CONSIDERATIONS

Of course every designer wants to plan for software that is easy to use, fast, small, maintainable, and compatible with other software systems, but as we learned in the previous section these attributes often conflict with one another. Therefore a designer must judiciously select when and where these attributes are going to be exchanged to gain the best overall mix. Accordingly, the designer has a "bank account" to draw upon to pay for these desirable attributes. A designer can trade disk storage, RAM storage, flexibility, portability, and convenience for speed, ease of use, and so forth, as shown in Figure 4-1.

There are no hard-and-fast rules for when to make a trade. Most designers learn the hard way, by making mistakes. Experience is perhaps the best teacher, but in this section we illustrate many of the typical exchanges that take place when designing and building a software product that must operate in a real-world environment of machines, operating systems, and marketing opportunities. In general, keep your design simple and direct and carefully consider both the data structures and algorithms to be employed in light of real-world considerations such as backups, audit trails, and finite memories.

KISS Principle

The KISS (Keep It Simple, Stupid) rule is one of the best rules for software designers because there are many ways to embellish almost any computer program. Yet, in many cases the embellishment does more harm than good. Let's look at a few examples.

A certain database application is to be designed that keeps a list of people who own automobiles. This list has several complicating requirements that must be satisfied during the operation of the application:

1. The list will, in general, grow to an undetermined size.

2. People buy and sell automobiles, so the list must be updatable.

3. Retrieval must be on-line and fast, and access must be on one key: name of owner.

4. Printed reports are to be sorted by owner names.

5. If the system crashes, the list must be restorable automatically.

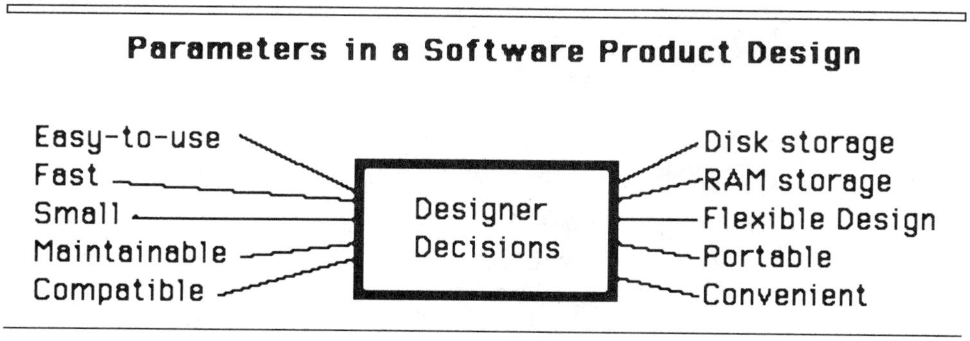

Parameters in a Software Product Design

Easy-to-use
Fast
Small
Maintainable
Compatible

Designer Decisions

Disk storage
RAM storage
Flexible Design
Portable
Convenient

FIGURE 4-1. Product design trade-offs

From these requirements we might conclude that the list should be

- Stored on a direct access storage device such as a disk
- Organized as a random access file so that updates can be made in place
- Accompanied by an index file so the list is indexed on NAME
- Printed via the NAME index
- Backed up periodically with its index file

This seems like a simple application of indexed file I/O, and in fact it is quite simple, but not as straightforward as might be thought. The complexity of this example is due to the last requirement that says the list must be recoverable.

Suppose the application is to run on a personal computer with one floppy disk drive and one hard (nonremovable) drive. Let's say the hard drive can hold 5,000 records. If we allow the application to add to the list until the hard disk fills up, there is no way to back up the system. The designer has two choices: limit file sizes to roughly one-half the disk capacity so the user can always make a backup copy on the same drive, or provide a mechanism to back up the list and its associated index file onto several floppy disks.

So what is the problem with these solutions? Both are technically sound but the designer must use up some of the "bank account" — through either inconvenience to the user (backing up onto several floppies) or limited usefulness of the application (using only one-half of the disk space). Furthermore, if the designer uses a "trick" to find the capacity of the hard disk, the application may lose some of its portability, maintainability, or both.

The analysis does not end there. The second requirement says the list must be updatable. On the surface, this seems easy to implement, but consider what happens when an update changes a NAME field in an indexed record. Since the list is indexed by NAME, this update changes not only the list file, but also the index file. What happens to the index file? We might delete the "old" NAME from the index file, and insert the "new" name. This causes a performance problem that is difficult to overcome. If the "old" record is kept in the list file, but marked as "deleted," the list and index files both increase in length and retrieval times increase. If the "old" record is erased from the list and index file, these files become fragmented and the application must perform "garbage collection" and "memory management" to clean out the files. Both of these solutions are undesirable because they either reduce the application's speed and compactness or make the application complex and difficult to maintain.

What should the designer do?

First, the degradation in performance caused by simply marking the "old" records as "deleted" and leaving them in the files may be acceptable. Second, the application must be able to back up the files periodically. The backup operation could also perform garbage collection and serve two purposes. This simple approach is probably the best, because more elaborate schemes violate the KISS principle.

To make things more realistic, suppose an added requirement stated that an audit trail of updates had to be kept as well. An **audit trail** *is a recorded history of what happened to a system during a given period of time*. If we had to keep track of all updates, for example, we might be tempted to keep all records in the index and list files. Probably a simpler and more powerful solution is to write an extra file, called a transaction file, after every update. The transaction file can be reset, periodically, by writing an archival backup copy to another disk, and then restarting from zero update transactions.

Now let us look at another problem lurking in this seemingly simple application. The third requirement emphasizes responsiveness — a fast lookup. How should the file system be designed? We have a choice here: the index file might be small enough to fit into RAM, thus making the application run very fast. Every lookup must access the index file, find a record number, and then access the list file. Searching the index file usually requires many accesses, so running the index out of RAM is an attractive opportunity to gain speed.

Alternatively, the index file can be directly accessed from its storage locations on disk. Recall that the index file must retrieve NAMEs in alphabetical order. Does this mean the index file must be sorted? A B-tree indexing scheme can be used to avoid sorting the file, but even this will not prevent multiple accesses of the file to find the right NAME. Indexing is perhaps the most time-consuming operation to be performed.

Again, the KISS principle leads us to sacrifice the speed aspect for simplicity, maintainability, and ease of use. First, the designer has little control over how much RAM is available in the user's machine. What happens when the application runs out of RAM space? Second, running out of RAM ultimately limits the size of the list file, and this limit will be reached by users sooner or later. When the limit is reached, a new version of the software will have to be released.

This example illustrates the class of problems encountered by most application software designers. We could have analyzed several variants of this class with similar trade-off issues. We briefly mention a few more here.

Sorting of files File sorting is so common among application programmers that it is often assumed that a sort will be done. Modern interactive systems dictate, "avoid sorting at all times" because sorts are slow and take too much disk space. Users do not want to wait for a sort before printing a report — better to use an indexing scheme as the previous example suggests. Also keep in mind that most disk sorts take roughly twice as much space to sort a file as the file itself takes. This limits the size of the file and makes sorting impractical for most desktop computers.

Hashed files Scatter-table techniques are often used to gain very rapid retrieval from direct access files. Clever hashing techniques need not be complicated, hence they are good candidates for the design of fast, compact, and maintainable software. Hashing does not guarantee order, however, so if your application needs to keep lists in order, slower indexing schemes are preferable. If order is not important then you will have to decide if extendability is important. Simple hash tables cannot be extended without sacrificing speed. (The hash table or index must be rehashed into a larger list when the table overflows.

This may incur unreasonable delays.) Extendable hashing techniques can grow with the application, but they are less understood and thus more complex to manage. Yet a correct, extendable hash technique can give better performance than the best file indexing schemes and can grow along with the data.

Arrays versus linked lists   For RAM memory, arrays are fast, simple, and supported by most programming languages. They also cannot be "stretched" during program execution (in most languages used for producing commercial-quality software). Furthermore, it is a big mistake to assume a certain maximum size array. For example, in an order-entry application, we might be tempted to assume that a user would never enter more than ten items in a single order. Accordingly, we might design the software to hold a maximum of ten items per order. What happens when a user tries to enter eleven items?

Instead of using fixed-length arrays to hold lists in RAM, we often use linked lists. They are allocated dynamically, and can grow to the size of RAM. There are two problems with linked lists, however. They are error-prone because pointers are error-prone, and they tend to slow down the application because they must be searched.

Arrays should only be used for keeping lists that are fixed in length, such as tables. Linked lists should be used whenever the list can grow. Performance can be realized by using simple binary tree structures — more elaborate schemes such as 2-3 trees are not necessary — to reduce searching times. Be sure to catch "Out of memory" errors, however, because RAM is finite.

This brief list of issues concerning data structures shows how important it is to consider carefully how the application uses RAM and disk space. Algorithms and data structures taken out of context can lead to a bad design. In general, be critical of more complex structures or algorithms when discussing design trade-off considerations with team members.

Algorithm Design

The KISS principle does not serve as well when discussing algorithm design because choosing algorithms requires extra caution, even more than choosing file and data structures. For example, a sorting algorithm that works well on a list of 100 numbers may hide intrinsically poor performance. Testing the application on 100 numbers may not reveal the performance problem: a list of 10,000 numbers takes 2 minutes to sort. A user attempting to sort 10,000 numbers may terminate the program in 30 seconds thinking the program does not work correctly.

Of course, most designers are aware of intractable algorithms for sorting, the "traveling salesperson" problem, the "knapsack" problem, and the famous "halting" problem. These theoretical problems can be used as benchmarks for deciding if a certain algorithm is impractical. Rather, we are concerned with less obvious problems that can arise because of poor algorithm design. Again, the designer must choose from among less-than-ideal options.

Consider the following example. A certain application was designed to read a Pascal source program file containing an arbitrary number of "includes." An "include file" is any text file that is included in the source code of a program by stating a metacommand, a comment that directs the compiler to read from the include file rather than the original source file. The example below shows one way to state an include file from within a Pascal program:

```
Program Sample (input, output);
{ $I Globals.Text}
begin
{ $I Body.Text}
end.
```

In this simple example, the compiler reads the program header, then it opens the Globals.Text file and reads from this file until the end-of-file is reached, or until a subsequent **include** metacommand is read. Similarly, the Body.Text file is opened and read when the $I metacommand is reached.

The application designed to read Pascal source programs worked most of the time, but not always. Sometimes it would crash due to an out-of-memory error. Why? Upon lengthy study it was discovered that the application used a recursive routine to handle the **includes**. Whenever an **include** directive, $I, was encountered, the routine would call itself and resume scanning the input text from the newly opened file. This worked most of the time, but failed whenever the number of nested **includes** exceeded ten deep. The application simply exceeded its stack space when ten recursive calls were made.

This problem can be solved by increasing the stack space, but is this the best solution? Increasing the stack space has two problems with it. First, it is wasteful of memory most of the time, and second, the same error will occur when a more deeply nested input is used. In short, increasing the stack size does not solve the problem. The solution is to replace the recursive routine with an iterative routine.

This example illustrates an inappropriate algorithm design and how it can cause problems long after the software is developed and released. Recursion is convenient for a programmer, but dangerous for the application and its users.

Our second example shows how insidious some designs are. Consider another application that stores all data in linked lists. One routine in the program searches a linked list for a number, and then passes this number to another routine that searches another linked list. The second search results in a string which is used by the first routine to search the first list again, and so on. When the routines are tested one at a time they perform nicely, because their searches take time proportional to the length of their list, say $O(n)$ for the first list of length n, and $O(m)$ for the second list of length m. The problem is that the combination of searching both lists takes $O(nm)$ instead of $O(n+m)$, which gives unacceptable performance. The algorithm must be redesigned to circumvent the $O(nm)$ search time.

It is common to design routines that use $O(n)$ algorithms but end up with $O(n^2)$ performance after combining routines. The careful designer must consider the consequences for overall performance of putting "simple" routines together.

The most common consideration when designing algorithms is the trade-off between memory and speed. Hash tables are a good example of this, because hash tables deliberately swap memory space for execution time. The time taken by a hash table to look up an entry is roughly,

$$1/(1 - \beta);$$

where

β = loading factor = fraction of the table that is full

The loading factor ranges from 0 to 1; at 0, retrieval time is minimal, and at 1 retrieval time is infinite! By setting β to approximately 0.8, retrieval time and wasted space are balanced. If the hash table is stored on disk, setting β to approximately 0.5 gives a better balance between disk retrieval time and wasted disk space.

USER INTERFACE DESIGN CONSIDERATIONS

The user interface is the most important single attribute of an application in terms of the application's appeal to the user. An outstanding program will fail to attract many users if it is confusing or difficult to use. Similarly, many mediocre programs have been purchased and used extensively by thousands of people because of a superior user interface. Because of this designers have begun to place greater and greater emphasis on user interface design. This emphasis has led in turn to the desirability of integrating interface design into overall system design. The traditional waterfall lifecycle model places requirements analysis at the leading edge of the process, but in modern design, requirements and user interface design interact back and forth, each one reacting to the other until both the requirements and the user interface are determined.

Besides turning the user interface specifications into requirements, user interface design is critical to achieving ease of use, convenience, efficiency, and other desirable attributes. The Macintosh style of user interface has proven to be a major force in user interface design because of its simplicity, power, flexibility, and most importantly, its consistency. Consistency reduces training effort because one application works much like another. This fact has convinced developers to adopt user interface standards.

A *standard user interface* uses consistent menus, windows, dialogs, and icons to convey meaning, reduce learning effort, and increase user efficiency, flexibility, and convenience. We will describe much of the Macintosh standard user interface by simple example in the next section.

The Macintosh user interface is *object-oriented*, meaning that the user is presented a collection of graphic objects and operates the application by manipulating the graphic objects. Menus are objects that can be selected, enabled, disabled, and so forth. Windows are objects that can be opened, scrolled, closed, and made inactive. Dialogs are special kinds of windows containing messages, data, and information of interest to the user. These objects are all manipulated by a mouse, a pointing and selecting device connected to the computer.

KEYBOARDS CONSIDERED HARMFUL

Most computer keyboards are modeled after the typewriter, a design that purposely fostered the QWERTY layout to slow down typists in the nineteenth century. An ergonomic keyboard is designed for maximum speed and comfort. Such a keyboard is curved to conform to the shape of a human hand, thus facilitating the positioning of fingers. The left side slopes down to the left, and the right side slopes down to the right to reduce muscular strain.

Source: Kroemer, K. H., "Human Engineering the Keyboard," Human Factors, 14(1), 1972, pp. 51–63.

An Ergonomics Keyboard

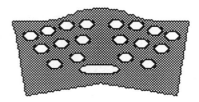

Source: Nakaseko, M., Grandjean, E., Hunting, W. and R. Gierer, "Studies on Ergonomically Designed Alphanumeric Keyboards," Human Factors, (1985), 27(2), pp. 175–187.

The mouse has a single button that can be "clicked" or "double-clicked." Depressing the mouse button while moving the mouse is called "dragging," and is used mainly to drag objects across the screen. Thus the user interface objects are selected by clicking, activated by clicking or double-clicking, and moved by dragging.

A second advancement in software development technique made by the Macintosh is essential to the design of every Macintosh application. Each compiled application consists of two parts: the *code fork* containing processing logic, and the *resource fork* containing the specification of user interface objects. The resource fork of an application is obtained by compiling the user interface object specifications into a binary resource file. The specification of an object is written in a high-level specification language — just like a source program — and is fed into RMaker, the resource compiler.

We will illustrate in the following sections the resource specification language used to specify user interface objects. Keep this in mind: a high-level resource language tells an application what the user interface objects look like when they appear on the screen. The high-level resource specification is converted into binary code by RMaker, but the logic of the application is converted into binary code by a Pascal, C, or other high-level language compiler. The linker combines these two binary files into one file called the application. Every application has two forks, a resource fork and a code fork, each provided by either RMaker or a compiler.

THE MOUSE THAT ROARED

The electronic mouse invented by Englebart caused a stir among computer system developers. Some said it detracted from usability while others claimed it was a major advancement in user interface design. A common complaint, for example, came from users of word processing software who disliked switching between the keyboard and the mouse: "the mouse may be good for graphics, but keyboards are better for text." This complaint contradicted the original experimental data collected by English, Englebart and Berman.

The early "mouse experiments" compared the performance of five selection devices — light pen, mouse, tablet, knee control, and joystick. For experienced users the mouse proved to be the fastest and least error-prone device, while the knee control and light pen were observed to be marginally faster than the mouse for inexperienced users. For all users the mouse was more accurate, with error rates roughly half of those for other devices. (The joystick was the poorest performer.)

Card et al. found improvements with repeated use of the mouse versus other devices in an independent study as follows: positioning time for a mouse decreased from 2.2 to 1.3 seconds versus 2.2 to 1.7 seconds for joystick. But decreases for keyboard "arrow keys" were less favorable: from 3.0 to 2.2 seconds with practice. Thus, even for text processing, the mouse roars past the keyboard as a selection device.

Sources: English, W. K., Englebart, D. C., and M. L. Berman, "Display Selection Techniques for Text Manipulation," IEEE Trans. Human Factors in Electronics, vol. HFE-8, no. 1, (March 1967), pp. 5–15.

Card, S. K., English, W. K., and B. J. Burr, "Evaluation of Mouse, Rate-Controlled Isometric Joystick, Step Keys, and Text Keys for Text Selection of a CRT," Ergonomics, vol. 21, no. 8, (Aug. 1978), pp. 601–613.

Menus

Menus appear at the top of the screen in a special region called the menu bar. Menus consist of a title and menu items. Each menu item contains a string and, optionally, specifications of command keys (keyboard equivalents). For example, the ⌘ N key combination does exactly the same function as the NEW item shown in the PROJECT menu, Figure 4-2.

The graphic objects we recognize as menus in the Macintosh menu bar are specified in the high-level resource language as follows: The first line specifies the kind of resource — MENU means the resource specifies a menu object, WIND for window, DLOG for dialog, and ICN for icon. The second line specifies the identifier name and number of the menu. If no name is given, the id number appears following a comma. Thus, the id ",257" means this is menu number 257. The title and all items in the menu follow the id. Optional command keys are specified after each item string. To give the item string special attributes, precede the item with a < character. For example,

```
Bold  <B/B
Quit  <U/Q
```

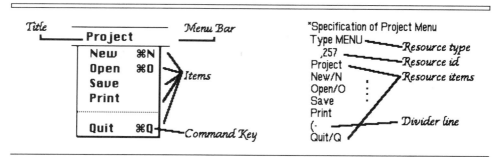

FIGURE 4-2. Graphical and textual specifications of a menu

The first example means to display the item in bold font, and the second example means to underline the "Quit" string. Both examples have corresponding command-key equivalents.

Menus are objects to be manipulated by the application program. But because all user interface objects are manipulated by their application code in exactly the same way — to enforce consistency — the Macintosh ROM contains all routines that are allowed to operate on menus, windows, and so on. These routines are access procedures defined on the state information which we see on the screen as a graphic object. Thus, the Macintosh interface system is an example of *object-oriented software*.

Windows

Windows were invented to simulate multiple display screens on a single CRT screen. A window is a graphic object for displaying text and graphics. Two kinds of windows are typically provided by a user interface system: tiled and overlapped. Tiled windows do not overlap one another and simply divide the screen into rectangular panels adjacent to one another. Overlapped windows are rectangular areas on the screen that may or may not overlap one another. The Macintosh supports overlapping windows, allowing multiple windows to appear partially or completely on the screen.

The high-level specification of a window gives the initial screen location of the window as a pair of coordinates. The upper left corner coordinate tells where the window is to be anchored, and the lower right corner tells how large the window is going to be when displayed, see Figure 4-3. The coordinate system of the Macintosh defines a two-dimensional plane ranging from −32K to +32K in both horizontal and vertical directions. The origin of this coordinate system is initially placed at the upper left corner of the physical screen. The location of any rectangle, such as a window or icon, is given by TLBR, which means:

TL = top, left corner

BR = bottom, right corner

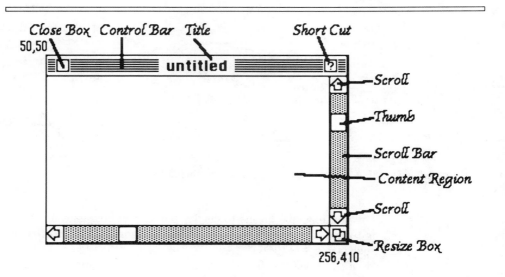

FIGURE 4-3. Graphical and textual specifications of a window

To read the coordinates of the window in the example,

50,50 256,410 = 50 down, 50 from left, 256 down, 410 from left

These four numbers are used to place the window on the screen. They give the initial location of the window. The application may allow the window to be moved or resized, changing these values.

Windows may optionally be dressed up with attributes such as a close box or control bar. A close box is used to discard the window. If the user clicks in the close box, the window is closed and removed from the desktop. A control bar allows the user to move the window by dragging with the mouse. The window may have a title, which appears in the control bar. The application must take care of these operations, since they are not automatic.

Windows may also contain controls such as scroll bars and a resize box. A vertical scroll bar indicates that text or graphics can be scrolled. A complete view of the contents can be obtained by moving the contents up or down within the content portion of the window. A resize box, or simply size box, is used to change the size of the window. Dragging the size box causes the window to become larger or smaller. Short cuts can be added to the window to do such things as rapidly resize the window — if the window is small, the short cut increases it to its fullest possible size, and vice versa. These operations must also be programmed into the application.

The high-level language specification of a window gives only an initial state: the id, the coordinates indicating where the window will appear on the screen, its title, what kind of window it is, and whether it has a close box (GoAway) or not (NoGoAway). Windows are initially invisible, and must be displayed on the screen at the appropriate time by the application.

Keep in mind that windows and menus are resources that become part of the application only after their specifications are compiled by RMaker and after they are combined with the application's code through the linker. Interestingly, the resources can be accessed in their compiled form even after the application has been delivered to the customer. The attributes of resources such as menus and windows can be changed by the customer. This is a very powerful maintenance tool because an English language application can be localized to virtually any languages with minimal effort.

Dialogs

Dialogs are special-purpose windows containing text, graphics, and controls. The application communicates with the user through various kinds of dialogs. There are two general kinds of dialogs: *modal*, in which the dialog must be dealt with before the user is allowed to continue, and *modeless*, in which the dialog can be sidestepped in order to do some other operation.

Dialogs contain various kinds of text, graphics, and controls, see Figure 4-4. A *control* is a graphic object that is manipulated by the mouse to cause direct, immediate action. The most common controls in the Macintosh are scroll bars, buttons, radio and check boxes, and static and editable text fields.

Buttons are small graphic objects labeled with text. Clicking the mouse on a button performs the action described by the text in the button. Some standard buttons are OK, Cancel, Open, Close, and Quit.

Radio boxes are small round buttons used to indicate one of many choices. That is, only one radio from among many radios should be selected. When clicking a radio with the mouse, the radio will be filled with a dot.

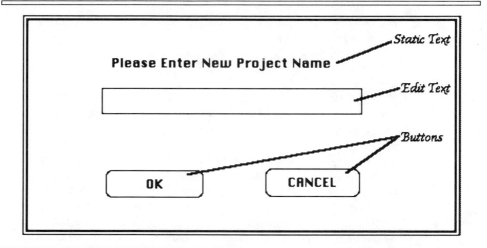

FIGURE 4-4. An example of a dialog

Check boxes are small squares used to indicate one or more options. That is, one or more of the choices represented by several check boxes can be selected by clicking the mouse. When selected, a check box is filled with an *X* mark.

The dialog shown in Figure 4-4 contains four controls: two buttons and two text fields. One text field is called a static text control because its contents cannot be changed by the user. Only the application can place text into a static text control. The other field is called an edit text control, indicating that the user is allowed to edit — enter, change, or erase — the text during program execution. Edit text controls appear as rectangles.

The high-level specification of a dialog box is given in two parts: the DLOG definition part defines the window containing controls, and the DITL (Dialog Item List) part defines the contents of the dialog. The items are numbered as in Figure 4-5. The rectangular coordinates of the items in the dialog are relative to the upper left corner of the DLOG window, *not* to the screen containing the dialog.

The software developer must write code to process most of the interactions that take place between the user and a dialog. For instance, the user can click on a button or select an edit text field and begin entering text. The application must be able to intercept either of these radically different operations on the dialog. Exactly how this is done will be discussed at length in a later chapter.

Alerts

Alerts are special-purpose dialogs that notify, warn, or stop the user. In the Macintosh user interface, alerts give applications a way to respond to errors in a consistent manner and in stages according to the severity of the error, the user's level of expertise, and the particular history of the error. A variety of alerts are provided:

```
Type DLOG
    ,300
50 50 250 450
Visible NoGoAway
1
0
300


Type DITL
    ,300
4        ;number of controls to follow
* 1 first item
BtnItem Enabled
144 71 171 164
OK

* 2     second item
BtnItem Enabled
142 223 170 313
CANCEL

*  3
StatText Disabled
31 75 51 330
Please Enter New Project Name

*  4
EditText Enabled
66 70 86 312
```

FIGURE 4-5. Specification for dialog in Figure 4-4

Note Alert notifies user of minor mistakes that will not have any disastrous consequences if ignored.

Caution Alert warns user of possible damage. The user is given a choice of whether or not to continue.

Stop Alert identifies a severe error which requires remedial attention from the user.

Each of these alerts is displayed on the screen with a corresponding icon signifying what kind of alarm is being given, see Figure 4-6. The user's response must then be analyzed by the application to decide what action to perform.

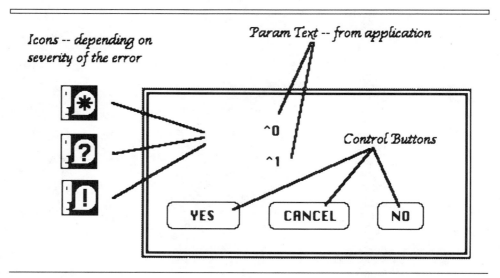

FIGURE 4-6. Modal alert

Alerts are dialogs, hence we can place controls in them the same way we place controls in dialogs. In addition, alerts contain an icon that identifies the alert's severity. One of the three icons — Note, Caution, or Stop — will appear in the upper right corner of the alert, depending on which alert routine is called from the application. (These routines are part of the Macintosh User Interface Toolbox: NoteAlert, CautionAlert, and StopAlert.)

Also, notice the ^0 and ^1 items in the alert box. These are placeholders for strings, error messages to be substituted into these placeholders during program execution. These "param texts" are filled with actual error messages by the application.

Since alerts are special-purpose dialogs, their high-level specifications are made of two parts: the ALRT portion and a DITL portion; see Figure 4-7. The ALRT portion has the usual title, location, and id information, but includes an additional number: 5555 in the example. This is the so-called staging information. Alerts go through stages, and up to four stages are supported by Macintosh alerts.

The first stage is defined by the right-most digit — the least significant 5 in this case — the second stage by the next digit, and so on. The fourth stage is defined by the most significant digit. These digits are actually hexadecimal numbers that tell which button is the default button, whether to display the alert or not, and how many beeps are to be sounded. We can decode the hexadecimal stage number by looking at its binary representation.

Hexadecimal 5 is actually binary 0101. Grouping the bits from left to right: 0 means button 1 is the default button. If the user simply presses the RETURN key, the application assumes button 1 was clicked. If this bit had been a 1, the default button would have been 2. Moving to the next bit, 1 means the alert box will be displayed on the

```
Type ALRT
,256           ;Alert id
50 50 214 456 ;location on screen
256        ;corresponding DITL id
5555       ;staging info: 4 stages, all 4 default to button 1, sound 1 beep

Type DITL
,256 ;Item list id
5     ;5 items to follow
*  1
BtnItem Enabled       ;YES button enabled
94 13 119 126    ;location relative to DLOG window
YES       ;text inside of button


*  2
BtnItem Enabled       ;CANCEL button enabled
94 151 119 271   ;location inside DLOG window
CANCEL       ;text inside of button


*  3
BtnItem Enabled       ;NO button enabled
94 295 119 373   ;location inside DLOG window
NO       ;text inside of button


*  4
StatText Disabled       ;Static text from running program
15 89 35 360 ;location of rectangle to contain text
^0       ;parameter 0 passed from program


*  5
StatText Disabled       ;Item 5 is a second text parameter
48 110 68 315   ;location of rectangle inside DLOG
^1   ;parameter 1 passed from program
```

FIGURE 4-7. Specification for alert in Figure 4-6

screen when one of the alert routines is called. A 0 here would result in a beep, but no alert would appear on the screen. Finally, the last two bits tell how many beeps to sound: 10 binary is 2 decimal, so two beeps will sound. If this had been 01, only one beep would sound, and so on.

This code is applied to each stage, thus the third time the alert is used in a row, the third stage number is used. In this example all stages are equal, but suppose the following staging information is given in the specification: F765. Stage one uses 5, as discussed above; stage two uses 6, and stage three uses 7. The default button is 1, the alert is displayed on the screen, and the beeper beeps three times. How many beeps are sounded in stage four?

Icons

An icon is a graphic object representing an operation or other object in the system. Icons are 32 pixels on a side and can be placed in menus, dialogs, windows, or anywhere the mouse can go. Icons can be simply ornamental or informational, or they can be selected, moved, sized, and inverted. Icons should be used to clarify the application.

Desktop icons — the CoCoPro icon is shown in Figure 4-8 — are defined by two 32-by-32 pixel bit maps. One bit map contains the icon itself and the other bit map contains a mask. Each bit in the icon is exclusive-or'ed with the corresponding bit in the mask when the desktop icon is selected. If the mask contains all 1s then the icon is inverted, as shown in Figure 4-8. If the mask contains some desirable pattern, then selecting the desktop icon causes the icon to change. Recall the rules for ex-or logic:

1 ex-or 0 = 1,
1 ex-or 1 = 0,
0 ex-or 0 = 0,
0 ex-or 1 = 1.

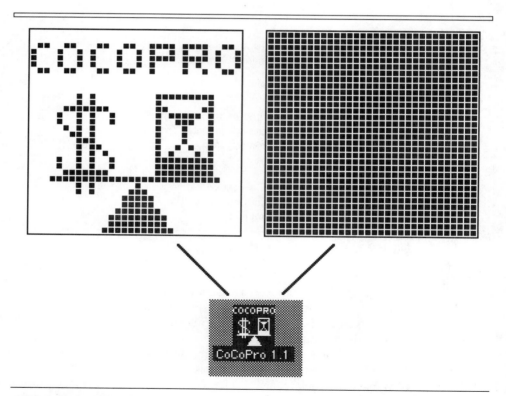

FIGURE 4-8. The CoCoPro icon

The high-level specification of an icon can contain either an icon alone, or the icon and its mask together, see Figure 4-9. Both patterns are given as hexadecimal numbers. The hex numbers are converted to pixels, or bits for black-and-white screens.

```
Type ICN# = GNRL
,128 (32)
.H
00000000
00000000
66333DE6
8944A529
8944BDE9
8944A149
66332126
00000000
00000000
00000000
01401FF0
01401010
07F01830
094817D0
09481390
05401110
03401110
01C01110
01601290
01501450
09481FF0
09481FF0
07F01FF0
1FFFFFF8
01408000
0141C000
0003E000
0003E000
0007F000
000FF800
000FF800
001FFC00
* below is the mask
FFFFFFFF
FFFFFFFF
FFFFFFFF
FFFFFFFF
FFFFFFFF
FFFFFFFF
FFFFFFFF

* etc. for 32 rows
```

FIGURE 4-9. Specification for icon in Figure 4-8

A simple icon is of type ICN (four characters including a space after the N), but a desktop icon containing a mask is of type ICN#. The first hexadecimal bit map defines the icon, and the second one the mask. In this example, the mask bits are all set to ones, so the mask will invert the icon when the icon is clicked.

The icon id number in this example is 128. The (32) tells the memory manager of the Macintosh how to allocate memory space. An icon can be purged from memory in the event that memory is needed for more useful purposes. In Figure 4-9 we have designated the icon as a purgeable resource. The remaining specification consists of 32 rows of 32 bits each for the icon, and a second 32-row by 32-column bit map for the mask.

The bit maps would be rather tedious and likely to contain errors if entered, one hexadecimal number at a time. This is also true of many of the other user interface objects we have discussed. Fortunately, CASE tools such as the Resource Editor, or ResEdit have been developed for creating and changing user interface objects. Actually, a variety of resource editors exist: REdit, ResEdit for general resources that have been compiled; IEdit, DEdit, and others for creating and editing high-level (textual) specifications of icons, dialogs, and windows; and ScreenEdit for creating and editing standard user interface objects.

ResEdit — a CASE tool provided by Apple Computer — is perhaps the most widely used tool for creating and editing user interface objects. ResEdit is also used to explore the internal structure of the Macintosh operating system. Much can be learned by experimenting with ResEdit. Be careful, however, because ResEdit can damage system files and cause an untimely death of the operating system.

FORM FOLLOWS FUNCTION

The software designer must know in advance what the application is going to look like, how it is going to "feel" to the user, and how it is going to fit in with existing software. This is a challenge for all but the most experienced, insightful designer: we have elaborated only a few of the pressing issues that must be considered by software engineers.

Two main points stand out:

1. Attributes of good software design compete with one another, and must be sorted out during the design process.

2. Form follows function.

We made a strong case for sorting out design issues at the beginning of the development phase and at every turn during design. But what do we mean by *form* and *function* in software design?

A beautiful building is designed to perform a certain function, and like a building, good software is both functionally and aesthetically pleasing. The pleasing qualities of software are more than "merely" aesthetic — they are essential. Software must compel users to use it, and this can only be achieved through thoughtful and artful user interface design. Thus the "form-follows-function" school of software design places great importance on principles of user interface design.

TEN HYPOTHESES FOR USER INTERFACE DESIGN

There are no hard-and-fast rules for user interface design, but Ledgard et al.[2] offer a collection of hypotheses to guide designers:

1. Inclusion of extraneous and redundant features interferes with usefulness of the system.

2. Inclusion of unknown features — undocumented commands, unrealized limitations of the system, or little-used parameters — interferes with the usefulness of the system.

3. Commands should be modeless, especially if they are layered or hierarchically organized. The meaning of a command should be consistent across layers.

4. The user should be alerted to any potentially damaging situations: alerts should caution, warn, and prevent irreversible error conditions.

5. Error messages should help, not scold the user. Messages should contain all information necessary to remedy the error condition.

6. Error condition correction should be easy and immediate.

7. Command formation rules should be simple and consistent.

8. First-letter "short-cut" commands are superior, but they must be unique.

9. Commands (menu items) should be based on meaningful natural-language phrases and composed of familiar, descriptive words with no abbreviations.

10. Be specific. Avoid generalizations in describing commands, giving help, prompting for input, and showing error messages.

Form-follows-function leads naturally to software designs that evolve from user interface specifications. If we capture how the system is going to work — its menus, windows, and dialogs — then we can identify the functionality of the system. For example, menu items typically contain verbs that define functions to be performed; dialogs typically contain modifiers that refine even further the functions to be performed.

Form-follows-function also implies direct manipulation interfaces instead of natural language interfaces. A direct manipulation interface is operated by manipulating graphic objects rather than telling the system what you want it to do with "language." For example, a direct manipulation system allows the user to drag a file icon to a wastepaper basket icon to remove the file from the system, rather than requiring the user to type a command such as ERASE <filename>. This is a controversial departure from traditional "command" languages that had been used by software designers for thirty years.

Direct manipulation also encourages WYSIWYG (What-You-See-Is-What-You-Get) interfaces. In a WYSIWYG system, commands, flags, and cryptic notations are replaced by an image of the actual or desired result. For example, a WYSIWYG word processor displays the document exactly as it will appear when printed. It is not necessary to format the document or actually print it to see how it will turn out. This is also controversial because experienced users complain that WYSIWYG interfaces are cumbersome and slow, while advocates claim the opposite. But the tide appears to be favoring WYSIWYG, direct-manipulation as the dominate form of user interface.

Color Guidelines

Concerning the use of color in displays, we summarize some observations made by Swezey et al.[5] and Foley et al.[6] relating to graphics and graphical user interfaces.

Color should be used conservatively to avoid clutter.

The maximum number of color codes is 11.

Color coding is most valuable in search tasks. From fastest to slowest the preferred colors are: red, blue, yellow, green, black, and white.

Color coding is not appropriate for situations that demand rapid and precise identification of objects in the interface.

Highlighting (inverse video or coloring) is valuable in general and necessary if key events are to attract a bored operator's attention.

Blinking is to be avoided or used sparingly.

Limit highlighting to one or two items at a time.

The same color should be used on all functionally related controls/buttons, up to a maximum of 8 colors. The hierarchy of colors for most efficient coding is: red, yellow, green, blue. If more colors are needed, then use red, yellow, two shades of green, two shades of blue, orange, and white, in this order.

Buttons should be at least 0.25 inches on a side, and grouped according to function. Avoid abbreviated labels, and use familiar phrases or words.

WYSIWYG ON TRIAL

Veteran computer users feel that the WYSIWYG principle of user interface design is just a fad. Productivity gains have been reported, however. In one experiment, learning time and performance of users working with a command line editor was compared to that of workers using a screen editor. The users of line editors required 17% more time to learn the editor, while the users of the screen editor were 40% more productive[3].

Nonetheless, results are mixed. In a second experiment, users of a spreadsheet program were given a choice between using a menu command versus a mouse to select spreadsheet cells. These users tended to favor menu selection over mouse clicking even though the mouse clicking operation was faster[4]. (The users were not aware of the speed advantage of mouse clicking, but perceived the menu selection as the most efficient method of cell selection.)

Regarding text coloring, spectral density (what the human eye can see best) is greatest in the yellow-green portion of the color spectrum, hence yellow characters on a green background are usually recommended. Otherwise the display should show bright (yellow or white) characters on a dark (green or gray) background.

Many of these observations are controversial because computer technology has outpaced human factors research. These principles can be seen in action in most modern software systems, however, and represent the best of what we know about user interface design.

Terms and Concepts

abstract data type	object-oriented design
alarm	packaging
audit trail	paradigm
bomb	param text
code fork	performance amortization
compact	prototype
consistent interface	ResEdit
control	resource fork
double-click	responsive
easy to use	RMaker
encapsulation	robust
error message	seamless interface
fast	short cut
KISS	standard user interface
modal	user interface
modeless	WYSIWYG
object	

DISCUSSION QUESTIONS

1. Make a list of the features of a good interface design. Describe how Macintosh menus, windows, dialogs, icons, and alerts satisfy (or do not satisfy) your list of features.

2. How would you propose to use color coding to improve the desktop model of the Macintosh?

3. Change the stage number of the example alert dialog (5555) so that item 2 becomes the default button instead of item 1. What is the hexadecimal value used in place of 5555, if this modification is used on the first stage only?

4. RAM memory is getting larger and cheaper, and accessing data from RAM is much faster than accessing from disk. When would you choose to load a disk file entirely into RAM when initializing an application to gain speed?

5. Read question four. Discuss when it might be appropriate to "buffer" or "swap" large sections of a disk file into and out of RAM memory to strike a balance between speed and size.

6. Binary files are typically more compact and faster to read/write than text files, yet text files are simple and compatible with most other software. When would you design an application to use text files instead of binary files? Give several examples that justify your design decision.

7. Explain the consequences of an application that uses a merge sort to sort disk files. Discuss the impact on size, speed, convenience, and usability of the application.

8. Why is recursion sometimes considered harmful? Give an example not cited in the text.

9. Early computer system designers were limited by technology. For instance, low-resolution color could be traded for high-resolution black-and-white, but high-resolution color was out of reach. If you were designing a computer system and you had to choose between black-and-white graphics with relatively high resolution or color graphics with relatively low resolution, which choice would you make, and why?

10. What characteristics make the mouse preferable to light pens, joysticks, and keyboards?

11. Make a list of desirable attributes of error messages. What criteria guide the design of an on-line help facility for an application?

REFERENCES AND FURTHER READING

1. Sackman, H., W. J. Erikson, and E. E. Grant. 1968. "Exploratory Experimental Studies Comparing Online and Offline Programming Performance." *Communications of the ACM* 11, no. 1 (January): 3–11.

2. Ledgard, H., A. Singer, and J. Whiteside. 1981. "Directions in Human Factors for Interactive Systems." *Springer-Verlag Lecture Notes in Computer Science* 103: 146–162.

3. Dunsmore, H. E. "Line and Screen Text Editors: Some University Experiment Results." In *Human-Computer Interaction*; ed. G. Salvendy, 57–164. New York: Elsevier Science Publisher.

4. MacLean, A., P. T. Barnard, and M. D. Wilson. 1985. "Evaluating the Human Interface of a Data Entry System: User Choice and Performance Measures Yield Different Tradeoff Functions." In *People and Computers: Designing the Interface*; eds. P. Johnson and S. Cook, 172–185. Cambridge: Cambridge University Press.

5. Swezey R. W., and E. G. Davis. 1983. "A Case Study of Human Factors Guidelines in Computer Graphics." *IEEE Computer Graphics and Applications* 3, no. 11 (November): 21–30.

6. Foley, J. D., V. L. Wallace, and P. Chan. 1984. "The Human Factors of Computer Graphics Interaction Techniques." *IEEE Computer Graphics and Applications* 4, no. 11 (November): 13–48.

5

Software Requirements Specification

PREVIEW

Software design begins with the Software Requirements Specification document — the SRS. In this chapter we list the attributes of an SRS document. We use tables, diagrams, and English descriptions to specify the user interface, functions, and data managed by an application.

These requirements must be verifiable — that is we must be able to confirm their existence, correctness, completeness, and so on, in a requirements review meeting prior to the next step — designing the system architecture. The need to examine the specification in considerable detail, change it when new requirements are added, and keep up with demands for current documentation leads to the need for automatic CASE tools. A DFD/DD CASE tool is described and used to specify the top levels of CoCoPro, the Development Project.

DFD/DD specification is only one of many representations possible, but because it is simple and automated, it is widely used by developers.

AN OVERVIEW

The previous chapters have provided preliminary tools for planning the development process. In this chapter the development itself is introduced. Several process models are available to guide development. Prominent among these are the waterfall model which is compatible with a strictly "top-down" approach, and the rapid prototyping model, which is compatible with an iterative approach. The waterfall model is the oldest and perhaps most mature model, but the rapid prototyping model has many advantages.

The waterfall approach will serve as the primary model for this chapter. In a subsequent chapter we modify portions of the waterfall approach by introducing rapid prototyping techniques where appropriate. In both cases we apply tools and techniques that are appropriate to specific phases of the software lifecycle.

The overall plan for a top-down, waterfall development process is as follows:

1. Start with the product description as given by the SCM Plan (see chapter three).
2. Capture the Software Requirements Specification (SRS) as described in this chapter.
3. Refine the SRS document into a System Architecture Specification (see chapters five, six, and seven).
4. Refine the System Architecture Specification into source code (see chapters eight and nine).
5. Implement the components, then the entire system per the refinements (see chapter nine).
6. Perform Unit, Functional, and System Verification and Validation (see chapters ten and eleven).

This ideal top-down approach is actually iterated rather than followed strictly from top (step 1) to bottom (step 6). Iteration is necessary because each phase must evolve from a baseline document. First, a baseline SCM, SRS, System Architecture, and so forth, is established from top to bottom. Then the team refines baseline as they become fully aware of the needs, complexities, and goals of the system. The team establishes subsequent baselines, and the process is repeated as many times as needed to complete the project.

Each iteration of the design is accomplished by a combination of techniques, intuition, and tools. CASE tools are of particular interest because they provide automated means of iterating the design. We use word processors to create and update the baseline SCM Plan; automated data flow diagramming software to capture and iterate the SRS documents; automated structure chart software to manage System Architecture Specifications; PDL (Program Design Language) tools to refine the System Architecture Specification into source code; interactive compiler and debugging tools to implement and test components of the system; and various testing techniques and tools to verify and validate the completed product.

The process can be explained in specific operational terms:

1. Use a special SRS document preparation tool or a word processor to list the functional and operational requirements of the Product. This list becomes the SRS Document.

2. Use a Data Flow Diagramming tool to define the overall system configuration. This configuration becomes the Preliminary Design.

3. Use a Structure Chart tool to refine the Preliminary Design specification. This spec becomes the System Architecture.

4. Use a PDL (Program Design Language) tool to refine each component of the System Architecture into pseudo-code.

5. Use a Programming Environment tool to implement the system of components. This creates the source code.

6. Use Testing tools to verify and validate the source code against the SRS Document. The result becomes the Product.

The development team will need various kinds of additional information along the way. To implement a compelling user interface, they will need information about the toolbox of the Macintosh. They will need guidelines for laying out source code so that it is easily maintained and modified later on by maintenance programmers. This information will be provided in the text as it is needed.

Once the traditional waterfall approach has been completed for the Development Project (CoCoPro), we return to the more advanced technique of Rapid Prototyping. We examine the advantages and disadvantages of rapid prototyping and show how to build a prototype of the Development Project using a prototyping tool developed by the author and his students. Additionally, we examine tools and techniques for maintaining large, complex systems. Finally, we briefly survey the most difficult part of the problem, marketing and supporting the product.

THE SRS DOCUMENT

Requirements analysis *is the process of studying user needs to arrive at a definition of software requirements.* A **requirements specification** *sets forth the requirements for a system or system component. Typically, this includes functional requirements, performance requirements, user interface requirements, design requirements, and development standards.* The requirements analysis phase of the software lifecycle is considered the first phase of the waterfall model and often ends with an inspection of the requirements specification (SRS) document. This document may be organized and formatted in various ways, but it typically has the following minimum contents:

Product Overview and Summary
Development, Operating, and Maintenance Environments
External Interfaces and Data Flow
Functional Requirements
Performance Requirements

Exception Handling
Early Subsets and Implementation Priorities
Foreseeable Modifications and Enhancements
Acceptance Criteria
Design Hints and Guidelines
Glossary of Terms

There is no universally accepted method for producing an SRS document, but standard attributes have been suggested by a number of organizations. For example, the IEEE Standard suggests the following attributes for all items listed in the SRS document.

Correct

The SRS must define a specific product that the user wants. Obviously, every software developer wants to produce a "correct" program. The problem is not so simple, however, because product correctness is relative to the user's needs. For example, the SRS might incorrectly specify that the product must compute the *mean* of a list of numbers, when the user needs the *median* value of the list. This SRS item is incorrect, not because the calculation incorrectly computes the mean value, but because the user wants the median value. This kind of error can only be found by careful inspection of the SRS document during a meeting with the users.

Complete

The SRS must: specify all requirements including responses to all inputs, conform to all standards, and define all terms. The important point here is the need to be thorough. For example, a word processor might satisfy all of the requirements listed in its SRS document, but if the SRS document fails to include the requirement that the product accept input data from a graphics program, then the SRS is not complete. One of the main purposes of the requirements inspection is to guarantee completeness.

Often the user is *not* the best source of information for collecting requirements items. Users have a tendency to think of new requirements only after they have used the system for awhile. This is one of the main reasons for rapid prototyping: to give the user an insight prior to building the system. As a result, the SRS document is subject to change while the product is in development. A moving target is difficult to hit, so only limited changes can be permitted. Even then, the changes must be incorporated carefully and systematically. An SRS baseline is established and followed until changes are introduced. Subsequent baselines are established to incorporate new requirements. Thus in practice, completeness of the SRS document is established by an evolutionary process.

Consistent

The SRS has no conflicting items. The most common inconsistencies are multiple or conflicting descriptions of an object. For example, one SRS item might say to add two numbers while another item might say to multiply them; a printed report might be described as tabular in one place and textual in another; or an item might specify that actions A and B are to be done in sequence while another item might specify that A and B occur in parallel. Inconsistencies can be detected in an SRS document by cross-referencing all terms, objects, functions, and actions defined for the product.

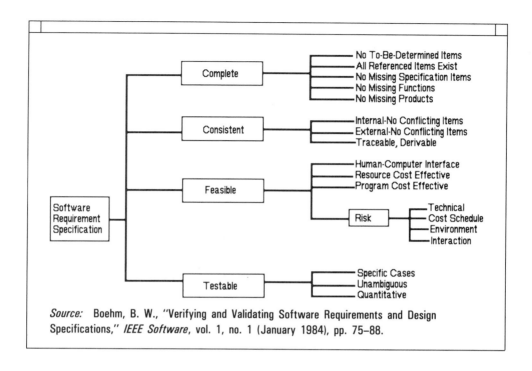

Source: Boehm, B. W., "Verifying and Validating Software Requirements and Design Specifications," *IEEE Software*, vol. 1, no. 1 (January 1984), pp. 75–88.

Unambiguous

Every requirement item must have one and only one interpretation. Unambiguous means concise and clear. The need for rigor is great, but the tendency in speccing is to be loose with definitions and requirements. For example, instead of stating "the product must degrade gracefully as the number of users increases," the requirement must be precise; "the product must respond in less than 1 second when up to 10 users are performing editing operations, and respond in less than 10 seconds when 20 users are performing compilation operations." Such specifications abound: round-off errors in numerical calculations must be specified; limitations on file and disk space must be quantified; and limitations on screen layouts must be provided in the SRS document. Much of the ambiguity of an SRS document can be eliminated by providing a glossary of terms, and replacing vague descriptions with precise measurements and exact amounts.

Functional

The SRS document must define what is required without specifying how the system is to work. Functional specifications enumerate what the system is supposed to do. For example, CoCoPro is supposed to 1) compute the effort and time needed to complete a software project, 2) store historical data on actual projects, and 3) calibrate the models to reflect the database of actuals. In addition, CoCoPro can print reports, adjust drivers, and save the adjustments. Functional specifications can be clearly defined by simply listing them.

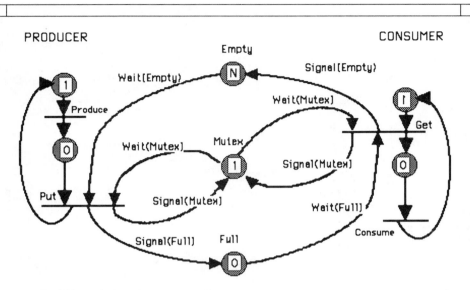

Petri Networks have been proposed as a means of specifying real-time concurrent systems because they are able to model states and transitions. A state is represented by a round "bubble" with an inflow and an outflow; a transition is represented by a straight line with one or more inflow and outflow arrows.

A system moves from a state to a transition and from a transition to a state, but never from state to state or from transition to transition. Transitions become executable routines in the software, and states become placeholders between actions where a certain property of the system can be guaranteed.

In the classical producer-consumer problem of operating system software, a "producer" process is a concurrent process (locus of control through some code) that attempts to fill a buffer with characters while another process called the "consumer" attempts to empty the same buffer. The two processes must be synchronized to avoid a race condition (Mutex), and to avoid either underflow (attempting to get a character when the buffer is empty) or overflow (attempting to put a character into a full buffer).

The WAIT primitive forces a process to be delayed until a condition is satisfied, for example, when the buffer is EMPTY and the SIGNAL primitive forces a process to resume execution after it has been delayed by a WAIT. The effect of WAIT and SIGNAL operations is to avoid indeterminism, overflow, and underflow.

Verifiable

The SRS document must tell how the developers and users can know when the product satisfies its requirements. The term *verifiable* is overloaded with meaning in software engineering. Even in the context of the SRS document it has been used by various people to mean different things. The standard definition states that a requirement item is

PSL/PSA

PROCESS DESCRIPTION: Process_Menu_In
This process takes In_Menu_Bar selections from the user and forwards them to each routine, which in turn handles the requested operation.
GENERATES: Menu_Id, Item_No
RECEIVES: In_Menu-Bar
SUBPARTS ARE: Do_Apple_Menu,
Do_Project_Menu, Do_CoCoMo_Menu,
Do_History_Menu, Do_Driver_Menu
PART OF: CoCoPro Application
DERIVES: Ram_Driver_Record,
Ram_Component_Record
USING: Do_Apple_Menu, Do_Project_Menu,
Do_CoCoMo_Menu,
Do_History_Menu, Do_Driver_Menu
PROCEDURE:

1. Repeat until user selects Project-Quit.

2. Poll for In_Menu_Bar event.

3. Computer Menu_Id, Item_No.

4. Call one ...
Do_Apple_Menu,
Do_Project_Menu,
Do_CoCoMo_Menu,
Do_History_Menu,
Do_Driver_Menu

5. Quit or Repeat.

HAPPENS: Each time application is launched
TRIGGERED BY: Initialization
TERMINATION CAUSES: Project_Quit,
Fatal Error
END.

PSL/PSA is a Program Specification Language/Program Specification Analysis system for producing an SRS document that can be processed automatically and checked for completeness, consistency, and so on. It resembles a very high-level language, complete with syntax and semantics.

Source: Teichroew, D., and E. A. Hershey III, "PSL/PSA: A Computer-Aided Technique for Structured Documentation and Analysis of Information Processing Systems," *IEEE Trans. Soft. Engr.*, SE-3, 1 (Jan. 1977), 41–48.

verifiable *if and only if there exists some cost-effective process with which a person or machine can check that the product meets the requirement.* Boehm[1] distinguishes between verification and validation as follows:

Verification: "Am I building the product right?"

Validation: "Am I building the right product?"

Here are some examples of requirements that cannot be verified:

1. "The product should have a good user interface." (The notion of a "good" user interface is subjective and cannot be verified since it is not defined.)
2. "The product should never crash." (It is theoretically impossible to prove whether or not a program will crash.)
3. "The product should produce an answer in 10 seconds, most of the time." ("Most of the time" is not a specific quantity.)

Clearly, there is no place in the SRS document for vague, qualitative terms such as "good," "usually," and "never."

DECISION TABLE: CONDITIONS, ACTIONS, AND RULES

Conditions	Rules						
Actions	1	2	3	4	5	6	7
New Project	Y	N	N	N	N	Y	Y
Open Project		Y	N	N	N		
Save Project			Y	N	N		
Print Project				Y	N	Y	
Quit Project					Y		Y
About Dialog							
Get Project Name	X	X					
Open Project File		X					
Save Project File			X		X		X
Print Project File				X		X	
Quit Application					X		X

Y = Yes, condition applies
N = No, condition does not apply
X = Do this action
   = Ignore, does not matter

A **decision table** *is a table of all contingencies that are to be considered in the description of a problem together with the actions to be taken for each set of contingencies.* A decision table usually contains a list of conditions, rules to apply when a condition is met, and actions to perform when a condition arises. Simple decision tables may merely list all the conditions that must be true at a certain state of the program.

> The example shown here lists conditions to be considered when operating the CoCoPro program: a New, Open, Save, or Print Project state might exist at some point in the program, or the program might be in the Quit state. A rule is activated and certain actions performed when one or more of the conditions arise.
>
> For example, if the conditions NEW PROJECT and PRINT PROJECT both arise, then rule 6 is applied, and action PRINT PROJECT FILE is performed. Notice how this specification prevents any action whatsoever when both NEW PROJECT and OPEN PROJECT conditions arise — there is no single rule for handling these two conditions at the same time. This illustrates the meaning of *disambiguous*: there is a single well-defined state, rule, and action for every possibility.
>
> The example also illustrates an *incompleteness* — there is no rule for activating the ABOUT DIALOG action as shown in the table. The ABOUT DIALOG row is empty, so no rule corresponds to this action. Such tables are valuable for checking specifications, but note the exponential growth in possible combinations. For N conditions, we must check 2^N possibilities. For this reason, decision tables work best for programming-in-the-small.

As a practical matter, verification is carried out at the end of each phase of the lifecycle. A phase is verified by inspection to determine if the product abides by the verification conditions set up by the previous phase. Requirement items are verified after design, implementation, and testing. Validation, on the other hand, must wait until the product is completed, then we can ask whether the product does what it was intended to do.

Typically, a checklist is all that is needed to verify and validate the functionality, performance, and robustness of a software product. However, as the last chapter made clear, there are many other attributes of high-quality software. These attributes may well appear in the SRS document along with a checklist for verifying the presence of the attributes.

Traceable

The origin and destination of each requirement item is known. Traceability is one of the most overlooked attributes of requirements specification. The idea is quite simple but implementation is difficult. For every item in the design, we want to be able to trace the implication of the item either forward or backward through the design. **Forward traceability** means *an item can be traced from one phase of the lifecycle to a subsequent phase*; **backward traceability** means *an item can be traced backward to an earlier phase*.

Traceability is extremely important because it is used during verification to explain why certain actions must be done, and it is important during maintenance because it is used to follow the implications of a change to the finished product. Various kinds of diagrams and charts are used to show traces in a design and implementation.

Several examples can be given to demonstrate traceability. Suppose a database system is being developed, and a requirement item states that the user must be able to retrieve a record in less than 2 seconds from a database containing one million records. A forward trace of this requirement might lead to a detailed design requirement for an indexing function that specifies, "The indexing software must be able to retrieve any record from a file of one million records in less than 1 second." The trace might be followed even further into the product by specifying the design of a B-tree structure: "The B-Tree indexing algorithm must operate on trees with a fan-out of 100 keys, because an average retrieval must be done in less than 100 milliseconds."

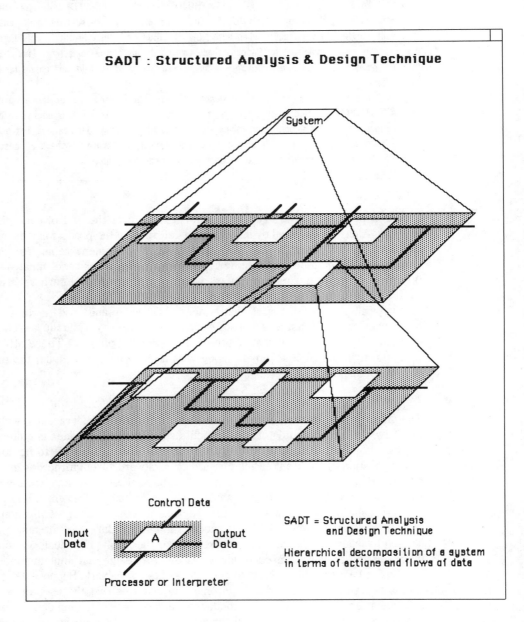

SADT : Structured Analysis & Design Technique

Control Data

Input Data — A — Output Data

Processor or Interpreter

SADT = Structured Analysis and Design Technique

Hierarchical decomposition of a system in terms of actions and flows of data

As a second example, consider a product that has been completed and is given a final inspection: a sample output contains a total at the end of the printed report. What requirement was responsible for specifying this total? If the requirement is backward traceable, we should be able to follow the trace from the report, to the system architecture, back to the preliminary design, and finally back to the SRS document. Perhaps the total appeared in the report because an item in the SRS document specified, "The product must compute a final balance by subtracting the debits from the credits."

Modifiable

Easy to change, and usable by maintenance programmers. Like the software product that the SRS document describes, the SRS document itself must be modifiable. Baseline SRS documents must facilitate change. When the users discover a new requirement, the SRS must be updated to a new baseline.

STRUCTURED ANALYSIS AND DESIGN: PRECURSOR TO SOFTWARE DESIGN

Structured Analysis and Design Technique is a general technique for designing any kind of system, including social, physical, hardware, and software systems. It was invented by Ross in the late 1960s and used for several decades to design large military systems involving many organizations, groups of people, machinery, and software.

SADT is applicable to software because it shares many of the features of good software design: complexity is controlled by using hierarchical structures, interfaces are clearly defined by flows, and functionality is specified by actigrams. An actigram defines an activity (a function) performed by the system. Actigrams connect inflows to outflows, as shown by data entering from the left side of the actigram box, and data leaving the right side of the actigram box. SADT diagrams are read from left to right just like normal text. However, SADT diagrams hide unnecessary detail through an orderly hierarchical structure as shown in the example.

Hierarchical decomposition — *a method of designing a system by breaking it down into its components through a series of top-down refinements* — is enforced by SADT. Hierarchical decomposition in SADT corresponds with functional decomposition in software design. Each actigram is refined by expanding it to another level. Each level is defined by another SADT diagram, and so forth, until the lowest level is reached. The "top" diagram is the most "abstract," while the "bottom" diagram is the most "concrete." Correspondingly, the top level hides the greatest amount of detail, while the lowest level exposes the greatest amount of detail. When used in the design of software, the process of concealing details at the top and incrementally revealing more detail as we uncover levels is called **information hiding**: *the technique of encapsulating software design decisions in modules in such a way that the module's interfaces reveal as little as possible about the module's inner workings; thus each module is a "black box" to the other modules.*

SADT is actually a complete philosophy of design containing many of the axioms of contemporary software development. For example, SADT diagrams are restricted to 6 or fewer actigrams, a rule that forces hierarchical decomposition on the user. The number 6 is thought to be the limit of "manageability" for humans. A humorous saying goes with SADT: "Everything worth saying about anything worth saying something about, must be expressed in six or fewer pieces."

Because SADT diagrams are capable of modelling any system of processes, each actigram is controlled and "interpreted" by two other entities: control information in the form of control data, and processor information in the form of people, machines, or software interpreters. For example, control data might be "enabling" information in the form of parameters — the state of a robot at some point in time — or perhaps parametric information — the size of a graphics screen. Processor information usually consists of an indication of whether an actigram is to be carried out by a machine or by a human. For example, a human might perform the function defined in an actigram (pressing the reset button, perhaps) or a machine might perform the function (averaging a list of numbers).

SADT diagrams have been automated in the form of a CASE tool. They have not found widespread use, however, perhaps because other graphical techniques are equally capable of describing software designs but are even simpler to use. These tools, whether they are SADT-based or not, form the starting point for most software specifications.

Source: Ross, D. T., "Structured Analysis(SA): A Language for Communicating Ideas," *IEEE Trans. Soft. Engr.*, SE-3, 1 (Jan. 1977), pp. 16–34.

One of the major uses of the SRS document is for maintenance, the enhancements and modifications that take place long after the product has been developed. As a result, the SRS document becomes a repository for the histories of a variety of activities. For example, suppose the product was modified to work with a new peripheral device. The modification activity becomes part of the history of the product. This history is incorporated into the SRS document to be read by a future generation of programmers. Similarly, the history of major bug fixes, ports to new hardware, and improvements to the software become valuable sources of information.

THE DEVELOPMENT PROJECT SRS

The Development Project is defined in the SCM Plan discussed in a previous chapter. In this section we will lay out the SRS — Software Requirements Specification — for the Development Project. Recall that the application to be implemented is the CoCoPro cost estimation program which was used earlier to estimate the time and effort needed to complete the development of CoCoPro itself. You may want to run this program again to become more familiar with its user interface and functionality.

Functional Requirements Specification

The first step is to make a list of the functional requirements for the top-most functions only. From an examination of CoCoMo and the "wish list" of users we can arrive at the following list:

Apple_About

CoCoPro must support desk accessories, and include its own "About CoCoPro..." item in the Apple-DA menu. When this menu item is selected, a single dialog will appear containing the program's identification, who wrote it, and an OK button for terminating the dialog.

Project

CoCoPro must be able to manage the estimation of costs for a single project at a time, and to create, load, save, and print other project data stored on disk. Thus, CoCoPro must provide the following functions:

New: Create a new project. Collect information from the user and compute estimates.

Open: Open an existing project file and read its contents into RAM — modify, compute estimates.

Save: Save the current project on disk, along with all of the information needed to calculate estimates.

Print: Print the current project.

Quit: Quit the application. Save the current project if it has been modified since the last save.

CoCoMo

CoCoPro must implement the model calculations of *Intermediate CoCoMo* for each of these modes:

Organic: Select the organic mode model.

Semi: Select the semi-embedded mode model.

Embedded: Select the embedded mode model.

Calculate: Compute the effort, MM, development time, TDEV, and distribution of effort and time over the development phases using standard Intermediate CoCoMo formulas and percentages.

History

CoCoPro extends the Intermediate CoCoMo model by storing actual project data in a file called the "History" file. History files contain effort and time estimates for past projects, along with their pertinent data such as the cost drivers assumed by the project.

See Storage Requirements Specification. One History file at a time is kept in RAM — the current file — but many files may be kept on disk. CoCoPro must provide the following functions on History files:

New: Create a new History file, give it a name and provide actual values.

Open: Open an existing History file and read it entirely into RAM.

Save: Save the current file on disk.

Print: Print the current History file.

Provide_Actuals: Capture actual project data from the user.

Calibrate: Calibrate the CoCoMo model by fitting a least-squares curve to the actual data.

Select_All: Select all projects in the History file for calibration.

Deselect_All: Reverse the "Select_All" operation.

Driver

CoCoPro must permit multiple sets of cost driver values to be used so that "what if" analysis can be performed. Each of the fifteen cost drivers defined by Intermediate CoCoMo may be modified by the user. A default file called CoCoPro.Drivers will be supplied and locked so that it is read-only. The default driver file will be used unless the user selects another file, or creates a new file.

Open: Open a driver file and read it into RAM.

Save: Save the current cost drivers in a disk file.

Change_Personnel: User can modify the Personnel cost drivers.

Change_Project: User can modify the Project cost drivers.

Change_Product: User can modify the Product cost drivers.

Change_Computer: User can modify the Computer cost drivers.

Show_Model_Params: Show all current cost drivers and coefficients of the CoCoMo models.

Storage Requirements Specification

We have made references to storage in the form of files, so we need a storage specification. The three kinds of files in the application are:

Report File

Stores all project information in report format, and is printed by the Project_Print function. This file is stored as an ASCII text file so it can be read and processed by other applications, such as a word processor. It contains the project name, CoCoMo mode, KDSI, MM, TDEV, average FSP, peak FSP, distribution of time and effort, and driver values used to calculate the estimates for each component in the project. A sample of a report file is given in Figure 5-1a to guide the designer and programmer during implementation.

Sample Report File

Component Name: Main Program

KDSI: 6.50
KEDSI: 6.50
MM: 9.04
Cost Per MM: 3000.00
TDEV: 5.77
Design Percent: 100.00
Code Percent: 100.00
Integration_Percent: 100.00
Average FSP: 1.57
Peak FSP: 1.90
Component Cost: 27119.82
Productivity: 719.03
Cost Per Instruction: 4.17

RELY	NOM	1.00
DATA	NOM	1.00
CPLX	LOW	0.85
TIME	NOM	1.00
STOR	NOM	1.00
VIRT	NOM	1.00
TURN	HI	1.07
ACAP	HI	0.86
AEXP	HI	0.91
PCAP	HI	0.86
VEXP	NOM	1.00
LEXP	HI	0.95
MODP	VHI	0.82
TOOL	VHI	0.83
SCED	NOM	1.00

Project Name: Development Project

Model: Organic

KDSI: 6.50
KEDSI: 6.50
MM: 9.04
TDEV: 5.77
Total Cost: 27119.82
Average FSP: 1.57
Peak FSP: 1.90
Productivity: 284.58
Cost Per Instruction: 4.17

Distribution:

	MM	TDEV
Plan	0.54	0.58
Design	1.45	1.10
Code	6.15	3.64
Integrate	1.45	1.04

FIGURE 5-1a. Sample report file

Sample History File

Project Name: One
Model: Organic

KDSI: 5.00
MM: 5.60
TDEV: 5.40

RELY	LOW	0.88
DATA	NOM	1.00
CPLX	NOM	1.00
TIME	HI	1.11
STOR	NOM	1.00
VIRT	NOM	1.00
TURN	NOM	1.00
ACAP	NOM	1.00
AEXP	NOM	1.00
PCAP	NOM	1.00
VEXP	HI	0.90
LEXP	NOM	1.00
MODP	LOW	1.10
TOOL	VLOW	1.24
SCED	HI	1.04

Project Name: Two
Model: Organic

KDSI : 6.00
MM: 9.00
TDEV: 8.60

RELY	NOM	1.00
DATA	NOM	1.00
CPLX	VHI	1.30
TIME	NOM	1.00
STOR	HI	1.06
VIRT	NOM	1.00
TURN	NOM	1.00
ACAP	NOM	1.00
AEXP	NOM	1.00
PCAP	LOW	1.17
VEXP	VLOW	1.21
LEXP	NOM	1.00
MODP	NOM	1.00
TOOL	NOM	1.00
SCED	NOM	1.00

. . . .etc. . . . . .

FIGURE 5-1b. Sample history file

History File

Stores all information pertaining to actual project data. These data are used to calibrate the model. This file is also stored as an ASCII text file and contains multiple records — one for each project — consisting of Project Name, mode, KDSI, MM, TDEV, and cost drivers assumed by the project. A sample of this file is also shown in Figure 5-1b to guide the designer and programmer.

Driver File

Stored as an ASCII file, this file contains all parameters assumed by the CoCoPro application: coefficients of the three modes (organic, semi-detached, and embedded), and all cost drivers stored as numerical values (three digits of significance in real format). The sample file is shown in Figure 5-1c for designer and programmer.

Sample Driver File

Organic
3.20
1.05
2.50
0.38

Semi-Detached
3.00
1.12
2.50
0.35

Embedded
2.80
1.20
2.50
0.32

RELY	0.75	0.88	1.00	1.15	1.40
DATA		0.94	1.00	1.08	1.16
CPLX	0.70	0.85	1.00	1.15	1.30	1.65
TIME		1.00	1.11	1.30	1.66
STOR		1.00	1.06	1.21	1.56
VIRT		0.87	1.00	1.15	1.30
TURN		0.87	1.00	1.07	1.15
ACAP	1.46	1.19	1.00	0.86	0.71
AEXP	1.29	1.13	1.00	0.91	0.82
PCAP	1.42	1.17	1.00	0.86	0.70
VEXP	1.21	1.10	1.00	0.90	
LEXP	1.14	1.07	1.00	0.95	
MODP	1.24	1.10	1.00	0.91	0.82
TOOL	1.24	1.10	1.00	0.91	0.83
SCED	1.23	1.08	1.00	1.04	1.10

FIGURE 5-1c. Sample driver file

These storage components have a counterpart in RAM when the application is running. That is, when the CoCoPro application is launched by the user, one of the first things it does is to open the default driver file called CoCoPro.Driver and read all of it into RAM. This file is always present, and always contains the values recommended by Boehm in the Intermediate CoCoMo model. Should the CoCoPro.Driver file be absent, an error message is displayed on the screen and the application terminates.

We also specified that each of the other two files must fit into RAM. This places a restriction on the size of these files, a restriction which we must clearly specify here. This requirement is complicated by the fact that the application can be run on a variety of hardware configurations. Disk and RAM capacities vary from one model of Macintosh to another.

We can estimate the upper limit on both disk drive and RAM capacities in tabular form as shown in Figure 5-2. A 400K disk drive can hold 500, 800, and 300 records of Report, History, and Driver information, respectively. This information might be

Requirements Analysis
Data Storage Capacity Chart

Store *Data*	*Disk* *(400K)*	*RAM* *(512K)*
Report File (Component Records)	500 Records	>125 Records
History File (History Actuals)	800 Actuals	>200 Actuals
Driver File (Driver Record)	300 Records	1 Record

Requirements Analysis
Speed Performance Chart

Data *Actions*	*Report* *(50 components)*	*History* *(50 actuals)*	*Driver* *(1 record)*
Read from disk file	1 min. 30 seconds	1 min.	5 seconds
Write to disk file	12 seconds	10 seconds	2 seconds
Calculate project result	10 seconds		
Calibrate actuals		11 seconds	
Print	5 min.	4 min. 45 seconds	12 seconds

FIGURE 5-2. Storage and performance requirements

apportioned to one file or the other, but not all files can be of these sizes at the same time. Thus, there may be five Report files totaling 5 records; one History file totaling 100 records; and two Driver files totaling 2 records on a single disk.

The more significant restriction is shown in the limitations due to RAM. We show an approximate limit of 125, 200, and 1 record, respectively, for Report, History, and Driver files in RAM in Figure 5-2. The application only needs 1 record of a Driver file at any point in time, so this restriction is of little concern. The Report file will contain a record for each component of a Project. The limitation of 125 records translates into a limitation of 125 components. Similarly, the History file is limited to 200 actuals, one for each record. These capacities are expressed in tabular form, as in Figure 5-2.

Trade-offs

A second concern surrounds the storage requirements specification: performance. We have made two design trade-offs of considerable importance in this example. First, we decided to run the application entirely out of RAM by requiring all files to fit into RAM. No file activity occurs except to copy each file entirely into RAM prior to accessing records of a given file. This decision was based on the desire for simplicity and speed of operation, with full knowledge that it sacrificed capacity.

The second trade-off was to write the files in ASCII text format to make them accessible to other applications, a desirable packaging attribute. But this leads to a slow system that wastes storage space, because text must be converted into numerical representation each time it is moved from disk to RAM, and then converted back each time it is moved from RAM to disk. Performance and compactness of disk storage has been sacrificed for compatibility with other applications.

Trade-offs are always difficult to gauge before implementation. In this case several reasons for making the trade-off were given:

- Disk storage capacity is not a major concern because the files are typically "small" and disk space can easily be purchased, if necessary.

- RAMs are getting larger, and in fact, a 1MB RAM system would hold perhaps more records that anyone would care to manage.

- Text files are slower, but not significantly slower. The exception is when the History file becomes very large, around 100 records. Thus, in most cases, speed of operation is not threatened.

- Conversion between text and numbers is rather easy and uncomplicated. The speed disadvantages are not obvious to a user.

- Simplicity was considered more important than the other factors, especially when considering the problems of maintenance, complexity of coding, and the rather limited advantage gained by requiring the application to run from direct access files.

This completes the storage requirements specification. We turn now to the specification of the system as a collection of interacting storage elements and operational functions. To do this, we must combine the functional and storage specifications and show how they fit together to comprise a system.

DATA FLOW DIAGRAM SPECIFICATION

Data Flow Diagrams (DFDs) are perhaps the simplest and most widely used method of documenting the specification of a software system. A **DFD** *is a graphic representation of a system, showing data sources, sinks, and storage; processes performed on data as nodes; and logical flow of data as links between nodes.* DFD is sometimes called a Data Flow Graph (DFG), data flow chart (DFC), or data flow document (DFD).

DFDs contain three important components:

1. *Bubbles*, the nodes representing processes or functions performed by the system.
2. *Storage*, the data sources and sinks which hold information.
3. *Information flow*, as indicated by links.

A system DFD specifies what functions are to be performed, what data is to be operated on, and what data is to flow among process bubbles and storage elements. We sometimes refer to the process bubbles as *actigrams*, and the flows as *datagrams*. A datagram flowing into an actigram shows an input flow; conversely, a datagram leaving an actigram shows an output flow.

DFDs show information flow rather than control flow. Therefore, unless the application is going to run on a parallel processor computer, the functions and flows in a DFD must be *sequenced* before they can be implemented on a serial computer.

DFDs are hierarchically structured, that is, each bubble of a DFD may be decomposed into a lower-level DFD. The input flows of the top bubble must equal the input flows of the lower-level DFD. Likewise, the output flows must match. When a DFD is checked for consistency of flows between two levels, we say the top bubble and the lower DFD are *leveled*. A *balanced DFD* is one where all input and output flows are leveled.

The storage elements of a DFD are decomposed into lower-level data definitions. A Data Dictionary (DD), is a repository of all storage elements, along with their definitions and components. A data element is decomposed into its components by simply listing the lower-level components with the data element in the DD.

Many dialects of DFDs have been proposed and implemented as CASE tools. For example, the Structured System Analysis (SSA) technique of Gane and Sarson; the Structured Analysis (SA) technique of Yourdon, Constantine, and DeMarco; and combinations of other techniques have been implemented as part of various CASE tools. An SSA DFD is shown in Figure 5-3 for the CoCoPro Development Project using Anatool for the Macintosh.

Although these techniques were known for many years, programmers were slow to use them. The principal reason was the fact that they were graphic rather than textual representations of systems. When the graphic workstation became inexpensive and widely available, the graphic specification techniques also became available. In the next section, we show how the Development Project is specified with such a tool.

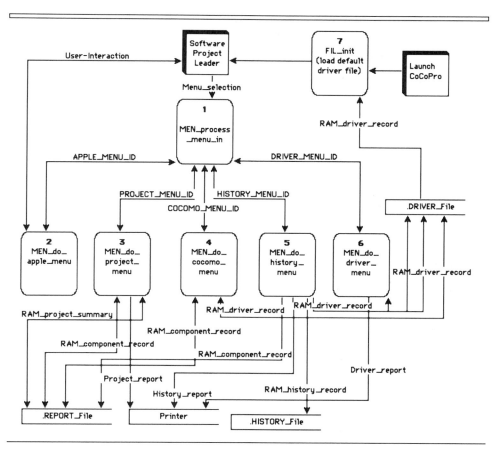

FIGURE 5-3. Top-level data flow diagram of CoCoPro

CoCoPro DFD

The top-level DFD of the CoCoPro application contains two boxes representing the user, a Software Project Leader who launches the application from the desktop and then operates the application by selecting menus. The User_Interaction flow specifies a data flow that takes place when the user activates any one of several Desk Accessories (DAs). Thus, CoCoPro must support DA selection.

The FIL_init process bubble is activated upon launching. This function opens the default CoCoPro.Driver file which contains the default driver values. The cost drivers are copied from the text file into RAM, converted to numerical values, and stored internally as indicated by the RAM_driver_record flow.

Process bubble 1, MEN_process_menu_in, controls the process of selecting a menu item. Recall that the menu items specified earlier mirror the functionality of the entire system. Thus, selection of any item in the PROJECT menu as indicated by the flow from process bubble 1 to process bubble 3, PROJECT_MENU_ID, causes the function represented by MEN_do_project_menu to be activated. Similarly, each menu selection corresponds to one of the process bubbles — each bubble is "reached" by one of the flows.

We can design the application's menu bar from the specification shown here. The menu bar will initially contain some items that are disabled (disabled items are not dimmed here) and other items that are active. A more detailed specification will be needed to determine which items are initially disabled, but the most general level of specification is already useful for designing the top-level portion of the application.

The top-level DFD includes the three data files and one storage element not previously discussed. (The Printer appears much like a write-only storage element.) Each of the three data files may be printed under program control. All files are copied entirely into RAM when needed and are shown as RAM_project_summary, RAM_component_record, Project_report, and so forth.

Notice the naming conventions. They have a specific meaning. Names are chosen to indicate *where the named entity is defined.* For example, all entities beginning with RAM_ are defined in the part of the system that deals with all operations on RAM; the MEN_ entities are defined in the part of the system that deals with all operations on MENUS, and so forth. Naming in a consistent manner like this is important for establishing traceability, a principal attribute of a good SRS document.

Each menu has several items as shown in the prototype menu of Figure 5-4. These items are activated by user selection. For example, if the user selects menu CoCoMo as shown in the prototype menu, this corresponds to Menu_Selection = COCOMO_MENU_ID in the DFD. When one of the items in the CoCoMo menu is selected, say CALCULATE, the process shown in bubble 4 is activated. To see what happens next, bubble 4 must be decomposed.

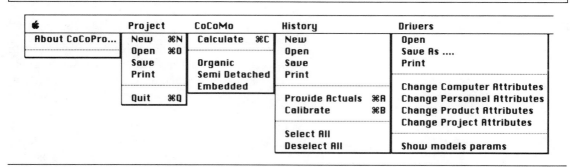

FIGURE 5-4. Menu prototype for CoCoPro

Bubbles are decomposed into other DFDs, as illustrated in Figure 5-5 by decomposing bubble 4 into a DFD containing bubbles 4.1, 4.2, ..., 4.6, and additional data flows. The decomposition is level, because all inputs/outputs to bubble 4 are also inputs/outputs to the lower-level DFD. Specifically, COCOMO_ID is the inflow, and RAM_component_record and RAM_driver_record are outflows at both levels.

At the second-level decomposition of bubble 4, we see additional process bubbles which may be decomposed even further. Bubble 4.1 divides the flow into two categories, one dealing with calculations and the other with selecting the mode. Notice again the naming convention: REP means REPORT. Process bubbles at the second level are defined in the Report part of the system, so their names begin with REP. Using this terminology helps to establish a working vocabulary for the system very early in the design process. Programmers will adopt this naming convention and use it throughout the development phase, leading to a traceable and maintainable system.

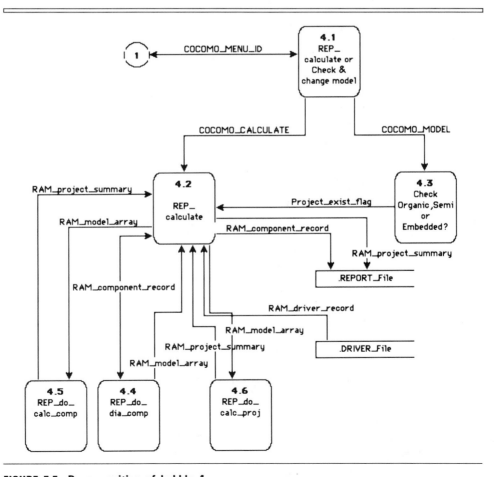

FIGURE 5-5. Decomposition of bubble 4

The second-level DFD specifies what steps to take to select a mode (4.3) and then compute the estimates we want (4.4, 4.5, 4.6). Greater detail is possible by decomposing these bubbles further, but we have not done so here. Many details remain to be clarified, however, even at this high level. To do so, we must provide additional specification in some formal or semi-formal language.

Informal Specifications

To illustrate the completeness attribute of requirements specification, suppose we embellish the DFD documents and menu prototype with English language descriptions of the system — both data flows and functional specifications. These embellishments serve as an informal specification complementing the DFD, DD, and tabular documents. The embellishment must provide information on INITIAL and FINAL states, and transformations that take place in between. For example, consider two of the bubble processes, one from each of the two levels.

Bubble 1: MEN_process_menu_in

INITIAL. All menu items are enabled except the following:

PROJECT
- SAVE

HISTORY
- SAVE,
- PROVIDE ACTUALS
- CALIBRATE
- SELECT ALL
- DESELECT ALL

All parameters are set to zero, initially, and all inputs are either blank or zero.

TRANSFORM. All menus are highlighted when selected, and remain highlighted until the operation completes.

All items are disabled when not available, enabled otherwise.

DA-About...
- always enabled,
- transition to bubble 2 when DA selected.

Project
- NEW, OPEN disabled when Report file is loaded; QUIT always enabled,
- transition to bubble 3 when PROJECT_MENU_ID selected.

CoCoMo
- CALCULATE enabled when a report is created or loaded; place check mark next to selected mode,
- transition to bubble 4 when COCOMO_MENU_ID selected.

History
- PROVIDE ACTUALS, CALIBRATE, SELECT ALL, DESELECT ALL enabled when History file loaded,
- transition to bubble 5 when HISTORY_MENU_ID selected.

Drivers
- Always enabled because a driver file is always loaded,
- transition to bubble 6 when DRIVER_MENU_ID selected.

FINAL.

Menus are available after each operation is completed.

Now, suppose we examine a specification for a second-level process bubble. This time, the bubble represents a final decomposition, so no additional levels of decomposition are required.

Bubble 4.3 Check Organic, Semi, or Embedded

INITIAL.

Highlight the CoCoMo menu.

TRANSFORM.

Place a check mark next to one of the following: Organic, Semi, Embedded.

Mode may be changed at anytime; current mode is used whenever CALCULATE is selected.

Update RAM copy of estimates.

FINAL. Remove highlighting from the menu.

These specifications must clarify what happens whenever the user attempts an impossible or incorrect operation or combination of operations. In addition, the specification may include user interface details such as the error dialogs, data entry dialogs, and so on. For example, file I/O is most prone to exceptions as shown in the next embellishment.

File specifications

INITIAL.

All files are TEXT files and are named according to a simple rule:
- Report file names end with .Report, History files with .History, and Driver files with .Driver.

A default file named CoCoPro.Driver always exists, and is write-protected.

The user will always be warned of the following conditions when manipulating files:
- File already exits — do you want to write over it?

- File has not been saved yet — do you want to save it?
- File read/write error — bad media, file, or format.
- File overflow — out of disk space, disk locked, etc.

TRANSFORM.

Read/Write entire file into RAM.
Use error dialogs as specified.
Append Project Name as prefix to all file names.

FINAL.

Close all files before exiting application.

These embellishments are refined through additional decompositions as we move on to other phases of development. We will come back to functional decomposition later, but for now, what about decomposition of the data flows and storage elements?

Most automated DFD tools include facilities for DD storage and management. The idea is to establish a vocabulary of procedure, function, constant, type, and variable identifier names which can be traced from specification to final product. Since it is impossible to identify and specify all named entities at the very top of the design, it is necessary to begin with the major processes and flows and refine these into a number of detailed entities.

The DD facilities of Anatool illustrate data decomposition. For example, the top-level flow called RAM_history_record is decomposed into eight lower-level data elements, see Figure 5-6.

```
RAM_history_record = Project_Name
                    + actual_model
                    + actual_KDSI
                    + actual_MM
                    + actual_TDEV
                    + Driver_levels
                    + Driver_Coef
                    + selected
```

The " + " signifies the components of RAM_history_record in much the same way that the RECORD structure of Pascal signifies separate components of a data structure. Structured System Analysis techniques use the following notation to signify various possibilities:

+   means "and ..." The data element is composed of several parts.

| means "or..." The component is optional, and may or may not appear in the structure.

{}   means "one or more..." The component may appear repeatedly in the data element.

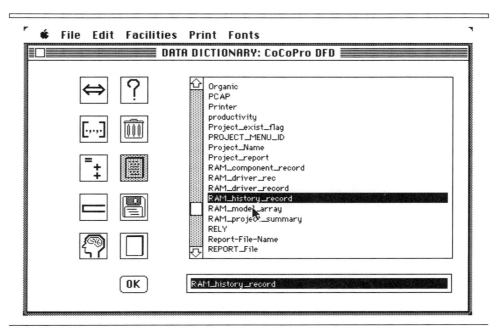

FIGURE 5-6a. Opening the data dictionary

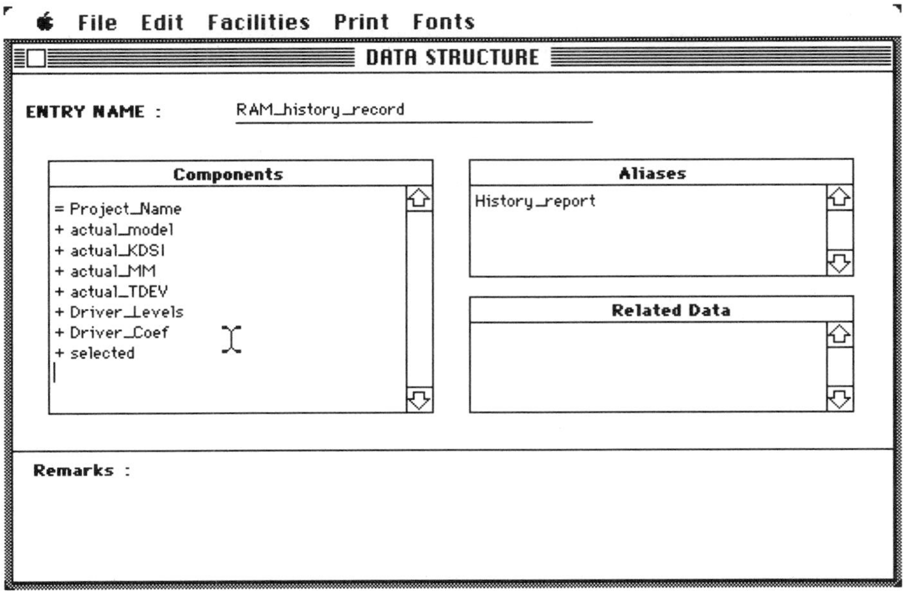

FIGURE 5-6b. The definition of RAM_history_record

For example, $A = B + \{C \mid D\}$ means the data element is composed of B and C, or B and D, or B and CD, or B and CC, or B and DD, or B and DC, etc. (The $\{\}$ are equivalent to the regular expression *.)

Each component may be decomposed into additional components. Data, like the bubbles which represent function, are decomposed level-by-level. The complete data dictionary is consulted by programmers during the implementation phase to guarantee a complete, consistent, traceable, and correct design.

REQUIREMENTS REVIEW

The SRS Document has two goals: to communicate with the user, and to guide further design and eventual implementation. Before going to System Design — the next step — we must pass a requirements review. The review is attended by all members of the team. The purpose of the review is to inspect the SRS document to verify that it achieves the intended goals and objectives. Accordingly, the review consists of:

- Stating goals and objectives of the entire system, including a brief review of the SCM and SQA documents as they pertain to the requirements
- Checking off the attributes of a good system design (easy to use, fast and responsive, small and compact, maintainable, packaged properly, appropriate trade-offs)
- Checking off the properties of a good SRS (correct, complete, consistent, unambiguous, functional, verifiable, traceable, modifiable)
- Early assessments — suggesting alternative approaches that might be cleaner or better, or that might somehow improve the design; assessing how the system will be tested.

We can illustrate the activities that take place in a requirements review by reviewing the CoCoPro SRS presented in this chapter. The review should not run more than two hours, and it should cover the topics listed below. The team leader should begin by verbally reciting the goals and objectives from the SCM Plan.

Goals and Objectives

The goal is to produce a commercial-quality CASE tool for computing software development cost estimates using the intermediate CoCoMo model. This product, called CoCoPro, will be able to retain actual data on previously completed projects and will be able to use this data to calibrate the intermediate cost models of Boehm to derive more accurate cost estimations. The CoCoPro software will be fully designed, documented, and implemented on the Apple Macintosh computer.

Good System Design

The team leader should next run down a list of specification attributes and argue that the requirements are "good" because the resulting system will be easy to use, fast and responsive, small and compact, maintainable, packaged properly, and appropriate trade-offs have been made. For example, the user interface — menus, dialogs, and so forth should be discussed to show how easy the system will be to operate; the performance specification table will be reviewed and discussed; the DFDs will be reviewed to show that the system is small and compact; and the various trade-offs will be discussed and evaluated. It is also appropriate to discuss the implementation language the team plans to use, other tools that are going to be used, and how the tools will impact maintainability, performance, and packaging.

QUESTIONS TO ASK AT A REQUIREMENTS REVIEW

- What is the overall design philosophy?
- Is the design philosophy consistently expressed across the system?
- Is the system properly structured?
- Are error handling and user interfaces consistent?
- Where might the system be subject to the greatest amount of change? Will change be easy?
- Are system resources sufficient — enough RAM, disk space?
- Have existing reusable components been identified and evaluated for possible use?
- Is the system adequately documented?
- Is the system maintainable? Why?
- Have the features been generalized? Too much? Not enough?
- How will the system be tested?
- How much will it cost to build?
- How long will it take to build?
- When will it be ready to use?
- What impact will it have on existing systems?
- Have any functions been accidentally left out?
- Are any requirements misinterpreted?
- Does the system interface properly with the outside world?
- Are there any timing problems? synchronization problems? deadlock?
- Are all mathematical formulae correct?
- Are all logical and Boolean expressions or conditions correct?
- Have all cases been considered?
- Can the system recover from errors?
- Is the system robust?
- Are performance estimates acceptable?
- Is it feasible?
- Does the team have the necessary tools? experience? personnel?
- Where are the weak points in the system?
- How will the system be verified?

Requirements Analysis Checklist
Functions/Verifiable

Required Functions \ Actigrams	DIA_about_cocopro	DIA_get_project_name	FIL_open	FIL_save	FIL_print	FIL_quit	REP_calculate	Check & Change Model	HISTORY_new	HIS_provide actuals	HIS_calibrate	HIS_select_all (true)	HIS_select_all (false)	DRI_show_model_param	DRI_change_computer_values	DRI_change_personnel_values	DRI_change_product_values	DRI_change_project_values
Apple_about	X																	
Project_new		X																
Project_open			X															
Project_save				X														
Project_print					X													
Project_quit						X												
CoCoMo_calculate							X											
CoCoMo_organic								X										
CoCoMo_semi								X										
CoCoMo_embedded								X										
History_new									X									
History_open			X															
History_save				X														
History_print					X													
History_provide_actuals										X								
History_calibrate											X							
History_select_all												X						
History_deselect_all													X					
Driver_open			X															
Driver_save as...				X														
Driver_print					X													
Driver_change_personnel																X		
Driver_change_project																		X
Driver_change_product																	X	
Driver_change_computer															X			
Driver_show_model_params														X				

FIGURE 5-7. CoCoPro requirements analysis checklist

Good SRS

The team leader should next review the attributes of a "good" SRS, showing why it is correct, complete, consistent, unambiguous, functional, verifiable, traceable, and modifiable. For example, the functional specifications can be checked against the process bubbles in the complete DFD as shown in a Functional/Verifiable checklist, see Figure 5-7. The DFD itself will be checked to make sure it is complete and that all functions have been included. The names of DD items will be checked to guarantee traceability, and all informal specifications will be checked for ambiguities.

Early assessments

Finally, the leader will discuss trade-offs — why they were important, what justifies each one, and what alternatives were considered. If a better way is discovered, then the requirements specification is redone, and a subsequent review held. For example, should the menu items be grouped together differently to improve ease of use? Is the information in the data files sufficient? Have we correctly defined each calculation? Are the formulas for least-squares calibration of actuals in the History file correct?

THE SEVEN SINS

Meyer[2] lists seven sins of the system specifier that should be avoided in an SRS document.

1. **Noise:** The presence of an item in the SRS that does not carry information relevant to any feature of the system under development.

2. **Silence:** The existence of a feature that is not covered by the SRS — an incompleteness in the SRS.

3. **Overspecification:** The presence of an item in the SRS that corresponds not to a feature of the system, but to a feature of a possible implementation. The specifier has gone too far in defining what the system is going to do versus how the system operates.

4. **Contradiction:** The presence of two or more items in the SRS that contradict one another — the specification is not consistent.

5. **Ambiguous:** The presence of and item in the SRS that makes it possible to make more than one interpretation of a feature of the system.

6. **Forward Reference:** The presence of items that refer to other items before those items are defined or discussed.

7. **Wishful Thinking:** The presence of items that cannot be validated — the use of undefined or poorly understood concepts such as "good," "approximate," "almost," and "most of the time."

We have surveyed the attributes of an SRS document and given several examples from the Development Project. The techniques advocated here are most appropriate for automated CASE tools:

- The use of decision tables, lists, diagrams, and informal — but unambiguous — English
- The use of graphical representations of the system — SADT and DFD
- Application of hierarchical decomposition of both function and data to control complexity
- Enforcement of "good" design practices via review of the SRS document

The DFD/DD approach has gained widespread acceptance as the starting point for software specification because of the widespread availability of low-cost workstations, and because it is easy to understand, use, and manipulate. In fact, the terminology of CASE tools is almost coincidental with the use of these representations. The dominance of DFD/DD representation should not be interpreted to mean that this is the only way to represent systems, however. Several other paradigms are not only possible, but equally viable.

The DFD/DD is an example of a class of representations called *data flow models*. Other classes are:

Data Structure Model

The system is represented by the form and content of its data, as in the Jackson Structured Design Methodology (JSD)[3]. For example, the processing steps of a program designed by this method mirror the shape of the data being processed.

Control Flow Model

The system is represented by control flow rather than data flow or structure. An example of this class is Software Requirements Engineering Methodology (SREM)[4].

Axiomatic Model

The system is represented by a collection of mathematical propositions called *predicates*. Each predicate states a condition which must be met by the system. This is the most formal representation possible, and is quite amenable to automation. Due to its formidable mathematics, however, few practitioners use it. An example of this class of models is found in [5].

We will return later to an analysis of data flow, data structure, control flow, and axiomatic modelling. Just keep in mind that the DFD/DD technique presented in this chapter is not the only technique available. The most useful techniques are the automated ones, however, and DFD/DD representations are widely available in the form of CASE tools.

Terms and Concepts

actigram	noise
axiomatic model	PDL
balanced	PSL/PSA
complete	requirements analysis
consistent	requirements specification
correct	SADT
datagram	SRS document
DD	SSA
decision table	system architecture
DFD	top-down
functional	traceable
hierarchical decomposition	unambiguous
information hiding	verifiable
modifiable	

DISCUSSION QUESTIONS

1. Specify the CoCoMo menu, with items Calculate, Organic, Semi, and Embedded, using a decision table. Give conditions, actions, and rules for each of the options.

2. How many combination of conditions are there for a decision table with two conditions in it? with three or four? with n? Why are decision tables limited to relatively small sets of conditions?

3. Devise a Petri Network for describing what happens to the Project menu when items are selected from it. Give transitions for each item and show that the menu eventually returns to its initial state after every item is selected.

4. Produce a SADT diagram equivalent to the two-level DFD diagram shown for CoCoPro. You need only provide the top-level diagram, and expand bubble 4 as illustrated in this chapter.

5. How do we know if the DFD given here for the CoCoPro system is complete? Can you convince yourself that the DFD is complete by looking at the Functional/Verifiable table discussed in the Requirements Review section? Why not? What do you need to verify that an SRS is complete?

6. Make a list of things we can do to make a design traceable. What does traceable mean? What portions of the development phase does traceability affect?

7. Why do we need to sequence the DFD specification of a system? Is sequencing necessary if the software is going to run on a computer with many processors?

8. Is it acceptable to connect two process bubbles to one another via several data flows? Can we connect two data storage elements together via a single data flow?

9. Draw a DFD for a system that you are familiar with. (Pick a relatively small system.)

10. Use a DFD CASE tool to duplicate the DFDs given here. Complete the DFD and DD for a fully specified CoCoPro system. How many levels deep is your specification?

11. Design a system and present it to the class in the form of a requirements review. What feedback did you get from your classmates?

12. What does the DD entry $X = \{A \mid B \mid C \}$ mean?

REFERENCES AND FURTHER READING

1. Boehm, B. W. 1984. "Verifying and Validating Software Requirements and Design Specifications." *IEEE Software* 1, no. 1 (January): 75–88.

2. Meyer, B. 1985. "On Formalism in Specification." *IEEE Software* 2, no. 1 (January): 6–26.

3. Jackson, M. A. 1975. *Principles of Program Design.* New York: Academic Press.

4. Alford, M. W. 1977. "A Requirements Engineering Methodology for Real-Time Processing Requirements." *IEEE Transactions on Software Engineering*, SE-3, no. 1: 60–69.

5. Dijkstra, E. W. 1976. *A Discipline of Programming.* Englewood Cliffs, NJ: Prentice-Hall.

6

Principles of Modular Design

PREVIEW

Modular Design is a well-known methodology in software design as well as in other disciplines. But because software is invisible, no widely accepted method has dominated the software development field, nor has one method become a "standard." Instead many methods are used.

We present a general discussion of modularity, what it is, what its problems are, and give a list of general design rules for producing "good" modular designs. Then we survey four main methods: Data Structure, as characterized by Jackson Structured Design; Functional Decomposition, as commonly practiced; Data Flow Design, as proposed by a variety of its advocates; and Object-Oriented Design, in the form of Object-Oriented Development proposed by Booch and others.

This survey provides a rational basis for selecting a method, reveals some surprising experimental results about modularity, and suggests a new methodology which is a combination of the last two methods surveyed.

MODULARITY

Decomposing a requirements specification into a system architecture is essentially the process of identifying modules and their interfaces. But in order to do this, we must understand *how* to identify modules and their interfaces — more than one method of decomposition is practiced among software engineers. We first define what is meant by

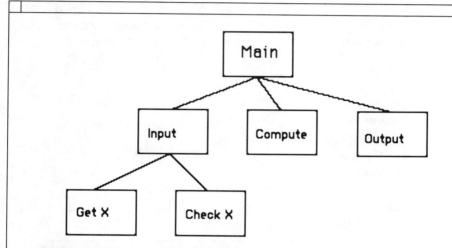

CLAIMED BENEFITS OF MODULAR DESIGN

Many have claimed that modularity is "good" for software design. For example, modular systems:

- Are easier to understand, test, and maintain
- Yield higher programmer productivity
- Help projects complete on time
- Increase program reliability.

The disadvantages of modular design are rarely pointed out. Modular design:

- Takes more computer time to develop
- Produces larger programs
- Requires difficult training for programmers
- Requires more effort to document.

Regardless of its "good" and "bad" qualities, the technique of modular decomposition is here to stay.

modularity, what it implies, and then survey four major decomposition technologies before resuming progress toward a solution to the Development Project.

Modularity — *the extent to which software is composed of discrete components such that a change in one component has minimal impact on other components* — is one of the most powerful techniques for combating software complexity. When applied to design, it is the software engineering equivalent of one of the oldest known problem-solving techniques: *divide and conquer*. The idea in modular design is to divide a large problem into smaller, more manageable, less complex, and better-understood subproblems. Each subproblem is divided into even simpler subproblems, and so forth, until "primitive" subproblems are obtained. The primitive problems are usually trivial either because a solution is known or because a solution can be easily found.

We used hierarchical decomposition of requirements as the starting point of the design of a large complex software system. Hierarchical decomposition is a divide-and-conquer technique used to solve the overall design problem. Modularity is simply a continuation of the decomposition process leading to implementation of code. In fact, the standard definition of a module is much more closely associated with implementation than with design. A **module** *is a program unit that is discrete and identifiable with respect to compiling, combining with other units, and loading; a logically separable part of a program.* Modular programming is a technique for developing a program as a collection of modules. But what constitutes a module, and how are modules derived from specifications? These are the questions we intend to answer in this chapter.

What Is a Module?

Most programming languages have syntactic structures for divide-and-conquer programming. FORTRAN uses the SUBROUTINE and FUNCTION constructs; Pascal and most block-structured languages implement **procedure** and **function** constructs; and LISP implements functions. These are not modules, however, unless they are *discrete* and *separable*. That is, they must be separately compilable, and they must somehow be identifiable as self-contained pieces of program. Furthermore, the notion of module often means a separately compiled piece of source code containing *one or more* functions or procedures. A FORTRAN subroutine may be separately compiled, but is limited to one function or procedure. A Pascal internal **procedure** is not separately compiled.

We make a distinction between functional and modular decomposition of a program. *Functional decomposition* is a method of program design in which the components of the program correspond to functions and subfunctions of the application. In a functional decomposition, it is highly likely that each program FUNCTION corresponds to a function of the application. For example, a program procedure called CALC_MM corresponds to the calculation of MM (effort in the CoCoMo model). The correspondence of application function with program decomposition is the key feature of functional decomposition.

"Call" Graph Structure
(Function Mapping)

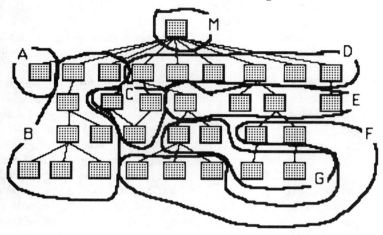

Uses Graph Structure
(Module Mapping)

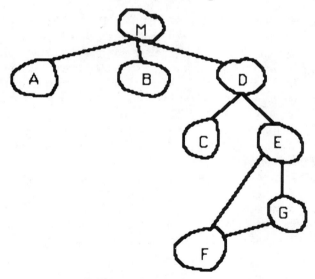

Module structure is not the same as function structure. The call graph shows how functions are called. The module uses graph shows how modules use one another.

Note the distinctions between *function* and *functional decomposition*, and between *module* and *modular decomposition*:

Function: A language construct — procedure or function to be "called" from within a program.

Functional Decomposition: A specific design technique — a system architecture that mirrors the application's functions.

Module: A separately compiled program unit containing one or more procedures, constants, types, and data.

Modular Decomposition: A general design technique which includes many forms of hierarchical decomposition.

These terms will be used throughout the discussion of this chapter. Furthermore, a module will be equivalent to a Macintosh Pascal **unit** — a separately compiled block of program containing its own data and procedure/function definitions. Units are used by main programs by including the interface part of a unit in the using program. Thus, every unit contains an *interface* part and an *implementation* part. (The implementation part may be null, in which case the unit defines data only.) Consider, for example, **unit** MENU_cocomo, which implements the menus of CoCoPro. This unit is stored in a file by the same name, and is compiled separately from all other source code, see Figure 6-1.

MENU_cocomo begins with a unit heading, **unit** MENU_cocomo and ends with the keyword **end**. The interface part begins with the keyword **interface** and ends with **implementation**, if an implementation section is present, and **end.** otherwise.

A unit may use other units; this is indicated by placing a **uses** statement in the interface part, following the **interface** keyword. A **uses** statement tells the compiler to include the interface specification of another unit in the current unit. Thus, MENU_cocomo uses GLOBAL_cocomo by reading the interface part of GLOBAL_cocomo during compilation. All names in the interface part of GLOBAL_cocomo are accessible to all units that use GLOBAL_cocomo.

It is very important to study how the interface and implementation parts of a unit are separated. The interface part specifies how modules are "glued together" or coupled. The degree and kind of coupling is critically important in designing a good modular system. Similarly, the implementation part defines the cohesiveness of the module. We will explore this attribute of modular systems more fully in order to devise good design rules for modular structure.

The interface part defines names that are *visible* and, by their absence in the interface part, names that are *opaque*. A visible name is known to any other module outside of the unit containing the name. An opaque name is known only to the unit in which it is declared. Visible names establish coupling among units, while opaque names are restricted to the unit in which they are defined. The rules for visible and opaque names are called *scoping rules*, and are very much like the scoping rules of block-structured languages.

The unit may have a private global procedure such as MEN_do_driver_menu, which is used by other procedures in the implementation part. The private procedure is invisible outside of the unit where it is defined.

```
unit MENU_cocomo;    {Unit = Module}

interface         {Every Unit has both interface and implementation parts}
  uses GLOBAL_cocomo;   {Uses another unit...}
  { Visible Const, Type, Var go here, if any }
  { Visible Procedures and Functions}
  procedure MEN_setup_menus;
  procedure MEN_process_menu_in (Menu_selection : longint);

implementation
  { Global to this unit, only...}
   const                    {    Invisible Constants   }
     MEMCOUNT = 5;              { Number of menus }
     APPLE_MENU = 1;           { Menu id numbers }
   { Other const declarations...}
   { Types, if any...}
  var                       {   Invisible Variables   }
   Mymenu : ARRAY[1..MEMCOUNT] OF MenuHandle;

  procedure MEN_do_driver_menu (Driver_item : integer);      {Invisible, global procedure }
   begin
   { Executable code goes here...}
   end; { MEN_do_driver-menu }

  procedure MEN_setup_menus;                              { Visible procedure definition }
   var
     index : integer;        { Local to this procedure, only}
   begin
     Mymenu[APPLE_MENU] := GetMenu(APPLE_MENU_ID);      { Get handles to menus and insert... }
     AddResMenu(Mymenu[APPLE_MENU], 'DRVR');             { into the array that holds all these... }
     Mymenu[PROJECT_MENU] := GetMenu(PROJECT_MENU_ID);  { menu handles. AddResMenu will... }
     Mymenu[COCOMO_MENU] := GetMenu(COCOMO_MENU_ID);    { add the desktop accessories under... }
     Mymenu[HISTORY_MENU] := GetMenu(HISTORY_MENU_ID);  { the apple menu. }
     Mymenu[DRIVERS_MENU] := GetMenu(DRIVERS_MENU_ID);
     For index := 1 TO MEMCOUNT DO                       { Insert menu handles to menu bar }
       InsertMenu(Mymenu[index], 0);
     DrawMenuBar;                                         { Show the menu bar}
   end; {MEN_setup_menus}

  procedure MEN_process_menu_in;
   var
     Menu_no : integer;      {menu number that was selected}
     Item_no : integer;      {item in menu that was selected}

   begin
   { Executable code for visible procedure...}
   end; { MEN_process-men-in }

end. {unit MENU_ }
```

FIGURE 6-1. The MENU_cocomo module

Observe how the visible procedures are declared twice: once in the interface part, and again in the implementation part. When defined in the implementation part, they do not have formal parameters, but they do have a body — the executable code. However, it is good practice to include the parameters in a comment in the heading of each implementation part procedure definition.

What Is Modularity?

How can we determine the best kind of problem decomposition, that is, modularity that compartmentalizes the application in such a way that it is simple, comprehendible, maintainable, and so forth. We know how to write a syntactically correct Pascal unit, but this does not guarantee that we know what to put in such units. We need *design rules* to guide the construction of modules.

We know several design rules from earlier discussions about good software practice. For example, modularity must enforce some sort of *encapsulation*, or isolation of functions and data. Encapsulation has to do with module cohesion or module strength. *Information hiding*, encapsulations that reveal as little as possible about the module's inner workings, has to do with module coupling.

Cohesion: The degree to which the tasks performed by a module are related. Also called *strength*.

Coupling: A measure of the interdependence or connectedness of modules in a program.

We examine each of these attributes of modules in some detail and derive a set of design rules based on what is "good" and "bad" about each attribute.

Module Strength

Module strength ranges over a spectrum of values. Actually, most modules exhibit some degree of all of the different kinds of cohesion. The stronger a module, the better. The best form of module strength depends on the method of design being used. The most frequently quoted form of "good" modular cohesion is called "functional," while "bad" cohesion is called coincidental. Here are some common forms of cohesion listed in order from worst to best.

Coincidental

The tasks performed by a module are only loosely related, at best. An example of a coincidental module is one containing all functions beginning with the letter A. A second module might contain all functions beginning with the letter B, and so forth. Although alphabetical order is a rational relationship in many circumstances, it has very little to do with how to form modules in software. Functions end up in a module by coincidence rather than by design. When a programmer attempts to locate an error or enhance the module by adding a function, coincidental cohesion makes the job more difficult than it need be.

TESTING FOR MODULE STRENGTH

How do you tell what kind of cohesion exists in a module or function? Stevens et al. proposed this test: Write a description of the module then ask the following questions:

1. Does the description have compound sentences, contain commas, or more than one verb? The module is probably performing multiple functions — communicational cohesion may be present.

2. Does the description refer to time? (First, next, last, after, when, start, etc. are some words that refer to time.) The module is probably bound by temporal cohesion.

3. Do the verbs refer to one object? If not, then the module is probably logically cohesive. For example, "Edit all data" has logical cohesion, but "Edit Date File" is probably functional cohesive.

4. Words such as "initialize" and "finish up" indicate temporal cohesion.

Functional cohesion is described by rather simplistic statements such as "calculate net balance," "copy file to backup," and "search table for key." Direct imperative language usually implies functional cohesion.

Source: Stevens, W. G., Myers, G., and L. Constantine, "Structured Design," *IBM Systems Journal*, 13, 2 (1974)

Logical

The tasks are related by the logic of the program. An example of a logical module is one containing all functions for computing the average, mean, and standard deviation of a list of numbers. This seems logical, but problems arise when the list is stored as an array of integers, then as a file of real numbers. The functions that work well on the array of integers fail on the file of real numbers. To do both, the module must be extended to contain two sets of functions — one set that works on the array of integers, and another set that works on the set of real numbers stored in a file. Had the modules been organized around the data structure instead of the logical operations, the enhancement would have been easier to accomplish. For example, one module might contain functions for array calculations while the other might contain functions for file calculations.

Temporal

The tasks are related because they are executed in chronological order. An example of a temporal module is one containing all functions related to initialization and termination of the application. Each time the application is launched, start-up functions are called; each time the application is terminated, epilog functions are called. Temporal modules are also common in real-time control software where functions are called during the same time interval. Once again, this structure is difficult to maintain because changes in other modules are usually related to initialization and termination functions, so the temporal module will also be affected.

Procedural

The tasks are done in a certain order as dictated by the application. An example of a procedural module is one containing all functions that work together to achieve an application step. For example, a paycheck is obtained by accessing the database, computing a gross income, calculating the deductions to obtain a net income, and then printing the check. If these four operations are implemented and grouped together as functions to be performed in the sequence indicated, they form a procedural module.

Communicational

The tasks are related by data interrelationships. A communicational module contains functions that all operate on the same data. Thus, a communicational module might contain functions for computing the average, mean, and standard deviation of a file of real numbers.

Functional

The module performs only one function. A functional module contains functions that perform one and only one function. Such a module would most likely contain only one visible procedure or function. For example, the paycheck module contains a visible function that prints a check, but it also contains opaque functions for accessing the database, then calculating gross and net pay.

Communicational and functional cohesion are the most desirable forms of module strength. But recall that different modular decomposition rules strive for different goals. The *functional decomposition* technique says that a good design is one that achieves functional strength in all of its modules. A *data decomposition* technique, which we will discuss in the next section, strives for communicational strength in all modules. A third approach called *object-oriented design* strives for a mixture of communicational and functional strength. In general, we can state the following design rule concerning modularity:

Module Strength Design Rule: Maximize module strength.

Of course each method of modularity will advocate a different measure of module strength. In all cases the idea is to increase the cohesiveness of modules according to some measure.

Coupling

Coupling measures two attributes of a modular system: *how* modules communicate via their interfaces; and how *much* they communicate via their interfaces. A module can communicate in a number of ways:

- **Passing Parameters:** This is the most obvious method of communication, but most programming languages do no provide sufficient mechanisms to pass types, constants, and so on, through parameter lists, so other mechanisms must be considered.
- **Side Effect:** This is the most common method used, but of course it is difficult to control. Typically, a global or common module is created to hold all global constants, types, variables, and procedures. If only one copy of the global data module is maintained, and the compiler checks for type conflicts, then control is possible and this method becomes not only practical, but desirable.

- **I/O:** A file produced by one module is read by another module. The two modules are coupled by the fact that a change in the file format by one module affects the other module. We must be careful to isolate the data types that allow for such changes. This form of coupling is perhaps the most difficult to control.

- **Visible Interface:** The interface part of a module is "used" by another module. This is the most common form of coupling for the purpose of passing data types and constants. Module 1 makes its types visible (exports the types) so other modules can import them. Module 2 imports types so it can create variables that are type compatible with module 1. This mechanism could be avoided if types were passed through the parameter list of a procedure, but in Pascal that is not possible.

- **Convention:** An "include" directive is used in two or more modules, creating an interface by textual inclusion. For example, suppose all global variables were stored in a text file called global_cocomo. Then all modules that make use of one or more of the names in global_cocomo simply specify a connection via the compiler "include" command:

    {**$include** global_cocomo}

This mechanism varies from one compiler to another, but the effect is the same. When the module is compiled, the compiler reads global_cocomo into RAM and replaces the include command with the actual text read from the file.

How do modules communicate? From the point of view of simplicity, no coupling is the best, but a system of modules that do not communicate is meaningless. Here are the forms of coupling found in practice, listed in order from best to worst:

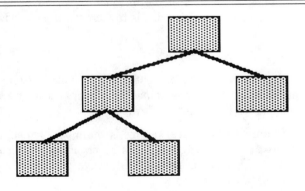

Data and Stamp Coupling

FIGURE 6-2. Data and stamp coupling

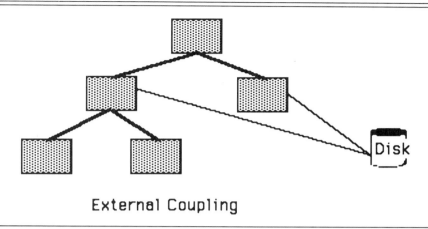

FIGURE 6-3. External coupling

- **Data Coupling:** All communication is done through well-defined parameter lists. Each module contains functions whose arguments define all channels of communication. The only names that are visible are listed in the parameter lists of all functions. There are no import or export interfaces, only parameters. Figure 6-2 illustrates data coupling.

- **Stamp Coupling:** Types cannot be passed via parameter lists in Pascal functions and procedures. As a result, the interface part of a unit allows constants, types, vars, and procedure names to be "passed" as visible names in the interface. This is a form of stamp typing — we say the module stamps the type of its variables on the using module. Figure 6-2 illustrates stamp coupling.

- **Control Coupling:** Control information such as a flag or switch is often passed between modules. For example, an error flag is returned by a file I/O function. If the function fails, the error flag indicates the failure, which affects what the calling program does after the call.

- **External Coupling:** A module uses an external file created by another module. The two modules are coupled by nature of the fact that both modules must know the format and content of the file. Similarly, two modules might communicate via "pipes," special files used in the Unix operating system that allow concurrent processes to communicate, see Figure 6-3.

- **Global Coupling:** Global side effects are often used in place of passing parameters. This reduces the number and amount of data explicitly passed between two modules. Unfortunately, global side effects are often abused and undocumented. However, as we will see in the next section, if we avoid the abuse, this method can be beneficial. In practice, global coupling is a necessary evil because of the tremendous number of constants, types, and variables that must be communicated throughout a large, complex system, see Figure 6-4.

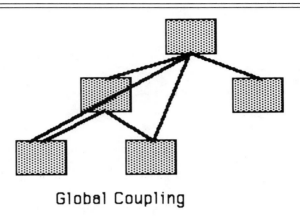

Global Coupling

FIGURE 6-4. Global coupling

- **Content Coupling:** Modules may contain functions that have multiple entry and exit points. This is not possible in Pascal, but in other languages multiple entry/exit points may cause the "state" of the data in a module to be in doubt. This form of coupling should never be allowed.

We summarize this brief overview of coupling by stating a second design rule:

Coupling Design Rule: Minimize coupling.

We can minimize coupling in Pascal **units** by applying five rules that are especially appropriate to Pascal:

1. Keep named entities such as functions, procedures, types, variables, and constants local to the function or procedure that created them, except when they must be used by other functions and procedures.

2. Pass variables via parameter lists, except when they are used by so many modules that they become pervasive.

3. Put pervasive entities such as functions, procedures, constants, types, and variables in one carefully controlled global module.

4. Build modules with well-defined interface and implementation parts. Make all names local first, then global to the module. Next, pass names via parameter lists, then via interface part, and finally, make names global by way of a single global module.

5. Use an encapsulation design rule that fits the situation (more on this later). There are several encapsulation rules with attractive benefits to the designer. We will advocate a combination of communicational and functional cohesion that places both function and the data on which it operates in the same module. When this approach is used, the encapsulation design rule is object-oriented.

Rules for Modular Design

The general idea of modularity has gained widespread acceptance among software engineers, but few studies have been made to verify commonsense faith in the benefits of modularity. Card et al. [1] did a preliminary study of the benefits of modular FORTRAN programming and found a number of interesting, counter-intuitive results. The results of this study are summarized here.

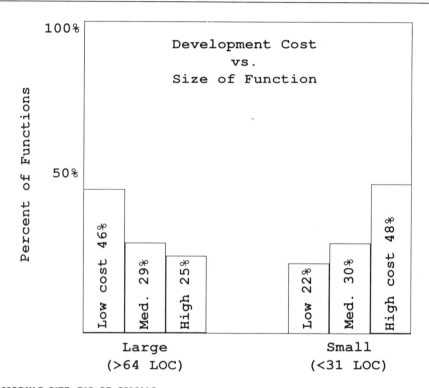

MODULE SIZE: BIG OR SMALL?

What is the optimal size of a module? Some say modules should be small and plentiful, while others say module size should be determined by the functions it is to perform.

Here we see evidence that suggests larger modules are less costly to develop. A FORTRAN application containing "large" and "small" subroutines indicated a lower cost for 46% of the large subroutines versus only 22% of the small ones. The reverse was true for costly subroutines — 48% of the small routines were high cost compared to only 25% of the large ones.

The cost per LOC (line of code) seems to increase as the subroutine size measured in LOC decreases.

FIGURE 6-5. Development cost versus size of function

Module Size

Arbitrary module size limitations can *increase* module development cost. Common wisdom has long advocated that modules should be kept small, typically, the size of a page (60 lines or so). This result suggests that during development, at least, larger modules cost less to develop per executable statement than smaller ones, see Figure 6-5. Note the emphasis on development cost. The study does not say anything about the effects of module size on maintenance costs. Nonetheless, this result suggests module sizes should be larger.

One reason given for writing small modules is that they are less error prone. The Card study does *not* verify this commonly held belief. This may be due to the way experiments are conducted, or simply because error rates are reported relative to LOC (Lines Of [executable] Code). A small module with one error has a higher fault rate (errors per LOC) than a large module with one error. The fault rates reported by practitioners do not measure the cause of an error, only its incidence.

Perhaps a more useful measure of module size is the "amount of information," "complexity," or some other quantity that considers "size" in terms of human cognitive values. For example, monolithic programs (monolithic means the program is written as one large text file with no modules) have been shown to be more difficult to write, understand, and maintain than modular ones, but experimental results have not conclusively shown how much modularization makes a monolithic program less costly, less error prone, and less difficult to maintain. Obviously, there is a limit to the number of modules that can be tracked by human programmers in any software system.

Module Strength

High module strength reduces fault rate. There is no widely accepted quantitative measure of module strength, but the kind of module cohesion discussed previously was used to classify modules according to the Module Strength Design Rule. Each module was identified as performing one or more functions as defined by the classes of functions shown below:

> Input/output
> Logic/control
> Algorithmic

Modules that clearly performed only one function were classified as high-strength, and modules that perform more than three functions were classified as low-strength modules.

Apparently, there is no relationship between module strength and development cost, see Figure 6-6. It cost the same to develop a "good" module as to develop a "bad" one as far as cohesion is concerned. Thus, developing high-strength modules is good practice.

Global Coupling

Global coupling *reduces* development cost for utility modules. This finding is counter to common wisdom, but probably in step with common practice. Pervasive names and pervasive modules are considered "utility" names, and are best managed by locating them centrally in a global module.

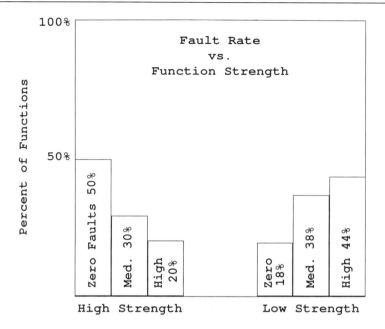

Function Strength

MODULE STRENGTH: HIGH OR LOW?

Is it really true that cohesion plays a role in reducing errors? In the study quoted here modules with high strength were less likely to contain errors regardless of their size.

Modules were considered "high-strength" if they had one function to perform; "low-strength" modules had three or more functions to perform.

Fifty percent of the high-strength modules were error-free compared to only 18% of low-strength modules. Only 20% of the high-strength modules had high fault rates, whereas 44% of the low-strength modules had high fault rates. (Fault rate was computed by dividing the number of faults found in a module by the LOC of the module.)

FIGURE 6-6. Fault rate versus function strength

Computer scientists have long been critical of global side effects in block-structured languages such as Pascal. They theorize that global side effect is a form of uncontrolled access that leads to errors. The commonsense rule states that all module coupling should be formal, even if it means long and unwieldy parameter lists. However, the data show that under certain restrictions, global access is actually less error prone.

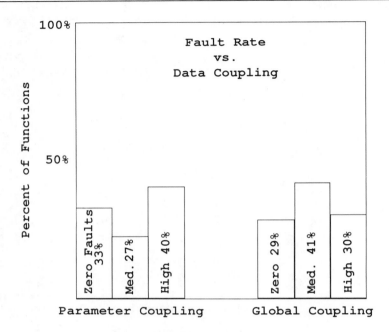

GLOBAL VS. NONGLOBAL DATA?

Global data used to be considered harmful, but the results of this study suggest otherwise. Apparently there are reasons to use global data modules in the development of reliable software.

While the number of error-free modules was nearly the same (33% versus 29%) for both parameter-passing data coupling and global data coupling, far fewer global coupled modules had high fault rates. Thus, highly error prone modules were those that used parameter coupling!

Global coupling is especially appropriate in languages like Pascal.

FIGURE 6-7. Fault rate versus data coupling

Global coupling via global data modules can be error prone if multiple copies of the global data module are allowed to appear in the system; see Figure 6-7. This can be avoided in most any language, however, by using the file "include" mechanism available in most modern compilers. For example, a Pascal or FORTRAN program can "include" the file containing the global data regardless of its status — as a block of text containing data constants, types, variables, and functions, or as a separately compiled unit with an interface part. Any time the single copy of the global data changes, all users of the module are granted immediate access to the new version.

While controversial among theoreticians, a global data module is nearly essential to practitioners. Without relying on a global data module, an application becomes very difficult to manage. The parameter lists of every module become very long — they would need to contain all global constants, for example — and the separation between global and local names becomes error prone, tiresome to establish and maintain.

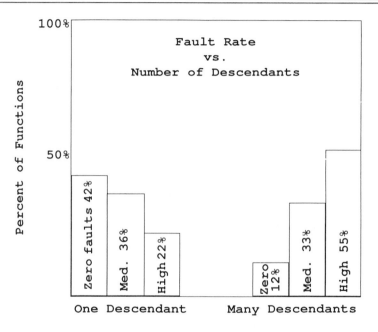

HOW MANY LEVELS?

A hierarchical modular program is composed in layers or levels. But how many levels are "good"? This question is complicated, because for a fixed number of modules and a fixed "fan-out" per module, the number of levels is also fixed.

In this study, modules were grouped according to the number of descendants: one, two to seven, and more than seven (many descendants). The fault rate for modules with more than seven descendants was many times higher than the fault rate for modules with only one descendant.

FIGURE 6-8. Fault rate versus number of descendants

Module Depth

Modules with many descendants are more error prone than modules with few descendants. By depth we mean the length of the chain of calls from the main program, through all intermediate modules, to the terminal module. This rule essentially supports the 7 ± 2 rule of Miller[2], which states that human cognitive abilities rapidly decay for more than 7 ± 2 "mental items." In terms of modules the rule states, "each module — excluding terminal modules — should call no more than 5 to 9 other modules."

In development, modules with more descendants tend to cost more per LOC than modules with fewer descendants, see Figure 6-8. In a large system this means an increase in the *fan-out* of the modules in the system. A commonly held belief states that "good system design encourages a small fan-out." This reason is usually based on the popular misconception that deep programs employ information hiding. However, information hiding has little to do with module depth.

Depth of calling sequence is a good overall measure of fault rate — better, in fact, than more complex measures involving counts of IF statements and operators. However, the *total number of faults* seems to increase with size, number of IFs, and number of operators, a phenomenon we will study again later.

Unreferenced Variables in Modules

Modules with many unreferenced (nonglobal) variables are more prone to error and thus more costly than those with fewer unreferenced variables. An unreferenced variable is any variable that could be accessed by a module, but is not. For example, a variable transmitted by the global module but not used by the receiving module is considered unreferenced. A variable might also be created locally in a module but not used by the module. Most compilers do not complain of such unreferenced local variables, yet the lack of referencing may indicate an error. Finally, a component of a data structure (**records** in Pascal, for instance) can be passed to a module, but not used.

We might be tempted to lay the blame for high fault rates from unreferenced variables to the negative aspects of global side effects. This is not the case; in fact, the opposite is true. Keeping (logically) related variables together in a global module — even if some are unreferenced — resulted in a lower fault rate, see Figure 6-9. The bulk of errors are due to unreferenced local and passed variables.

This result also points out a subtle difference between information hiding and layering. A layered or leveled system of modules can fail to enforce information hiding. A modular system enforces information hiding only if strict access is enforced. Data is allowed to flow from one level to the other only through explicit constructs such as import/export mechanisms, or through calling conventions that shield variables at one level from modules at another level. This is a subtle but important concept, which we will revisit.

Module Reuse

Reusing modules as much as possible reduces cost and fault rate. A module is reusable if it can be used in another application. A *custom module* is a module that has been hand-crafted from specifications, whereas a reused module has been copied, perhaps modified, and then used in place of a custom module. Reusability has been touted as the most important software technology of the 1980s and 1990s, because it is the only known

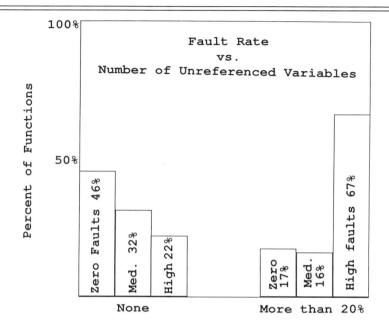

Number of Unreferenced Variables

IMPROPER DATA COUPLING

Modules that are data coupled to other modules may or may not reference the imported data. There are a variety of explanations for this, but many of the explanations lead to errors. In general, the presence of unreferenced variables in the calling sequence suggests a lack of proper information hiding.

Modules with no unreferenced variables contained fewer errors, in fact, 46% had no errors. Modules with more than 20% of unreferenced (nonglobal) variables showed a high fault rate — 67% had a high number of errors. In fact, only 17% of the modules with 20% or more unreferenced variables were error-free.

This finding supports a design concept called object-oriented design, which we will cover in detail later in this chapter.

FIGURE 6-9. Fault rate versus number of unreferenced variables

technology for achieving several orders of magnitude of improvement in both productivity and quality. Quality factors of 5- to 10-fold have been quoted for real systems [3], and productivity improvements ranging from 5- to 100-fold are expected in future systems. Ada projects have reported improvements in productivity that lower the exponent in CoCoMo estimates below 1.0! This means larger applications are more cost effective per line of code than smaller projects.

If the trend is toward reusability, then why is this technology not widely used already? Woodfield et al.[4] list several problems to be overcome before reusability becomes widespread:

- Software personnel untrained in reuse do not correctly identify reusable modules. They either do not accurately estimate the effort saved by using existing modules versus writing custom modules or else fail to match up the requirements with the module. Woodfield et al. found a threshold of 70% — that is, if the effort required to reuse an existing module is more than 70% of the effort required to write a custom module, the custom approach is chosen. (Intuition would suggest a threshold of 100%.)

- Untrained software personnel are influenced by the wrong factors when deciding whether to use an existing module or to write a custom module. Rather than focusing on the effort needed to use an existing module, they are often influenced by the size of the module. Size is not the most important factor, however, because a large piece of code might be used without modification, thus saving enormous effort. However, percentage of modification and its relationship to effort is often overlooked by programmers when deciding whether to reuse an existing module.

Summary of Design Rules

- Maximize module strength. Use CASE tools that generate high-strength modules.
- Minimize coupling. Use CASE tools that generate low-coupled modules.
- Do not arbitrarily limit module size. The application determines module size and content.
- Centralize pervasive data in a single global module.
- Limit module call chains to a depth of 7 ± 2 descendants.
- Eliminate unreferenced (nonglobal) variables. Use CASE tools that enforce information hiding.
- Reuse modules as much as possible. Use CASE tools to find, modify, and incorporate existing modules.

DATA STRUCTURE DESIGN

We have examined a number of rules for modular decomposition, but we have not yet described exactly how to decompose a specification into a system architecture. Many design rule-based techniques have been proposed for this process. We describe four methods beginning here with the method of Data Structure Design [5,6]. The best-known Data Structure Design technique was proposed by Jackson, and bears his name[5,7]. Jackson Structured Design (JSD) is a scientific method of decomposing a system into modules based on "function follows form." In JSD, the "shape" of an application program is determined by the "shape" of the input and output data structures.

Jackson describes his method:

- It depends little on inventiveness or cleverness on the part of the software engineer.
- It is based on rational principles. Each step may be checked against these principles.
- It is teachable. Two or more designers using JSD will come up with the same system architecture.
- It is practical, simple, and easy to understand, and it can be implemented easily.

JSD is unique among design rule-based decomposition techniques because it is "repeatable," that is, programs that solve a given problem all look alike. Since the "shape" of a JSD program is determined by its input and output data, all programs with identical input and output data have the same shape. None of the other techniques have this property.

JSD: The Method

JSD is applied in eight steps:

1. Draw *logical structure diagrams* for all input and output data. A logical data structure is composed of only three building blocks: 1) concatenation (one component is connected to another component), 2) iteration (one or more instances of a component appears repeatedly), and 3) selection (only one from an array of possible choices of components appears in the logical data structure).

2. Make one-for-one *data correspondences* between components of the logical structure diagrams drawn in step 1. This is especially important to do between input and output structures, because the correspondence is used by the program under design to "map" the input data onto the output data. This mapping is the basis for the "function follows form" of JSD.

3. Using concatenation, iteration, and selection, as with the logical structure diagrams, draw a program structure diagram based on the logical structure diagrams and their correspondences. The correspondences will be used to combine data components into a "chunk" to be processed by a particular section or "chunk" of program. Data chunks usually correspond with places in the program where related processing is done, hence the correspondences.

4. Step 3 will not always work nor will it always accommodate the entire program. Therefore, wherever a single program chunk cannot be produced directly from the data correspondences and data chunks, produce two program chunks that communicate via an intermediate data chunk (newly introduced). This problem arises because the input data structures do not always map easily onto the output data structures — a "structure clash" occurs.

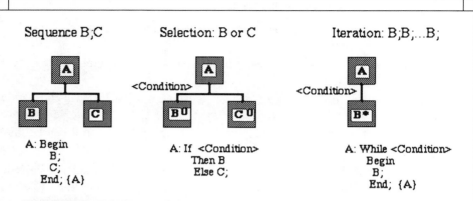

Sequence B;C

A: Begin
    B;
    C;
End; {A}

Selection: B or C

A: If <Condition>
    Then B
    Else C;

Iteration: B;B;...B;

A: While <Condition>
    Begin
    B;
    End; {A}

JSD BUILDING BLOCKS

The building blocks of JSD programs and data structures are identical. A "chunk" is denoted by a rectangular box containing a title or meaningful phrase. The chunks are "glued" together by using three composition rules:

Sequence Programs execute chunks in sequence, one following the other, left to right in the diagram. In a data structure diagram, sequence is replaced by concatenation, in which one data structure component follows another, left to right.

Selection Programs execute either one chunk or the other, but not both. The choice between alternatives is determined by a <condition> or test. If the condition is TRUE one branch is taken, otherwise, the other branch is taken. This construct can be generalized to a multiple-choice selection construct by simply adding branches to the basic building block. The small O appearing in the upper right corner of the box indicates selection rather than sequence. Data structure chunks may be selected by indicating either one or another "optional" component in the data. For example, an output data structure consisting of a report may have multiple lines. Optionally, a line may contain a heading or a row of values.

Iteration Programs execute loops — **While**, **Repeat**, **For** loops in Pascal. A loop predicate or loop counter is used to determine how many times a loop is repeated. The <condition> indicates what must be TRUE on each iteration of the loop in order to continue through the loop. Data structures contain iterated components. For example, a file contains zero or more records. Each record is identical in format, but possibly contains different values. Iteration is distinguished from selection or sequence by placing an * in the upper right corner of the box representing either a program or data chunk.

Programs and data are represented *logically* by these building blocks. That is, the actual implementation may vary from one program or data structure to another. For example, an iterated data structure might be implemented as a file in one application and as a linked list in another application. Similarly, an iterative structure may indicate a **For** loop in one place, and a **While** loop in another place of the same program.

The logical separation between structure and implementation is an illustration of data abstraction. Purposefully separating the structure of both program and data from implementation provides a major intellectual advantage over lower-level techniques such as flowcharting.

5. Identify appropriate conditions (logical expressions) for each iteration and selection program chunk. These conditions correspond to the test predicates in **If**, **While**, **Repeat-until**, and **Case** statements in Pascal, for example. A program chunk might repeatedly read a record from an input file until the end-of-file marker is reached. The condition for this program chunk is: **Until EOF** (input).

6. Make a list of basic operations (functions as specified by the SRS document) that must be done by the application. These operations need not be in any order, and they can be written in plain English. They should be checked against the SRS Functional Specifications for completeness, correctness, and so on.

7. Allocate the basic operations to the program structure diagram. Place each operation in the block corresponding to the program chunk that must perform the operation. It may be necessary to add more detail to the program structure diagram. Add enough new program chunks to "use up" all basic operations from your list.

8. The program structure diagram constitutes the system architecture of the application. It may be necessary to refine the modules in the JSD program structure diagram into lower-level modules, but the basic program structure is fixed at this stage. The program may be implemented in a variety of ways; most likely, you will want to refine each module into *pseudo-code* first, then proceed on to writing each module in some high-level programming language.

A key feature of these rules is *correspondence*, the matching between components of separate data structures. In order for two components to correspond, they must satisfy the following rules for a match:

- The data chunks are in the same processing order in both structures. Processing one before the other is avoided by this order property.
- Iterated data chunks have the same number of components in the correspondence.
- The output chunk is derived from the input chunk.

The correspondence between data chunks is shown in the logical data structure diagram as a line connecting the matching chunks. In the example of Figure 6-10, an input file is printed in report form as an output file. The input file consists of iterated records — zero or more. The output file consists of a report heading concatenated to a report body, concatenated to a report "tail" consisting of a tally. The input/output correspondences are shown by two lines connecting matching chunks.

Each record of the input file corresponds to a line of output in the body of the report file. The input records are processed in the same order as the lines of output; there are as many lines of output as records in the file; and the output lines are derived from the input records.

In this example, the corresponding data chunks are simply merged into single blocks to obtain the program structure chart. The merge produces a simple tree structure representing the "shape" of the application. This is the system architecture of this simple

Data Structure: Input/Output

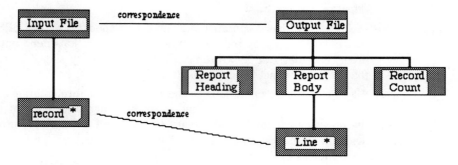

Input: R;R;...R;   Output: Head;Body:Line;Line;...Line;Count;

Correspondence => Same order + Same Number of Each + Ouput is derived from Input

Program Structure

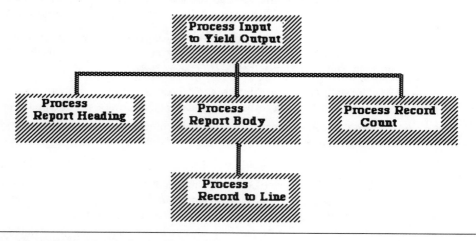

FIGURE 6-10. JSD specification of simple input/output

application. Note here that "function follows form." Each chunk representing sequence, iteration, or selection in the data diagram also represents sequence, iteration, or selection in the program structure diagram.

The correspondence is not always obvious, see Figure 6-11. Suppose a report file is produced that contains only a subset of the input file. For example, a "factory employee" report contains only the "factory employee" records, while the "office employee" records are not printed. This illustrates the importance of the rule, "output is derived from input" in making a correspondence.

Data Structures: I/O Correspondence

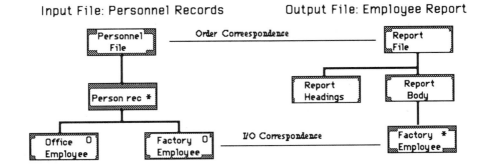

Program Structure

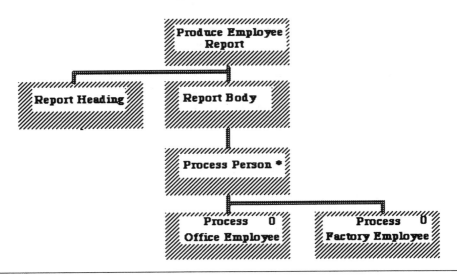

FIGURE 6-11. I/O correspondence in JSD

Further, the correspondence rule is not always strictly applied to input and output structures. For example, if a program processes multiple input files, the multiple input files must be mapped into a single structure before they are matched with the output file(s). Thus, multiplicity of inputs is a source of difficulty when resolving the "structure clash."

In addition, program structure is influenced by functions to be performed but not reflected in any of the data structures. For example, initializations are usually needed in a typical program, yet the initializations are not evident from examination of either input or output data.

Functionality is captured in JSD by simply making a list of the basic operations to be carried out by the application. The list of basic operations need not be in order — the program structure will take care of that — but they should be complete and consistent according to the specifications document. JSD does not provide much help in identifying a missing operation.

A third concern has to do with refinement of the JSD program structure. The technique does not guarantee a concise structure, only a predictable one. By *concise* we mean the structure is neither redundant nor overly detailed, as illustrated by solving the following "two-file merge" problem shown in Figure 6-12. In this problem, two ordered files are merged into a single ordered file. Each record of the two input files and the single output file contains a key that uniquely identifies the record.

The two-file merge problem requires extra effort to resolve the data structure clashes before arriving at a final compact structure. First we make two correspondences between input files A and B. The correspondences are used in a subsequent refinement to derive a more concise structure in which the corresponding data chunks are coalesced into one.

The coalesced structure contains a tree of selections that can be combined to make the structure more concise. The two-level tree of selections is compacted into a one-level tree of four selection options. But the reduced data structure is only a starting point for the final version of the program structure; see Figure 6-12. The final program structure consists of the data structure "core" and additional chunks representing all of the functions to be performed, see Figure 6-13.

The list of basic operations together with the reduced data structure show that there are more basic operations than chunks. Many operations can be allocated to one chunk, but in the end we must add more chunks to the program structure, see Figure 6-13. Operations 1, 4, 5, 12, and 13 are not represented in the reduced and merged data structure diagram, so we must add a new chunk to the data structure and allocate these operations to it. The same steps are taken to add operations 6, 2, and 3 as a "post processing" step; operation 11 as a "patch" to the structure for accommodating an overall counter; and the other operations as refinements to the lowest level chunks.

Included with the basic operations are the conditions to be satisfied by the selection and iteration chunks. Notice in this example that only one matching key is merged per "match." If one of the files has duplicates, the duplicate record is skipped. If file A, for example, contains records with identical keys, the duplicate key will not be processed correctly. To correct this oversight, we would have to change the input file structure to include the possibility of an iterated record in either input file A or B. This change propagates to the program structure with the result that a new program structure must be created to solve the extended two-file merge problem. This is left as an exercise for the reader.

Two Input Data Structures: Merge

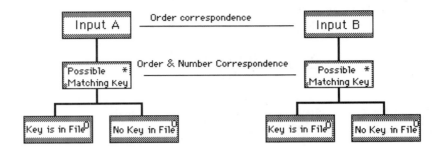

Merged Input Data Structures

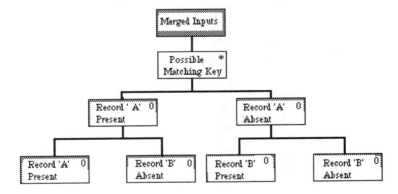

Reduced Merged Data Structure

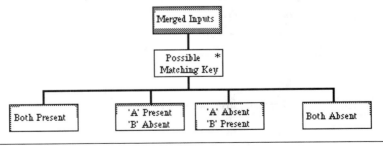

FIGURE 6-12. Two input data structures: merge

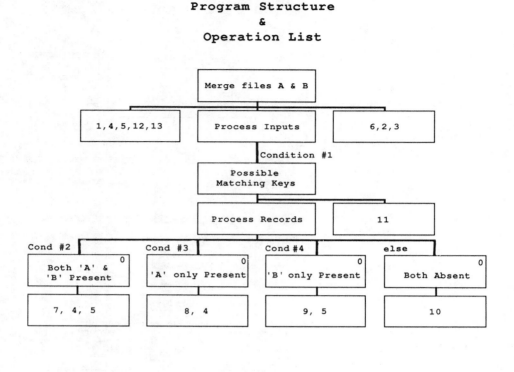

Program Structure
&
Operation List

Merge files A & B

| 1,4,5,12,13 | Process Inputs | 6,2,3 |

Condition #1
Possible Matching Keys

| Process Records | 11 |

Cond #2	Cond #3	Cond #4	else
Both 'A' & 'B' Present 0	'A' only Present 0	'B' only Present 0	Both Absent 0
7, 4, 5	8, 4	9, 5	10

Operations

1. Open Files
2. Close Files
3. Halt
4. Read a record from file A
5. Read a record from file A
6. Print totals
7. Add 1 to running total
8. Add 1 to 'A' total, only
9. Add 1 to 'B' total, only
10 Add 1 to 'Both A & B total, only
11. Add 1 to key counter
12. Initialize all totals
13. Initialize key counter to 1

Conditions

#1. Until end of both files
#2. 'A' key = 'B' key
#3. 'A' key <'B' key
#4. 'B' key < 'A'key

FIGURE 6-13. Program structure and operation list

Structure clashes occur for a number of reasons, which are a source of difficulty when applying JSD:

- Ordering clash — correspondences cannot be made because chunks are not in order.

- Boundary clash — this occurs when there is a mismatch between the data structure and a physical output device structure. For example, a mismatch between records in a file and lines per page on a printer.
- Interleaving clash — this problem is related to the boundary clash problem, but occurs in multiprogramming or parallel processing systems where the order of access to a file is difficult to control.

These problems are solved using a technique called *inversion*, but we will not delve into that technique here[7].

Experience with JSD

JSD has been widely applied to data processing problems and is perhaps the best technique to use when input and output files are processed in batches. While the technique has been adapted to interactive and real-time programming, it is probably not the best technique to use in these environments. Also, the technique appears to be rather mechanical and rigorous, but in fact this is not the case. Typical designs must be reworked and refined as much with JSD as with other techniques[8].

JSD tells how and why to decompose a system into modules, but it does not follow the Cohesion Design Rule. Sometimes JSD modules exhibit strong functional cohesion and sometimes they do not. JSD modules often show communicational cohesion, but the technique does not intrinsically support high-strength modularity. Similar comments apply to coupling. Since the program structure is a model of the shape of the data rather than the functionality of the application, interfaces are not the main emphasis. We do not know, for example, what the interface specifications are, nor what data is supposed to flow from one module to the other in the merge problem used here to illustrate JSD.

The main advantage of the JSD method is its basis for making modules: every programmer who applies the technique produces the same basic program structure. This is a valuable contribution to software engineering, and if we can achieve this predictability in a system's architecture, we should strive to do so.

A set of CASE tools to support JSD are available. PDF is a graphics editor for drawing structure diagrams and entering lists of operations; SPEEDBUILDER is a series of tools for managing the JSD process; and JSD-COBOL is a preprocessor for automatically inserting access control and testing mechanisms into COBOL source code applications[7].

FUNCTIONAL DESIGN

JSD enforces neither functional cohesion within modules nor low coupling between modules. What technique supports the desirable levels of cohesion and coupling? Functional design, FD, or structured design is perhaps the oldest known methodology for enforcing these desirable attributes in a system architecture. The functional design technique has been called various names: structured programming, hierarchical decomposition, modular decomposition, functional decomposition, and so forth[9]. It is widely practiced and is taught in undergraduate courses in programming.

FD: The Method

The design rules of FD are loosely described as:

- State the intended function (the problem to be solved).
- Successively refine the function into layers or levels.
- Connect the refined functions, check, refine further, recheck until a satisfactory solution is obtained.

These rules are not very explicit nor do they tell how to decompose, refine, connect, check, and so on. The major weakness of FD is the fact that anyone can do it without much concern for the result. Unlike JSD, the results of FD are unrepeatable.

The "shape" of an FD system may not be predictable, but the amount of coupling and module strength can be controlled quite well in FD. The CoCoPro application is partially specified in FD form to illustrate the close relationship between program "shape" and application function, see Figure 6-14. The illustration is, of course, only one of many different ways to decompose CoCoPro — a different decomposition is given in the next chapter. The FD tree is essentially a *call graph*, a graph where "A calls B" is represented by an arc from module A to module B.

The modular structure of the CoCoPro FD design closely parallels the list of functions given by the SRS Functional Specification. The advantage of this feature cannot be overemphasized: the program's system architecture ought to be easily checked against its requirements. In the illustration, CoCoPro is decomposed in a simplistic manner. Each menu title corresponds with a top-level function, and each menu item corresponds with a second-level function. In reality this is too simplistic, and misses several important functions specified in the requirements document. (For example, the requirements document given earlier specify several initializations that must be performed when the application is launched.)

The simplistic FD represents a first approximation to the final design. Additional refinements and iterations are typically carried out during the design phase. For example, the simplistic decomposition shown in Figure 6-14 will go through several modifications, enhancements, and corrections. These changes may not be realized until a complete FD decomposition is carried out, checked, and then repeated. Thus, FD usually involves iteration. In fact, it is sometimes modified into a form of *iterative design*. Any design methodology that involves repeated passes over the design is considered an iterative design methodology. FD iterative design means constructing a call graph of all major components of the system from top to bottom, then repeating the design until final approval is obtained from a design review meeting.

Experience with FD

FD often leads to good system architecture. It sometimes leads to logical cohesion instead of functional cohesion, and it occasionally leads to *telescoping* — defining smaller and smaller modules which are not independent but in fact have strong coupling with each other by way of the fact that they all belong to the same calling sequence. This is also related to the depth-of-calling-sequence problem explored earlier. Module depth beyond 5 to 9 levels was shown to be error prone.

Partial Functional Decomposition of CoCoPro

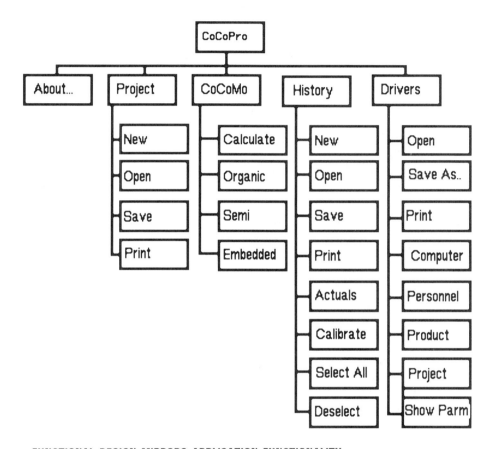

FUNCTIONAL DESIGN MIRRORS APPLICATION FUNCTIONALITY

The functional decomposition of CoCoPro is (partially) shown here as a layered system. The top layer is the application itself. The second layer corresponds to the menus in the menu bar, and the third layer corresponds with the items in each menu. This correspondence between layers in the system architecture and the functionality of the application is one of the strongest features of FD.

Advocates of FD have long claimed it reduces errors, decreases maintenance costs, and improves programmer productivity. The problem with this method, however, is that it does not guarantee the improvements claimed by its advocates. As a result, the claimed improvements have been sporadic, and have not been realized by every software development group that has adopted FD. A more scientific technology is needed.

FIGURE 6-14. Relationship between FD and application functionality

The fact that the potential number of decompositions seems almost infinite makes applying FD more of an art than a science[8]. The method does not give much guidance for decomposing modules, what size they ought to be, nor how they ought to connect to one another.

While FD is easy to learn, simple to apply, and has some good qualities as a software design methodology, it is far too simplistic. Perhaps FD is most important as a bridge between various other techniques. In the next two sections we will explore advanced techniques that use FD in addition to other techniques to overcome the weaknesses of both FD and JSD.

DATA FLOW DESIGN

Data flow design (DFD) was proposed by Constantine, Yourdon, Myers, and others[10]. Early versions were called *composite design* and *structured systems analysis*. The method gained popularity in the early 1980s principally because it is simple and straightforward, and more recently, because it is easily computerized. In its computerized form, it makes an easy-to-use CASE tool. We used DFD in earlier chapters to specify the top-level requirements of an application. The top-level specification of CoCoPro is given in the previous chapter as a DFD diagram.

DFD: The Method

DFD is an application of functional decomposition with the addition of rules for connecting functions. Functions are identified, refined in levels, and connected by drawing data flows between them. These "connectivity rules" provide control over coupling, thus circumventing the coupling problems of FD. Module strength is preserved by decomposing the data flow "process bubbles" into functionally cohesive modules.

DFD works through the decomposition of a problem into a data flow diagram containing actigrams and datagrams, described in chapter five. Actigrams are called *processes* (sometimes *bubbles*) and datagrams are called *flows*. The DFG also contains storage elements where "static information" resides while it is waiting to be processed. Programmers typically follow six steps when applying the DFD method:

1. The application is modelled as a data flow graph (DFG) complete with processes, flow, and storage elements.

2. A "central process" is identified among the processes in the DFG.

3. The DFG is transformed into a tree-structure with the "central transform" as its root.

4. Processes are decomposed by a form of functional decomposition which divides modules into three classes: inputs, transforms, and outputs. Inputs and outputs are sometimes called, respectively, *afferent* and *efferent* processes.

Data Flow Diagram and Potential Central Bubbles

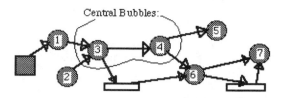

Transformation to Control Flow

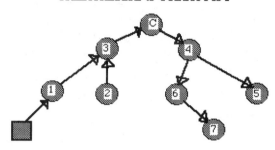

Decomposition into Functions

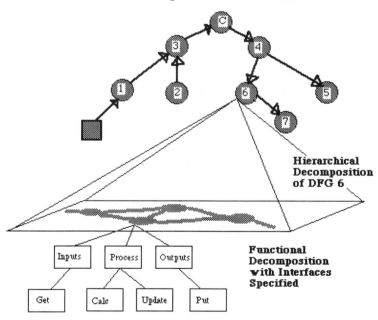

FIGURE 6-15. Transformation from data flow to control flow

5. Processes are refined to some arbitrary level where they are converted to text in the form of a PDL (program design language). PDL is a kind of pseudo-code, which expresses the algorithmic content of a module as sequences, iterations, and selections.

6. The PDL "minispecs" are converted to the application code by transcribing them into some programming language.

A diagrammatic view of these steps in Figure 6-15 shows how the DFG is "molded" into modules. The DFD is transformed into a tree structure; the bubbles of the tree are hierarchically decomposed into other DFGs; at some level, the DFGs are decomposed into modules using a restricted form of FD; and finally, the modules are transformed into pseudo-code. DFGs do not hold sequencing information so they do not tell in what order each module is activated. The sequence information is obtained by transformation: the central transform bubble is used as an "anchor" to establish a sequencing order. The DFG is converted from "parallel" data flow into "serial" control flow by transformation at some level in the decomposition. We have shown this transformation from data flow to control flow at the top DFG level, but the transformation to control flow may not be useful until several levels below the top. For example, activation of subsystems in a menu-driven application may be nondeterministic. That is, a user may choose to select any one of several menus at random, rather than in some predetermined way. This nondeterminism shows up in the DFG as a "don't care" data flow. Such "don't cares" need not be transformed into sequential control flow.

At a certain level (usually after three or four levels of DFG decomposition) each bubble is refined into modules by a restricted form of FD. The method of Gane and Sarson[11] suggests an FD that specifies the coupling of modules. In addition, the FD follows a "standard" format with input functions placed visually on the left side, solution functions in the center, and output functions on the right side of the FD diagrams. This form of refinement is represented graphically as a *structure chart*. A structure chart shows a system's functions and interfaces, and shows the architecture as connected functions.

A "standard" FD decomposition is shown in Figure 6-16 with a *commander function* at the root of the tree; input or *get functions* on the left; transform or *solution function(s)* in the center; and output or *put functions* on the right. Function interfaces are shown as data or control information flows among the tree-structured functions. An interface containing data is shown with an "open" arrow and an interface containing control information such as a flag is shown with a "closed" arrow.

The structure chart defines the system interface and the functional decomposition of the application. It represents the *detailed design* of a system, and as such is subject to inspection. A review of the detailed design must check the structure chart against the SRS document for consistency, completeness, correctness, and so on. The technique is iterative — many passes over the structure chart may be required before a final structure chart is derived.

The next step in the DFD approach is to write miniature specifications for each function in the structure chart. These minispecs are actually pseudo-code specifications for

Standard Functional Decomposition

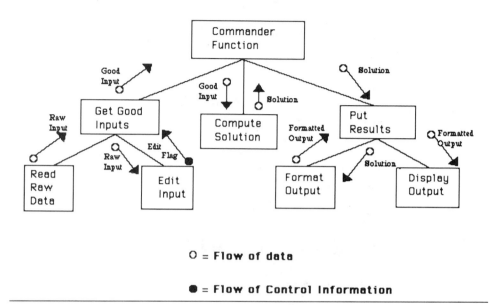

O = **Flow of data**

● = **Flow of Control Information**

FIGURE 6-16. Standard functional decomposition

the yet-to-come source code, see Figure 6-17. A minispec shows the input/output flows as defined by the interface specifications in the structure chart, and the algorithmic component of each function. Typical minispecs contain either English language or "structured English" statements. When some form of structured English is used in defining a minispec, we say the specification is in a PDL, or program definition language (also, procedure description language, pseudo-code definition language, and PRISM definition language).

In systems such as that in Figure 6-17, the minispec is written first, and the CASE tool generates the structure chart. That is, the DFG is decomposed hierarchically down to some level, say level 4. The bubbles at level 4 are then refined into functions by writing a PDL minispec for each process bubble. The minispec contains interface information and structured English specifications of the process. The CASE tool converts this specification into a structure chart showing all interfaces and functions. The next chapter will elaborate on this approach.

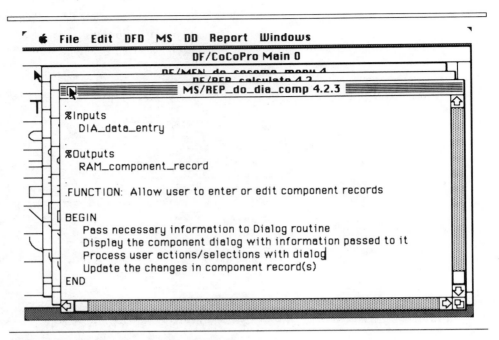

FIGURE 6-17. Minispecs of REP_do_dia_comp routine

Experience with DFD

There are several difficulties with using DFD. First, drawing the DFG is somewhat of an art: the result is unpredictable. This is also a problem with FD, nor is the problem solved with DFD. Second, finding a "central transform" is an art, usually done by visual inspection of the DFG. Third, the number of levels of refinement is neither well defined nor well understood by most designers. When do you stop refining process bubbles and begin writing PDL minispecs? Finally, refinement of PDL minispecs is an art — how many levels and what guidelines should be followed when writing the minispecs? Yet, these problems have not prevented this method from gaining popularity. In fact, CASE tools are widely available to support DFD, including graphic editors that permit a designer to organize and draw the DFG on a screen, enter PDL minispecs, build a data dictionary of data flows and storage elements, and in general manage the details of a system architecture based on DFD.

OBJECT-ORIENTED DESIGN

It is doubtful whether the object-oriented design approach should be called a design technique as opposed to a programming technique. Object-oriented programming (OOP) is an important method of programming. It has greatly influenced not only the design of programming languages, but also methods of program implementation[12,13]. We could delay discussion of this field until the chapter on implementation, but we introduce it here because this programming technique is rapidly evolving into a design technique.

Booch[14] advocates a low-level design technique called object-oriented development (OOD). Booch's development technique is the forerunner of a complete design methodology which is still evolving. Its principles are not easily applied to design, but in terms of a programming language they can be stated as follows:

- The entities to be manipulated by a program are called *objects* and they are manipulated by sending and receiving messages to and from one another.

- Objects are *instances* — concrete entities derived from prototype entities containing both *state* and *functionality*. The state portion of an object consists of its data values, and the functional portion consists of an object's methods — procedures which perform the functions defined for the object.

- Objects are created by "cloning" them from prototypes called *classes*. A class is a generalized object consisting of methods and data values.

- Objects *inherit* methods (operations) from their parent class. Inheritance is important because it enhances code reusability.

- Object-oriented software systems are constructed as a system of communicating objects, each object taking its data values and operations from a well-organized collection of classes.

The main difference between OOD and other techniques is its emphasis on objects and their decomposition, rather than on functional or data structure decomposition. Instead, OOD combines function and data into a whole: objects contain or encapsulate both data and function. This hoisting feature of OOD is a very powerful force for designing systems with high communicational cohesion, low coupling (with its corresponding desirable information hiding), and ease of maintenance.

According to Booch[14], OOD is an approach to software design in which a system is decomposed by identifying data/function encapsulations called objects, and arranging these objects into a whole by defining messages that connect objects together. OOD is an improvement over other techniques because it:

- Effectively addresses the need for proper data abstraction and information hiding.

- Is equally valid for sequential and parallel, or highly concurrent, systems.

- Offers advantages for maintenance — objects do not change as often as data or function.

OOD: The Method

The method's steps are loosely defined by Booch[14] as follows:

1. Identify the objects and their attributes. For instance, in the Macintosh user interface, the menu bar, windows, and dialogs are all objects with attributes such as menu titles and menu items; window title, scrolls, and resize boxes; and buttons. In addition, an application typically manipulates objects such as disk files, RAM tables, and other data structures. The first step is to identify objects that are meaningful to the application; if a payroll system operates on a file called PAYCHECKS, then PAYCHECKS is identified as one of the objects in the application.

2. Identify the operations required by each object. All objects encapsulate both data and function. In this step you must identify the functions performed on the objects. These functions characterize the behavior of each object. Menus are pulled down, windows are opened, closed, resized, and scrolled. The PAY-CHECKS object is probably opened, closed, updated, read, written to, and backed up. This step attempts to identify *all* operations on all objects, but of course additional operations are discovered at various stages of development.

3. Establish the visibility of each object in relation to other objects. Objects interact by "calling" the operations on other objects and by allowing other objects to "call" operations on themselves. In this step you must establish the behavior of objects as a system of interacting parts. For example, the PAYCHECKS object may use the DIRECT_FILE object to implement a direct access file. The visibility of DIRECT_FILE to PAYCHECKS, and the converse, must be established before we know how these two will behave. Suppose, for example, PAYCHECKS needs to call OPEN_DIRECT_FILE, READ_DIRECT_FILE, and CLOSE_DIRECT_FILE — all operations defined on DIRECT_FILE. This means DIRECT_FILE must make the three operations *visible* to outside objects such as PAYCHECKS.

4. Establish the interface of each object. In step three we establish the dependence of one object on another. In this step we specify the interfaces that make the dependency possible. For example, when PAYCHECKS calls OPEN_DIRECT_FILE it sends a message to object DIRECT_FILE that tells what "service" is needed, and how to return the desired information. This is essentially a protocol for passing parameters. The input parameters in this example might well be the name of the file and its status. The output parameters might be the returned file number and an error flag. The types of interface variables establishes a protocol — passed by value or passed by reference.

5. Implement each object. This is where OOD excels. Once the objects, their operations, data, and interactions are known, we can easily implement objects in a variety of languages. Special object-oriented languages might be used, or more conventional languages such as Pascal, Ada, or C might be adapted to the OOD style. For example, in Macintosh Pascal, we can use the unit structure to encapsulate state, function, and interface information. The implementation portion of a unit contains the data and function as global declarations (data) and procedure/function declarations (function). The interface portion contains the OOD interface specification.

While it appears a simple matter to apply these five steps to actual problems, the steps are not very helpful in guiding software engineers in *how* to identify objects and operations, or *how* to establish visibility and interfaces. Like many other design techniques, OOD leaves much of the creative part of design up to the individual. Perhaps the only way to learn the OOD technique is to study examples.

OOD of CoCoPro

The OOD of a portion of CoCoPro is shown in Figures 6-18 and 6-19. We use a variation of the notation proposed by Booch[14] to draw the objects and their interactions for the top-level CoCoPro system, and then refine one of the objects at the top (CALCULATE_cocomo) into a lower-level OOD network. The top-level OOD network starts with an object called MAIN, see Figure 6-18.

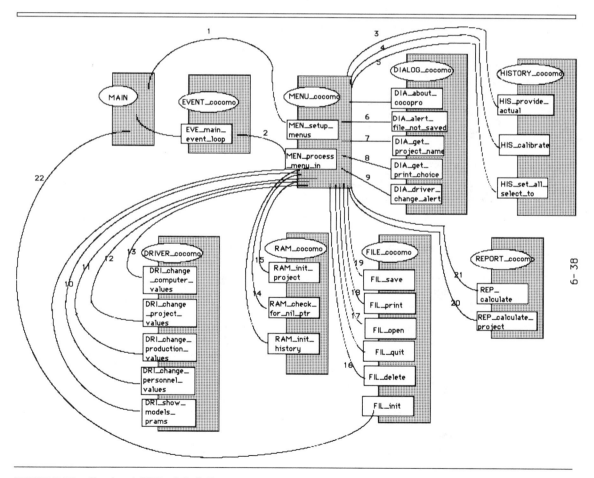

FIGURE 6-18a. Top-level OOD of CoCoPro

LIST OF PARAMETERS FOR TOP-LEVEL GRAPH

ARC Number	Parameters
1	Default_ok
2	Menu_selection
3	HIS_model, HIS_empty
4	HIS_model
5	HIS_boolean
6	Filetype, Alert_button
7	Project_name, Name_ok_flag
8	button
9	Change_type, Alert_button
10	DRI_changed
11	DRI_changed
12	DRI_changed
13	DRI_changed
14	Project_nil, History_nil
15	project
16	filename
17	fopen, ok_flag
18	filename, Show_SFGetfile
19	original_name, ok_flag
20	REP_model, REP_show_results
21	REP_model, REP_empty
22	Default_ok

FIGURE 6-18b. Parameters for top-level graph

In the diagram, a rectangle represents an object, or **unit** in Macintosh Pascal. An elliptical insert in the box contains the name of the object — the unit and file name in Pascal. The rectangles inserted in an object contain the names of access procedures or methods defined on the object. Methods are implemented in Pascal by simply writing a function or procedure corresponding to each method. Methods are also visible to outside objects, hence they appear in the interface portion of a unit.

An object manipulates other objects through the visible access procedures or methods defined for external objects. That is, a visible procedure can be called from another object. This is shown in the OOD network as a line drawn from the body of an object (from the unit's implementation part), to an access procedure of another object. For example, in the CoCoPro network, MAIN manipulates objects EVENT_cocomo, FILE_cocomo, and MENU_cocomo by calling procedures which are defined in these units. MAIN calls EVE_main_event_loop in **unit** EVENT-cocomo, FIL_init in FILE_cocomo, and MEN_setup-menus in **unit** MENU_cocomo. These manipulate other objects, and so forth.

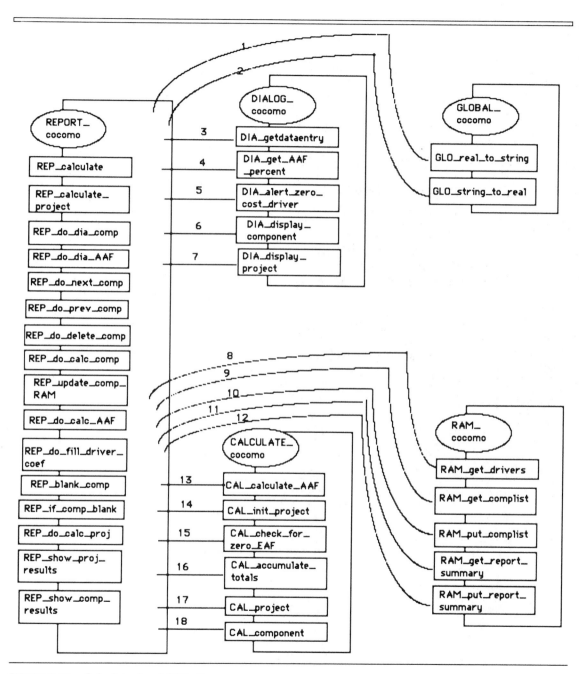

FIGURE 6-19a. Calculate_level OOD diagram

Experience with OOD

The OOD network is reminiscent of a DFD because it does not tell what order to perform these access procedure calls. There is no explicit sequencing information given in the network, only the relationship among objects. This is why OOD works equally well for serial and concurrent software. Sequencing a serial program through its calls must be done explicitly in the actual code.

The interface portion of the OOD network is specified separately as a table of data flows. For example, the specification of interfaces for the top-level OOD network of CoCoPro is shown in Figure 6-18b.

These interface specifications are incomplete, but they provide a starting point for the complete specification. A complete specification is one that will compile with a Pascal **unit** and will provide all of the necessary constants, types, and variables used by each **unit**. This "uses" relationship is part of the "establishment of visibility" in the system of objects. We will return later to this difficult but important topic.

The OOD network is hierarchical in the same way that other diagramming techniques are hierarchical. An OOD design can be decomposed into a system of layers or levels. For example, the CALCULATE object (unit) is refined into a subnetwork as shown in Figure 6-19a. The interface specification for this subnetwork is given in Figure 6-19b.

LIST OF PARAMETERS FOR CALCULATE_LEVEL GRAPH

ARC Number	Parameters
1	real_string, value, decimal_places
2	real_string, value
3	DataEntry, button, first
4	AAF_percent, button
5	Non_zero
6	DIA_comp_Rec
7	DIA_proj_Rec
8	driver_record
9	RAM_first_component
10	RAM_first_component
11	RAM_report_summary_record
12	RAM_report_summary_record
13	parameters
14	project_totals
15	component
16	project_totals
17	project_in, project_totals
18	component

FIGURE 6-19b. Parameters for calculate_level graph

This subnetwork is a partitioning of the overall top-level network. If we were able to isolate one or more objects as a hierarchical decomposition, the subnetwork would be a hierarchical subnetwork; but in this example we merely separated the functions of the application according to the menus. Calculate is done by selecting the CALCU-LATE item under the CoCoMo menu.

Hierarchical decomposition is not an obvious trait of OOD. This is troublesome because OOD networks tend to become large "spaghetti" diagrams. Secondly, like DFD decomposition, there are no clear-cut rules for deciding where to subdivide or knowing how many levels are "correct."

A DESIGN GUIDE

This brief survey of design methodologies has served to illustrate the strengths and weaknesses of existing design methodologies. The goal of all of these methods is to derive a system architecture to be used during the implementation phase. This architecture must be verifiable in terms of the SRS document and changeable during implementation and maintenance. It must also ensure "good" software engineering practices. These are difficult goals to achieve together and none of the methods proposed are optimal for all of these goals.

Bergland[8] surveys three of the techniques discussed here and draws five conclusions:

1. **There is no complete methodology for partitioning big problems.**
   Hierarchical decomposition and divide-and-conquer techniques are good in the abstract, but when a real-world problem is encountered we cannot find its "top" (see chapter one), or else the diagrams and documents produced to describe the large system overwhelm the designer. There is still no method for coping with the complexity of size.

   The sheer size of many problems *is* the problem: We need methods of decomposition that hide certain details when a design is viewed from one perspective, but hides other details when viewed from another perspective. Techniques that encapsulate both data and function (OOD) offer hope in this respect. CASE tools that manage the details, revealing only those we want to see at a given time, offer more hope. DFD tools are a step in this direction because they provide separate views of a large system through data dictionaries and DFGs.

2. **The best techniques are those that lend themselves to automation.**
   Many methods exist besides those surveyed here, but when do we apply any given technique? Finite State Machine, FSM, and Petri Network models are the basis for methodologies that we have not covered, yet these methods may apply to certain situations. How do we evaluate these situations and know when to apply which technique?

   Generally speaking, the best techniques are the ones that lend themselves to automation. A model is only as good as its implementation as a CASE tool will allow. CASE tools are the vehicles by which technology is transmitted. If this assumption is valid, then the DFD methodology is the best technique simply because of its widespread availability. However, OOD technology also lends itself to automation. We can conclude that DFD and OOD are the strongest methods surveyed here. Other techniques are best used in very special circumstances.

3. **There are no guidelines for combining methods when appropriate.** The best method may actually be a combination of methods, but how do we know which methods to apply and when to combine them? Again, the answer lies in automation. Two or more techniques will be used together only if their files are mutually accessible. If a DFD tool can access and use information produced by an OOD tool, then they are the "correct" choice to make when combining methods. CASE tools that do not work in concert with one another will not be selected by software engineers looking to combine methods.

4. **None of the methods discussed so far help with the number-one problem in software engineering: maintenance.** Design tools are, however, indirectly harmful or helpful to maintenance. A poorly designed system is more difficult to maintain than a well-designed system. Nonetheless, design tools do not always promote the best interests of the maintenance programmer. For example, OOD networks are not easily followed, nor are they self-descriptive.

5. **None of the methods guarantee incremental correctness of the design.** By this we mean that each step in the design process represents an increment from some baseline. These increments must guarantee overall correctness, yet a step may introduce an inconsistency, incorrectness, or fault in the design. For example, DFD decomposition into a structure chart does not guarantee that the structure chart implements a correct refinement of the bubble diagram above the structure chart.

CASE tools incorporate some checking — leveling in DFGs, for example, and checks on the data dictionary of a design to make sure all data dictionary entries have been used. The DFD technique is the most advanced for this kind of automatic checking. However, specification languages exist that do a better job of generating test cases than DFD tools provide (DFDs typically do not generate test cases from DFGs, but such cases can be generated from the minispecs).

Bergland goes on to suggest a hybrid approach to design. A similar hybrid between DFD and OOD is offered in the next chapter. Bergland's recommendations:

1. Identify reusable components to be used in the application, such as toolboxes for windows, icons, menus, and file subsystems. These components, along with the features of a particular high-level language, form the basis for a "virtual machine." The application will be developed "on top of" this virtual machine.

2. Use a DFD method to map the system requirements into a DFG. The DFG is virtually machine dependent because it depends on the reusable components established in step one. For example, when designing for the Macintosh, the DFG is patterned after menu and mouse toolbox routines. (A "main event routine" is used to intercept events on the desktop. This approach to the desktop impacts the way the system must be designed.)

3. Refine the DFG in a variety of ways: If the subsystem is "business data processing-like" the JSD method may fit. Use the JSD method whenever the solution is likely to be strongly influenced by the input/output data structures. If the system is highly concurrent, use either the DFD or OOD technique. The OOD technique is especially appropriate if there are many synchronization or "race condition" problems to be solved. On the other hand, the DFD technique is useful for partitioning a system into many "parallel" parts, because it does not bind the design to a sequential ordering. The DFG is useful for describing parallel flows while OOD is good for encapsulating access procedure and shared data, thus controlling race conditions.

A major problem arises when combining the DFD and OOD techniques. DFD defines a functional decomposition of a system while OOD defines an object-oriented decomposition. In terms of programming, DFD maps every function or procedure into its own unit, a separately compilable file. On the other hand, functions and procedures in an OOD design are clustered around the data they operate on. How do we transform the scattered unit structure of DFD into a clustered system of units per the OOD method?

In the next chapter we propose a hybrid approach that combines the advantages of these two techniques into a single technique we call Object-Oriented Data Flow Design, OODFD. The idea of OODFD is to use the DFD description of a problem as a starting point, transforming the DFG into an OOD network by clustering the functions in the structure chart. When certain design rules are followed, a structure chart can be converted into an object-oriented system architecture with the following advantages:

1. The simplicity and ease of use of the DFD CASE tool is retained, especially during the early stages of requirements specification and design.

2. The module strength and coupling properties of FD are retained by using a restricted form of decomposition resulting in a structure chart.

3. Components of the system are properly encapsulated to provide information hiding and data abstraction mechanisms by converting the structure chart into an OOD network. The transformation process produces a mapping of functions into objects. This vital information is used by the development team during the coding phase.

Terms and Concepts

afferent	procedural
call graph	temporal
central process	commander function
class	composite design
cohesion	correspondence
coincidental	coupling
communicational	content
functional	control
logical	data

global	modularity
stamp	module
custom module	custom
data correspondence	depth
data structure design	reuse
design rules	object
DFD	object-oriented
divide and conquer	OOD
efferent	opaque
encapsulation	ordering clash
fan-out	PDL
FD	pseudo-code
functional decomposition	put function
functional design	reusability
get function	scoping rules
implementation part	solution function
information hiding	state
inheritance	strength
instance	structure chart
interface	structure clash
inversion	structured systems analysis
iterative design	telescoping
JSD	unit
logical structure diagram	unreferenced variable
method	visible
minispec	

DISCUSSION QUESTIONS

1. List the four design methods surveyed in this chapter, along with the advantages and disadvantages of each.

2. Implement the merge application design from the JSD diagrams. Did you have to make modifications to the design after you wrote the first version of the program? Discuss the viability of JSD for this problem.

3. Modify the merge application design given in JSD form so that files with multiple, identical-keyed records can be merged successfully. Remember that the files are initially sorted, but the duplicate keys must now be modeled by a different data structure diagram. Show all of the diagrams resulting from your design.

4. Design an application for merging two sorted files together as stated in question 3. Use FD to design your system. Now, test your design by comparing it with the list of design rules given at the end of the first section of the chapter.

5. Solve question 3 using the DFD method. How many bubbles do you have? How many levels? What does your structure chart look like?

6. Use the OOD methodology to design the merging program given in question 3. What are the objects? Show your OOD network. How does your network compare with the actual code produced to solve this problem?

7. Discuss the viability of each of the following design methods when designing a word processor application: JSD, DFD, and OOD. Assume the word processor produces one text file at a time. Also, assume the word processor is capable of standard operations such as moving a paragraph and so on.

8. Write a JSD data structure diagram corresponding with the following Pascal file structure:

```
type persons=record
               age : integer;
               sex : (male, female);
               case t of 1: factory; 2: office; 3: admin end;
             end;
var
     theFile : file of persons;
```

9. Give an OOD network for a personal computer system in which the objects consist of a keyboard, screen, a disk drive, a printer, and a mouse. Assume the following operations are visible for each object: Keyboard ⇒ GetChar; Screen ⇒ PutChar, Clear, NewLine, GoToCursorLocation; Disk ⇒ Initialize, CreateFile, OpenFile, ReadFileRecord, WriteFileRecord, CloseFile, DisposeFile; Printer ⇒ PrintChar; and mouse ⇒ ButtonDown, ButtonUp. Draw a general OOD network that shows how these objects are connected to one another. (For example, when a keyboard key is pressed, the GetChar method of Keyboard gets the character and sends it to the "Main" object of the computer system; the main object most likely sends the character message to the PutChar method of Screen to have it displayed.)

10. Find the central transform for the DFG below, and convert this DFG into a tree, then rewrite it as a structure chart. Show all interfaces and modules pertaining to the original DFG.

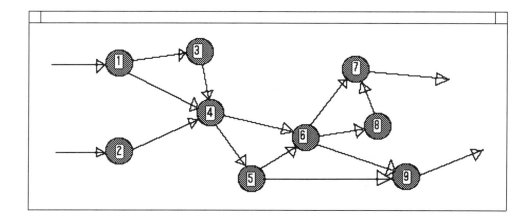

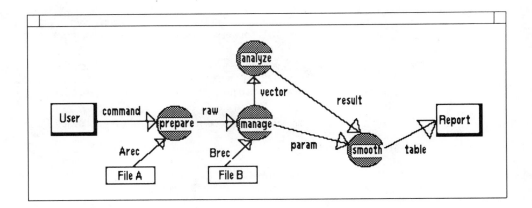

11. Convert the above DFD design into a structured design using the restricted FD method proposed for DFD. Show all interfaces and modules corresponding to the original design in your structure chart.

REFERENCES AND FURTHER READING

1. Card, D. N., V. E. Church, and W. W. Agresti. 1986. "An Empirical Study of Software Design Practices." *IEEE Transactions on Software Engineering* SE-12, no. 2 (February): 264–271.

2. Miller, G. A. 1956. "The Magical Number Seven, Plus or Minus Two: Some Limits on Our Capacity for Processing Information." *Psychology Review* 63: 81–87.

3. Tracz, W. (ed). 1987. "Reusability Comes of Age." *IEEE Software* 4, no. 4 (July).

4. Woodfield, S. N., D. W. Embley, and D. T. Scott. "Can Programmers Reuse Software?" *IEEE Software* 4, no. 4 (July): 52–59.

5. Jackson, M. A. 1982. *System Development*. Englewood Cliffs, NJ: Prentice-Hall.

6. Warnier, J. D. 1974. *Logical Construction of Programs*. New York: Van Nostrand-Reinhold.

7. Cameron, J. R. 1986. "An Overview of JSD." *IEEE Transactions on Software Engineering* SE-12, no. 2 (February): 222–240.

8. Bergland, G. D. 1978. "Structured Design Methodologies." *Proceedings of Fifteenth Annual Design Automation*. Reprinted in *IEEE Computer* 14, no. 10 (October 1981): 13–37.

9. Baker, F. T. 1975. "Structured Programming in a Production Programming Environment." *IEEE Transactions on Software Engineering* SE-1, no. 2 (June): 241–252.

10. Myers, G. J. 1978. *Composite/Structured Design*. New York: Van Nostrand-Reinhold.

11. Gane, C., and T. Sarson. 1979. *Structured Systems Analysis: Tools and Techniques*. Englewood Cliffs, NJ: Prentice-Hall.

12. Shaw, M. 1984. "Abstraction Techniques in Modern Programming Languages." *IEEE Software* 1, no. 4 (October): 10–18.

13. Cox, B. 1984. "Message/Object Programming: An Evolutionary Change in Programming Technology." *IEEE Software* 1, no. 1 (January).

14. Booch, G. 1986. "Object-Oriented Development." *IEEE Transactions on Software Engineering* SE-12, no. 2 (February): 211–222.

7

System Architecture

PREVIEW

System architecture is the major factor that determines the "shape" of a software system, but system architecture can be viewed in a variety of ways. We first examine some of the points of view that can be used to reveal the underlying structure of a large, complex software system.

As a specific example, we trace the design of the Development Project (CoCoPro) using a set of DFD CASE tools called PowerTools. We show the DFG, DD, and structure chart of a major portion of CoCoPro.

Then we introduce the notion of combining OOD with DFD to derive a design methodology called OODFD — Object-Oriented Data Flow Design. This technique provides the final step in design, and identifies the modules to be implemented by the programming team.

But how good are CASE tools? In the final section of this chapter, we critically evaluate the tools used to produce the example design. The result? While an immature technology, CASE offers hope for improvements in software development productivity.

ARCHITECTURAL VIEWS

The final step in design prior to coding consists of documenting an overall **program architecture** — *the structure and relationships among the components of the computer program*. A "good" program or application system architecture should be based on an appropriate model of how components are connected and related to one another. Therefore, an interconnection model along with a language for describing component interconnections is needed.

The purpose of this chapter is twofold: to investigate the topic of interconnection models and how they are used to construct an overall system architecture, and to show how to map the system architecture into a collection of tasks to be performed by human programmers. Interconnection models provide a basis for CASE tools, especially maintenance tools. Further, the mapping from system architecture into tasks provides a solid base for beginning the implementation phase.

The previous chapter discussed several design methodologies based on decomposition strategies. These decomposition strategies often incorporate an interconnection model as a side effect of the design process. An **interconnection model** *is any pair of sets: a set of components, and a set of relations that define various interactions among components*[1]. One of the goals of any design methodology is to control the growth of complexity through divide-and-conquer techniques. In the current context, a major goal is to control complexity arising from interaction among the "conquered" components. As the number of components grows, so does the complexity of their interactions. A "good" system architecture must prevent unbounded growth in complexity of size. This control pays off in general ease of maintenance.

SOFTWARE CONNECTIONS

Software components such as separately compiled modules, functions, and their corresponding interfaces are often represented in the form of graphs. The nodes of the graph represent components — functions, procedures, packages, units, and so on. The arcs in the graph represent some relation such as "calls": function A calls function B.

The architecture of a software system is essentially a graph of some form, either an interconnection graph showing what routine calls another, or a graph showing a relationship of interest to designer or maintainer. Different graphs show different relationships, thus rendering different views of the system.

The JSD, FD, and OOD methodologies certainly incorporate interconnections among modules and their corresponding interface specifications. In JSD the interconnection model is represented by a structure diagram for data and a corresponding program structure diagram for the application. In FD, the interconnection model is a simple "call graph" where components are functions, and the "calls" relation is shown by drawing arcs from one function to another. The OOD methodology employs a graph structure to document the module interconnections among objects. These methodologies provided control over the design complexity, but they are not always suitable for controlling coding and maintenance complexity. We can (and will) use design methodologies as interconnection models, but in addition, we may need to use other models, especially for the purpose of exposing interconnections of interest to maintenance programmers. What kinds of interconnection models are there, and how do they benefit the software engineer?

Perry[1] divides interconnection models into three categories:

1. **Module**, such as OOD
2. **Syntactic**, such as FD
3. **Semantic**, such as Predicate Graph

These models form the basis for most design and maintenance tools commonly available to designers, implementors, and maintainers of software systems. How do we represent a system architecture using each of these kinds of models, and what purpose do they serve?

Module Interconnection

The module interconnection graph shows relationships among separately compiled modules; see Figure 7-1a. For example, the MAKE utility of UNIX and PC-DOS operating systems describes the dependency of one separately compiled module on other

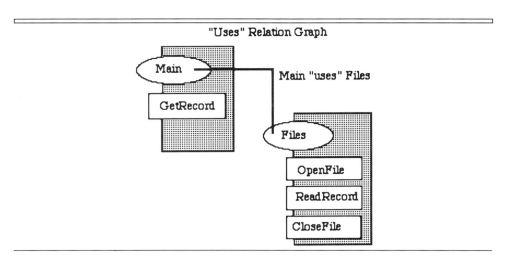

FIGURE 7-1a. Module Interconnection

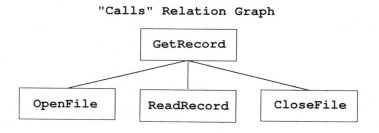

FIGURE 7-1b. Syntactic Interconnection

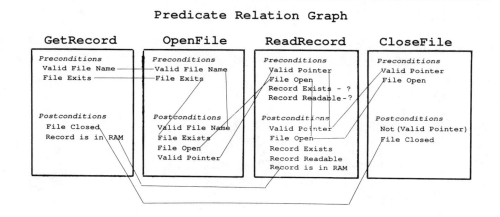

FIGURE 7-1c. Semantic Interconnection

modules. When one module is changed and compiled, it may cause a change in another module. The MAKE utility automatically recompiles all "depends on" components. Because of this automated tool, developers have come to rely on this form of module interconnection graph.

Any implementation of a system that employs an include directive to bind modules together establishes a dependency among components. The include directive is used in C, Pascal, and FORTRAN compilers to encourage modularity. It is a mechanism commonly used to implement a system, but it often troubles maintenance programmers because includes may obscure the effects of a change. The module interconnection graph documents the most obscure dependency, hence it is extremely useful to maintenance programmers.

Module interconnection is "good" for design and implementation, but "bad" for maintenance programmers. A CASE tool for automatically drawing graphs with the following relations can be used to overcome the maintainer's problem:

uses: A graph showing which modules are used by other modules.

defines: A graph showing where a named entity is defined, for example, procedures, constants, and variables.

referenced: A graph showing where a named entity is referenced, e.g. where it is used.

flow: A graph showing import/export flows from/to modules.

These are but a few of the "cross-reference" tools used by programmers to "understand" large and complex systems. They are all based on module interconnections of some sort.

Syntactic Interconnection

The syntactic interconnection model is based on function and procedure level descriptions rather than on module level descriptions, see Figure 7-1b. A syntactic interconnection model focuses on smaller components: it describes the relationships among the syntactic elements of the programming language used to implement the system. As such, this kind of model is of more use to a maintenance programmer than it is to a designer.

We have shown an FD graph as an example of a syntactic interconnection model, but other graphs are often used to expose the fine-grained structure of an application. A "calls" graph shows what function calls another function, but an "is called by" relation shows what functions call a given function. Other relations may be applied to any syntactic element including types, constants, structures, procedures, functions, parameters, import/export variables, and coupling via files:

is used at: A graph showing everywhere a certain name is used (referenced).
is changed at: A graph showing everywhere a certain name is assigned a value.

These kinds of cross-references are especially useful for change management, static analysis of the application for performance or testing purposes, and for version control.

The syntactic model is very much like the module interconnection model, except the syntactic model operates at a level of much greater detail. This usually means the syntactic model works from the actual finished source code. Hence, it is a tool for maintainers. On the other hand, the module interconnection models are used by designers who have not yet produced source code. A module interconnection graph might be a good starting point for a syntactic interconnection graph. The module graph could be produced by the designer and passed on to the coder, who would evolve it into a coding document. This would then be used with other tools to generate useful cross-reference graphs for maintenance programmers to use.

Semantic Interconnection

Perry[1] introduces a new model based on what the programmer *intended* rather than what the program might actually do! The idea in semantic modeling is to express the "meaning" of a program in terms of predicates, assertions that are either true or false at some point in a program, see Figure 7-1c. These predicates give meaning to the components of a program.

Two kinds of predicates are employed in the semantic model: a precondition specifies what must be true before a certain program component is run; a postcondition specifies what must be true after the component completes. These pre- and postconditions establish generalized relations among components, which propagate through the system. If the propagation of "truth" is disrupted by a change in some component, the disruption shows up as a "false" condition.

As an illustration, consider the propagation of "truth" from one precondition to another by three functions: OpenFile, ReadRecord, and CloseFile. These three functions are used to get a record of data from a disk file into RAM. The sequence of pre- and postconditions that must propagate "truth" are listed below in the order they are "executed."

We begin with the assumptions Valid File Name and File Exists, which are preconditions stating that we assume the user has given a valid file name and the file we want to read actually exists. When the OpenFile routine is called, these preconditions are passed to it.

OpenFile does not change the truth in Valid File Name and File Exits. In addition, OpenFile establishes new truth in the form of postconditions File Open and Valid Pointer. These are passed on when the main routine calls ReadRecord to fetch the record into RAM.

Now, ReadRecord assumes two preconditions that are not passed to it, directly: Record Exists and Record Readable. These two conditions are assumed by the ReadRecord routine. If at most one of these is false, the chain of "truth" is broken, and the semantic interconnection fails. These conditions are specifications to be enforced by both developer and maintainer. Typically, the ReadRecord routine checks for both of these conditions, and reports an error if either condition is false.

One of the postconditions of the calling routine, Get Record, is satisfied by ReadRecord. If the operation succeeds, then Record is in RAM is true after ReadRecord runs. This postcondition from ReadRecord is connected to the postcondition of Get Record. The second postcondition of Get Record is supplied by the postcondition File Closed, from CloseFile.

The pre- and postconditions along with the components of a simple Get Record subsystem form a graph structure which models the semantics of the subsystem. The predicates are linked by arcs from one condition to another condition, thus forming a network of pre- and postconditions. The interesting feature of this network is that it represents what the subsystem is supposed to do, not necessarily what it does. This information is very valuable to maintenance programmers who were probably not part of the original development team.

All of the interconnection models treat a software system as a coupled system. That is, the graphs depict different forms of coupling. The coupled components establish various kinds of relations among the components. If we change the kind of coupling to be exposed, the relationship among components is also changed, leading to a different graph. In short, these various graphs provide different views of the system's architecture.

Views of Software

A **view** *is a mapping from the artifact (source code, design document, or whatever) onto an abstraction of the artifact (graph, specification document, or whatever).* We can think of a view as a simplification of a complex system that lets us understand only a certain aspect, without cluttering details. A programmer *views* a program from various vantage points — each vantage point reveals something special about the system.

To illustrate this seemingly vague idea, consider an analogy with a construction project, see Figure 7-2. A house can be viewed from several different aspects. One view of a house is the elevation — a drawing of what the house will look like when it is completed and sitting on the lot. The elevation is used by builders to get the owner's attention and to show the owner what the ultimate result is likely to be. The elevation is an abstraction of what the house actually contains, because the elevation does not expose the plumbing, electrical wiring, or heating ducts. Yet this rendition of the house is very important to both builder and owner. The elevation of a house plan is much like a specification of a user interface for a software application.

A second view of a house is its internals, one abstraction of which is the floor plan. The floor plan of a house is similar to an application's system architecture. The software architecture might express the coupling of modules (modular interconnection model), the coupling of functions (syntactic interconnection model), or the coupling of meanings (semantic interconnection model). Similarly, the floor plans of a house might emphasize the spacial relationship among rooms, windows, power outlets, vacuum outlets, and so forth.

A third view of a house is a more detailed view of its internals. One such abstraction is the schematic drawing of the heating system, including furnace and ducts. This drawing is probably used by both implementor (carpenter or heating system installer), and maintainer (repair person). The drawing is far more detailed than any other view of the house. Similarly, the source code of an application is far more detailed than any other document used to describe the application. Yet source code is still a level of abstraction above the actual machine code of the application itself.

The final view of a house is the house itself. The "real thing" is as concrete as possible, just like the machine code of an application. This view is sometimes needed to debug a very difficult program, thus it is of value to both developer and maintainer.

Elevation - House

User Interface - Application

Floor Plan - House

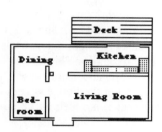

System Architecture - Application

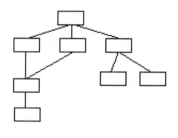

Heating System - House

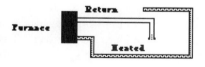

Implementation - Application

```
Procedure wDisplay ( a, b : list );
    var i : counter;

    begin
    For i := 1 to a do
      {.....code....}
    End;
```

**Completion - Actual House
(Photo)**

Completion - Actual Application

FIGURE 7-2. Views of a house versus views of an application

ARCHITECTURE OF COCOPRO

In the remainder of this chapter we will combine all that we have learned thus far into a single, quite complete example that shows how the CoCoPro application was designed and implemented. The example will be given slightly out of order from the way it was constructed, because presenting the results before the details will make the example easier to understand.

We will use Iconix PowerTools from Iconix Software Engineering, Inc. — a CASE tool for design — to automatically generate the software. PowerTools consists of several design and analysis tools:

CoCoPro: This tool is provided as part of PowerTools. It produces cost and time estimates of the application under development. (This is the Development Project application we are going to design and partially build.)

FreeFlow: A DFD/DD (Data Flow Design/Data Dictionary) graphic editor for entering DFG specifications of an application. This tool supports DeMarco data flow analysis, integrated data dictionary and minispec editing.

FastTask: A finite-state machine editor for use in real-time control software design. We will not be using this tool in this example, because CoCoPro is not a real-time application.

PowerPDL: A tool for converting minispecs into intermediate form. This tool reads the PDL files created in FreeFlow and produces files containing a tree-structured graph and PDL listing. Listings include a table of contents and a cross-reference of data definition and reference. These files are used by SmartChart to produce a structure chart.

SmartChart: This tool reads the files created in PowerPDL and produces a structure chart in the form of a tree-structured graph and a PDL listing. A language-sensitive editor is incorporated so the designer can become coder. The language-sensitive editor provides templates of source code such as Ada™ and Pascal. A programmer can use SmartChart to add source code to the PDL pseudo-code minispec, thus generating a source code version of the application.

These tools are used in the order given here. First, CoCoPro is used to estimate effort and time. The information obtained from CoCoPro is fed into a management tool such as MicroPlanner to track software development progress. Then FreeFlow is used to draw a DFG and construct a DD. The minispecs are processed by PowerPDL to obtain intermediate files which are read by SmartChart. Assuming no errors or inconsistencies, SmartChart is used to functionally decompose to the code level. Templates are used to produce the source code which is then compiled, tested, and validated.

Of course this is oversimplified, because errors and oversights occur and the process is actually iterative. Assuming no problems occur, however, we end up with the application source code and design documents, which can be used for validating the application, maintaining the finished product, and generating updates from baseline documents.

In summary, PowerTools produces the following outputs:

- DFG, the flow diagrams of your application
- PDL, the specification of each function in the application
- DD, the system data dictionary
- FSM, the finite state machine diagrams in tables and matrices
- FD, the functional design of your system in the form of a structure chart
- Reports, the PDL listings, program source code listings, and consistency check reports

The consistency check reports will reveal the following inconsistencies:

- unnamed or unconnected flows, processes, or stores in the DFG
- identical stores appearing on multiple levels of the DFG
- unbalanced I/O for each process bubble in the DFG
- undefined, circularly defined, or self-defined terms in the DD

Before we provide details of the Development Project design using PowerTools, it will be useful to show the results we are striving for. Consider first the modular interconnection graph of CoCoPro in Figure 7-3. This graph shows the "uses" relation among all modules in the finished application. There are eleven separately compiled modules, each with a name that reflects its object-oriented purpose. The MAIN module is very simple, and merely initializes the system upon launch, and then passes control to the EVENT module. EVENT handles all events, of which MENU selections are of the highest interest. Thus, MENU processes all menu selections by passing control on to the appropriate module. Utility modules CALCULATE, RAM, and DIALOG provide low-level services as their names imply. All but MAIN use GLOBAL, a module containing all global constants, types, variables, and procedures.

You will notice that PowerTools does not enforce modular decomposition. Instead PowerTools enforces functional decomposition in the spirit of DFD. How then do we obtain a modular decomposition like the one presented here? To get a modular architecture, we must combine the DFD and OOD techniques. Watch as we develop a hybrid technique called *OODFD* as part of this example. (See the end of chapter six for an overview of OODFD.)

The system architecture of CoCoPro is shown as a "uses" graph because each of the modules shown in the graph uses something from the modules they point at. CoCoPro is written in Pascal, and the "uses" relation is actually implemented with the **uses** statement. Each module is implemented as a Pascal **unit**, and each **unit** consists of an interface part (the visible part) and an implementation part. The arrows in the graph represent the **uses** statement in each **unit**.

This structure has been simplified, because we have not provided labels on the graph. If the labels were provided, they would list the constants, types, variables, and procedures made visible by each unit. Thus, the interface part is represented by an arrow. In Pascal, no distinction is made between "import" and "export" names. Consequently, the interface information can flow both ways.

System Architecture - CoCoPro Application

USES Relation Graph

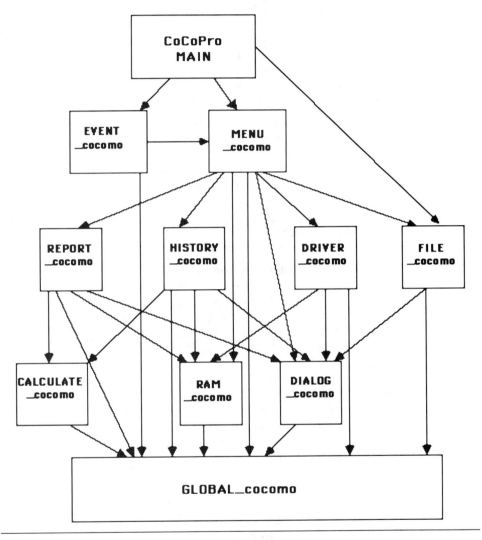

FIGURE 7-3. Modular interconnection graph of CoCoPro

We claim this architecture is object-oriented. In fact, an OOD graph is given for CoCoPro in the previous chapter. (Compare these two architectures. You will notice they are exactly the same graph, but drawn in a different form.) The basis for our claim is the following:

- Each module encapsulates both state and function, that is, storage and procedures for operating on the storage. EVENT encapsulates the event queue and its operations; MENU encapsulates the menu bar and its menus; REPORT encapsulates the output report objects; HISTORY encapsulates actual project histories as an object; DRIVER encapsulates the cost drivers as an object; FILE encapsulates application files as objects; CALCULATE encapsulates the storage that holds the calculated values; RAM encapsulates RAM storage; DIALOG encapsulates each dialog box as an object; and GLOBAL encapsulates all global names as a single object.

- Operations are clustered around the storage they manipulate, thus all operations on FILEs, for instance, can be located in the module called FILE; all operations on DIALOGs are in DIALOG, and so forth.

- Objects inherit the operations defined by these modules through an adaptation of Pascal. The state of an object is passed as a variable parameter to all processing functions in a module. Thus, substitution of one "instance variable" for another achieves the effect as inheritance, although it is not true inheritance in its strictest form. This programming technique is achieved by convention, not by enforcement by the Pascal compiler.

The system architecture shown in Figure 7-3 can therefore be interpreted in two ways: as a modular decomposition where each module employs communicational cohesion, and global, data, and external coupling; or as an object-oriented design where each module is an instance of an object, and messages are passed among the objects. The problem with both of these interpretations is that we have not presented a mechanical method for combining functions and data into modules of either kind. We return to this question later.

As we have stated before, a *modular* decomposition of a software system is not the same as a *functional* decomposition. Consider the system architecture of CoCoPro when expressed as a functional decomposition, see Figure 7-4. The "call" graph of a functional decomposition contains greater details of the structure of CoCoPro, but it does not tell how functions are combined into modules. The view of CoCoPro shown by the "call" graph is different from the view shown by the "uses" graph.

Because of its size, this graph is shown on several pages. Also, only a portion of the entire CoCoPro "call" graph is shown. The shaded functions indicate a top-down refinement of all functions needed to implement the calculation portion of CoCoPro. MAIN calls EVE_main_event_loop, which calls either DealWthMouseDowns or DealWthKeyDowns, which calls MEN_process_menu_in, and so forth until the lowest level is reached. The calculations are done in REP_do_calc_comp which computes estimates for one CoCoMo component and then displays the results.

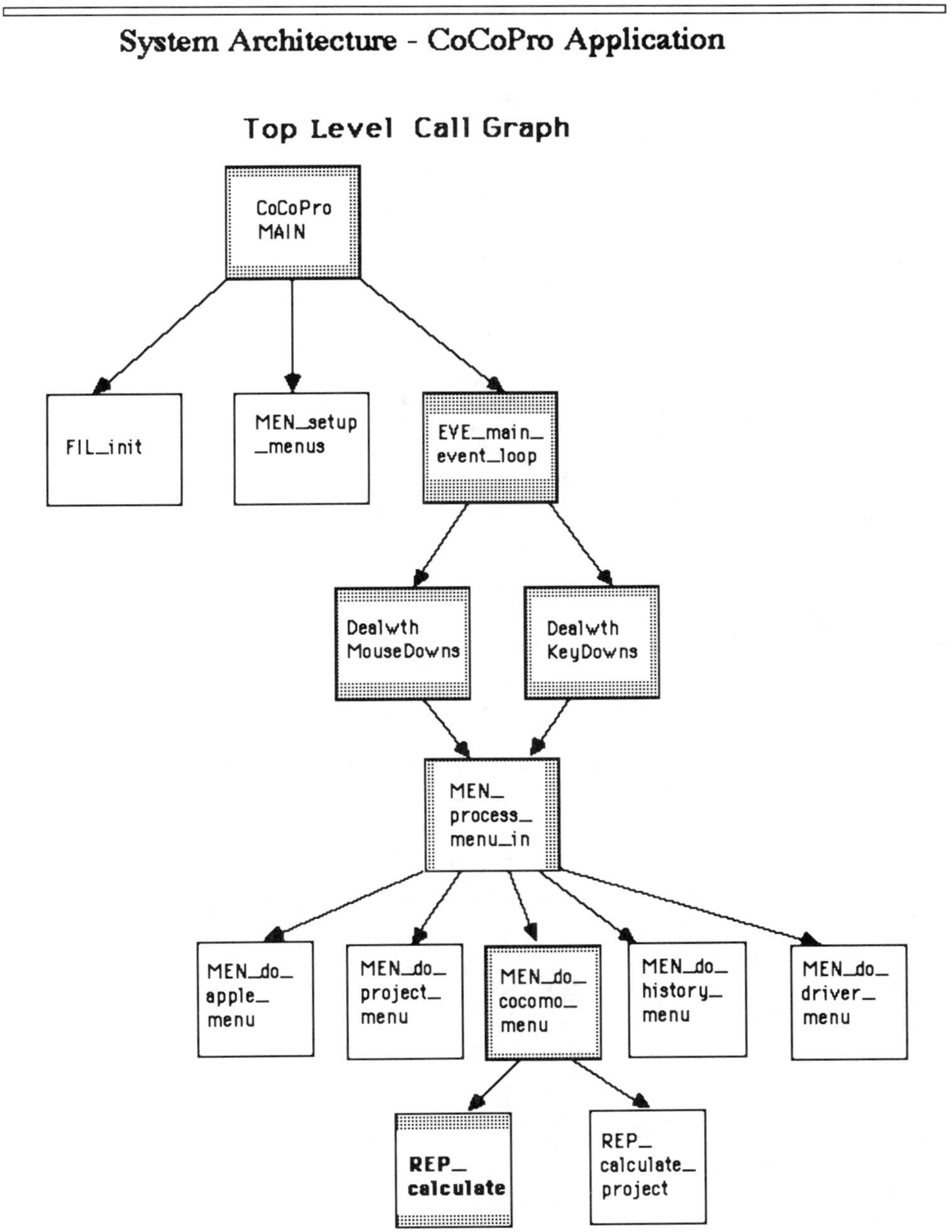

System Architecture - CoCoPro Application

Top Level Call Graph

FIGURE 7-4a. Top-level call graph

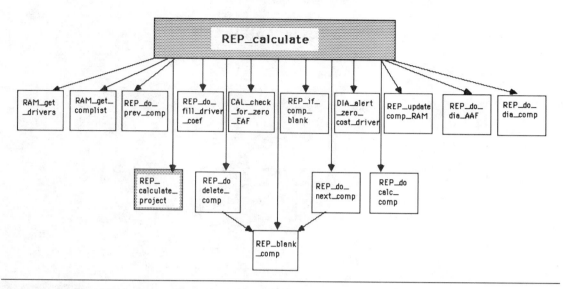

FIGURE 7-4b. REP_calculate call graph

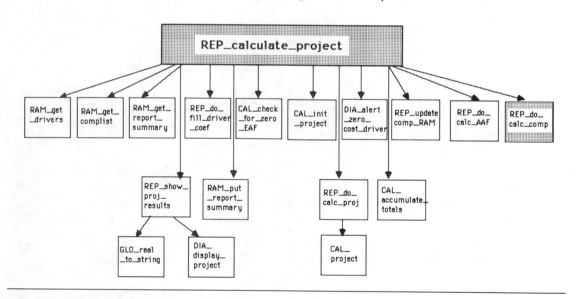

FIGURE 7-4c. REP_calculate_project call graph

REP_do_calc_comp Call Graph

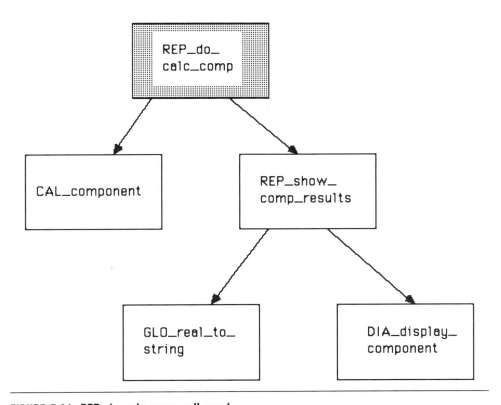

FIGURE 7-4d. REP_do_calc_comp call graph

The refinement is 11 levels deep — too deep according to the 7 ± 2 law. This classical problem with FD is called *telescoping*. Although this structure shows strong functional cohesion, the coupling effects are not well represented because:

- External coupling may exist, in which functions are coupled by having access to the same file. Since this design combined OOD with its communicational cohesion, this architecture does not suffer from external coupling problems, but the point is that this graph does not provide a view that would expose external coupling even if it existed.

- Global coupling may exist — in fact it does in this example — but the architecture does not show this. In addition, showing all interface information by labeling the arcs in the graph would hopelessly clutter the graph, rendering it useless. While revealing greater detail, FD may actually overwhelm the design with too much detail. This is another reason to use the encapsulating power of OOD to control interface complexity.

- The levels of nesting (descendant call chain) tends to be long. This partial architecture shows 11 levels, but CoCoPro is a relatively small application (roughly 7K lines of Pascal source code). What happens in a large application?

These objections notwithstanding, this view of a system is perhaps the most commonly used by designers and maintainers. It is simple, direct, and mirrors the way the application runs. The functional view is one of many valuable and useful views of a system's architecture. Take a minute to examine all of the graphs shown in Figure 7-4.

Now, we can plunge into the details of the design of CoCoPro using OODFD. We begin by using PowerTools and end by transforming the structure chart produced by PowerTools into a hybrid OOD architecture.

DESIGN OF COCOPRO

In this section, we show how to produce design and code documents of CoCoPro using three Iconix Software Engineering PowerTool tools in the following order (see Figure 7-5):

1. **FreeFlow**. DFG, DD, and minispec files are produced containing data flow graph, data dictionary, and PDL pseudo-code, respectively. The DFD is refined in levels, each level is balanced (inputs equal outputs across levels), and minispecs provided for all processes.

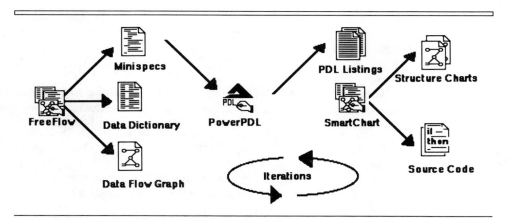

FIGURE 7-5. The power tool case tool set

2. **PowerPDL**. Using minispecs from FreeFlow, and coupling information provided by the designer, PowerPDL produces PDL listings (documentation), and preparatory information for SmartChart.

3. **SmartChart**. Using coupling information from PowerPDL, and minispecs from FreeFlow, SmartChart produces the system architecture as a structure chart and (optionally) the source code of each function in the system. The initial design may be modified at this point, reflecting the iterative nature of design. If so, minispecs for altered or new process bubbles are added to the specification, a new PDL file is generated and processed by PowerPDL, and then SmartChart used again to produce a fully specified architecture.

First, we draw a Data Flow Diagram as a collection of hierarchical decompositions, each level consisting of a DFG as described in the previous chapter. The top-level DFG is called the *context diagram* and defines the interface between the real-world and the CoCoPro software system, see Figure 7-6. The context diagram consists of only one process bubble and one or more external entities. The single process bubble is decomposed into additional DFGs with the lowest level process bubbles representing the primitive functions of the system, see Figure 7-7.

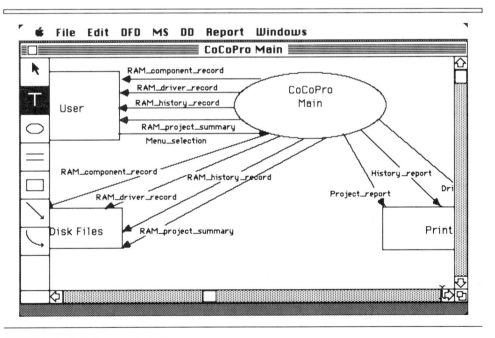

FIGURE 7-6. CoCoPro context diagram

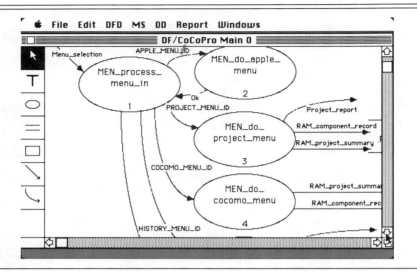

FIGURE 7-7a. Top level of CoCoPro

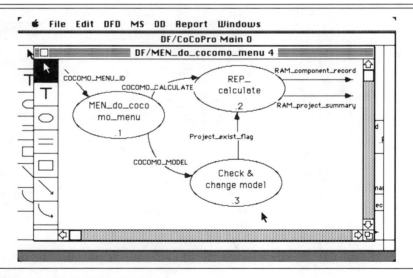

FIGURE 7-7b. Level 2 of bubble 4

As we decompose each DFG, we create names for all flows, storage entities, and process bubbles. These names and their attributes are captured and stored in the DD, a data dictionary which establishes a system vocabulary. The DD entries are decomposed into structured data elements much as the process bubbles are decomposed into lower-level DFGs.

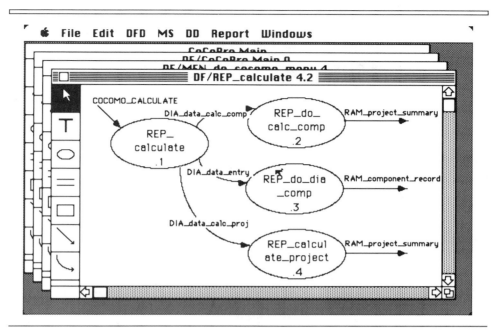

FIGURE 7-7c. Refinement of process bubbles

A primitive function is any component that needs no additional refinement. Primitive functions are specified by writing minispecs in PDL. These minispecs are the pseudo-code specifications used to guide the writing of source code for each module. Typically, the primitive functions corresponding to the lowest-level process bubbles constitute the building blocks of the entire system. For this reason, they may be used in more than one place in the system. DFD does not facilitate reuse, so you must be alert in looking at the cross-reference information produced by PowerPDL (discussed later).

Furthermore, you must write minispec specifications for each nonprimitive process bubble in the DFD to specify the sequencing order of the entire system of modules. This is a departure from the traditional DFD technique where a "central transform" bubble is first identified, and then "input" and "output" (efferent and afferent) processes identified. Instead, sequencing and "call" graph information is gleaned from the PDL minispecs. These minispecs can be entered from FreeFlow or SmartChart. If entered in SmartChart, the PowerPDL compiler must be run before the revised "call" graph can be viewed from within SmartChart. This gives rise to an iterative process as shown in the flowchart for PowerTools.

PowerPDL is a kind of specification compiler that combines all minispecs into a single file and computes a tree-structure representation of the system. PowerPDL analyzes the minispecs and constructs a "call" graph for the entire system. Since the CASE tool does not allow cycles, the "call" graph is actually a tree. The tree starts with the first minispec function having no higher-level function calling it and at least one function that it calls. The primitive functions are the terminal or leaf nodes of the call graph.

SmartChart is a kind of editor that draws the structure chart corresponding to the tree produced by PowerPDL, and permits entry of additional minispecs (to specify the internal nodes of the "call" tree). In addition, SmartChart permits entry of actual source code in one of several programming languages. Language-sensitive templates are provided by SmartChart to speed entry of the source code.

If changes occur either to update the design or to add in the specification of each internal node of the "call" tree, the modified structure chart must be recompiled through PowerPDL before it can be "browsed" by SmartChart. Typically, changes to the minispecs made in SmartChart are cycled back through PowerPDL, then the output from PowerPDL is used by SmartChart to construct an updated structure chart.

FreeFlow

To illustrate, suppose we trace the design of a portion of the CoCoPro architecture beginning at the context diagram, through the menu processing subsystem, and finally down to the levels that deal with performing the basic calculations of CoCoMo. So as not to cloud the main ideas, we will skip over some of the perfunctory steps needed to operate FreeFlow.

CoCoPro operates in an environment consisting of its user, various disk files, and a printer, see Figure 7-6. This environment defines the boundary between CoCoPro and the "real world." It also defines the boundary of the design. CoCoPro does not use telecommunications, networking, or other devices. Specification at this level constitutes a starting point for the system.

Here we see data flowing between user and CoCoPro, CoCoPro and disk files, and CoCoPro and the printer connected to the machine. The user enters data into RAM (see RAM_component_record, RAM_driver_record, etc.), and makes menu selections (see Menu_selection). CoCoPro produces information that is stored in driver, history, and report files. The various files are printed upon request.

The example we want to trace through the design starts with the CoCoPro Main process bubble and involves the Project_report data flow. Watch these entities as we construct DFG and DD entries. It may be helpful to study the call graph for CoCoPro given earlier as you study the screen dumps from FreeFlow.

FreeFlow™ 1.3

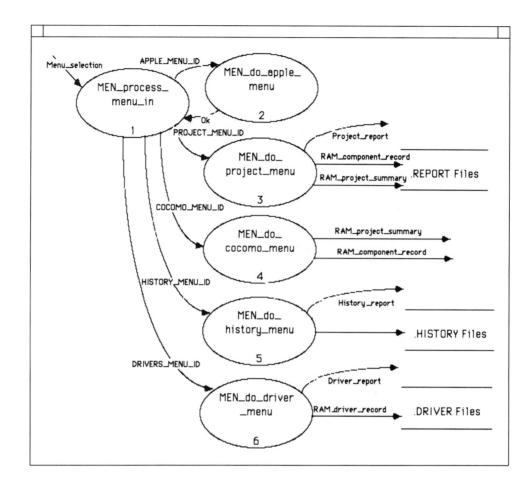

The user sends Menu_selection to CoCoPro Main in the form of a menu selection event. The selection is passed to a function called MEN_process_menu_in as shown in the zero level DGD, see Figure 7-7a. Notice how each process bubble is numbered 1, 2, 3, ... FreeFlow automatically numbers each process bubble as it is created. Levels are indicated by a decimal system to indicate subordination. Thus, process bubble 1.2.1 is at the third level in the hierarchy.

Notice also the in-flows and out-flows at level zero. Project_report is an outflow that we will refine later in the data dictionary. This level is said to be balanced if the flows from the context diagram are the same as the inflows and outflows of the zero level DFG.

Next, notice the functional decomposition. Process bubble MEN_do_cocomo_menu is of particular interest because we will trace it through several levels of decomposition until reaching the primitive functions that actually do the CoCoMo calculations.

Process bubble 4 is refined into the DFG shown for MEN_do_cocomo_menu (Figure 7-7b), which is in turn refined into 4.2 and 4.3, see Figure 7-7c. Only the refinement for process bubble 4.2 is shown here, but both process bubbles are refined further.

Keep in mind that these diagrams are drawn with a mouse by selecting a tool from the palette displayed on the left side of the screen. The icons are obvious: a cursor for selecting bubbles, storages, and flows; T for text entry; bubble, storage, terminal box, and arrows for drawing the DFG itself. FreeFlow combines graphics and text much like other computer-aided design tools.

Process bubble 4.2 is composed of bubbles 4.2.1, 4.2.2, 4.2.3, and 4.2.4. The last three are primitive functions because they are not refined further. These three primitive functions perform the calculations necessary for computing estimates one component at a time, displaying the estimates in a dialog, and then computing the project totals. We can specify the actions of these primitive functions in a minispec. Before we do so, let's go back and add an entry into the DD to show how we hierarchically decompose data storage and data flow entities.

To add an entry to the data dictionary, pull down the DD menu and select Add Definition as shown in Figure 7-8. Once a DD item is in the DD, double-clicking the storage or flow element in the DFG will re-open the DD and display the entry, see Figure 7-9a.

Every DD entry is composed of components — some unique and some repeating. The symbols for sequence, iteration, and selection in a data structure are given below. These are very similar to the symbols used in JSD to describe data structure diagrams and composite data:

= composed of, e.g. Project_report is composed of....
+ together with, e.g. RAM_project_summary together with....
{ } iteration, e.g. one or more of RAM_component_record....
[ ] selection, e.g. select one from the list. List elements are separated by |.
( ) optional, e.g. zero or one occurrence of the enclosed element.
' ' literal, e.g. '1.5'.
* * comments, e.g. *this is a comment*.

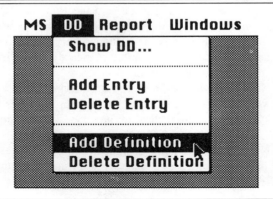

FIGURE 7-8. Adding a data dictionary item

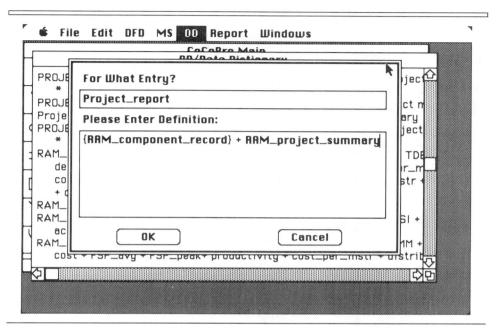

FIGURE 7-9a. Adding Project_report to DD

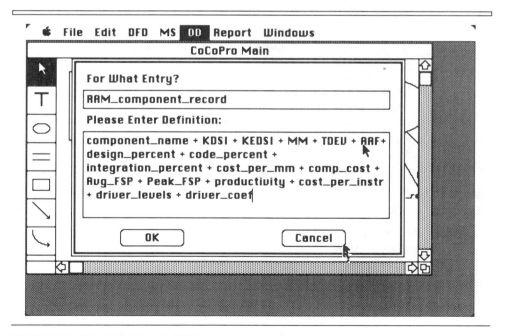

FIGURE 7-9b. The definition of RAM_component_record

For example, the definition of Project_report is given in several levels as (see Figure 7-9b):

```
Project_report = {RAM_component_record} + RAM_project_summary
RAM_component_record = component_name + KDSI + KEDSI + MM + TDEV + AAF
   + design_percent + code_percent + integration_percent + cost_per_mm + comp_cost
   + Avg_FSP + Peak_FSP + productivity + cost_per_instr + driver_levels + driver_coef
RAM_project_summary = project_name + model + KDSI + KEDSI + MM + TDEV + cost + FSP_avg
   +.FSP_peak + productivity + cost_per_instr + distribution
```

Each of these terms may in turn be decomposed into more detailed definitions. The data entry dialogs for two DD entries are shown in Figure 7-9, but additional dialog interactions are needed to completely specify all data storage and flow entities in the design.

The entire DD can be displayed in a scrollable window by selecting the Show DD... item from menu DD, see Figure 7-10a. This produces a complete listing of all definitions, see Figure 7-10b.

Each entry in the DD defines not only a vocabulary word to be used throughout the system, but also an interface element. The flow entries are destined to become part of the interface between communicating modules, and the storage entries define data structures that will most likely be propagated throughout major parts of the system. Accordingly, it is very important to use these names consistently throughout the design, coding, and testing phases.

As an illustration, the word Project_report is introduced here at a rather high level of abstraction. Even so, it will persist throughout the design and on into the coding stage. The design must be traceable. Anyone ought to be able to follow vocabulary words from design, through coding, testing, and revision. It would be a mistake to allow the word Project_report to be renamed Project_data in one part of the system, Project_info in another part, and some other alias in yet another part of the system. Even worse, it would be a mistake to permit the word Project_report to be called theProject in a function written by one programmer, and Project_stuff by another programmer in a second function. This kind of freedom becomes very costly because we lose control of traceability in the system.

Because traceability is so important, the DD must be readily available to all team members. More importantly, it must be used like any other dictionary — to provide official definitions of terms used by the development team.

Minispec Definitions

Let us now complete the functional decomposition of the DFG. Recall that we refined a portion of the DFG to trace the design of the calculation processes. To complete the specification of this trace, we must describe what each process bubble does. The PDL pseudo-code language is used to write minispecs.

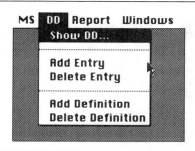

FIGURE 7-10a. Viewing the DD

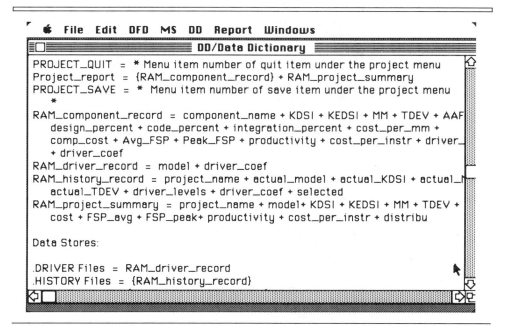

FIGURE 7-10b. The complete DD of CoCoPro

When in FreeFlow, shift + double-clicking function bubble 4.2.2 causes the interface specifications shown in the first screen for MS/REP_do_calc_comp 4.2.2 to appear, see Figure 7-11a. This is the top half of the minispec which is automatically generated from the data flows provided by the DFG. The PDL pseudo-code language uses "%" to signify a pseudo-code keyword, and uses a period as a separator (any comment can be placed on a line beginning with a period in column one).

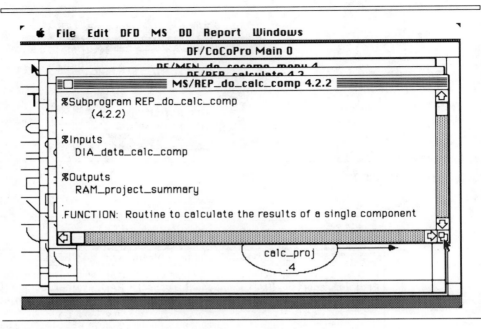

FIGURE 7-11a. Interface part of REP_do_calc_comp minispec

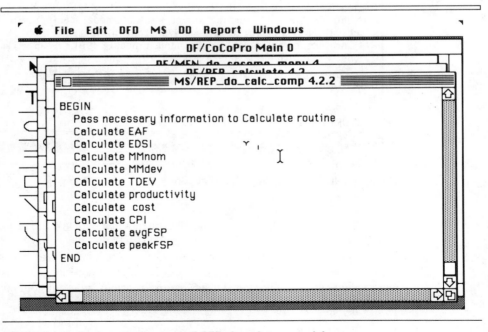

FIGURE 7-11b. Implementation part of REP_do_calc_comp minispec

The **%subroutine** keyword specifies the heading of a function. The **%inputs** and **%outputs** keywords signify the list of inputs and outputs assigned to the function by the DFG. The phrase beginning with the keyword **.function** is simply a header for writing a commentary that tells what the function does.

The pseudo-code description of actions performed by the function is placed between a **begin-end** pair, see Figure 7-11b. The actions in this case are the simple calculations done by CoCoPro to produce cost estimates and values of interest: MMdev, TDEV, avgFSP, and so on. Notice that each statement in the minispec is a mixture of PDL keyword (shown in uppercase) and any English phrase (shown in lowercase). Data entities are either upper- or lowercase, and should match exactly with the spelling and case of DD entries.

PDL is a structured pseudo-code language, so iteration and selection are also allowed. The **loop** construct signifies iteration, and the **if** construct is used for selection. A second example is shown in Figure 7-12 which illustrates looping in the minispec for process bubble 4.2.4.

Branching and case selection control structures are also provided so that any kind of processing action can be described in PDL.

In addition to specifying processing steps, interface coupling (via **%input** and **%output** specifications), and call graph structure (via explicit reference to function names in the PDL pseudo-code specification), the minispec must specify external functions that are used, but not defined. For example, the Macintosh toolbox routines are used, but are not defined by the CoCoPro system. Hence, OpenDeskAcc, and other toolbox routines must be declared as an **%external** function, see Figure 7-13.

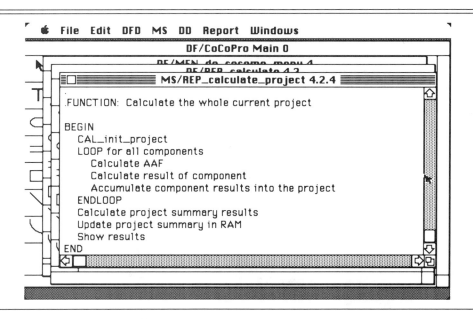

FIGURE 7-12. Minispec of REP_calculate_project

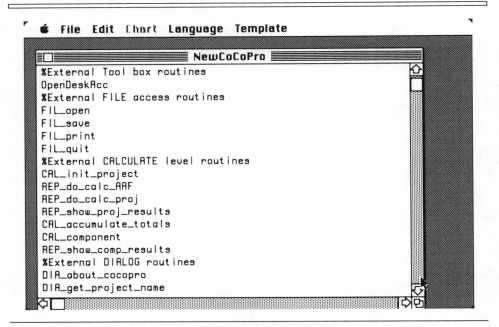

FIGURE 7-13. Interface to unspecified externals

You may want to postpone the definition of other functions as well. For example, the file processing functions, FIL_open, FIL_save, FIL_print, and FIL_quit functions may be defined later in SmartChart. Similarly, CALCULATE and user DIALOG routines are shown as externals in the example. These must be specified before a complete system architecture can be drawn.

Finally, the design is ready to be "compiled" and passed on to the PowerPDL report generator. This is done by selecting the Create PDL from MS item under the MS menu (MS = minispec), see Figure 7-14.

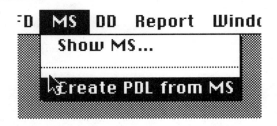

FIGURE 7-14. "Compiling" a design

PowerPDL™ 1.3

PowerPDL

PowerPDL is a tool for two basic functions: compiling the specifications created by either FreeFlow or SmartChart into a form that can be viewed as a structure chart, and generating reports that are extremely valuable for documenting, tracing, and checking the design for problems.

Compiling minispecs can be done from FreeFlow, as illustrated in Figure 7-4, or PowerPDL. If you iterate between PowerPDL and SmartChart, then select the "Compile PDL" action from within PowerPDL each time you modify a minispec.

The reports generated by PowerPDL are placed in a single "PDL Listing" file:

Table of Contents. This gives a table of contents for all other reports in the PDL listing.

Primitive Process Specifications. This contains a complete listing of all minispecs, written in PDL.

Data Cross-Reference. This list gives all interface coupling among functions, indexed by DD item name.

Subprogram Nesting Tree. This gives an indented listing of all functions, and the functions each calls. This is the "call" graph architecture of the system expressed in textual form. Recursive calls are listed with an * in front of the function name.

The CoCoPro PDL listings shown in Figure 7-15 are incomplete, but illustrate the ideas.

SmartChart

The purpose of SmartChart is twofold: to display the structure chart (the system architecture) and permit modifications to be made; and to facilitate implementation in Pascal, Ada, and so on. The structure chart is obtained from compiling in PowerPDL, and is used as a navigational aid. Changes in the system architecture may be made, but the entire system description must be compiled in PowerPDL to effect the changes.

SmartChart™ 1.3

Iconix Software Engineering **Power PDL™**
NewCoCoPro **Aug. 23, 1987**
Table of Contents **Page 1**

FIGURE 7-15a. Table of contents for CoCoPro design

Iconix Software Engineering   Power PDL™
NewCoCoPro   Aug. 23, 1987
Primitive Process Specifications   Page 3

Tool box routines
  OpenDeskAcc

FILE access routines
  FIL_open
  FIL_save
  FIL_print
  FIL_quit

MEN_process_menu_in
.   (1)
.
.
INPUTS:
  Menu_selection
  Ok
.
.
OUTPUTS:
  DRIVERS_MENU_ID
  HISTORY_MENU_ID
  COCOMO_MENU_ID
  PROJECT_MENU_ID
  APPLE_MENU_ID
.
.Function: Process Menu selections
Begin
    SELECT by Menu_selection
     APPLE_MENU_ID:
        MEN_do_apple_menu
     PROJECT_MENU_ID:
        MEN_do_project_menu
     COCOMO_MENU_ID:
        MEN_do_cocomo_menu
     HISTORY_MENU_ID:
        MEN_do_history_menu
     DRIVERS_MENU_ID:
        MEN_do_driver_menu
    End Select
End

MEN_do_apple_menu

.   (2)
.
INPUTS:
  APPLE_MENU_ID
.
OUTPUTS:
  Ok

FIGURE 7-15b. Primitive process for CoCoPro

```
.
.Function:  Process menu selection in apple menu
Begin
  Select of Menu item
    APPLE_COCOPRO_ABOUT:
      DIA_about_cocopro
    Apple_item:
      OpenDeskAcc
  End Select
End

.
REP_calculate
.     (4.2)
.
INPUTS:
  Project_exist_flag
  COCOMO_CALCULATE
.
OUTPUTS:
  RAM_project_summary
  RAM_component_record
.
.Function:  Process actions for calculate
Begin
  Select by dialog action
    DIA_data_calc_comp:
      REP_do_calc_comp
    DIA_data_entry:
      REP_do_dia_comp
    DIA_data_calc_proj:
      REP_calculate_project
  End Select
End

.
REP_do_calc_comp

.     (4.2.2)
.
INPUTS:
  DIA_data_calc_comp
.
OUTPUTS:
  RAM_project_summary
.
.Function:  Routine to calculate the results of a single component
Begin
  Pass necessary information to Calculate routine
  CAL_component
  REP_show_comp_results
End
```

FIGURE 7-15b (Continued).

Iconix Software Engineering   **Power PDL™**
NewCoCoPro   **Aug. 23, 1987**
DATA ITEM CROSS REFERENCE LIST   **Page 36**

APPLE_COCOPRO_ABOUT
  is an input to DIA_about_cocopro   on page 11

APPLE_MENU_ID
  is output from MEN_process_menu_in   on page 9
  is an input to MEN_do_apple_menu   on page 10

COCOMO_CALCULATE
  is an input to REP_calculate   on page 19

COCOMO_MENU_ID
  is output from MEN_process_menu_in   on page 9
  is an input to MEN_do_cocomo_menu   on page 18

COCOMO_MODEL
  is an input to Check & change model   on page 23

DIA_data_calc_comp
  is an input to REP_do_calc_comp   on page 20

DIA_data_calc_proj
  is an input to REP_calculate_project   on page 22

DIA_data_entry
  is an input to REP_do_dia_comp   on page 21

DIA_recalculate_button
  is output from HIS_calibrate   on page 26

DRIVERS_MENU_ID
  is output from MEN_process_menu_in   on page 9
  is an input to MEN_do_driver_menu   on page 29

DRIVER_group_item
  is an input to DRI_change_values   on page 31

Driver_report
  is output from MEN_do_driver_menu   on page 29

DRIVER_SHOW_PARAM
  is an input to DRI_show_model_param   on page 30

DRI_comp
  is output from DRI_change_values   on page 31
  is an input to DRI_change_computer_values   on page 32

DRI_pers
  is output from DRI_change_values   on page 31
  is an input to DRI_change_Personnel_values   on page 33

FIGURE 7-15c. Cross-reference for CoCoPro design documents

```
MEN_process_menu_in
MEN_do_apple_menu
 DIA_about_cocopro
  *DIA_about_cocopro
 OpenDeskAcc
MEN_do_project_menu
 DIA_get_project_name
  *DIA_get_project_name
 FIL_open
 FIL_save
 FIL_quit
 FIL_print
MEN_do_cocomo_menu
 REP_calculate
  REP_do_calc_comp
   CAL_component
   REP_show_comp_results
  REP_do_dia_comp
   DIA_getdataentry
  REP_calculate_project
   CAL_init_project
   REP_do_calc_AAF
   REP_do_calc_comp
    CAL_component
    REP_show_comp_results
   CAL_accumulate_totals
   REP_do_calc_proj
   REP_show_proj_results
 Check & change model
  REP_calculate_project
   CAL_init_project
   REP_do_calc_AAF
   REP_do_calc_comp
    CAL_component
    REP_show_comp_results
   CAL_accumulate_totals
   REP_do_calc_proj
   REP_show_proj_results
```

FIGURE 7-15d. Call structure of CoCoPro

MEN_do_history_menu
    FIL_open
    FIL_save
    FIL_print
    HIS_provide_actuals
    HIS_calibrate
    HIS_set_all_select_to
MEN_do_driver_menu
    FIL_print
    FIL_open
    FIL_save
    DRI_show_model_params

FIGURE 7-15d (Continued).

The structure chart can be displayed through a window with navigational controls to pan and zoom, see Figure 7-16. Pan is controlled by placing the dotted rectangle over the desired region of the structure chart "call" graph. The selected region will be zoomed up to full size. Other levels of magnification are possible as illustrated in Figure 7-17.

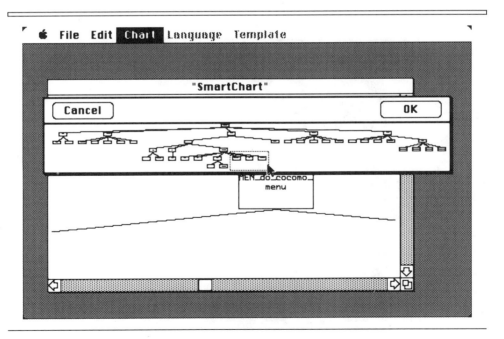

FIGURE 7-16. Structure chart display of CoCoPro

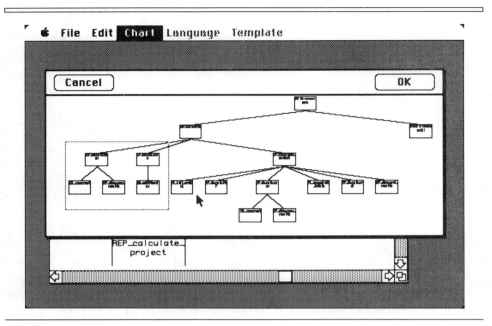

FIGURE 7-17a. Zoomed view of CoCoPro structure chart

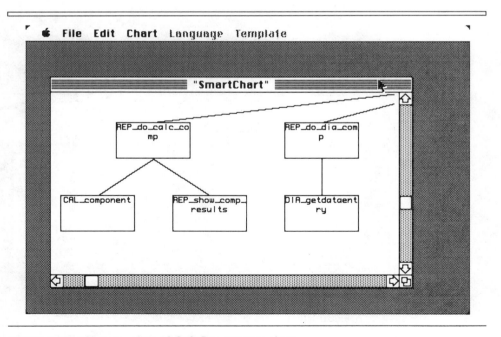

FIGURE 7-17b. Close-up view of CoCoPro stucture chart

The structure chart display is an excellent tool for gaining an understanding of the overall system architecture. Accordingly, the structure chart is extremely valuable for maintenance programmers. However, there is a tendency for the chart to become outdated, especially if changes to the source code are not documented in the structure chart. Such inconsistencies must be avoided by synchronizing design document versions with source code document versions. For this reason, SmartChart promotes a linkage between

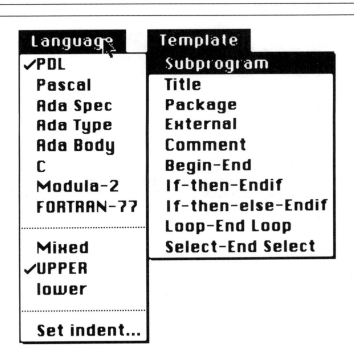

LANGUAGE SELECTION

The Language Menu controls the contents of the Template menu. Here we see the possibilities: PDL, Pascal, Ada, C, Modula-2, and FORTRAN.

Selecting PDL causes items for selecting templates for PDL to appear in the Template menu. Similarly, selecting Pascal, for example, causes templates for Pascal to appear in the Template menu.

Templates speed coding and remove many syntax errors before the source code is compiled.

Below is a template for PDL Subprograms, the building blocks of the structure chart we developed in the CoCoPro example.

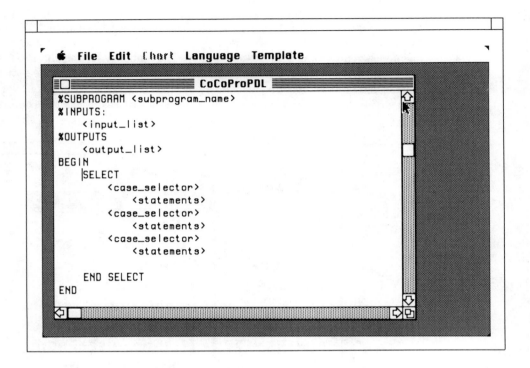

PDL pseudo-code specifications and actual source code for all modules. When embedded in the source code of a module, PDL pseudo-code looks like comments. When stripped out of the source code and recompiled by PowerPDL, the PDL minispec pseudo-code permits automatic updating of the structure chart and PDL Listings. The ability to update the design in this way is very powerful, because it encourages programmers to do their duty: keeping the design documentation up to date with the implementation.

After the design phase has been approved (through the Design Inspection process), the implementation phase can begin. Implementation is accomplished by coding in SmartChart to guarantee that coding is governed by the design, and that design documentation is kept in sync with coding changes. A variety of language templates may be used to speed up coding.

This completes the example, a complete design of CoCoPro. The result is a documented design that incorporates many of the desirable features we were looking for: low coupling through interface specifications and hierarchical decomposition, high functional cohesion through functional decomposition, and the orderly control of system complexity through the application of DFD methodology, DD specifications, PDL pseudo-code specifications, and report generation.

The design can be improved, however. As it stands, the design consists of many functions spread throughout the system. There is little information hiding and the system architecture lacks communicational cohesion. Recall that communicational cohesion improves the strength of modules (collections of functions) by forcing data constants, types, and variables to be clustered together in a more maintainable structure.

The current functional architecture lacks a good modular architecture. Recall that functions are not modules — modules are *collections* of functions that can be separately compiled. To get a modular architecture, we must combine functions according to some rule that enforces strength of module, low coupling, information hiding, ease of maintenance, and so forth.

Modular structure also provides a team structure. Each programmer can be assigned one or more modules to implement, test, and compile separately. Each separate *compiland* can then be given a version number, and added to the library of components. Furthermore, since each module has a well-defined interface part, other programmers can reuse appropriate functions selected from the library of modules.

OBJECT-ORIENTED DATA FLOW DESIGN

The DFD architecture of CoCoPro can be easily converted into an OODFD (Object-Oriented Data Flow Design) by grouping functions together to form objects. We must be careful to form objects that enhance the communicational strength of the modules that contain functions, however. Not just any formation will do.

What features of a collection of modules enhance communicational cohesion and encourage information hiding?

The principle of *data abstraction* provides a clue. **Data Abstraction** *is the result of extracting and retaining only the essential characteristic properties of data by defining specific data types and their associated functional characteristics, thus separating and hiding the representation details.*

> **Principle of Data Abstraction:** Information hiding is achieved and access to hidden information is properly controlled by encapsulating data along with all of the allowable operations on the data. The encapsulation must provide for a visible part — the interface to the data — and a complete encapsulation of the private part, the implementation details. Implementation details consist of both data representation and processing steps.

We make this important concept clear by taking an example from Pascal. Consider the following trivial data type:

```
type
  Blob = 1..10;
var
  X, Y : Blob;
```

In abstract data terminology, we call Blob a simple *class*, and X and Y *objects*, or instances of the class. The Pascal compiler provides the allowable operations on X and Y, hence they are not explicitly shown. We will come back to the notion of explicit operations later. But for now, consider what operations are allowed on objects X and Y.

Pascal allows addition, subtraction, and multiplication of X and Y:

```
X + Y
X − Y
X * Y
```

But Pascal does not allow assignment to an integer from a real:

```
X := R;
```

Furthermore, division is not defined, but allowed to make conversion to a real number convenient:

```
R := X/Y;
```

The integer division operations are allowed:

```
X := X mod Y;
Y := X div Y;
```

These are some of the operations allowed on integer objects X and Y. They are the access procedures defined on X and Y. But, suppose we want to define new access procedures on X and Y that are not part of Pascal? Can we do so?

Suppose, for example that we want to include an operation called **gcd** — this operation computes the greatest common divisor of two integer objects. If Pascal included such an operation, it might be used as follows:

```
X := X gcd Y;
```

This is *not* possible in Pascal, however. Instead, we must define a function to extend the operation of **gcd** to integer objects X and Y. We might do so like this:

```
function gcd (X, Y : integer);
begin
  while X < > Y do
  if X > Y
    then X := X − Y
    else Y := Y − X;
  gcd := X
  end; { gcd }
```

This piece of code rightfully belongs with the class of objects that it modifies. That is, **gcd** is designed to work with integer objects X and Y, hence it should be clustered with X and Y. We might imagine an extension to Pascal that permits this form of clustering. Programming languages that allow types and their operations to be clustered together are called *object-oriented programming languages* because they use the Principle of Data Abstraction. An object-oriented version of Pascal called Object Pascal does exist. In Object Pascal, the class called Blob includes both type and access procedure information.

```
type Blob = object (integer);     {integer is the superclass of Blob}
   iObj : integer;                        {iObj is an instance variable — also the representation of Blob}
   function Blob.gcd (i, j : integer);        {Blob.gcd is the gcd operation on objects of type Blob}
        begin
          while X < > Y do
          if X > Y
          then X := X − Y
          else Y := Y − X;
          gcd := X
          end; {Blob.gcd}
   {Other operations on Blob go here...}
end; {Blob}

var X, Y : Blob;          {create templates for objects X and Y}
........
begin
   new(X);                {instantiate X and Y as objects...}
   new(Y);
.......
X := Blob.gcd (6, 32);   {apply an access operation}
......
end.
```

This simple example illustrates the Principle of Data Abstraction as it is applied to
the design of a programming language. We are interested in applying the Principle to
design, and then implementing the design by forcing the programming language to abide
by object-oriented rules. In Pascal, this means using the **unit** structure of Macintosh
Pascal to implement abstract data types, and then instantiating these units to create
objects.

Simply stated, an OODFD system architecture is obtained by equating units with
objects, and message-passing with procedure calls. Each unit contains an encapsulated
abstract data type, i.e. data and the operations defined on the data. The OOD structure
shown for CoCoPro in the previous chapter illustrates the design obtained if we group
functions together into units per the OODFD methodology.

The following objects are easily identified in CoCoPro. The name of each unit was
chosen to suggest the name of the object. Similarly, every variable that is created in
object A, for example, is prefixed with the first three letters of unit A's name. This naming convention is more than aesthetic, it is *essential* for maintaining traceability of the
interface and implementation parts of the architecture. Notice also, these names are identical to the names defined in the data dictionary.

The objects and their names are:

MAIN/GLOBAL.   The main program is an object containing Globals as data
(state), and global procedures as operations. We have retained the separation
of GLOBAL from other parts of the system to ensure a single copy of the
global data. This is in keeping with the modularity concepts described earlier.

EVENT.   The event queue used by the Macintosh to hold events until they are processed by the application is an abstract data type with operations defined by **unit** EVENT. This unit also uses lower-level event queue operations defined in the Macintosh toolbox.

MENU.   All menu bar operations are encapsulated in this unit. The menu bar is the data, and the operations on menus are the access procedures which define allowable operations on **Menu**.

DIALOG.   All dialogs are processed by this module. Dialogs are specified in the associated resource file, but this module handles all dialog interactions.

HISTORY.   All access to the history files (objects) is via this module.

DRIVER.   All access to the cost drivers is via this module.

REPORT.   All access to the report files is via this **unit**.

RAM.   This module accesses RAM, memory management, allocation, and so on.

FILE.   A low-level unit that handles all access to disk files. Each of the many disk files created by CoCoPro is an object, hence this unit implements a class of objects, and passing variables to the access procedures in this unit effectively implements the instantiation of multiple objects from this single "class." While this is stretching Pascal to the limits to implement an object-oriented design, the effects are much the same as the effects of using an object-oriented programming language.

CALCULATE.   All calculated variables are encapsulated here, and all calculations on these variables are clustered around these variables.

These units define the entire architecture of CoCoPro. These are also the units that must be implemented, tested, and maintained by the programming team. A responsibility matrix can be drawn up from this list to assign programming responsibilities. Such a list might look like the Product WBS, Activity WBS, or Responsibility Matrix given in chapter three.

CASE PRODUCTIVITY

Is CASE technology useful? Does it improve programmer productivity and lower software lifecycle costs?

The answer to this question is still emerging, but the following facts can be given in support of CASE tools. First, we can use CoCoPro to learn that the cost drivers for automated tools show a marked decrease in development costs when automation is used. The benefits become larger as the application becomes larger. Hence CASE tools are most beneficial for very large software projects.

Forte[2] lists some specific reasons why CASE is here to stay:

- Software is becoming more complex, larger, and the expectations for high quality are greater. Manual methods of software development cannot keep up with the demands of complexity, size, and quality.

- CASE tools catch errors early in the lifecycle. Early error detection and correction is one of the most powerful means of reducing cost and improving quality.
- Most software is developed by teams, not individuals. CASE tools provide a focus of attention for groups that must coordinate, communicate, and interact over time.
- Inexpensive graphic workstation hardware has made the personal workstation a profound productivity tool. CASE tools take advantage of such cost-effective "platforms."
- Competition in the CASE market has driven the cost of CASE software down to compelling levels — some large organizations *require* programmers to use the CASE approach.

CASE tools are gradually encompassing the whole software lifecycle, but the example shown here is heavily oriented toward the early phases. Requirements, Preliminary Design, and Detailed Design are easily documented with tools such as PowerTool. Coding, testing, and maintenance tools must be integrated into the whole lifecycle, however, before major advances are realized.

The following list of CASE tools suggests the extent of full lifecycle support:

Requirements Check	Simulation	Documentation
Design Check	Code Reuse	Configuration Check
Prototyping	Performance Check	Reporting
Editing	Source Code Control	WBS chart
Code Generation	Project Management	Conversion
Compiling	Interface Control	
Debugging	Cost Estimating	

The approach taken in this chapter is rather traditional because it is based on the Waterfall Model of the software lifecycle. Earlier, we mentioned Rapid Prototyping as an alternate lifecycle model. Prototyping is discussed in a later chapter, but the concept of prototyping should be considered in this evaluation.

If prototyping were used in place of DFD, OODFD, or one of the other methods of program construction, the outlook would be radically altered. In prototyping, a designer is able to quickly produce a running version of the final software product. The prototype can then be validated without the need for DFD, DD, and so forth. This approach has much to offer, and in fact, prototyping may replace traditional techniques over time.

Prototyping is a kind of CASE tool based on an alternate model of the lifecycle. Generating applications from prototypes is a promising technology that can lead to several orders of magnitude of improvement in software development. When it fully matures, prototyping will offer an alternative method of automatically constructing software systems for certain classes of applications. (Most likely, both methods of program construction will coexist, each one having advantages over the other for specific applications.)

Regardless of the approach — Waterfall or Prototyping based — the key to CASE technology lies in the potential for automating *forward* and *backward* development. Forward development means an application is constructed from the requirements phase, through the design and coding phase, and then finally to the maintenance and operational phase. We have been illustrating forward development for most of this book.

Backward development means an application is (re)constructed from the operational and maintenance phase, backward through the coding and design phase, and then finally back to the requirements phase. Why are we concerned with backward development? *Change* is the answer.

Every good software system must accommodate change. Software products *evolve*, they don't pop into existence overnight. Users gain new insights into an application only after using it for some time. New techniques and methods of processing information force software products to go through various enhancements. For example, the capability of most word processors grows with each release of the application.

When software is modified, the new version impacts user's manuals (documentation), source code, test cases, design, and in many cases, the original requirements. These artifacts must be updated in accordance with the modification. How can the documentation, design, and requirements document be updated along with the source code? A backward development process is initiated each time the application is modified.

CASE tools often implement both forward and backward development tools. This facilitates software evolution. For example, a change in the source code might trigger corresponding changes in the DFG, DD, and pseudo-code. In extreme cases, the list of functional and storage requirements might be updated after the source code is enhanced to provide a new report or processing function. Backward development can save many years of programmer time and effort.

CASE tools that support forward and backward development allow iterative design, coding, and maintenance to occur throughout the entire lifecycle. Such systems often incorporate expert systems technology in the CASE tools. A simple expert system tool, for example, can deduce that all modules that *use* a certain variable must be altered whenever the type of the variable changes. Similarly, the tool might be "smart" enough to automatically change the operations on the variable to avoid type conflicts. For instance, when a variable changes from **real** to **integer**, it will change the allowable operations also.

Terms and Concepts

architecture	OODFD
backward development	postcondition
call graph	precondition
class	predicate graph
compiland	principle of data abstraction
context diagram	program architecture
cross-reference	semantic interconnection
data abstraction	syntactic interconnection
external function	unit
forward development	uses graph
interconnection model	view
object-oriented language	

PROJECTS

Each of the following projects are to be done by one team. The projects must be fully documented from requirements analysis through detailed design. Each project must be completed using automated tools and in accordance with the guidelines discussed in the previous chapters:

- CoCoMo estimates of time and effort must be given on a component basis
- Project controls must be established with baselines for:
   SCM documentation
   SQA planning
   SRA documentation
   Complete CPM diagram with resource and scheduled time (calendar)
- Use DFD, FD, or OODFD system architecture and detail design documentation
- Use WBS and responsibility matrix for all members of the team
- Complete user interface "mock-up" showing what the user will see on the screen
- Create a short user's manual showing how the system will operate
- Activity logs must be kept by all members of the team giving activities done, times, and dates

The documents listed above must be provided on diskette as well as in bound hardcopy reports. The team leader will be expected to present each design in a one-hour Design Review — a walk-through of the design — presented to the other members of the team.

1. **CASE Tool for Source Code Quality Assessment**
   Read 3-6 in the list of references to obtain a collection of program quality measures. Select the "best" measures from these papers that you believe can be successfully applied to Macintosh Pascal source programs and units and design a system for computing these measures. Your application must be easy to use, effective, and interactive. Before you do your design, discuss the techniques you plan to use.

2. **CASE Tool for Editing Data Flow (Bubble) Diagrams**
   Design a system for editing, drawing, saving, and printing data flow diagrams similar to the DFGs described in this chapter. Your system must support multiple windows, scrolling, resizing, and zooming. Bubbles must be selectable by single- and double-clicking to see their contents. Also, the arcs connecting bubbles must be selectable. When a bubble is single-clicked, it can be changed, moved, or deleted. When a bubble is double-clicked, it opens a dialog containing information about the bubble: name, size, and documentation text. When an arc (data flow) is single-clicked, it can be repositioned on the screen. When double-clicked, an arc opens a dialog containing name, size, and documentation text. Complete diagrams must be saved to disk, restored from disk, and printed on the printer.

3. **Project Management System**

Design a system for tracking and controlling a software project involving a team of programmers. The system uses the following information:

- Names of programmers, responsibilities, schedule of completion dates, time estimates, and other information that can be obtained from CoCoPro.

- Modular decomposition of the software to be implemented: names of modules, interfaces, and other information obtained from an object-oriented view of the software system architecture.

- Project constraints in the form of CPM information — what must be done (documentation, testing, coding, integration), and what order it must be done in (coding before testing and so forth) information that can be obtained from MicroPlanner, for example.

The system must be interactive and must allow the project manager to change time and effort estimates as the project evolves. For example, each time a subproject is completed, the completion time and effort is recorded, the information updated, and so forth.

The system should provide printed reports containing information on what each programmer has done and is currently doing, and whether each project is on schedule, delayed, or ahead of time. The reporting subsystem should alert the project manager to any problems or delays.

Most likely, you will want to implement a small database system for storing this information. The database subsystem should allow indexed access to personnel, project, and task information.

4. **System Architecture Tool**

Design a CASE tool for Macintosh Pascal that reads an entire source program system, computes the uses relation, call relation, and object-object relation for the entire system. Display each relation, graphically, in separate windows, with the call graph in one window, uses graph in a second window, and object-oriented message-passing graph in the third window. When the user double-clicks a node or arc in any of the graphs, a fourth window appears and displays the text corresponding to the graphical item selected. For example, if a node in the uses graph is selected, the text from the corresponding unit appears; double-clicking an arc in the call graph window causes the source code containing the "call" to appear in the (fourth) text window.

This is essentially a navigational aid to maintainers of large systems. Your design should consider possible "large-scale" problems such as the size of text files, and the placement and management of large graphs in small windows.

REFERENCES AND FURTHER READING

1. Perry, D. E. 1987. "Software Interconnection Models." *Proceedings of the Ninth International Conference on Software Engineering*, March 30 – April 2, 1987: 61–67.
2. Forte, G. (ed). 1987 *CASE Outlook* 1, no. 1, (July) (Portland, OR).

3. Redish, K. A., and W. F. Smyth. 1986. "Program Style Analysis: A Natural By-Product of Program Compilation." *Communications of the ACM* 29, no. 2 (Feb. 1986), 126–133.

4. Berns, M. G. 1984. "Assessing Software Maintainability." *Communications of the ACM* 27, no. 1 (January): 14–23.

5. Berry, R. E., and B. A. E. Meekings. 1985. "A Style Analysis of C Programs,"*Communications of the ACM* 28, no. 1 (January): 80–88.

6. Rees, M. J. 1982. "Automatic Assessment Aids for Pascal Programs." *ACM SIGPLAN Notices* 17, no. 10 (October): 33–42.

8

Programming Cliches

PREVIEW

Every programmer has a "bag of tricks" that are used day-in and day-out to accelerate the production of code. These "tricks" are cliches — essential fragments of code that are used in nearly every application.

The Macintosh and similar computer systems encourage the use of cliches through standardization of user interface, toolbox routines, and packages for such recurring operations as file I/O. But before any programmer can take advantage of the leverage offered by such standards, a thorough understanding of the system is needed.

We describe the fundamental software architecture of the Macintosh, and then describe in great detail the cliches for handling menus, windows, dialogs, alerts, and file I/O. Complete examples of these most important routines are given along with illustrations of the user interface objects as they would appear on the screen. A short example of how to drag an object on the screen is also given.

THE MACINTOSH SYSTEM

Recall the Personnel Attributes of CoCoMo: expertise in the programming language, machine, and application domain are very important to decreasing overall time and effort. The purpose of this chapter is to gain expertise in both the machine and the software needed to do a high-quality commercial system. The Macintosh computer serves as a good example of the kind of hardware and software that the modern software engineer must master before embarking on the implementation phase. Thus, we begin with a brief introduction to Macintosh internals.

Macintosh programming is radically different from programming traditional machines. This is due to the radically different user interface of the machine, which is characterized by *direct manipulation*. In direct manipulation, the user communicates with the application by directly interacting with graphic representations of the objects to be manipulated. These objects — menus, windows, dialogs, icons, and other graphic objects defined by the application — are metaphorical rather than literal. Graphic metaphors require graphic interaction, whereas the tradition of computing has been aimed at literal interaction.

In a literal computer system, textual commands are typed into the system's *command line interpreter*. For example, to copy a file from one disk volume to another, we might enter the command:

```
copy fileA, c:fileB
```

Users not familiar with this "pidgin English" must study a manual before such commands make sense. Furthermore, while these commands may please an English-speaking user, they must be completely replaced with other phrases to be useful to French, Italian, or Japanese users. This creates not only major training problems for users, but expensive maintenance problems for developers.

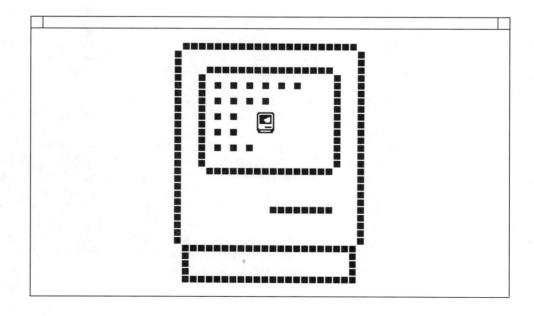

A metaphorical computer, on the other hand, communicates in the universal language of pictures. But because the pictures are metaphorical — icons, if you will — users must intuitively understand their meaning. Sometimes the meaning of an icon is not obvious in any language, causing the user to miss the intended meaning. This is where the importance of direct manipulation comes in. When the meaning of an icon is in doubt, the user need only experiment briefly with the object to "get it."

The notion of direct manipulation changes how applications are constructed. In fact, this notion changes how computer systems are constructed, beginning with the hardware (graphics), extending to the operating system ("finders" in place of command line interpreters), and finally, radically altering the way application software is constructed.

System Resources

A *resource file* is a file containing objects and their specifications. Resource files are assigned icons which can be seen on the metaphorical desktop if the resource file is made visible. Resource files can contain data, specifications, or both.

Resource files consist of two parts: the *data fork* and the *resource fork*. The data fork can contain any kind of data: text, constants, pictures, and so forth. For example, a document created by a word processor is stored in the data fork of a resource file. Similarly, pictures created by a paint program are stored in the data fork of one or more paint documents.

The resource fork contains the application's code, specifications of graphic objects, text (such as prompts and error messages), and information used by the operating system. For example, a word processor or paint program is stored as code, windows, dialogs, strings, and icons in the resource fork of the program's resource file. Double-clicking the resource file icon causes the resource fork to be "launched" — loaded into memory and started running.

Resource files can be studied with the ResEdit tool. (See Appendix A.) Resource files contain other information that is discussed later in this chapter. To become familiar with the Macintosh system, examine the DeskTop and System files with ResEdit. Other resource editors are available, such as REdit, that perform similar functions. Keep in mind that a resource file is stored in *binary* form. We call this the *compiled resource*. It is also possible to represent the *text* form of a resource in a high-level language. Do not confuse these two forms of the same thing.

The DeskTop file is an invisible resource file which is written onto every volume by the format operation. It is a table of contents to all other resource files on the volume. Whenever an application is launched, the resource file containing the application is looked up in the DeskTop file. This "lookup" is called *finding* the application, and is done by the Finder, MultiFinder, or equivalent desktop management programs.

A **finder** *is a special resource file containing code to manage the user interaction with the system*. In short, a finder is a "command interpreter" of the graphical user interface. A finder reads menu selections, mouse clicks, and keystrokes made by the user and "interprets" them according to the desktop metaphor. When an icon is double-clicked, for example, a finder such as MultiFinder intervenes to find the resource file in the DeskTop table of contents corresponding to the double-clicked icon. When found, the icon is matched up with the location of the resource file on the disk volume. Then one of two things can happen.

If the icon represents a resource of type APPL (application), the resource fork of the application is "launched" — its code resource is loaded into main memory and the application is started. If the icon represents a resource file of some other type, MultiFinder looks for the *creator* of the selected resource. If a creator can be found, the creator's resource file is launched, and the selected resource file is passed on to the running application.

This mechanism is not only interesting, but essential to understand before constructing Macintosh software. This points to an important feature of the Macintosh system: every resource file is "tagged" with two flags of information that the MultiFinder relies on:

Creator: A four-letter word that uniquely identifies what resource file created the resource.

Type: Another four-letter word that (nonuniquely) identifies the resource file as belonging to a class of objects. This information is used by the application to filter out all noninteresting resource files to prevent inadvertent use of illegal resources.

Creator signatures (the 4-letter word) must be unique, so they should be registered with Apple Computer Corp. to guarantee their uniqueness. Type signatures can be anything, but TEXT, PICT, and others have been commonly accepted for text files and so forth. Most word processors, for example, create TEXT files.

The creator and type signature of any resource file can be changed by selecting the File-Info menu item from within ResEdit. While this permits an application to read files it should not, it also may cause the application to fail.

MultiFinder and DeskTop together form the fundamental structure of the Macintosh system, see Figure 8-1. A double-clicked icon is looked up in the DeskTop file for a corresponding application resource. The application is launched by reading its code resource into main memory. The application can then read the remaining resources stored in its resource fork into memory through a series of calls to ROM or System toolbox routines. These resources occupy heap space in memory as shown in Figure 8-1. For example, a dialog box on the screen is a graphic representation of a resource object stored in a linked list of resources held in main memory.

The System file contains system resources such as the control panel window, self-portraits, error messages, and "drivers." The best known drivers are DAs — Desk Accessories — located under the "Apple menu." These resources of type DRVR are activated by pulling down the Apple Menu. The System file also contains FONT resources, fonts used by all applications. DAs and Fonts are added and removed from the System file by using a tool called Font/DA Mover or by dragging a FONT or DRVR icon onto the System icon.

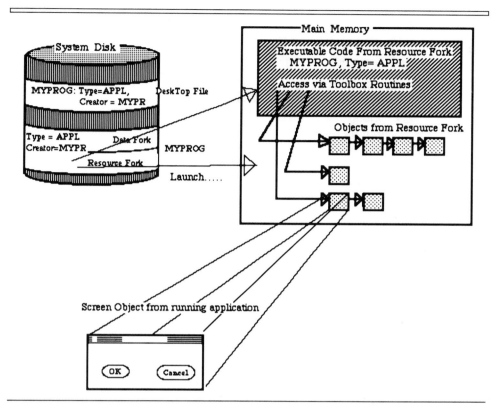

FIGURE 8-1. Architecture of an application

Every application must have a creator and type. It should also have an icon, its representation on the metaphorical desktop. This information is provided in the resource fork through a mechanism called *bundling*. The application bundle contains creator, type, and icon linkages. When a resource file is created by a compiler or linker, copied, or some way introduced into the system, the finder looks at the bundle bits of the resource fork and uses them to update the DeskTop. The resource's creator, type, and icon are copied into the DeskTop file along with all other information needed to launch the resource.

Similarly, whenever a disk volume window is opened (corresponding to listing the files on the disk) the finder must read the icons from the DeskTop and display them in the window. Thus, information about each resource file must be copied from the resource file into DeskTop. But first, the programmer must provide the bundle bit information to the application through its resource file.

As an illustration, consider the text resource file, Flow.R, shown in Figure 8-2. This file is compiled into Flow.rsrc, and then linked together with the compiled source code for Flow.pas, to obtain an application resource file. The Flow.R text file shown here is typical of most resource specifications.

```
*****************************************
* Resource file for the bubble flow project
*     Written by Sherry Yang.
*     This file is: Flow.R
*     Output file is: Flow.rsrc
*****************************************
* Asterisk lines are comments
* First line is the name of compiled resource file
* produced by RMaker

flow.rsrc

Type BUBL = STR
 ,0
bubble flow Version 0.1 August 5, 1987

Type FREF
 ,128
  APPL 0

Type FREF
 ,129
  TEXT 1

*****************************************
* Bundle bits
*****************************************

Type BNDL
 ,128
  BUBL 0
  ICN#
  0 128
  FREF
  0 128
```

```
*****************************
* Below is the icon and mask resource
* for the application icon.
* Notice the number 128 matches the
* ICN# in the bundle.
*****************************

Type ICN# = GNRL
 ,128 (32)
.H
00000000
0001C000
00022000
00041000
00080800
00080800
00080800
00041000
00022000
0007F000
000C1800
00180C00
00200600
00C00300
01800180
078001C0
0C400220
10200410
20100808
20100808
20100808
10200410
08400220
078001C0
00000000
00000000
3D03C248
21042248
21042248
39042248
21042250
21E3C3E0
* below is the mask
FFFFFFFF
FFFFFFFF
FFFFFFFF
...etc...
```

FIGURE 8-2. A portion of a resource fork

First, the application is given a creator signature, BUBL. This is also used to identify the application. Thus, BUBL is declared a string, 'STR '. (This is a four-letter word. Notice the trailing blank.)

```
Type BUBL = STR
,0
bubble flow Version 0.1 August 5, 1987
```

Next, the resource is given a type signature, APPL (application). This is done through the resource type called FREF (file reference). Any number will do — the finder renumbers the resources to make sure they are uniquely numbered in DeskTop. These two FREFs tell the Finder that resources numbered 128 and 129 are application and TEXT documents, respectively. That is, 128 is "mapped" into zero, and 129 is mapped into 1:

```
Type FREF
,128
APPL 0

Type FREF
,129
TEXT 1
```

These two FREFs become important in the next section where the bundle bits are set. We want to "map" the ICN# resource onto the APPL 0 FREF and, if we had a different icon for files created by Flow, map another ICN# onto the TEXT 1 FREF.

```
Type BNDL
,128
BUBL 0
ICN#
0 128
FREF
0 128
```

BNDL resource number 128 tells the finder to give the creator signature BUBL to resource 128 (which maps to APPL 0), and ICN# 128 to BUBL 0 (which maps to APPL 0). If, in addition, we had wanted to link ICN# 129 to the documents created by this application, then we would have written the following:

```
Type BNDL
,128
BUBL 0
ICN#
0 128 1 129
FREF
0 128 1 129
```

In addition, the resource file would have to contain an icon numbered 129 so the finder can match this icon with all documents created by BUBL.

Icon number 128 is given as a hex bit map. Thus, .H means "hexadecimal": both icon and mask are included as 32×32 pixels each. The code (32) refers to the purge-ability of the resource during program execution, and can be ignored for now. The hex bit map is typically generated by a tool rather than entered by hand.

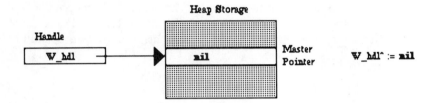

Initially, W_hdl points to nothing............................

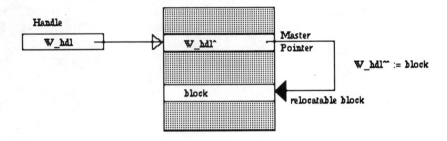

Data is stored in a block pointed at by Master Pointer ......

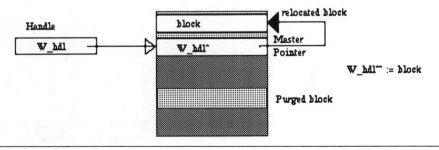

When memory is compacted, blocks can be moved to other locations.....

FIGURE 8-3. Memory management by handles

Memory Management

Graphical objects come and go in any application. This means memory must be managed behind the scenes. Unfortunately, the activities of the memory manager can often interfere with the activities of the application. Consequently, application programmers must understand the rudiments of Macintosh memory management.

Resources are stored in the heap section of main memory. Whenever memory gets fragmented or full, the memory manager examines the heap to find purgeable resources. Icons, windows, and other transient data structures become candidates for purging, or at least moving. Moving a block of data can free up a larger section of memory, thus making it possible to allocate space that would otherwise be lost to fragmentation.

If blocks were simply moved around in the heap, references to them would become inconsistent, see Figure 8-3. If a block is moved, all references to a purged block must be changed to point to the new location. But there may be more than one reference to a purged block. Instead of finding all references to all purged blocks, the memory manager uses an additional level of indirect addressing called *handles*. A **handle** *is a pointer to a pointer*. Handles overcome the need to update all references to a certain block whenever it is moved or purged.

Handles are themselves allocated to the heap, but they are anchored in the heap and cannot be purged or moved. Because they are anchored, handles should be allocated to the heap before any other block is allocated, otherwise the handles themselves might cause fragmentation of memory. It would be poor form to allocate an immovable handle in the middle of the heap, thereby dividing the heap into two smaller pieces.

The toolbox routine moremasters is used to allocate space for 64 masters per call.

Handles are written as variables with two up-arrows in Pascal (two asterisks in C). Thus, we use the following extended notation in Pascal:

```
type
  aThing = record

          ...
          end;

aThingPtr  = ^aThing;
aThingHandle = ^aThingPtr;
var
  aPtr       : aThingPtr;    {points to something}
  aThingHdl : aThingHandle; {points to a master}
  aThingRec: aThing;
begin
   moremasters; {allocate 64 blank spaces}

   ...
   aPtr := aThingPtr (aThingHdl^);     {type coercion, e.g. casting}
   aThingRec := aThingHdl^^;           {double dereference the handle}

   ...
  end.
```

There are several points to emphasize in this example. First, the master pointers are allocated by calling moremasters once for each group of 64 pointers you want to allocate. The application programmer must estimate how many pointers are needed, and issue enough calls to moremasters to generate sufficient numbers of pointers.

Second, data is strongly typed in Pascal, but a handle is a handle. Therefore a nonstandard feature is added to Macintosh Pascal that allows type coercion. Using a type name much like a function name is interpreted as a type casting operation. Thus, aThingPtr is a type, and aThingPtr (*) coerces (*) into data of type aThingPtr. The ^ operator means to dereference a pointer, and since a handle is a pointer to a pointer, the ^^ operator means to dereference a handle.

This may seem like an unnecessary detail, but application programs fail unexpectedly if memory management is not taken care of by the application. The reason: applications must be able to *react* to, rather than *control*, a stream of nondeterministic events. This places Macintosh applications closer to real-time control programs than traditional application programs. Every Macintosh application resembles an operating system. The resemblance centers on the *event queue* and a corresponding *event loop*.

Events

Because every application must respond to (unexpected) events, every application must incorporate one or more event loop. An **event loop** *is a section of code that iterates and tests for the existence of an event*. Events consist of key-presses, mouse-down, mouse-up, and disk activities.

The Macintosh operating system places events in a queue. An event queue is a list of events and associated information. It is processed by taking an event off, processing it, and then returning to ask if another event is waiting.

Event loops occur in various parts of an application. A *main event loop* usually handles the major activities of an application such as menu selection, window activation, and mouse clicking. Every application typically has one main event loop, but it is possible for an application to incorporate more than one. It is also common for an application to contain a number of minor event loops. A minor event loop is usually implemented in the form of a *filter function*, a function that is repeatedly called by a toolbox procedure to process a stream of "microevents." An example of a filter function is any function written to handle the "microevents" that occur when the screen cursor passes over a dialog. The coordinates of the cursor are handed to the filter function, where the cursor is interrogated. If the coordinates fall inside an editable text item in the dialog, the filter function should change the cursor to a blinking edit text cursor. If the cursor falls outside the text edit item, the filter function should change the cursor to an arrow. Other examples of minor event loops are: scrolling a page of text in a window, closing the window, and selecting a file name of a certain type.

The main event loop is the heart of an application. It polls the event queue and performs the corresponding actions as needed. The diagram in Figure 8-4 showing the main event loop illustrates what every application must do. First, if the user clicks an inactive window, two events are generated: one to activate the new window, and another to deactivate the "old" window. (The "old" window is the previously active window.) Windows are resources that are copied from the resource fork of the application's resource file and stored in a linked list in the heap. When a window is clicked, the linked list of window records is searched for the window record corresponding to the graphic object selected. When found, this record is brought to the front of the linked list and designated the *active window*. Of course the previously designated active window must be redesignated as an inactive window. Thus, an activate event is generated so the application can activate the selected window, and another activate event is generated so the application can deactivate the "deselected" window.

Next, the application's main event loop may obtain a "current event" from the event queue such as a click in the menu bar. The application must interpret the event in an appropriate way, such as dealing with the menu bar selection. For example, if the menu

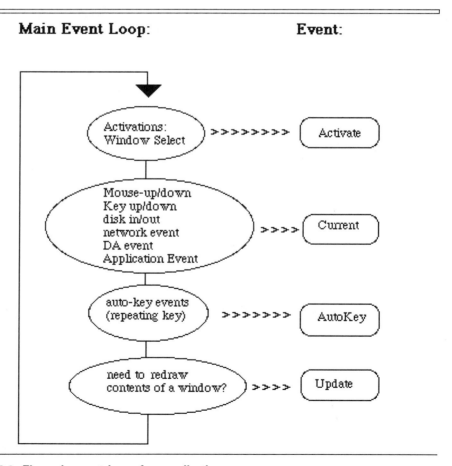

FIGURE 8-4. The main event loop of an application

bar has been selected, a mouse-down event will be passed to the application. The mouse-down event is interrogated, and if the mouse was clicked in the menu bar, the application must find out which menu was selected. These steps are actually done by calling the appropriate toolbox routines such as GetMenuBar, GetNextEvent, and so forth. A collection of programming fragments called *cliches* is given in the next section, which demonstrates these operations.

The autokey event is generated for repeating key strokes. This happens whenever the user holds down a keyboard key for a period of time that exceeds the Control Panel setting for the keyboard. Once again, the application must interpret this event. If the application is a word processor, for example, the repeat key might be interpreted by inserting the same character into the word processor document at a location specified by the blinking cursor.

The update event is generated each time a graphic object on the screen needs to be redrawn. For example, when a dialog box overlaps a window then disappears, the area under the dialog box must be redrawn. If the window contains text, the text must be redrawn along with the window, window controls, and any other parts of the window that were covered up by the overlapping dialog. The update event can also be generated by the application whenever it is appropriate to redraw something.

These are the principle activities of the main event loop, but they are not the only activities. If your application deals with communications, networks, external devices, and so on, then it should be prepared to handle other events. The nature of the events depends on the application.

PROGRAMMING CLICHES

A cliche is a trite or overused expression or idea. In programming, a cliche is a fragment of code that is so useful and common that it becomes trite. Programming cliches are especially trite to redesign and rewrite, hence they should be readily available for reuse.

Natural language cliches lose their impact with overuse, but programming cliches have an opposite effect on programmers. They become more forceful and commonplace as their utility increases. Nobody wants to reinvent the obvious, hence programming becomes a process of combining cliches, crafting new algorithms and data structures, and devising ways to make the program robust, compact, and fast. In fact, studies have shown that one of the major differences between expert and novice programmers is the ability of experts to remember and use cliches.

Cliches are even more important to Macintosh programmers because of its standardized user interface. The user interface of a certain Macintosh application must look and feel much like the interface of all other Macintosh applications. This is not only aesthetically pleasing but economically important, because it reduces the cost of training people to use every new application. Consequently, a standard user interface becomes a standard "language," similar to textual languages such as Pascal.

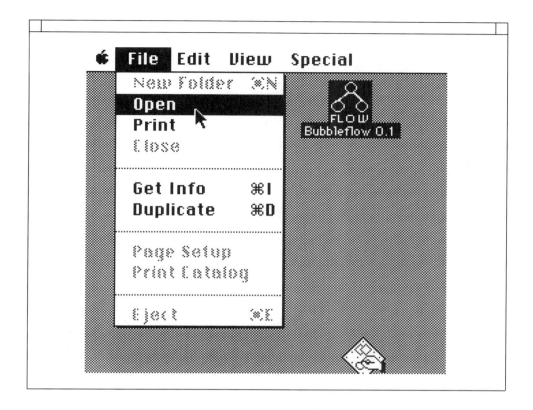

Learning to design applications in a standard user interface "language" is made doubly difficult by the existence of hundreds of reusable routines — the Toolbox routines — that each programmer must know about and be able to use properly. This burden can be lessened by cataloging and using a collection of programming cliches for doing standard things such as managing windows, menus, icons, and so on.

In this section we explore the Macintosh Toolbox routines in greater detail, and begin the process of building a library of programming cliches. We will supply code that works on monochrome machines, but the reader should know that most of these cliches can be easily converted to color machines by replacing monochrome names with color names; for example, NewWindow is replaced by NewCWindow, ShowWindow by ShowCWindow, and so forth. Similarly, a MultiFinder version of these cliches can be obtained by inserting WaitNextEvent into the main event loop of a Finder application.

We will illustrate these cliches by using the Bubble Flow example, an application containing menus, windows, and some graphics. In later sections, we will present additional cliches for doing other standard things with the Macintosh user interface routines.

The Structure of an Application

An application program consists of a main program which first calls one or more initialization procedures to set up memory pointers, initialize the toolbox managers in ROM, and create the initial state of the desktop. The main program then calls a procedure that implements the main event loop. The main event loop is run until a termination flag is set. Then the main event loop exits, followed by program termination. (Some programs may incorporate an epilog procedure for "cleaning up" before returning control to the finder. For example, the epilog might write text to the clipboard.)

An example of this is shown for the Bubble Flow application (the resource file for this application was given earlier, and may be consulted along with this code); see Figure 8-5. The comment statements at the beginning of this program tell who wrote it, who modified it (if anyone), and the dates of implementation and modification. This information is extremely important, because it can be tied to revisions and used during maintenance. In addition, the comments outline the top level of the program, forming a kind of table of contents or directory to the remaining parts of the program. Additional "table of contents" information is found in the **uses** statement:

```
uses
    GLOBAL_flow, CLOCK_flow, MENU_flow, EVENT_flow, DIALOG_flow, DRAW_flow, WINDOW_flow;
```

All modules used by the main program are listed here. Each module implements an object — an entity with state and function — and is named accordingly. GLOBAL_flow contains all global data and the operations on them; CLOCK_flow encapsulates the system clock and contains functions to initialize and interrogate the system clock; MENU_flow encapsulates menus and all the access procedures for operating on menus; EVENT_flow, DIALOG_flow, and WINDOW_flow encapsulate all state and function information having to do with the event queue, dialogs, and windows.

The naming convention established by this program is also very important because proper adoption of names establishes a vocabulary for all programmers implementing, or later, maintaining the system. Notice the modules are named after the objects that they encapsulate: DIALOG, WINDOW, MENU, and so on. Also, notice the suffix _flow appended after each name. This identifies each module with the program. These names are identical to the file names used: DIALOG_flow is stored in file DIALOG_flow.pas, WINDOW_flow is stored in WINDOW_flow.pas, and so forth.

Furthermore, variables that are visible outside of the module that defines them are named so that their ownership can be easily identified. We have used the first three letters of every module name in the name of every visible identifier. These three letters are appended to the beginning of procedure, function, constant, type, and variable identifier names. Thus, the procedures that are called from the main program can easily be identified and located in the corresponding module:

```
MEN_setupMenus;        {Menu routine to set up menu bar}
GLO_changeCursor;      {Change back to the arrow cursor}
DIA_aboutFlow;         {Display the about dialog}
WIN_setupLimit;        {Window routine that set up the limit of the windows}
```

```
{= = = = = = = = = = = = = = = = = = = = = = = = = = = = = = = = = = = = = = = = = = = = = = = =}
{   WRITTEN BY: SHERRY YANG                                                        }
{   CREATE DATE: AUG. 13, 1987                                                     }
{   LAST MODIFIED DATE: SEPT. 19, 1987                                             }
{= = = = = = = = = = = = = = = = = = = = = = = = = = = = = = = = = = = = = = = = = = = = = = = =}
{                 Flow.pas calls the following initialization routines:            }
{ — moremasters: ROM TOOLBOX ROUTINE FOR ANCHORING MASTER POINTERS                 }
{ — GLO_putUpClock: CHANGE CURSOR TO A WATCH...INDICATES A DELAY                   }
{ — GLO_changeCursor: CHANGE CURSOR TO AN ARROW                                    }
{ — GLO_initFinishedFlag: INITIALIZE THE PROGRAM TERMINATION FLAG                  }
{ — CLO_initClickTime: INITIALIZE TIME FOR DETECTING DOUBLE CLICKS                 }
{ — MEN_setupMenus: READ MENUS FROM RESOURCE FORK AND DISPLAY IN MENU BAR}
{ — DIA_about_flow: DISPLAY THE 'ABOUT DIALOG' UPON LAUNCHING THE PROGRAM }
{ — WIN_setupLimit: SETUP THE SCREEN SIZE, DRAG, RESIZE, AND GROW AREAS            }
{     FOR WINDOW                                                                   }
{ — EVE_mainEventLoop: THE HEART OF THE SYSTEM, HANDLES ALL EVENTS                 }
{= = = = = = = = = = = = = = = = = = = = = = = = = = = = = = = = = = = = = = = = = = = = = = = =}
program bubbleflow;
  uses
     GLOBAL_flow, CLOCK_flow, MENU_flow, EVENT_flow, DIALOG_flow,
     DRAW_flow, WINDOW_flow;

begin
     Moremasters;            {Tool box routines to get more handles}
     GLO_putUpClock;         {Global routine to put up a watch cursor}
     MEN_setupMenus;         {Menu routine to set up menu bar}
     GLO_changeCursor;       {Change back to the arrow cursor}
     DIA_aboutFlow;          {Display the about dialog}
     WIN_setupLimit;         {Window routine that set up the limit of the windows}
                             {drag area and grow area by getting the screenBound}
     GLO_initFinishedFlag;   {Initialize the global finished flag}

     CLO_initSecondClick;    {Initialize secondClick time for double clicks}
     EVE_mainEventLoop;      {Main event loop in the Event unit}
end.
```

FIGURE 8-5. Main program of the Bubble Flow application

If a maintenance programmer wants to know where the MEN_setupMenus procedure is located, the three-letter prefix MEN tells the programmer to look in file
MENU_flow.pas.

Obviously, the remaining letters in each name should tell what the identifier means: procedures should show action, hence they should be verbs or verb phrases; and function names, constants, types, and variables ought to be nouns (people, places, or things). Perhaps DIA_aboutFlow should have been named DIA_DoAboutFlow; otherwise, the names shown here are all "action names" because these are procedures.

The body of the main program should be as brief as possible. Its purpose is to guide the maintenance programmer into the appropriate location for making a change. Here we see many initialization steps followed by a call to the main event loop routine.

```
moremasters;            {Toolbox routine to get more handles}
GLO_putUpClock;         {Global routine to put up a watch cursor}
MEN_setupMenus;         {Menu routine to set up menu bar}
GLO_changeCursor;       {Change back to the arrow cursor}
DIA_aboutFlow;          {Display the about dialog}
WIN_setupLimit;         {Window routine that sets up the limit of the windows}
                        {drag area and grow area by getting the screenBound}
GLO_initFinishedFlag;   {Initialize the global finished flag}
CLO_initSecondClick;    {Initialize secondClick time for double clicks}
EVE_mainEventLoop;      {Main event loop in the Event unit}
```

Moremasters allocates 64 master pointers to be used by handles; GLO_putUpClock changes the cursor arrow to a watch, indicating that the user must wait; MEN_setUpMenus writes the menu bar along with all of the items in each menu; GLO_changeCursor changes the watch back into a pointing arrow cursor; DIA_aboutFlow puts up the "about dialog" which tells the user who wrote the application; WIN_setupLimit establishes the features of all windows to be used, partially by reading the resource fork of the resource file; GLO_initFinishedFlag sets the application's halt flag to False (when it is set to True, the application's main event loop terminates, and the application returns control to the finder); and CLO_initSecondClick initializes a counter so that the application can distinguish between a single and double click of the mouse.

EVE_mainEventLoop is where the application spends most of its time. This loop is repeated until the halt flag is set to True. Events such as mouse clicks, window activation/deactivation, and menu selection are each processed independently from within the main event loop.

The simple example shown here for program FLOW does not completely conform to the standard desktop user interface, however, because several features are missing. An application can be launched from the desktop in several ways:

Double-click the Application

Single-click the Application, followed by selection of File-Open

Double-click one of the files created by the Application

Single-click one or more files created by the Application, followed by selection of File-Print

The first two methods are usual for starting the application. When either one of these methods is used, the finder launches the application as we have discussed before.

The second two methods are most interesting: when one or more resource file(s) lacking code resources are double-clicked, the finder attempts to find the creator of the file(s). If the creator is found, the file(s) are remembered by finder and passed on to the application. The application must open or print these files as necessary.

Suppose two word processing document files are selected and the File-Print menu item selected. The finder launches the creator of these data files and passes the number of files selected (two), their type, and name to the application. The application must then print the files, one at a time, or else display an error alert. After the application has processed the files, it returns control to the finder.

Alternately, suppose a word processor document is double-clicked. The user obviously wants to launch the application and load the document simultaneously. In this instance, the file type and name is passed to the application where the application is responsible for loading the file. If the application cannot load the file, an error alert should be shown.

These operations are facilitated by toolbox routines to get the type, number, and names of the files passed to the application. For example:

CountAppFiles (message, Count): Returns the launch operation and number of files selected.

GetAppFiles (Number, Info): Returns file type and name, given the file number.

ClrAppFiles (Number): Removes file number from list of passed files.

In addition, toolbox constants AppPrint, and so on, indicate which operation is being attempted by the finder. These constants are used to guide the application.

The application must process these requests immediately after initialization, but before the main event loop takes over. The reader is given an opportunity to enhance FLOW using the global startup routine shown here.

Procedure GLO_DoStartUp is self-explanatory, but a few points should be made, see Figure 8-6. There are two application dependent procedures called from within GLO_DoStartUp that must be replaced if the cliche is used in another application. The DoNew and OpenFile routines can be supplied or replaced as needed.

Furthermore, this example assumes that the application always processes TEXT files. This may not be true, in which case the routine must be modified. In fact, the application may process more than one type of data file. All types must be processed and handled accordingly.

Additionally, GLO_DoStartUp uses two alert dialogs to communicate with the user. These are assumed to be in the resource fork as Alert IDs 101 and 102. The StopAlert toolbox routine is used to display both alerts, but the application must provide resource definitions. Note also the use of the toolbox routine ParamText to insert the filename into Alert 102 during program execution.

One more note: the use of the ExitToShell toolbox routine may be unwise, because some applications may need to perform epilog operations — cleanup operations such as writing a scrap file to the clipboard or closing files. The ExitToShell immediately exits the application without regard for termination processing.

```
procedure GLO_DoStartUp;
const
  CantPrintID = 101;                    {Resource Id of "Can't Print" Alert}
  WrongTypeID = 102;                    {Resource Id of "Wrong File Type" Alert}
var
  theMessage : INTEGER;                 {User selects File-Open or File-Print?}
  nDocs      : INTEGER;                 {Number of documents selected by Finder}
  thisDoc    : INTEGER;                 {Index number of document}
  docInfo    : AppFile;                 {Startup information about one document}
  ignore     : INTEGER;                 {Item code returned by alert}

begin {GLO_DoStartup}
    {Get startup message and number of documents from finder}
    CountAppFiles (theMessage, nDocs);
    {Did user choose Print in Finder?}
    If theMessage = AppPrint
          then  begin                            {Can Print or Give Alert, here...}
                    ignore := StopAlert (CantPrintID, NIL);      {Post alert}
                    ExitToShell                          {Return to Finder}
                end {If-Then}
          else if nDocs = 0              {Can do File-New or File-Open...}
                    {...do same as if File-New}
                    then DoNew              {--Application Dependent--}
                    else begin               {...do same as if File-Open}
                    {Loop through documents}
                    for thisDoc := 1 to nDocs
                      do begin
                        {Get startup information}
                        GetAppFiles (thisDoc, docInfo);
                        With docInfo do
                          if fType = 'TEXT'      {Could be of any type, but...}
                            then begin           {...for text processing...}
                              OpenFile (fName, vRefNum);      {--Application Dependent--}
                              ClrAppFiles (thisDoc)            {Tell finder we have it...}
                            end {With-If-Then}
                            else begin  {Filter out non-TEXT types}
                              {Substitute file name into text of alert}
                                ParamText (fName, '', '', '');
                                ignore := StopAlert (WrongTypeID, NIL) {Post alert}
                            end {With-If-Else}
                      end {For loop}
                    end{...do same as if File-Open}
end; {GLO_DoStartup}
```

FIGURE 8-6. Source code for GLO_DoStartUp

Briefly, GLO_DoStartUp accepts the file information passed to it from the finder, decides what is required (Printing, Opening, or simply nothing), and then either displays an alert or does the requested operation. In this example, it shows an alert instead of printing when File-Print is selected. If the application normally prints a document, this part of the routine would have to be changed to handle the print operation.

Main Events

While many similarities exist between main event loops, every application has its own loop. For this reason, and to gain concreteness, we describe a main event loop for program FLOW.

FLOW simply permits one or more scrollable windows, as shown in Figure 8-7, to be opened, and a round "bubble" to be drawn inside each window. The window can be scrolled, resized, closed, and moved around on the desktop.

If the user presses the mouse button while pointing at a bubble in a window, the application must detect the difference between a single and double click. A single click must cause the bubble to be inverted (turned black if it is white, and white if it is black). A double click must cause the bubble to "open up," displaying a dialog or performing some other action. This operation is left as an exercise for the reader.

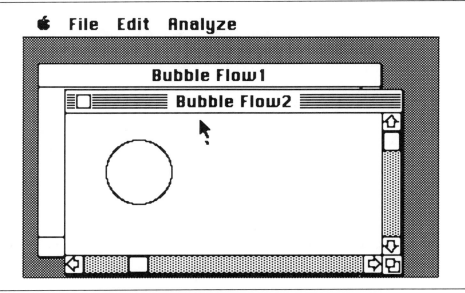

FIGURE 8-7. Running Bubble Flow

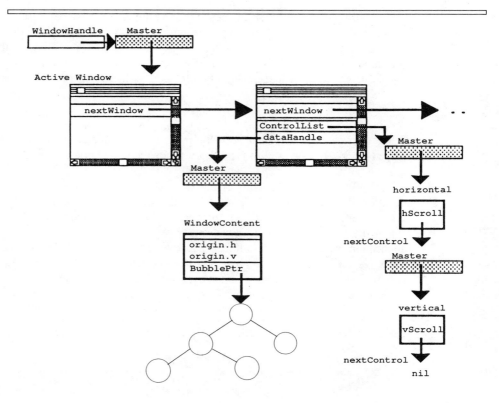

Data Structure of the Bubble Flow Window System

FIGURE 8-8. Window data structure for FLOW

The window data structure is shown for FLOW with several windows open at the same time, see Figure 8-8. The idea is to keep everything associated with each window together. The bubble diagram and scroll bars are linked to each window that contains them. This is accomplished through a window record established by the toolbox "window data structure." Of course, this structure uses handles to ensure proper memory management.

The main event loop is responsible for intercepting the MouseDown, KeyDown, Activate, and Update events generated by the user; see Figure 8-9. A processing routine is called to handle each one of these major events. The names of these routines are self-descriptive:

EVE_dealWithKeyDowns
EVE_dealWithMouseDowns
EVE_dealWithUpDates
EVE_dealWithActivates

EVE_mainEventLoop is the only procedure that is visible outside of **unit** EVENT_flow; see Figure 8-10. All constants, types, and variables (state information) are hidden within the unit. Nearly all other modules are used by EVENT_flow, however, including GLOBAL_flow, CLOCK_flow, MENU_flow, DIALOG_flow, DRAW_flow, and WINDOW_flow.

MAJOR EVENTS IN FLOW

It is easy to get lost in details when reading the main event loop code. The big picture is this: when an event occurs, it is placed on the event queue and then processed according to this outline.

MouseDown: User points and clicks.
  InSystemWindow: User selected a DA.
  InMenuBar: User has selected a menu item.
    AppleMenu: About... and DAs.
    FileMenu: New, Open, Close...Quit.
    EditMenu: Cut, Paste...
    AnalyzeMenu: FLOW operations.
  InContent: User selected a FLOW window.
  InGrow: User selected a window's grow box.
  InDrag: User drags a FLOW window.
  InGoAway: User to close a FLOW window.
KeyDown: User presses a keyboard key.
  InCharacter: Does nothing, for now.
  CommandKey: Menu selection shortcut.
    AppleMenu: About... and DAs.
    FileMenu: New, Open, Close...Quit.
    EditMenu: Cut, Paste...
    AnalyzeMenu: FLOW operations.
ActivateEvt: Window activated/deactivated.
UpDateEvt: Window refreshed.

FIGURE 8-9. Major events in FLOW

```
{ =============================================== }
{              BUBBLE FLOW PROGRAM --- EVENT UNIT            }
{              WRITTEN BY: SHERRY YANG                       }
{              CREATE DATE: AUG. 13, 1987                    }
{              LAST MODIFIED DATE: SEPT. 28, 1987            }
{ =============================================== }

unit EVENT_flow;
interface
  uses
    GLOBAL_flow, CLOCK_flow, MENU_flow, DIALOG_flow, DRAW_flow, WINDOW_flow;
  procedure EVE_mainEventLoop;

implementation
  procedure EVE_dealWithKeyDowns (event : EventRecord);
{ ---------------------------------------------------------- }
{ CHECKS IF A COMMAND KEY MENU OPTION IS SELECTED      }
{ IF SO, CALL MENU ROUTINE TO PROCESS THE SELECTION.  }
{ ---------------------------------------------------------- }
  var
    chCode : integer;                        { Integer value of the character pressed }
  begin
    chCode := BitAnd(event.message, CharCodeMask);      { extract character code }
    if BitAnd(event.modifiers, CmdKey) = CmdKey THEN
      begin
        MEN_doProcessMenuIn(MenuKey(CHR(chCode)));      { process menu equivalent of character pressed }
      end;
  end;

  procedure EVE_dealWithMouseDowns (event : EventRecord);
{ ---------------------------------------------------------- }
{ CHECK TO SEE WHERE MOUSE CLICK OCCURRED           }
{ CALL APPROPRIATE ROUTINES TO HANDLE THE EVENT.    }
{ ---------------------------------------------------------- }
  var
    windowPointedTo : WindowPtr;       { Pointer to the window selected by user }
    mouseLoc : Point;                  { Location of the mouse }
    windowLoc : integer;               { Which part of window pointed to }
    tempWindowPeek : WindowPeek;       { Temporary variable to hold pointer to WIN_currentWindow }
    tempDrawingHandle : WIN_drawingDataHandle;   { Temporary variable to hold the actual drawing data handle }
    actualDrawingRect : Rect;                     { The dimension of the drawing rect not including scroll bars }
  begin
    mouseLoc := Event.Where;           { Location of mouse click is returned by event queue }
    windowLoc := FindWindow(mouseLoc, windowPointedTo);  { Toolbox routine tells which window }
    case windowLoc of
```

FIGURE 8-10. Event unit of Bubble Flow

```
InMenuBar:
  MEN_doProcessMenuIn(MenuSelect(mouseLoc));        {Menu Selection}

InSysWindow:
  SystemClick(event, windowPointedTo);              {DA windows}

InContent:
  begin
    if windowPointedTo < > FrontWindow
      then SelectWindow(windowPointedTo);           {Make window active first}
    GlobalToLocal(event.where);                      {Convert to window coordinates}
    actualDrawingRect := windowPointedTo^.portRect; {Compute dimension of the drawing rect not including scroll bars}
      actualDrawingRect.bottom := actualDrawingRect.bottom - (SBARWIDTH - 1);
      actualDrawingRect.right := actualDrawingRect.right - (SBARWIDTH - 1);
    tempWindowPeek := WindowPeek(windowPointedTo);   {Type cast to windowPeek type}
    Hlock(tempWindowPeek^.dataHandle);               {Locking handle before manipulatng window data}
    tempDrawingHandle := WIN_drawingDataHandle(tempWindowPeek^.dataHandle); {Cast generic handle to data handle}
    if not PtInRect(event.where, actualDrawingRect)  {Click in Drawing rect or Scrolls?}
      then WIN_doProcessInControl(windowPointedTo, event.where)  {Scrolls}
      else if DRA_inBubble(tempDrawingHandle^^.drawingRecord, event.where)  {Click inside Bubble?}
            then begin
              if CLO_doubleClick then DIA_displayBubbleInfo              {Double Click...}
                else DRA_invertBubble(tempDrawingHandle^^.drawingRecord); {Single Click...}
            end
            {If click elsewhere in the window while the bubble is highlighted, then unhighlight the bubble}
            else if tempDrawingHandle^^.drawingRecord.bubbleHighlighted
                  then DRA_invertBubble(tempDrawingHandle^^.drawingRecord);
    Hunlock(tempWindowPeek^.dataHandle);
  end;

InGrow:
  begin
    if windowPointedTo < > FrontWindow
      then SelectWindow(windowPointedTo);            {Make window active}
    WIN_doProcessInGrow(windowPointedTo, event.where); {Resize the window}
  end;

InDrag:
  WIN_doDragWindow(windowPointedTo, event.where);    {Move the window}
InGoAway:
  begin
    if windowPointedTo < > FrontWindow
      then SelectWindow(windowPointedTo);            {Make window active}
    if TrackGoAway(windowPointedTo, event.where)     {Lock onto close box}
      then WIN_doCloseWindow(windowPointedTo);       {Remove window}
  end;
```

FIGURE 8-10 (Continued).

```
      otherwise;                          {Ignore all other events}
    end; {CASE}
  end; {dealWithMouseDowns}

  procedure EVE_dealWithUpdates (event : EventRecord);
  {-----------------------------------------------------------------------------}
  {REFRESH CONTENTS OF THE ACTIVE WINDOW                      }
  {-----------------------------------------------------------------------------}
  var
     updateWindow : windowPtr;            {Points to the window that needs update}
  begin
    updateWindow := WindowPtr(event.message); {Cast event data into window pointer}
    WIN_doUpdateWindow(updateWindow);     {Redraw window, scrolls, etc}
  end;

  procedure EVE_dealWithActivates (event : EventRecord);
  {-----------------------------------------------------------------------------}
  {MAKE WINDOW ACTIVE AND INACTIVE                            }
  {DEPENDING ON WHETHER IT IS AN ACTIVE OR INACTIVE EVENT.    }
  {-----------------------------------------------------------------------------}
  var
    targetWindow : WindowPtr;                      {Points to the window that needs to be made active or inactive}
  begin
    targetWindow := WindowPtr(event.message);    {Cast event data into window pointer}
    if Odd(event.modifiers)                       {Odd = Activate, Even = Deactivate}
      then WIN_doActiveWindow(targetWindow)   {Make the window active...}
      else WIN_doDeactiveWindow(targetWindow); {Make the window INactive...}
  end;

  procedure EVE_mainEventLoop;
  {-----------------------------------------------------------------------------}
  {PROCESS ALL PENDING EVENTS ON THE EVENT QUEUE              }
  {TERMINATE ONLY WHEN USER SELECTS QUIT FROM THE FILE MENU.  }
  {-----------------------------------------------------------------------------}
  var
    event : EventRecord;                 {Holds the current event information}
  begin
    repeat
      SystemTask;                        {support Desk Accessories}

      if GetNextEvent(EveryEvent, event) then

        case event.what of

          MouseDown:
            EVE_dealWithMouseDowns(event);
```

FIGURE 8-10 (Continued).

```
    KeyDown:
      EVE_dealWithKeyDowns(event);

    ActivateEvt:
      EVE_dealWithActivates(event);

    UpDateEvt:
      EVE_dealWithUpdates(event);

    otherwise
      ;
    end;
  Until GLO_finished;  {terminate the program}
  end;  {mainEventLoop}

end.
```

FIGURE 8-10 (Continued).

Careful study of the source code reveals much about the event-driven nature of user-friendly software design. These designs are radically different from traditional applications, which force users into various modes of operation. In event-driven systems, the user dictates what happens next, not the software. Accordingly, the software must be able to respond to numerous events, in any order. This leads to the nondeterministic behavior of such applications.

Menus

The main event loop uses a great number of other modules, and several are important enough to be added to the list of cliches. Menus and windows are used by nearly every application. The sample menu unit shown in Figure 8-13 can be easily adapted to other applications, and the sample window unit described in the next section is general enough to be modified and reused in most applications requiring a scrollable text or graphics window.

We examine **unit** MENU_flow (which contains the menu bar as its state information) and the two operations, SetUpMenus and doProcessMenuIn, forming its functional part. In addition, the unit contains several hidden functions that are application dependent. One procedure must be written for each menu (Apple, File, Edit, Analyze). These procedures in turn call other procedures that carry out the intended operation.

The menus are created in SetUpMenu. This routine reads the resource fork of the application and extracts the specification of the initial state of each menu item — see the excerpt from the FLOW.R file shown in Figure 8-11.

* A FANCY RESOURCE FILE FOR FLOW

```
Type ICON = GNRL
 ,257
.H
00000000
0001C000
...etc...
21E3C3E0

Type MENU
* Apple Menu \14 is the apple symbol
,256
 \14

About Bubble flow...
(–

* the file menu
 ,257
File
New/N < B ^ 1
Open/O
Save/S
Print/P
(–
Quit/Q

* the edit menu
 ,258
Edit
Delete/D
Change/C
Unknown1

* the Analyze menu
 ,259
Analyze
Unknown1 < I
Unknown2 < U
Unknown3 < S
```

Legend:
```
< I = Italic,      < U = Underscore,      < S = Shadow
< B = Bold,        < O = Outline
/x  = Command key x, where x = keyboard key
^i  = menu has icon # 256 + i
!   = menu has check mark
(   = menu item is disabled
```

FIGURE 8-11. Excerpt from FLOW.R file

Several interesting features of resource files are shown by this example. First, each item has a display code associated with it. These codes are appended to the menu item string. For example, /Q means to associate the Command-Q pair with a short cut menu selection operation. Instead of pulling down and selecting File-Quit, the user may use the Apple-Command key in combination with the Q key to do the same thing.

Similarly, appending <I to an item means to display the item as an italicized string of characters. Similar codes can be used to make the menus more meaningful to the user.

The results of these enhancements to the menus of FLOW are shown in Figure 8-12. Of particular interest is the File-New menu showing the desktop icon of the application. How was this done?

The ^1 appended to the resource specification of this menu item means to use ICON resource item number 257 (256 + 1) in the menu item. Notice that ICON number 257 is simply a copy of the application's icon.

More than one appended code can be used. The File-Menu item has three appended codes: /N meaning to permit the command-N shortcut; <B meaning to make the string boldfaced; and ^1 meaning to use ICON number 257.

The unit named MENU_flow shown in Figure 8-13 encapsulates the identifiers corresponding to menu resource IDs, an array of handles that point to the menus once they are brought into memory, and the procedures for manipulating the menus. In particular, if the resource IDs are changed, then the encapsulated constants must also be changed.

The object-oriented module uses GLOBAL_flow, DIALOG_flow, DRAW_flow, and WINDOW_flow as well. This unit would also use one or more other units containing processing functions that are called when each menu item is selected. We have not included these calls in the cliche.

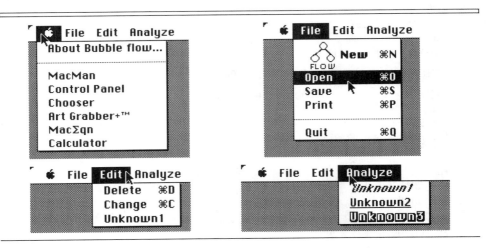

FIGURE 8-12. The Apple, File, Edit, and Analyze menus

```
{=================================================}
{BUBBLE FLOW PROGRAM --- MENU UNIT                }
{WRITTEN BY: SHERRY YANG                          }
{CREATE DATE: AUG. 13, 1987                       }
{LAST MODIFIED DATE: AUG. 13, 1987                }
{=================================================}

unit MENU_flow;

interface
  uses
    GLOBAL_flow, DIALOG_flow, DRAW_flow, WINDOW_flow;

  PROCEDURE MEN_setupMenus;
  PROCEDURE MEN_doProcessMenuIn (menuSelection : longint);

implementation
{----------------------------------------------------------------------------------}
{CONSTANTS FOR MENU UNIT                                                            }
{These constants are used by the menu unit and menu unit only for handling menu     }
{selections and item selections within a menu.                                      }
{----------------------------------------------------------------------------------}
  const

    MEMCOUNT = 4;              {Number of menus}
    APPLE_MENU = 1;            { Array subscripts of menu handle array}
    FILE_MENU = 2;
    EDIT_MENU = 3;
    ANALYZE_MENU = 4;

    APPLE_MENU_ID = 256;       {Menu resource IDs}
    FILE_MENU_ID = 257;
    EDIT_MENU_ID = 258;
    ANALYZE_MENU_ID = 259;

    APPLE_FLOW_ABOUT = 1;      {Dialog APPLE_FLOW_ABOUT id}

    FILE_NEW = 1;              {File menu item list number}
    FILE_OPEN = 2;
    FILE_SAVE = 3;
    FILE_PRINT = 4;
    FILE_QUIT = 6;

    EDIT_DELETE = 1;           {Edit menu item list number}
    EDIT_CHANGE = 2;
    EDIT_UNKNOWN1 = 3;

    ANALYZE_UNKNOWN1 = 1;      {Analyze menu item list number}
    ANALYZE_UNKNOWN2 = 2;
    ANALYZE_UNKNOWN3 = 3;

  var
    myMenu : ARRAY[1..MEMCOUNT] OF MenuHandle;  {Array of Menu handles}
```

FIGURE 8-13. Menu unit of Bubble Flow application

```
    PROCEDURE MEN_doAppleMenu (appleItem : integer);
{------------------------------------------------------------------------------------------------}
{PROCESS THE ITEM HIT IN THE APPLE MENU. APPLE MENU CONSISTS OF EITHER        }
{THE ABOUT BUBBLE FLOW..., OR DESKTOP ACCESSORIES.                            }
{------------------------------------------------------------------------------------------------}
    var
      DAName : str255;                        {Name and reference number used in}
      DARefnum : integer;                     {Desktop Accessories}
    begin
      if appleItem = APPLE_FLOW_ABOUT
        then DIA_aboutFlow                    {Display About dialog}
        else if appleItem < > 2
          then begin                          {If the item hit is DA}
            GetItem(myMenu[APPLE_MENU], appleItem, DAName);  {Activate Desktop Accessories}
            DARefnum := OpenDeskAcc(DAName);
          end;  {DA}
    end;  {MEN_doAppleMenu}

    procedure MEN_doFileMenu (fileItem : integer);
{------------------------------------------------------------------------------------------------}
{PROCESS THE ITEM HIT IN THE FILE MENU.                                       }
{------------------------------------------------------------------------------------------------}
    begin
      case fileItem of

        FILE_NEW:
          begin WIN_setupWindow; end;         {Open a window}

        FILE_OPEN:
          begin   {Do nothing for now} end;   {Open a File}

        FILE_SAVE:
          begin   {Do nothing for now} end;   {Save a File}

        FILE_PRINT:
          begin {Do nothing for now} end;     {Print Contents of a window}

        5:
          ; {Dash Line}

        FILE_QUIT:
          begin GLO_setFinishedFlag; end; {Set the finish flag to terminate the program}

      end;  {CASE}
    end;  {MEN_doFileMenu}

    procedure MEN_doEditMenu (editItem : integer);
{------------------------------------------------------------------------------------------------}
{PROCESS ITEM HIT IN THE EDIT MENU, INCLUDING DELETE, CHANGE, ETC.            }
{------------------------------------------------------------------------------------------------}
```

FIGURE 8-13 (Continued).

```
    begin
      case editItem of
        EDIT_DELETE:
          begin  {Do nothing for now} end;
        EDIT_CHANGE:
          begin  {Do nothing for now} end;
        EDIT_UNKNOWN1:
          begin  {Do nothing for now} end;
      end;
    end;  {MEN_doEditMenu}

    procedure MEN_doAnalyzeMenu (analyzeItem : integer);
    {-------------------------------------------------------------------------}
    {PROCESS THE ITEMS IN ANALYZE MENU -- THIS IS UP TO YOU!                  }
    {-------------------------------------------------------------------------}
    begin
      case analyzeItem of

        ANALYZE_UNKNOWN1:
          begin  {Do nothing for now} end;

        ANALYZE_UNKNOWN2:
          begin  {Do nothing for now} end;

        ANALYZE_UNKNOWN3:
          begin  {Do nothing for now} end;

      end;  {CASE}
    end;  {MEN_doAnalyzeMenu}

    procedure MEN_doProcessMenuIn;
    {-------------------------------------------------------------------------}
    {CALLED FROM THE EVENT UNIT TO HANDLE USER MENU SELECTIONS.               }
    {FIRST GET THE HIWORD AND LOWORD OF MENU SELECTION TO DETERMINE           }
    {THE MENU ITEM WITHIN THAT MENU. THEN CALL ONE OF FOUR                    }
    {PROCEDURES, DEPENDING ON THE MENU SELECTED TO HANDLE                     }
    {-------------------------------------------------------------------------}
    var
      menuNo : integer;        {menu number that was selected}
      itemNo : integer;        {item in menu that was selected}

    begin
      if menuSelection < > 0 then
        begin
          menuNo := HiWord(menuSelection);        {Get the menu that was selected by user}
          itemNo := LoWord(menuSelection);        {Get the item within the menu that was selected by user}

          case menuNo of

            APPLE_MENU_ID:
              MEN_doAppleMenu(itemNo);            {Process item selected in apple menu}
```

FIGURE 8-13 (Continued).

```
          FILE_MENU_ID:
             MEN_doFileMenu(itemNo);          {Process item selected in file menu}

          EDIT_MENU_ID:
             MEN_doEditMenu(itemNo);          {Process item selected in edit menu}

          ANALYZE_MENU_ID:
             MEN_doAnalyzeMenu(itemNo);       {Process item selected in analyze menu}

        end; {CASE}

        HiliteMenu(0);                        {unhilite after processing menu}

      end; {If-Then}

   end; {MEN_doProcessMenuIn}

procedure MEN_setupMenus;
{-----------------------------------------------------------------------------------}
{CALLED FROM THE MAIN PROGRAM...                                                    }
{GET MENU RESOURCES FROM THE RESOURCE FILE AND DRAW THEM IN MENU BAR                }
{-----------------------------------------------------------------------------------}
   var
      index : integer;                        {Temporary index used for inserting menus}
   begin
      myMenu[APPLE_MENU] := GetMenu(APPLE_MENU_ID);  {Get handles to menus and insert into the array that holds
                                                      all them}
      AddResMenu(myMenu[APPLE_MENU], 'DRVR');        {DAs are in System File. Type is 'DRVR'}
      myMenu[FILE_MENU] := GetMenu(FILE_MENU_ID);    {All other menus depend on Application}
      myMenu[EDIT_MENU] := GetMenu(EDIT_MENU_ID);
      myMenu[ANALYZE_MENU] := GetMenu(ANALYZE_MENU_ID);

      for index := 1 to MEMCOUNT do           {Insert menu handles into menu bar}
         InsertMenu(myMenu[index], 0);                {0 means to insert at end of list}

      DrawMenuBar;                            {Show the menu bar}
   end; {MEN_setupMenus}

end. {END MENU UNIT}
```

FIGURE 8-13 (Continued).

As an example, follow what happens when the user selects File-New from the menu bar of FLOW. The EVE_mainEventLoop routine responds to a MouseDown event by calling EVE_dealWithMouseDowns. The EVE_dealWithMouseDowns procedure selects the InMenuBar case because the location of the mousedown event was in the menu bar. The MEN_doProcessMenuIn procedure is called from the InMenuBar case of EVE_dealWithMouseDowns.

Inside of MEN_doProcessMenuIn, the high-order word of the long word returned by the event queue contains the menu number, and the low-order word contains the item number within the menu selected. The menu number is used to select the FILE_MENU_ID case, which calls MEN_doFileMenu.

The MEN_doFileMenu routine uses the item number passed to it to select the FILE_NEW case. This case calls the WIN_setupWindow routine inside of unit WINDOW_flow, where a new window is created according to the data structure shown in Figure 8-8.

After this sequence is completed and a new window is created, the main event loop is executed again, picking up another event from the event queue. This "next event" is used to carry out another sequence of case selections leading to possibly some other actions. After perhaps thousands of iterations of the main event loop, the user terminates the application by selecting File-Quit, which calls GLO_setFinishedFlag.

Windows

Although lengthy, the window cliche is one of the most frequently used modules. Rather than reinvent it each time a text or graphic window is needed by an application, we recommend that programmers reuse the complete unit given in Figure 8-14. This unit is taken from FLOW, but the reader can clearly identify the places where it can be altered to adapt it to other purposes.

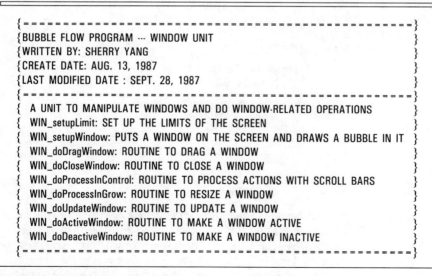

```
{ ============================================================ }
{BUBBLE FLOW PROGRAM --- WINDOW UNIT                           }
{WRITTEN BY: SHERRY YANG                                       }
{CREATE DATE: AUG. 13, 1987                                    }
{LAST MODIFIED DATE : SEPT. 28, 1987                           }
{ ============================================================ }
{  A UNIT TO MANIPULATE WINDOWS AND DO WINDOW-RELATED OPERATIONS }
{  WIN_setupLimit: SET UP THE LIMITS OF THE SCREEN             }
{  WIN_setupWindow: PUTS A WINDOW ON THE SCREEN AND DRAWS A BUBBLE IN IT }
{  WIN_doDragWindow: ROUTINE TO DRAG A WINDOW                  }
{  WIN_doCloseWindow: ROUTINE TO CLOSE A WINDOW                }
{  WIN_doProcessInControl: ROUTINE TO PROCESS ACTIONS WITH SCROLL BARS }
{  WIN_doProcessInGrow: ROUTINE TO RESIZE A WINDOW             }
{  WIN_doUpdateWindow: ROUTINE TO UPDATE A WINDOW              }
{  WIN_doActiveWindow: ROUTINE TO MAKE A WINDOW ACTIVE         }
{  WIN_doDeactiveWindow: ROUTINE TO MAKE A WINDOW INACTIVE     }
{ ============================================================ }
```

FIGURE 8-14. Window unit of Bubble Flow application

```
unit WINDOW_flow;
interface
  uses
    GLOBAL_flow, DRAW_flow, DIALOG_flow;
{-------------------------------------------------------------------------------------}
{WINDOW HANDLE, POINTER AND RECORD TYPE THAT HOLDS INFORMATION ABOUT A WINDOW  }
{-------------------------------------------------------------------------------------}
  type
    WIN_drawingDataHandle = ^WIN_drawingDataPtr;  {Handle to WIN_drawingData}
    WIN_drawingDataPtr = ^WIN_drawingData;         {Pointer to WIN_drawingData}
    {Record used to hold the drawing information and the current origin of the window}
    {Record referred through dataHandle field of the window record}
    WIN_drawingData = record
        theOrigin : Point;       {Horizontal and vertical coordinates of origin of window}
        drawingRecord : DRA_bubbleRecord;
      end;

  procedure WIN_setupLimit;
  procedure WIN_setupWindow;
  procedure WIN_doDragWindow (var WIN_currentWindow : WindowPtr; location : Point);
  procedure WIN_doCloseWindow (var WIN_currentWindow : WindowPtr);
  procedure WIN_doProcessInControl (var windowPointedTo : WindowPtr; location : Point);
  procedure WIN_doProcessInGrow (windowPointedTo : WindowPtr; location : Point);
  procedure WIN_doUpdateWindow (var updateWindow : WindowPtr);
  procedure WIN_doActiveWindow (targetWindow : WindowPtr);
  procedure WIN_doDeactiveWindow (targetWindow : WindowPtr);

implementation
{-------------------------------------------------------------------------------------}
{CONSTANTS FOR WINDOW UNIT                                                             }
{These constants are used by the window unit for window resource number,              }
{and scroll bar numbers, and numbers to control scroll, etc.                          }
{-------------------------------------------------------------------------------------}
  const
    WINDOW_ID = 601;                        {Window number in the resource file}

    VER_SCROLL_ID = 601;                    {Scroll bar numbers in the resource file}
    HOR_SCROLL_ID = 602;

    DRAG_LEFT_OFFSET = 4;                   {Setting the location/size for drag area by}
    DRAG_RIGHT_OFFSET = 4;                  {specifying the offset from the screen coordinates}
    DRAG_TOP_OFFSET = 24;
    DRAG_BOTTOM_OFFSET = 4;

    GROW_LEFT_OFFSET = 60;                  {Setting the size/location for resize box by}
    GROW_RIGHT_OFFSET = 0;                  {specifying the offset from the screen coordinates}
    GROW_TOP_OFFSET = 40;
    GROW_BOTTOM_OFFSET = 0;
```

FIGURE 8-14 (Continued).

```
      DOWN_SCROLL_AMOUNT = 10;                        {Amount to scroll for page down and page up on the scroll bar}
      UP_SCROLL_AMOUNT = -10;
      NUMBER_OF_PIXELS_PER_UNIT_OF_MOVE = 10;

      H_OFFSET = 20;                                  {Constants used for offset of new window}
      V_OFFSET = 20;
      TITLE_BAR_HEIGHT = 18;
      MENU_BAR_HEIGHT = 20;

      STRING_ID = 1001;                               {Resource file string type id}
      TITLE_BAR_STRING_INDEX = 1;                     {Title bar string id in the resource file}
var
  {---------------------------------------------------------------------------------}
  {A list of global variables of WINDOW_flow unit.                                  }
  {---------------------------------------------------------------------------------}
      dragArea, growArea, screen : Rect;             {Limits of the window}
      theDiagramWindowPointedTo : WindowPtr;         {Current pointer to the diagram window selected by user}
      screenHeight, screenWidth : integer;      {Screen size}
      windowCount : integer;                    {Global variable to keep track how many windows have been opened}
      {windowCount is used to determine the position of the window on the screen. Used in the offsetWindow routine}
      actualDrawingRect : Rect;                           {Temporary variable used to hold the dimensions of the actual}
      {actualDrawingRect is used for drawing -- minus the width of scroll bars}

  procedure WIN_setupLimit;
  {---------------------------------------------------------------------------------}
  {SET UP THE LIMIT/ SIZE OF THE SCREEN AS WELL AS INITIALIZE windowCount.          }
  {THIS IS PART OF THE INITIALIZATION ROUTINE CALLED BY THE MAIN PROGRAM            }
  {---------------------------------------------------------------------------------}
  begin
    screen := ScreenBits.Bounds;
    SetRect(dragArea, screen.left + DRAG_LEFT_OFFSET, screen.top + DRAG_TOP_OFFSET,
            screen.right - DRAG_RIGHT_OFFSET, screen.bottom - DRAG_BOTTOM_OFFSET);
    SetRect(growArea, screen.left + GROW_LEFT_OFFSET, screen.top + GROW_TOP_OFFSET, screen.right, screen.bottom);
    screenHeight := screen.bottom - screen.top + 1;
    screenWidth := screen.right - screen.left + 1;
    windowCount := 0;  {Initialize counter to be used in the offsetWindow routine}
  end  {WIN_setupLimit};

procedure WIN_offsetWindow (whichWindow : WindowPtr);
  {---------------------------------------------------------------------------------}
  {CALLED FROM WIN_setupWindow TO STACK UP MULTIPLE WINDOWS                         }
  {---------------------------------------------------------------------------------}
  var
  {Temporary variables used by the procedure to compute offsets}
  windowWidth, windowHeight, hExtra, vExtra, hMax, vMax, windowLeft, windowTop : integer;

  begin
    with whichWindow^.portRect do
```

FIGURE 8-14 (Continued).

```
     begin                              {Get window dimensions from portRect}
       windowWidth := right - left;
       windowHeight := bottom - top;
       windowHeight := windowHeight + TITLE_BAR_HEIGHT       {Adjust to title bar}
     end;

   hExtra := screenWidth - windowWidth;                   {Find excess screen width and height}
   vExtra := screenHeight - (windowHeight + MENU_BAR_HEIGHT);

   hMax := (hExtra div H_OFFSET) + 1;                      {Find maximum number of windows}
   vMax := (vExtra div V_OFFSET) + 1;                      {that would fit on the screen}

   windowLeft := (windowCount mod hMax) * H_OFFSET;        {Calculate offset}
   windowTop := (windowCount mod vMax) * V_OFFSET;
   windowTop := windowTop + TITLE_BAR_HEIGHT + MENU_BAR_HEIGHT;

   MoveWindow(whichWindow, windowLeft, windowTop, FALSE);    {Move window to new location}
   end;  {WIN_offsetWindow}

procedure WIN_moveScrollBar (var WIN_currentWindow : Windowptr);
{----------------------------------------------------------------------------------------------------}
{UPDATE SCROLL BAR                                                                                   }
{CALLED AFTER SETTING UP THE WINDOW AND EVERYTIME THE SCROLL IS PRESSED                               }
{----------------------------------------------------------------------------------------------------}
   var
     tempWindowPeek : WindowPeek;            {Temporary variable to hold the windowPeek of the WIN_currentWindow}
                                             {WindowPeek is a pointer to the window record}
   begin
     tempwindowPeek := windowPeek(WIN_currentWindow); {Type cast window pointer to a window peek,}
     with WIN_currentWindow^.portRect do

     begin
     {Horizontal and vertical scroll bars are maintained as a linked list inside the window record field called controlList}
       HideControl(tempWindowPeek^.controlList);                      {First in the control list is the horizontal scroll bar}
       MoveControl(tempWindowPeek^.controlList, -1, bottom - (SBARWIDTH - 1));
       SizeControl(tempWindowPeek^.controlList, (right + 1) - (left - 1) - (SBARWIDTH - 1), SBARWIDTH - 1);
       ShowControl(tempWindowPeek^.controlList);

       HideControl(tempWindowPeek^.controlList^^.nextControl); {Second in the control list is the vertical scroll bar}
       MoveControl(tempWindowPeek^.controlList^^.nextControl, right - (SBARWIDTH - 1), -1);
       SizeControl(tempWindowPeek^.controlList^^.nextControl, SBARWIDTH - 1,
                                      (bottom + 1) - (top - 1) - (SBARWIDTH - 1));
       ShowControl(tempWindowPeek^.controlList^^.nextControl);

     end; {WITH}

   end; {WIN_moveScrollBar}
```

FIGURE 8-14 (Continued).

```
procedure WIN_setupWindow;
{------------------------------------------------------------------------------------------------}
{PUTS UP A WINDOW ON THE SCREEN, OFFSETS ITS POSITION TO LAYER EFFECT FOR        }
{MULTIPLE WINDOWs. THEN IT DRAWS CONTROL (SCROLL BARS, GROW ICON FOR RESIZING    }
{SETS THE TITLE OF THE WINDOW TO BE THE STRING "DIAGRAM WINDOW" PLUS THE         }
{CURRENT windowCount, AND DRAWS A BUBBLE IN IT. ALL INFO. ON THE WINDOW IS       }
{SAVED IN THE WINDOW RECORD AND MAY BE REFERENCED BY TYPE CASTING THE WINDOW     }
{POINTER TO A WINDOW PEEK TYPE.                                                  }
{------------------------------------------------------------------------------------------------}
  var
    tempWindowDrawingHandle : WIN_drawingDataHandle; {Temporary variable to hold the actual drawing data handle}
    tempWindowPeek : WindowPeek;        {Temporary variable to hold the windowPeek of WIN_currentWindow}
    diagramWindowPtr : WindowPtr;       {Temporary variable to hold the window pointer}
    tempPort : Grafptr;                 {Temporary variable to hold the current graf port}
    currentWindowTitle, stringWindowCount : str255;   {Temporary variables to hold the parts of the window title}
    windowTitle : str255;               {Temporary variable to hold the window title}

  begin
    GetPort(tempPort);                              {Save current port}

    diagramWindowPtr := GetNewWindow(WINDOW_ID, NIL, Windowptr(-1)); {Get window from resource file}
    windowCount := windowCount + 1;                 {Increment windowCount and incorporate}

    NumToString(windowCount, stringWindowCount);    {it in the title bar of the window}
    GetIndString(windowTitle, STRING_ID, TITLE_BAR_STRING_INDEX);     {Get the title from the resource file}
    currentWindowTitle := concat(windowTitle, stringWindowCount);
    SetWTitle(diagramWindowPtr, currentWindowTitle);   {Put title in window's Title Bar}

    WIN_offsetWindow(diagramWindowPtr);             {Offset window for layer effect}
    ShowWindow(diagramWindowPtr);                   {Show window on screen}

    SetPort(diagramWindowPtr);                      {Use the new window's coordinates}
    ClipRect(diagramWindowPtr^.portRect);           {Clip its rectangle}

    tempWindowPeek := WindowPeek(diagramWindowPtr); {Type cast to window peek for storing information in the window}
    tempWindowPeek^.dataHandle := NewHandle(Sizeof(WIN_drawingData)); {Get a new dataHandle, to draw bubble}
    Hlock(tempWindowPeek^.dataHandle);              {Lock the handle before storing information}
    tempWindowDrawingHandle := WIN_drawingDataHandle(tempWindowPeek^.dataHandle); {Cast the actual data handle}

    DRA_drawBubble(tempWindowDrawingHandle^^.drawingRecord);        {Draw a bubble in the window}
    DRA_setPositionRect(tempWindowDrawingHandle^^.drawingRecord);   {Set up the position rect of the bubble}

    tempWindowDrawingHandle^^.theOrigin.h := 0;     {Initialize the origin}
    tempWindowDrawingHandle^^.theOrigin.v := 0;
    Hunlock(tempWindowPeek^.dataHandle);            {Release handle}
```

FIGURE 8-14 (Continued).

```
    {Scroll bars are maintained as a linked list in the window record}
    tempWindowPeek^.controlList := GetNewControl(HOR_SCROLL_ID, diagramWindowPtr);  {Get from resource fork}
    tempWindowPeek^.controlList^^.nextControl := GetNewControl(VER_SCROLL_ID, diagramWindowPtr);
    tempWindowPeek^.controlList^^.nextControl^^.nextControl := nil;
    ShowControl(tempWindowPeek^.controlList);
    ShowControl(tempWindowPeek^.controlList^^.nextControl);  {Window now has scrolls}

    DrawGrowIcon(diagramWindowPtr);                         {Draw resize box}

    WIN_moveScrollBar(diagramWindowPtr);

    SetPort(tempPort);                                     {Restore port saved earlier}

  end;

procedure WIN_doDragWindow;
{-----------------------------------------------------------------------------------------------}
{DRAG A WINDOW.                                                                                 }
{-----------------------------------------------------------------------------------------------}
  begin
    DragWindow(WIN_currentWindow, location, dragArea);         {Toolbox routine to drag a window}
  end;  {WIN_doDragWindow}

procedure WIN_doCloseWindow;
{-----------------------------------------------------------------------------------------------}
{CLOSE A WINDOW.                                                                                }
{-----------------------------------------------------------------------------------------------}
  var
    tempWindowPeek : WindowPeek;      {Temporary variable to hold the windowPeek of the WIN_currentWindow}
                                      {WindowPeek is a pointer to the window record}
  begin
    tempWindowPeek := WindowPeek(WIN_currentWindow);           {Type cast to a window peek type}
    DisposeControl(tempWindowPeek^.controlList^^.nextControl); {Dispose the memory held by the controls}
    DisposeControl(tempWindowPeek^.controlList);
    DisposeWindow(WIN_currentWindow);                          {Dispose the memory held by the window}
  end;  {WIN_doCloseWindow}

procedure WIN_scrollBits;
{-----------------------------------------------------------------------------------------------}
{SCROLL THE BUBBLE IN THE WINDOW. THIS IS DONE BY FIRST OFFSET THE WINDOW                        }
{RECT (PortRect), THEN RESET THE ORIGIN TO (X,Y), REDRAW THE BUBBLE,                             }
{THEN SET THE ORIGIN BACK AGAIN TO 0,0                                                           }
{WARNING: THIS USES TWO SETS OF COORDINATES -- CONFUSING --                                      }
{-----------------------------------------------------------------------------------------------}
  var
    oldOrigin : point;                     {Temporary variable to store the old origin}
    horOffset, verOffset : integer;    {Holds the horizontal and vertical offset, how much to move horizontally and vertically}
    tempWindowPeek : WindowPeek;  {Temporary variable to hold the windowPeek of the WIN_currentWindow}
    tempDrawingHandle : WIN_drawingDataHandle;  {Temporary variable to hold the actual drawing data handle}
    updateRegion : RgnHandle;                   {Region used in scrollRect}
```

FIGURE 8-14 (Continued).

```
      begin
      tempWindowPeek := WindowPeek(theDiagramWindowPointedTo);        {Type cast to a windowPeek type}
      Hlock(tempWindowPeek^.dataHandle); {Lock the handle before manipulating information in the window}
      {Type cast a generic handle to an actual data handle...}
      tempDrawingHandle := WIN_drawingDataHandle(tempWindowPeek^.dataHandle);
      oldOrigin := tempDrawingHandle^^.theOrigin;                {Find the current location of the scroll bars}
      {The head of controlList is the horizontal scroll bar, and nextControl is the vertical scroll bar}
      tempDrawingHandle^^.theOrigin.h := NUMBER_OF_PIXELS_PER_UNIT_OF_MOVE
                                  * GetCtlValue(tempWindowPeek^.controlList); {horizontal scroll...}
      tempDrawingHandle^^.theOrigin.v := NUMBER_OF_PIXELS_PER_UNIT_OF_MOVE
                                  * GetCtlValue(tempWindowPeek^.controlList^^.nextControl); {vertical scroll...}
      horOffset := oldOrigin.h - tempDrawingHandle^^.theOrigin.h; {Find the offset, or how much to scroll the window}
      verOffset := oldOrigin.v - tempDrawingHandle^^.theOrigin.v;
      updateRegion := NewRgn;                {A region handle is needed for ScrollRect. See Inside Macintosh for details}

      with theDiagramWindowPointedTo^.portRect do        {Re-draw the contents of the window's rectangle}
        SetRect(actualDrawingRect, left, top, right - SBARWIDTH, bottom - SBARWIDTH);
      ScrollRect(actualDrawingRect, horOffset, verOffset, updateRegion);

      SetOrigin(tempDrawingHandle^^.theOrigin.h, tempDrawingHandle^^.theOrigin.v);        {Reset origin}

      {Offset the content of the region}
      OffsetRect(updateRegion^^.rgnBBox, tempDrawingHandle^^.theOrigin.h, tempDrawingHandle^^.theOrigin.v);
      ClipRect(updateRegion^^.rgnBBox);

      {Redraw relative to the new origin}
      DRA_offsetPositionRect(tempDrawingHandle^^.drawingRecord, horOffset, verOffset);
      DRA_redrawBubble(tempDrawingHandle^^.drawingRecord);
      DisposeRgn(updateRegion);

      InvalRect(actualDrawingRect);                        {Force update on the window Rect}
      Hunlock(tempWindowPeek^.dataHandle);

      SetOrigin(0, 0);                        {Set origin back to 0, 0}
      ClipRect(theDiagramWindowPointedTo^.portRect);
    end; {WIN_scrollBits}

    procedure WIN_scrollUp (control : ControlHandle; code : integer);
    {--------------------------------------------------------------------------------------------------------------------}
    {SCROLL THE WINDOW UP ONE CONTROL UNIT.                                                                              }
    {--------------------------------------------------------------------------------------------------------------------}
      begin
        if code = inUpButton then
          begin
            SetCtlValue(control, GetCtlValue(control) - 1);
            WIN_scrollBits;
          end;
      end; {WIN_scrollUp}
```

FIGURE 8-14 (Continued).

```
procedure WIN_scrollDown (control : ControlHandle; code : integer);
{------------------------------------------------------------------------------------------------------}
{SCROLL THE WINDOW DOWN ONE CONTROL UNIT.                                                              }
{------------------------------------------------------------------------------------------------------}
  begin
    if code = inDownButton then
      begin
        SetCtlValue(control, GetCtlValue(control) + 1);
        WIN_scrollBits;
      end;
  end; {WIN_scrollDown}

procedure WIN_pageScroll (control : controlHandle; code, scrollAmount : integer);
{------------------------------------------------------------------------------------------------------}
{SCROLL THE WINDOW UP OR DOWN 10 CONTROL UNITS.                                                        }
{FOR THIS VERSION OF THE PROGRAM, A PAGE IS JUST AN ARBITRARY UNIT.                                    }
{------------------------------------------------------------------------------------------------------}
  var
    mousePoint : Point;                       {Holds the location of the mouse at a given time}
  begin
    repeat
      GetMouse(mousePoint);
      if TestControl(control, mousePoint) = code then  {User holds mouse down...}
        begin
          SetCtlValue(control, GetCtlValue(control) + scrollAmount);
          WIN_scrollBits;
        end
    until not StillDown;
  end; {WIN_pageScroll}

procedure WIN_doProcessInControl; {var windowPointedTo: WindowPtr; location: Point}
{------------------------------------------------------------------------------------------------------}
{DETERMINE WHICH PART OF SCROLL BAR WAS PRESSED AND CALL APPROPRIATE                                   }
{ROUTINES TO SCROLL EITHER ONE UNIT, 10 UNITS (IN THIS EXAMPLE, WE USE THAT                            }
{TO DENOTE AN ARBITRARY PAGE ) OR TO THE LOCATION OF THE THUMB.                                        }
{REFER TO INSIDE MACINTOSH -- CONTROL MANAGER SECTION -- FOR MORE DETAIL.                              }
{------------------------------------------------------------------------------------------------------}
  var
    ignored : integer;                            {Temporary dummy variable}
    whichControl : ControlHandle;                  {The control handle returned by FindControl toolbox call}
    controlType : integer;                         {The control type returned by FindControl toolbox call}
  begin
    theDiagramWindowPointedTo := windowPointedTo;       {for use in the scrollBit routine}
    {Find which control user selected and where in the control to process}
    controlType := FindControl(location, windowPointedTo, whichControl);
    case controlType of
```

FIGURE 8-14 (Continued).

```
        inUpbutton :
          Ignored := TrackControl(whichControl, location, @WIN_scrollUp);     {Scroll up as long as user has mouse down}

        inDownButton :
          Ignored := TrackControl(whichControl, location, @WIN_scrollDown); {Scroll down as long as user presses mouse}

        inPageUp :
          WIN_pageScroll(whichControl, controlType, UP_SCROLL_AMOUNT); {Page up -- user has mousedown in grey area}

        inPageDown :
          WIN_pageScroll(whichControl, controlType, DOWN_SCROLL_AMOUNT); {Page down -- user pressing in grey area}

        inThumb :
          begin
            Ignored := TrackControl(whichControl, location, NIL);     {User is dragging thumb}
            WIN_scrollBits;
          end;

        otherwise
            ;
        end
    end; {WIN_doProcessInControl}

  procedure WIN_doProcessInGrow; {(var windowPointedTo : WindowPtr ;location : Point)}
  {---------------------------------------------------------------------------------------}
  {RESIZE THE WINDOW AND SET UP APPROPRIATE PROCEDURE FOR                    }
  {UPDATING THE WINDOW AFTER A RESIZE IS DONE.                               }
  {---------------------------------------------------------------------------------------}
    var
      newSize : longInt; {Newsize holds the horizontal and vertical window size change as a result of GrowWindow toolbox call}
    begin
      newSize := GrowWindow(windowPointedTo, location, growArea);{Get newsize of the window from GrowWindow toolbox call}
      if newSize < > 0 then
        begin
          GLO_putUpClock;              {Wait...}
          SizeWindow(windowPointedTo, Loword(newSize), Hiword(newSize), true);
          WIN_moveScrollBar(windowPointedTo);     {Adjust scroll bars to new size}
          DrawGrowIcon(windowPointedTo);          {Put up grow icon}
          InvalRect(windowPointedTo^.portRect);  {Force update on the newly sized window}
          GLO_changeCursor;           {...Revert to arrow}
        end;
    end; {WIN_doProcessInGrow}

  procedure WIN_doUpdateWindow;                    {(var updateWindow : WindowPtr)}
  {---------------------------------------------------------------------------------------}
  {UPDATE THE WINDOW, WHICH INVOLVES MOSTLY REDRAWING THE INFORMATION IN THE WINDOW  }
  {---------------------------------------------------------------------------------------}
```

FIGURE 8-14 (Continued).

```
var
  tempPort : WindowPtr;                    {Temporary variable that holds the current grafport}
  tempWindowPeek : WindowPeek;             {Temporary variable to hold the windowPeek of the WIN_currentWindow}
  tempDrawingHandle : WIN_drawingDataHandle; {Temporary variable to hold the actual drawing data handle}
  tempRect : Rect;                         {The drawing Rectangle}
begin
  GLO_putUpClock;                 {Waiting...}
  GetPort(tempPort);              {Save current port}
  BeginUpdate(updateWindow);      {Begin update}
  SetPort(updateWindow);
  tempWindowPeek := WindowPeek(updateWindow);      {Type cast to windowPeek type}
  EraseRect(updateWindow^.portRect);               {Erase what was there, before}
  tempRect := updateWindow^.portRect;              {Compute the drawing rectangle to put bubble in}
  tempRect.bottom := tempRect.bottom - SBARWIDTH;
  tempRect.right := tempRect.right - SBARWIDTH;
  Hlock(tempWindowPeek^.dataHandle);        {Redisplay and redraw stuff in the window}
  tempDrawingHandle := WIN_drawingDataHandle(tempWindowPeek^.dataHandle); {Type cast to actual data handle}
  OffsetRect(tempRect, tempDrawingHandle^^.theOrigin.h, tempDrawingHandle^^.theOrigin.v);
  ClipRect(tempRect);                      {Make tempRect the clipping region of the window}
  SetOrigin(tempDrawingHandle^^.theOrigin.h, tempDrawingHandle^^.theOrigin.v); {Restore the current origin X, Y}
  DRA_redrawBubble(tempDrawingHandle^^.drawingRecord);        {Redraw the bubble}
  Hunlock(tempWindowPeek^.dataHandle);
  SetOrigin(0, 0);                         {To draw controls and growbox}
  ClipRect(updateWindow^.portRect);
  DrawControls(updateWindow);
  DrawGrowIcon(updateWindow);
  EndUpDate(updateWindow);                 {End update}
  SetPort(tempPort);                        {Restore port saved earlier}
  GLO_changeCursor;                        {...Restore arrow}
end; {WIN_doUpdateWindow}
procedure WIN_doActiveWindow;    {(targetWindow : WindowPtr);}
{-----------------------------------------------------------------------------------------}
{MAKE WINDOW ACTIVE BY SHOWING ALL CONTROLS.                                              }
{-----------------------------------------------------------------------------------------}
var
  tempWindowPeek : WindowPeek;             {Temporary variable to hold the windowPeek of the WIN_currentWindow}
begin
  SetPort(targetWindow);
  tempWindowPeek := WindowPeek(targetWindow);              {Type cast to windowPeek type}
  DrawGrowIcon(targetWindow);
  ShowControl(tempWindowPeek^.controlList);               {Horizontal scroll bar}
  ShowControl(tempWindowPeek^.controlList^^.nextControl); {Vertical scroll bar}
end; {WIN_doActiveWindow}
```

FIGURE 8-14 (Continued).

```
procedure WIN_doDeactiveWindow;     {(targetWindow : WindowPtr);}
{-------------------------------------------------------------------------------------------}
{MAKE WINDOW INACTIVE BY HIDING CONTROLS.                                                   }
{-------------------------------------------------------------------------------------------}
  var
    tempWindowPeek : WindowPeek;        {Temporary variable to hold the windowPeek of the WIN_currentWindow}
  begin
    tempWindowPeek := WindowPeek(targetWindow);     {Type cast to windowPeek type}
    HideControl(tempWindowPeek^.controlList);
    HideControl(tempWindowPeek^.controlList^^.nextControl);
  end; {WIN_doDeactiveWindow}
end.
```

FIGURE 8-14 (Continued).

Dialogs

Dialogs are special-purpose windows for entering input data into an application, observing computed values, editing values, and exercising control over the application. Dialogs can be modeless or modal. A *modeless* dialog permits events to occur outside of the dialog, such as pulling down a menu while the modeless dialog is on the desktop. A *modal* dialog, on the other hand, prohibits any other event until the user has disposed of the dialog.

Dialogs are used in almost all programs and support a variety of options. We will illustrate the most common options with an example that does nothing useful, but shows how to write a modestly sophisticated dialog that can be adapted to most real-world situations. The sample dialog unit shows how to:

- Implement a modal dialog containing icon, static and editable text, control buttons (push, radio, checkbox).
- Filter the minor events occurring in the dialog, that is, how to change the cursor and invert the icon while the user is scanning the dialog.
- Enter, edit, and get both text and numerical values from the user.
- Respond to push buttons.

We have thrown in some purely pedagogical "extras," such as *hiliting* — the process of making a control active/deactive by making it appear bright or dim in the dialog; and the process of drawing pictures in the dialog, an icon which can be manipulated by the user. (The word *hiliting* is a corrupted form of *highlighting*. Computer jargon is famous for corrupting natural language.)

First, a brief discussion of the theory of dialogs. Because dialogs are special windows, they look like windows. But the similarity does not go very far, because modal dialogs intercept the flow of events to the main event routine, something that windows do not do. In fact, when a dialog is made active, the dialog manager intercepts events and passes them on to the dialog routine called by the application. The intercepted events are processed by a minor event loop established by the dialog routine.

The minor event loop may be part of the application code if a *filter procedure* is specified. A filter procedure is any application routine that processes minor events such as keyboard inputs, mouse activities, disk activities, and so forth. In the sample, a filter routine called ShowFilter is used to change the arrow cursor into an IBeam — a text cursor — whenever the cursor passes over a data entry field. ShowFilter also inverts an icon whenever the cursor passes over the icon in the sample dialog.

If no filter procedure is specified in the application, then all minor events are processed by the dialog manager's filter routine. A standard feature of the dialog manager's filter routine is that it assumes item number one of the dialog to be an OK button, and that pressing the RETURN key is identical to pushing the OK button.

In the sample module described in Figures 8-15, 8-16, and 8-17, a single dialog is processed by an access procedure called DIA_ShowDialog. This routine uses an opaque filter procedure called ShowFilter to modify the cursor and icon during filtering. In addition, we describe only the actions of a modal dialog. The toolbox routine ModalDialog is called to process this dialog.

```
Type STR#
,1001
1
Bubble Flow

Type DLOG
SampleDialog,600
Sample Modal Dialog
50 50 200 320
InVisible NoGoAway
16
0
600

Type DITL
SampleItems,600
10
BtnItem Enabled
95 15 110 100
OK

BtnItem Enabled
120 15 135 100
Cancel

IconItem Disabled
5 15 37 47
257
```

FIGURE 8-15. Sample dialog module

StatText Disabled
15 100 35 300
^0

StatText Disabled
42 8 62 145
Edit w/Default

EditText Enabled
40 150 60 225
Default

StatText Disabled
64 6 84 148
Edit/No Default

EditText Enabled
65 150 85 225

RadioItem Enabled
89 154 104 220
Radio

ChkItem Enabled
108 154 123 220
Check

Type ALRT
CautionAlert,600
50 50 200 320
700
4577

Type DITL
CautionStuff,700
2
BtnItem Enabled
10 150 30 200
OK

StatText Disabled
75 10 90 230
Bad Input!

FIGURE 8-15 (Continued).

The sample dialog contains ten items: two push buttons (OK and CANCEL); an icon copied from the resource fork (#257); a static text field, which is inserted into the dialog when the dialog is displayed (^0); two data entry fields called EditText items (one to receive text and the other to receive numerical data); a radio button; and a checkbox item, see Figure 8-15.

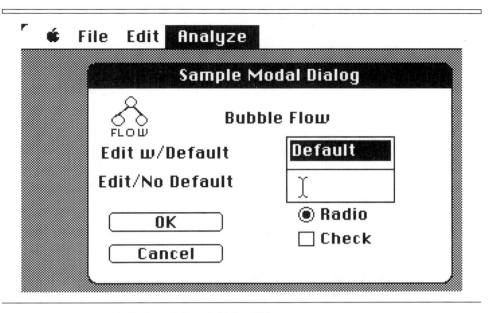

FIGURE 8-16. Graphical display of SampleDialog,600

FIGURE 8-17. Graphical display of CautionAlert,600

The dialog is nontrivial, because it must begin with a default entry in the first editable field, the radio button enabled and selected, and the checkbox item disabled. Furthermore, when the radio is selected, the checkbox must be hilited (enabled) and when the enabled checkbox is selected, a check mark is placed in the box. The radio and checkbox controls must toggle, so that when clicked a second time, the check mark disappears, see Figure 8-16.

Finally, this nontrivial dialog has an error alert associated with it. When the user selects CANCEL instead of OK, a Caution alert box appears, as shown in Figure 8-17. The first time the alert appears, three beeps are heard. On the fourth time, no beep is heard.

The dialog and alert structure is specified in the resource text shown in Figure 8-15. Carefully study this specification and compare it with the objects shown in Figures 8-16 and 8-17 before you study the source programs.

The DIALOG module is mostly glue code — instructions for pulling together the toolbox routines in some meaningful way, see Figure 8-18. We have used routines to load the dialog into RAM from the disk resource fork, access items within the dialog, and manipulate controls such as buttons. The most difficult part to understand is the interaction between ModalDialog and ShowFilter. When ModalDialog is called, it passes control to ShowDialog, which handles minor events for awhile. Then ShowFilter terminates and passes control back to ModalDialog. If ShowDialog returns FALSE, ModalDialog continues to handle the minor events. If ShowFilter returns TRUE, ModalDialog terminates, also. ModalDialog is activated once for each event, including a single keypress or mouse-down event.

```
unit DIALOGS;
interface
  procedure DIA_showDialog (var aString : Str255;
    var aNumber : longint;
    var Result : boolean);          {TRUE= OK button, FALSE = Cancel button}
implementation
{----------------------------------------------------------------}
{CONSTANTS FOR DIALOG UNIT                                       }
{----------------------------------------------------------------}
  const
    ICON_ID = 3;                    {Icon in upper left corner is item #3}
    EDIT_DEFAULT_TEXT_ID = 6;       {First Edit Text Field is item #6}
    EDIT_NUM_ID = 8;                {Second Edit Field -- numeral -- is item #8}
    HILITE_ON = 0;                  {Brighten control}
    HILITE_OFF = 255;              {Dim control}
  function ShowFilter (theDialogPtr : DialogPtr;
            var theEvent : EventRecord;
            var itemHit : integer) : boolean;
```

FIGURE 8-18. Dialog unit in Bubble Flow application

```
var
  MouseLocation : Point;              {Where the cursor is at all times}
  itemHdl : Handle;                   {Returned by GetDItem}
  itemType : integer;                 {Returned by GetDItem}
  iconRect, StringRect, NumRect : Rect;   {Working Rects}
  IconHdl : Handle;                   {Used to Brighten or Dim icon}
  TextCursor : CursHandle;            {Temporary to get IBeamCursor}
begin
  ShowFilter := false;                {ModalDialog handles events when ShowFilter is False}
  {Get Rect's of icon, aString and aNumber from GetDItem...}
  GetDItem(theDialogPtr, EDIT_DEFAULT_TEXT_ID, itemType, itemHdl, StringRect);
  GetDItem(theDialogPtr, EDIT_NUM_ID, itemType, itemHdl, NumRect);
  GetDItem(theDialogPtr, ICON_ID, itemType, IconHdl, iconRect); {Get iconRect}
  case theEvent.What of
    nullEvent :              {User is just scanning the dialog...}
      begin
        GetMouse(mouseLocation);{Where is cursor, now ?}
        if PtInRect(mouseLocation, IconRect) then
          begin
            InvertRect(iconRect);                    {Icon inverts when pointed at}
          end
        else
          PlotIcon(iconRect, IconHdl);               {Restore as original}

        if PtInRect(mouseLocation, StringRect) or PtInRect(mouseLocation, NumRect) then
          begin
            TextCursor := GetCursor(IBeamCursor);   {Change to IBeam}
            SetCursor(TextCursor^^)
          end
        else
          begin
            SetCursor(arrow);                        {Revert to Arrow}
          end;
      end; {nullEvent}
    KeyDown, AutoKey :     {Keyboard action ?}
      begin
        {Ignore Keys: User must Push OK or CANCEL button to exit Dialog}
      end;
    otherwise
      ;
  end; {CASE}
end; {ShowFilter}
```

FIGURE 8-18 (Continued).

```
procedure DIA_showDialog;
  const
    SHOWDIALOG_ID = 600;      {Resource ID of the dialog}
    WARNING_ID = 600;         {Resource ID of Caution Alert}
    OK_ID = 1;                {OK button is item #1}
    CANCEL_ID = 2;            {Cancel button is item #2}
  {Items 3,4,5 are Icon, "BubbleFlow" message, and Edit/w Default, resp.}
    RADIO_ID = 9;             {Radio is item # 9}
    RADIO_ON = 1;             {Turn-on Radio}
    RADIO_OFF = 0;            {Turn-off Radio}
    CHECK_ID = 10;            {Check box is item # 10}
    CHECK_ON = 1;             {Turn-on Check box}
    CHECK_OFF = 0;            {Turn-off Check box}
    STRING_LIST_ID = 1001;    {String from Resource}
    BUBBLE_FLOW_MSG = 1;      {Message: 'Bubble Flow'}
  var
    theDialogPtr : DialogPtr;     {Points to the dialog in RAM}
    itemHit : integer;        {Which item ?}
    theString : Str255;           {From Resource Fork}
    ItemType : integer;       {Type returned by GetDItem}
    itemRect : Rect;              {Rectangle returned by GetDItem}
    TextHdl : Handle;             {Text item returned by GetDItem}
    Check_itemHdl : Handle;       {Check box handle returned by GetDItem}
    Radio_itemHdl : Handle;       {Radio handle returned by GetDItem}
    itemHdl : ControlHandle;      {Handle returned by GetDItem, then cast}
  begin
    theDialogPtr := GetNewDialog(SHOWDIALOG_ID, NIL, Pointer(-1)); {Put it in Front}
    {Set up Dialog before it is displayed}
    GetIndString(theString, STRING_LIST_ID, BUBBLE_FLOW_MSG);           {Get text from 'STR#' resource}
    ParamText(theString, '', '', '');                                  {Insert theString into theDialog}
    SellText(theDialogPtr, EDIT_DEFAULT_TEXT_ID, 0, 255);              {Select the default -- reverse video --}
    GetDItem(theDialogPtr, RADIO_ID, itemType, Radio_itemHdl, itemRect); {Get itemHdl of radio}
    SetCtlValue(ControlHandle(Radio_itemHdl), RADIO_OFF);              {Initially, deselect radio}
    GetDItem(theDialogPtr, CHECK_ID, itemType, Check_itemHdl, itemRect); {Get itemHdl of checkbox}
    SetCtlValue(ControlHandle(Check_itemHdl), CHECK_OFF);              {Initially, deselect checkbox}
    HiliteControl(ControlHandle(Check_itemHdl), HILITE_OFF);          {Dim checkbox }
    ShowWindow(theDialogPtr);                                          {In case the INVISIBLE bit is set in resource fork}
    SetPort(theDialogPtr);                                             {Work in the Dialog coordinates}
    repeat
      ModalDialog(@ShowFilter, itemHit);              {Filtered Modal Dialog}
      case itemHit of

        RADIO_ID :
          begin
            itemHdl := ControlHandle(Radio_itemHdl);        {Cast reference to radio}
            if GetCtlValue(itemHdl) = RADIO_ON then
```

FIGURE 8-18 (Continued).

```
                begin
                   SetCtlValue(itemHdl, RADIO_OFF);              {Reverse Selection}
                   HiliteControl(ControlHandle(Check_itemHdl), HILITE_OFF);  {Dim checkbox}
                end
             else
                begin
                   HiliteControl(ControlHandle(Check_itemHdl), HILITE_ON);  {Hilight checkbox}
                   SetCtlValue(itemHdl, RADIO_ON);
                end;
             end;

       CHECK_ID :
          begin
             itemHdl := ControlHandle(Check_itemHdl);       {Cast reference to radio}
             if GetCtlValue(itemHdl) CHECK_ON then

                SetCtlValue(itemHdl, CHECK_OFF)            {Reverse Selection}
             else
                SetCtlValue(ItemHdl, CHECK_ON);
          end;

       otherwise
          ;
       end; {Case}

    until itemHit in [CANCEL_ID, OK_ID];
    Result := (itemHit = OK_ID);            {Returns TRUE if OK, FALSE if CANCEL}
    if Result then                          {Return aString and aNumber, if valid}
       begin
          {EDIT_DEFAULT_TEXT_ID }
          GetDItem(theDialogPtr, EDIT_DEFAULT_TEXT_ID, itemType, TextHdl, itemRect);
          GetIText(TextHdl, aString);             {Returns aString}
          {EDIT_NUM_ID }
          GetDItem(theDialogPtr, EDIT_NUM_ID, itemType, TextHdl, itemRect);
          GetIText(TextHdl, theString);
          StringToNum(theString, aNumber);       {Convert to Long Integer}
       end
    else          {Return null and 0}
       begin
          aString := '';
          aNumber := 0;
          itemHit := CautionAlert(WARNING_ID, NIL);  {Tell user, values may be bad}
       end;

    DisposDialog(theDialogPtr);                    {Remove from screen and RAM}

  end; {DIA_showDialog;}

end.
```

FIGURE 8-18 (Continued).

A brief explanation of the process of putting up a dialog and filtering it follows.

When DIA_showDialog is called, Toolbox routine GetNewDialog copies the dialog's specification into RAM, and since its Visible bit is set, the dialog does *not* appear on the screen. Instead, the specification is modified on the fly: string 1 of STR# resource 1001 is copied from the resource fork into the BUBBLE_FLOW_MSG field of the dialog; the EDIT_DEFAULT_TEXT field is selected (you can see this from the dialog because it is reversed white on black); the radio and check control items are deselected; and the disabled checkbox is dimmed to indicate that the user cannot select it.

The modified dialog in RAM is now displayed on the screen, and the current graphics port is selected so that the application can draw into the dialog. The minor event loop can now be entered and dialog events processed.

Since the sample illustrates a modal dialog, the ModalDialog toolbox routine is called with ShowFilter as the filter routine. If we had not desired a filter routine, a nil pointer would have been used in place of the @ShowFilter pointer. ModalDialog and ShowFilter return the number of the item selected by the user when the minor event loop executed.

In ShowFilter, preparations are made to handle several events: the nullEvent occurs when the user has done nothing; the KeyDown and AutoKey events occur when the user presses a keyboard key. Since ShowFilter is concerned with only the icon and the two editable fields, the graphic locations of these three items in the dialog are retrieved and stored in Rect structures.

ShowFilter handles one event at a time, the event passed to it by ModalDialog. If no event has occurred, the nullEvent case simply examines the location of the mouse to see if it is in the rectangle containing the icon or in either of the two fields. If in the icon rectangle, that rectangle is inverted, causing it to "flutter" while the cursor is pointed at the icon. If the cursor is in one of the two editable fields, the cursor is changed from an arrow to an IBeam, indicating that the user can edit the field of text.

When ShowFilter terminates, control returns to ModalDialog, where input characters or button pushing events are processed one at a time. Suppose, for example, that the user presses the radio button. Looking in the DIA_ShowDialog routine once again, we see that this event is processed by one of the case clauses following the call to ModalDialog. The control is turned on if it had been off, or is turned off if it had been on. Also, the Checkbox control is enabled or disabled, accordingly. The HiliteControl toolbox routine toggles the Checkbox between enabled (bright) and disabled (dim) states.

ModalDialog is called repeatedly until the user presses either OK or CANCEL. If OK is pressed, the text in the first field is passed back as a string and the text in the second field is converted into an integer before being passed back. If CANCEL is pressed the Caution Alert is displayed to warn the user, and the return parameters are set to harmless values.

Finally, the dialog is removed from the screen and from RAM. All space taken up by the dialog and its various items is reclaimed by the memory manager. Alternately, the dialog could have been removed from the screen, but not from RAM.

Obviously, additional dialogs require additional routines in this unit to process user interactions. This sample can be used as a guide for writing similar dialog processing code.

File Processing

A complete description of file processing is beyond the scope of this book. Instead, we illustrate a fundamental cliche, the basis for more sophisticated file processing. The FILE_flow unit contains a simple open and close access procedure, see Figure 8-19. These two procedures are very simple. They only work on a text file, and they read the entire file into memory during the FIL_doOpen operation, and they write the entire file to disk during the FIL_doClose operation. Partial file I/O operations are left as an exercise for the reader.

```
unit FILE_flow;
interface

{Access Procedures -- visible outside of object -- forfile objects}
procedure FIL_doOpen (Where : Point;             {Location of SFGetFile Dialog}
                var fName : Str255;               {Returned File Name}
                var Length_Of_File : LongInt;     {Number of bytes in File -- to RAM}
                var DataHdl : Handle);            {Handle to RAM holding file}

procedure FIL_doSave (Where : Point;             {Location of SFPutFile Dialog}
                Length_Of_File : LongInt;         {Number of bytes in RAM -- to File}
                var DataHdl : Handle);            {Handle to RAM holding file}

implementation
  var
    FileRefNum : integer;      {The object -- a file}

  procedure FileIOErr (result : OSErr);
  {--------------------------------------------------------------------------------------------------------------}
  {Opaque operation which handles all file I/O errors. Calls an error alert #600. Must be enhanced to handle all possibilities  }
  {--------------------------------------------------------------------------------------------------------------}
    const
      FILE_ERROR_ID = 600;       {Resource Id of error alert}
    var
      void : integer;            {Temporary for StopAlert}
    begin
      if result < > noErr then
        void := StopAlert(FILE_ERROR_ID, NIL);
    end; {FileIOErr}

procedure FIL_doOpen;
{--------------------------------------------------------------------------------------------------------------}
{Gets file name from SFGetFile Dialog, Opens File, Reads entire file into RAM, and Closes File. Returns Length and Handle  }
{--------------------------------------------------------------------------------------------------------------}
```

FIGURE 8-19. File unit in Bubble Flow application

```
    var
      theReply : SFReply;                  {Returned by SFGetFile}
      theTypeList : SFTypeList;            {For Filtering the names}
      result : OSErr;                      {Error message number}
    begin
      theTypeList[0] := 'TEXT';          {Filter out all but text files}
      SFGetFile(Where, 'Not Used', nil, 1, theTypeList, NIL, theReply); {Return theReply...}
      if theReply.good then           {...unless, of course, the user selected CANCEL}
        begin
          result := FSOpen(theReply.fName, theReply.vRefNum, FileRefNum); {Open, Return FileRefNum}
          if result = noErr then
            begin
              result := GetEOF(FileRefNum, Length_Of_File);              {Return Length of file in bytes}
              if result = noErr then
                begin
                  HLock(DataHdl);                                        {Lock RAM, Read ENTIRE file into RAM}
                  result := FSRead(FileRefNum, Length_Of_File, DataHdl^); {Read into RAM}
                  HunLock(DataHdl);
                  result := FSClose(FileRefNum);                         {Close, when done}
                end;
            end; {Read}
          FileIOErr(result);               {Could have had an error result somewhere along the way...}
        end; {SFGetFile}

    end; {FIL_doOpen}

procedure FIL_doSave;
{------------------------------------------------------------------------------------------------------------}
{Open or Create File, Write entire file from RAM to disk, Close File. Does not Return Error Messages, however.  }
{------------------------------------------------------------------------------------------------------------}

    var
      theReply : SFReply;      {Returned by SFGetFile}
      result : OSErr;          {Error message number}
      FileInfo : FInfo;        {From File Control Block}

    begin
      SFPutFile(Where, 'Save as ...', 'Default File Name', NIL, theReply);    {Display Dialog, Return theReply}
      if theReply.good then                                                  {User could select CANCEL}
        begin
          result := GetFInfo(theReply.fName, theReply.vRefNum, FileInfo);     {Does File already Exist?}
          case result of

            noErr : {File exists, already, check its type...}
              begin
                result := ord(FileInfo.fdType < > 'TEXT');                    {Make sure it is of correct type}
              end; {noErr}
```

FIGURE 8-19 (Continued).

```
        FNFErr :                                          {FNFErr=File Not Found Error}
          begin {Create a new file...}
            result := Create(theReply.fName, theReply.vRefNum, 'BUBL', 'TEXT'); {Creator='BUBL', type='TEXT'}
          end;
        otherwise
          ;
        end; {Case}
        if result = noErr then        {Either it exists, or was created...}
          begin
            result := FSOpen(theReply.fName, theReply.vRefNum, FileRefNum); {Return FileRefNum}
            if result = noErr then
              begin
                HLock(DataHdl);
                result := FSWrite(FileRefNum, Length_Of_File, DataHdl^);      {Write from RAM}
                HunLock(DataHdl);
                if result = noErr then
                  result := FSClose(FileRefNum);        {The WHOLE thing was in RAM, now it is on Disk}
              end; {Write & Close}
          end; {Open}

        FileIOErr(result);                              {result could be an error condition...}
      end; {SFPutFile}

    end; {FIL_doSave}

  {End of Unit}
  end.
```

FIGURE 8-19 (Continued).

The most important aspect of this illustration is the use of two standard user interface dialogs, one for opening a file and another for selecting a file to save into, see Figure 8-20. The SFGetFile and SFPutFile toolbox routines should always be used to capture the user's selection. An application should never force the user to enter a filename without telling what choices are available.

These two toolbox routines produce a standard dialog recognized by every user as a standard file "minifinder." The toolbox takes care of everything else including disk initialization and errors in the event that a bad diskette is inserted into the drive. This not only saves much time and effort on the part of the application programmer, but also presents an understandable interface to users.

Files are unstructured. They are simply long strings of characters, including carriage returns, line feeds, and so forth. When a file is opened, a file pointer is positioned at the beginning of the file, ready to read the first character. If an FSRead operation is intended, one or more characters are copied into a buffer in RAM pointed to by a data handle. The RAM space must be allocated from the application's heap prior to the read operation.

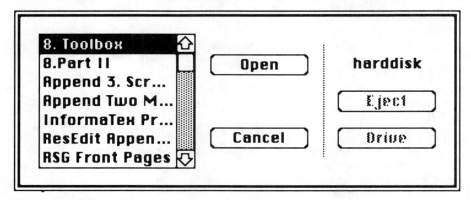

SFGetFile Dialog

Every file is opened by first selecting the desired file from all files that match the requested type. This is done by viewing every file of a given type through a dialog containing a "minifinder" window.

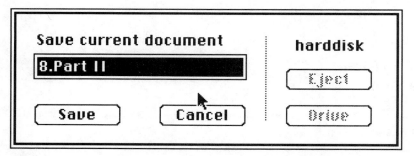

SFPutFile Dialog

Each time a file is saved to disk, the user should be told what the assumed name is, shown here as "8.Part II," and given an opportunity to change the name, volume, and so on.

FIGURE 8-20. Standard file dialog

If an FSWrite operation is intended, one or more characters are copied from the RAM buffer pointed at by the data handle, and the characters are copied to the disk file. (Actually, the action does not always take place immediately following the execution of the procedure. Sometimes the buffer must be "flushed" to force the data onto the disk.) The RAM pointed at by the data handle must be released to reclaim the heap space.

The simple FILE_flow cliche does minimal checking for errors and assumes the entire file will fit into RAM. Additional file operations such as paging segments of the file into memory on a "demand page" basis, indexing, and record I/O (with records per the usual

Pascal technique), must be supplied by the application programmer. A number of commercially available "file systems" should be (re)used, however, rather than starting from the primitives shown in Figure 8-19.

Printing and other forms of input and output are done very much like file I/O. For example, speech output is done by opening a pseudo-file to the speech device. An excerpt from a speech cliche is similar to ordinary file output, see Figure 8-21.

Direct Manipulation

Direct manipulation of user interface objects — dragging, for instance — is one of the best forms of "user friendliness." A brief cliche shows how to drag a graphical object drawn in a window. Consider the single "bubble" described earlier in the FLOW sample program.

A rectangle is any rectangular area in a window (or any graphic drawing area, also known as a port). Rectangles are defined by their upper left and lower right corner coordinates. Rectangles are used to draw "connected" objects such as circles and squares, and "enclosed" objects. Regions, on the other hand, may be disconnected collections of drawings such as two or more squares, circles, or irregular objects. Bounded regions are collections of drawings with a known, encompassing boundary. Regions can be directly manipulated by "dragging" them using the toolbox routine DragGrayRgn.

```
var
    numCharacters : integer;              {How many chars to say}
    result : SpeechErr;                   {Result code}
    theSpeech : SpeechHandle;             {Handle to Speech Manager}
    SoundOut : Handle;                    {Output from Speech Manager}

begin
    result := SpeechOn('', theSpeech);    {Initialize the Speech Manager}
    ...                                   {Do other things, like get English words to say...}
    SoundOut := NewHandle(0);             {Get some heap space for Speech Manager}
    result := Reader(theSpeech, dataHandle^, numCharacters, SoundOut);  {Convert English to Phonemes}
    result := MacinTalk(theSpeech, SoundOut);  {Say it out loud}
    ...                                   {Do other things appropriate for the application}
    SpeechOff(theSpeech);                 {Close Speech Manager}
    DisposHandle(SoundOut);               {Reclaim heap space}
    ...
end;
```

FIGURE 8-21. Speech I/O example

```
begin
    DragObject := NewRgn;                                      {Allocate heap space}
    OpenRgn;                                                   {Capture drawing in heap space}
    FrameOval(Object.bubblePositionRect);                     {Must be a framed object}
    CloseRgn(DragObject);                                      {Got it!}
    SlopRect := DrawingRect;                                   {Use the whole thing}
    LimitRect := SlopRect;                                     {Not very fancy}
    OffSet := DragGrayRgn(DragObject, MouseLocation, LimitRect, SlopRect, 0, nil);
    DisposeRgn(DragObject);                                    {Reclaim heap space}
    EraseRect(Object.bubblePositionRect);                     {Erase original object}
    {Compute new location of object, and re-draw it}
    OffSetRect(Object.bubblePositionRect, LoWord(OffSet), HiWord(OffSet));
    FrameOval(Object.bubblePositionRect);                     {Re-draw in the new position}
end;
```

FIGURE 8-22. Dragging example

DragGrayRgn is given a region containing an object to drag, its location, and some boundaries, including a limit boundary that defines the rectangular area on the screen where the object can be dragged, and a "slop" rectangle, which prevents pieces of a large object from being "slopped" over the edge of the limit rectangle. Since DragGrayRgn only manipulates regions, it is often necessary to map a rectangle to a region. This technique is demonstrated using toolbox routines OpenRgn and CloseRgn to capture the object in a draggable region called DragObject, see Figure 8-22. The object is passed to this cliche as Object.bubblePositionRect: a rectangle containing the circular bubble. The location of this rectangle is changed to the new location of the dragged object.

GRABBAG: A PROGRAMMER'S DATABASE

Keeping track of thousands of cliches that might be useful in any number of applications can be a difficult and time-consuming part of the software development process. In fact, unless the library of cliches is easily accessible, programmers may not even bother to

use a cliche to avoid re-inventing it. Clearly, programmers need an on-line database of cliches and other useful fragments that is easy to understand, quick to access, and always present. GrabBag is an example of a simple programmer's database containing the cliches discussed in the previous sections of this chapter.

In this section we illustrate only a portion of GrabBag's cliches, and show how a programmer uses the GrabBag desk accessory to quickly look up and copy pieces of code into a new application. The collection of reusable components includes initialization routines useful for starting an application; event processing code used to handle user interaction events; menu, window, dialog, and alert routines; and a number of other helpful cliches.

The network structure of GrabBag is an interesting feature. Cliches are organized in a directed acyclic graph structure that permits a hierarchical search for each cliche, see Figure 8-23. This structure makes it quick and easy to find the right cliche, read it, and if it is useful, copy it into an editor.

The hierarchical structure of GrabBag databases consists of categories and modules at each node of the structure and access paths at each arc. A category (shown as rectangular boxes in Figure 8-23) is a classification or index used to classify the group of cliches underneath it. A module is shown simply as a named "leaf" in the tree-like directed acyclic graph. (The graph is acyclic because it is possible that more than one path leads to a module from the root of the "tree".)

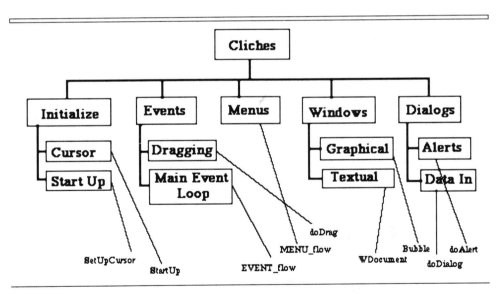

FIGURE 8-23. Directed acyclic graphic structure of GrabBag

A database is searched by clicking on appropriate categories and following the path leading to a module. When a module is found, it is displayed. The code in a module can be copied into the system Clipboard and pasted into any other application. Thus, a programmer can find and copy the desired source code routines into any text editor.

GrabBag databases are searched by clicking on categories listed in two windows, see Figure 8-24. The window on the left contains a "trace" of previously selected categories: clicking on one of these causes backtracking to previous nodes of the graph. The window on the right contains a list of optional categories: selecting one of these moves the search forward. For example, clicking on DRAGGING causes the next level in the hierarchy to be accessed. Eventually the path leads to a module containing code. The programmer can select from one of several options, see Figure 8-25.

Modules can be modified in place, but the database is "read-only." That is, all changes are ignored by the database. But the modifications can be copied into a work file and used by another application.

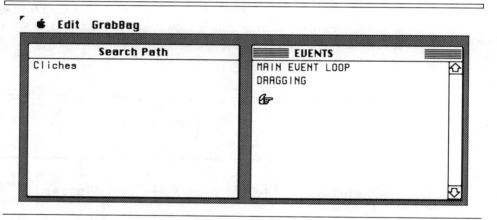

FIGURE 8-24. Navigating a GrabBag database

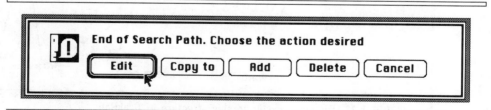

FIGURE 8-25. Operations allowed on a reusable module

The programmer's database is maintained by a separate administrative application that permits addition of categories, extension of the database by splitting categories, linking categories to existing modules, and so forth, see Figure 8-26. For example, a new link might be added from a category to a module so that searching is much faster. In some cases, a direct link from a high-level category to a low-level module can shorten the time taken to find a frequently reused module.

The database can be extended in two ways: by adding new modules and by adding new categories. When a new category is added, it can be inserted at the lowest level in the directed graph, or it can be added to the interior of the graph. When added to the interior, an existing node is modified by inserting the new category into the node. The new category must have at least one module attached.

A node can be split whenever the granularity of categories seems inadequate to classify the modules properly. Thus, the database may start off containing broad classifications such as MENU and DIALOG, and end up over time containing more narrow categories such as MENU HILIGHT, MENU DISABLE, MENU SELECT, and DIALOG SHOW, DIALOG DISPOSE, and so forth.

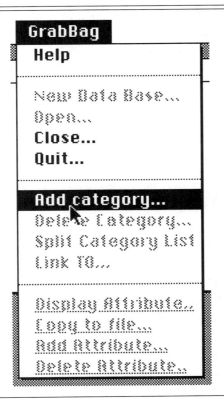

FIGURE 8-26. GrabBag database operations

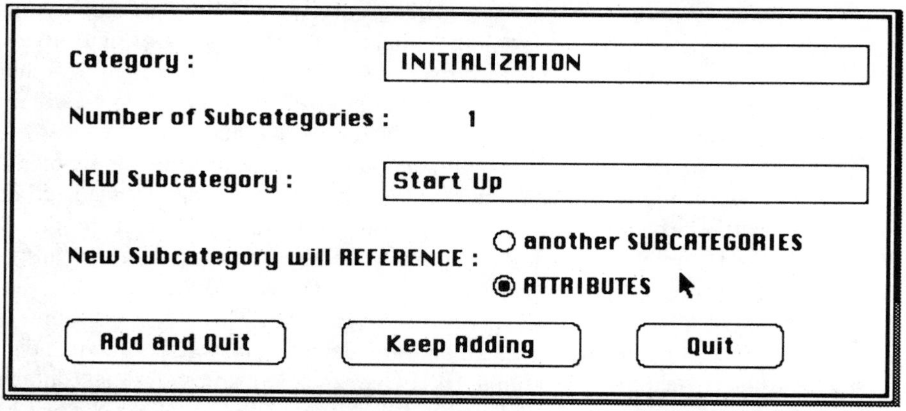

FIGURE 8-27. Adding a category to GrabBag

The dialog shown in Figure 8-27 illustrates how the database administration program captures a category. The program builds an internal list structure representing the directed acyclic graph. This "index" is saved along with the text of all cliches in the database. Different databases can be created for different programming languages, classes of applications, and so on.

CLICHE PROGRAMMING

The Macintosh radically altered the way software is developed because of the high demands it places on the programmer to write applications that use a standard interface. The impact of user interface standardization is directly responsible for:

- Direct manipulation in place of lexical command languages
- User-directed control of the application, leading to event-loop style of programming
- International "universality" of the interface, leading to the idea of a resource file that is easily altered even after the application is compiled
- Organization of files according to creator and type, so that confusion is lowered
- Common acceptance of a "high standard" of excellence in the user interface, thus forcing applications to be more sophisticated

These factors mean that every application is expected to do certain things, such as menus, windows, and direct manipulation wherever possible. Further, intuitive operations are the rule, not the exception. The impact on programmers is extreme. To offset the high level of effort needed to produce such demanding applications, programmers have devised cliches, highly useful but routine pieces of code, for doing all sorts of "standard" things.

Cliches go beyond the standard user interface routines found in the toolbox. They are collections of medium-level routines likely to be found in every application. In the Macintosh environment, as in most systems that adopt a standard user interface paradigm, cliches can be very powerful in reducing development time and cost.

Cliches and Reusable Components

Using reusable components at any level of programming can dramatically improve programmer productivity if the reusable components can be easily accessed and understood. Access is provided by a programmer's database such as MacMan (see Appendix B), and GrabBag. However, the accessed cliche must be easily understood, because it most likely will need modification. The utility of GrabBag is tied to the ability of programmers to comprehend the source text of each cliche. In the next chapter we will examine techniques for writing code that is easy to understand, and therefore of greater value to the maintenance and development programmer. In subsequent chapters we will describe even more advanced tools for program comprehension (see page 406).

Terms and Concepts

active window
bundle
cliche
command line interpreter
compiled resource
creator
DA
data fork
direct manipulation
event loop
event queue
filter function

finder
handle
hiliting
launch
main event loop
modal dialog
modeless dialog
multifinder
resource file
resource fork
type

DISCUSSION QUESTIONS

1. What is a main event loop, and why is it needed in a system like the Macintosh?

2. Write a program to enter data into a file consisting of three fields: NAME, SEX, and AGE. Specify the menu and dialog to be used in the application as a text resource file. Draw a picture of the screen display showing how the menu and dialog will appear in the running application.

3. Explain how hiliting and disabling menu items can be used to approximate a hierarchical menu system.

4. What is the purpose of modal and modeless dialogs?

5. Write a program that opens a window, draws a rectangular box in the window, and then allows the user to drag the box around within the window. Implement scroll bars for both horizontal and vertical pan. What happens in your program when the user drags the rectangle beyond the bounds of the viewing area?

6. Modify an existing application program by changing all menu items: 1) Change the words and phrases used in the menus; 2) Add icons to one or more of the menu items; and 3) Change the attributes of at least one menu item so that it contains bold letters. (Hint: Use a resource editor like ResEdit — see Appendix A.)

7. Implement one of the projects listed in chapter seven.

8. Design and implement an Alert that goes through four different stages of beeping and defaulting.

9. Explain how a user can get a non-TEXT file to become recognized as a TEXT file by some word processing application. Explain the difference between file Creator and Type signatures.

10. How is a double-click detected by an application? How does an application know the difference between one and two clicks of the mouse?

REFERENCES AND FURTHER READING

1. 1988. *Inside Macintosh*, 5 vols. Reading, MA: Addison-Wesley Pub. Co.

9

Implementation

PREVIEW

We introduce the programming environment, a CASE tool for coding. This tool is an integrated editor, compiler, linker, and debugging system that keeps track of details like the build order of an application, syntactic errors, and which statement is executing.

We then emphasize the importance of coding standards and of writing maintainable code. Observation of a handful of simple coding conventions can greatly improve the lot of the maintenance programmer.

Structured programming and structured programs are shown to be different things. A structured program is an artifact of the process of structured programming. However, there are many forms of structure in a program. We show that an SESE-structured program is reducible according to certain rules that govern the power of a programming language.

Finally, we present another CASE tool for checking the style of a source program and making qualitative recommendations for improvement.

PROGRAMMING SUPPORT ENVIRONMENTS

The **implementation phase** of the waterfall model of the software lifecycle *is the period of time during which a software product is created from design documents and debugged.* Recall that **implementation** is defined as *a realization of an abstraction in more concrete terms: a machine-executable form of an application program, or a form of a program that can be translated automatically to machine-executable form.* Implementation is the *process* of translating a design into code and debugging the code. The *artifact* of implementation is the application's source code.

A well-planned and carefully controlled implementation phase obeys one or more **implementation requirements** — *any requirement that impacts or constrains the implementation of a software design.* For example, design descriptions, software development standards, programming language requirements, and software quality assurance standards are often specified prior to coding to guarantee a successful implementation. *The requirement imposed in this book is simply to code for maintainability.* Exactly how this is achieved is the focus of the last half of this chapter.

Implementation is usually done under the umbrella of a CASE tool such as a Program Support Environment (PSE). A **program support environment** *is a tool for producing the principle artifact of an application — its source code.*

This is *not* a generally accepted definition of PSE. In fact there are many alternate definitions of a PSE, some of which are discussed below.

The standard definition given by the IEEE supports the modern view of a PSE as an integrated set of tools: *an integrated collection of tools accessed via a single command language to provide programming support capabilities throughout the software lifecycle. Typically, the environment includes tools for designing, editing, compiling, loading, testing, configuration management, and project management*[1].

Charette[2] defines a software engineering environment more generally: *the process, methods, and automation required to produce a software system.* This broad definition might also satisfy our definition for CASE. We use a much more restricted definition which concentrates on the code production phase of the lifecycle.

Birrell and Ould[3] consider UNIX a universal environment for program development, while the Ada environment called APSE (Ada Program Support Environment) is centered on a database containing programs and other objects of interest to the programmer. These definitions are tied to a particular implementation, and are not general.

Tully[4] adds that a PSE is more than a collection of tools. A PSE must provide a means for exchanging information among the tools, projects, and programmers. He lists nine attractive features of a PSE:

1. Universality — the PSE must work with diverse languages, application domains, and methods.
2. Adaptability — the PSE must be configurable so adaptable instances of the PSE are possible.
3. Openness — the PSE can be extended by adding new tools after the PSE is generated.
4. Reuse — the PSE must support indexing and accessing of reusable modules.

EVOLUTION OF PROGRAMMING ENVIRONMENTS

Programming tools began to emerge soon after the first computer hardware was constructed. First, simple coding tools such as line editors, assemblers, cross-reference listing generators, and loaders were invented, followed by high-level languages, operating systems, linkers, and breakpoint-based binary debuggers.

The overall balance of software to hardware costs changed from 15:85 in 1955 to 85:15 by 1985. As the "programming problem" began to account for more and more of the cost of system implementation, "workbench" tools such as MAKE, screen editors, linking loaders, and symbolic debuggers began to appear. These tools accelerated the steps needed to recompile after a modification, observe program behavior during execution, and debug separate modules effectively.

By the late 1970s, early *programming support environments* (PSE) began to appear. They combined syntax-directed editors, interpreters, incremental compilers, and integrated debugging tools into a coordinated "suite" of productivity enhancers. While syntax-directed editing was found to be overly restrictive by most programmers, the notion of a programming environment was widely accepted and progress toward further integration of tools began.

Integrated PSEs became widely used in the 1980s — incorporating a single "shell" consisting of edit-compile-link-go steps with built-in MAKE and automatic debugging tools. The edit tool performs syntax checking as each statement is entered, performs compiling and linking incrementally, and processes the program in memory, so execution is immediate. Such PSEs give the illusion of a seamless, interpretive development environment.

Full-Lifecycle Integrated PSEs are still evolving today. They encompass requirements, design, coding, testing, and maintenance phases. Some systems are capable of *reverse engineering* — backward development of the specifications documents after modifications to the source code.

---

5. Self-Control — the PSE must guarantee correctness and consistency of operation.

6. Database — the PSE should enclose a database which is used to store and manipulate program artifacts.

7. Quality — the PSE must enhance the quality of the software products produced from it.

8. User Attractiveness — programmers must want to use the PSE.

9. Market Attractiveness — the PSE must quantitatively improve programmer productivity.

Tully's list is far too ambitious to be realized in the near future, but it does give an idea of the goal of all PSEs. In the meantime, less comprehensive PSEs are being used by programmers to enhance coding productivity. We describe one representative PSE widely used by Macintosh programmers.

Think Pascal Programming Support Environment

Think Pascal (TP) is a Pascal program support environment for the Macintosh personal computer[5]. TP supports the full toolbox of the Macintosh and integrates editing, compiling, linking and loading, testing and debugging, and project management tools.

The editing tool is a free-style, multi-window, syntax-checking editor fully integrated into the PSE so that errors can be pointed out by the PSE during execution. Source code can be directly entered into an editing window or imported from any text file. Syntax errors are indicated as soon as the statement is entered into the source program. However, the editor is not a syntax-directed editor — the programmer can enter any syntactic structure. Errors are flagged by outlining the offending tokens.

The compiler incrementally translates applications into one of two forms: as an encapsulated application run under the control of the PSE; and as a stand-alone "launchable" application that resides on the desktop like all other applications. Desk accessories can also be constructed. A resource file can be associated with the application through a "run time option," thus allowing application resources such as windows and dialogs to co-exist with the windows and dialogs of TP.

Modifications force recompiling and automatic linking of only those Pascal **unit**s that are affected by the modified unit. This facility is implemented through the PROJECT, a list of units provided by the programmer in the order they must be compiled and linked. The PROJECT facility only partially implements an automatic MAKE; the programmer must provide the initial list of units in the proper order.

Linking and loading is done "behind the programmer's back" and is transparent. Each time a unit is compiled, it is linked to the unit(s) that "uses" it. If a unit has previously been linked, and no modifications have been made to it, the compile and link step is skipped.

Testing and debugging is done with the assistance of a number of symbolic and low-level tools. Applications can be run in several modes: GO mode runs the application while it is being monitored by TP to catch errors and so forth; STEP runs the application in single step mode, one statement at a time; GO-GO runs the application in sprints, full speed to the next STOP breakpoint; TRACE uses a pointing "finger" to point out each statement as it is executed. Additional, low-level debugging tools are also provided but will not be discussed here.

The focal point of all TP applications is the PROJECT, which is controlled by the PROJECT menu containing NEW, OPEN, CLOSE, ADD, REMOVE, BUILD & SAVE AS..., VIEW OPTIONS..., RUN OPTIONS..., and SOURCE OPTIONS..., see Figure 9-1.

An existing or new project is loaded into the PSE by selecting OPEN or NEW from this menu. A **project** *is a collection of Pascal source code units in TP*. The purpose of a project is twofold: 1) to establish an order property among the units so that dependent

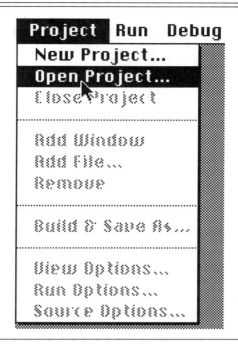

FIGURE 9-1. The Project menu.

units can be compiled after the units they depend upon are compiled, and 2) to maintain currency among units so that only dependent units are recompiled when a modification takes place in one or more of the units in the project.

You might think of a project as an inverted call graph or tree with the units represented as nodes and the "uses" dependency represented as arcs. The "leaves" of the uses tree are nodes that depend on no other nodes; the internal nodes depend on other nodes and have other nodes dependent on them. The project listing places independent units at the top of the list and the main program, which depends on everything else, at the bottom of the list. Thus, the "build order" of a project is the order in which its units are compiled.

For example, BubbleFlow presented in previous chapters is a project consisting of nine units and the toolbox interfaces called MacPasLib and MacTraps. (These names have been changed in later versions of TP.) The independent units are GLOBAL_flow and CLOCK_flow so they are listed and compiled first, see Figure 9-2. FLOW.pas is the

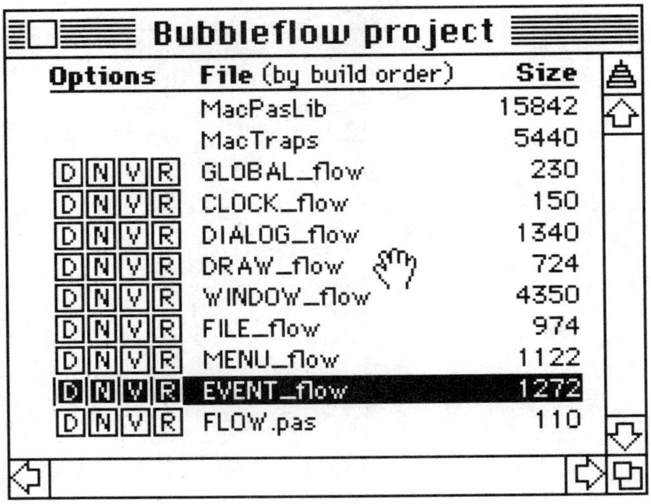

The build order of a project specifies which units are to be compiled first. This order is given by the programmer, who uses the hand shown above to drag the units into place.

The options list specifies D = debug turned on, N = names for low-level debugging, V = numerical overflow detection, and R = range error detection.

The size column tells how large each unit is in bytes. The Macintosh limits each unit to a 32K byte segment, hence an upper bound limits the size of each compiland.

FIGURE 9-2. The Bubble Flow project

main program, so it is listed last. The "hand" icon is shown, too. It is used to move the units around on the screen and to change the order of compiling by "grabbing" and moving any unit.

The project listing also maintains a partitioning of code into segments. A segment equals 32K bytes of memory. Executable applications are divided into segments to conserve memory space by limiting the size of branch instructions (16, 24, or 32 bit addresses take 2, 3, or 4 bytes to hold the target address). The programmer must "pack" units together to make segments of 32K or less bytes in size. To do this, select the upper right corner icon (Tower of Hanoi symbol), and the project reveals another side of itself, see Figure 9-3.

Units are moved from one segment to another to achieve a packing as close to 32K as possible. In this example, the whole application fits into one segment of 31,558 bytes, total. When more than one segment is required, the programmer must decide which segments each unit is to occupy.

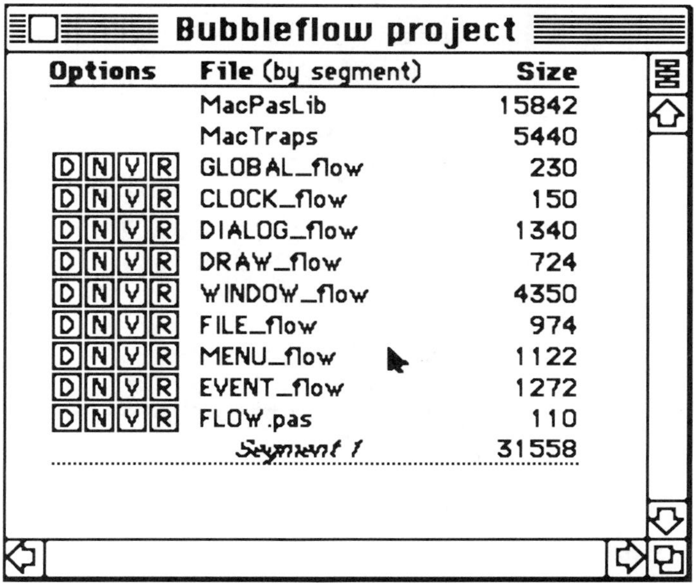

FIGURE 9-3. Segment 1 of Bubble Flow project

The Project information can be changed by VIEW OPTIONS... to include filename, debug options, code size (as shown in Figure 9-4), and unit name, volume name, and date file last saved, as shown in the VIEW OPTIONS dialog. In addition, the programmer can select font and type size. The project window can be observed during program execution, if desired, and is very useful during debugging because each unit may be "pointed at" when activated, see Figure 9-5.

FIGURE 9-4. View options

Bubbleflow project

Options	File (by build order)	Size
	MacPasLib	15842
	MacTraps	5440
D N V R	GLOBAL_flow	230
D N V R	CLOCK_flow	150
D N V R	DIALOG_flow	1340
D N V R	DRAW_flow	724
D N V R	WINDOW_flow	4350
D N V R	FILE_flow	974
D N V R	MENU_flow	1122
D N V R	EVENT_flow	1272
D N V R	FLOW.pas	110

FIGURE 9-5. Watching Bubble Flow execute

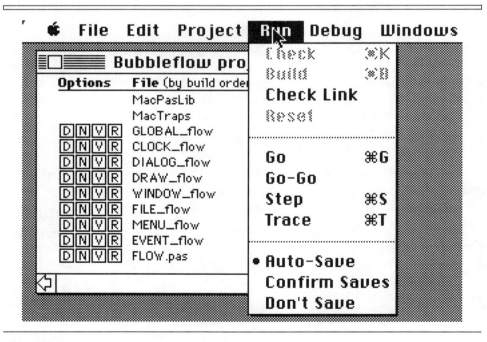

FIGURE 9-6. Running Bubble Flow

The BUILD AND SAVE AS... item in the Project menu is used in the final step of program development. Once debugged and validated, an application is separated from TP by building and saving a stand-alone application. The BUILD AND SAVE AS... mode selection causes the entire project to be recompiled (taking out all debugging and inter-ruption traps from the code), and linked with its resource fork to make a "launchable" desktop application.

Alternately, the application is run from within TP by selecting one of the many run options provided under the Run menu; see Figure 9-6. These permit full-speed execu-tion, stopping at breakpoints, resuming, and single stepping through the application one statement at a time.

GO causes all modified units to be compiled and linked automatically, followed by execution of the application. The TP menus disappear and the application's menus appear in the menu bar. The application's resources are displayed over the TP resources, and a small "bug spray can" appears in the upper right corner of the menu bar. Clicking on this bug suspends the application, and the TP menus reappear. In most cases, the application can be resumed after modifications.

GO-GO is a variation on GO that depends on breakpoints being set. These are placed in the source file by dragging small STOP signs into the source file next to the statement where the breakpoint will occur, see Figure 9-7.

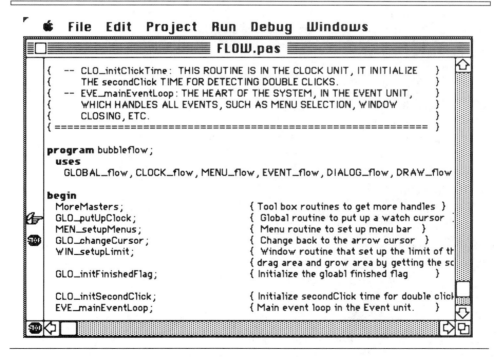

FIGURE 9-7. Break points are STOP signs

FIGURE 9-8. The Debug menu

STEP is selected each time a single statement is executed. One statement is performed for each selection of STEP. This is an extremely useful mode whenever the program's execution is studied in minute detail, but it is slow. The GO-GO mode should be used until a short piece of code is isolated, then the STEP mode used to "zero in" on the error.

TRACE is perhaps the most useful and educational tool. When TRACE is selected, a pointing finger appears next to each statement as it is executed. (In the Project window, this finger points to each unit as it is activated.) Each statement is identified as the active statement, in turn, and the whole program can be viewed in execution. It is particularly instructive to watch the main event loop of an application execute in trace mode.

AUTO-SAVE, CONFIRM SAVES, and DONT SAVE are switches that tell TP what to do after each modification to a unit. The AUTO-SAVE switch setting causes TP to automatically save each modified unit; CONFIRM SAVES lets the programmer decide each time whether to save or not, and DONT SAVE simply doesn't replace the original with its modified version.

Debugging tools let you watch the application run as suggested above, using the TRACE mode of execution, observing variables change values as the program executes.The D = debug option must be turned on inside the Project window, however, and the proper settings of AUTO-SHOW FINGER, STOPS IN, STEP INTO CALL, and BREAK AT A-TRAPS selected under the Debug menu, see Figure 9-8.

Stops can be inserted anywhere in the source code listing by dragging a stop sign into the left margin of the source code and running GO-GO, see Figure 9-8. The application will be suspended prior to the statement with the associated stop sign. The application

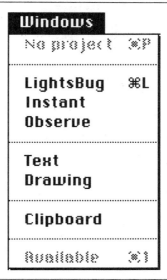

FIGURE 9-9. The Windows menu

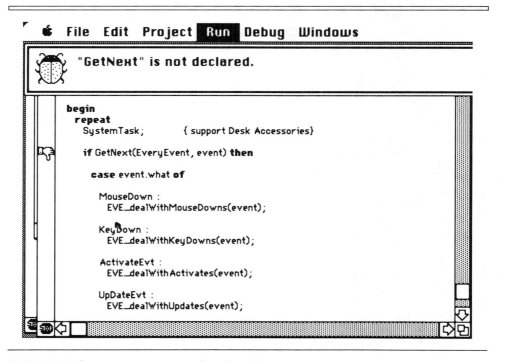

FIGURE 9-10. Error messages appear in a bug alert

can be resumed by selecting GO-GO a second time. This method is good to use when trying to isolate an error somewhere in the program by divide-and-conquer techniques.

To observe the changing values of a variable, open the Observe window by selecting Observe from the Windows menu, and then enter the name of the variable, see Figure 9-9. The value of the variable will remain "undefined" until the program enters the range of the variable. The value is shown changing as the program executes. To "freeze" the action, use GO-GO and stops. Also, TRACE causes the program to run slowly enough to see the variable change values.

When errors occur, the finger will appear as a "thumbs down" icon, and will point to the statement that failed, see Figure 9-10. If only the Project window is open at the time of failure, the thumbs down icon will point to the unit containing the defective statement. Double clicking on this unit causes the editor to fetch the source code, check it, and point to the defective statement. Typically, an error message also appears at the top of the screen indicating the problem. For example, an undeclared identifier such as "GetNext" results in an error message and a thumbs down pointer to the defective statement.

CODING STANDARDS

Maintainability — the ease of maintaining a functional unit according to prescribed requirements — is of central concern during coding. We know that coding is a relatively minor portion of the overall cost of developing and delivering a software product, but a small investment in coding for maintainability yields major benefits during the maintenance and enhancement phases. Therefore, writing maintainable code is high on the SQA list.

High-quality coding goes beyond efficiency. Programmers must balance coding efficiency against other demands such as the time and corresponding cost to write the code, debug and test the code, explain the code to others, and modify the code[6].

These and other effects are often overlooked by individual programmers, who may be too heavily influenced by programming-in-the-small. A good software development group needs to follow coding standards that restrict or constrain individual programmers for the benefit of the entire team.

General Coding Rules

Generally speaking, coding is the process of creating an understandable artifact admirable for its clarity, compactness, and efficiency. In practice, however, these are often conflicting goals. When a conflict arises, use common sense and follow these rules.

Code for Maintainability

Implication: Accommodate change.

One thing is true for all software systems — they go through many changes, modifications, and enhancements. Even small "throw-away programs" originally designed for one-time use often end up living a long life and experiencing more than one version.

The Macintosh system software enforces many rules that other systems do not, hence we list methods for accommodating change that may be useful in other systems.

Divide the Code into Attributes

In addition to modular decomposition and object-oriented detailed design, every program can be compartmentalized into relatively independent parts. These parts can be changed without causing major propagation of changes throughout the other parts. For example, cosmetic attributes such as screen forms and printer formats can be parameterized and set aside in a "configuration file" which is used by the running program. The resource fork of every Macintosh application serves this purpose. The resource fork concept can be implemented by other means in other systems.

Separate Text from Logic

This is the same idea again. However, this simple idea is often overlooked by busy programmers. All text — error messages, help screens, I/O prompts — should be separated from the application code and placed in a separate "resource" file. The text attributes of an application can then be changed with minimal impact on the logic of the application. Foreign language translation can be done after the code is written, and cosmetic enhancements can be carried out without extensive recompilations of the application. Prompts and error messages can be accessed and displayed by a basic set of access procedures, just like all well-behaved objects.

Strive for Flexibility

The code should be able to withstand unexpected change: turnover in programming personnel, porting of the application to another system, correction of bugs, anomalies, and user interface inconveniences. Parts of the application may even be submitted to a library of reusable components and used by many other programmers over a long period of time.

Start Early Thinking about Quality Control

Implication: Accommodate testing.

If you are serious about quality, then the software product must be written to be tested. (We explore testing strategies in greater detail in a later chapter.) Consider the testing a procedure or module will undergo at each stage: unit, functional, module, and system integration testing. When testing questions are asked early in the implementation stage, they have a major influence on coding style. Here are some methods of addressing this rule.

Instrument Your Code with Hooks

Conditional compiler commands that are activated from the compiler can be imbedded in the source code. For example, a SORT routine might be written with a hook to test if the list is actually in ascending order after it is sorted. For example, the $IF metacommand for a certain compiler might permit a conditional compile on switch $SETF as follows:

```
$IF $SETF THEN Assert_Ascending (List, ErrorFlag);
```

When the compiler metavariable $SETF is False, this line is ignored, but when $SETF is true, the invocation of testing routine Assert_Ascending is compiled into the source code. Routine Assert_Ascending returns ErrorFlag = True only if List is in ascending order. This hook is easily turned on/off to perform a simple, yet effective test of the SORT routine.

Devise Test Cases Early

We have emphasized the need for design and code inspections in previous chapters, but the concern here is for programmer-devised tests used by individual programmers to locate and remove bugs at the function and procedure level. A clever programmer will have devised the Assert_Ascending hook illustrated above *before* writing the SORT routine. Even if the SORT routine is taken from a library of reusable components, the test case should be prepared and run as soon as possible.

Never Discard Test Cases

Tests are valuable throughout the full lifecycle of a product. **Regression testing** *is the process of running old test data through the system after each modification to assure that old test cases are still valid.* Modifications often introduce new bugs into a polished system, and regression testing is the best method for detecting these new problems. Keep the test cases, along with the corresponding test data and the source code, so they can be reused.

Test cases and test data files can be described in documentation and incorporated in the coding method. For example, a consistent file-naming convention can be used to identify all test data files associated with a unit. Suppose the unit is named CLOCK_flow, and it is stored in source code file CLOCK_flow.unit. If we use conventional names, then the files containing documentation, test data, and so forth are known, because they all have consistent and previously agreed-upon names:

CLOCK_flow.pas contains the test harness program. Run this program to test the unit.

CLOCK_flow.test1, CLOCK_flow.test2,... CLOCK_flow.test9 contain test data for the unit's procedures.

CLOCK_flow.doc contains the documentation describing CLOCK_flow.unit.

Never Wait to Document

Implication: Don't separate documentation from programming.

Programmers hate to document their code, but the project is not complete until program documentation is finished. If documentation is part of coding, then the project is more likely to be completed on time. Good project managers are wise to reward good documentation. Great project managers enforce documentation standards requiring certain minimal comments suggested by Pfleeger[6]. Documentation should list:

What the code does
Who wrote it
Where the code fits into the overall system

When the code was written and revised
Why the code exists
How the code uses data structures and algorithms

Here are some additional tips on documentation.

Keep Running Logs

Each programmer should keep notes, news, and change-request information in an electronic file called a "programmer's log." These logs are invaluable to new programmers, as well as to the study of project dynamics. We have given several examples of the revealing nature of programmer logs in previous chapters. Logs are also helpful to the programmer who wrote them because they contain reminders that are useful when documenting the final version of the code.

Make Someone Responsible

Every successful development team includes a documentation specialist, as suggested by the *Development Team*. The Test and Documentation programmer is responsible for collecting and organizing all programmer documentation. If file-naming conventions are used as indicated earlier, the documentation files can be easily collected and formatted into an understandable document.

Combat Complexity with Consistency

Implication: Adopt standards and conventions.

Use Consistent Version Controls

Versions should be numbered in some consistent manner, such as 2.3A1 for version 2, release 3, of alpha test program number 1. In this example, alpha test program 2 of version 2, release 3 is numbered 2.3A2, and beta test program is called 2.3B1, and so forth. When the program is released, it will be called version 2.3. Subsequent minor fixes of the program will result in version 2.4, 2.5, and so forth.

A version is a major enhancement, so 2.3 is derived from 1.X, where X is the last release of version 1. Thus, version 1.0 is the first version and release of the program; 2.0 the next version containing major enhancements and fixes, and so forth.

An automated version control or configuration management control system is used to manage the source code corresponding to each change. CASE tools for version control are not described here, but in brief, they provide methods for making a new compiled application from the properly marked source code modules. Thus, when version 2.3 is compiled, the version control system extracts the proper version 2.3 modules to be compiled and linked into the application.

Use Consistent Coding Conventions

Consistent coding conventions contribute a great deal to reduction in complexity, but enforcing such conventions is difficult, because programmers do not like to be told how to write code. It took ten years to convince programmers to eliminate GOTO branching in their programs. There are many other similar complexity-reducing techniques which have yet to be widely used. Clearly, proper commenting, careful use of nesting, and simplicity of algorithm design are a few obvious guidelines. We list a few of the less obvious complexity-reducing guidelines below.

Use Meaningful Names. Use meaningful names of constants, types, variables, procedures, functions, and files everywhere. Be consistent in naming; for example, use the naming conventions described in the previous chapter so that the origin of every identifier can be traced through its name.

Use verbs for procedure names, because procedures are action statements.

Use nouns for constant, type, variable, and function names, because these are "persons, places, and things."

Prefix the names of all visible identifiers with the first few letters of the module name that defines them, for example:

```
const PromptSize = 80;
type   PromptRec = record
                        PromptInt : integer;   {Number of prompt line}
                          PromptStr : Str255; {The prompt herself}
                 end;
   var PromptItem : integer;   {working stiff}
   procedure PromptShow (PromptIs : PromptRec);
```

Obviously, the constant, type, variable, and procedure above is defined inside a unit called Prompt. These identifiers are visible outside the unit. In a large program, these names may appear in thousands of locations scattered throughout the program. Regardless of where they are, the naming convention identifies these as belonging to unit Prompt.

Avoid abbreviations and incorrect spellings. This improves comprehension of the program by maintenance programmers. Use uppercase letters or the underscore symbol to designate compound words and phrases. For example, use:

Count instead of kount
ListFiles versus listfiles
TextFile in place of txtf

Avoid using literals. Replace them with resources or manifest variables. For example, write:

```
for Index := 1 to StringMaxLength do
```

instead of the cryptic,

```
for I := 1 to 255 do
```

and declare StringMaxLength as a manifest constant in the interface part of module Strings.

```
Const StringMaxLength = 255; {Upper limit on size of strings}
```

This is placed in the interface part of the unit in which it is defined. More on this later.

Adopt a Clear, Understandable Style. Use indentation, parentheses, and spacing as a weapon against ambiguity. This is especially important for clarifying difficult sections of code. Here are some specific recommendations.

Indentation is used to convey meaning:

```
if (A = 5) and (B < A)
  then if (B > 1) then A := 0
                  else A := 1;
```

The nested statements above are equivalent to the non-nested statements below, but one is obviously less ambiguous than the other (the answer is left as an exercise for the reader):

```
if (A = 5) and (B < A) then if B > 1 then A: = 0 else A: = 1;
```

Boolean expressions should be in parentheses and spaced to make their meaning clear. The following loop is difficult to understand:

```
while A + B < C and C > 10 and not EOF(F) do
```

but simple insertion of parentheses and spacing shows immediately what the loop means:

```
while ((A + B) < C)
      and
      (C > 10)
      and
    (not EOF(F))
  do
```

The same idea applies to even simple assignment statements. The following is an example taken from a novice programming class. (The longer an assignment statement is, the more spacing and parentheses are needed.)

Instead of the usual,

```
Root := ( B - sqrt(B*B - 4*A*C)/(2*A) ),
```

use the improved version,

```
Root := (B - sqrt(B*B - 4*A*C)
              /
           (2*A));
```

This version is easier to follow, and exposes one of the most common errors in programs for solving the quadratic equation: dividing by 2 instead of (2*A).

This kind of indentation may not be permitted by certain editors, such as the Think Pascal editor.

Adopt an Assertive Style of Coding. By *assertive*, we mean code that is easy to make assertions about. This will help the maintenance programmer form hypotheses about your program and, when testing the hypotheses, to discover your true meaning. For example, loops and **if** branching are especially prone to error, so use assertions to show what you really intend the program to do:

```
I := 1;                              {Start searching at front of list}
while   (Key < > List[I])           {Miss...}
            and
        (not List[I].occupied)       {no collision}
            and
        (I < = TableLength)          {no overflow}
    do I:=I+1;                       {Increment through whole list}
{Assert: K=List[I] or List[I].occupied or I>TableLength}
```

Anyone can understand the intent of this loop without knowing the algorithm or application. The assertion comment at the end of the loop is derived by logical complement of the Boolean expression in the loop. That is, the loop terminates only if the assertion is true, otherwise the program is trapped in the loop forever!

In English, this loop must terminate for one or more of the reasons given by the assertion:

"Either, the Key matches List[I], or the *I*th item in List is occupied, or the search reaches the end of the List."

Apparently, this loop performs some kind of search on a list, and when the loop terminates, the assertion is true. This assertion makes a claim about the programmer's intent, based on the semantics of the program.

Reduce Intermodule Coupling. We have offered the guideline several times already, but it is advice that nonetheless bears exploring in greater detail. A good system minimizes coupling by limiting the number of names and values passed among modules and procedure/function items.

Consider two communicating modules X and Y; X contains procedure A:

1. All constants, types, variables, procedures, and functions defined in procedure A of module X should be confined to procedure A, and where possible, constants, types, variables, procedures, and functions should be passed explicitly through the parameter list of procedure A, except,

2. Constants, types, variables, procedures, and functions that are used in more than one procedure or function defined in module X should be defined in the implementation part of X, only, except,

3. Constants, types, variables, procedures, and functions that are defined in module X, but used by another module, should be defined in the interface part of X; and all modules that use them must do so by referencing the interface part of module X. This means a **uses** statement is required to couple the two modules.

4. Constants, types, variables, procedures, and functions defined in the interface part of module X and used by more than one other module, say Y1, Y2, . . ., Yn, should be inserted as close to the using modules Yi as possible. Therefore, such an interface is placed at the global level of the application program as a last resort, only.

Rule 1 is preferred all the time, but in most languages, especially Pascal, this means encapsulation of all constants, types, variables, and procedure/function names within units. The only means of communication between two units would be by "message passing" via the parameters in a procedure call. (In fact this is the basis of pure object-oriented languages such as SmallTalk.)

Unfortunately, this is not possible in Pascal, because types cannot be passed as parameters in a procedure call, for example. In addition, interface information is needed to compile units separately. Hence, rules 2 and 3 are often needed to make encapsulation work.

The philosophy of these rules is "force encapsulation where possible, and when it is not possible, incrementally ease up on the rules." But the rules are often ignored by even experienced programmers. An example will illustrate one of the most common flaws.

Unit MENU_flow is the menu manager unit for BubbleFlow, the example described earlier. It illustrates good coding style because it uses consistent naming conventions, meaningful names, and most importantly, it obeys the coupling rules discussed above, see Figure 9-11.

The first temptation in writing such a unit is to declare the constants, types, variables, and procedures at the main program level. The reason for this is that we tend to think these are used by every other function in the system. After all, menus are "global" to the application.

If we cluster all access to the menus in this unit, then all procedures that have a right to manipulate menus are encapsulated inside this unit. Thus, following rule 1, we try to place the constants and so forth in an access procedure (either MEN_setupMenus or MEN_doProcessMenuIn). But this fails because two procedures need access to the constants, etc.

Rule 2 says to put the names in the implementation part, which is where they ended up. But why does this level of coupling work? We should examine rules 3 and 4 as well.

Rule 3 says the constants, etc. should be placed in the interface part of the unit, but here we see that only the access procedures need appear in the interface part. Hence, only the access procedures are visible outside this unit. If any other unit needed one of the constants, etc., then we would be forced to place them in the interface part. Apparently this is not the case here.

Rule 4 says to place **uses** statements in units so that the interfaces are made accessible to other units. We see that unit MEN_flow uses other units, hence it has a **uses** clause.

The placement of *instance variables* inside the implementation part of this unit is especially informative. This is an example of near-total data encapsulation. MyMenu holds all references to the menus of the entire application, yet it is invisible to any other units. The only way a menu item can be manipulated is via calls to the access procedures defined in the interface part of MENU_flow.

PARTIAL LISTING OF UNIT MENU_FLOW

Unit MENU_flow;
 Interface
   Uses GLOBAL_flow, DIALOG_flow, DRAW_flow;
 Procedure MEN_setupMenus;
 Procedure MEN_doProcessMenuIn (menuSelection : longint);

Implementation
 CONST

  MEMCOUNT = 4; {Number of menus}

  APPLE_MENU = 1; {Menu id numbers}
  FILE_MENU = 2; {handle array}
  EDIT_MENU = 3;
  ANALYZE_MENU = 4;

  APPLE_MENU_ID = 256; {Menu id in the resource file}
  FILE_MENU_ID = 257;
  EDIT_MENU_ID = 258;
  ANALYZE_MENU_ID = 259;

  APPLE_FLOW_ABOUT = 1; {APPLE_FLOW_ABOUT id}

  FILE_NEW = 1;   {File menu item list number}
  FILE_OPEN = 2;
  FILE_SAVE = 3;
  FILE_PRINT = 4;
  FILE_QUIT = 6;

  EDIT_DELETE = 1;   {Edit menu item list number}
  EDIT_CHANGE = 2;
  EDIT_UNKNOWN1 = 3;

  ANALYZE_UNKNOWN1 = 1; {Analyze menu item list number}
  ANALYZE_UNKNOWN2 = 2;
  ANALYZE_UNKNOWN3 = 3;

Type
 Data = ARRAY[1..3200] OF char;

Var
 myMenu : ARRAY[1..MEMCOUNT] OF MenuHandle; {Menu handles}
 Where : Point;
 fName : Str255;
 DataPtr : ^Data;

FIGURE 9-11. Partial listing of unit Menu_flow

If non-object-oriented design techniques had been used, the declaration of MyMenu would most likely have been made global to the whole application. The logic of such a decision is that this important and all-pervasive variable needs to be available from many parts of the application. However, object-oriented design reduces coupling by fully encapsulating such instance variables.

A second possibility is to pass MyMenu to other parts of the application via parameters of procedures. This is a poor idea again, because it broadens the coupling among modules and exposes MyMenu to unauthorized and hidden modifications. Changes in the implementation part of MENU_flow may conflict with hidden modification done to MyMenu in other parts of the program. With the encapsulation shown, changes to the implementation have restricted effects on MyMenu.

The consequences of the structuring rules given here lead to very limited and controlled propagation of change throughout the system after each modification. Object-oriented programs that carefully limit interfaces reduce complexity and are much easier to maintain. This brings up the value of the next coding rule.

Localize Side Effects at Every Level

Implication: Minimize coupling.

What other techniques can be used to reduce complexity in the interface? Major improvements that go beyond object-oriented design can be realized using various forms of *decoupling*. Several points merit additional attention:

Decouple Interface and Implementation Specifications

A simple coding technique can be used to separate interface an implementation specifications of modules, even in programming languages that do not have modularity features. The $INCLUDE metacommand of most compilers can be used to separate these two parts into distinct files. The compiler then sews them back together during compilation.

Decouple Text, I/O Formats, and Code

Remove all literals from the code and encapsulate them in either resource forks or in separate units that access the literals stored in "configuration files." This is the idea behind the Macintosh resource fork, but the same idea applies to other systems.

These rules for decoupling parts of a program limit or *localize* side effects of changes in remote parts of the code. A small change to a report format can often be made without recompilation of the program! But how is this done in a conventional programming language such as Pascal? Here is a suggestion.

Partition the application's source code into files that contain each of the "attributes" discussed above. Use a standard file-naming convention as below. F and G are the names of a program and unit, respectively:

F.PAS   Source code file containing a Pascal program. Typically a main program or test program.

G.INT   The interface specification for object F (unit F).

G.IMP   Implementation part of G.

G.DOC   Documentation part of G.

G.NEW   News, notes, and bug reports for G.

G.TST   A test data file for G.

G.ERR   Error messages for G.

G.HLP   Help messages for G.

G.FRM   Format rules and configurations for G.

Every separately compiled unit has a corresponding set of files containing these attributes (and maybe more attributes such as graphics, sound, and so forth). Whenever all interface specifications, for example, are printed as a report, a single command such as Print all .INT files is issued to get every interface in the application.

The combination of these rules and object-oriented design is called *maintainable object (M-Object) coding* because it results in a maintainable application.

Reuse as Much as You Can

Implication: Adapt what you can from other programmers.

The best unit, procedure, function, or whole program is one that you do not need to write. Taking code from someone else (legally) is the most cost-effective solution to the coding phase, but it must be tempered by the knowledge that all code is not easily adapted to new purposes.

A database of reusable source code should be established and maintained for all programmers to use. This database classifies reusable modules according to the function they perform, how they perform it, and details of implementation (language, operating system, algorithm, data types, etc.). Prieto-Diaz and Freeman[7] give a pseudo-code algorithm that illustrates the process of locating and adapting a reusable module, see Figure 9-12.

SOME REUSE TECHNOLOGIES

- Subroutine Libraries
- Software IC
- Software Building Blocks
- Reusable Components
- Parts-Based Programming
- Salvageable Software
- Software Repositories
- Object-Oriented Programming
- Software Factory
- Software Synthesis
- Application Generators
- 4GLs
- Automated Assistant

Source: Tracz, W., Tutorial #1: Software Reuse Update, IEEE COMPCON Spring '88, San Francisco, CA.

REUSE COMPONENT ALGORITHM[7]

begin
  search library
  if identical match
    then terminate — reusable component is found
    else
      collect similar components as a set
      for each component in the set:
        compute degree of match
      end
    rank and select the best component
  end if
end

FIGURE 9-12. Reuse component algorithm[7]

Of course this algorithm leaves the details undefined — "matching," "degree of match," "rank," and "modify" are undefined operations. Many methods have been proposed that use different definitions of these operations, but currently no single method has gained widespread use.

WHAT MAKES CODE REUSABLE?
- Following Standard Conventions
- Management Encouragement
- No Language Tricks in Code
- Portable Code
- Reliable Code
- Strong Cohesion, Weak Coupling
- Well-Defined Interfaces
- Generality
- Robustness
- Conceptual Integrity
- Separate Compilation
- Readable Code

Source: Tracz, W., Special Issue on Reusability, *IEEE Software*, vol. 4, no. 4 (July 1987), pp. 6–73.

The effects of reuse on quality are still being studied, but early indications are that dramatic improvements can be realized. Lenz et al.[8] report the number of errors per line of code was about 9 times better during function test and 4.5 times better during component and system test than systems that do not use reusable building blocks. These results were obtained on projects consisting of 10%-25% reusable components.

Despite these advantages, programmers have difficulty using reusable code, as we reported earlier. Woodfield et al.[9] studied programmer performance and reusability and found that untrained users tend to consider component size an important feature when deciding whether or not to reuse a component. This caused many programmers to avoid using large components indiscriminately. In fact, selection should be based on percentage of modification required to adapt the component to its new use. Furthermore, when attempting to use the more meaningful selection criteria, users failed to accurately estimate the effort required to adapt the component. Clearly, our understanding of this important approach toward reducing errors while improving programmer productivity needs more research.

STRUCTURED PROGRAMMING

Structured programming has thoroughly permeated software development technology, and yet many practitioners do not fully understand it. Therefore, it is worthwhile to study the development and principle of structured programming apart from coding style and standardization.

Many definitions exist for the term *structured programming*:

. . . programs that can be mathematically proven correct . . . [Dijkstra]

. . . programs obtained by stepwise refinement . . . [Parnas]

. . . programs in which the first error is never encountered during its use . . . [Mills]

. . . well-defined development technique using top-down design and implementation and strict use of structured program control constructs . . . [IEEE]

These definitions fail to distinguish, however, between the process and the artifacts of software development. Furthermore, they do not tell how to produce a structured program. A structured program is a *reducible* program; while structured programming is a *process* per the IEEE definition. We have spent considerable effort on structured programming as process. In this section, we concentrate on the artifact called a structured program, and define what we mean by reducibility.

Reductionism

Reductionism is a concept with a two thousand-year history in the annals of science. In simplistic terms it means that "things" in the universe can be understood by reducing them to elementary parts. Matter is made up of molecules, molecules are reducible to atoms, atoms are reducible to subatomic particles, and so forth. This idea caught the imagination of computer scientists in the mid-1960s and has evolved into what we now call structured programming. Reductionism in programming leads to structuralism, and so we say a program is structured if it can be reduced.

A program is **reducible** *if and only if every segment defined by flow of control through the program can be replaced by a single-entry-single-exit construct.* Each single-entry-single-exit (SESE) construct must itself be reducible into smaller SESE constructs or into fundamental constructs with SESE flow of control.

SESE reducibility is an intriguing idea. Every program ought to be reducible, but is it possible to write *any* program in such a restricted fashion? Theoretically, all computable functions can be written as an SESE program, so it is possible to write all programs as structured programs. Practically, SESE programs may require additional variables or added statements to force them into SESE reducibility. We illustrate these concepts with several examples.

Consider the (nonsensical) algorithm given below that has some "difficult" control flow properties. This problem is called SCAN, and it serves only to illustrate the properties of SESE reductionism. (The reader could "optimize" the problem away by simplification, but this is not the point.)

SCAN: Sequentially search an array A of size N, starting from element 1, and:

1. Output "Done," if every element of A is greater than zero.

2. Output the location of the first element of A that was found to be zero, and terminate.

3. When the first element less than zero is encountered, increment it by 1 and begin scanning once again from the first element.

Flowcharts of this algorithm in both structured and unstructured form reveal some interesting properties of structured programming. A first attempt at writing an SESE reducible version will probably fail because of the convoluted nature of the specification. Yet we know that an SESE version is theoretically possible.

The algorithm is given in both unstructured and structured form in Figures 9-13 and 9-14. Figure 9-15 shows the unstructured flowchart after an attempt to reduce it by identifying concatenated and nested SESE chunks of code. The reduction fails in the case of the unstructured flowchart because we cannot find an SESE chunk — see the piece of code with two entry points. However, the structured version is reducible as shown by the SESE-partitioned flowchart in Figure 9-16. This example shows how to test a program to see if it is structured.

1. Identify the deepest level nested control block and draw a box around it. This becomes a chunk, which can be replaced by a single "node" in the flowchart.

2. Repeat finding the deepest level nested chunks, until all have been found and reduced to a single node. Move up a level of nesting and repeat for all revised chunks at this new level.

3. Repeat at all levels of nesting. Treat concatenated chunks of code as a single node by "coalescing" them into a single node.

4. When the entire flowchart has been reduced to a single node with one entry and one exit point, the flowchart has been reduced. If it is not possible to reduce the flowchart to a single node, the flowchart is not structured.

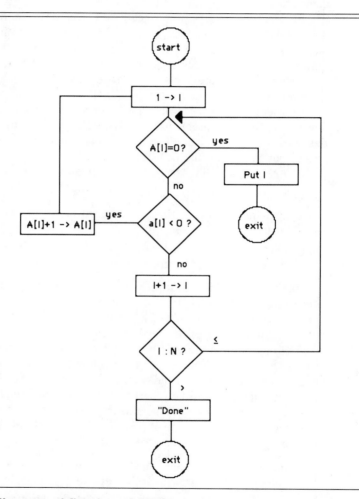

FIGURE 9-13. Unstructured flowchart of SCAN

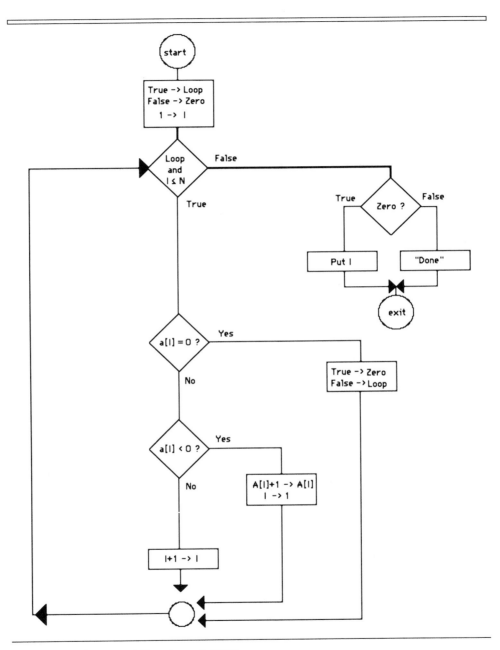

FIGURE 9-14. Structured flowchart of SCAN

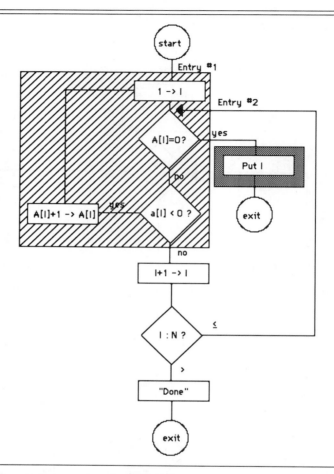

FIGURE 9-15. An attempt to reduce unstructured SCAN

Why is it not possible to reduce the unstructured flowchart as shown in Figure 9-15? The principal difficulty is branching — either forward or backward (loop). A forward branch may cause multiple entries into a chunk while a backward branch often causes both multiple entry and multiple exit. Such overlaps in branches are called knots. A **program knot** *is any flow of control path through a program that crosses over another path when drawn on a semi-infinite two-dimensional plane such as a flat piece of paper, where all backward and forward branching is drawn on the same (left or right) side of the paper.*

The knot in the unstructured version of the example is clearly shown by the crossing lines: the two backward branches cross one another when drawn on the same side of the paper. It is also clear that this is not the case with the structured version.

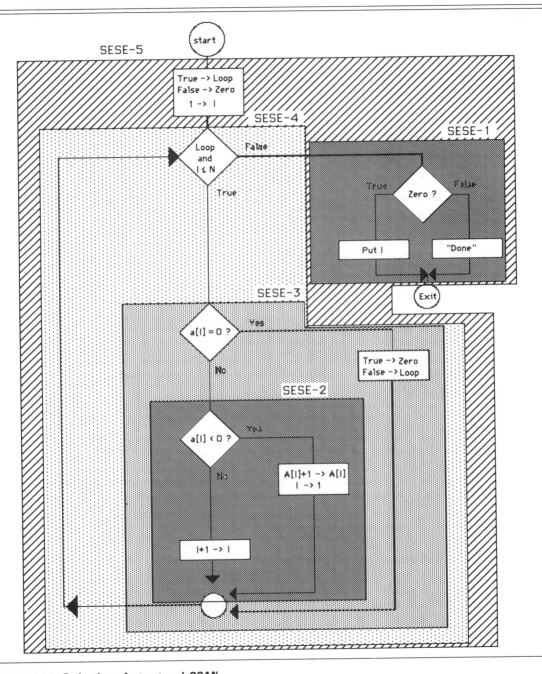

FIGURE 9-16. Reduction of structured SCAN

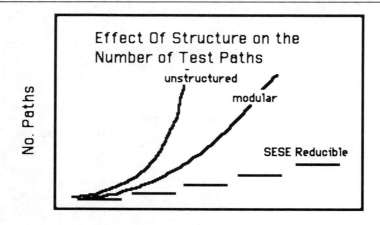

FIGURE 9-17. Structure and testing

A properly nested flowchart has no multiple entries or exits caused by branching — there are no knots in the flow of control of the program. This is always the case for structured programs, because only concatenation and nesting of control paths are allowed. The question naturally arises, what is the significant difference between the two versions of the example?

The Power of Languages

The sample program demonstrates the different *power of expression* in two languages. We can measure expressive power of programming languages by comparing their semantic power: the *semantic power* of language A is greater than the semantic power of language B *if the algorithms in A can be expressed in fewer statements and variables than in language B.* We assume the primitive operations of both A and B are identical. That is, both languages contain the same operations such as addition, square root, Boolean comparison, and so forth.

If languages A and B have the same primitive operations, then how can one be more powerful than the other? The answer lies in the expressiveness of their control structures. Comparing the flowcharts of the two versions of SCAN reveals a startling fact — the unstructured version implements SCAN in fewer "statements and variables" than does the structured version. Hence, a language containing GOTOs is more powerful than a language lacking the GOTO control construct.

We call languages with GOTOs L-structured because they contain GOTO labels. Languages with only single-entry-single-exit constructs are called SESE-structured. SCAN illustrates the following fundamental principle:

Principle of Structured Programming: Every program can be expressed in an SESE-structured language, however, conversion of an L-structured program into an equivalent SESE-structured program may require more statements and variables.

The L-structured version of SCAN contains five primitive operations (assignment), and three test predicates; the SESE-structured version contains nine primitive operations (assignment), and five test predicates (we have counted the compound predicate 'loop and $L \leq N$' as two tests). In addition, the SESE-structured version uses two additional variables, Loop and Zero, to signify an internal state of the program. Additional flag variables such as these are common in SESE-structured programs because they remove knots.

It would appear that structured programming is less efficient than unstructured programming. This is a naive impression, however, because unstructured programs are often the result of poor design, and poor design leads to redundancies and inefficiencies. Practical results suggest that structured programs are frequently shorter and more compact than unstructured programs. The major point, however, is that structured programs are less costly. In one carefully controlled study, structured programs were shown to have 3.5 times fewer bugs in unit testing, and were 5 times easier to maintain. This is due to reduction of complexity in the form of fewer decision predicates and fewer paths through the SESE-structured program.

Programmers often complain that SESE structure is too restrictive. The Principle of Structured Programming says that SESE-structured languages are weaker than L-structured languages, so in a way programmers are correct in complaining. In fact, adoption of SESE-structured programming is a vote for weaker languages. Critics say that human programmers cannot be trusted with powerful languages such as L-structured FORTRAN, BASIC, and COBOL. This is because the maintenance costs are too high, see Figure 9-17.

Another illustration will show why SESE structure is perhaps too restrictive. This example also shows a hidden facit of semantic power which has not been elaborated: the power of nesting control constructs. Suppose a certain program contains a control path that nests into three loops as shown in Figure 9-18. At level 3 an error is possible that is handled by abandoning the normal flow of control and exiting to the body of the first loop. This might occur, for example, if an alternate path is to be attempted to recover from the error.

This kind of flow of control can occur within a single procedure as shown in Figure 9-18, or throughout a whole system of procedures. When error conditions are passed out of one procedure to be handled by another procedure, this is called *control coupling*. Within a single procedure, however, the result is a knotted control path.

Of course this program can be written as an SESE-structured program, but this requires an extra flag variable and extra branching at the end of the two inner loops to test for the existence of an error condition. These variables and tests can mount as the number of error conditions increase, a perplexing situation to most programmers attempting to write structured code.

```
while p do
 while q do
  while t do

   ...

   if ERROR then Goto Level 1;

   ...

  end; {While t}
 end; {While q}
Level 1: Fix_Error;

 ...

end; {While p}
```

FIGURE 9-18. Branching of nested structures

The problem illustrates the power of nesting and the need for breaking out of nested constructs prematurely. Pure SESE-structured languages are too weak to handle breakouts of this kind, so another, more powerful class of languages has been proposed. A **Repeat-Cycle SESE-structured language** *is a language containing SESE structures plus additional structures for gracefully exiting from nested loops.* In a Repeat-Cycle SESE-structured language, control can leave 1, 2, ..., *n* nested loops, and cycle back again.

Typically, an error condition requires exiting from some nested level, and then entering at some other nested level to retry one of several operations. Thus, a case selection construct follows the terminated loop, see Figure 9-19.

```
while p do
 while q do
  while t do

   ...

   if ERROR then BREAK(Err, 2);

   ...

  end; {While t}
 end; {While q}
case Err of
Err1: ...
Err2: ...
 ...
end; {Case}
...
end; {While p}
```

FIGURE 9-19. Repeat-cycle structure

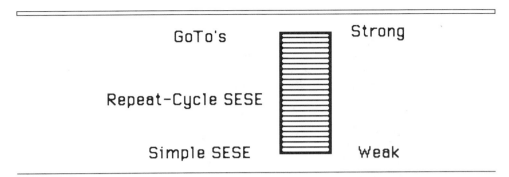

FIGURE 9-20. The hierarchy of language power

In this version of the error-handling program, a BREAK command is used to set the error number in variable Err and branch 2 levels out to the end of the second level **while** loop. Here, the value of Err is tested by the case statement, and the appropriate action is taken. When the case statement ends, the outer loop is repeated.

A similar situation is possible using a CYCLE(j) statement. Here the inner loop is terminated by branching out j levels, and resuming the outer loop. This construction might be used to retry the same control path again.

These constructs seem to be GOTOs in disguise, but keep in mind that the branching is restricted to SESE structure. Hence, these programs retain their reducibility. This means they are still easier to test and maintain, and yet they overcome some of the criticisms leveled at the SESE-structured programmer.

The class of Repeat-Cycle SESE-structured languages are more powerful than the class of SESE-structured languages, but still not as powerful as the class of L-structured languages, see Figure 9-20.

A hierarchy of control structures shows that L-structured languages are the most powerful (and dangerous), while the Repeat-Cycle SESE languages are of intermediate power. The SESE-structured languages are the least powerful, but the safest.

Control structures like case, repeat-until, for-loop, and procedure call do not increase the semantic power of a language. However, these constructs have other virtues that make them valuable. In most programming, the SESE structures are sufficient and the most reliable. In some cases, the extra power of Repeat-Cycle control is desirable. Rarely is the power of GOTO needed, and far too frequently, GOTOs introduce errors and reliability problems. The powerful L-structured languages are too powerful for day-to-day use.

A CASE TOOL FOR STYLE ANALYSIS

Style is a CASE tool for analyzing a source code program and making recommendations for improving its readability and clarity[11]. It uses several metrics and "rules of thumb" to give advice on how to improve coding[12–21].

Principles of Style

According to Lake[11], **programming style** *is the effective structuring and arrangement of programs to increase readability and maintainability without degrading performance.* More specifically, style means coding according to a set of principles. In *Style*, these principles are turned into guidelines that can be checked automatically.

Economy

Careful or thrifty measures taken to provide the code as concisely as possible.

- Avoid superfluous actions or variables in the program.
- Avoid variable name overloading (for instance, use of the same variable name in more than one context).
- Use the least possible number of variable names.
- Minimize the size of the program.
- Minimize the execution time of the program (maximize the speed).
- Avoid module redundancy and repetition.
- Check for the negative side effects of global variables.

Modularity

Partitioning of code into meaningful and cohesive functions.

- Break up lengthy or complex passages or subprograms into smaller, better defined program segments.
- Align physical and logical functions.
- Minimize the number of activities in a module.
- Allow no more than one logical function in a module.
- Check for replication of code.
- Avoid long modules.

Simplicity

Absence of complexity, intricacy, or artificiality.

- Use a simple or straightforward algorithm.
- Use a simple data structure; consider the complexity level appropriate for the intended user or reader.
- Make consistent use of data structures and variable names.
- Avoid complex data structures.
- Avoid tricky or complex programming segments.

ADDITIONAL COMMON STYLE GUIDELINES[14–15]:

Use library functions.
Avoid temporary variables.
Parenthesize to avoid ambiguity.
Choose variable names that won't be confused.
Avoid the FORTRAN arithmetic IF.
Avoid unnecessary branches.
Use the good features of a language; avoid the bad ones.
Don't use conditional branches as a substitute for a logical expression.
Use DO-END and indenting to delimit groups of statements.
Use IF-ELSE to emphasize that only one of two actions is to be performed.
Use DO and DO-WHILE to emphasize the presence of loops.
Make your programs read from top to bottom.
Use IF ... ELSE IF ... ELSE IF ... ELSE ... to implement multiway branches.
Use the fundamental control flow constructs.
Avoid THEN-IF and null ELSE.
Avoid ELSE GOTO and ELSE RETURN.
Follow each decision as closely as possible with its associated action.
Choose a data representation that makes the program simple.
Don't stop with your first draft.
Make the coupling between modules visible.
Each module should do one thing well.
Make sure every module hides something.
Don't patch bad code — rewrite it.
Use self-identifying input. Allow defaults. Echo both on output.
Make sure all variables are initialized before use.
Don't stop at one bug.
Use debugging compilers.
Initialize variables with executable code.
Watch out for off-by-one errors.
Take care to branch the right way on equality.
Avoid multiple exits from loops.
Make sure your code "does nothing" gracefully.
Test programs at their boundary values.
Program defensively.
10.0 times 0.1 is hardly ever 1.0.
Don't compare floating point numbers just for equality.
Make it right before you make it faster.
Keep it right when you make it faster.
Make it clear before you make it faster.
Let your compiler do the simple optimizations.
Don't strain to reuse code; reorganize instead.

> Make sure special cases are truly special.
> Keep it simple to make it faster.
> Don't diddle code to make it faster — find a better algorithm.
> Instrument your programs. Measure before making "efficiency" changes.
> Make sure comments and code agree.
> Don't just echo the code with comments — make every comment count.
> Don't comment bad code — rewrite it.
> Use statement labels that mean something.
> Format a program to help the reader understand it.
> Indent to show the logical structure of a program.
> Document your data layouts.
> Don't over-comment.

Structure

Organization of elements, parts, or constituents in a system.

- Write an orderly, well-organized program.
- Write an easy-to-read program.
- Make use of transitional parts and program components clear to the reader.
- Use a straightforward algorithm.
- Arrange program parts consistently with the meaning of the application.
- Make the program level appropriate for the reader.
- Write clearly — don't be too clever. Don't sacrifice clarity for efficiency.
- Write simply and directly.
- Let the machine do the "dirty" work such as repetitious functions or existing library functions.
- Replace repetitive expressions with calls to a common function.
- Check parameter passing to ensure effective use.
- Check for deeply nested structures.
- Use effective and illustrative indentation.
- Use single-entry-single-exit (SESE) source code.

Documentation

Degree of self-descriptiveness of a program.

- Make effective and adequate use of comments.
- Ensure effective use of variable names.
- Ensure consistency in the use of block documentation versus in-line documentation.

- Document the program thoroughly and consistently.
- Use meaningful variable names.
- Use descriptive and meaningful comments.

Layout

Arrangement, plan, and formatting of the program.

- Make effective use of programming space (horizontal and vertical) to assist reader comprehension.
- Make effective use of the physical arrangement of the program layout to assist comprehension, readability, clarity, and structure.
- Parenthesize to enhance logical and physical clarity.
- Make concise and effective use of space.

Style Metrics

Style reads a program, computes a number of counts, and uses these counts to decide if a certain principle of style has been violated. The counts are based on a **metric** — *a number representing some feature of a program.*

Devising metrics is a highly controversial topic in software engineering. Assigning meaning to the metrics is even more speculative, so quantitative thresholds are assigned by the user of *Style*. Default thresholds are provided by *Style* for beginner, intermediate, and advanced programmer levels. The following metrics and their meanings are used to produce the associated message.

Economy

- SUPER VAR (Superfluous variables): A superfluous variable is any variable that does not provide useful results, such as an intermediate variable that does not enhance the readability of the program. This measure is estimated from the ratio of the total number of variables to the number of executable lines of code (TOTAL VAR/EXEC LOC).

    The message is "A larger than usual number of variables was used in this module. See if the number of variables can be reduced."

- OVER VAR (Overloading variables): A variable name is "overloaded" when it is used in more than one context. Variable overloading is estimated by counting the number of lines between uses of a variable. If the line count exceeds some constant value, then the variable is 'estimated' as being used for a different context (OVER VAR).

    The message is "Some variable was used for several different purposes in this module. You should use more variable names."

- TOTAL VAR (Total number of variables): Use the least number of variables possible. If the total number of variables is greater than some constant, a message is issued.

  The message is "This module seems to contain an unusually high number of variables. Try to reduce the number of distinct variables."

Modularity

LONG MOD (Long modules): Check for modules with more than n (say 50) and less than m (say 10) lines of source code ($m > \text{EXEC LOC} < n$).

The message is "This module contains too few (many) lines of code."

MOD SIZE (Module size): Check all functions/procedures for a complexity measure greater than 10, where complexity is defined as the number of conditionals such as IF/DO and WHILE/REPEAT/CASE.

The message is "The logic of this module is too complex. There are so many control paths that it may be difficult to test. The module should be divided into several modules."

LOG FUNC (More than one logical function in a module): Check for functions that perform more than one logical function. This measure is estimated by counting number of I/O and arithmetic statements (I/O and ARITHMETIC) in the same module.

The message is "This module has more than one logical function. These should be separate modules."

PARAM PASS (Parameter passing): Minimize the number of parameters passed. Count the number of parameters being passed (PARAM COUNT) to determine if the number of parameters passed is greater than n.

The message is "Too many parameters are being passed to the module. This makes it difficult to keep them straight. Either make some of the parameters global or else modify the module."

Simplicity

CLARITY (Write clearly — don't be too clever and don't sacrifice clarity for efficiency): See MOD SIZE.

The message is "The logic of this module is too complex. There are so many paths through it that it may be difficult to test."

PAREN (Parenthesize to avoid ambiguity): Check extended lines of code for use of parentheses. Any line of source code, either an assignment or logical statement (IF statement), which contains more than n words, or more than m operators should contain parentheses (NOT PAREN & MAX SOURCE $> n$ or NUM OPER $> m$).

The message is "This module contains long lines of source code without parentheses. Include parentheses to make the statements more understandable."

NUM PAREN (Check for the number of operators in an expression to determine the number of parentheses): There should be one set of parentheses for every logical operator. Count the number of operators in each logical expression to determine if the number of parentheses is sufficient (NUM OP and PAREN).

The message is "This module has an expression with many logical operators. Include parentheses to make the statements more understandable."

IF THEN (Avoid unnecessary branches): Check for an IF-THEN-ELSE statement with no executable statement on one of its alternatives.

The message is "This module contains IF-THEN-ELSE statements with null branches. These empty paths make the program more complex than necessary."

GOTO (Avoid unnecessary GOTOs): Check for the ratio of GOTO statements to all source code (COUNT(GOTO)/EXEC LOC) and total number of GOTOs (COUNT(GOTO)). If the ratio is greater than 5% or if the number of GOTOs is greater than four for any module, then print a message.

The message is "This module contains too many GOTO statements. Reduce the number of GOTO statements for a less complex module."

NEST SUB (Check subprogram nesting): A deeply nested subprogram structure complicates the structure of the module. Count the number of embedded subprograms. There should be no more than four levels of nesting (NEST SUB).

The message is "This module is complicated because it contains too many levels of nesting. Reduce the nesting by using a CASE statement or breaking it into modules."

AVG NEST (Average nested level): The average level of nesting for each LOC should not exceed n. Count the nesting level of each line of code and take a weighted average (the nesting level times the number of lines at that level divided by the total number of lines in the module). Check for an average nesting level greater than n (SUM(NESTED LEV)/TOTAL NESTED $> n$).

The message is "This module contains too much nesting. Reduce the nesting level."

MAX NEST (Compute the maximum nesting level): Find the maximum nesting level of any line in each module. Count the nesting level of each line of code to determine the maximum nesting level (MAX NEST).

The message is "This module contains extreme nesting. Reduce the nesting levels by a CASE statement or break it into modules."

Structure

ELSE NULL (IF-THEN-ELSE statements with a null condition): Do not allow null conditions in an IF-THEN-ELSE.

The message is "This module contains IF-THEN-ELSE statements with a null condition."

ELSE AND (Check for ELSE GOTO and ELSE RETURN): Control the use of a branch from an ELSE condition and a return from an ELSE condition. Check for a RETURN or GOTO condition in IF-THEN-ELSE (IF-THEN-ELSE).

The message is "This module has GOTO or RETURN statements from an IF-THEN-ELSE statement."

MULTI IF-ELSE (The use of multiple GOTOs to replace a complex IF-THEN-ELSE): Use IF...ELSE IF...ELSE IF...ELSE... or a CASE statement to implement multiway branches rather than using GOTOs. Check for complex IF-ELSE-IF-ELSE... conditions (MULTI IF-ELSE).

The message is "This module contains multiple GOTO statements. Multiple GOTO statements could be replaced with IF-THEN-ELSE statements or with a CASE statement."

Documentation

CONSISTENT (Thorough and consistent documentation): This measure is estimated by checking for consistent use of in-line versus block comments in all modules.

The message is "Commenting is not consistent. Both in-line and block comments should be used in this module."

HEADER (Use of a header block of comments after the beginning of a function or procedure): This checks for the existence of comments at the beginning of a module. It does not measure the effectiveness of the comments (HEADER).

The message is "This module does not contain a block comment. Each module should contain a block comment at the beginning that describes what the module does."

COMMENTS (Variables are described by comments): Ensure that all variables are properly and thoroughly documented. This measure is estimated by computing the ratio of executable lines of code to comments (EXEC LOC/COMMENTS). If the ratio is less than a percentage n (say 10%) or greater than a percentage m (say 80%), output a message.

The message is "There are too few (many) comments in this module."

MEANINGFUL VAR (Meaningful variable names): Check for meaningful variable names. This measure is estimated by checking for variable names with a word length less than n (say 3) characters or greater than m (say 32) characters (VAR LEN).

The message is "Some of the variable names in this module are short and are not meaningful."

ADEQUATE (Effective and adequate comments): Estimate the ratio of the number of words used in the comments (NUM WORD / COMMENTS) to ensure adequate comments. If the ratio is less than a percentage n (say 10%) or greater than a percentage m (say 80%), output a message.

The message is "There are too few (many) comments in this module. Consider removing some and making the remaining comments more meaningful."

OVERCOMMENT (Don't use excessive comments): Overcommenting is a subjective measurement depending on the expertise of the maintenance programmer and on the level of understanding of the program. This measure is estimated from the average number of words in each comment (AVG COMMENTS), and checked against an upper and lower bound, $n < \text{AVG COMMENTS} > m$ (for values such as $n = 50$ and $m = 3$).

The message is "The comments in this module are too short. Try adding some depth and meaning to your comments. (The comments in this module are too long. The comments are overpowering the actual code.)"

Layout

VERTICAL (Effective use of programming space, both horizontal and vertical, to assist with program comprehension): This measure is estimated by computing the ratio of blank lines to comments on the page (BLANK/COMMENTS).

The message is "There are too few (many) blank lines per comments in this module. Use blank lines to make comments more visible."

AVG COMMENTS (Compute the average number of comments as an estimate to enhance clarity): This measure is estimated by comparing the average number of words in comments with the number of executable lines of code (AVE WORDS/LOC).

The message is "The comments in this module are too short. Trying adding some depth and meaning to your comments. (The comments in this module are too long. The comments dwarf the actual code.)"

SPACE (Concise and effective use of space): This measure is estimated by comparing the ratio of blank lines to the number of total lines with threshold n (BLANK/LOC $> n$).

The message is "Make more use of blank lines to separate parts of the program."

MAX BLANK (Maximum number of blank lines): The maximum number of consecutive blank lines should not exceed some value (say 10). Check for any modules with more than 10 consecutive blank lines (MAX BLANK).

The message is "There are too many blank lines in this module. Consider reducing the number."

A QUESTION OF STYLE

Program support environments increase programmer productivity by decreasing the edit-compile-link-run-edit cycle. In the case of Think Pascal, this is done by automatic conversion of as much of the source code as possible, as soon as possible. Thus, statements are checked for syntactic correctness and tokenized as soon as entered. These tokenized statements are then translated to memory-resident executable code as soon as a unit is entered. Additional speed is obtained by keeping the application project up to date by compiling only those units that have changed since the previous compilation. A final speed enhancement is made possible by linking the units "on the fly" (as they are compiled).

The dataflow diagram in Figure 9-21 shows how an application is constructed with the TP PSE. Resources (menus, windows, dialogs, icons) are entered into a separate text file and compiled with RMaker. The binary resource file is linked into the final application implicitly.

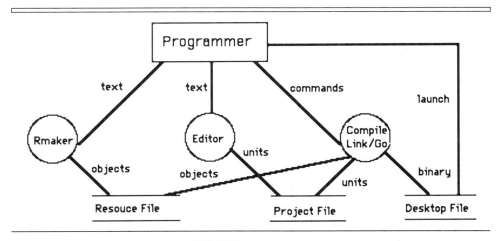

FIGURE 9-21. Dataflow diagram of LSP PSE

The programmer then enters the source text into a window — one window for each unit — and it is immediately checked for syntactic errors. Each unit is added to the project file where it is compiled and linked following each modification. The application can then be executed in one of two ways: by selecting either GO or LAUNCHING.

When running the application by selecting GO, the application is run under the umbrella of TP. This permits tracing, observation of variables, and the use of debugging tools. When LAUNCHED, the application must be recompiled as a stand-alone application. Stand-alone applications are launched directly from the desktop like all other applications.

Programming environments are ideal for handling the artifacts of coding, but the process of coding requires careful thought and a complete understanding of the full software lifecycle. We know that a modest investment in coding style can return big benefits later in the lifecycle, when the source code must be enhanced and repaired. Therefore, it is imperative to observe a number of stylistic conventions.

There are many rules for coding style — we listed over 100. Writing maintainable code is easy: simply write clearly and concisely so that someone else can quickly understand and modify your code. In most cases, the original programmer will not be around during maintenance. Therefore, the code must be self-documenting.

A major opportunity exists for reducing effort, time, and errors in coding by using reusable components. In one empirical study of system software (over 20,000 lines of code), it was observed that over 92% of the code performed identifiable "small-scale functions" of 1) searching a data structure, 2) moving a data structure, 3) initializing a data structure, 4) translating the contents of a data structure, and 5) comparing two similar data structures[21]. The data structures, in this empirical study, were arrays, linked lists, and strings. A major savings of time and effort would have resulted from reuse of a simple abstract data type that encapsulated these three data structures.

Maintaining existing code is currently a multibillion dollar activity, and a variety of CASE tools continue to become available for automating some of the chores of the maintenance programmer. We devote an entire chapter to the topic. The careful and considerate programmer can significantly impact the high cost of maintenance with or without a maintenance CASE tool.

Terms and Concepts

APSE	L-structure
assertive style	localize
breakpoint	make utility
build order	metric
decoupling	M-object coding style
economy of style	modularity of style
implementation phase	programming style
implementation requirement	program support environment
instance variable	project
knot	PSE
layout style	reducible program

regression testing   simplicity of style
repeat-cycle SESE language   structure of style
semantic power   structured programming
SESE-structure   style

DISCUSSION QUESTIONS

1. What is the primary goal(s) of implementation? How does implementation interact with design and maintenance?

2. What is reusability? How does it impact implementation? design? maintenance? testing?

3. What is structured programming? What is a structured program? Is it possible to write a structured program without structured programming? Is it possible to use structured programming as a process, and obtain a structured program as an artifact?

4. Rewrite the following code as an SESE-reducible program (FORTRAN, anyone?):

```
DO 10 I = 1,15
  IF (A .EQ. B) GOTO 12
10 CONTINUE
  GOTO 30
12 ...etc...
  GOTO 40
30 ...etc...
40 STOP
```

5. What is semantic power? Describe how the semantic power of a programming language is increased by the ability to use predicates and nesting in a program.

6. Write a LightSpeed Pascal program to solve the quadratic equation: $A X^2 + B X + C = 0$. Be sure your solution considers all possible conditions: $A = 0$; $B = 0$; real and imaginary solutions. Use the programming environment to trace the execution of this program.

7. For problem 6, draw the flowchart of the program and show that it is SESE-structured by reducing it to a single chunk.

8. For problem 4, draw the flowchart of the FORTRAN program and show its knots. How many knots does it have?

9. Make a list of coding style conventions and tell why they enhance readability and comprehension of source code. (Make up your own list — don't use the conventions listed in this chapter.)

10. What is regression testing, and how do the file-naming conventions of the M-object coding style help in regression testing?

11. Give a build order for CoCoPro (the sample program). See the uses graph in previous chapters.

12. Write a reusable object called a LIST that encapsulates a linked list with operations for INITIALIZE, INSERT, SEARCH, DELETE, and COMPARE. How might this object be useful to another programmer? How might LIST be classified for easy identification and retrieval?

REFERENCES AND FURTHER READING

1. Institute of Electrical and Electronics Engineers, Inc. 1983. *Glossary of Software Engineering Terminology. ANSI/IEEE std 729-1983.* New York: IEEE.

2. Charette, R. N. 1986. *Software Engineering Environments: Concepts and Technology.* New York: McGraw-Hill.

3. Birrell, N. D., and M. A. Ould. 1985. London: Cambridge University Press.

4. Tully, C. J. 1987. *Prospects for Future Environments, Proceedings of the Ninth International Conference on Software Engineering, March 30 – April 2, 1987*: 340–341. Monterey, CA: IEEE.

5. Symantec Corporation. 1986. *Lightspeed Pascal User's Guide and Programmer's Reference.* Bedford, MA: Symantec Corp.

6. Pfleeger, S. L. 1987. *Software Engineering: The Production of Quality Software.* New York: Macmillan.

7. Prieto-Diaz, R., and P. Freeman. 1987. "Classifying Software for Reusability." *IEEE Software* 4, no. 1 (January): 6–16.

8. Lenz, M., H. A. Schmid, and P. F. Wolf. 1987. "Software Reuse Through Building Blocks." *IEEE Software* 4, no. 4 (July): 4–42.

9. Woodfield, S. N., D. W. Embley, and D. T. Scott. 1987. "Can Programmers Reuse Software?" *IEEE Software* 4, no. 4 (July): 58–59.

10. Emery, J. E. 1979. "Small-Scale Software Components." *ACM SIGSOFT Notes* 4, no. 4 (October): 18.

References to Style

11. Lake, A. 1988. *Style: A Tool for Evaluating Programming Style.* Corvallis, OR: Oregon State University.

12. Berry, R. E., and B. A. E. Meekings. 1985. "A Style Analysis of C Programs." *Communications of the ACM* 28, no. 1 (January): 80–88.

13. Conte, S. D., H. E. Dunsmore, and V. Y. Shen. 1986. *Software Engineering Metrics and Models.* Redwood City, CA: Benjamin/Cummings.

14. Kernighan, B. W., and P. J. Plauger. 1974. "Programming Style: examples and counter examples." *ACM Computing Surveys* 6, no. 4 (December): 303–319.

15. Kernighan, B. W. and P. J. Plauger. 1978. *The Elements of Programming Style.* New York: McGraw-Hill.

16. Ledgard, H. F. 1975. *Programming Proverbs.* Rochelle Park, NJ: Hayden.

17. McCabe, T. J. 1976. "A Complexity Measure." *IEEE Transactions on Software Engineering* SE-2, no. 4 (December): 308–320.

18. Meekings, B. A. E. 1983. "Style Analysis of Pascal Programs." *ACM SIGPLAN Notices* 18, no. 9 (September): 45–54.

19. Oman, P. W., and C. R. Cook. 1987. "A Paradigm for Programming Style Research." Corvallis, OR: Oregon State University.

20. Rees, M. J. 1982. "Automatic Assessment Aids for Pascal Programs." *ACM SIGPLAN Notices* 17, no. 10 (October): 33–42.

21. Redish, K. A. and W. F. Smyth. 1986. "Program Style Analysis: A Natural By-Product of Program Compilation." *Communications of the ACM* 29, no. 2 (February).

10

SQA: Testing and Debugging

PREVIEW

Software quality control of the implementation phase is achieved by various methods of verification: 1) the social interactions of programmers doing code reviews, 2) formal mathematical "proof" techniques, and 3) informal debugging and formal testing. We survey these technologies followed by detailed recommendations for debugging and testing.

Expert debuggers are shown to be much more productive than novices. Fortunately, debugging skill can be acquired through training.

Formal testing is based on the concept of program coverage — various coverage measures have been proposed, but which one is best? We show how to analyze a program, generate test cases from a coverage measure, and select test data values from test cases. These values force the program to execute its paths, conditions, and I/O.

Few CASE tools are in widespread use, but they can greatly reduce the time, effort, and cost of formal testing. However, there is reason to believe that human code reading is as effective as a CASE tool. Which is best, code review or CASE tool?

SOFTWARE QUALITY ASSURANCE

We have stressed the importance of software quality control throughout this book, but now the time has come to show how it is achieved. There are two stories: one about process and another about artifact. First, we survey the process and discuss the documentation items that typically accompany activities surrounding quality assurance. Then we look at tools and techniques for inspecting the artifacts of quality — the programs themselves. A variety of techniques are used to examine source programs: inspection, proof of correctness, and testing. In this chapter, we study testing. Formal methods such as proof of correctness are studied in the next chapter.

The Review Process

Recall from earlier chapters that SQA involves two fundamental activities: verification and validation. These are so closely tied together that they are abbreviated as V&V. **Verification** — *the process of determining whether or not the products of a given phase of development fulfill the requirements of the previous phase* — asks, is the software right?, while **validation** — *the process of evaluating the application at the end of development to ensure compliance with the requirements* — asks, is this the right software?

Verification has other definitions, which are used interchangeably by software engineers. For example, the ANSI/ASQC A3-1978 definition is, *the act of reviewing, inspecting, testing, checking, auditing, or otherwise establishing whether or not items, processes, services, or documents conform to requirements.* This just about covers everything in SQA!

Others give it a very specific definition: *the process of formally proving the correctness of a program.* This definition presumes a specific approach to verification. We will use the broader definitions since they allow a greater choice of tools.

SQA JARGON

SQA is filled with jargon, some of which is decoded below:

CDR critical design review
PDR preliminary design review
SDD software design description
SQA software quality assurance
SQAP software quality assurance plan
SRR software requirements review
SRS software requirements specification
SVVP software verification and validation plan
SVVR software verification and validation report

For a complete definition of terms used by software engineers and testers, see IEEE Standard for Software Quality Assurance Plans[1].

Small programs need little in the way of group SQA activity because, as we learned earlier, they are best developed by one individual. As the development activity increases in size (lines of code, number of programmers, and magnitude of the computing problem), the development process becomes more of a social process.

THE WALK-THROUGH

Inspection by walk-through has proven to be extremely effective in software quality control. Inspection meetings are run by a moderator who is typically a coworker rather than a supervisor, and must be limited to two hours in duration, not more than twice per day[2].

Get the big picture (whole team). The designer describes the overall problem and then the specific module to be inspected. The stage is set for the third part by noting whether this is a rework inspection or a new piece of code. Documentation is given to all members of the inspection team.

Prepare a brief (individual members). Using data provided beforehand, the team members study the design and/or source code to understand it. They are given a checklist to fill out and return when the whole team reconvenes.

Find errors (whole team). The implementor describes how the design will be implemented (I_1) or how the coding was done (I_2). Each logic decision is discussed at least once, and if the inspection is I_2, then every branch in the program is discussed. The discussion is opened up to the other members of the inspection team. The team tries to find errors. When errors are found, they are recorded. No solutions are discussed; only the errors are noted and recorded by the moderator for follow-up.

Rework the module. The implementor removes the defects. If more than 5% of the design code is reworked, the inspection must be done again. If 5% or less is reworked, the moderator can approve the inspection without reconvening the team.

Follow-up rework. The moderator must guarantee the correction of every error, resolution of every concern, and settlement of every issue raised during the previous inspection meeting. If there are fewer than 5% errors, then the inspection is completed.

Effectiveness. Russell[3] reports significant advantages of the inspection technique when used on large programs over a long period of time. His conclusions are based on over 2.5 million lines of imbedded real-time software systems. Over 42,000 product defects were eliminated, proving the walk-through to be 2 to 4 times more effective (faster) than any single form of testing. His conclusions are:

1. Properly applied inspection techniques can detect approximately 1 software defect per person-hour invested.

2. Inspection finds software defects from 2 to 4 times faster than software testing.

3. Inspection uncovers errors which may not be detected at all by testing techniques, for instance missing or extra code anomalies.

4. Inspection can enhance testing by removing up to 80% of the code defects before testing starts.

In particular, SQA becomes a group activity, complete with overhead in the form of meetings, documentation, and other forms of human social activity. We concentrate only on the minimum recommended core SQA activities called **reviews** — *formal meetings at which the preliminary or detailed design of a system is presented to the user, customer, or other interested parties* (the developers!) *for comment and approval*[1]. These meetings are also referred to as *inspections, walk-throughs,* and *audits*[1]:

SRR

The SRR is held to ensure the adequacy of the requirements stated in the SRS. It answers the questions, will the completed application satisfy the customer?

PDR

The PDR is held to evaluate the technical adequacy of the preliminary design as stated in the SDD. It answers the question, will the completed application meet technical goals for speed, storage, functionality?

CDR

The CDR is held to decide if the detailed design as given in the SDD satisfies the requirements as stated in the SRS. It asks, have we overlooked something in the transformation of the requirements into a software architecture?

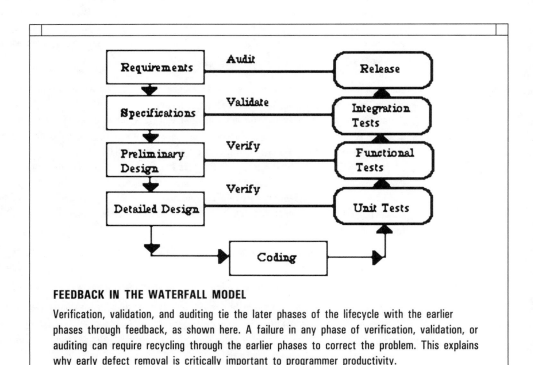

FEEDBACK IN THE WATERFALL MODEL

Verification, validation, and auditing tie the later phases of the lifecycle with the earlier phases through feedback, as shown here. A failure in any phase of verification, validation, or auditing can require recycling through the earlier phases to correct the problem. This explains why early defect removal is critically important to programmer productivity.

SVVR

The SVVR is held to evaluate the adequacy and completeness of the verification and validation methods defined in the SVVP. It asks, if we apply our V&V plan, will it yield a stringent test of the system?

Functional Audit

This audit is held prior to release of the software to verify that all requirements have been met. This is a final check on the requirements specification per the SRS document.

Physical Audit

This audit is held to verify that the software and its documentation are consistent and ready to deliver. This is a final check on the package itself to make sure everything is in the box, ready to be shipped.

In addition, most software development groups establish software configuration controls (version and release control), bug reporting methods, technical support systems, and information management systems to record information on the process itself. The information management system for self-assessment is very important to "close the loop" and get information about the process of development. This information is used to improve the process in the following ways:

Anomaly Tracking

Bugs and other anomalies in the product are recorded and analyzed. Software quality can be improved in subsequent projects by learning from past mistakes. For example, if the majority of errors reported by users occurred in one module of an earlier system, the team can learn why, and correct the problem in the next project.

Evaluation of Tools

Past performance with CASE tools can be evaluated, and if certain tools are productivity enhancers, they can be used again; if not, they can be dropped. For example, cost estimation tools such as CoCoPro can be evaluated for accuracy, and weights adjusted to improve their predictive ability.

Evaluation of Process

The process itself can be studied in retrospect. For example, reviews of test cases may turn out to be too time-consuming. If so, the formal review can be dropped in favor of informal, individual reviews.

Methods of Verification

The old adage about a glass of water being half full or half empty applies to verification. We can seek absolute perfection by attempting to show that a program is correct, or alternately, we can attempt to find all errors that exist. **Correctness** *is the extent to which software is free from design and coding defects.* The goal of mathematical methods of verification is to prove the absence of all errors, while the goal of formal testing is to show the presence of any errors. Figure 10-1 gives a taxonomy of methods of verification.

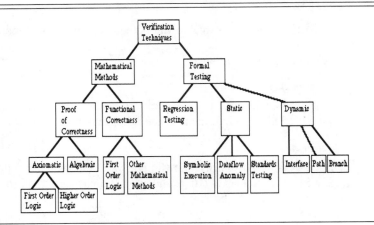

FIGURE 10-1. Taxonomy of verification techniques

The difference between "absence of errors" and "presence of errors" may seem indistinguishable at first, but in practice there is a major difference in these two approaches. For one thing, we know that mathematical methods have theoretical limits, per Manna and Waldinger[4].

Correctness of Specifications: We can never be sure that the specifications are correct. This is a kind of "halting problem" paradox that goes as follows: Suppose person or machine A writes a specification S1, and claims that it is correct. Now suppose person or machine B checks the specification for correctness. If B says that S1 is correct, how do we know B is telling the truth? If we invite person or machine C to check on B, how do we know that C is telling the truth? We can add person or machine D, E, F, . . ., to check the correctness of everyone before, but we have no "oracle of truth" to verify any of the persons or machines is itself correct, and therefore telling the truth.

Intractability of Verification: No verification system can verify every correct program. This argument is similar to the preceding one, except we divide all programs into two categories: all correct programs in one category, and all defective programs in a second category. Now, we analyze only the correct programs using our "perfect" verification system. If it tells us that all programs are correct, it may be a coincidence; if it finds one program that it claims is incorrect, then it may be due to a defect in the verification system, itself. How do we know? If we add person or machine B to verify the verification system, we run into the same paradoxical "who is checking the checker" problem as before. Therefore, it is impossible to build a perfect verification system, because when we use it to verify itself, we run into the halting problem.

Correctness of Tools: We can never be certain that a verification system is correct. This is a consequence of the previous argument. The unfortunate truth is that we cannot build provably correct tools any more than we can build provably correct programs. (A program is a program is a program. Or a rose by any other name. . . .)

Technical Limitations: Logical limitations are inherent in the verification process, and cannot be surmounted by any technical innovation. Faster computers with infinite memory cannot solve these problems because they are not technical problems. These limitations are due to paradoxes, which are intractable by their very nature.

So, if theoretical limitations are so severe, why do we care about the mathematical approach? First, the study of mathematical methods is valuable in its own right because it shows how to think logically about programming. It provides a basis for program structure (no GOTOs, assertive programming), and it provides an intellectual way of writing concise, clear, and maintainable code.

Second, there are cases where it is essential to guarantee the total correctness of a program, and even if the technique is impossible, it can generally be used to advantage in special cases. For example, mission-critical software (for a manned mission to Mars or for control of transportation systems) must work every time it is used. Wherever human life is endangered, mission-critical software must be thoroughly verified.

Mathematical Methods

Verification by mathematical means attempts to prove **total correctness**, *a designation indicating that a program's output assertions follow logically from its input assertions and processing steps, and that, in addition, the program terminates under all specified input conditions.* An **assertion** *is a logical expression specifying one or more conditions that the program must satisfy in order for the program to be correct.*

There are two broad categories of mathematical methods for finding total correctness. The proof of correctness approach models the source code directly. That is, proof of correctness techniques rewrite the program in a mathematical form and then attempt to prove that the abstracted program is correct by using theorem-proving techniques. In the axiomatic approach, first order (or higher order) logic is used to model the source code program. Certain predefined axioms are assumed to be true for each programming language construct. These axioms represent the semantics of the language constructs. For example, one axiom represents the meaning of an **if** statement, and another axiom represents the meaning of a **while** loop. Because this is a large topic, we delay additional details until the next chapter.

The algebraic approach to proof of correctness uses equational algebra as the model language instead of equational logic. Specifically, each language construct is modeled by a function. For example, assignment statements are modeled by an equation that computes the value of a variable; loops are replaced by a function that computes the same side effects as the original loop, and so forth. This topic is also expanded in greater detail in the next chapter.

The functional correctness technique really does not prove the program, but instead proves the algorithm underlying the program. Functional correctness is checked by building a mathematical model of the algorithm and then showing that the model is correct by any number of mathematical means. For example, a program that sorts a list in ascending order by means of the merge-sort algorithm is proved by showing that the merge-sort algorithm correctly rearranges the list into ascending order. We must accept on good faith that the program carries out the algorithm properly.

Formal Testing

In contrast, formal testing is less ambitious than mathematical methods, because it attempts to reveal the presence of as many errors as possible rather than to prove the absence of all errors. Hence, testing can never guarantee that all errors have been found. Indeed, testing is imperfect, but theoretically feasible! The goal of formal testing is to find methods of testing that are as reliable as possible, that is, techniques that find high percentages of errors.

Regression testing is a special form of verification that uses data from an earlier test to reveal the presence of errors that may have been introduced by enhancement or maintenance of the original code. **Regression testing** *is the selective retesting to detect faults introduced during modification . . . to verify that modifications have not caused unintended adverse effects, or to verify that a modified system still meets its specified requirements.*

Most developers use static analysis and dynamic testing to reveal the presence of errors. **Static analysis** *is the process of evaluating a program without executing it.* Static analysis can be as rudimentary as desk checking, code auditing by walk-throughs, and inspection by a code reader, or it can be done by sophisticated CASE tools that read and analyze the source code automatically.

Symbolic execution *is a technique in which program execution is simulated using symbols rather than actual values for input data, and program outputs are expressed as logical or mathematical expressions involving these symbols.* For example, the following (incorrect) program for computing the absolute value of input VAL can be rewritten as a symbolic program:

```
function ABS(VAL : integer) : integer;
  begin
  if VAL < 0 then ABS := -VAL;
end; {ABS}
```

We replace the actual variables with symbolic values, such as ϕ for VAL, and $\overset{\circ}{a}$ for ABS. Then we simulate the execution of ABS by forward substitution of ϕ and $\overset{\circ}{a}$ for VAL and ABS. The result in this simple example is two possible mathematical expressions involving the symbols:

$$\overset{\circ}{a} = \text{``undefined''} \text{ if } \phi \geq 0; \text{ or } \overset{\circ}{a} = -(\phi) \text{ if } \phi < 0.$$

Symbolic execution results in a very large number of mathematical expressions from even simple programs. CASE tools have been constructed to automatically compute the formulas, but test results have not been as robust as with other techniques. This problem limits the utility of symbolic execution.

Dataflow anomaly checking *is a static analysis technique based on examination of the flow of data values through the program.* Each variable is traced through the program, and anomalies are recorded. For example, all variables should be assigned one, and only one, value before they are used.

A trace of each variable is made by marking the variable as u = undefined, d = defined, and r = referenced for each appearance of the variable in the code. All variables start out as undefined unless they are inputs; they are marked with a d when entered as an input or assigned a value during program execution; and they are marked with an r when used in a calculation or output statement.

To illustrate, suppose we analyze the anomaly in the absolute value function. VAL is defined by being an input parameter, then referenced twice — once in the Boolean expression VAL < 0, and again in the assignment to ABS.

Dataflow of VAL: drr if VAL < 0; dr if VAL ≥ 0.
Dataflow of ABS: ud if VAL < 0; u if VAL ≥ 0.

Patterns $u...$, $rd...$, and $ur...$ are anomalies, because they reveal possible errors. The ABS function has an error in it because of the $u...$ anomaly that says ABS is undefined for certain inputs of VAL. The function should define ABS for both legs of the **if** statement. The pattern $rd...$ says that a variable is referenced before it is used — another error. The pattern $ur...$ says a variable is used before it is defined — a third error.

CASE tools have been constructed to do automatic dataflow analysis[5]. In addition, CASE tools have been constructed to check for other anomalies like branches that may never be taken, arithmetic precision errors (**if** A = 0 **then**... may never occur exactly if A is a real number), and mismatched parameters in the interface part of a module.

STATIC ANALYSIS TOOLS

Some of the information-collecting tools for static analysis are:

1. Syntactic error messages: compiler warnings.

2. Statement occurrence histogram.

3. Cross-reference maps and tables.

4. Identifier usage patterns.

5. Procedure usage analysis.

6. Unreachable code.

7. Coding convention violations.

8. Mismatched parameter lists.

9. Module/procedure size.

10. Metrics.

Dataflow anomaly checking is a good technique for individual programmers desk checking procedures prior to running. It is also a valuable technique to use with older languages like FORTRAN that do little or no type checking. The technique is of little value for modern languages, however, when used under the umbrella of a program support environment such as the one described in chapter nine.

Standards Checking

Standards checking is similar to dataflow anomaly checking because it reads the source code automatically and checks for violations of programming standards. For example, the checker might count the number of comment statements per executable statement like the style analyzer described in chapter nine, or it might look for violations in language use (one-way branches, formats, and variable names). This tool is of less value to programmers who use modern languages and program support environments.

Dynamic testing *is the process of evaluating a program by executing it.* Once again, this can be rudimentary — simply running the program under normal or elaborate conditions. A **dynamic analyzer** *is a CASE tool for evaluating a program by monitoring the execution of the program.* A variety of monitoring techniques are implemented in the form of a dynamic analyzer.

The major difficulty in dynamic testing is to select test cases and corresponding test data that sufficiently exercise the code. In fact, the number of test cases can be so large that complete testing might take decades to finish, even on a very fast computer. Therefore, methods have been devised that reduce the number of test cases examined. These methods are based on various types of *test coverage measures*, a subset of program components that must be exercised in order to satisfy a test. A test based on *statement coverage*, for example, must execute all statements of a program at least once during the test.

Interface Testing

Interface testing is conducted to ensure that program or system components pass information or control correctly to one another. An interface test is based on the interface coverage measure. Therefore, test data that force all interfaces to be executed at least once is adequate for an interface test. While this may seem like a simple test to perform, the problem is complicated by additional factors such as how to select the test data. For example, do we execute each interface once, once for each set of possible actual parameters, or once for each procedure? As it turns out, interface testing is not very effective, especially when using a modern language compiler that checks interface coupling.

Path Testing

Path testing is a method of dynamic testing in which every path through the program is executed once. Path coverage means we must execute every path through the program at least once to satisfy the test. Once again, this technique appears to be good, but how do we select input values that force the program through every path? How many paths does the program have, and is it feasible to test them all?

The simple ABS function has two paths through it, which are easily forced by selection of two values for VAL. We need use only one positive and one negative (or zero) value for VAL:

TEST CASE 1: VAL = +2
TEST CASE 2: VAL = −1

The resulting values should be (2, 1), otherwise the ABS function fails the test.

Branch Testing (also Decision-Decision Testing)

Is a method in which every branch condition is executed once, but only one path after the decision is taken. The coverage measure here is the Booleans embedded within **loop**, **if**, and **case** statements. Every Boolean is executed at least once, but only one branch is taken. This method reduces the number of paths tested, but it may also reduce the number of errors revealed. Once again, how do we select test data that forces the program to "visit" every Boolean?

Branch coverage of function ABS is simple — we need only execute the **if** Boolean once. Therefore, either one of the test cases above will do:

TEST CASE 1: VAL = +2

While all branches is covered by this test, only one of the paths is covered. Clearly, branch testing is a major compromise over path testing. However, branch testing takes only half as much computer time.

Many other testing techniques have been suggested and implemented as CASE tools. For example, *mutation testing* creates an altered version of the program in order to evaluate the adequacy of test data. A program Boolean might be reversed, or a calculation altered to study its effect on the program. Obviously, if the result is the same for both original and mutation, the test data is not adequate.

DEBUGGING

Testing is characterized as a more formal process than debugging. Debugging is typically an individual, personalized activity, whereas testing is more formal and often involves the whole team. Therefore, these two modes of quality control will be studied separately. We first examine debugging, and then return to the problem of testing.

Debugging is the process of locating, analyzing, and correcting suspected faults. Debugging is much more focused on revealing errors, rather than verifying requirements.

Debugging is difficult for several reasons: 1) programmers often develop wrong models about the way their program should work, and hence overlook many errors; 2) on-line and interactive debugging tools as found in modern program support environments are often difficult to understand and may not supply the information needed by a programmer; 3) the program changes as errors are found and removed, making it difficult for a programmer to retain an understanding of the program; 4) the programmer must keep track of too many details; and 5) debugging requires many problem-solving skills which may require training to learn and use[6].

HOW TO DEBUG

Nanja[6] has shown that most programmers do not fully understand the debugging process. Here is a simple algorithm for finding bugs:

1. Employ a simple hierarchical search for bugs — do not read the program from beginning to end like a book.

2. Look for syntax errors first, because they are the easiest to find and fix; and they may be related to deeper errors.

3. Gain an overall understanding of the program by concentrating on the most-probable errors first — **if** and loop control structures, I/O, long assignment statements, and finally Boolean expressions.

4. Beware of debugging aids and tools that are counterproductive. Poor tools are not a substitute for a disciplined approach.

Most of the difficulties listed above can be overcome by understanding the process and by adopting a debugging strategy based on knowledge of where bugs hide in code, and how they can be flushed out. One of the most productive approaches to debugging is based on the theory of the most-probable errors (MPE) in software.

Most-Probable Errors

Pareto (1848–1923) was an Italian economist who claimed that "80% of the problems can be found in 20% of the system." Known as Pareto's Law or the 80/20 Rule, this observation is often quoted in software engineering because it explains many phenomena. In particular, it explains testing: 80% of the errors can be found in 20% of the code; 80% of the effort is used to find the final 20% of the errors; and so forth.

Poston[7] defines **MPEs (Most-Probable Errors)** *as the most frequent mistakes (actions or inactions) that result in a fault in a work product (plan, specification, program, and so on)*. As we will show, this is a most useful principle in testing and debugging.

If we can identify which parts of a program are responsible for the MPEs then we can reduce the overall effort of debugging by concentrating on these parts. The challenge, then, is to understand the processes that lead to errors, to identify the artifacts containing them, and to concentrate on these artifacts. Where are errors in software systems?

Remember that an *error, failure, fault, bug,* or *anomaly* is any discrepancy between a computed, observed, or measured value or condition and the true, specified, or theoretically correct value or condition[1]. Most often, errors are the result of a human action: the omission or misinterpretation of user requirements, incorrect translation into design and/or code, or incorrect implementation of algorithms in code, for example.

COMMON ERROR CATEGORIES

Design:
Code does not match specs
Identifiers do not match data dictionary entries
Module structure does not match detailed design specs
Wrong algorithm, wrong data structure
Missing requirements/specs/component

Computation:
Incorrect operand in expression
Incorrect placement of parentheses
Sign convention error
Unit or data conversion error
Underflow/Overflow
Incorrect/inaccurate assignment
Loss of precision/accuracy
Missing calculation

Logic:
Incorrect operand in expression
Logic activities out of sequence
Checking wrong variable or condition
Missing test
Loop iterates wrong number of times
Duplicate tests

Data Input & Output:
Wrong format
Incorrect protocol (communication)
Wrong device
Wrong file
Wrong location in file

Data Handling:
Missing initialization
Wrong initial values
Incorrect flag setting
Incorrect bit manipulation
Wrong format, type, scale, operation
Subscripting error
Pointer dereferencing errors

Interface:
>   Wrong procedure called
>   Procedure invocation error
>   Wrong parameter type, value, order
>   File format/access error
>   Module interfaces don't match

Other:
>   Performance/timing problems
>   Memory limits exceeded
>   Synchronization error
>   I/O and CPU timing error

Errors are introduced at various stages of the lifecycle. Errors introduced during implementation can be classified into various *error categories*, the set of classes into which errors might fall. If errors are observed to occur more often in one category than in another, we can form a theory about the MPEs; from this theory, we can deduce where the errors are likely to be found. One such error category is shown in the sidebar on this and the previous page.

An *error model* can be constructed from error data and the theory of MPEs. Such a mathematical model is used to predict or estimate the number of remaining errors, required test time, and similar characteristics of software.

Boies and Gould [8] studied the rate of errors encountered during translation from a programming language into object code, and concluded that translation errors are *not* a major problem in software development, see Table 10-1. They instrumented a mainframe computer system with measurement tools to observe the number of times a compiler or assembler found errors. In this experiment, program runs were divided into three categories: 1) no translation errors, 2) one or more errors, and 3) the translator found so many errors or such severe errors that it was unable to continue.

TABLE 10-1. Translator error rates

Translator Error Rates in Percentages[8]

Language	0 Errors	≥ 0 Errors	Failed
FORTRAN	78	16	6
PL/I	73	17	10
Assembler	62	12	26

TABLE 10-2. Translator versus execution error rates in student programs

Compile Time Error Rates		Execution Time Error Rates	
Error Category	Percentage of Total	Error Category	Percentage of Total
Assignment	26.0	Arithmetic faults	3.5
Statement sequence	22.0		
Identifiers	14.8		
DO iteration	6.8		
Punctuation	6.6		
I/O statements	5.6	I/O operations	64.2
Reference/definition	5.4	Reference/definition	31.3
Format statements	4.6		
Branch statements	2.4		
All others	5.8	All others	1.0

In 78% of the cases, FORTRAN programs compiled with no errors. Assembler language syntax errors were the most frequent, but almost two-thirds of the runs were successful. In addition, most syntactic errors can be easily remedied, and the translation attempted again. Modern program support environments make translation errors even less of a problem.

Errors were observed and classified by Moulton and Muller [9] to reveal MPEs in student FORTRAN programs; see Table 10-2. In this study, both compile time and execution time errors were tabulated and compared. Clearly, there is a major difference between these two major classifications. For inexperienced students, compile time errors in assignment statements, statement sequencing, and identifiers are a major difficulty, while almost all of the execution errors stemmed from I/O and reference/definition errors. (In FORTRAN, most reference errors occur in array subscripts.)

The student data is most interesting because it distinguishes the great difference between compile and execution phase errors, but it is biased toward novice programmers. Few software engineers are novices, so we should look at data collected from experienced programmers. This was done by Young[10], who compared novice and

TABLE 10-3. Novice and advanced programmer performance

Error Rates (in Percentages) for Beginner and Advanced Programmers				
Category	Beginner	(First Run)	Advanced	(First Run)
Syntax	12	22	17	31
Semantic	41	45	21	28
Logic	35	21	51	34
Clerical	5	8	4	6
Other	7	5	7	1

advanced programmer performance, see Table 10-3. Young also collected error data from "first run" and "subsequent run" cases. This method factored out the effects of syntax error removal in the first run of a program.

Young's subjects were classified "beginners" or "advanced" by years of experience as programmers. (This classification could be challenged, because years of programming may not be equivalent to capability.)

Again, Young's data supports the conjecture that syntax errors are not a problem. However, it is interesting to note that advanced programmers experienced a higher rate of syntax errors than novices. Perhaps experienced programmers pay less attention to the language, and more attention to the problem to be solved.

Semantic errors occur during program execution and are associated with misinterpretation. Logic errors occur during execution as well, and are associated with the algorithm. Clerical errors range from punctuation to documentation problems.

Both groups committed major errors in semantics and logic. Beginners were, however, roughly twice as likely to commit a semantic error as were advanced programmers. Apparently, as programmer experience increases, semantic errors decrease.

Interestingly, the rate of logic errors for advanced programmers is half again as high as it is for beginners. It seems as if the advanced programmer's error rate simply shifts from semantic to logic errors.

TYPICAL EXECUTION ERRORS

Semantic:
- Uninitialized variables
- Improperly shared variables
- Array subscript out of range
- Improper program termination
- Improper linkages and parameter passing
- Improper data formats
- Overflow/Underflow
- Incorrect address calculation

Logic:
- Misuse of compound Boolean expressions
- Misuse of nested **if** statements
- Incorrect exit from procedure
- Improper handling of flags, return codes, etc.
- Errors in complicated computational sequences

Clerical:
- Spelling, terminator, alignment, typing errors
- Wrong documentation, listing, problem definition
- Mistaking zero for the letter 'O'

A more detailed analysis by Young shows that 47% of the semantic and logic problems encountered by advanced programmers were due to incorrect keyword usage, wrong variable, operator, or constant, in contrast to 28% for beginners. The second most-frequent error rate for advanced programmers was 12% in "wrong statement sequences." The second most-frequent error rate for beginners was 14% in "missing statements." These figures lead to the following conclusions:

Error Discovery

Experience does not help reduce errors in the first run of a program.

Language-Based Problems

Beginners fail to understand both problem and programming language, while advanced programmers fail to adequately understand the problem or algorithm.

Intrinsic Complexity

Beginners underestimate the complexity of a program, while advanced programmers get bogged down in the specific details and logic of the solution.

In both groups, techniques for error prevention, detection, and repair are needed. Advanced programmers and beginners alike can benefit from learning how to avoid problem areas and where to look for potential errors.

Young suggested a mathematical model for computing the number of errors remaining after running the program R times. The parameters of this equation vary depending on the level of programmer.

$$PE = P_0 \, X^R,$$

where

P_0 = first-run coefficient. Young suggests 0.442 for beginners; 0.728 advanced, 0.479 combined.

X = programmer expertise. Young suggests 0.702 for beginners; 0.595 advanced, 0.678 combined.

R = number of trial runs during debugging and testing.

PE = proportion of errors remaining after R runs. $0.0 \leq PE \leq 1.0$

This equation does not tell how many errors remain in a program, only the fraction of total errors remaining. However, it can be used to estimate when to stop testing by solving for R:

$$R = [\text{Log}(PE/P_0)]/(\text{Log } X),$$

where R is rounded up to the nearest integer.

Using the parameters for the combined model and setting $PE = 10\%$ remaining errors, we get $R = 4$. Hence, 90% of the errors can be found by running the program 4 times.

TABLE 10-4. Relative error-proneness in PL/I

Relative Error-Proneness in PL/I[10]

Construct	Percentage of Defects	REP
Allocation	16	0.9
Assignment	29	0.7
Iteration	10	1.1
I/O Formats	6	1.5
Other I/O	8	1.1
Parameters/Subscripts	5	0.6
if-then-else	5	5.0
Delimiter (end)	4	3.3

Perhaps more important for identifying the MPEs of a program is Young's relative error-proneness (REP) measure and the data collected to support a rudimentary theory of MPE; see Table 10-4.

REP_j = (Percent errors due to construct j)/(Frequency of appearance of construct j in the program)

The REP number measures the error-proneness of a language construct by computing the ratio of the frequency of occurrence of faulty program statements to the total frequency of occurrence of the construct. The frequency of occurrence of each language construct can be approximated by computing an average over many programs. The percentage of errors per construct can also be found by observation. When this was done for PL/I programs, the MPE for a class of applications was found as follows:

The **if-then-else** and **end** constructs are highly error-prone and are therefore the source of the MPEs. Input/Output constructs are next in line, and loops are the third most probable source of errors. Interestingly, assignment statements are relatively "safe" when compared with their occurrence in a "typical" program. We can summarize these results even more succinctly:

First MPE: Loop and Branch constructs containing tests of Booleans are the source of the most-probable errors. These constructs should be checked first and most closely. Second MPE: Input/Output constructs are next most likely to have errors, so they should be checked next and carefully analyzed.

These guides are useful in testing, too. But this single source of empirical data is not sufficient to support an entire theory of MPE. REP numbers are probably biased by many factors such as the type of application, programmer's experience, and the programming language used. For example, Endres[11] studied errors in an operating system and found that most were caused by a poor understanding of the dynamic behavior of operating systems in general, and process representation in particular. While Endres did not compute REP numbers, he reports the error rates in Table 10-5.

TABLE 10-5. Expert strategy for debugging

Poor Understanding

Error Rate %	Cause of Error
17	Dynamic behavior and interprocess communication
12	Functions provided by the operating system
10	Machine configuration and architecture
3	Output listings and formats
3	Diagnostics
1	Performance

Implementation Bugs

Error Rate %	Cause of Error
8	Initialization of fields and tables
8	Counting and calculations
7	Addressing (pointers)
7	References to names
5	Bad patches (misplaced instructions)
2	Masks and comparisons
1	Range limits
16	Others: spelling, documentation, interface, etc.

Endres also supported Pareto's Law by observing that 80% of the errors were concentrated in 20% of the modules. In addition, he observed two other phenomena which have become legendary in debugging:

- After a certain point, it is better to throw away and rewrite an old module than to save and patch it.
- Any change produces at least one additional error, but usually only one.

Expert Debugging

The preceding analysis gives some ideas on where errors are likely to be found, and it suggests a strategy for debugging, see Figure 10-2. We know that debugging performance can be greatly improved by practice and careful cultivation of technique. Nanja[6] performed several protocol studies of experts and novices in the act of finding and correcting seeded errors in small programs. His experiments revealed several useful results:

- Experts employ a comprehensive approach to debugging, in which they first attempt to understand the program and then use this knowledge to find bugs, instead of working on isolated parts of the program.
- Experts correct multiple errors before rerunning the program. This increases their productivity by repairing "batches" of errors all at the same time.

- Experts are efficient. They modify fewer statements and introduce fewer new bugs into the program than do novices. This is probably a consequence of experience and heuristic knowledge of programming. Experts gain an intuitive sense of what happens when a program is modified — as we have seen, bug fixes tend to lead to other bugs.

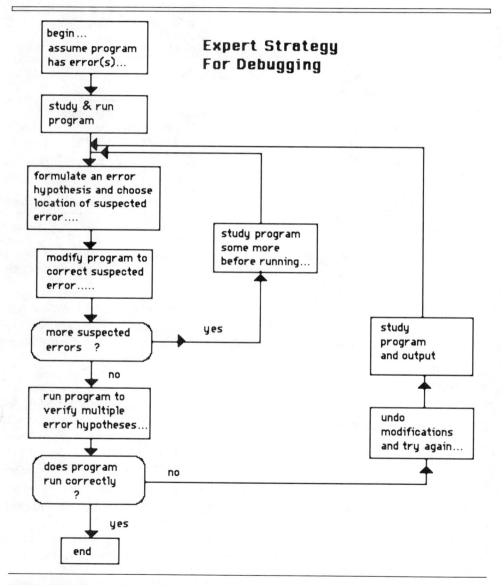

FIGURE 10-2. Expert debugging strategy

· Experts were better at recognizing and locating the source of errors than novices. Again, this is perhaps due to experience and an intuitive sense of what is wrong with a program when a certain behavior is observed.

In addition, an expert debugger's behavior is characterized by top-down comprehension of the program versus beginning-to-end; by correction of both semantic and logical errors at the same time versus trial-and-error correction of semantic errors only; by use of on-line debugging aids and mental execution versus embedded write statements and hand simulation of program execution; and by systematic isolation of errors versus trial-and-error isolation.

Nanja recommends the expert strategy shown in the flowchart as the best known approach to debugging, but keep in mind that his experiments were biased. His subjects were students instead of professional programmers, the programs were small, and the testing tools were simple. Nonetheless, this is a first step toward a more thorough understanding of debugging.

Nanja's study begs the question of what constitutes a "good" on-line debugging tool. Curiously, not much is known about which debugging aids work and which do not.

One inconclusive experiment revealed some surprising results. The time to find the cause and fix a seeded bug was recorded for programmers constrained by various "hints" as shown in Figure 10-3. One group had no hints in the form of aids; a second group was told the error category; a third group was given a sample I/O listing without correct

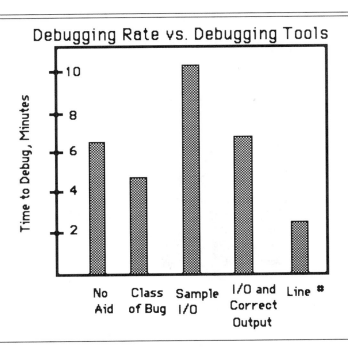

FIGURE 10-3. Relationship of debugging rate to debugging tools

answers; the fourth group was given both I/O listing and correct answers; and a final group was told which line contained the bug, but not what the bug was.

These results suggest that on-line debuggers that highlight the erroneous statement are most useful, followed by knowledge of the error category. This is not surprising, and is what most program support environments provide, but it is surprising that a sample I/O listing without correct answers is counterproductive. No aid is better than sample I/O. Sample I/O with the correct answer is not much better than no aid at all, and is inferior to knowledge of the error category.

FORMAL TESTING

Program testing has been known ever since programming began. In a 1950 manual written by Alan Turing, testing was defined as the extreme form of experimental correctness checking. The current interest in testing began in 1972, however, with a conference and the publication of a book by Hetzel[12].

Testing *is the process of exercising or evaluating a system or system component by manual or automated means to verify that it satisfies specified requirements or to identify differences between expected and actual results.* Of course, an error is a "difference between expected and actual results," so one major purpose of testing is to reveal errors, as stated before. Testing is different from debugging, however, because it serves as a means of verification of specifications as well as a method of correctness checking.

Goodenough and Gerhart[13] published the first paper that attempted to provide a theoretical foundation for testing. The centerpiece of their paper is a "fundamental theorem of testing" which established the properties of testing:

> **Fundamental Theorem of Testing:** Given program F with input data domain D, output requirement $OK(d) = OUTPUT(d,f)$, and test data selection criterion C, $OK(d)$ **iff** COMPLETE **and** RELIABLE **and** VALID **and** SUCCESSFUL, where d is a subset of D; OK, COMPLETE, RELIABLE, VALID, and SUCCESSFUL are predicates.

PRINCIPLES OF PROGRAM TESTING

Miller[14] lists some principles of testing:

SEPARABILITY A whole program can be tested by testing its parts.

REPEATABILITY The same result must be obtained each time the same part is tested with the same test data.

MEASURABILITY The results of testing must be measurable: it must be possible to determine when testing is done, that errors have been found, and so on.

FINITENESS All test cases must produce a result in a finite length of time.

UNIQUENESS Two identical tests are no better than either one of them.

This theorem says that no errors are present in a program tested with input data d, if and only if the test is COMPLETE, RELIABLE, VALID, and SUCCESSFUL. Obviously, we need to know what C, COMPLETE, RELIABLE, VALID, and SUCCESSFUL mean before we can interpret this theorem.

The data selection criterion C is a consequence of the coverage properties of the program (branches, paths, segments, and so on) — the parts that must be exercised to constitute a thorough test. For a test to be RELIABLE, C must ensure selection of tests that consistently reveal some, if not all, errors. For example, a test designed to reveal branching errors is RELIABLE if it reveals one or more faulty branch predicates.

A thorough test is a COMPLETE test. Specifically, COMPLETE is TRUE if the test exercises the whole program according to the coverage criterion implied by C. For example, the test might exercise all paths, branches, and data conditions for all possible values in D. In general, COMPLETE-ness is impractical, leading to a test condition problem.

Test Condition Problem: What are the test conditions (predicates) and their combinations used in the test to make the test COMPLETE?

Practically speaking, we use a coverage measure to estimate the completeness of a test. TER's (Test Effectiveness Ratios) are measures of COMPLETENESS. For example:

TER_0 = (Number of statements exercised)/(total executable statements in program)

TER_1 = (Number segments exercised)/(total number of segments in program)

TER_2 = (Number branches exercised)/(total number of branches in program)

The goal of all test methods is to maximize the TER and exercise as much of the program as possible. Unfortunately, TERs of 100% are impractical for all but the simplest programs — the number of possibilities is enormous in typical applications.

C is VALID if and only if for every error in a program there is a complete set of test data capable of revealing the error. Think of VALID this way: divide all test data into two sets, one containing data that tests the program and claims that no errors are present, and the other containing data that tests the program and reveals an error. Look at each input to the program taken from the second set. Do they drive the program to an error? If so, and the second set is not empty, C is VALID.

A test is SUCCESSFUL if it produces the correct output. Therefore, we can state the theorem in simple terms as, "a test of program F using test data d, selected by criterion C, shows no errors present when the test is thorough, the test reveals errors when they exist, for every error the test finds it, and the test produces correct output."

The fundamental problem of testing is to derive suitable test data to "force" the program. Test data selection is done by attempting to satisfy a coverage criterion. We can do this in a number of ways. Each method is responsible for a certain kind of testing technique, some more reliable than others. In the remainder of this section, we investigate some of these techniques.

Structure-Based Testing

One way to reduce the enormous number of possibilities in large software systems is to use structured testing techniques. We can, for example, use the inherent modular structure of the application to divide testing into parts. Then, by the principle of separability, we can be reasonably sure that the whole system is reliable if its parts are reliable.

Structure-based testing treats each function in the system as a black box. The functions are exercised in a variety of ways, each corresponding to partial coverage of the whole system of functions. Miller[14] lists the coverage levels of various structure-based testing:

S_0. Select test data that invokes all functions at least once. Unfortunately, this test is insufficient, because it does not fully exercise the entire system. S_0 does little more than test each function individually, as in unit testing.

S_1. Select test data that exercises all invocations of all functions at least once. This is the minimum useful system level test. Unlike S_0, this test forces every "call" to be executed at least once. Thus, if function A is invoked from three different places in the application, three calls are executed for function A.

S_2. Select test data that exercises all invocations of all functions at least once as in S_1, but in addition, each function is called several times — once for each actual parameter that is a logical expression. In this test, a function may be called more than in S_1, because it may have one or more logical expression (Boolean) parameters. A variation on this test is to include calls for each possible outcome of the Boolean expression. For example, if the actual parameter is A or (B and C), then the function must be called $2^3 = 8$ times to cover all possibilities.

S_D. Select test data that exercises every module down to a certain prescribed decision level, d. This measure tries to execute the most complex parts of a system.

Typical Test Result Summary [14]

Application Characteristics

Functions	128
Statements	60,881
Test Cases	1,544
Coverage Measured	89%

Testing Results

Coding Violations	1,296
Program Errors	190
Total Anomalies	1,486
Statements/Anomaly	40.96%
Error Rate per Statement	2.44%

S_t. Select test data that executes all calling chains from top to bottom of the call graph. This test tries to cover all paths leading to the application's functions.

S_3. Reduce the bulk of test data by selecting one test for each equivalence class of tests. An *equivalence class* is a set of test cases that produce the same result. It may be difficult to group test cases into equivalence classes, but if possible, the number of tests required to cover the system is greatly reduced.

Note that these test coverage strategies may hide a number of difficult and time-consuming problems associated with finding test cases, generating test data, and managing the results. For example, system testing may require loading a large file to exercise a "Disk Full" condition or running lengthy calculations to force a "Numeric Overflow" error message.

Unit Testing

Miller[14] lists coverage measurers for testing individual functions:

C_0. Select test data that forces execution of all statements in a program at least once. While most programmers think this is sufficient, it typically leaves out many conditions and interactions that may cause problems. This is not a recommended test coverage measure.

C_1. Select test data that forces execution of all segments in the unit. This is the coverage recommended and used by most experts in testing. A segment is defined as a straight-line piece of SESE code. This means each branch and each loop of a program is exercised at least once. However, a loop body may be executed only once, rather than the number of times indicated by the loop's parameters.

Coverage Analysis of a Small Function

Function Characteristics

Lines of COBOL test	2,391
Sentences	767
Segments	371

Coverage Measure

Initial coverage achieved	63%
Final coverage achieved	87%

Testing Results

Error Rate (% of sentences)	3.9%
Total Errors found	30
Untested segments	6

C_*.   Select test data that forces extended testing beyond C_1. For example, iterating loops more than one time; boundary testing with loop upper/lower limits; forcing all outcomes of Boolean expressions in loop and branch predicates; and forcing data to take on boundary values such as zero, maximum-integer, and maximum-floating point values.

Practical dynamic testing is based on C_1 coverage. The goal of C_1 testing is to achieve a TER_1 value of 100%, but 85% is acceptable in practice. Miller[14] gives a list of guidelines for the practicing software test engineer:

- The number of segments in a typical program unit is approximately 25% of DSI (recall that one DSI = one line of delivered source instructions). Thus, a 500-line unit will contain approximately 125 segments.

- No more than one test per segment is normally required, with approximately 2–8 segments being "retired" per test. Thus, out of the 125 segments expected in a 500 DSI unit, 16–63 runs are likely to be needed to thoroughly test the unit.

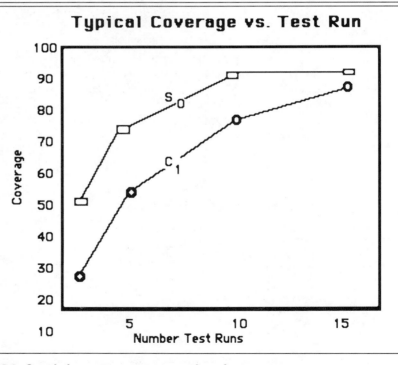

FIGURE 10-4. Cumulative coverage versus number of test runs

- While $TER_1 = 85\%$ is relatively easy to achieve, 100% may require some other test coverage technique. Exception testing and special value testing may be required. TER_1 values of 25–50% in initial testing are not unusual. Additional runs are required to bring the coverage ratio up to 85%.

The plot of cumulative coverage versus number of test runs in Figure 10-4 shows a near-linear increase in coverage as the number of tests increase. Notice that the last 10% coverage is increasingly difficult to obtain. For this reason, practitioners usually rely on a variety of test methods. But which methods complement one another?

Test Data Selection

Coverage measures such as S_1 and C_1 described in the previous sections give a theoretical basis for test case selection, but the theory does not recommend actual test data. How is test data obtained? The actual values used in a test run are obtained by forcing the program to execute a certain path, segment, or branch. We show how to select test data values according to some coverage criterion by examining several examples.

First, we look at a small unstructured FORTRAN program fragment, and then we take on a more difficult SESE-structured Pascal program. It will become clear why SESE-structure greatly reduces the complexity of program testing. Even so, it is often necessary to resort to heuristic rules for selecting "good" test data values.

The FORTRAN program in Figure 10–5 has several branches and GOTOs, giving rise to a knotted control flow graph as shown by the crossed control paths in (a). The knot occurs in the GOTO 30 and GOTO 40 branches. The knot in the program is responsible for an additional segment that we must consider when deriving test data. Regardless, seven segments can be identified and used to draw the DD-graph, a control-flow graph that connects the decision-to-decision points together. In this DD-graph, GOTOs and IFs are treated as segments, and straight-line code is lumped together into a single segment.

The DD-graph in (b) can be studied to identify paths as shown in (c). Actually, there are too many paths to enumerate if the GOTO 10 in S7 is exercised more than one time. Multiple passes through S7 are likely, but we cannot predict the number in advance. Therefore, we have listed only the three most obvious basic paths through the program fragment to show how path analysis in unstructured programs quickly becomes an insurmountable problem.

Having abandoned path analysis we attempt to reduce the number of possibilities by pruning the DD-graph. Suppose segment coverage is tried, leading to the reduced graph shown in (d). This graph has only three paths that force all segments to be executed. While this reduction may lead to uncovered segments, it does greatly reduce the number of possibilities. Each test case corresponds to one of the paths:

CASE 1. Force the program to exercise segments S1, S2, and S3.
CASE 2. Force the program to exercise segments S1, S2, S4, and S5.
CASE 3. Force the program to exercise segments S1, S2, S4, S6, and S7.

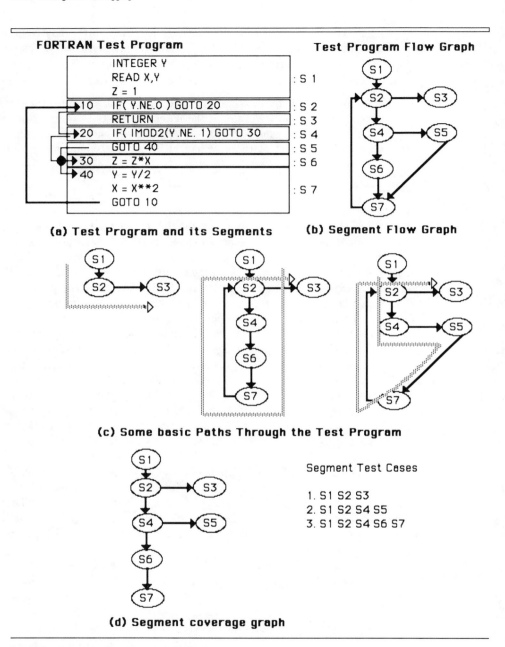

FIGURE 10-5. Example of test data selection

Test data values are derived from these test cases by simple enumeration of the Booleans, noting that S2 and S4 are the only segments containing Booleans: S1 contains (Y .NE. 0) and S4 contains (IMOD2(Y) .NE. 1). The first test is obvious; the second test is FORTRAN notation for deciding if Y is even or odd. Therefore, we can obtain the following test values corresponding to each test case:

CASE 1: (Y .NE. 0)
CASE 2: (Y .NE. 0) and (Y even/odd)
CASE 3: same as CASE 2

The number of tests are reduced even further by combining redundant tests into equivalence classes and simplifying as below.

Test Case 1': Y = 0
Test Case 2': (Y $\neq$ 0) and (Y odd)
Test Case 3': (Y $\neq$ 0) and (Y even)

Now, we can generate test data:

Test Data 1: Y = 0
Test Data 2: Y = ± 1
Test Data 3: Y = ± 2

The program is tested in three runs using these values. Note that we do not even know what the program does! Test data can be so mechanically derived that it is not necessary to understand the function of the program. However, someone must know the correct output values so that the program can be validated.

This example illustrates the overall process of test data selection, but it is far too simple to be convincing. In addition, interest in testing unstructured code is dwindling. The next technique illustrates a form of structured testing advocated by McCabe[15] and illustrated by Li[16]. McCabe's structured testing methodology relies on SESE-structure to force all paths through the program created by decision-decision segments. However, unlike full path analysis, McCabe's test case design procedure is based on his complexity measure. The technique is a modified path analysis technique that limits the number of paths through the program to McCabe's complexity metric, which is computed as (b + 1), where b is the *cyclomatic number* equal to the number of **if** and **loop** predicates in the program. The end result is that every statement, branch, and Boolean condition is covered. However, because the program is SESE-structured, the number of tests is bounded by the relatively small number, b.

In this method, the SESE-structured program graph is drawn as shown in the example of Figure 10-6. Each node of the graph corresponds to a Boolean decision (**if** and **loop** predicates). The arcs correspond to all possible outcomes of *individual* Boolean tests. Thus, some DD paths are represented by multiple arcs, one for each Boolean test.

Test-Case Design for McCabe's Complexity-based Coverage[16]

1. Draw the modified DD-graph as shown in Figure 10-6, where multiple arcs represent all possible outcomes of compound Boolean expressions and/or case-constructs.

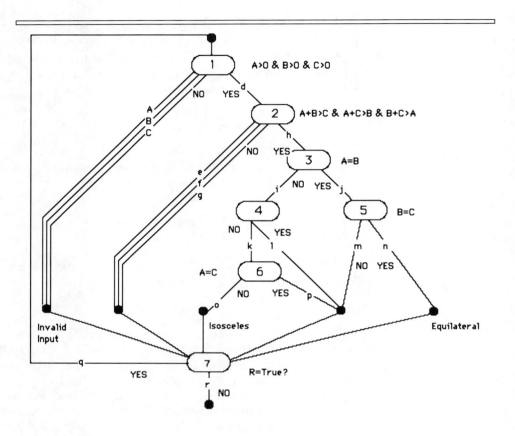

```
PROCEDURE TRIANGLE( A,B,C : integer ) ;
begin

Repeat
  READ ( A, B, C );
  If (A>0) and (B>0) and (C>0)
    Then if ((A+B)>C) and ((A+C)>B) and ((B+C)>A)
            Then if (A=B) then if (B=C) then WRITE( 'Equilateral' )
                                          else WRITE( 'Isosceles ' )
                          else if (B=C) then WRITE( 'Isosceles')
                                          else if (A=C) then WRITE( 'Isosceles')
                                                          else WRITE( 'Scalene')
            else WRITE( 'Not a triangle')
    else WRITE( 'Invalid input ' ) ;
  READLN( R );
  until R=False
  end;
```

FIGURE 10-6. McCabe structured testing example

2. For loops, exercise the "loop back" arc by selecting any arbitrary condition that forces the loop to be executed once.

3. The number of test cases is $(b + 1)$, where b is the number of decision conditions in the modified DD-graph. In the example, $b = 11$ because there are 11 paths through the graph excluding the single loop back representing the repeat loop. When the repeat loop is included, McCabe's complexity number equals 12, the number of tests to be performed.

The sample program is supposed to compute the type of right triangle given the lengths of the three sides, *A*, *B*, and *C*. The program prints a message that tells the type of triangle: isosceles, if two sides are of equal length, equilateral if all three sides are of equal length. The comparisons are repeated as long as the user requests continuation.

Let's look at a few of the paths selected for the PROCEDURE TRIANGLE. The first test is a compound Boolean expression. If the test succeeds, the YES branch is followed from node #1 of the graph, otherwise one of the three NO arcs are followed.

NO at #1 implies: $(A \leq 0)$ or $(B \leq 0)$ or $(C \leq 0)$.

Arc *A* represents the condition $(A \leq 0)$; arc *B* represents $(B \leq 0)$, and arc *C* designates the final condition, $(C \leq 0)$. Similarly, the path labeled 1-*d*-2-*h*-3-*i*-4-*k*-6-*p*-7-*r* (node number followed by arc letter) is forced by selecting data that makes the following true: $A > 0$, $B > 0$, $C > 0$, $A + B > C$, $A \neq B$, $B \neq C$, $A = C$, and $R =$ False.

The test cases corresponding to paths through the procedure can be documented, analyzed, and grouped into equivalence classes by listing them in a **decision table** — *a table of all contingencies that are to be considered in the description of a problem together with the actions to be taken for each set of contingencies*[1]. In testing, a decision table consists of a matrix with the test cases across the top and conditions, plus actions listed down the left side of the matrix. The conditions are Boolean conditions from the predicates of the program, and the actions are the anticipated outputs from the test run. The entries in the condition portion of the matrix signify the Boolean truth of a condition, and the entries in the action portion signify whether an action is to be done.

The decision table for PROCEDURE TRIANGLE is shown in Table 10-6. Note the twelve cases, and the Booleans taken directly from the program. It is possible to reduce this table by combining certain cases; for example, the repeat condition can be merged with any one of the other cases.

The decision table is readily used to generate test data by satisfying each of the twelve columns under *Cases(Paths)*. The first column (case 1) matches columns 2–5 in the first six entries. Duplicate conditions exist for a number of other entries. We can take advantage of these duplicates and group the test data into input equivalence classes. These simplified cases are listed below:

Valid Inputs.

Integer $A > 0$
Integer $B > 0$
Integer $C > 0$
$A + B > C$

$$A + C > B$$
$$B + C > A$$
$$R = \text{TRUE}$$
$$R = \text{FALSE}$$

Invalid Inputs.

Integer $A < 1$
Integer $B < 1$
Integer $C < 1$
A, B, C not integers
$A + B \leq C$
$A + C \leq B$
$B + C \leq A$

TABLE 10-6. Decision table for PROCEDURE TRIANGLE

Decision Table for McCabe's Test Case Selection[16]

Conditions:	Cases					(Paths)						
	1	2	3	4	5	6	7	8	9	10	11	12
A > 0	Y	Y	Y	Y	Y	Y	Y	Y	N	Y	Y	Y
B > 0	Y	Y	Y	Y	Y	Y	Y	Y		N	Y	Y
C > 0	Y	Y	Y	Y	Y	Y	Y	Y			N	Y
A + B > C	Y	Y	Y	Y	Y	N	Y	Y				Y
A + C > B	Y	Y	Y	Y	Y		N	Y				Y
B + C > A	Y	Y	Y	Y	Y	Y		N				Y
A = B	Y	Y	N	N	N							Y
B = C	Y	N	Y	N	N							Y
A = C	Y		Y	N								Y
R = TRUE	N	N	N	N	N	N	N	N	N	N	N	Y

Actions												
Triangle?	X	X	X	X	X							
Equilateral	X											
Isosceles		X	X	X								
Scalene					X							
Not a triangle						X	X	X				
Invalid input									X	X	X	
Repeat												X

Y = yes, N = no, X = do this action, blank = does not matter

LI'S SUGGESTED VALUES

Isosceles:
$A = 4, B = 1, C = 4, R = $ FALSE
$A = 999, B = 999, C = 1, R = $ FALSE
$A = 1, B = 3, C = 3, R = $ FALSE

Equilateral:
$A = 1, B = 1, C = 1, R = $ FALSE

Scalene:
$A = 2, B = 3, C = 4, R = $ FALSE

Invalid A:
$A = -1, B = 1, C = 4, R = $ FALSE

Invalid B:
$A = 1, B = -1, C = 4, R = $ FALSE

Invalid C:
$A = 1, B = 1, C = -999, R = $ FALSE

Noninteger A:
$A = 1.9, B = 1, C = 4, R = $ FALSE

Noninteger B:
$A = 1, B = 1.9, C = 4, R = $ FALSE

Noninteger C:
$A = 1, B = 1, C = 0.99, R = $ FALSE

Not a Triangle:
$A = 1, B = 1, C = 2, R = $ FALSE
$A = 2, B = 1, C = 1, R = $ FALSE
$A = 1, B = 2, C = 1, R = $ FALSE

FIGURE 10-7. Suggested values for each expected outcome

These revised conditions can be used in a variety of ways. For example, we could attempt to generate actual input values from these conditions by solving a set of simultaneous equations. But perhaps the simplest solution is to select arbitrary values that force each condition to be true or false. Li[16] suggests values corresponding to each expected outcome, see Figure 10-7.

Plugging these values into the program forces all possible paths in the modified DD-graph to be executed. In addition, bad input errors are forced by entering nonintegers and lengths that cannot be sides of a triangle. In the act of testing, procedure TRIANGLE is improved, leading to the unit containing TRIANGLE shown in Figure 10-8.

Test Values Selection

The two examples emphasize how to construct test cases, but the selection of test values from these cases is somewhat vague and arbitrary. Where did the actual input values come from? In addition, the test data were still rather simple. What is the rule for creating files and arrays of values? The theory of test data selection breaks down in this respect. The answer can be found, however, in empirical studies.

Duran[17] empirically evaluated a number of testing strategies versus a nonstrategy called random testing. In random testing, inputs are chosen from a distribution. No coverage strategy or test case analysis is made. This seemingly meaningless method of test data selection is better than might be expected. According to Duran, ". . . a moderate number of random test cases used in the experiments on the average achieved 97% of segment testing, 93% of branch testing, 57% of structured path testing. . . . The unexecuted branches tend to be those which provide handling of exceptional cases. This suggests that random testing should be augmented with extremal/special values testing."

Test Module:

```
unit Triangle;
interface
  procedure Triangle (VAR A, B, C : integer);
implementation
  procedure Triangle;
   var
     Reply : char; {User answers 'y' or 'Y'}
     R : Boolean;
  begin
   repeat
    Writeln('Enter 3 integers');
    Readln(A, B, C);
    if (A > 0) and (B > 0) and (C > 0) then
     if ((A + B) > C) and ((A + C) > B) and ((B + C) > A) then
      if (A = B) then
       if (B = C) then
         Writeln('Equilateral')
       else
         Writeln('Isosceles')
      else if (B = C) then
         Writeln('Isosceles')
      else if (A = C) then
         Writeln('Isosceles')
      else
         Writeln('Scalene')
     else
       Writeln('Not a triangle')
    else
      Writeln('Invalid input');
    Write('Enter Y for more:');
    Readln(Reply);
    R := ((Reply = 'y') or (Reply = 'Y'));
   until R = False;
  end;{Proc Triangle}
end. { Unit Triangle}
```

Test Harness Program:

```
program triangle;
 uses
  triangle;
 var
  a, b, c : integer;
 begin
  Triangle(a, b, c);
 end.
```

FIGURE 10-8. TRIANGLE unit

Perhaps the most encouraging empirical evidence for selecting test data values using the most simpleminded approach is given by DeMillo, Lipton, and Sayward[18] who observed a coupling effect:

> **The Coupling Effect:** Test data that distinguish any program differing from a correct one by only simple errors is so sensitive that it also implicitly distinguishes more complex errors. In other words, complex errors are coupled with simple errors.

The coupling effect is good news for programmers because it says that simple test data selection is effective in finding both simple and complex errors. The coupling effect gives four simple rules for test data value selection. These four rules are effective at finding all kinds of errors in programs, whether they are due to shallow or deep defects in the code:

> Arrays as subscripts in programs that manipulate arrays, include array values that are outside the size of the array. This will catch range errors caused by using array elements as subscripts in the same or other arrays.

> Negative domains include test values that are negative, especially array element values.

> Nonunique domains include test values that are repeated, especially array values.

> Degenerate domains include test values that are degenerate, such as zeros and constants. This will catch boundary value errors and "off-by-one" errors.

Examples of applying these rules to selection of values for array $A[1..N]$:

$A[1..1] = \{2\}$ Value outside range of subscripts
$A[1..2] = \{-1, -2\}$ Negative domain
$A[1..2] = \{-1, -1\}$ Nonunique domain
$A[1..5] = \{0,0,0,0,0\}$ Degenerate domain

These rules are useful in both testing and mathematical verification discussed in the next chapter. Combined with the coverage techniques described here, they provide individual programmers a basis for unit testing.

CASE TOOLS FOR TESTING

A variety of CASE tools exist for program testing. These tools range from early verification of specifications to code inspection tools. For example, $\mathbb{T}$ is a CASE tool that automatically generates test cases from a specification document written in a formal specification language[19]. TCAT and a variety of C_1 coverage analysis tools are available in the form of a workbench[20]. These tools implement techniques described in this chapter, plus many more features not discussed here.

CASE tools for testing reduce the cost per defect uncovered from thousands of dollars per defect to less than \$2,000/defect, and in many situations very large systems can be tested for less than \$1,000/defect. Instead of taking weeks, test tools reduce the time to verify large complex software to a matter of days or hours.

SOME CASE TOOLS FOR CODE VERIFICATION

CASE tools for testing are among the oldest known CASE tools, yet these tools were not widely accepted by early software engineers. Here is a list of tools suggested in the mid-1970s. Most have never been implemented, but many inspired modern test techniques.

Automated Testing Analyzer: Tells percentage of coverage in terms of TER.

Static Analyzer: Reads the program for anomalies, language standards violations, and potential "trouble spots."

Dynamic Assertion Processor: Programmer inserts assertions about the program in comments. Checks assertions and reports violations.

Test Difficulty Estimator: Tells which procedures are the most difficult (easiest) to test. Used by management to allocate resources wisely.

Self-metering Instrumentation: Programmer inserts probes into source code to meter running program. Execution time behavior is collected and reported.

Test Case Guide: Helps programmer construct test cases by suggesting conditions, paths, and so on.

Test Data Generator: Generates test data by automatic analysis of program coverage.

Automatic Test Facility: Management tool for tracking and recording tests and test results.

Automatic Modification Analyzer: Analyzes a program for potential impact of proposed program changes on testing process. Retesting may be a consequence.

Source: Miller, E. F., "A Service Concept for Software Auditing," *Proc. NSF Software Auditing Workshop*, January 1976. San Francisco, CA. IEEE Catalog # EHO 180-0 Order #365.

CASE tools for testing have not been widely accepted, however, because of their cost and a dearth of trained programmers. Some CASE tools are difficult to understand and use. However, the emergence of graphic workstations has accelerated acceptance of these tools. In this section, we illustrate the state of the art in unit testing of procedures.

Vigram

Vigram is a program visualizer that reads a Pascal source code unit and displays the code in a compact, visual form, one procedure at a time. The main goal of Vigram is to increase source code comprehension so that it can be understood, tested, and reused. We are concerned with using Vigram to understand and test Pascal units by generating a visual chart of source code procedures, but it is also used for other purposes.

Vigram is both an editor and an analyzer of source code. A palette of SESE-structured constructs is displayed at the top of the editing window in the form of icons representing each of the Pascal statement types, see Figure 10-9. Specifically, **const**, **type**, **var** data declarations are indicated by the first three icons in the palette; assignment, **if**, **repeat**, **while**, **case**, **for**, and **with** constructs are drawn in the next seven icons;

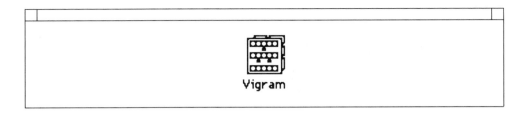

Macintosh Toolbox routines are shown as a toolbox icon; user-defined procedure calls, I/O statements, and an EXIT are each represented in the last three icons.

A program is composed of these icons by two composition rules: 1) concatenation and 2) nesting. All Pascal statements can be composed as combinations of concatenation and nesting. In Vigram, concatenation is shown by simply stacking icons next to one another, left to right across the page. If the page is too narrow to display a long procedure, the icons are stacked row by row down the page.

Nesting of structures — **type** and **var** statements as well as **if, case, repeat, while, for,** and **with** statements — is indicated by a *nesting box* drawn immediately below the icon that hides the level below. To see the next level, double-click the nesting box and the next level of program structure is drawn in a subsequent window. The top level of procedure TRIANGLE is shown as an illustration. Notice the row of icons for variable declarations and the third icon representing the topmost **repeat** statement.

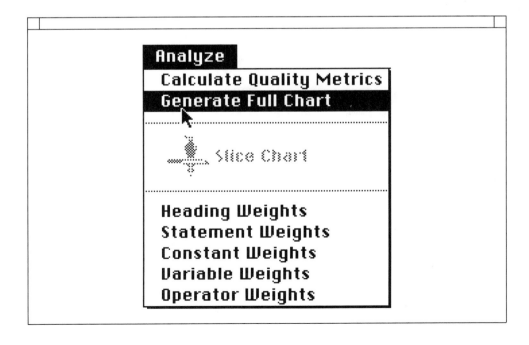

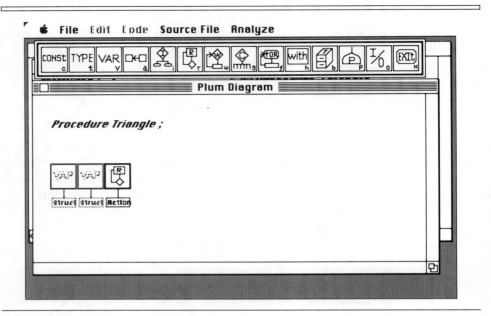

FIGURE 10-9. Example of a Vigram display

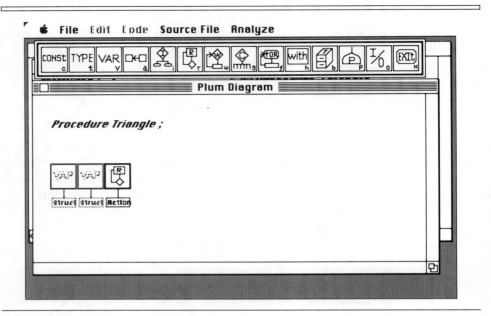

FIGURE 10-10. Specifying a program slice

The first two icons in the example are dimmed to indicate a program slice. *Program slicing* is a technique for suppressing details of a program by dimming uninteresting statements while emphasizing other statements. In this example, we are interested in all constructions containing predicates, because these tell how to test the procedure.

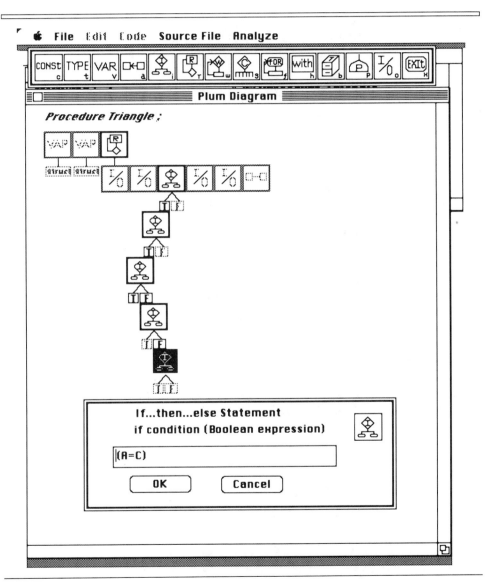

FIGURE 10-11. Fully sliced version of TRIANGLE

Program slicing is carried to the fullest extent in Vigram. Slices can be made on one or more control statements, variables, and combinations of statements and variables, see Figure 10-10. Slices cut across nested levels of hierarchy as illustrated by the fully sliced TRIANGLE procedure shown in Figure 10-11. In this example, we sliced on **case**, **for**, **if**, **while**, and **repeat** statements to expose all predicates needed to derive test cases. The diagram shows the highlighted path from top to bottom of the series of **if** statements in TRIANGLE. The final **if** statement contains a test: $(A = C)$. This is obtained in a dialog when the **if** icon is double-clicked to see its contents. Vigram was designed for program understanding, but it can compute a variety of factors about the program.

Those factors are discussed in chapter twelve. The computations of interest here, however, are the ones that pertain to testing. Vigram computes the McCabe cyclomatic number b to get the number of paths through the procedure. Then it analyzes these paths to generate the path predicates needed to get the test cases described in the previous section. For procedure TRIANGLE, the path analysis done by Vigram produces predicates from an analysis of the decision tree corresponding to the b conditions, see Figure 10-12.

From the information in Figure 10-12, Vigram enumerates the predicate paths; see Figure 10-13.

These predicate paths can be converted into test cases by separating Boolean expressions, factoring out redundant tests, and selecting values with the help of the coupling effect. The results are similar, but not exactly the same as the results obtained by complexity-based testing.

$P_1 : A > 0$ and $B > 0$ and $C > 0$
$\quad A + B > C$ and $A + C > B$ and $B + C > A$
$\quad A = B$
$\quad B = C$

$P_2 : A > 0$ and $B > 0$ and $C > 0$
$\quad A + B > C$ and $A + C > B$ and $B + C > A$
$\quad A = B$
$\quad B \neq C$

$P_3 : A > 0$ and $B > 0$ and $C > 0$
$\quad A + B > C$ and $A + C > B$ and $B + C > A$
$\quad A \neq B$
$\quad B = C$

$P_4 : A > 0$ and $B > 0$ and $C > 0$
$\quad A + B > C$ and $A + C > B$ and $B + C > A$
$\quad A = B$
$\quad B \neq C$
$\quad A = C$

$P_5 : A > 0$ and $B > 0$ and $C > 0$
$\quad A + B > C$ and $A + C > B$ and $B + C > A$
$\quad A \neq B$
$\quad B \neq C$
$\quad A \neq C$

$P_6 : A > 0$ and $B > 0$ and $C > 0$
$\quad$ **not** $A + B > C$ and $A + C > B$ and $B + C > A$
$\quad A = B$
$\quad B \neq C$
$\quad A = C$

$P_7 :$ **not** $(A > 0$ and $B > 0$ and $C > 0)$

$P_8 : R =$ False

$P_9 : R \neq$ False

FIGURE 10-12. Predicate paths in procedure TRIANGLE

Predicate Paths in Procedure TRIANGLE

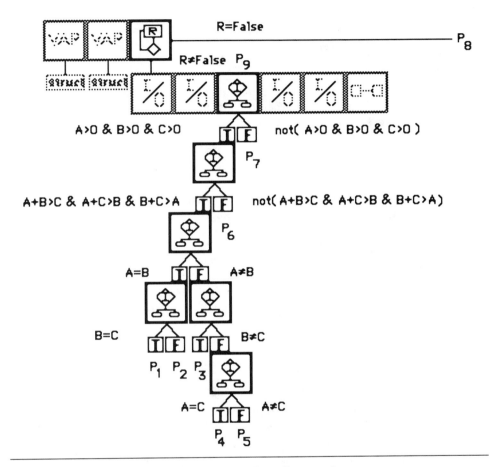

FIGURE 10-13. Vigram enumeration of TRIANGLE predicate paths

WHAT WORKS?

The Inspection technique has been shown to be the most powerful and effective technique for assuring quality of code. However, code inspection requires time and training. Russell[3] estimates the time to inspect and correct code to be proportional to the size of the application as follows:

Elapsed Time = 3 KDSI days

but notes that the effectiveness of defect detection is highly correlated with inspection pace. Inspecting 150 lines of code per hour produces the greatest number of defects per KDSI. The rate drops off quickly when the pace is increased (37 defects per KDSI were reported at 150 lines of code per hour, versus only 8 defects per KDSI when the pace was 750 lines per hour).

Programmer performance can be greatly enhanced by adopting a debugging strategy that facilitates program understanding and looks for the most-probable errors first. Clearly, programmer experience is directly related to debugging skill, but much of this skill can be learned.

Verification of software divides into two major approaches: mathematical and empirical. The mathematical approach is characterized by proof of correctness techniques discussed in the next chapter. Empirical approaches are characterized by debugging and formal testing.

Formal testing focuses on verification of the structure of code, especially from the point of view of satisfying specifications. While debugging seeks to remove errors, testing seeks to reveal errors. There are two fundamental approaches to testing: static analysis and dynamic testing. Dynamic testing is sometimes called *program forcing* because most dynamic testing techniques force the subject program to exercise certain paths, conditions, and calculations.

Modern programming languages attempt to shift the errors from execution time failures to compile time failures because of the ease in detecting and correcting compile time errors. Strong typing, range checking, and simplified I/O are several advances in programming languages that have contributed to the shift from execution errors to compiler errors. Accordingly, static analysis has largely become a feature of advanced compilers.

DYNAMIC TESTING METHODS AND THEIR SUCCESS RATES[22]

Path Testing (64%): Execute every path through the program once.

Special Value Test Data (61%): Use limited test data based on boundary values, zeros, degenerate arrays, and so forth.

Symbolic Execution (61%): Execute program symbolically using symbol manipulation instead of actual test data.

Structured Composition (43%): Construct program modules and test using stubs (partially completed modules) in a top-down fashion.

Standard Specifications (25%): Check program against programming standards.

Branch Testing (21%): Execute every if-then-else condition once, but take only one path or the other.

Anomaly Analysis (14%): Check undefined variables and anomalous control structure.

Interface Consistency (7%): Test I/O and parameter-passing values.

The basis of all dynamic testing techniques is test coverage. Each measure of coverage dictates the method of test case analysis, which in turn dictates the method of test data selection. The coupling effect can be used to generate simple values that are likely to reveal deep errors. Taken together, coverage and test data selection determine the reliability of each test technique. A good question is, which test technique is best?

Dynamic testing may not find all errors as shown in the sidebar. The best technique reported by Howden succeeded in finding fewer than two-thirds of the errors. When all test methods were used in combination, 93% of the errors were revealed[22]. This points to the importance of multiple coverage testing.

Alternatives

Coverage techniques that reduce the number of test cases have been proposed. For example, overlapping paths can be collapsed into one, or the fact that test data for one run often covers most of the paths exercised by another run can be exploited, so fewer values need to be entered in the program[21,23]. While additional improvements are always being made, testing is basically limited to revealing errors rather than proving the absence of errors.

Indeed, the best technique may not be based on automated coverage. Basili and Selby[25] compared testing results obtained by reading code in a review setting versus formal testing by functional and statement coverage techniques, and found that code reviews were better than the two formal test techniques. A formal software review technique where professional and student programmers read code by stepwise refinement was compared with functional and structural testing. The group of professional programmers detected more errors and had a higher error detection rate than did functional or statement coverage testing. In addition, code reading detected more interface errors than did the other methods, and code readers were better able to estimate the percentage of errors detected.

While the study by Basili and Selby did not compare all coverage techniques with code reviews, their results should remind the practicing software engineer to use code reviews as well as formal testing techniques. The best approach is to use every available tool and technique to verify the soundness of the application.

Bug Estimates

Formulas for estimating error densities in software are valuable because they can be used to estimate when to stop testing. These formulas are usually based on some probability density function or exponential model, such as the formula by Young mentioned earlier in this chapter.

Stetter and Lipow[24] developed a simple but accurate bug estimation formula based on Halstead's software metrics work (Halstead's metric is described in chapter twelve):

B = Number of errors (bugs)

LOC = Lines of Executable Code

K = Constant equal to the average number of operators and operands used per line of code. Estimates of K range from 3 for assembler languages to 8 for high-level languages.

To simplify the formula, let $N = K*P$ be the average number of operators and operands in the program, and the number of bits in N is written as $V = \log_2(N)$. Since we are looking for an estimate of the number of errors per line of code, let $\partial = B/P$ be the error density. Finally, it is thought that programmers make about 3,000 mental discriminations between each error (see chapter twelve), so the constant of mental discrimination, $D = K/3,000$. Thus, the simplified formula:

$$\partial = D \log_2[(8N)/(1 + 8\,V - 9\log_2(V))]$$

Using this formula with $K = 3$, a 10,000 line program is expected to have 115 bugs! The number of bugs in a high-level language of 10,000 lines increases to 316, assuming $K = 7.5$. If we assume that a line of code in a high-level language equals 5 lines of code in assembler, the error density in high-level language programs is approximately 1.8 times lower than assembler language programs.

Terms and Concepts

anomaly
assertion
audit
branch testing
bug
code reader
correctness
coupling effect
coverage
DD-graph
DD testing
debugging
decision table
dynamic analyzer
dynamic testing
error
error category
error model
fault
functional audit
inspection
interface testing

most-probable error
mutation testing
Pareto's Law
path testing
physical audit
program forcing
program slicing
regression testing
REP
review
semantic error
slicing
static analysis
symbolic execution
TER
test coverage
testing
validation
verification
walk-through
80/20 Rule

DISCUSSION QUESTIONS

1. Code review, formal testing, and mathematical correctness checking are three distinct methods used to verify software. Explain what each of these are, and compare them in terms of reliability.

2. Perform a code review by walk-through on procedure TRIANGLE with two other programmers. Write a short report based on the walk-through format given in this chapter. List the length of time taken, what questions were asked, and what answers were given.

3. Explain how anomaly tracking might be used to construct a list of MPEs.

4. Is it theoretically possible to guarantee the absolute correctness of a program? Explain your answer.

5. Generate test cases for the ABS function, and use complexity-based testing to reveal the error. What can you say about the effectiveness of this method?

```
function ABS(VAL : integer) : integer;
begin
  if VAL < 0 then ABS := -VAL;
end; {ABS}
```

6. Generate test cases, test data, and finally, exercise procedure MERGE. Is it correct? (Hint: MERGE takes two ordered lists, $L1[1..N]$ and $L2[1..M]$, and merges them into a single ordered list $LOUT[1..N + M]$. The procedure is correct if LOUT contains all elements of L1 and L2, in ascending order.)

```
procedure MERGE( L1, L2 :list; var LOUT : listout);
  var I, J: integer;
  begin
    I := 1; J := 1; {Start with first elements}
    while (I <= N) and (J <= M) do
      begin
        LOUT[I+J-1] := min(L1[I], L2[J]); {Take smallest of the two}
        if L1[I] < L2[J] then I := I+1 else J := J+1
      end; {while}
    for I := I to N do LOUT[I+J-1] := L1[I]; {copy trailing elements}
    for J := J to M do LOUT[I+J-1] := L1[J];{if J>M, this is skipped}
  end; {MERGE}
```

7. The following code for searching an ordered list of length N, using a form of binary search, has a bug. Use the techniques described in this chapter to debug this function. Give the corrected function along with your list of errors found.

```
function BINARY (Key : integer; List : lists) : integer;
  var Y, Z : real; {subscripts}
  begin
    if (List[1] <= Key) and (Key <= List[N])
      then
        begin
          Z := N;
          Y := -N;
          while (Y < -1) and (List[trunc(Z)] <> Key) do
```

```
          begin
            Y := Y/2;
            if Key < = List[trunc(Z + Y)] then Z := Z + Y;
          end; {while}
          BINARY := trunc(Z) * ord(List[trunc(Z)] = Key); {0 or 1 times trunc (Z)}
        end {if-then}
      else BINARY := 0 {not in list}
    end; {BINARY}
```

8. What is an MPE? Make a list of MPEs from your own experience.

9. What is a semantic error? a logical error? Compare syntactic, semantic, and logical errors in terms of compile, load, and program execution phases.

10. How many bugs are there in a Pascal program containing 20,000 lines of code? How many segments are there in 20,000 lines of code if it is considered a single monolithic fragment? What formulas did you use to compute these estimates? Why?

11. How many runs of a program are required to detect and remove 50% of its errors? How did you compute this? What assumptions did you use?

12. What are the characteristics of an expert debugger? Can expert debugging be compared with structured design and coding? How might the "rules" of expert debugging be used in a code review?

13. How important is knowledge of error category to debugging?

14. What is the difference between debugging and testing? What is the purpose of each?

15. What is the difference between COMPLETE and RELIABLE in the theory of testing? How are these two concepts measured? (Hint: explain what 90% complete and 50% reliable mean.)

16. Does McCabe's complexity-based test case generation work on unstructured programs?

17. Draw the DD-graph for the BINARY function listed in question 7. List the path predicates of this graph.

18. Give a decision table corresponding to the test cases generated by questions 7 and 17.

19. Use the coupling effect and complexity-based case analysis to test procedure QSORT and the procedure it calls, SWAP. Assume that the stack operators InitStack, Push, Pop, and StackSize are correct. This code is supposed to sort a list of numbers into ascending order. Does it?

```
procedure QSORT(var List : Lists);
  var L, R, NewL, NewR : indexes;
  begin
    InitStack; Push (1, M);   {Initialize a pushdown stack and put (1, M) on the top of the stack}
    repeat
      Pop(L, R); {take (L, R) from the top of the stack}
      repeat
      SWAP(L, R, NewL, NewR); {Swap elements until list is partitioned}
      if NewL < R then Push(NewL, R);
      R := NewR;
    until (L > = R);
    until StackSize = 0;
  end; {QSORT}
```

```
procedure SWAP(L, R : integer; var NewL : integer; var NewR : integer);
var Mid : Datatype; {Some kind of structure with scalar key}
begin
  NewL := L; NewR := R; Mid := List[(L+R) div 2]; {approx. midpoint of list}
  repeat
    while List[NewL].Key < Mid.Key do NewL := NewL+1;
    while List[NewR].Key > Mid.Key do NewR := NewR-1;
    if NewL <= NewR then
      begin
        Exchange(List[NewL], List[NewR]); {Swap two elements}
        NewL := NewL+1; NewR := NewR-1;
      end; {if-then}
  until NewL > NewR;
end; {SWAP}
```

20. Under what conditions might the following loops fail? (Failure is defined as nontermination, or abnormal termination of the loop.)

    (a) **repeat** X := X+5 **until** X>20; (b) **while** X>0 **do** X := X/3;
    (c) **repeat** X := X+5 **until** X>Y; (d) **while** X>0 **do** X := X/Y;
    (e) **while** (X>Y) **and** (X>Z) **do** X := X/2; (f) **while** X>Y **do** X := X*Y;

21. How might you measure the effectiveness of a CASE tool for testing? What should such tools do?

22. Is code review an effective verification technique? Which is better, code review or formal testing? Why?

23. Draw a Vigram iconic representation of the program in question 19. Draw separate diagrams for each of the two procedures.

24. What is program slicing? Slice the Vigram diagram obtained in question 23 on **if** statements. Slice it on **repeat**, **if**, and **while** statements. What is the value of slicing?

REFERENCES AND FURTHER READING

1. IEEE. 1983, 1984. "IEEE Standard for Software Quality Assurance Plans," *ANSI/IEEE Std 730-1984*, and "IEEE Standard for Software Test Documentation," *ANSI/IEEE Std 829-1983*.

2. Fagan, M. E. 1976. *Design and Code Inspections and Process Control in the Development of Programs, IBM TR 0.2763 (June 10,1976)*. Poughkeepsie, NY: IBM.

3. Russell, G. W. In press. "Experience with Inspections in Ultra Large Scale Software Developments."

4. Manna, Z, and R. Waldinger. 1978. "The Logic of Computer Programming." *IEEE Transactions on Software Engineering* SE-4, no. 3 (May).

5. Fosdick, L., and L. Osterweil. 1976. "Dataflow Analysis in Software Reliability." *ACM Computing Surveys* 8, no. 3 (September): 305–330.

6. Nanja, M. 1988. "An Investigation of the On-Line Debugging Process of Expert and Novice Student Programmers." PhD Thesis, Oregon State University.

7. Poston, R. 1987. "Preventing Most-Probable Errors in Planning." *IEEE Software* 4, no. 4 (July): 86–87.

8. Boies, S. J., and J. P. Gould. 1974. "Syntactic Errors in Computer Programming." *Human Factors* 16, no. 3: 253–257.

9. Moulton, P.G., and M. E. Muller. 1967. "DITRAN — A Compiler Emphasizing Diagnostics." *Communications of ACM* 10, no. 1 (January): 50–52.

10. Young, E. A. 1974. "Human Errors in Programming." *International Journal of Man-Machine Studies"* 6, no. 3: 361–376.

11. Endres, A. 1975. "An Analysis of Errors and Their Causes in Software Programs." *IEEE Transactions on Software Engineering* SE-1, no. 2 (June): 140.

12. Hetzel, W. C. 1973. *Program Test Methods*. Englewood Cliffs, NJ: Prentice-Hall.

13. Goodenough, J. B., and S. L. Gerhart. 1975. "Toward a Theory of Test Data Selection." *IEEE Transactions on Software Engineering* SE-1, no. 2 (June): 156–173.

14. Miller, E. 1988. "Tutorial #4: Software Quality Control." *COMPCON '88, Feb. 29–Mar. 4, 1988, San Francisco, CA* (Available from Software Research Associates, San Francisco, CA).

15. McCabe, T. E., 1983. "Structured Testing: A Testing Methodology Using the McCabe Complexity Metric." In *Structured Testing*; ed. T. E. McCabe: 19–47. Silver Spring, MD: IEEE Computer Society Press.

16. Li, E. Y. 1988. "Test Case Design: An Evaluation of Existing Techniques." Technical report, School of Business, California Polytechnic State Univ.

17. Duran, J. W., and S. C. Ntafos. 1984. "An Evaluation of Random Testing." *IEEE Transactions on Software Engineering* SE-10, no. 4 (July): 438–444.

18. DeMillo, R.A., R. J. Lipton, and F. G. Sayward. 1978. "Hints on Test Data Selection: Help for the Practicing Programmer." *IEEE Computer* 11, no. 4 (April): 34–41.

19. Poston, R. 1987. *The Letter* T 1, no. 1 (September). Tinton Falls, NJ.

20. Miller, E. 1987. *Testing Techniques Newsletter* 10, no. 1 (Winter 1987/1988), Available from Software Research, Inc., 625 Third Street, San Francisco, CA, 94107-1997.

21. Prather, R. E., and J. P. Myers, Jr. 1987. "The Path Prefix Software Testing Strategy." *IEEE Transactions on Software Engineering* SE-13, no. 7 (July): 761–766.

22. Howden, W. E. 1978. "Theoretical and Empirical Studies of Program Testing." *IEEE Transactions on Software Engineering* SE-4, no. 4 (July): 293–298.

23. Chusho, T. 1987. "Test Data Selection and Quality Estimation Based on the Concept of Essential Branches for Path Testing." *IEEE Transactions on Software Engineering* SE-13, no. 5 (May): 509–517.

24. Stetter, F. 1986. "Comments on 'Number of Faults per Line of Code,'" *IEEE Transactions on Software Engineering* SE-12, no. 12 (December): 1145.

25. Basili, V. R., and R. W. Selby. 1987. "Comparing the Effectiveness of Software Testing Strategies," *IEEE Transactions on Software Engineering* SE-12, no. 12 (December): 1145.

11

SQA: Mathematical Verification

PREVIEW

Mathematical verification of arbitrary programs is an intractable problem, but the theory of program proving provides a powerful basis for precise and rigorous examination of the deep structure of algorithms and their implementation in source code.

Two approaches are studied: 1) algebraic modeling, which attempts to model a program as a set of mathematical equations, and 2) proof by assertion checking, which attempts to model the state of a program through first order logic.

The algebraic approach blends testing with formal verification. Each program statement is represented as a mathematical formula. Inputs are the "forcing functions" to the program's equations, and the solutions to the equations are the program's output values.

The program proving approach uses predicates to model program states — assertions about the program before and after execution of each statement. The collection of predicates forms a logical system of equations. The anticipated output values, conditions on inputs, and the system of predicates form a theorem. Proving the theorem is equivalent to proving the program.

MATHEMATICAL METHODS OF VERIFICATION

Mathematical techniques for verifying the correctness of computer programs have been studied since the early 1960s. Perhaps the first paper describing the concept of programs as mathematical objects which can be "proven" and "transformed" much like traditional mathematical equations was published by Floyd in 1967[1].

Nonetheless, mathematical verification has not been widely used. One reason is that it cannot be fully automated, so there are no CASE tools available to perform automatic verification by mathematical methods. Another reason is due to the level of formalism shrouding the subject.

THE TAUTOLOGY OF PROVING

Many tasks in computing are shown to be impossible because they are equivalent to a logical contradiction. For example, the impossibility of proving an arbitrary program correct, or even building an automatic "proving program" has been shown to be equivalent to Turing's Halting Problem.

A simple demonstration of the concept of "impossibility" is to "prove" the following system of assertions:

$S1$: Sally says, "John always tells lies."

$S2$: "Sally always tells the truth," says John.

H : $S1$ and $S2$ are correct.

We attempt to prove H by direct substitution as follows:

Assume $S1$ is true. This implies that $S2$ is not true, which implies that $S1$ is false, a contradiction.

Assume $S2$ is true. This implies that $S1$ is true, but if $S1$ is true, then $S2$ is false, again a contradiction.

Given only $S1$ and $S2$, we cannot prove whether John and Sally are liars. We say the problem is undecidable because it is impossible to decide who is lying, and who is telling the truth.

Such problems arise in proving arbitrary programs. (A syntactically correct program is arbitrary if we have no knowledge of it ahead of time.) For example,

$S1$: According to John, Sally is always right.

$S2$: According to Sally, program P is correct.

H : Is program P correct?

If we assume $S1$ is true, H can be shown to be true. If we assume $S1$ is false, H can be shown to be false. It is impossible to decide which is the case.

Conceptually, we know that an arbitrary program can never be proven correct. Yet techniques for mathematically analyzing programs are very useful for reasoning about a program, deriving properties of a program that are useful in studying performance and algorithmic structure, and finally, revealing the presence of errors, much as in testing. Therefore, mathematical methods belong in the software engineer's tool kit of techniques.

In the previous chapter we divided the mathematical approach into two broad areas: proof of correctness and functional correctness techniques. Functional correctness techniques are useful in studies of algorithms, while proving is useful in verification. Therefore, we discuss proof of correctness only, because proving deals directly with the artifact of interest — source code.

Proof of correctness is further divided into axiomatic and algebraic techniques. The axiomatic technique is usually based on first order logic. Specifically, the most widely known axiomatic technique is called the **inductive assertion method** — *a proof of correctness technique in which assertions are written describing program inputs, outputs, and intermediate conditions, a set of theorems is developed relating satisfaction of the input assertions to satisfaction of the output assertions, and the theorems are proved to be true*[2].

The inductive assertion method — also called proof by induction — is actually a modeling technique. A logical model of the program is made by assigning assertions to each statement or statement group in the program, and then using a variety of proof techniques to "derive" the proof. The advantage of this method is that it is very logical and rigorous. The disadvantage is that the model may not represent the actual program, and even if it does, deriving the proof may be difficult.

The other approach, the algebraic technique, models the program as a system of algebraic equations, and then solves the equations in much the same way that an engineer solves a set of differential equations describing a physical phenomenon. The advantage of this approach is that it very closely relates to the actual program. The equations are nearly identical to the statements of the program, and the methods of solving the equations are identical to the methods used in applied mathematics. The disadvantage is that the resulting equations may not be easy to solve.

Most software engineers and programmers find the literature on formal proofs and verification by mathematical modeling arcane and difficult to understand. Accordingly, these techniques are usually ignored. In reality, the methods are rather rudimentary and make good sense, once they are understood. The problem is one of pedagogical approach rather than difficulty of subject matter. Therefore, we first derive a technique based on more traditional algebraic methods, and then use the same ideas to derive a logical basis for proof of correctness. By separating the ideas from the notation and tools, we hope to overcome resistance to these methods.

In both algebraic and axiomatic approaches, the central difficulty with analyzing programs is, once again, loops and branches. Both techniques use models of loops and branches that are often difficult to formulate and even more difficult to solve. This is another reason to use simple control constructs and SESE structure to implement a software system. Without SESE structure, the task of verifying even the smallest program is extremely difficult.

ALGEBRAIC MODELING

Algebraic modeling assigns an algebraic equivalent to each construct in the language, and then uses composition rules to analyze the model. In effect, the algebraic equivalent is a meaning we assign to the programming construct. In other words, the algebraic equivalent is a representation of the semantics of the construct. Semantics is the relationships between symbols and their meanings, so the goal of assigning algebraic equivalents is to model the programming constructs as closely as possible with an algebraic symbol that describes what the construct does.

Perhaps the best way to explain this approach is to define algebraic equivalents for SESE structures used by Pascal. We intend to rewrite a Pascal source program as a set of algebraic equations, and then transform each program component into an equivalent reduced component that performs the same computation. For example, the two segments below compute the same results for variable A:

(a) $B := 10; C := 5; A := B + C$;
(b) $A := 15$;

The computation in (b) is equivalent to the computation in (a) as far as the final value of A is concerned. However, (b) is much simpler than (a). We say (b) is a reduced form of (a), and methods for performing such reductions are called program transformations.

A second example illustrates a more difficult transformation on a program component that computes the value of X. The transformed component produces an equivalent result, but one component is more complex than the other:

```
(a) X := 5; I := 0;
       while I < N do
         begin
           X := X + 1;
           I := I + 1
         end
(b) X := N + 6;
```

The idea underlying a transformational theory of software verification is demonstrated by these two examples. We seek a set of rules for transforming program components like those of example (a) into simpler program components like those of example (b). Why? Because the transformed components are easier to verify; yet they perform the same computation as the more complex (original) components.

Assignment Statement Transformation

Let s_i be a concatenated sequence of assignment statements:

$$\{s_1; s_2; ..; s_n\}$$

The braces are used to indicate serial execution of statements s_i. The semicolon designates concatenation. Let T_s be an assignment transform. Thus,

$$T_s \{s_1; s_2 ;..; s_n\} \sim \{s_1; s_2 ;..; s_n\}$$

The square bracket metasymbols indicate arbitrary execution order of statements s_i. They are strictly a notational device — we do not care about what order the assignment statements are executed, only that they can be executed in any order.

The purpose of transform T_s is to simplify the original sequence of statements by removing data dependencies from the original sequence. A data independent version is easier to verify than a data dependent version. Consider, for example, the following (untransformed) sequence of assignment statements:

(a) $\{A := 5; B := A + 3; C := A + B\}$

This sequence is data dependent because the value of B depends on the value of A, and the value of C depends on both A and B. The data dependencies of (a) can be removed by forward substitution of the values of A and B into the expressions used to compute B and C, respectively. An equivalent version of (a) is derived by forward substitution as follows:

$$T_s \{A := 5; B := A + 3; C := A + B\} \sim \{A := 5; B := 5 + 3; C := 5 + 8\}$$

If we carry out the expression evaluations, the resultant values of A, B, and C are immediately verified. In this example, the sequence of assignment statements were transformable into data independent form by T_s because the data dependencies were simple. However, the sequence of assignment statements shown below are not easily transformed:

$\{A := 5; B := B + 3\}$

T_s cannot transform this sequence because the definition of B is computed recursively. Therefore, the forward substitution transform is restricted to simple, single-assignment sequences (SSA) only. A **simple, single-assignment sequence** *is a sequence of assignment statements in which left-hand side variables are distinct (only appear once on the left-hand side), and the right-hand side expressions do not contain recursively defined variables.*

The T_s transform applies to SSA segments of program code. All other segments must be transformed into SSA sequences before T_s can be used. The following counterexamples illustrate the difficulty of transforming non-SSA sequences.

$\{Y := Y + 1; I := I/2\}$

We cannot simplify Y or I because they are both defined recursively. Recursive expressions are not always easy to detect. Consider the following:

$\{X := 1 - B; B := 1 - X\}$

This example becomes a recursive sequence of assignments when $X := 1 - B$ is forward substituted into $B := 1 - X$. The result $\{X := 1 - B; B := B\}$ is impossible to reduce to a data independent form.

This kind of recursion is typically found in program loops. Perhaps we can find a loop transformation that simplifies such expressions.

Iteration Transformation

Consider the following simple **while** component:

X := 0; **while** X < N **do** X := X + C;

This loop repeatedly performs a test and a recursive assignment statement. We rewrite the body of the loop as follows to show the state of the computation on the tth pass through the loop.

X_0 := 0; **while** X_{t-1} < N **do** X_t := X_{t-1} + C;

The first pass corresponds with $t = 1$, the second $t = 2$, and $t = 0$ corresponds to the initial state, before the loop is entered. Therefore, X_0 is the initial value of X and X_t is the value of X after the loop has executed t times. If the loop terminates after $(t' - 1)$ iterations, the value of X is $X_{(t'-1)}$.

We seek a transformation that reduces the component above to a computationally equivalent component containing $X_{t'}$ but without the troublesome loop. In other words, the transform must replace the loop with the values computed by the loop. Thus,

T_w {X_0 := 0; **while** X_{t-1} < N **do** X_t := X_{t-1} + C} ~ {X := C* Ceiling(N/C)}

where Ceiling(x) is the nearest integer greater than or equal to x, and t' is to be found.

How is $X_{t'}$ computed? In this case, T_w computes a *loop functional* that terminates the loop. A loop functional is a series of computations that find t' such that the loop test is false. That is, we seek a functional that forces $(X_{t'-1} < N)$ to become $(X_{t'-1} \geq N)$, and in the process makes the loop terminate. To find the loop functional, we ask, what value of $(t' - 1)$ makes the loop stop?

The body of the **while** loop component must be converted into an iterative equivalent. This is done by solving the recurrence relation:

$X_{t+1} - X_t$ = C; (X_0 is given)

This is a first order difference equation with solution:

X_t = X_0 + C*t (t = 0, 1, 2, ...)

The solution X_t is substituted into the loop to replace the recursive expression:

X_0 := 0; **while** X_{t-1} < N **do** X_t := X_0 + C*t;

The initial value of X_0 := 0 can be forward substituted into the body of the **while** loop, and the loop test can be rewritten. Thus,

while C*(t-1) < N **do** X_t := C*t;

Now, the loop terminates prior to the t' iteration when $(C(t' - 1) \geq N)$. Hence, $(t' - 1) \geq (N/C)$. But $(t' - 1)$ must be an integer, and (N/C) is possibly a real-valued

FINITE DIFFERENCES

Transforming loop bodies from recursive to iterative form is done by solving finite difference equations. The simplest of these equations are of the form:

$$(a_k E_k + a_{k-1} E_{k-1} + \ldots a_0) X_t = 0$$

where a_i are constants and E_i is an operator that shifts X in t:

$$E_1 X_t = X_{t+1};\ E_k X_t = X_{t+k}, \text{ and so forth.}$$

For example, when $k=2$, $a_2 = 1$, $a_1 = 2$, $a_0 = -3$, the finite difference equation is,

$$(E_2 + 2E_1 - 3) X_t = 0, \text{ or } X_{t+2} + 2X_{t+1} - 3X_t = 0$$

The general solution to this equation is obtained by solving the polynomial obtained from the coefficients:

$$X_t = b_0 + b_1 \beta_1{}^t + b_2 \beta_2{}^{t+1} + \ldots b_k . \beta_k{}^{t+k-1}$$

where b_0 is obtained from boundary values, e.g. $X_0, X_1, \ldots X_k$, and $\beta_1, \ldots \beta_k$ are the roots of the polynomial,

$$a_k \beta^k + a_{k-1} \beta^{k-1} + \ldots a_0 = 0$$

For example, to get the roots of the polynomial from above, solve the equation:

$$\beta^2 + 2\beta - 3 = 0, \text{ which has roots } \beta_1 = 1 \text{ and } \beta_2 = -3.$$

The general solution is $X_t = b_0 + b_1 + b_2 (-3)^{t+1}$. From boundary conditions, we can find b_0, b_1, and b_2. Suppose, for example, that $X_0 = -1$ and $x_1 = 2$. We solve for coefficients $b_0 + b_1$ and b_2 as follows:

$$X_0 = -1 = (b_0 + b_1) - 3b^2 \text{ and } X_1 = 2 = (b_0 + b_1) + 9b_1$$

Solving these simultaneous equations yields values:

$$b_0 + b_1 = -1/4 \text{ and } b_2 = 1/4.$$

The particular solution is $X_t = (-1 + (-3)^{t+1})/4$

Note how the solution oscillates between positive and negative values.

---

number with a fractional part. We can replace (N/C) with Ceiling(N/C) and drop the inequality relation. Thus, $(t' - 1) = \text{Ceiling}(N/C)$, or simplifying and solving for t' that terminates the loop, we get $t' = \text{Ceiling}(N/C) + 1$.

The loop termination value of X after $t' - 1$ iterations (and before the t' iteration) is $X_{t'-1}$.

$$X_{t'-1} := C*(t'-1) = \text{final value of } X$$

Thus,

$$X_{t'-1} := C*\text{Ceiling}(N/C)$$

As a check, suppose $N = 10$ and $C = 3$. The loop terminates after 4 iterations.

$$t' - 1 = \text{Ceiling}(10/3) = 4$$

The termination value of X is,

$$X_{t'-1} = X_4 = 3*(4) = 12.$$

This is the solution we are looking for. Notice that we have succeeded in removing the loop. That is, we have transformed the loop into a simpler expression that does not involve recursion. Therefore, the transformation of the **while** loop computes t' and determines the proper value of X after the loop terminates.

$T_w \{X := 0; \text{ \textbf{while} } X < 10 \text{ \textbf{do} } X := X + 3;\} \sim \{X := 12\}$

This leads to a formal definition of T_w.

Loop Functional

T_w : Let LHS_0 and LHS_t be the initial and loop body statements, respectively,

$LHS_0; \text{ \textbf{while} } p \text{ \textbf{do} } LHS_t$

where t is an artificially induced loop counter and p is the loop predicate. If there exists a loop functional $LF(p)$ which determines the value of $t' = $ number of times p is tested, then,

$T_w \{LHS_0; \text{ \textbf{while} } p \text{ \textbf{do} } LHS_t\} \sim \{LHS_{t'}\}$

This transformation may not always be simple to find. The loop functional is usually a difference equation whose solution yields t'. The solution to the difference equation may be extremely complex, however.

Once the value of LHS_t is obtained through the solution of a recurrence equation, the value t' can be found by solving for a t such that the loop predicate is false. That is,

not p implies t'

In effect, finding the functional $LF(p)$ is equivalent to finding a loop *invariant*. The term invariant denotes the fact that the computed results no longer depend on the iterations of the loop. Finding a loop invariant means finding a replacement for the repeating loop. Thus, an invariant is a noniterative function that computes the same values as the loop. Finding loop invariants is fundamental to mathematical verification.

Let us illustrate the technique of finding a loop invariant using a Pascal function containing an error. LOCATE is supposed to return the location of character CH in string X, but the following attempt to verify LOCATE reveals the error.

```
function LOCATE (X : string; CH : char) : integer;
var
  I, N : integer;
  DONE : Boolean;
begin
  I := 1;
  N := LENGTH (X);
  repeat
    DONE := X[I] = CH;
    I := I + 1;
  until (DONE) or (I > N);
  if DONE
    then LOCATE := I    {correction: I-1}
    else LOCATE := 0;
end;
```

For convenience, we abbreviate repeat-until with a $\mathbb{U}$ and **if-then-else** with an $\mathbb{IF}$ and horizontal bar separating **then** and **else** clauses. As before, t is an artificially induced loop counter.

$\{I_0 := 1; N := \text{LENGTH(X)}; \text{DONE} := X[I]_{t-1} = \text{CH}; I_t := I_{t-1} + 1\}; \mathbb{U}_{\text{DONE or } (I_t > N)}; \mathbb{IF}_{\text{DONE}}$

$$\left\{ \begin{array}{c} \text{LOCATE} := I_t \\ \rule{3cm}{3pt} \\ \text{LOCATE} := 0 \end{array} \right\}$$

The $\mathbb{U}$ component terminates when (DONE) or ($I_t > N$) is true. The values of I_t refer to the values of I on the tth pass through the repeat-until loop.

We seek a loop invariant by finding a loop transformation functional that reduces the loop to a nonrecursive form. The loop body can be rewritten in iterative form as follows:

$I_t := I_0 + t$ where, $t = 1, 2, \ldots$

Hence, by forward substitution of $I_0 := 1$ into the loop, we get

$I_t := t + 1;$

Since $I_{t-1} = t$ and $N := \text{LENGTH}(X)$, we get (by forward substitution):

$$\{\text{DONE} := X[t] = \text{CH}; I_t ::= t + 1\}; \mathbb{U}_{\text{DONE or } (t + 1 > \text{LENGTH(X)})}; \mathbb{IF}_{\text{DONE}} \left\{ \begin{array}{c} \text{LOCATE} := t + 1 \\ \rule{3cm}{3pt} \\ \text{LOCATE} := 0 \end{array} \right\}$$

We can forward substitute the value of DONE into $\mathbb{U}$ and $\mathbb{IF}$, but quickly run into a problem with further reductions, because we do not have values for X[t]. Before going any further, we need values to *force* the transformed program. What values should we use?

The theory of test data selection described in the previous chapter can be used to select forcing values. Clearly, the predicates on $\mathbb{U}$ and $\mathbb{IF}$ should be used:

$t' = \text{LENGTH}(X)$
$X[t'] = \text{CH}$

The forcing value of t' is substituted into the expression for LOCATE. In this example, t' should be equal to the value of the index that points to a matching CH. But, the resulting value of LOCATE is off by one. This substitution reveals an error in the program when ($X[t]' = \text{CH}$), because LOCATION should be t' instead of $t' + 1$. This error can be corrected by replacing LOCATE $:= I$ with LOCATE $:= I - 1$. The tth character is found in $X[t]$ of the corrected version, instead of $X[t+1]$.

Similar calculations can be carried out by forcing the case where $t' = \text{LENGTH}(X)$. The **else** clause of the $\mathbb{IF}$ construct is exercised by this value, because DONE is False, resulting in LOCATE $:= 0$. When no match is found, the function returns zero.

Loop Transformation Rules

Loop transformations are carried out as follows:

1. Introduce a loop counter, say t, in every recursive statement within the loop body.

2. Convert all recursive statements to iterative form by solving the equivalent finite difference equations. The iterative equations are invariants.

3. Perform all forward substitution transformations permitted, and simplify the reduced program.

4. Find a loop functional that terminates the loop. This is usually done by computing a final value of the loop counter, say t', such that the loop terminates. In the case of **while** loops the loop predicate is false; in **repeat** loops the predicate is true when the loop stops.

5. Replace the loop with its equivalent computation. This is done by computing the final value (termination value) of the loop body using the results of Step 4.

A shorthand notation was used in the previous example for convenience. Other convenient symbols for looping in Pascal are:

$$T_w \{\text{while } p \text{ do } s\} \sim \mathbb{W}_p\{s\}$$
$$T_f \{\text{for } <\text{interval}> \text{ do}\} \sim \mathbb{F}_{<\text{interval}>} \{s\}$$
$$T_r \{\text{repeat } s \text{ until } p\} \sim \{s\}\mathbb{U}_p$$

Choice Transformation

The choice transformation is the most difficult to use, because every **if-then-else** and **case-of** component creates two or more paths through the program. These paths tend to rapidly increase in number, requiring a large number of forcing values to examine all possible executions of the program.

The following transformation rules attempt to reduce the number of paths created by the **if-then-else** and **case-of** components. Unfortunately, they often do not succeed in reducing the number of paths. We must often resort to careful selection of forcing values to simplify the majority of programs containing choice components.

The T_{if} transform divides the flow of control into two paths. The upper path is taken when the choice predicate is true, and the lower path taken when the predicate is false.

$$T_{if} \{\text{if } p \text{ then } s_{true} \text{ else } s_{false}\} \sim \{ \begin{array}{c} \{p\} \ s_{true} \\ \rule{3cm}{0.3cm} \\ \{\text{not } p\} \ s_{false} \end{array} \}$$

We can sometimes use p and **not** p to simplify s_{true} and s_{false}, respectively. Forward substitution of the relation p or **not** p may lead to a simplification as illustrated by the absolute value function below:

```
function ABS (var X : real) : real;
begin
  if X < 0
    then ABS := -X
    else ABS := X
end;
```

The transformed function yields two paths:

$$T_{if} \{\text{if } X < 0 \text{ then ABS} := -X \text{ else ABS} := X\} \sim \left\{ \frac{\{X < 0\} \{ABS := -X\}}{\{X \geq 0\} \{ABS := X\}} \right\}$$

Suppose we introduce an artificial variable $S > 0$ and rewrite the relations in the transformed **if-then-else** component as follows:

$$\sim \left\{ \frac{\{X = -S\} \{ABS := -X\}}{\{X = S\} \{ABS := X\}} \right\} \text{ where } S > 0$$

Forward substitution of the artificially introduced values of X give the simplification we seek:

$$\sim \left\{ \frac{\{ABS := S\}}{\{ABS := S\}} \right\} \sim ABS := S \text{ where } S > 0$$

Hence, the two paths have been reduced to a single path. Unfortunately, this trick does not always work for **if-then-else** components. In general, we must force one path or another even though forcing may weaken the analysis.

As before, we seek a transformation that reduces the difficulty of the program in terms of verification. If possible, an algebraic model of the program is derived that can be solved in closed form. The closed form solution is then forced so we can observe the way the solution responds to its inputs. When a closed form solution is not possible, we force all of the paths through the program by carefully selecting values. We use the coupling effect of testing, complexity-based testing, and whatever method that reduces the number of paths to be examined.

As an example, a program for finding the maximum element of a list $X[1..N]$ is modeled. We can reveal an error in MAXIMUM by applying the transform theory.

```
procedure MAXIMUM (X : array [1..N ] of integer; var MAX, LOC : integer);
var BIG, I : integer;
begin
  BIG := X[1];
  for I := 1 to N do
    if BIG < X[I]
      then begin BIG := X[I]; LOC := I end;
  MAX := BIG;
end;
```

The **if-then-else** transform yields an abbreviated program:

$$\{BIG_0 := X[I]\} \; \mathbb{F}_{(I := 1..N)} \left\{ \frac{\{BIG_{t-1} < X[I]\} \{BIG_t := X[I]; LOC_t := I\}}{\{BIG_{t-1} \geq X[I]\}} \right\} \{MAX := BIG_N\}$$

The **for** loop counter I runs over the values $1..N$. When $I = 1$, the artificially introduced counter $t = 1$, and so on until $I = N$, $t = N$. The value of I becomes undefined outside the **for** loop, but t is defined ($t = N$).

This example demonstrates the difficulty of verifying programs containing **if-then-else** branches. The only way out of this difficulty is to force the program to execute both paths through the loop. In this case we employ the coupling effect. Three cases are used:

Arrays as subscripts: This program does not use arrays as subscripts to (other) arrays. So we choose a simple "identity" function. Let

X[I] = I where I is **in** [1..N]

Negative domain: Include simple negative values, so let

X[I] = −I where I is **in** [1..N]

Nonunique domain and degenerate domain: Include repeated values and degenerate values (e.g., zero). These two cases are combined:

X[I] = 0 when I is **in** [1..M−1] + [M+1..N]
    = 1 when I is M

First, we perform the transformation of MAXIMUM using $X[I] = I$ as forcing data.

TEST 1: (X[I] = I)

Note that when $t = 1$, $BIG_0 \geq 1$; so $BIG_1 = BIG_0 = 1$. Then, when $t > 1$, we observe that $BIG_t = t$ and $BIG_{t-1} = t-1$. These observations lead to a simplification in the transformed and abbreviated program:

$$\sim \mathbb{F}_{(t \text{ in } [2..N])} \quad \{ \frac{\{t-1 < t\}\ \{BIG_t := t;\ LOC_t := t\}}{\{t-1 \geq t\}} \}\ \{MAX := BIG_N\}$$

Since $(t − 1) < t$ is always true, the **if-then-else** expression reduces to the true-clause only. Thus,

$\sim \mathbb{F}_{(t \text{ in } [2..N])}\ \{\{BIG_t := t;\ LOC_t := t\}\}\ \{MAX := BIG_N\}$

The **for** loop terminates with $(t' − 1) = N$, and $BIG_N = N$, $LOC_N = N$, leading to functional transformation of the **for** loop as follows:

$\sim \{BIG_N := N;\ LOC_N := N\}\ \{MAX := BIG_N\}$

and forward substitution yields the final result:

$\sim \{LOC_N := N\}\ \{MAX := N\}$

We conclude that the first test case certifies a correct program. The largest element of $X[I] := I$ is N, and it is found in LOC: $= N$.

TEST 2: (X[I] = −I)

The abbreviated version of MAXIMUM with this input is:

$$\{BIG_0 := -1\} \ \mathbb{F}_{(I := 1..N)} \ \{ \ \frac{\{BIG_{t-1} < -I\} \ \{BIG_t := -I; \ LOC_t := I\}}{\{BIG_{t-1} \geq -I\}} \ \} \ \{MAX := BIG_N\}$$

Notice that when $t = 1$; $I = 1$ so that $BIG_0 < (-1)$, becomes $-1 < (-1)$ when forward substitution is applied, which is false. Thus, $BIG_1 = BIG_0 = (-1)$. Furthermore, when $t > 1$, $I = t$, and the test $BIG_{t-1} < (-t)$ is also false. In other words, $BIG_{t-1} \geq (-t)$ is always true leading to execution of the false-clause of the **if-then-else** component. The loop transforms into:

$\sim \ \{BIG_0 := (-1)\} \ \{BIG_N := BIG_0\} \ \{MAX := BIG_N\}$

Finally, forward substitution yields

$\{MAX := (-1)\}$

The resulting value of MAX is correct, but the value of LOC is undefined. Hence, the program contains an error. This error is corrected by defining LOC as shown below.

```
procedure MAXIMUM (X : LIST; var MAX, LOC : integer);
   var
   BIG, I : integer;
   begin
     BIG := X[1];
     LOC := 1; {correction}
     for I:=1 to N do
     if BIG < X[I]
        then begin BIG := X[I]; LOC := I end;
     MAX := BIG;
   end; {MAXIMUM}
```

Now, we perform a final test using repeated zeros and a single maximum of one.

TEST 3: (X[I] = 0; I ≠ M; X[M]=1

When $M = 1$, we get

$\{BIG_0 := 1; \ LOC_0 := 1\}; \ \mathbb{F}_{(I := 1..N)} \ \{ \ \{BIG_t := BIG_{t-1}\} \ \}; \ \{MAX := BIG_N\}$

because $\{BIG_{t-1} < X[I]\} \sim \{1 < X[I]\}$ which is always false. The resulting output values are $\{LOC := 1; \ MAX := 1\}$. This is the correct answer.

When $M > 1$, we notice that every pass through the loop executes the false-clause of the **if-then-else** component until the $X[M]$ element is compared. Then the true-clause is executed once. BIG becomes 1 and subsequent passes through the loop execute the false-clause again. Thus, the abbreviated program transforms into:

$\sim \ \{BIG_N := 1; \ LOC_N := M\}; \ \{MAX := BIG_N\}$

The third test succeeds, so we are confident in the correctness of the program.

As a final illustration of this technique of mathematical verification, suppose we analyze a procedure containing all three "difficult to analyze" constructs: loops, **if-then-else**, and array data types. Procedure MERGE takes two ordered lists as inputs and merges them into a single ordered list according to the following plan:

1. Let L1 and L2 be two ordered lists, and LOUT the output of MERGE.

2. Repeat the following until one or the other list is exhausted:
   (a) Compare elements of L1 and L2.
   (b) Copy the smallest element to LOUT.
   (c) Update list counters in L1 and L2.

3. Copy the trailing elements from the list that was not exhausted in Step 2 into the output list LOUT.

4. The output list LOUT is in order and of length equal to the sum of the lengths of L1 and L2.

This plan is implemented in procedure MERGE as shown in Figure 11-1. The lists are of length N, M, and NPLUSM. The variables I and J keep track of the locations of elements to be copied into LOUT next. The MIN function returns the smallest value of its two arguments.

MERGE PROCEDURE OPERATES ON TWO ORDERED LISTS

```
procedure MERGE (L1, L2 : LIST; var LOUT : LISTOUT);

var I, J : integer;

begin
  I := 1; J := 1;
  while (I < = N) and (J < = M) do
    begin
      LOUT[I+J-1] := MIN(L1[I], L2[J]);
      if L1[I] < L2[J]
        then I := I+1
        else J := J+1
    end;
  for I := I to N do LOUT[I+J-1] := L1[I];
  for J := J to M do LOUT[I+J-1] := L2[J];
end; {merge}
```

FIGURE 11-1. Procedure MERGE

It is important to note that only one of the **for** loops is executed in the procedure. Either I exceeds N, or J exceeds M when this point is reached. The executed **for** loop simply copies the trailing elements into LOUT as specified in Step 3 of the plan.

The most challenging segment in procedure MERGE is the **while** loop. Let's begin the analysis by representing this loop with a mathematical equivalent. First, we use a mathematical trick to remove the **if-then-else** from the loop body. The trick is based on the property of the ORD function, which returns 0 if its argument is false, and 1 if its argument is true. That is,

{**if** L1[I] < L2[J] **then** I := I+1} ~ {I := I + ORD(L1[I] < L2[J])}
{**if** L1[I] < L2[J] **else** J := J+1} ~ {J := J + ORD(L1[I] ≥ L2[J])}

That is, the successive value of I and J is determined by comparison of L1 and L2. In the case L1[I] < L2[J], we add 1 to I, otherwise, we add 1 to J. The two expressions are computationally equivalent, but the version that employs ORD simplifies verification. Now we can rewrite the **while** loop in transformed notation:

$$\sim \{I_0 := 1;\ J_0 := 1\};\ \mathbb{W}_{(I_{t-1} \leq N \text{ and } J_{t-1} \leq M)} \left\{ \begin{array}{l} \text{LOUT}[I_{t-1} + J_{t-1} - 1] := \text{MIN}(\text{L1}[I_{t-1}], \text{L2}[J_{t-1}]) \\ I_t := I_{t-1} + \text{ORD}(\text{L1}[I_{t-1}] < \text{L2}[J_{t-1}]) \\ J_t := J_{t-1} + \text{ORD}(\text{L1}[I_{t-1}] \geq \text{L2}[J_{t-1}]) \end{array} \right\}$$

To obtain a loop invariant, we must replace the recurrence formulas with an equivalent iterative form for I_t and J_t. Using $I_0 = 1$ and $J_0 = 1$, we get a solution that depends only on the values of L1 and L2.

$$I_t = 1 + \sum_{s=1}^{t} \text{ORD}(\text{L1}[I_{s-1}] < \text{L2}[J_{s-1}])$$
$$J_t = 1 + \sum_{s=1}^{t} \text{ORD}(\text{L1}[I_{s-1}] \geq \text{L2}[J_{s-1}])$$

The value of I_t is equal to one greater than the number of times L1[I_{s-1}] is less than L2[J_{s-1}]. A similar observation is true for J_t. But how do we get such counts? Before we can go further, we must select values for L1 and L2 that force values for ORD. We look at two sets of values.

TEST 1: L1[1..N] = 0; L2[1..M] = 0

This simple, repeated, and degenerate case should work even if nothing else does! These values cause ORD to return zero in the formula for I_t, and one in the formula for J_t. Using $I_0 = J_0 = 1$, yields an abbreviated version of MERGE:

$$I_t = 1 + \sum_{s=1}^{t} 0 = 1, \text{ and } J_t = 1 + \sum_{s=1}^{t} 1 = t + 1$$
$$\sim \{\mathbb{W}_{(1 \leq N) \text{ and } (t \leq M)} \{\text{LOUT}[t] := 0;\ I_t := 1;\ J_t := t + 1\}\}$$

This loop terminates when $(t' \leq M)$ is false. That is, $t' > M$ implies $t' = M + 1$. Completing the transformation of the loop:

LOUT[1..M] := 0; I := 1; J := M + 1

This result can be combined with the remainder of the program which simply copies array L1 into the remaining elements of LOUT[I + M..N + M].

for I := 1 **to** N **do** LOUT[I + M] := L1[I];

In this example, MERGE first copies M zeros from L2 into LOUT, and then copies N zeros from L1 into the remaining N elements of LOUT. Hence, we conclude that the procedure works for this degenerate list.

TEST 2: (L1[*I*] := 2*I*; L2[*J*] := 2*J*−1)

The purpose of this test is to study MERGE when the data values alternate back and forth. When the ascending lists alternate, $\text{ORD}(\text{L1}[I_{s-1}] < \text{L2}[J_{s-1}])$ becomes $\text{ORD}(\text{odd}(s))$, and $\text{ORD}(\text{L1}[I_{s-1}] \geq \text{L2}[J_{s-1}])$ becomes $\text{ORD}(\text{even}(s))$, where odd(s) is true if s is an odd integer, and even(s) is true if s is an even integer. Therefore,

$$I_t = 1 + \sum_{s=1}^{t} \text{ORD}(\text{odd}(s)) = 1 + \text{Floor}(t/2) \text{ and } J_t = 1 + \sum_{s=1}^{t} \text{ORD}(\text{even}(s)) = 1 + \text{Floor}((t+1)/2)$$

where Floor(x) is the integer part of x. Then,

$$\text{MIN}(\text{L1}[I_{t-1}],\ \text{L2}[J_{t-1}]) = t, \text{ and } I_{t-1} + J_{t-1} - 1 = t$$

The transformed loop becomes:

$$\sim \{ \mathbb{W}_{(1+\text{Floor}((t-1)/2)\ \leq\ N\ \text{and}\ (1+\text{Floor}(t/2)\ \leq\ M)} \left\{ \begin{array}{l} \text{LOUT}[t] := t \\ I_t := 1 + \text{Floor}(t/2) \\ J_t := 1 + \text{Floor}((t+1)/2) \end{array} \right\}$$

LOUT correctly copies the values in order for as long as the loop repeats. The remaining question is whether the loop terminates as expected. Two cases are considered.

CASE A: 1+Floor((t'−1)/2) > N

Case A corresponds with termination of the loop because all elements of L1 are copied into LOUT. The smallest value of t' that satisfies this condition is $t' = 2N + 1$. The loop is performed $(t'-1)$ times (it fails before the t'th pass). The values of I and J at $(t'-1) = 2N$ are $I_{t'-1} = (1+N)$ and $J_{t'-1} = (1+N)$.

The remaining elements of LOUT are obtained from the remainder of L2. Note that $I + J - 1 = 1 + N + J - 1 = N + J$. Thus, the **for** loop becomes

        for J := N+1 **to** M **do** LOUT[N+J] := L2[J];

CASE B: 1+Floor(t'/2) > M

Case B is the mirror image of Case A except it models the program when L2 is copied into LOUT, first. The smallest value of t' that terminates the loop is $t' = 2M$. Therefore, the **while** loop is performed $(t'-1) = 2M-1$ times. The termination values of I and J are $I_{t'-1} = M$, and $J_{t'-1} = M + 1$. This time, however, $I + J - 1 = I + M + 1 - 1 = I + M$ and the **for** loop that copies the remainder of L1 is executed $(N-M+1)$ times. Thus,

        for I := M **to** N **do** LOUT[I+M] := L[I];

This example illustrates the formalism of functional transformations that simplify the control structure of a program. This approach is sufficiently strong to nearly constitute a proof of the program's correctness. Unfortunately, it does not always succeed in transforming the program in question into its simplest form. To overcome this weakness, we force values to assist in making the transformation.

The ideas underlying the transform theory are simple: (1) apply forward substitution wherever possible, (2) reduce loops to straight-line code segments wherever possible using the loop transformation, (3) remove branching choice components wherever possible by forcing values, and (4) attempt to simplify the resulting transformed program to a collection of simple, single-assignment statements.

PROOF OF CORRECTNESS

Proof of correctness *is a formal technique used to prove mathematically that a program satisfies its specifications*[2]. This is done by describing both specifications and the program itself in the form of assertions. An **assertion** *is a logical expression specifying one or more conditions that the program must satisfy in order for the program to be correct.* The theory of proof of correctness by assertion is very similar to the theory of mathematical transformation studied in the previous section. However, the mathematical tools are different. Specifically, predicate logic is used rather than algebraic equations.

Proof of correctness attempts to prove **total correctness** — a *designation indicating that a program's output assertions follow logically from its input assertions and processing steps, and that, in addition, the program terminates under all specified input conditions.* We learned in chapter ten that this is theoretically impossible to do for arbitrary programs, because:

We can never be sure that the specifications are correct.

No verification system can verify every correct program.

We can never be certain that a verification system is correct. The unfortunate truth is that we cannot build provably correct tools anymore than we can build provably correct programs.

These limitations are inherent in the verification process, and cannot be surmounted by any technical innovation.

If theoretical limitations are so severe, why do we care about proof of correctness? First, it is valuable in its own right because it shows how to reason about programming. It provides a basis for program structure (no GOTOs, assertive programming), and it provides an intellectual way of writing concise, clear, and maintainable code.

Second, there are cases where it is essential to guarantee the total correctness of a program, and even if the technique is impossible, it can generally be used to advantage in special cases. Remember mission-critical software, which must work every time it is used.

Because of its intellectual power, proof of correctness has contributed to the advancement of software engineering by providing a basis for structured programming, abstract data types, and object-oriented design. These are ample reasons to study the topic even if its practical application is limited.

The Very Idea

The most widespread method of proof of correctness is based on the use of predicates — first order logic propositions — to model a program and its inputs. We make assertions about each part of the program in the form of predicates. Then the system of predicates is shown to yield the result we want. For example, to prove that the output of function ABS is greater than zero for all negative inputs, a predicate model of the program is used to formulate a theorem. Proving the theorem leads to the desired conclusion that the outputs are always greater than zero.

```
function ABS(VAL : integer) : integer;
begin
  if VAL < 0 then ABS := -VAL
              else ABS := VAL
end; {ABS}
```

Assumption: Assert #1: VAL < 0;   Assert #0: ABS > 0
Theorem: (Assert #1) and (Correct (function ABS)) implies (Assert #0).

In this simple example, assuming Assert #1 is T (T means *True*, and F means *False* in this chapter), and the predicate Correct(x) is T leads to the desired conclusion. Substitution of function ABS for x requires that we prove Correct(function ABS) is T. This is what we mean by "proof of correctness."

Now, we need to represent each Pascal construct by a meaningful predicate. In the previous section we used algebraic models to attach meanings to each construct. In "proof by assertion," we write predicates that quantify the semantics of each construct. The "predicate models" of proof by assertion are assumed to be valid representations of each Pascal construct, hence they are called *axioms*. For this reason, proof by assertion is also sometimes called the axiomatic approach to program proving.

After all program statements are replaced by assertions derived from the program, and the axioms of proof by assertion, we use theorem proving techniques to derive the

Rules of Predicate Logic

p	q	p and q	p or q	not p	p implies q	p iff q
T	T	T	T	T	T	T
T	F	F	T	F	F	T
F	T	F	T	T	T	F
F	F	F	F	T	T	T

p, q are predicates which evaluate to T or F
T = True, F = False
iff = if and only if

desired conclusions. For example, to prove the theorem above, we apply the axioms and assertions in the most direct fashion — forward substitution of Assert #1 into the theorem:

(Assert #1: VAL $<$ 0) **and** (**function** ABS : **if** VAL $<$ 0 **then** ABS := -VAL) **implies** (ABS $>$ 0)
(ABS $>$ 0) **implies** (Assert #0).
QED.

We conclude Correct (**function** ABS) is T from this proof. Note we cannot conclude that the program runs without crashing, only that the program is correct relative to its specifications. In this case the specifications are given as Assert #1. If this specification does not properly model all the possible values that can be passed to ABS, then the proof is incomplete. This is called partial correctness, and is the best that we can do in most circumstances.

Partial correctness *is a designation indicating that a program's output assertions follow logically from its input assertions and processing steps*[2]. We seek partial correctness of procedures and functions. To achieve this more modest goal, we must prove two things: 1) the procedure/function terminates, and 2) when it terminates, the output assertion is T (True).

The assertions in partial correctness checking are of two kinds: *pre-conditions* and *post-conditions*. A pre-condition is an assertion that specifies the state of the program prior to execution of the statement following the pre-condition. A post-condition is an assertion that specifies the state of the program following execution of the statement immediately preceding the pre-condition. The post-condition of one statement becomes the pre-condition of the next statement in sequence. A proof usually consists of a chain of pre- and post-conditions that leads from an input assertion to a final assertion.

Assignment Axiom

Assignment statements, and any concatenated sequence of SESE-structured statements, can be modeled as before, where s_i are statements:

$S \sim \{s_1; s_2; ..s_n\}$

The braces are metasymbols used to indicate serial execution of statements s_i. The semicolon designates concatenation. S is a series of statements.

Each statement s_i consists of a left-hand-side, *lhs*, and a right-hand-side, *rhs*,

lhs := rhs

We assign a pre-condition, *pre*, and post-condition, *post*, to each statement to model the state of the program during execution:

pre [lhs := rhs] post

This leads to the first axiom in the axiomatic approach to program proving. T_s is the assignment axiom:

T_s : {pre [lhs := rhs] post} $\sim$ {pre **implies** post}

For example, suppose the assignment statement

{C := A + B}

is to be verified. We need pre-condition and post-condition assertions:

pre = {B ≥ 8 and A = 5}; post = {C ≥ 13}

Using T_s yields the desired result:

{B ≥ 8 and A = 5} [C := A + B] {C ≥ 13} ~ {B ≥ 8 and A = 5} **implies** {C ≥ 13}

This is T.

Composition Axiom

The series of statements in an SESE-structured program are modeled by pre-conditions and post-conditions as expected:

T_+ : {pre [s_1; s_2] post} ~ {(pre **implies** intermediate) **and** (intermediate **implies** post)}

where *pre*, *post*, and *intermediate* are assertions.

In the previous section we modeled the following sequence of assignment statements as a series of algebraic equations. Now, suppose we write a series of predicates which model the computational behavior of the sequence:

{A := 5; B := A + 3; C := A + B;}

Assume:

pre_1 = T; $post_1$ = {A = 5}; pre_2 = {A = 5}; $post_2$ = {B ≥ 8}; pre_3 = {B ≥ 8 and A = 5}; $post_3$ = {C ≥ 20}.

Prove:

Correct (series) **implies** (C ≥ 20)

Again, forward substitution is sufficient to derive the (incorrect) conclusion.

s_1 : {T} [A := 5] {A = 5} ~ {T} **implies** {A = 5}	This is T.
s_2 : {A = 5} [B := A + 3] {B ≥ 8} ~ {A = 5} **implies** {B ≥ 8}	This is T.
s_3 : {B ≥ 8 and A = 5} [C := A + B] {C ≥ 20} ~ {B ≥ 8 and A = 5} **implies** {C ≥ 20}	This is F.

The *pre* and *post* assertions establish a chain of assertions leading from the input specification assertion to the output assertion. However, forward substitution is rarely powerful enough to prove more realistic programs. Therefore, the idea of a chain of assertions may not always be valid. For example, we will require proof by induction to prove the correctness of loops.

Branching Axiom

In addition to *pre* and *post* assertions, branching and looping axioms must consider the predicate of the statement. Thus, the **if-then-else** axiom must include the test predicate, and the **while** axiom must include the loop test predicate.

Secondly, the *post* condition must be invariant with respect to the branch taken. That is, *post* must be identical for the **if-then** as well as the **if-else** path through the **if-then-else** statement. This gives rise to the branching axiom:

T_{if} : {pre [if C then S_t else S_f] post} ~ {((pre **and** C) **implies** post) **or** (pre **and not** C) **implies** post)}

As an example, we can prove function ABS with this axiom.

```
function ABS(VAL : integer) : integer;
begin
if VAL < 0 then ABS := -VAL
            else ABS := VAL
end; {ABS}
```

pre = $\{-\infty \leq VAL \leq +\infty\}$
post = {ABS ≥ 0}
C = VAL < 0

So, we must prove:

$\{\{-\infty \leq VAL \leq +\infty\}$ [if VAL < 0 then ABS := -VAL else ABS := VAL] {ABS ≥ 0}}
~ {(($\{-\infty \leq VAL \leq +\infty\}$ **and** VAL < 0 **implies** {ABS ≥ 0})
or ($\{-\infty \leq VAL \leq +\infty\}$ **and not** (VAL < 0)) **implies** {ABS ≥ 0})}

This becomes, after simplification:

~ {(VAL < 0 **implies** {ABS ≥ 0})
or ((VAL ≥ 0) **implies** {ABS ≥ 0})}

And one more simplification:

$\{-\infty \leq VAL \leq +\infty \}$ **implies** {ABS ≥ 0}

which is what we expect from an ABS function.

Looping Axiom

Looping, like branching, requires a test predicate. But, instead of holding the post-condition invariant with respect to the loop test, we hold the pre-condition invariant. Why? Recall that the problem with looping is the difficulty we have in modeling recursive statements within the loop. To circumvent this difficulty, we require that the pre-condition be an invariant. This, in turn, permits mathematical induction to be used as a proof technique. The induction technique is analogous with finding a closed-form solution to the algebraic recursion equations in the previous section.

The axiom for **while** loops is given below; the reader can deduce the equivalent axiom for **repeat** and counting loops:

T_w : {invar [**while** C **do** S] (invar **and not** C)}
~ {(invar **and** C) **implies** (invar **and not** C)}

MATHEMATICAL INDUCTION: A REVIEW

Loops built around invariants are proven correct by mathematical induction. Recall the technique:

1. State the conjecture to be proven.

2. Give the initial case.

3. Assume the general case.

4. Prove the inductive (next step) case using the initial case and the general case as givens.

Example:

1. Conjecture $\sum_{i=1}^{n} (i) = n(n+1)/2$

2. Given $\sum_{i=1}^{1} (i) = 1$

3. Assume general case $\sum_{i=1}^{k} (i) = k(k+1)/2$

4. Prove inductive case $n = k+1$

$$\sum_{i=1}^{k+1} (i) = (k+1)(k+2)/2$$

Proof: Add $(k+1)$ to both sides of general case given in the assumption of step 3:

$$\sum_{i=1}^{k} (i) + (k+1) = k(k+1)/2 + (k+1)$$

The left-hand side becomes the left-hand side of the desired result:

$$\sum_{i=1}^{k+1} (i) = k(k+1)/2 + (k+1)$$

The right-hand side becomes the desired result:

$$\sum_{i=1}^{k+1} (i) = (k+1)(k+2)/2$$

QED.

This technique is used in proving by constructing a loop invariant as the conjecture to be proven, and then using the pre- and postcondition assertions as follows:

1. Conjecture Loop Invariant

2. Given Pre-condition assertion

3. Assume kth iteration through loop is correct

4. Prove Postcondition results from loop termination — the inductive step being that loop iteration does what the conjecture states.

Notice that the pre-condition designated here by *invar* is unaltered by the loop. This is why it is an invariant — the truth value of the loop pre-condition is not altered by the loop.

Secondly, note that the loop test C is true while the loop executes and false in the post-condition. Thus, when proving such loops we must show that the loop terminates, for instance, that it is possible to force **not C**, and that the loop invariant is preserved by the terminating loop.

Loop invariants are *not* easy to find. In fact, the best way to obtain a loop invariant is to start with the invariant before the loop is written. This approach is called *formal structured programming*, because of the way loops are designed by formal proof techniques. In the formal approach, the loop invariant is derived from specifications, and then the code derived from the invariant. If this form of top-down design is not followed, we may end up with loops that have no discernible invariant.

Suppose, for example, we want to design and implement a function for computing $Z = X^N$ where N is an integer assumed to be greater than zero. The obvious method of calculating an exponential when no exponential function is available is to iteratively multiply X. The loop for doing this can be derived from the invariant:

1. *Conjecture* Loop Invariant: $V_I = \{(Z = X^I)$ **and** $(0 \leq I \leq N)\}$
2. *Given* Pre-condition assertion: $V_0 = \{(Z = 1)$ **and** $(I = 0$ **and** $0 \leq N)\}$
3. *Assume* kth iteration through loop is correct: $V_k = \{(Z = X^k)$ **and** $(0 \leq k \leq N)\}$
4. *Prove* $V_N = \{(Z = X^N)$ **and** $(0 \leq N)\}$. First, prove V_{k+1} is derived from V_k and looping. Then set $I = N$.

Not only can the function be written from this format, but the proof is almost immediate. First, the code derived from the invariant V:

```
function POWER (X : real) : real;
var I : integer; {Loop counter = Invariant index}
    Z : real; {Intermediate = answer}

begin
    Z := 1.0; I := 0; {pre = V₀ = (Z = 1) and (I = 0 and 0 ≤ N)}
    while (I < N) do

      begin
        Z := Z * X; {assume k-th pass : Vₖ = {(Z = Xᵏ) and (0 ≤ k ≤ N)}

        I := I + 1
      end; {while}
    POWER := Z;    {post = Vₙ = (Z = Xᴺ) and (0 ≤ N)}

end; {POWER}
```

This code mirrors mathematical induction very closely. This is exactly the point — if you write the loop as a proof by induction, then actually carrying out the proof is rather simple. In fact, in this simple example, we only need to show that pass $k = I + 1$ through the loop keeps the invariant intact, and that substitution of $I = N$ does two things: 1) terminates the loop, and 2) yields the post-condition. Clearly, the loop terminates because (N < N) is false — **not** C. Then, because the induction is true, direct substitution of $I = N$ into the post-condition gives a correct answer for Z. The value of Z is a desirable by-product of proving the loop.

In more formal terms, we can plug the invariant formula and the loop test predicate into the **while** loop axiom to obtain:

T_w : {invar [**while** C **do** S] (invar **and not** C)}
~ {(invar **and** C) **implies** (invar **and not** C)}

First, substitute the pre-condition version of the invariant, V_0 into the "before loop" invariant:

T_w : {(Z = 1) **and** (I = 0 **and** 0 ≤ N) [**while** C **do** S] (invar **and not** C)}
~ {((Z = 1) **and** (I = 0 **and** 0 ≤ N) **and** C) **implies** (invar **and not** C)}

Next, replace C with the loop predicate — complementing the predicate to obtain **not** C:

T_w : {(Z = 1) **and** (I = 0 **and** 0 ≤ N) [**while** (I < N) **do** S] (invar **and** (I ≥ N))}
~ {((Z = 1) **and** (I = 0 **and** 0 ≤ N) **and** (I < N)) **implies** (invar **and** (I ≥ N))}

Finally, replace the post-condition invar with V_N:

T_w : {(Z = 1) **and** (I = 0 **and** 0 ≤ N) [**while** (I < N) **do** S] ((Z = X^N) **and** (0 ≤ N) **and** (I ≥ N)}
~ {((Z = 1) **and** (I = 0 **and** 0 ≤ N) **and** (I < N)) **implies** ((Z = X^N) **and** (0 ≤ N) **and** (I ≥ N))}

To prove the theorem, we show that the loop terminates because iteration (induction) results in ($I = N$), and then we show that iteration drives the loop invariant to the final value we seek. Both of these are shown by generalizing the loop body and induction.

$S_k = \{Z_k := Z_{k-1} * X ; I_k := I_{k-1} + 1\}$

and so, from solving the difference equations (see the previous section):

$S_k = \{Z_k := Z_0 * X^k; I_k := I_0 + k\} = \{Z_k := X^k; I_k := 1 + k\}$

Thus, S_k is exactly the assumed invariant V_k and substitution of $k = N$ proves both points:

$S_N = V_N = \{Z_N := X^N; I_N := 1 + N\}$

The loop terminates because $(1 + N) \geq N$ satisfies the **not** C part of the post-condition. The loop "converges" to the final value, because $S_N = V_N$. QED.

Loop Invariant Technique

The loop invariant proof technique can be summarized as follows:

1. Approximate the post-condition from the problem statement. If application specifications are given in formal notation, the invariant can often be found from a formal spec.

2. Invent a loop test C and then write a skeleton that reduces the loop test to **not** C. This may take several attempts by trial and error. Keep in mind that **not** C is part of the post-condition, so the post-condition is a good place to look for hints about C.

3. Approximate a pre-condition based on the loop test, the post-condition, and the problem. The pre-condition is a first attempt to understand and discover the loop invariant. Again, this may require several trial-and-error revisions.

4. Adjust the pre-, post-, and loop termination conditions to make them satisfy the initial, final, and problem specification conditions.

5. Modify, looking for an invariant that is true before, during, and after the loop.

We can demonstrate this process by example. Suppose we derive a software division algorithm for a computer that cannot do hardware divides. Such a machine is also unlikely to be able to multiply, but we assume that the machine can shift (divide and multiply by 2). Algorithm *qdiv* computes $q = (a/b) \pm e$, where a and b are integers, and e is an error bound. The result, q, is a real-valued fraction, for example, $0 \le a \le b$, and $e > 0$.

We attempt to derive post- and pre-conditions from the top-level specification:

pre [qdiv] post

From the problem specifications:

pre $= (0 \le a \le b)$ and $(e > 0)$
post $= (a/b - e) < q \le (a/b)$

EXAMPLES OF LOOP INVARIANTS

Compute the maximum element in array A[1..N]. That is, compute X = MAX(A):
The invariant for this problem is $V_I = \{(X = max(A[1..I])) $ **and** $ (1 \le I \le N)\}$

Sort array A[1..N] into ascending order using QSORT.
Let L[1..N] and U[1..N] be index place holders.
The invariant is $V_M = \{(A[L[1], U[1], (A[L[2]..U[2]]), ... A[L[M]..U[M]])$ are disjoint and sorted$\}$
Initially, M = 1, L[1] = 1, U[1] = N. When done, M = 0 and A[1..N] is sorted.

Search array A[1..N] for key K, using binary search. Assume A is in ascending order.
Let L[1..N] and U[1..N] be index place holders.
The invariant is $V_I = \{A[L..U]$ and $(L \le I \le U)\}$

The machine has no divide capability so we remove all divisions, except where they can be done by shifting.

This is achieved by multiplying post by b:

post = ((a − b*e) < b*q ≤ a)

Now for deriving C, the loop predicate. The approach is one of successive approximation as follows. We initially set a variable, ϵ to 1, and then proceed to reduce the error between the desired result and the current result. As we do so, ϵ is reduced in size until it is below the acceptable error, e.

0 < ϵ < e

We begin the successive approximations by setting q to zero, ϵ to 1, and looping. Each iteration of the loop reduces the current error, ϵ, by shifting:

```
begin
  q := 0;
  ε := 1; {e < 1, so this is a safe initial value}
  while (ε > 0) do {Since e > 0, ε > 0, too}
  begin
    ε := ε/2; {shifting is the only way}
  end
end;
```

This satisfies step 2 of the procedure. We have a skeleton loop that is a first approximation to a loop containing an invariant that 1) terminates the loop, and 2) reduces the error to a "small" amount, with the corresponding hope that the approximation is calculated as a by-product. But, the desired result, q, is not yet incorporated into the function.

A second attempt adds q to the assertions in anticipation of finding a way to compute q by successive approximation. The assertions are deduced from the specifications above, leading to a better approximation to the loop invariant.

Substituting the value of ϵ into *post* does not change the truth value of *post*. Thus, the form of *post* suggests a more general assertion:

a < b*(q + ϵ) ≤ a + b*ϵ

This leads to a more complete function for *qdiv*:

```
function qdiv(a,b,e : real) : real;
var q, ε : real; {fractions, only − less than 1.0}
begin
{Assert (0 ≤ a < b) and (e > 0)}
  q := 0; ε := 1;
  while (ε > 0) do
    begin   {Assert a < b*(q+ε) ≤ (a + b*ε)}
    ε := ε/2; {shifting is the only way}
    end
{Assert a < b*(q+e) ≤ (a + b*e)}
qdiv := q; {return q}
end; {qdiv}
```

The value of q remains at $q = 0$ throughout the loop, but this "improved version" reveals some structure and a rudimentary invariant. Note, especially, the assertion in the loop. If this is *True*, we can increase q by a small amount, say $q := q + \epsilon$. If the assertion is *False*, we iterate one more time to reduce ϵ by a small amount, say $\epsilon := \epsilon/2$. In this way, we "correct" the value of q such that the assertion is *True* while at the same time the successive values computed for q become closer to the exact result. This is expressed in the form of code:

```
function qdiv(a,b,e : real) : real;
var q, ε : real; {fractions, only — less than 1.0}
begin
{Assert (0 ≤ a < b) and ( e > 0)}
  q := 0; ε := 1;
  while (ε > e) do    {replace 0 with e}
    begin {Assert a < b*(q+ε) ≤ (a+ b*ε)}
    ε := ε/2; {shifting is the only way}
    if (a < b*(q+ε)) and (b*(q+ε) ≤ (a+ b*ε)) then q := q+ε;
  end;
{Asset a < b*(q+e) ≤ (a+ b*e)}  {This follows from above}
qdiv := q;   {return q}
end; {qdiv}
```

This version looks very close to the final form. What is the invariant, and does the function correctly compute the desired value, q? The invariant seems to be V_p;

1. *Conjecture* Loop Invariant: $V_p = \{a < b*(q+p) \le (a+ b*p)\}$
2. *Given* Pre-condition assertion: $V_1 = \{a < b \le (a+b) \text{ and } (q = 0)\}$
3. *Assume* kth iteration through loop is correct: $V_k = \{a < b*(q+\epsilon) \le (a+ b*\epsilon)\}$
4. Prove $V_N = \{a < b*(q+e) \le (a+ b*e)\}$

We substitute these into the proper assertions in the loop axiom:

T_w : {invar [**while** C **do** S] (invar **and not** C)}
$\sim$ {(invar **and** C) **implies** (invar **and not** C)}

The axiom for function *qdiv* is:

T_w : {$a < b \le (a + b)$ **and** (q = 0) [while ($\epsilon >$ e) **do** S] ($a < b*(q+e) \le (a+ b*e)$ **and** ($\epsilon \le$ e)}
$\sim$ {($a < b*(q+\epsilon) \le (a+ b*\epsilon)$ **and** ($\epsilon >$ e)) **implies** (($a < b*(q+e) \le (a+ b*e)$ **and** ($\epsilon \le$ e))}

The proof need only examine the invariant form (the $\sim$ part) and note that successive values of ϵ are computed as $\epsilon_k = (1/2)^k$ where k is the loop counter. As k increases, ϵ decreases, ultimately forcing the loop to terminate (the first requirement).

$$\lim_{k \to \infty} \epsilon_k = 0$$

But, the loop terminates for some k such that $\epsilon \leq e$. Simplifying the axiomatic form leads to a tautology:

$\sim \{((a/b)\cdot\epsilon < q \leq (a/b) \text{ and } (\epsilon > e)) \text{ implies } ((a/b)\cdot e < q \leq (a/b) \text{ and } (\epsilon \leq e))\}$

Thus, when the loop terminates, the required answer is returned by function qdiv:

$(a/b)\cdot e < qdiv \leq a/b$

This is within the stated bounds specified in the problem statement. QED.

DESK CHECKING

Algorithmic errors can be found by formal proof of correctness checking. Perhaps more important, demonstration of correctness in this way is more rigorous and precise than other forms of checking. Consequently, these formal methods lead to deeper understanding of both program and algorithm.

We know that total correctness checking is an unrealistic goal, because it is theoretically impossible to verify arbitrary programs. Perhaps even more important to software engineers is the practical reality of mathematical verification techniques:

1. The proof may take more time than to write the original program.

2. The proof may be larger and more complex than the original program.

3. Formal techniques may not find errors in design, interfaces, interpretation of specifications, in syntax and semantics of the programming language, or in the application's documentation.

4. The proof may itself be incorrect.

So why bother? Formal proof techniques are effective methods of desk checking single functions and procedures. *Desk checking* is the activity performed by a single programmer during the implementation and debugging of a procedure. Careful and thoughtful desk checking can lead to high productivity because it is a method of early defect removal.

Formalism has a major impact on the way programmers think and write code. Assertions, in the form of pre-conditions and post-conditions, tie together artifact and process. When the process of design and implementation is geared toward precise methods, the result is a certain style of programming artifact. *Assertive programming* — the use of assertions to document what the programmer intended — is illustrated in the following example.

Assertive Programming

Assertive programming is a practical application of the mathematical method of correctness as it is used in desk checking and maintenance. Consider, for example, the hashing function QHASH, which is designed to search a scatter table of length N to find a matching key, *LookKey* in Figure 11-2. This routine assumes a table of type TABLE from the declaration below:

```
type
   TABLE = array[0..N-1] of record
                           Key : integer; {Unique element identifier}
                           Occupied : boolean; {T if element has something stored in it, F otherwise}
                           Info : string; {The stored information}
                 end; {TABLE}
   var T : TABLE; {An instance of TABLE}
```

The data structure is further assumed to be initialized so that all $I = [0..N-1]$ elements are not occupied, the key field is null, and the info field is empty:

```
T[I].Key := Null;
T[I].Occupied := False;
T[I].Info := Empty;
```

We want to desk check this routine before running it to make sure all conditions are considered. The focus of attention is the loop. Does it always terminate? Does it examine all locations of the scatter table? What about worst-cases? We use assertive programming to analyze the function.

In order for the loop to terminate, the assertion **not** C must be true at some point in the program's execution. In this case, **not** C is the logical complement of the loop predicate:

```
Assert: (T[Probe].Key = LookKey) or (not T[Probe].Occupied) or ((Probe+Quotient) mod N = Home)
```

QUOTIENT-OFFSET SCATTER TABLE HASHING FUNCTION

```
function QHASH(LookKey : integer; T : TABLE; N : integer): integer;
const Null = -1; {terminator}
var Home, Quotient, Probe : integer;
begin
   Home := LookKey mod N; Probe := Home;
   Quotient := LookKey div N;
   while (T[Probe].Key <> LookKey)
            and
         (T[Probe].Occupied)
            and
   ((Probe+Quotient) mod N <> Home)
      do Probe := (Probe + Quotient) mod N;
   if T[Probe].Key = LookKey
         then QHASH := Probe {Found}
         else QHASH := Null {Not found}
end;{QHASH}
```

FIGURE 11-2. Hashing function QHASH

The first factor is obvious: if the lookup key *LookKey* matches the key stored in the table, the loop terminates and the search is successful. We can quickly dispense with this case, because the routine behaves as we want.

The second factor is more subtle and requires an understanding of the algorithm. This is the case when the search fails. The idea is to terminate the search as soon as the first empty element is encountered. According to the theory of hashing, the sought after key is not in the table if we run into an empty element before finding a match. This feature of hashing is partially responsible for its speed — the search can halt before comparing all elements in the table, even when the table does not contain the desired key. Thus, the loop terminates when **not** $T[Probe].Occupied$ is true, and QHASH returns *Null* as the answer.

The third factor is even more subtle. This is the case when the search has examined all elements and is not able to find the desired key. According to theory, the search cycles through all elements of T in N probes. However, the search bounces around from one element to another in seemingly random order. This makes the problem of desk checking very challenging even though this is a relatively simple fragment of code.

Here is an opportunity to use the formal techniques studied in this chapter. We can show that QHASH is inadequate because of a subtle error that may result in an infinite loop! What we want to know is, will the loop terminate if the table is full and the key is not in the table? In answering this question, we gain a deeper understanding of the algorithm and its implementation.

In this special case, the loop terminates if $((Probe + Quotient) \bmod N = Home)$. Using the algebraic loop invariant technique, we rewrite this in parameterized form, where t is the loop counter:

$$(Probe_t + Quotient) \bmod N = Home$$

and inside the loop we get a recurrence relation to solve in closed form:

$$Probe_t = (Probe_{t-1} + Quotient) \bmod N$$

which has solution:

$$Probe_t = (Probe_0 + Quotient*t) \bmod N$$

and since $Probe_0 = Home$,

$$Probe_t = (Home + Quotient*t) \bmod N$$
$$\text{where } t = 0, 1, \ldots$$

Substitution of this solution into the loop predicate and solving for a t' that makes the loop terminate yields the following:

$$(t'-1) \, Quotient \bmod N = 0$$

There are two interesting cases to examine.

1. Quotient **mod** N = 0

It is possible that *Quotient* = 0, when (*LookKey* **mod** N = 0). The loop never terminates when *Quotient* = 0 corresponding to an error in QHASH! This error is corrected by inserting a simple test:

if Quotient **mod** N = 0 **then** Quotient : = 1; {1 or any i > 0, but not a multiple of N}

This "fix" may have been obvious after careful reading of the function, but the next case is even more subtle.

2. (*t'*-1) **mod** N = 0

The loop counter t starts at 1 and increments by 1 for each pass through the loop, but we are interested in only the smallest value of (t'-1) that makes (t'-1) **mod** N = 0. The first time this happens is for (t'-1) = **N**. Therefore, t' = N + 1. That is, the loop iterates N times — seemingly once for each element of the table. This conclusion, however, overlooks the most subtle error of them all. Do the N probes into T compare unique elements? How can we show that the value of $Probe_t$ scans all elements?

We desk check QHASH to make sure that every element of T is searched before returning to location *Home*. To do this we compute the length L of a search path from *Home* and then back again. If the length is equal to the size of the table, N, and we already know that the loop iterates N times, then each iteration must examine a unique element. On the contrary, if $L < N$, then some of the elements of T must be skipped while others are examined more than once.

From number theory we know that the number of numbers in the interval [0..N-1] generated by the recurrence relation

$$Probe_t = (Probe_{t-1} + Quotient) \bmod N$$

is

$$L = N/gcd(N, Quotient)$$

where *gcd* is the greatest-common-divisor function. That is, $gcd(N, Quotient)$ = 1 if N and *Quotient* are relative primes. In fact, the largest value of L is when $gcd(N, Quotient)$ = 1, yielding the desirable $L = N$.

The easiest way to force this condition for arbitrary *Quotient* > 0 values is by setting N to a prime number. This is why QHASH is also called a prime-division hashing function. Setting the table length to the nearest prime number equal to the desired table size fixes the remaining problem.

To show that this theory actually works, consider the following. Let N = 6, and *LookKey* = 13. The number of numbers generated is L = 6/gcd(6, 2) = 3, because 13 **div** 6 = 2. This yields a partial scan of the table as follows:

$$Probes = \{1, 3, 5, 1, 3, 5, \ldots\}$$

In this case, only $T[1]$, $T[3]$, and $T[5]$ are searched, and $T[0]$, $T[2]$, and $T[4]$ are ignored. Fortunately, the *Home* element is searched a second time, ending the loop.

On the other hand, if $N = 7$ (nearest prime), we get much better results as follows. Using *LookKey* = 13 as before, *Quotient* = 13 **div** 7 = 1. Clearly, $L = 7$, so this yields a full scan of the table in the following order:

Probes = { 6, 0, 1, 2, 3, 4, 5, 6, . . .}

The point is clear: formal methods are valuable tools for desk checking, and though it is impossible to prove the correctness of an arbitrary program, it is nonetheless possible to gain an understanding of the deeper and more subtle structure of the code itself. This may be the only way to remove subtle and hard-to-find errors early in implementation.

Terms and Concepts

assertion
assertive programming
axiom
desk checking
finite differences
formal structured programming
forward substitution
induction
inductive assertion

loop functional
loop invariant
loop transform
partial correctness
post-condition
pre-condition
predicate
proof of correctness
total correctness

DISCUSSION QUESTIONS

1. Verify the following program fragment using the theory of transforms. Under what conditions on A and B will the program be guaranteed to terminate?

```
program WHIZ;
var A, B : integer;
begin
  READLN(A, B);
  while A < B do A := A + 3
end.
```

2. Verify the MERGE program using the following test data to aid in transformation:

$L1[I] = I$; $I = 1$ to N
$L2[J] = J$; $J = 1$ to N
$M = N$

3. List some problems encountered in attempting to verify the following code fragment for computing the greatest common divisor.

```
while X <> Y do
  if X > Y
    then X := X-Y
    else Y := Y-X
```

4. Use $X = 1$ and $Y > 1$ to analyze the program fragment of question 3. Is the fragment correct?

5. What is the final value of Y as a function of C and X in the following code fragment?

```
Y := C;
while Y > X do Y := Y/2;
[Hint: Solve the recurrence relation Y_{t+1} - (1/2)*Y_t = 0]
```

6. Verify the MAXIMUM procedure using the following forcing values

$N = 5, X[I] = I^2 - 3, I = 1$ to 5

7. The following code for searching an ordered list of length N, using a form of binary search, has a bug. Use the techniques described in this chapter to reveal the bug in this function. Give the corrected function along with the list of errors you found.

```
function BINARY (Key : integer; List : lists) : integer;
    var Y, Z : real; {subscripts}
    begin
      if (List[1] <= Key) and (Key <= List[N])
        then
          begin
            Z := N;
            Y := -N;
            while (Y < -1) and (List[trunc(Z)] <> Key) do
              begin
                Y := Y/2;
                if Key <= List[trunc(Z+Y)] then Z := Z+Y;
              end; {while}
            BINARY := trunc(Z) * ord(List[trunc(Z)] = Key); {0 or 1 times trunc(Z)}
          end {if-then}
        else BINARY := 0 {not in list}
    end; {BINARY}
```

8. Under what conditions might the following loops fail? (Failure is defined as nontermination, or abnormal termination of the loop.)

(a) **repeat** X := X+5 **until** X > 20;
(b) **while** X > 0 **do** X := X/3;
(c) **repeat** X := X+5 **until** X > Y;
(d) **while** X > 0 **do** X := X/Y;
(e) **while** (X > Y) **and** (X > Z) **do** X := X/2;
(f) **while** X > Y **do** X := X*Y;

9. The MERGE function was designed without consideration for an axiomatic approach to proving programs. Can you find a loop invariant for it? Does it have one?

```
procedure MERGE(L1, L2 : list; var LOUT : listout);
var I, J : integer;
begin
I := 1; J := 1; {Start with first elements}
while (I <= N) and (J <= M) do
```

```
begin
    LOUT[I+J-1] := min(L1[I], L2[J]); {Take smallest of the two}
    if L1[I] < L2[J] then I := I+1 else J := J+1
  end; {while}
  for I := I to N do LOUT[I+J-1] := L1[I]; {copy trailing elements}
  for J := J to M do LOUT[I+J-1] := L1[J]; {if J>M, this is skipped}
end; {MERGE}
```

10. Give loop invariants for **function** MIN, which computes the smallest element in array $A[1..N]$. Use the axiomatic approach, and then write the function in Pascal or C.

11. What is desk checking? How does mathematical verification help in desk checking? If it is impossible to prove a program correct, then why do we need formal mathematical proofs?

12. What is wrong with this hashing function? Find the anomalies by desk checking and then repair the function. Finally, prepare some test data to verify that the routine executes correctly.

```
function QHASH(LookKey : integer;
               T : TABLE; N : integer) : integer;
const
  Null = -1; {terminator}
var
  Home, Quotient, Probe, tCount : integer;
begin
  Home := LookKey mod N; Probe := Home;
  Quotient := LookKey div N; tCount := 0;
  while (T[Probe].Key < > LookKey)
            and
        (T[Probe].Occupied)
            and
          (tCount < > N)
    do
    begin
      Probe := (Probe + Quotient) mod N;
      tCount := tCount + 1
    end; {While}

if T[Probe].Key = LookKey
   then QHASH := Probe {Found}
   else QHASH := Null {Not found}
end; {QHASH}
```

REFERENCES AND FURTHER READING

1. Floyd, R. W. 1967. "Assigning Meanings To Programs." In *Mathematical Aspects of Computer Science*; J. T. Schwartz, ed. Providence, RI: American Mathematical Society.

2. Institute of Electrical and Electronics Engineers, Inc. 1983, 1984. *IEEE Standard for Software Quality Assurance Plans. ANSI/IEEE Std 730-1984,* and *IEEE Standard for Software Test Documentation. ANSI/IEEE Std 829-1983.* New York: IEEE, Inc.

12

Metrics

PREVIEW

The study of metrics is perhaps the most controversial of all topics in software engineering, because it attempts to bridge the gap between software as artifact and software as process.

Two broad classes of metrics have been proposed based on their origins: 1) software science metrics, which attempts to model fundamental properties of software, and 2) empirical metrics, which attempt to measure, but not explain, the phenomena of software as a process. Metrics from both classes strive to explain *processes* through examining the *artifacts* of programming.

Halstead's pioneering work in software science set the stage for years of research into fundamental properties of software development. Unfortunately, Halstead's theorems have not been convincingly verified by experimental results. Even so, the metric bearing his name continues to intrigue software engineers.

McCabe's metric and other "empirical" measures continue to be refined and used to evaluate everything from "quality" to expected number of bugs. McCabe's cyclomatic complexity is the most promising because it is easy to apply, and it is useful in software testing.

THE SEARCH FOR RELIABLE METRICS

Many experiments have been performed and perhaps even more papers written in an attempt to quantify software, complexity, number of bugs, reliability, programmer effort, and the many other properties of programs that have been discussed in previous chapters. Directly counted quantities such as lines of code, cyclomatic complexity, and number of input/output variables are called *metrics*, a number computed by direct measurement of the program as artifact. Metrics are devised to account for certain observations such as the number of bugs, the effort and time required to write a program, and so forth.

The goal behind work in metrics is to discover and measure fundamental attributes of software in order to understand both process and artifact. For example, "complexity" might be measured and then controlled in a large-scale system of modules. Another metric might be used to help maintenance programmers understand and modify an existing program.

To date, none of the metrics discussed here or in other books and papers has succeeded in revealing any deep truths about software. Indeed, the study of metrics has created controversy over their value in many CASE tools. However, metrics provide an alternative view of software that may some day lead to deep understanding of programming-in-the-large. For the time being, metrics should be used with caution, because there is no solid proof that they actually measure deep structure of software systems.

Origins of the Species

Almost all studies of metrics are derived either from Halstead or from studies inspired by his pioneering work[1]. Halstead set out to derive the fundamental laws of software through an information theoretic derivation of "effort" and "difficulty." According to Halstead, programming is governed by laws of *software science*. These laws are subject to "forces of software development" as measured by counting the number of operators and operands in a program. From simple counts of the number of operators and operands, Halstead and his students have constructed a detailed theory of the forces operating within a software system. The analogy with Newton's laws of nature is very strong in Halstead's theory.

After Halstead's early work, many other metrics were introduced in an attempt to quantify complexity, which we have defined as the degree of complication of a system or system component, determined by such factors as the number and intricacy of

PLAGIARISM IN STUDENT PROGRAMS

Halstead's counts have been used for a wide variety of measures in programming. For example, Halstead's metrics were used to detect cheating in programming classes[2].

An experiment was conducted where the following metrics were tested and compared. The goal was to find a simple metric that revealed a plagiarized program by assigning a signature to each student's program. The signature was obtained by reading each program and assigning the following counts:

- lines of executable code
- total lines of code
- keyword counts
- count of real variables
- count of integers
- count of all variables
- count of assignment statements
- count of operators (Halstead N_1)
- count of operands (Halstead N_2)
- count of unique operators (Halstead n_1)
- count of unique operations (Halstead n_2)

While Halstead's N_1 was the strongest single factor, careful statistical analysis (factor analysis) failed to indicate any significance in Halstead's measures. There appeared to be nothing unique about Halstead's metrics in detecting plagiarism.

interfaces, the number and intricacy of conditional branches, the degree of nesting, the types of data structures, and other system characteristics. For example, Gannon et al.[3] proposed metrics for object-oriented Ada programming:

- Component Access Metric, CAM, equal to the ratio of NL/LOT, where NL = count of the number of accesses of objects with nonlocally defined data types, and LOT = lines of text in a module. The purpose of CAM is to measure a module's resistance to change.
- Package Visibility Metric, PVM, measures the visibility of each module to other modules in the system. The Used count equals the number of modules where information from a module is accessed or changed. The Current count for a module is the number of modules where the module is visible. These counts measure the degree and kind of coupling in a large system.

In an informal study, Gannon et al. concluded that programmers who had little experience with object-oriented programming failed to properly control system complexity through control of coupling. These metrics have not been widely used, however, perhaps because they are specific to Ada.

Halstead's metrics are based on a theoretical derivation, while Gannon's metric is one of many based on observation and the desire to measure "common sense" attributes of "good" software. In general, metrics are based on two approaches: 1) theoretical models derived from fundamental "laws" of software such as Halstead's metric, and 2) empirical models based on practical considerations such as nesting, number of branches, and module coupling.

HALSTEAD'S THEORY

Halstead developed a model of programs based on information theory that has an interesting property: it analyzes a program by counting the number of operator and operand symbols. It ignores other considerations, such as the number of executable paths or the complexity of the problem being solved. Instead, features such as "program difficulty" and expected number of bugs are obtained by counting only four parameters called the *directly counted software parameters*.

Halstead's Metric

Directly counted software parameters are obtained directly from a program listing:

N_1 Total number of operators appearing in the module.
N_2 Total number of operands appearing in the module.
n_1 Number of distinct operators used in the module.
n_2 Number of distinct operands used in the module.

```
function QUAD(A, B, C : real; var X, Y : real);
begin
  ReadLn (A, B, C);
  X := B ** 2 - 4 * A * C;
  A := 2 * A;
  if X > = 0 then begin
    X := SQRT(X);
    Y := (X - B) - A;
    X := (- X - B) / A;
    WriteLn (X, Y);
  end
  else begin
  WriteLn ('NO REAL SOLUTION');
  X := 0; Y := 0
  end;
end; {QUAD}
```

FIGURE 12-1. Function QUAD

The small segment of program shown as QUAD in Figure 12-1 illustrates how to obtain directly counted software parameters. First, we remove the formal parameters from consideration: **function** QUAD is not counted as part of the directly counted parameters.

Second, we ignore the keywords — for instance, **if, then, begin, end,** and **else** are not counted.

Next, we construct a list of operators and operands and count them. Operators are: $:=$, $*$, $-$, $+$, $>=$, $()$, SQRT, $/$, etc. Operands are A, B, C, X, 2, 4, 0, etc.

This list includes the number of *distinct* operators and operands counted as well as the total number of operators and operands counted — see the table of directly counted parameters for QUAD in Table 12-1.

Other rules for defining the directly counted parameters have been studied[4]. It was discovered that the method of counting has a dramatic effect on the actual numbers computed but that a consistent use of one counting method produces suitable measures.

The length of a program is the sum of its operators and operands. Thus,

$$N = N_1 + N_2 = 58$$

Furthermore, we define the size of a *program's vocabulary* as the sum of its distinct operators and operands. Thus,

$$n = n_1 + n_2 = 19$$

It is claimed that a program is of the "right" size when the programmer has carefully used the vocabulary of operators and operands to construct the program. A sloppy programmer will produce a program that is too long. This notion of "proper selection" is at the root of Halstead's theory of software science.

TABLE 12-1. Directly counted parameters from QUAD

Directly Counted Parameters for QUAD

Operators	Count	Operands	Count
WriteLn	2	A	6
ReadLn	1	B	4
$>=$	1	C	2
SQRT	1	X	9
$()$	5	2	2
$-$	4	4	1
$:=$	7	0	3
$*$	3	Y	3
$**$	1	"NO REAL SOLN"	1
$/$	2		
Totals:			
$n_1 = 10$	$N_1 = 27$	$n_2 = 9$	$N_2 = 31$

Software Science

Software science *is a collection of theories about properties of software which are based on universal laws of software as process.* Science deals with nature as opposed to artificial worlds created by humans. Therefore, the phrase "software science" is in itself controversial because it implies that there are natural laws governing the properties of software. Indeed, Halstead tried to discover the deep structure of software as process, and quantify both structure and process as a collection of "equations of motion" analogous with Newtonian laws of motion.

Halstead viewed programming as a nondeterministic process of selecting operators and operands from a predetermined list, see Figure 12-2. Suppose, for example, there are four operators to choose from. Assuming all operators are equally likely to be chosen, and that a binary decision tree properly represents a human's mental discrimination. One of the four operators can be selected in $\log_2 4 = 2$ yes/no answers to the question, Does selecting this group of operators move me closer to the one I need to use? In general, $\log_2 n_1$ mental discriminations are needed to select from a total of n_1 operators.

If all n_1 operators are eventually selected, then a total of $n_1 (\log_2 n_1)$ mental discriminations are used. In general, $\mu_1 (\log_2 n_1)$ discriminations are needed to select μ_1 operators, but Halstead's software science is based on a theorem that states that the "proper value" of μ_1 is n_1.

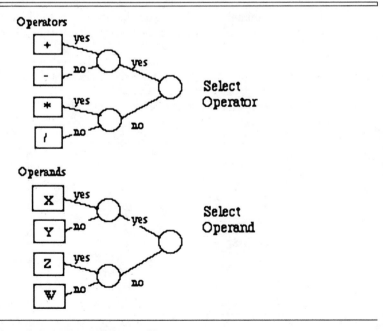

FIGURE 12-2. Selection of operators and operands

Similarly, it takes $n_2(\log_2 n_2)$ total discriminations to select the operands of a program. This gives a total of $n_1 \log_2 n_1 + n_2 \log_2 n_2$ discriminations needed to construct a program. This result is one of the first theorems of software science.

Program Length

A program is *proper* if its length N is L, where

$$L = n_1 \log_2 n_1 + n_2 \log_2 n_2$$

and $N = N_1 + N_2$ is the directly counted length of the program.

The term *proper* refers to the "goodness" of a program, a feature which is not well defined, but which will take on meaning as Halstead's theorems unfold. Here, the term means that the programmer has been careful in choosing the operators and operands of the program.

The Program Length theorem may be difficult to accept at first glance. Suppose we compare the length N with the proper length L using the data provided by procedure QUAD.

$$N = N_1 + N_2 = 58 \text{ (directly counted)}$$
$$L = n_1 \log_2 n_1 + n_2 \log_2 n_2$$
$$= 10 \log_2 10 + 9 \log_2 9$$
$$\approx 61.75 \quad \text{(expected)}$$

This agrees reasonably well with the directly counted value, hence the program is proper. But the numbers do not explain why the metric works! One explanation comes from psychological studies of cognitive behavior in humans. According to the theory of *chunking*, humans cope with complexity by grouping concepts into manageable clusters called chunks. Miller[5] claims that the number of items in a chunk should not exceed 7 ± 2. The magical number seven has found its way into many areas of software engineering as a consequence of Miller's hypothesis.

Chunking might explain the close fit between Halstead's Program Length metric and the directly counted value N. If properly used, chunking reduces the value of L to that approximating N. For example, QUAD uses psychological chunking in defining the values of variable X. X groups together B, 2, 4, A, and C into a single expression. Additionally, X is modified into a "larger" chunk in the subsequent steps involving SQRT, and the final calculated value of X. Both of these groupings contribute to a reduction in the length variable L. A second example of chunking is illustrated by operator chunking in the SQRT routine and in the replacement of $2*A$ with A.

"Impurities" in a program may be the cause of an improper module according to Fitzsimmons and Love[6]. According to Halstead's theory of software science, program impurities are:

1. Cancellation of operators: $A/2 + B/2$ instead of $(A + B)/2$.

2. Overloaded operands, for example, the same operand might be used to represent two or more quantities in a program.

3. Ambiguous operands: two different operands representing the same quantity in a program.

4. Common subexpressions: $A(I+1) := A(I+1)+10$.

5. Unnecessary replacements.

6. Unfactored expressions.

Extensions of Software Science

Halstead's theory of software science has been validated by experiments and refuted by counterexample, but mostly it has been extended by a number of theorems from Halstead and others. The resulting metrics, implemented in the form of various CASE tools, are surrounded by controversy. We do not take sides, but instead try to provide a balanced view of the theory.

Halstead attempted to link various cognitive aspects of programming to a number of additional measures. For example, he postulated that the difficulty of writing any program in a given programming language is related to a metric called *volume*, a measure that is proportional to the number of decisions required to choose each of the directly counted operators or operands in a program.

Program Volume

The number of decisions needed to write a program is proportional to V, where $V = N(\log_2 n)$. Volume V is measured in bits.

For example, the volume of procedure QUAD is:

$$V = 58 \ (\log_2 19)$$
$$\approx 246.38 \text{ bits}$$

The problem with program volume, V, is that it does not take into consideration the programming language. A high-level language should implement a program with fewer decisions than a low-level language requires. Is it possible to normalize V to a minimum volume for a given algorithm?

Suppose V^* is the volume of the most compact representation of an algorithm in some programming language. A lower-level implementation of the same algorithm requires more operands and operators leading to higher value of V relative to V^*. In short, an algorithm can be implemented in various levels, each level imposed by a programming language.

Program Level

The program level of an implemented algorithm depends on the representation of the algorithm in a language. The level LEV is the ratio of minimum program volume V^* to program volume, V. That is, $LEV = V^* / V$.

Elshoff and Halstead studied a *quality* metric using LEV and the estimated minimum volume V^*. In software science, program quality is a function of the number of input/output variables and program volume.

Program Quality

A program (representation of a given algorithm) is of low quality, that is, it has impurities, if its level LEV' is significantly lower than the directly counted level, LEV, where

$LEV' = V' / V$

$V' = (2 + p) \log_2 (2 + p) =$ an estimate of minimum program volume

$p =$ number of input/output parameters for the algorithm

Again, for procedure QUAD, $p = 5$ input/output parameters: (A, B, C, X, Y). Plugging these numbers into the formula for LEV' yields:

$LEV' = ((2 + 5) \log_2 (2 + 5)) / 246.38 \approx 0.079$

This means the representation of QUAD is not especially high level. We must keep in mind, however, that level is relative to a minimum encoding of the algorithm. The best we can do is obtain $LEV = 1.0$. QUAD is of modest quality when compared with the level of other programs.

Quality is judged relative to the volume of other programs written in the same programming language. If quality is lowered, volume is increased in a kind of "conservation of agony." Halstead, in fact, discovered such a conservation law.

Conservation laws are useful static measures of program quality because they measure the quality of information encoding. A "good" program is one that has been compactly encoded in some representation. If impurities creep into the implementation, then the quality suffers. This loss in quality manifests as a violation of the conservation law.

Halstead's Conservation of Volume

Level and volume are conserved for a given algorithm. That is,

$(LEV) * (V) =$ constant

This conservation law holds for particular representations of a certain algorithm. If we compare the quality of an algorithm in Fortran with other Fortran representations of the same algorithm, the constant remains unchanged. However, if we switch to assembly language as a form of representation of the same algorithm, the constant changes. The constant, then, is actually a quantitative measure of *language level*.

TABLE 12-2. Average language level

Average Language Level	
Language	*Level (avg. λ)*
English prose	2.16
PL/I	1.53
ALGOL 58	1.21
FORTRAN	1.14
Assembler	0.88

Source: Fitzsimmons and Love[6], p. 9.

Programming Language Level

$$\lambda = LEV* (V*)$$

It should take less volume to encode a program in a high-level language than in a low-level language. Thus, λ should be larger for Fortran, say than for an assembler language. This phenomena has been observed in actual programs and in English prose as shown in Table 12-2.

V is defined in terms of mental effort so the advantage of encoding an algorithm in a high-level language must be in reducing mental effort. Let E be the mental effort expended to understand a program at some level, LEV. Then effort is directly related to volume and indirectly related to language level:

$$E = V / LEV$$

And $\lambda = LEV^2 *V$, so the mental effort in terms of V, $V*$, and LEV is:

$$E = (V*)^3 /\lambda^2$$

This result says that programming effort is defined in terms of the number of mental discriminations needed to implement an algorithm in a programming language with level λ. For example, from Table 12-3, PL/I takes less effort to represent an algorithm than Fortran. In fact, PL/I requires about 1.8 times less effort than Fortran, and 3.0 times less effort than CDC Assembler. Conversely, we might be tempted to say that PL/I is three times as "high level" as CDC assembler language. These observations are quantified in Table 12-3 where "effort" has been normalized to English prose. The results give quantitative meaning to the qualitative phrase "high-level language."

Finally, Halstead hypothesized that difficulty is inversely proportional to program level LEV. Difficulty D is often claimed to be a measure of program complexity, but the claim is controversial.

$$\text{Program Difficulty } D = 1/LEV = (n_1 *N_2)/(2N_2)$$

TABLE 12-3. Normalized language level

Normalized Language Level

Language	Effort
English prose	1.00
PL/I	2.00
ALGOL 58	3.19
FORTRAN	3.59
Assembler	6.02

Applications of Software Science

Many claims have been made about the value of Halstead's software science. We survey only a few of the most interesting results. The theory is amazingly diverse and has found application in every branch of software engineering ranging from cost estimating to testing.

Time and Effort

A variety of formulas have been derived from Halstead's theorems for estimating programming time and effort. Perhaps the simplest formula was proposed by Halstead and his students. It assumes that programming time is directly proportional to mental effort E, and indirectly related to the speed of thinking.

TDEV = E / S, where S = number of mental discriminations per second

S is called *Stroud's constant* after the psychologist who measured the rate of making mental discriminations in human thinking processes. Stroud estimated S to range from 10 to 20 discriminations per second. Fitzsimmons and Love recommend $S = 18$[6].

Using $S = 18$ and the numerical results from procedure QUAD:

$$TDEV = E / 18$$
$$= (V^*)^3/\lambda^2 * 18$$
$$= (19.65)^3 / 1.53^2 * 18$$
$$= 7587.31 / 42.14$$
$$= 180 \text{ seconds} = 3 \text{ minutes}$$

This is an estimate of the time to code procedure QUAD, given that the algorithm is known and understood. This does not account for time to design the algorithm, and is thought to be limited to small coding problems.

Schneider[7] extended the effort formula E to model the software development process and obtain another method of estimating time and effort to develop large systems. Using least-squares estimators and data obtained from completed systems, Schneider obtained effort and time-to-complete estimates for modularized Fortran and Assembler software development.

These formulas are very similar to the formulas studied earlier, but they take into consideration the language used and the number of modules in the software architecture. In Schneider's model, improvements of productivity can be achieved by using a higher-level language.

$$\text{Effort}_{mm} = 28 \text{ KDSI}^{1.83} \quad \text{Fortran}$$
$$= 59.8 \text{ KDSI}^{1.83} \quad \text{Assembler}$$
$$\text{TDEV} = 2.47 \text{ E}_{mm}^{.35} \quad \text{months}$$

We find little similarity, however, in comparisons with numerical results obtained from Schneider's formulas and Putnam's or Boehm's CoCoMo model. Perhaps the most interesting feature of this result is in showing a connection between Halstead's theory and the models of time and effort derived by other means.

Program Bugs

The same psychological reasoning behind the effort formulas has been used to estimate the number of bugs in software. In this derivation, Stroud's constant and an empirical number called the *mean free path to an error* is used to estimate the number of faults in a piece of code. The mean free path to an error is the average number of mental discriminations per fault, E_0. Think of E_0 as the number of mental discriminations made without committing an error. Then on the very next discrimination, the programmer makes the wrong decision, which results in a bug.

The number of bugs in a program is directly related to the program volume and indirectly related to the mean free path to an error:

BUGS = K V / E_0 where K is a constant.

Halstead recommends setting $K = 1$, and $E_0 = 3,200$[1], but Ottenstein[8] recommends $E_0 = 3,000$. In this case, the bug count is estimated very simply by the formula,

BUGS = V / 3,000

For QUAD, this amounts to 246.38 / 3,000 $\approx$ 0 bugs.

Comparisons of this model with actual bug count data showed high correlations in Ottenstein[8], but poor results were reported by Basili et al.[9]. In addition to the BUG formula above, Ottenstein derived formulas for the average time to locate and correct a bug (4 hours), and the average number of computer runs needed to verify a program (2 * BUGS), based on the assumption that one run is needed to reveal each bug, and a second run needed to verify that the bug has been fixed. Basili et al. compared Halstead's metric E and B with other metrics and found that the correlations were rather low, leading to conclusions:

1. None of the metrics satisfactorily explained the errors incurred during software development.

2. Neither software science E, cyclomatic complexity, nor *LOC* relates convincingly with actual effort.

3. Strongest correlations were observed for single modules from individual programmers.

4. Number of revisions correlates better with development errors than with E, *BUGS*, cyclomatic complexity, or *LOC*.

A more sophisticated model of BUGS (developed after the one above) derived by Lipow and modified by Stetter[11] is supported by an empirical study by Lipow[10], see Figure 12-3. This model is language-dependent and requires an estimate of a constant (K is not the same as the K in Halstead's BUGS metric). Here, K ranges from 3 to 8. For most high-level languages, $K = 7.5$ is recommended.

D = K / 3,000 ($K = 7.5$ for a high-level language like Fortran)

N = average number of operand and operators, e.g. average value of $(N_1 + N_2)$

V = $\log_2(N)$

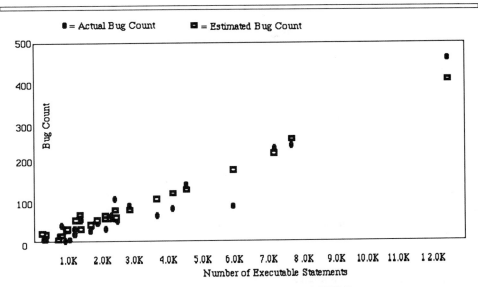

EMPIRICAL EVIDENCE THAT BUG ESTIMATION FORMULAS WORK

Data collected by TRW and reported by Lipow[10] shows close correlation between actual and predicted faults using bug estimation formulas developed by Lipow and Stetter[10,11]. Square boxes are estimations and round points are from actual programs.

FIGURE 12-3. Fault rate versus LOC

$$LOC = \text{Lines of executable code}$$
$$\partial = BUGS/LOC$$
$$= D \log_2 [(8N)/(1+8V - 9 \log_2 (V))]$$

EMPIRICAL METRICS

A variety of metrics have been proposed as a consequence of Halstead's original work. These metrics are based on pragmatic considerations more than on a theory of software science. A sampling of proposed measures is listed to illustrate their diversity.

In this section we examine McCabe's cyclomatic complexity measure and several other metrics which have been proposed in the literature. We survey the literature on the usefulness of these metrics and examine their shortcomings. As before, the conclusion will be somewhat negative because of the inconclusive evidence obtained by controlled experiment. Nonetheless, these metrics yield insights into the nature of software as process.

```
┌─────────────────────────────────────────────────────────────────────┐
│ ┌─────────────────────────────────────────────────────────────────┐ │
│ └─────────────────────────────────────────────────────────────────┘ │
│                                                                      │
│     EMPIRICAL METRICS                                                │
│         Lines of Code, LOC                                           │
│         Statement Count                                              │
│         Module Count, MOD                                            │
│         Average LOC per module                                       │
│         McCabe's Cyclomatic complexity                               │
│         Program Graph Node Count                                     │
│         Program Graph Edge Count                                     │
│         Number of Procedure Calls                                    │
│         Number of "Function Points"                                  │
│         Number of Interfaces                                         │
│         Information Flow: Fan-in and Fan-out                         │
│         Nesting level of Control Constructs                          │
│                                                                      │
└─────────────────────────────────────────────────────────────────────┘
```

McCabe's Cyclomatic Complexity

McCabe[12] reasoned that function size in functional decomposition needs to be determined by a measure of complexity instead of LOC or some other arbitrary measure. Therefore, he approached the problem of representing program complexity by abstracting the program into its flow graph. For example, the flow graphs of the two versions of SCAN (see chapter nine, Implementation) are shown in Figure 12-4. Recall that SCAN was written in two forms: 1) an unstructured version with GOTOs, and 2) an SESE-structured version.

The flow graph representation of a program is constructed by grouping together regions of code, as described for complexity-based testing. Each node corresponds to a region of code; each edge corresponds to flow of control. In unstructured SCAN, two edges intersect, giving rise to a knot. In SESE-structured SCAN, no edges intersect, leading to a simplification in calculation of the cyclomatic complexity metric.

The strategy proposed by McCabe is to:

1. Define program complexity as the number of linearly independent paths $V(G)$ through the program graph, G.

2. Control the size of a function by setting an upper limit to $V(G) - V(G) \leq 10$ is recommended by McCabe.

3. Use $V(G)$ as a basis for verification by testing — see chapter ten.

What is the meaning of "linearly independent" paths in G? This is the basis of the cyclomatic complexity metric. Consider the following mathematical definition from graph theory:

Cyclomatic Number.   The cyclomatic number $\varsigma(G)$ of program graph G with n vertices, e edges, and p components is $\varsigma(G) = e - n + p$.

Cyclomatic Complexity Metric.   The cyclometric complexity $V(G)$ of program graph G with n vertices, e edges, and p components is $V(G) = e - n + 2p$.

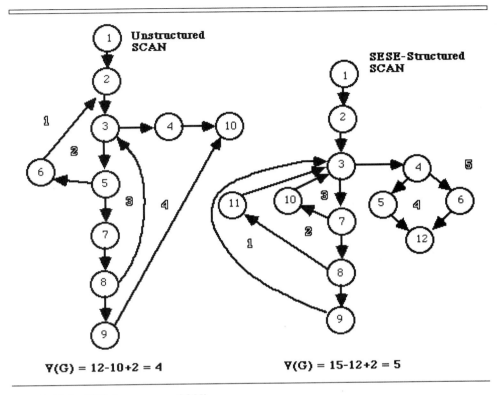

FIGURE 12-4. $V(G)$ for program SCAN

When analyzing a single program function or procedure, $p = 1$, hence p is the number of procedure/function components of a software system. Therefore, in a single function, $V(G) = e - n + 2$. Furthermore, the value of $V(G)$ in an SESE-structured program is exactly the number of predicates π plus one, or $V(G) = \pi + 1$.

These definitions are obtained from analyzing the number of linearly independent paths through a program flow graph, G. Consider the SESE-structured graph of SCAN. It contains $\pi = 4$ branching predicates, hence it has cyclometric complexity $V(SCAN)$ $= 4 + 1 = 5$. It also contains five **linearly independent paths** — *paths which can be used to construct all possible execution paths* through SCAN. The five paths are:

1. $1->2->3->4->6->12$

2. $1->2->3->4->5->12$

3. $1->2->3->7->10$

4. $1->2->3->7->8->11$

5. $1->2->3->7->8->9$

Of course these are exactly the basic paths in the cyclomatic tree which we used earlier to generate test cases for software testing. They are even more significant in complexity metric research, however, because they represent the fundamental structure of the software procedure/function. The implications of this observation are listed by McCabe[12]:

- $V(G) \geq 1$, meaning that complexity is always present at some level.
- $V(G)$ is the maximum number of linearly independent (basic) paths in G. It is the size of the basis set of paths from which all other paths can be constructed.
- Inserting or deleting nonbranching statements in G does not affect $V(G)$.
- G has only one path if and only if $V(G) = 1$.
- Inserting a new edge in G increases $V(G)$ by one.
- $V(G)$ depends only on the decision structure of G.

This last point should be expanded: in testing, we counted all simple predicates in the program rather than merely counting the number of **if**, **while**, **repeat**, and **case** statements. For example,

if (A = B) **and** (C < 3) **then** ...

becomes,

if (A = B) **then if** (C < 3) **then**...

for a total of 2 predicates. The cyclomatic complexity metric usually counts the compound predicate as only one predicate. Thus, $V(G) = \pi + 1 = $ "number of **if**, **while**, **repeat**, and **case** statements" + 1 for structured Pascal procedures and functions.

A shortcut method can be used to find $V(G)$ as shown in the program graphs of SCAN. Imagine the exit node being connected to the entry node by a single "loop back." For example, in unstructured SCAN this is done by drawing an edge from node 10 to node 1; in SESE-structured SCAN the connection is from node 12 to node 1.

Now, count the number of enclosed spaces inside the graph. That is, find all "fenced in" regions of the planar graph and mark them as a basic cycle. The first enclosed region is the one created by the loop back from exit to entry node. This is the " + 1" in the formula, $\pi + 1$. Next, find all other enclosed regions. For example, in unstructured SCAN there are 4 regions numbered 1, 2, 3, 4. Similarly, there are five regions in SESE-structured SCAN numbered 1, 2, 3, 4, 5.

Interestingly, the SESE-structured version of SCAN is *more* complex than the unstructured version. This is because the unstructured version has fewer linearly independent paths in its basis set. But this observation can be misleading because a greater number of paths can be constructed from the basis set of the unstructured version than the structured version. The paths that can be constructed for unstructured SCAN are listed here to illustrate that a low value of $V(G)$ does not always mean that the number of paths in a less complex program is less than the number of paths in a more complex program:

1. $1->2->3->4->10$ (basic)

2. $1->2->3->5->7->8->9->10$ (basic)

3. $1->2->3->5->6$ (basic)

4. $1->2->3->5->7->8$ (basic)

5. $1->2->3->5->7->8->3->5->6$ (nonbasic)

Path 5 should be made up of basic paths, but due to the knot in the flow graph, it is not possible to construct path 5 from basic paths. That is, path 5 = path 4 $->$ $3->5->6$, and $3->5->6$ is *not* a basic path. In terms of testing, unstructured SCAN is just as complex as SESE-structured SCAN — both programs have five cases to consider.

A second observation can be made about $V(G)$ and structured programs. Notice that $V(G)$ = 5 SESE regions exist in the SESE-structured version of SCAN. These correspond to exactly the number of reductions needed to show that SESE-structured SCAN is a structured program. That is, in five steps, SCAN can be reduced to a single SESE module as demonstrated in chapter nine. The order of reductions are given below:

3 or 4 first, 2, 1, and 5

Thus, cyclomatic complexity number $V(G)$ equals the number of steps needed to reduce a structured program to the most elementary SESE form. This ties the intuitive notion of complexity in a structured program to a quantitative value. Thus, $V(G)$ is a measure of the "structuredness" of a software function.

McCabe claimed that $V(G) \leq 10$ should be enforced by programmers to reduce errors. If a function exceeds $V(G) = 10$, McCabe recommends that it be divided into smaller, less complex functions to force a lower complexity number. This results in an increased value of p, so that the overall complexity is still high, but the complexity of individual functions is reduced.

The usefulness of $V(G)$ in predicting software reliability is still in question. Schneidewind[13] performed one of the earliest studies of cyclomatic complexity and concluded that "complexity measures serve to partition structures into high or low error occurrence according to whether the complexity measure values are high or low, respectively." Schneidewind concluded that $V(G)$ was no better than other metrics such as program size in LOC in predicting software reliability, but that $V(G)$ was easy to calculate, and it facilitates testing. As a consequence, $V(G)$ has been widely used by many software engineers.

In a later study, Li[14] found that $V(G)$ correlated well with program size LOC, Halstead's metric, and several other metrics when used to analyze Fortran programs. Li suggests that cyclomatic complexity bridges the gap between measures of volume, such as Halstead's metric, and measures of control flow, such as McCabe's metric. Accordingly, Li introduced the idea of a hybrid approach in which a volume metric such as Halstead's V is used first to categorize software into "simple" and "complex" and then a control flow metric such as $V(G)$ be used to examine each group in more detail.

Other Metrics

Evangelist[15] examined Halstead's E, McCabe's $V(G)$, information flow into and out of functions, nesting level, and LOC metrics in terms of "good" programming practices. He found conflicting results as summarized in Table 12-4. For example, the programming rule that recommends "Avoid **else goto**.." structures results in replacing:

```
1: read(a);              with      read(a);
   if a>b1 then                    while a>b1 do
     if a>b2 then s1                 begin
       else goto 1                     read(a);
     else goto 2                       if a>b2 then s1
   goto 1                           end;
2: ...
```

This change reduces the number of statements ($<$ LOC), but the number of conditions is unchanged. Therefore this improvement is reflected in only one of the metrics. Only LOC is reduced, and the reduction is for the wrong reason, because it does not measure simplification of flow of control.

TABLE 12-4. Sensitivity of metric to program structure

	Sensitivity of Metric to Program Structure				
	Halstead's E	*McCabe's V(G)*	*Info Flow*	*Nested Level*	*LOC*
Call Library Function	<	<	<	<	<
Avoid temporary variables	< >	< >	<	>	< >
Replace redundant expressions	< >	< =	=	< =	< >
Modularize	< >	< =	< =	< >	< >
Check inputs	>	>	=	>	>
Initialize variables	>	> =	> =	>	>
Avoid unnecessary branching	<	=	=	<	<
Avoid multiple exits	>	>	>	>	>
Combine logical expressions	<	>	=	< >	<
Delimit statement groups	< >	=	=	< >	=
Use **while** loops	< >	=	=	< >	<
Use **if...else-if...**	<	=	=	<	<
Avoid **...else goto...**	< >	=	=	< >	<
Parenthesize	>	=	=	>	=
Format for readability	=	=	=	=	=
Indent	=	=	=	=	=
Use meaningful names	=	=	=	=	=

Legend:
< means the programming practice reduces the numerical value of the metric
> means the metric is increased
= means the metric is unchanged
< > means that the metric may be increased or decreased

Source: Evangelist[15].

Evangelist concluded that none of the metrics performed better than LOC, and rules that reduce the size of a program also reduce its complexity, see Figure 12-8. For this reason, hybrid approaches to measuring "goodness" of programs are recommended. In addition, empirical measures that attempt to reveal the quality as well as the quantity of software produced by individual programmers have been proposed.

The Berry-Meekings style metrics used in the CASE tool called **Style** is an example of a metric which is designed to evaluate and rate a program according to established conventions of "good" programming[16]. The Berry-Meekings metric is a weighted sum of program qualities as listed below with their weights given in parentheses. A score of 0 is poor, while 100 is excellent.

+ Module length (15)
+ length of identifiers (14)
+ percentage of comment lines (12)
+ percentage of indentation spaces to all characters in the program file (12)
+ percentage of blank lines (11)
+ average number of nonblank characters per line (9)
+ average number of spaces per line (8)
+ percentage of symbolic constants used (8)
+ number of reserved words used (6)
+ number of INCLUDE files used (5)
+ number of GOTOs used (−20)

With the exception of GOTOs, these weights add up to 100. Vigram, a CASE tool for computing metrics, computes these numbers and summarizes them as a single Berry-Meekings metric (see next section in this chapter).

Harrison and Cook[17] attempted to use the Berry-Meekings metric to identify potential "trouble spots" in programs. They reasoned that a poor style might imply poor programming in general. Such programs are thought to be unreliable. As it turns out, the hypothesis could not be supported by empirical evidence.

Redish and Smyth[18] propose a similar style metric implemented as a CASE tool for students. They obtained positive results when their CASE tool was used to teach beginners and intermediates "good" programming style. The stylistic factors of Redish and Smyth are:

- Economy: avoid redundancy.
- Modularity: use procedures to break up long passages.
- Simplicity: keep it simple, use straight forward algorithms.
- Structure: keep the program code well organized.
- Documentation: use comments.
- Layout: use horizontal and vertical white space to improve readability.

A number of factors proposed by Redish and Smyth are incorporated into Vigram, see next section. They are extensions to the counts proposed by Berry and Meekings.

Berns[19] proposed a weighted sum metric for computing the Index of Difficulty of Fortran programs, and implemented it in the form of a CASE tool called MAT. Each syntactic unit of Fortran is assigned a weight, which is used to measure the difficulty of each unit. A program is scanned and the weighted sum of all units appearing in the program is computed. The resulting Index of Difficulty is used as a score to determine the quality of the program. Again, it is assumed that troublesome programs can be identified by their lack of syntactic quality.

The weights assigned by Berns and coworkers are somewhat arbitrary, being based only on experience and intuition. For Fortran and the set of weights used by Berns, a score less than 1,200 is considered acceptable. Berns reports scores near 10,000 for handwritten Fortran programs. In addition, MAT is credited with discovering errors that were overlooked during testing.

A sample of the syntactic units and their scores is shown in Figure 12-5. These are not the complete listing. See Berns[19] for a complete listing of weights for Fortran. A listing of weight categories for Pascal is given in the next section, which describes Vigram.

SOME WEIGHTS USED IN MAT[19].

Identifiers:

Parameter	1.00
Variable	0.85
Array	1.50
Function	2.00

Constants:

Logical	0.0
Integer	0.0
Real	0.05

Operators:

OR, AND	0.25
NOT	1.00
Relational	0.20
/	0.30
*	0.25
**	0.50

Statements:

Assignment	0.00
CALL	1.00
Do	7.00
Else	0.00
Else if	4.00
Goto	10.00
If	5.00
Read	3.00

FIGURE 12-5. Sample of syntactic units and their weights

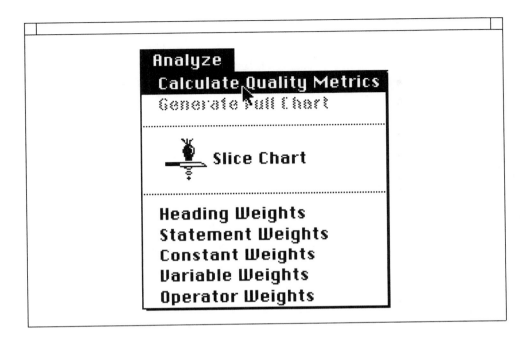

VIGRAM: A CASE TOOL FOR COMPUTING METRICS

Vigram was discussed in an earlier chapter but we did not disclose all of its capability. In addition to being a tool for understanding functions by graphically displaying SESE elements, Vigram is able to compute a number of metrics including some of those discussed in the previous sections.

Selecting Calculate Quality Metrics from the Analyze menu of Vigram causes the application to compute Berry-Meekings, Halstead, Berns' Weight of Difficulty, McCabe IF Count, number of comment words, number of indentation tabs, number of simple variables, and number of structured variables, as well as other metrics. A display dialog appears as shown in Figure 12-6 for the procedure TRIANGLE investigated earlier in chapter ten.

Vigram computes the Halstead E, V, and D metrics and counts the number of **if** statements used in McCabe's metric. However, Vigram does not compute $V(G)$ directly. In addition, Vigram initially sets all weights to 1 rather than the weights recommended by Berns for Fortran. Both of these limitations can be overcome by adjusting the weights to compute either $V(G)$ or Berns' metric as shown in the sequence of screen displays of Figure 12-7. To obtain McCabe's $V(G)$, set all weights to zero except the weights corresponding to the control statements **if**, **case**, **while**, and **repeat**. The sample procedure in Figure 12-10 produces $V(G) = 6.00$ as shown in Figure 12-8.

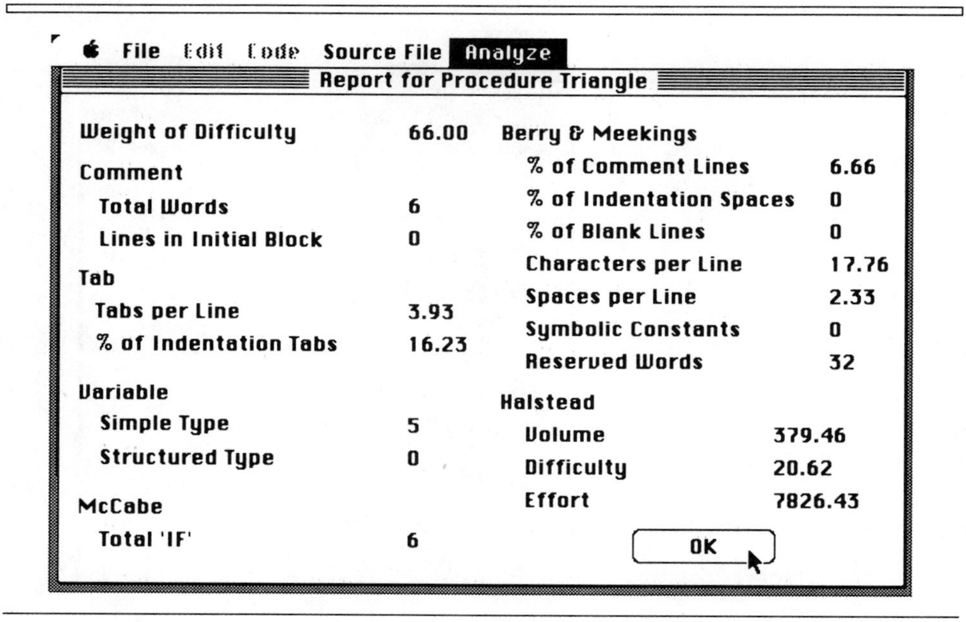

File   Edit   Code   Source File   Analyze

Report for Procedure Triangle

		Berry & Meekings	
Weight of Difficulty	66.00		
Comment		% of Comment Lines	6.66
Total Words	6	% of Indentation Spaces	0
Lines in Initial Block	0	% of Blank Lines	0
		Characters per Line	17.76
Tab		Spaces per Line	2.33
Tabs per Line	3.93	Symbolic Constants	0
% of Indentation Tabs	16.23	Reserved Words	32
Variable		Halstead	
Simple Type	5	Volume	379.46
Structured Type	0	Difficulty	20.62
McCabe		Effort	7826.43
Total 'IF'	6		

OK

FIGURE 12-6. Metrics computed by Vigram

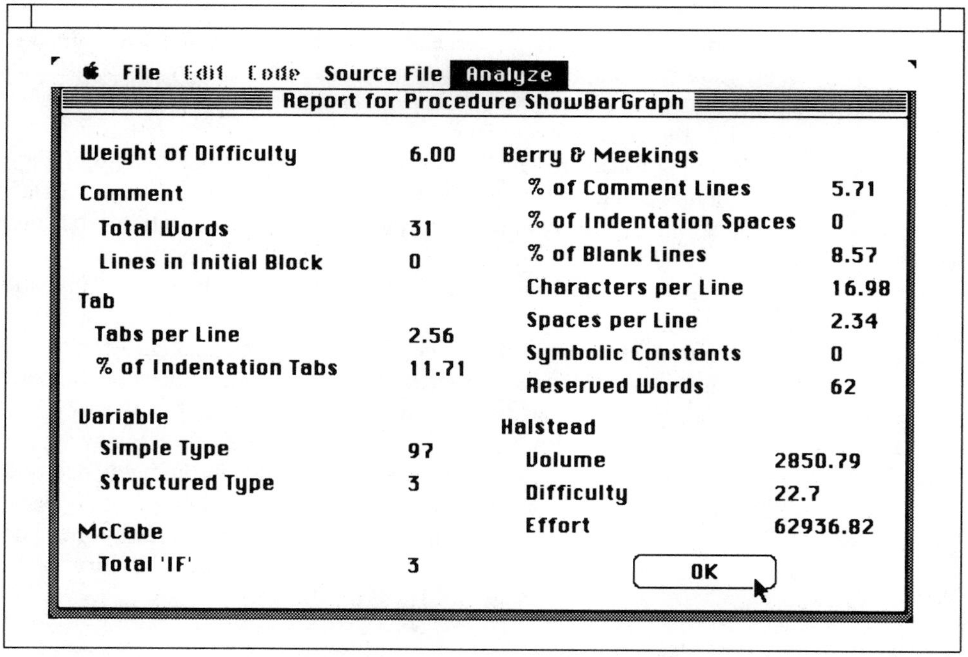

File   Edit   Code   Source File   Analyze

Report for Procedure ShowBarGraph

		Berry & Meekings	
Weight of Difficulty	6.00		
Comment		% of Comment Lines	5.71
Total Words	31	% of Indentation Spaces	0
Lines in Initial Block	0	% of Blank Lines	8.57
		Characters per Line	16.98
Tab		Spaces per Line	2.34
Tabs per Line	2.56	Symbolic Constants	0
% of Indentation Tabs	11.71	Reserved Words	62
Variable		Halstead	
Simple Type	97	Volume	2850.79
Structured Type	3	Difficulty	22.7
McCabe		Effort	62936.82
Total 'IF'	3		

OK

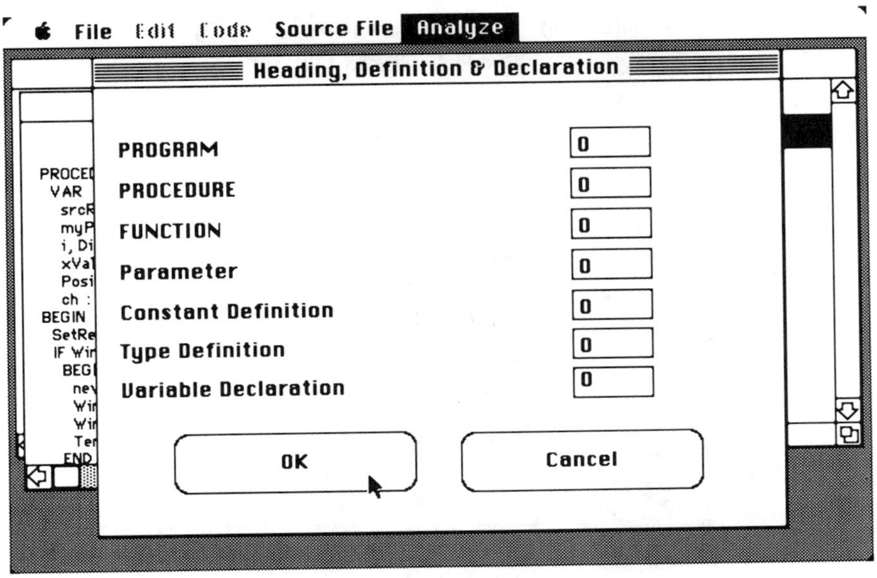

FIGURE 12-7a. Setting heading, definition, and declaration

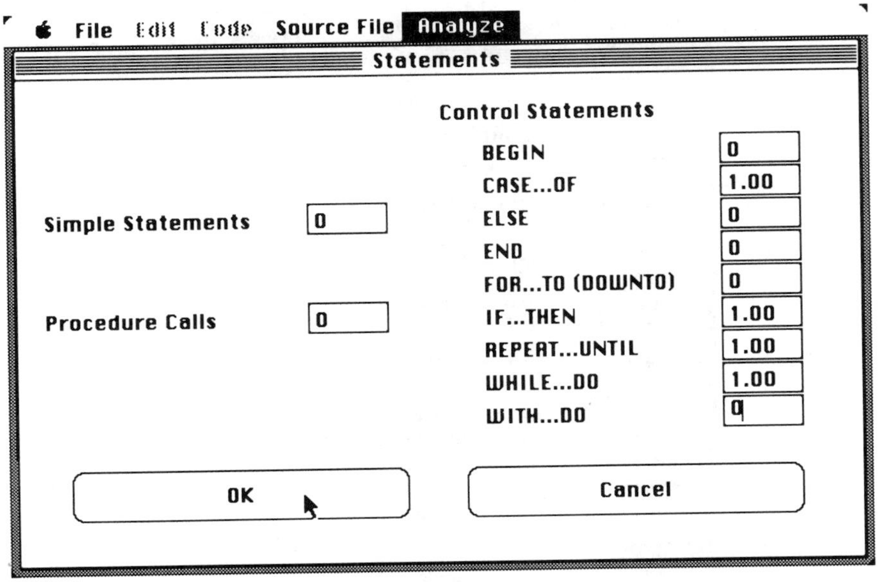

FIGURE 12-7b. Setting statements

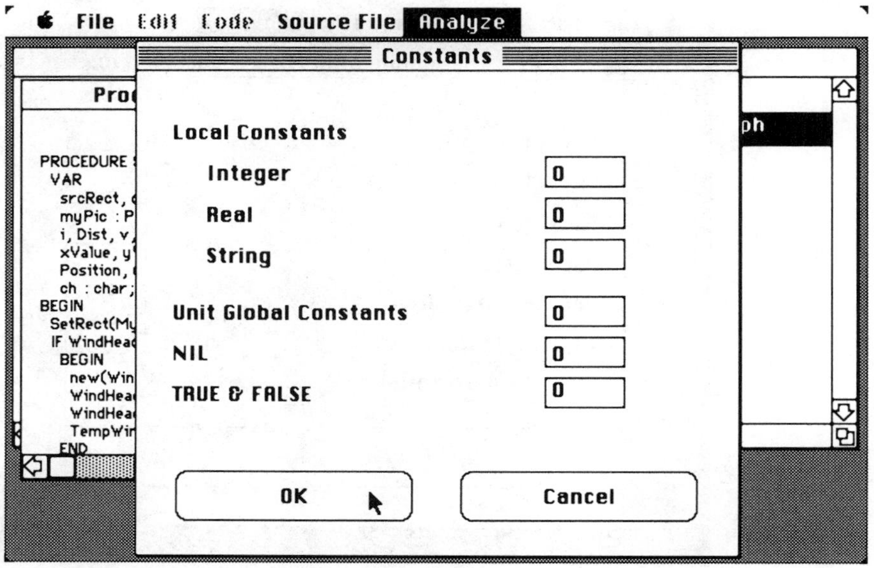

FIGURE 12-7c. Setting constants

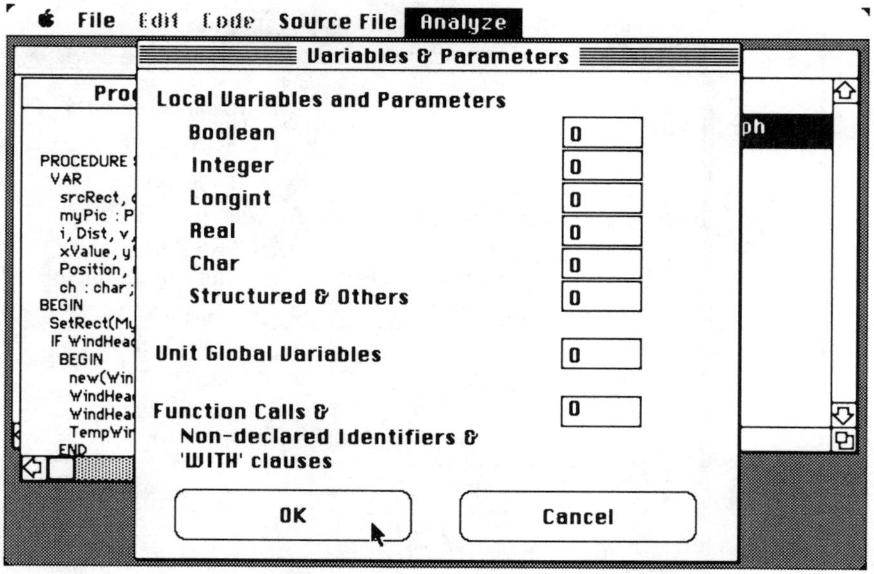

FIGURE 12-7d. Setting variables and parameters

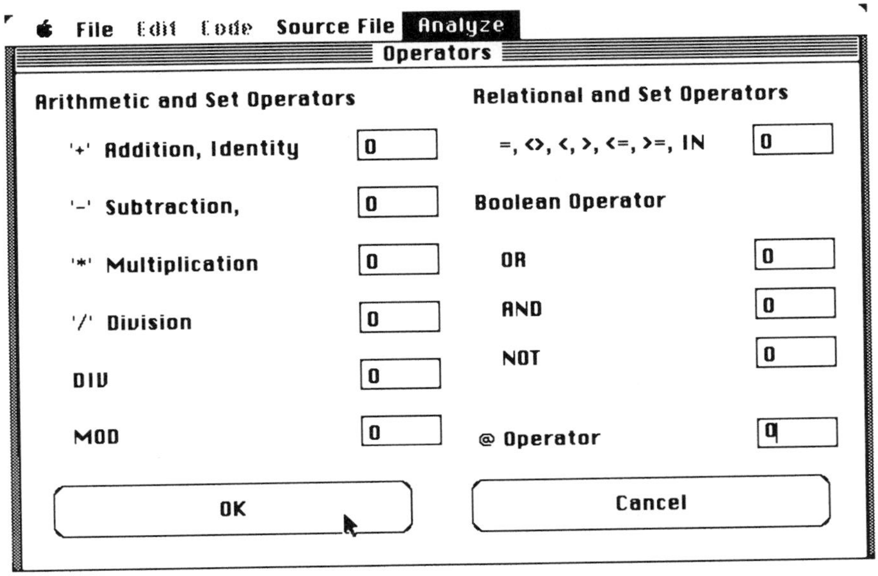

FIGURE 12-8. $V(G)$ as computed in Figure 12-8

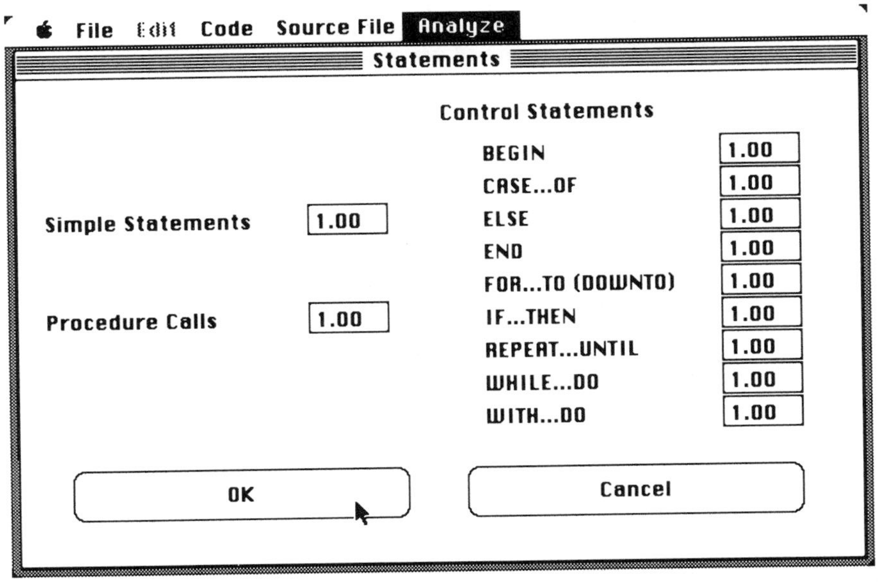

FIGURE 12-9a. Setting all weights to 1.00

```
  File  Edit  Code  Source File  Analyze
       Report for Procedure ShowBarGraph
Weight of Difficulty      355.0    Berry & Meekings
Comment                              % of Comment Lines      5.71
   Total Words            31         % of Indentation Spaces  0
   Lines in Initial Block  0         % of Blank Lines        8.57
Tab                                  Characters per Line     16.98
   Tabs per Line          2.56       Spaces per Line         2.34
   % of Indentation Tabs  11.71      Symbolic Constants      0
                                     Reserved Words          62
Variable
   Simple Type            97       Halstead
   Structured Type        3          Volume              2837.40
                                     Difficulty          22.27
McCabe                               Effort              63196.60
   Total 'IF'             3                    OK
```

FIGURE 12-9b. Metrics calculated based on 12-9a

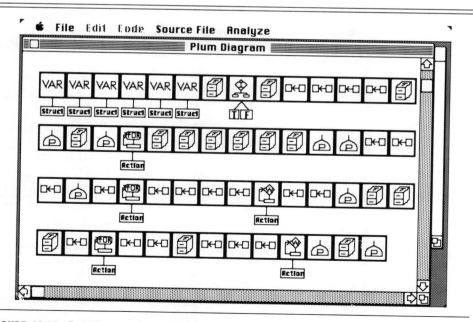

FIGURE 12-10. Full Vigram of sample procedure

The weights can also be set to 1, as shown in Figure 12-9a. When all weights are set to 1 and the metrics calculated once again, the result is as shown in Figure 12-9b. In this version, Berns' Weight of Difficulty metric increases to 355 — far below the upper limit of 1,200 recommended by Berns. From the Vigram diagram of the sample procedure in Figure 12-10, it is easy to agree that the score of 355 is within reason, because the diagram does not appear to be "complex."

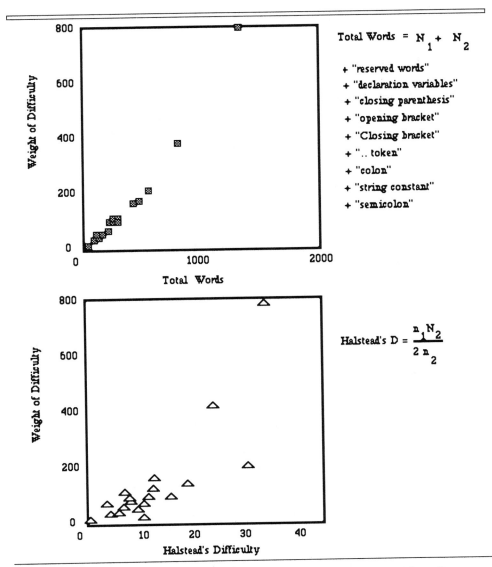

FIGURE 12-11. Correlation of weight of difficulty versus total words and Halstead's metric difficulty

Perhaps the most interesting use of Vigram's metric analysis is in studying code produced by individual programmers. As an illustration of this novel feature, consider results obtained by running 19 procedures chosen at random from Vigram, itself. When compared with one another, the correlations between Weight of Difficulty and number of "words" (e.g. length of procedure) appears stronger than the correlation between Weight of Difficulty and Halstead's Difficulty metric, (see Figure 12-11)! Data like these certainly add to the controversy of complexity metrics research.

Vigram is an investigation tool. It is used to study individual programming style, to pinpoint trouble spots in individual functions, and as a tool for understanding existing functions for the purpose of modifying and reusing them. Whether the metric calculations can be used to deduce specific details about a certain function remains in question.

METRICS THAT (SOMETIMES) WORK

Evangelist[15] lists a number of metrics for measuring complexity and style and claims they are "improper indices of program quality," and that many commonly used style rules do not fully cover "complexity" features of actual software.

According to Evangelist, none of the metrics performs better than the length of the program as measured by LOC. This conclusion is supported by the empirical evidence obtained from Vigram when used to analyze itself. However, the table produced by Evangelist should be of interest to programmers, because it links quantitative measures with qualitative guidelines. In addition, the study of metrics, like many topics in software engineering, adds to our understanding of software as process.

There is some evidence to support the claim that error-prone functions can be identified by McCabe's $V(G)$ metric. Functions with a high $V(G)$ are often more likely to be unreliable — to contain more errors per line of code — than functions with low $V(G)$.

There is also evidence that various style metrics can be used successfully to identify programs written by one programmer from programs written by another programmer. This may be useful, especially if one style leads to more errors than another. Currently, however, there is no evidence to support this conjecture.

Siefert[20] surveyed 238 people in 100 software development groups located in 11 different countries to find out what software engineers were doing with metrics, see Figure 12-12. Of the 26 qualified responses to Siefert's questionnaire:

- 12 groups were using no metrics of any kind.
- 14 groups from three countries were using some kind of measurements.
- The most frequently used metrics were not ranked the same as the most important metrics. This can be seen by comparing the two lists: Most Frequently Used vs. Importance Rating. These lists were obtained from the 14 groups using metrics.

The following is a short description of some metrics reported in Siefert's survey, but not discussed in this book:

Fault density — Count the number of faults per N lines of code.
Defect density — Count the number of defects per N lines of code.

MOST FREQUENTLY USED METRIC	IMPORTANCE RATING
Fault density	Failure counting
Defect density	Failure rate
Error distribution	Combined hard/software availability
Cumulative Failure Profile	Cumulative Failure Profile
Test Coverage	Cyclomatic complexity
Failure rate	Defect density
Cyclomatic complexity	Error distribution
Functional test coverage	Test Coverage
Graph-theoretic complexity	Functional test coverage
Failure counting	Graph-theoretic complexity
Fault-days number	Mean time to failure
Entries/Exits per module	Source listings and documentation
Software Science Difficulty	Fault density
Mean time to failure	Fault-days number
Source listings and documentation	Entries/Exits per module
Combined hard/software availability	Software Science Difficulty

FIGURE 12-12. Siefert's survey

Error distribution — Use normal distribution to predict number of errors.

Cumulative Failure Profile — Use Parabolic distribution to predict number of errors.

Failure rate — Count failures over program execution time.

Fault-days number — Count number of days per fault. (Used for version release decision.)

In the final analysis, metrics are used if 1) they are shown to be meaningful, and 2) they are implemented as a CASE tool that automatically computes a meaningful metric with minimum effort on the part of programmers. Because cyclomatic complexity is rated modestly high in both rankings, and because it is easily implemented in the form of a CASE tool that is easy to use, it is most likely the preferred metric. In addition, cyclomatic complexity is useful in testing — an added incentive to adopt it.

Other measures such as failure counting and fault-days number should not be ignored. Much can be learned from collecting and analyzing these numbers, but collection is not a simple matter. A concerted effort is needed to guarantee that these counts are collected and organized in a database. Analysis of the database of counts cannot be performed until some time after the application software is in the field. However, the information gained from such an ad hoc analysis may be useful in future projects.

Terms and Concepts

chunking
complexity
directly counted parameters
language level
linearly independent program paths
mean free path to an error
metric
program difficulty

program impurities
program length
program quality
program volume
proper program
software science
weight of difficulty

DISCUSSION QUESTIONS

1. Define complexity, difficulty, style, and quality as they pertain to programs as artifacts. Discuss the validity of the definitions given here for these terms.

2. Is it possible for McCabe's $V(G)$ to be larger for an unstructured version of a program versus the same program that has been rewritten using only SESE structures? Explain.

3. What is the relationship between π and the number of SESE chunks in an SESE-structured program? Explain the relationship between $V(G)$ and SESE-reducibility.

4. What is the relationship between $V(G)$ and test case generation?

5. Compute Halstead's E, V, D, and McCabe's $V(G)$ metric using a source program assigned by your instructor. Which of the metric values do you think represents the "complexity" of the program? Why?

6. Use Vigram to analyze at least five procedures you have written. Use a scatter diagram like the ones shown in this chapter to show that one or more of the measures calculated by Vigram are correlated — or are not correlated. Explain your results.

7. Why do you think the study of software metrics is controversial?

8. Compute $V(G)$ for flow graphs that model the following single-control structures: 1) **if**, 2) **while**, 3) **repeat**, 4) **case**. Why is **for** excluded? Which construct is "most complex"?

9. Does a knot increase, decrease, or leave unchanged the cyclomatic complexity of a program flow graph? Explain your answer.

10. Why is Halstead's Program Length metric a function of the logarithm of program operators and operands? Why not a power of two? Square-root? Explain.

11. Assuming Halstead's conservation law, $LEV*V = $ constant, what happens to effort, E, when the value of level doubles? Remember to "obey" the conservation law.

12. Compute the effort predicted by both CoCoMo and Halstead's equations (as extended by Schneider) to produce 35,000 lines of FORTRAN source code. Use nominal cost drivers in CoCoMo. How do the two cost estimating models compare? Explain.

13. How many bugs are expected in a 10,000 line FORTRAN program, according to formula BUGS? How does this formula compare with other formulas for estimating program bugs?

14. When applying Halstead's metric to Pascal, should the **const**, **type**, and **var** statements be counted? What about the parameters passed to a procedure? How does Halstead's metric count the interface part of a unit?

15. Compute $V(G)$ for fragment A and compare it with the total $V(G)$ of fragments B and C. Note that fragments B and C implement the same algorithm as fragment A.

A: **while** X $<>$ Y **do**   B: **while** X $<>$ Y **do**   C: **if** X $<$ Y **then** Y := Y-X **else** X := X − Y;
　if X $<$ Y　　　　　　"call" C
　　then Y := Y − X
　　else X := X − Y

Explain why cyclomatic complexity is a basis for deciding the "proper" size of a function.

16. Does cyclomatic complexity take nesting of control structures into consideration? What about data structures?

17. Propose a metric for measuring the complexity of data structures. Can Vigram weights be adjusted to compute your measure?

18. What are the goals of metrics research? Is it a fruitful avenue of study?

REFERENCES AND FURTHER READING

1. Halstead, M. 1977. *Elements of Software Science*. New York: Elsevier/North Holland.

2. Berghel, H. L., and D. L. Sallach. 1984. "Measurements of Program Similarity in Identical Task Environments." *SIGPLAN Notices* 19, no. 8 (August): 65–76.

3. Gannon, J. D., E. E. Katz, and V. R. Basili. 1986. "Metrics For Ada™ Packages: An Initial Study." *Communications of ACM* 29, no. 7 (July): 616–623.

4. Elshoff, J. L. "An Analysis of Some Commercial PL/I Programs." *IEEE Transactions on Software Engineering* SE-12, no. 2 (June): 113–120.

5. Miller, G. A. 1956. "The Magical Number Seven Plus or Minus Two: Some Limits on Our Capacity for Processing Information." *Psychological Review* 63: 38–46.

6. Fitzsimmons, A., and T. Love. 1978. "A Review and Evaluation of Software Science." *Computing Surveys* 10, no. 1 (March): 3–18.

7. Schneider, V. 1978. "Prediction of Software Effort and Project Duration — Four New Formulas." *ACM SIGPLAN Notices* 13, no. 6 (June).

8. Ottenstein, L. M. 1979. "Quantitative Estimates of Debugging Requirements." *IEEE Transactions on Software Engineering* SE-5, no. 5 (September): 504–514.

9. Basili, V. R., R. W. Selby, and T-Y Phillips. 1983. "Metric Analysis and Data Validation across Fortran Projects." *IEEE Transactions on Software Engineering* SE-9, no. 6 (November): 652–663.

10. Lipow, M. 1982. "Number of Faults per Line of Code." *IEEE Transactions on Software Engineering* SE-8, no. 4 (July): 437–439.

11. Stetter, F. 1986. "Comments on 'Number of Faults per Line of Code.'" *IEEE Transactions on Software Engineering* SE-12, no. 12 (December): 1145.

12. McCabe, T. J. 1976. "A Complexity Measure." *IEEE Transactions on Software Engineering* SE-2, no. 4 (December): 308–320.

13. Schneidewind, N. F. 1979. "An Experiment in Software Error Data Collection and Analysis." *IEEE Transactions on Software Engineering* SE-5, no. 3 (May): 276–286.

14. Li, H. F. 1987. "An Empirical Study of Software Metrics." *IEEE Transactions on Software Engineering* SE-13, no. 6 (June): 697–708.

15. Evangelist, M. 1984. "Program Complexity and Programming Style." *Proceedings of the International Conference on Data Engineering, Los Angeles, CA. April 24–27, 1984*: 534–541.

16. Berry, R. E., and B. A. E. Meekings. 1985. "A Style Analysis of C Programs." *Communications of ACM* 28, no. 1 (January): 80–88.

17. Harrison, W., and C. R. Cook. 1986. "A Note on the Berry-Meekings Style Metric." *Communications of ACM* 29, no. 2 (February): 123–125.

18. Redish, K. A., and W. F. Smyth. 1986. "Program Style Analysis: A Natural By-Product of Program Compilation." *Communications of ACM* 29, no. 2 (February): 126–133.

19. Berns, G. M. 1984. "Assessing Software Maintainability." *Communications of ACM* 27, no. 1 (January): 14–23.

20. Siefert, D. M. 1988. "Software Reliability Measurement: An Industry Benchmark Assessment." Englewood, OH: NCR.

13

Maintenance

PREVIEW

Accommodating change, writing clear code and documentation, walk-throughs and reviews, formal and informal testing, and emphasis on early defect removal have been emphasized throughout this book because of their dramatic impact on lowering software lifecycle costs. The question answered by this chapter is, What techniques apply to the maintenance task, what CASE tools are useful, and how do we apply them?

In the first section of the chapter we list critical issues of software maintenance. In section two we illustrate how DD — a CASE tool that implements many of the recommendations of section one — is used to aid in maintenance.

Various mathematical models of software reliability are surveyed, and three specific models developed in detail. These models are useful for measuring software quality and estimating when to stop testing.

Finally, we provide an algorithm for maintenance as process. In this algorithm it is noted that the most effective techniques for improving reliability and productivity are human ones — design and code walk-throughs, documentation, and programmer experience.

THE NATURE OF MAINTENANCE

Maintenance — *the modification of a software product after delivery to correct faults, improve performance, improve functionality, or to adapt the product to a changed environment* — is the final phase of the waterfall software lifecycle. However, as we have learned in earlier chapters, maintenance is a major factor in the overall software development process, because it is costly and extends over a long period of time.

The maintenance phase can be further divided into *corrective*, *adaptive*, and *perfective* maintenance. Obviously, corrective maintenance aims to fix bugs; adaptive maintenance aims to change the application software to accommodate some change in the environment, for instance, altering the application so that it runs on a new computer, operating system, or network; and perfective maintenance aims to improve the application by satisfying requests from users, rewriting documentation, improving efficiency, or improving ease of use.

A *user enhancement* is essentially a new requirement added after the application has been delivered. Such requirements usually originate after a period of use, because the user gains insight into the system and realizes the value of a new feature, capacity, or convenience. Many change requests are satisfied by minor enhancements such as printing new reports.

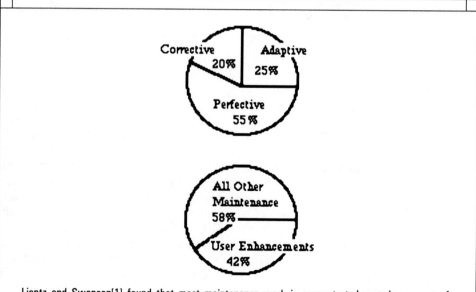

Lientz and Swanson[1] found that most maintenance work is concentrated on enhancement of existing systems. Adaptive and perfective maintenance often involves changing the system to meet new requirements suggested by the users. Thus, user enhancement accounts for nearly half of the work.

One of the major advantages of *prototyping* (see chapter fourteen) is that it avoids many after-delivery requests for enhancements. With prototyping, a user may try out the application during the requirements specification phase. This early exposure gives the user insight into the final system far in advance of completion. This is particularly true of data processing systems where experience with the prototype is helpful in designing it.

Boehm[2] lists several maxims regarding the impact that maintenance has on software development and delivery:

- Finding and fixing a software problem after delivery is 100 times more expensive than finding and fixing it during the requirements and early design phases. Use rapid prototyping where possible, and careful requirements and design specification elsewhere.

- For every dollar you spend on software development you will spend two dollars on software maintenance. Software development that emphasizes maintainability may cost more, but the costs are fully repaid during maintenance.

- Software development and maintenance costs are primarily a function of the number of source instructions in the product. This has been confirmed experimentally, even when compared with metrics such as Halstead's E [3]. Therefore, use the highest order languages possible to reduce maintenance costs.

- Only about 15% of software product development effort is devoted to programming. Pay particular attention to the full lifecycle, including maintenance.

- Walk-throughs catch 60% of the errors. The inspection technique has been the most cost-effective to date for assuring software quality. Fagan[4] gives a detailed account of the inspection process. It is interesting to note that approximately one-third of the time spent in a walk-through consists of design reconstruction — through discussion, conversation and so forth; another third of the time is spent on mental simulation — tracing the logic of the code. The remaining one-third is devoted to locating errors and suggesting fixes.

- Many software phenomena follow Pareto's law: 80% of the contribution comes from 20% of the contributors:
    - 20% of the modules contribute to 80% of the cost.
    - 20% of the modules contribute 80% of the errors.
    - 20% of the errors consume 80% of the cost to fix.
    - 20% of the modules consume 80% of the execution time.
    - 20% of the tools experience 80% of tool usage.

Laws like these abound in software engineering. Vessey and Weber[5] studied 447 operational COBOL programs in one Australian and two American organizations to determine how program complexity, style, programmer quality, and number of times a program was released affected corrective maintenance. The results of this study are listed here:

- Systems that minimize the number of interfaces among their subsystems tend to survive longer. What this means in software maintenance terms is that, to survive for a long time, programs must import energy from their environment to arrest entropy. (Imported energy takes the form of maintenance.)

- Corrective maintenance does not seem to constitute a very important activity. Adaptive maintenance is far more important. But corrective maintenance tends to introduce more errors, leading to a small likelihood that a program will successfully execute after a minor modification.

- Little difference was observed between the corrective maintenance rates of moderately versus highly complex programs. Complexity was measured by counting the number of interfaces among modules. Simple programs required less corrective maintenance than moderately or highly complex programs.

- Modular programs seem to experience less corrective maintenance than monolithic programs.

Why Is Maintenance a Challenge?

Maintainability — *the ease with which a software system can be corrected when errors or deficiencies occur, and can be expanded or contracted to satisfy new requirements*[7] — has been the constant emphasis throughout this book. Why, then, is maintenance a problem? Schneidewind[8] lists the challenges of software maintenance:

- Most software was produced prior to the adoption of modern programming practices.

- It is difficult to determine what effects a change in the program will have.

- It is difficult to relate specific programming actions to specific parts of the program.

- It is difficult to maintain programs that were written without maintenance in mind.

In addition, poor maintenance practices themselves aggravate the problem of maintenance. For example, in the process of maintaining an existing system, maintenance programmers often:

- Add, rather than replace functions
- Improperly tie a new function into the old system
- Give in to time and economic pressures to "get the system out"
- Patch, rather than discard and start over

ESTIMATING PROGRAM MAINTENANCE EFFORT

Scott[6] proposed an empirical method for estimating the effort to modify an existing program. Besides being an interesting method of estimation, the factors in Scott's technique suggest possible sources of difficulty in the maintenance process.

First, estimate the time to make the change, then add or subtract the following percentages from the original estimate. For example, if the original estimate is E, then add $0.5 * E$ to the estimate if the programmer is inexperienced.

Factor	Situation	Impact
Experience	Programmer has lots of experience with system or type of program	−30%
	Programmer has little experience with system or this type of program	+50%
Enthusiasm	Programmer can hardly wait to get started	−10%
	Programmer equates maintenance with a trip to the dentist	+20%
Expertise	Programmer can guess what the program does	−20%
	Programmer is easily upset by unusual identifier names	+20%
Life	Programmer recently got married, divorced, etc.	+10%
Documentation	Program has "standard" documentation	−20%
	Program has no documentation	+10%
	Program has obsolete documentation	+30%
Size	Program is less than 500 lines	−20%
	Program is about 1000 lines	+ 0%
	For each 1000 lines add...	+10%
Complexity	Program contains database calls	+20%
	Program contains matrix manipulation, math, etc.	+20%
	Program is "complex"	+50%
Structure	Program is structured	−20%
	Program is unstructured	+20%
Language	Program follows naming and style guidelines	−10%
	Program follows individual naming and style conventions	+20%
History	Program has had little or no maintenance	−10%
	Program has been maintained by many programmers	+20%
Users	Program is used by one person or department	+ 0%
	For each additional user department add...	+10%
Communication	User is in a different building	+10%
	User is in a different city	+20%
User Expertise	User is new to the position	+10%
	User is new to department	+20%
	User is new to company	+40%
Constancy	User has been known to make changes:	
	during requirements phase	+10%
	during design phase	+20%
	during build/test phase	+40%
	during install phase	+80%

These and other factors lead to difficulty in maintenance:

- Maintenance programmers cannot trace the process that created the software product.
- Changes are not adequately documented.
- Programmers lack adequate CASE tools for automating the process of change.

Schneidewind lists needed and existing tools for maintenance:

- Structure diagrams, showing 1) procedure, 2) control, 3) data, 4) I/O, and 5) data flow structure
- Reports of ripple effects on 1) changing a predicate, 2) changing program versions, and 3) changing identifier types, names, etc.
- Uses, Calls, and Interface Graphs of entire system
- Data traces: origins, uses, and modifications of all variables in program
- Control traces showing how each section of code can be reached from program entry point
- Storage of control program versions, test data for regression testing, and other "important" information
- Restructuring: convert unstructured code into structured code

In the next section, we describe a CASE tool incorporating many of these features. However, CASE tools that incorporate "intelligence" in the form of rules governing change to an existing program are still in their infancy. Such tools would assist the maintenance programmer, giving advice and warnings about harmful effects of change to the program.

A CASE TOOL FOR MAINTENANCE

Maintaining a large software system is very similar to keeping track of any other large system containing many items of interest. Accordingly, a database approach to maintenance is appropriate, where the entries in the database are facts about a single program. These facts are well organized, promoting easy browsing, understanding, and modification.

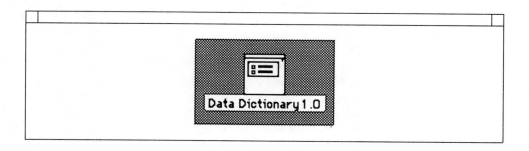

Maintenance tools exist that analyze the impact of a change, extract identifier names and list them in alphabetical order, perform dataflow analysis, check for programming style and standards violations, compute a variety of complexity metrics, restructure unstructured source code, display the structure of an application, and that generate documentation automatically[9]. DD is a CASE tool for maintenance that creates and manipulates a dictionary-like database containing cross-references to names used in the source code of an application. The cross-references are obtained by running the source code through DD. The output from DD is a collection of *relations*:

- Module Map Relation: Contains a listing of the static lexical structure of the application's source code.
- Defined Relation: Contains a list of all identifiers in the system, and tells where each is defined.
- Referenced Relation: Contains a list of all identifiers and tells where each is used.
- Uses Relation: Contains a list of all modules and what identifiers each module uses.
- Interface Relation: Contains a list of all modules and functions, and lists their interfaces.

An identifier is any name — function, procedure, variable, constant, type, parameter, and unit name — appearing in a program. An identifier is *defined* when it is declared; *used* when it is referenced in another statement; and *is used by* a function or procedure each time the function or procedure references the identifier. Interfaces in Pascal are established by unit interface parts, parameter lists, and side effects. A module here is equivalent to a unit.

When DD reads an existing system it produces a central "data dictionary" containing all of the information necessary to generate any of the five relations. Then when the user requests one or more of the relations, a text file is written. The text file can be viewed as a report, or the user can display the text file in graphic form. Programmers browse these tree-like graphs to gain an understanding of the application. The graph then becomes a useful index to the database. Modifications of the source code are done directly on the source code.

As an example of how DD solves a maintenance problem, suppose an identifier declaration is changed. For example, identifier OPEN_FLAG is changed from a Boolean to an integer. What is the ripple effect caused by this change? We can use the Referenced Relation, which contains an alphabetical listing of all identifiers, to find all locations of references to OPEN_FLAG. The "Where it is used" field lists all places that are affected by a change in OPEN_FLAG. These places can be investigated and changed also, to complete the modification.

A second example illustrates the usefulness of the Referenced Relation in making changes to functions and procedures. Suppose a certain function is modified so that it requires an additional parameter in its function heading. Using the Referenced Relation, we quickly find the function, and all of the places where it is used. These places must be changed as well as the function heading.

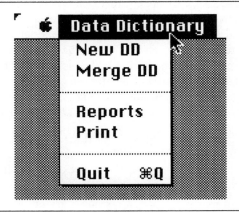

FIGURE 13-1. DD main menu

Using DD

DD is simple to use. To create a new database for an entire application or any subsystem of units, select the NEW DD item in the Data Dictionary menu, see Figure 13-1. This causes DD to read the source code and write a file containing all of the information needed to construct one or more relation.

    Selecting the REPORTS item leads to a choice of relation, see Figure 13-2. Selecting one of the relations — Module Mapper, Referenced, Uses, Interface, or Defined — leads to the creation of a text file containing the relation. The text file can be printed, or displayed in a window, or a graphic representation of the relation can be displayed in a window. When a graphical representation is shown, clicking on nodes of the graph allows a maintenance programmer to navigate the relation at high speed.

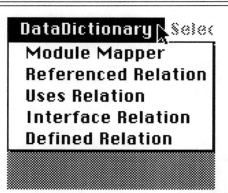

FIGURE 13-2. DD report menu

To illustrate, we construct a database for a graphics program called Paint.pas. First, the text relations are shown, followed by the graphical equivalents of these textual relations.

Even though Paint.pas is a relatively small application (under 5 KDSI), the database and relations created by DD are rather large. The graphical representations reduce the size and difficulty of navigation, but even these representations are rather large and cumbersome. Maintenance is a challenging problem, indeed.

Module Mapper lists the units and procedures/functions within units in the order they appear in the application. Names are indented to show lexical nesting and scope of the program. The nesting level is given along with an average nesting level at the end of the report, see Figure 13-3.

The graphic representation of the Module Map shown in Figure 13-4 displays each name as a labeled node, and each nested level as an arc between nodes. A node can be selected by clicking on it; a path from root to the selected node is shown in the window on the right side. The complete graph can be scanned by scrolling or by a search mechanism (under the SelectNode menu).

```
------------------MODULE MAPPER------------------

SYSTEM NAME = Paint.pas
<MODULE/FUNCTION/PROCEDURE>                      <LEVEL>
=================================================================

PROGRAM Paint                                       1
  UNIT PaintGlobals                                 1
  UNIT InitPaint                                    1
    PROCEDURE init                                  2
    PROCEDURE Init                                  2
  UNIT Drawing                                      1
    PROCEDURE InitPalette                           2
    PROCEDURE SaveScreen                            2
    PROCEDURE RestoreScreen                         2
    PROCEDURE SetMode                               2
    PROCEDURE SetStyle                              2
    PROCEDURE Draw                                  2
    PROCEDURE PutMenu                               2
    PROCEDURE MakeRect                              2
  PROCEDURE MySaveDrawing                           2
  PROCEDURE FileCmd                                 1
  PROCEDURE PaintCmd                                1
  PROCEDURE UpdateCursor                            1
  PROCEDURE TopLevel                                1
  END.
  ------------------------------------------------
  AVERAGE LEVEL                                     2
```

FIGURE 13-3. Module map of Paint application

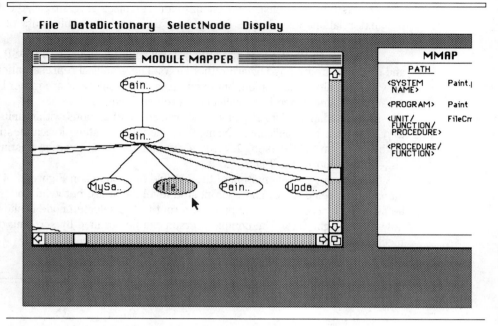

FIGURE 13-4. Visualization of module map

The Referenced relation is too long to list entirely here, see Figures 13-5 and 13-6. It cross-references all names used in the program starting with constants. Each name is listed each time it appears in a function/procedure. Thus, *AppleMenu* is used three times in routine *Init*. Toolbox names are listed as _PREDEFINED, and interface information is given in the *Import* column.

The Uses relation lists all modules (units) in alphabetical order followed by the name of the constant, type, or variable used in the module, followed by the function, procedure, or module within the unit that uses the name, see Figures 13-7 and 13-8. Specific information is provided as a code in parentheses: for identifiers in the middle column, P = passed, V = variable. For the function/procedure names appearing in the last column, P = procedure, F = function, and M = module.

The Uses relation is useful to maintenance programmers when a module is changed. The list of identifiers used by a module can be compared with the same list obtained after modification. Dead variables should be removed, for example. Errors may even be discovered before the revised module is tested. Often, identifiers are accidentally removed or ignored during maintenance. This "sin of omission" is especially difficult to find and is a common cause of newly introduced errors following a maintenance operation.

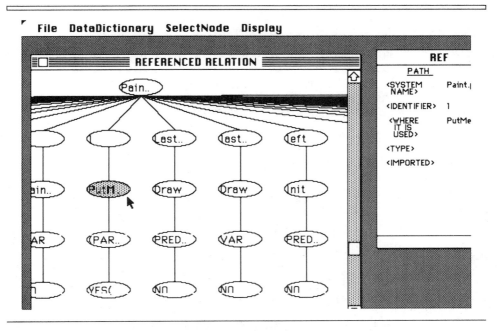

FIGURE 13-5. Visualization of referenced relation

Graphic representation of a relation condenses the information so it can be more easily comprehended and navigated. Even so, the graph can become large and incomprehensible. A Reduce-to-Fit feature in DD gives an overview of a graphically displayed relation as shown in Figure 13-9 for the Uses relation. The rectangle inside the reduced form identifies the current position of the full-scale window display.

The Interface relation contains structure chart information as discussed in earlier chapters. This relation is especially useful for observing the coupling of functions. It gives an alphabetical listing of all function/procedure names (along with the module they come from), the names of all function/procedure routines called, and coupled data flow in the form of "send and receive" parameters, see Figures 13-10 and 13-11.

The coded information, P = passed, I = imported refers to the "inflow" and "outflow" of values. In Pascal, this corresponds to pass-by-value or pass-by-reference parameter passing.

The Defined relation lists all identifiers in the entire application, followed by the name of the module/function/procedure where each is defined (declared), followed by the identifier's attributes — type and *visibility*. An identifier is *visible* if it can be referenced from outside the module/function/procedure. An invisible identifier is totally encapsulated within the lexical unit where it is defined. See Figures 13-12 and 13-13.

```
------------------------------REFERENCED RELATION------------------------------
SYSTEM NAME = Paint.pas
           <IDENTIFIER>    <WHERE IT IS USED>    <TYPE>    <IMPORTED>
================================================================================
```

IDENTIFIER	WHERE IT IS USED	TYPE	IMPORTED
0	PaintCmd	_PREDEFINED	NO
0..22000	Draw	_PREDEFINED	NO
0..4	SetStyle	_PREDEFINED	NO
1	SetMode	_PREDEFINED	NO
1	Paint	_PREDEFINED	NO
1..5	PaintGlobals	_PREDEFINED	NO
11	InitPalette	_PREDEFINED	NO
3	Init	_PREDEFINED	NO
5	SetStyle	_PREDEFINED	NO
5	Init	_PREDEFINED	NO
6	InitPalette	_PREDEFINED	NO
6..10	SetStyle	_PREDEFINED	NO
7	InitPalette	_PREDEFINED	NO
7	Init	_PREDEFINED	NO
AppendMenu	Init	_PREDEFINED	NO
AppleMenu	Init	VAR	NO
AppleMenu	Init	VAR	NO
AppleMenu	Init	VAR	NO
AppleMenuID	Init	CONST	NO
b	PutMenu	(PARAM)	YES(P)
black	Init	_PREDEFINED	NO
BlockMove	SaveScreen	_PREDEFINED	NO
BlockMove	RestoreScreen	_PREDEFINED	NO

```
...........................(Section cut here because of length) ...........................
```

IDENTIFIER	WHERE IT IS USED	TYPE	IMPORTED
I	PutMenu	(PARAM)	YES(P) (Selected in graphical representation)
LastEndPt	Draw	_PREDEFINED	NO
lastEndPt	Draw	VAR	NO
left	Init	_PREDEFINED	NO

```
...........................(Section cut here because of length) ...........................
```

IDENTIFIER	WHERE IT IS USED	TYPE	IMPORTED
UnloadSeg	TopLevel	_PREDEFINED	NO
UpdateCursor	TopLevel	PROCEDURE	NO

```
================================================================================
    TOTAL REFERENCED IDs = 348   TOTAL INVISIBLE = 247   AVERAGE INVISIBLE = 0.710
                 TOTAL YES(P) = 24      AVERAGE YES(P) = 0.069
                 TOTAL YES(I) = 72      AVERAGE YES(I) = 0.207
                 TOTAL YES(E) = 5       AVERAGE YES(E) = 0.014
   U = Unit   E = Export   I = Import   P = Parameter   M = Mainprogram
```

FIGURE 13-6. Referenced relation of Paint application

```
-----------------------------------USES RELATION-----------------------------------

SYSTEM NAME = Paint.pas
          <MODULE>              <WHAT IT USES (Referenced)>        <FROM WHERE>
======================================================================================

              Drawing                    v(P)                    SetMode(P)
              Drawing                    h(P)                    SetStyle(P)
              Drawing                  endPt(P)                  Draw(P)
              Drawing              OldScreenBits(V)              Draw(P)
              Drawing               ResourceID(P)                PutMenu(P)
              Drawing                    l(P)                    PutMenu(P)
              Drawing                    t(P)                    PutMenu(P)
              Drawing                    r(P)                    PutMenu(P)
              Drawing                    b(P)                    PutMenu(P)
              Drawing                    mr(V)                   PutMenu(P)
              Drawing                    h(V)                    PutMenu(P)
              Drawing                    i(V)                    InitPalette(P)
              Drawing                    r(P)                    MakeRect(P)
              Drawing                 startPt(P)                 MakeRect(P)
              Drawing                  endPt(P)                  MakeRect(P)
              Drawing                    t(V)                    MakeRect(P)
              Drawing                    ps(V)                   SetStyle(P)
              Drawing                 oldRect(V)                 Draw(P)
              Drawing                 newRect(V)                 Draw(P)
              Drawing                 startPt(V)                 Draw(P)
              Drawing                lastEndPt(V)                Draw(P)
              Drawing                HPosition(V)                Draw(P)
              Drawing                VPosition(V)                Draw(P)
              InitPaint                  r(V)                    Init(P)
              InitPaint                  i(V)                    Init(P)
              InitPaint                  h(V)                    Init(P)
              InitPaint              PaletteSize(V)              Init(P)
              InitPaint               MinWsize(V)                Init(P)
              InitPaint               MinWslop(V)                Init(P)

          ...........................(Section cut here because of length) ...........................

              Paint                      r(V)                    MySaveDrawing(P)
              Paint                 oldClipRgnH(V)               MySaveDrawing(P)
              Paint                      c(P)                    FileCmd(P)
              Paint                      c(P)                    PaintCmd(P)
              Paint                      i(V)                    PaintCmd(P)
              Paint                      j(V)                    PaintCmd(P)
              Paint                     pt(V)                    UpdateCursor(M)
              Paint                    hPos(V)                   UpdateCursor(M)
              Paint                    vPos(V)                   UpdateCursor(M)
              Paint                     pt(V)                    TopLevel(M)
              Paint                  menuCode(V)                 TopLevel(M)
              Paint                   event(V)                   TopLevel(M)

          ...........................(Section cut here because of length) ...........................

======================================================================================
      TOTAL USES IDs = 127
```

FIGURE 13-7. Uses relation of Paint application

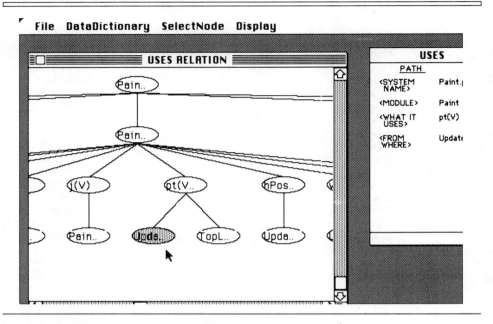

FIGURE 13-8. Visualization of Uses relation

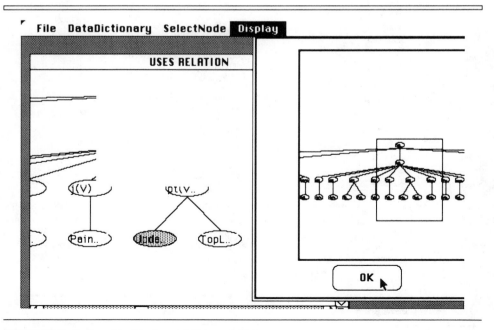

FIGURE 13-9. Reduced-to-fit view of Uses relation

```
-------------------------------INTERFACE RELATION-------------------------------

SYSTEM NAME = Paint.pas
<MODULE>
        <PROCEDURE/FUNCTION>        <CALLS>        <SENDS>              <RECEIVES>
================================================================================

/*Drawing*/
                        SetMode         *****           v
                        SetStyle        *****           h
                        Draw            *****           endPt
                        PutMenu         *****           ResourceID
                        PutMenu         *****           l
                        PutMenu         *****           t
                        PutMenu         *****           r
                        PutMenu         *****           b
                        PutMenu         SetRect         mr                   *****
                        PutMenu         SetRect         l                    *****
                        PutMenu         SetRect         t                    *****
                        PutMenu         SetRect         r                    *****
                        PutMenu         SetRect         b                    *****
                        PutMenu         GetIcon         ResourceID           *****
                        PutMenu         SysBeep         20                   *****
                        InitPalette     SetRect         ModeRect             *****
                        InitPalette     SetRect         0                    *****
                        InitPalette     SetRect         LineRect             *****
                        InitPalette     SetRect         PatternRect          *****

        ...................................(Section cut here due to length) ...................................

/*InitPaint*/
                Init    _IMPORTEDIDENT      PaintGlobals         AppleMenu
                Init    NewMenu             AppleMenuID          *****

        ...................................(Section cut here due to length) ...................................

                Init    AppendMenu      'Undo;(-;New;Save;(-;Quit     *****
                Init    DisableItem         UndoItem             ***** (Selected in graphical representation)
                Init    _IMPORTEDIDENT      PaintGlobals         PaintMenu
                Init    NewMenu             PaintMenuID          *****
                Init    NewMenu             'Paint'              *****

        ...................................(Section cut here due to length) ...................................

/*Paint*/
        MySaveDrawing           SetClip         Drawing                  *****
        MySaveDrawing           SaveDrawing StringOf('Drawing',DrawingNum:1 *****
        MySaveDrawing           SetClip         Palette                  *****
        MySaveDrawing           _IMPORTEDIDENT  PaintGlobals             DrawingNum
        FileCmd                 *****           c
        FileCmd                 _IMPORTEDIDENT  Init                     UndoItem
        FileCmd                 _IMPORTEDIDENT  PaintGlobals             NewItem
        FileCmd                 SetClip         Drawing                  *****
        FileCmd                 SetClip         Palette                  *****

        ...........................(Section cut here because of length) ...........................
```

FIGURE 13-10. Interface relation of Paint application

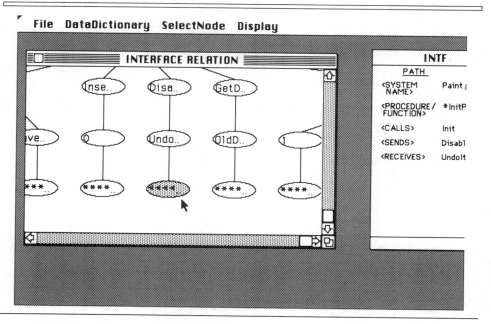

FIGURE 13-11. Visualization of Interface relation

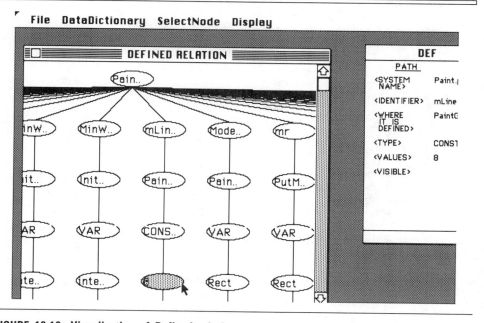

FIGURE 13-12. Visualization of Defined relation

--------------------------------DEFINED RELATION--------------------------------

SYSTEM NAME = Paint.pas

<IDENTIFIER>	<WHERE IT IS DEFINED>	<TYPE>	<VALUES>	<VISIBLE>
AppleMenu	PaintGlobals(U)	VAR	MenuHandle	NO
AppleMenuID	PaintGlobals(U)	CONST	100	NO
b	PutMenu(P)	(PARAM)	integer	YES(P)
BSize	PaintGlobals(U)	CONST	20	NO
c	FileCmd(P)	(PARAM)	integer	YES(P)
c	PaintCmd(P)	(PARAM)	integer	YES(P)
CurrMode	PaintGlobals(U)	VAR	integer	NO
CurrPattern	PaintGlobals(U)	VAR	integer	NO
CurrPenSize	PaintGlobals(U)	VAR	integer	NO
Draw	Drawing(U)	PROCEDURE	*****	YES(E)
DrawCursor	PaintGlobals(U)	VAR	Cursor	NO
Drawing	PaintGlobals(U)	VAR	RgnHandle	NO
DrawingNum	PaintGlobals(U)	VAR	integer	NO
endPt	Draw(P)	(PARAM)	Point	YES(P)
endPt	MakeRect(P)	(PARAM)	Point	YES(P)
event	TopLevel(M)	VAR	EventRecord	NO
FileCmd	FileCmd(U)	PROCEDURE	*****	NO
FileMenu	PaintGlobals(U)	VAR	MenuHandle	NO
FileMenuID	PaintGlobals(U)	CONST	101	NO
h	SetStyle(P)	(PARAM)	integer	YES(P)
h	PutMenu(P)	VAR	Handle	NO
h	Init(P)	VAR	CursHandle	NO
HBoxes	PaintGlobals(U)	CONST	11	NO

..................................(Section cut here due to length) ....

ps	SetStyle(P)	VAR	PenState	NO
pt	UpdateCursor(M)	VAR	Point	NO
pt	TopLevel(M)	VAR	Point	NO
PutMenu	Drawing(U)	PROCEDURE	*****	YES(P)
Quit	PaintGlobals(U)	VAR	boolean	NO
QuitItem	PaintGlobals(U)	CONST	6	NO
r	PutMenu(P)	(PARAM)	integer	YES(P)
r	MakeRect(P)	(PARAM)	Rect	YES(P)
r	Init(P)	VAR	Rect	NO
r	MySaveDrawing(P)	VAR	Rect	NO
ResourceID	PutMenu(P)	(PARAM)	integer	YES(P)
RestoreScreen	Drawing(P)	PROCEDURE	*****	YES(E)
SaveItem	PaintGlobals(U)	CONST	4	NO
SaveScreen	Drawing(P)	PROCEDURE	*****	YES(E)
r	MySaveDrawing(P)	VAR	Rect	NO
TopLevel	TopLevel(M)	PROCEDURE	*****	NO
UpdateCursor	UpdateCursor(M)	PROCEDURE	*****	NO
vPos	UpdateCursor(M)	VAR	integer	NO

FIGURE 13-13. Defined relation of Paint application

```
-----------------------------------------------------------------------------
TOTAL DECLARED IDs = 126    TOTAL INVISIBLE = 97    AVERAGE INVISIBLE = 0.770
                   TOTAL YES(P) = 17      AVERAGE YES(P) = 0.135
                   TOTAL YES(I) = 0       AVERAGE YES(I) = 0.000
                   TOTAL YES(E) = 12      AVERAGE YES(E) = 0.095
                   U = Unit   E = Export   I = Import   P = parameter   M = mainprogram
```

FIGURE 13-13 (Continued).

Codes are used in this relation to aid the maintenance programmer. In the second column (WHERE IT IS DEFINED) U = unit, M = main program, P = procedure, and F = function. In the last column (VISIBILITY) $YES(P)$ = passed-by-referenced, and $YES(E)$ = exported tell the maintenance programmer that a change in the computed value of a parameter may affect another function.

This relation is usually very large because it lists the entire collection of names used in all parts of the application program. Accordingly, the Reduce-to-fit option is frequently used to navigate the relation. The graph can be reduced to fit onto one or more pages by selecting the REDUCE TO FIT item under the DISPLAY menu. A three-by-five array of pages appears as shown in Figure 13-14. Clicking on the pages needed sets the size of the display area.

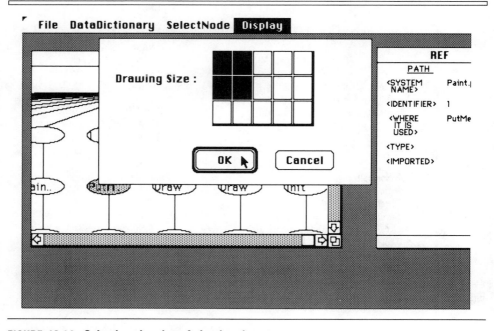

FIGURE 13-14. Selecting the size of the drawing area

SOFTWARE RELIABILITY

Programs need maintenance for two reasons: they contain bugs, and they must change over time to meet new requirements. In this section we examine the first problem — buggy software — but from a slightly different perspective. Many program bugs or faults lurk in application code for a long time before they are discovered. Such faults are not easy to find, and are usually discovered by the end-user rather than the developer. The incidental discovery of software faults during use of the application leads to the question of software reliability. **Reliability** *is the ability of a system to perform a stated function for a stated period of time.* **Software reliability** *is the probability that an application will not cause the failure of a system for a specified time under specified conditions.* The probability is a function of the inputs to the application, the use of the application, and the existence of faults in the application software. Let $\text{Prob}(F, \Delta T)$ be the probability that a failure will be encountered in time ΔT due to fault F. The reliability of an application is then given by

$$1 - \sum_i \text{Prob}(F_i, \Delta T)$$

where the summation is over all faults.

Software reliability is different from hardware reliability because software does not wear out like mechanical or electrical devices. In a physical device like a computer, reliability is usually related to wear and tear on the parts of the system. In software, there is no wear and tear. Instead, software reliability is related to the nature of use, inputs, and density of bugs. A certain application may be used for years without encountering an error simply because an error exists in a rarely traveled path of the software.

Software reliability is essentially a measure of the quality of design and implementation of an application. If properly designed and correctly implemented, an application should run without failure for all inputs and all uses. If we accept this model, then reliability of software should increase with use because the probability of failure decreases. (Hardware reliability typically decreases with use because of wear and tear.) It is nonetheless possible for reliability to initially increase as the bugs are worked out of an application, then decrease as the software is enhanced to incorporate new functions. Accordingly, the study of software reliability is complicated by these influences.

Mathematical Models

Various reliability models have been proposed to explain the phenomenon of software reliability, see Figure 13-15. Perhaps the earliest work in reliability modeling of computer programs is attributed to Shooman, Littlewood, Jelinski and Moranda, and Musa [10]. Many of the models in use today bear the names of these early researchers. Goel places these models in four categories as shown in Figure 13-15[11]. These four categories each represent a different approach to software reliability modeling.

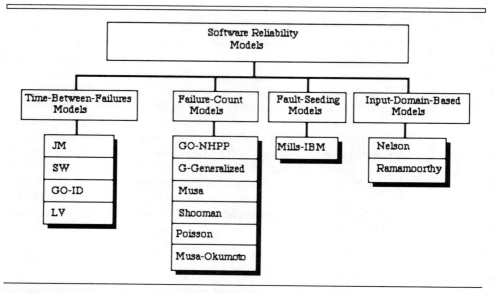

FIGURE 13-15. Four categories of reliability models

- Times-Between-Failures Models: This class of models attempts to study the time between failures by estimating the number of faults remaining in the program. Usually, the estimate is obtained by selecting a probability distribution and then fitting actual data to the distribution. The JM (Jelinski-Moranda), SW (Schick-Wolverton), GO-ID (Goel-Okumoto Imperfect Debugging), and LV (Littlewood-Verrall) models fall into this class.

- Failure-Count Models: This class of models attempts to study the number of faults per unit of time, rather than the elapsed time between faults. Again, a probability distribution is selected and observed data used to fit the distribution and obtain estimates of the parameters of the distribution. The GO-NHPP (Goel-Okumoto Nonhomogeneous Poisson Process), G-Generalized (Goel Generalized), Musa execution time, Shooman Exponential, Generalized Poisson, and Musa-Okumoto Logarithmic Poisson Execution time models fall into this class.

- Fault-Seeding Models: In this class, programs are seeded with faults and then tested. The number of seeded errors and indigenous errors are counted. These counts are used to estimate the total indigenous errors remaining. The Mills-IBM technique is the best-known method of reliability prediction in this class.

- Input-Domain-Based Models: This class of model is closely related to software testing. A set of test cases is used to generate a set of test data. The program is tested with these inputs and the number of errors counted. An estimate of the program reliability is obtained from the observed failures during testing.

ASSUMPTIONS IN RELIABILITY MODELS

Time-Between-Failures

- Times between failures independent of one another
- Equal probability of occurrence of faults
- Faults are independent of one another
- Faults are removed after occurrence
- No new faults introduced by correction

Fault-Count

- Testing intervals independent of one another
- Testing during intervals is homogeneous
- Independent number of faults in intervals

Fault-Seeding

- Seeded faults are randomly distributed
- Equal probability of detecting indigenous and seeded faults

Input-Domain-Based

- Input profile distribution is known
- Random testing is used
- Input domain can be partitioned into equivalence classes (separate paths tested)

In the next two sections we examine several of the Time-Between-Failures and Failure-Counting models in detail. Consult the references for an evaluation of these and other models not fully covered here.

Time-Between-Failures Models

The earliest reliability models are based on the simple assumption that the reliability of a program is proportional to the number of remaining errors. Each error is fixed as soon as it occurs, so the reliability is proportional to the number of errors remaining at the end of a period of time.

The occurrence of single errors is modeled by computing a *hazard function*, which relates the failure rate to the time intervals between errors. The methods in this class differ principally in their hazard functions.

The JM Model

The JM (Jelinski-Moranda De-eutrophication) model is one of the earliest software reliability models[12]. According to this model, the software failure rate is proportional to the number of remaining errors. The failure rate is expressed as a hazard function

$$Z(t_i) = C_{JM} [N - (i-1)]$$

where C_{JM} is a curve-fit constant of proportionality, N is the total number of errors initially in the application, and t_i is the time between failures $(i-1)$ and (i).

For example, assuming $N = 100$ and $C_{JM} = 0.01$, the failure rate at interval 3 is $Z(t_3) = 0.01 [100 - 2] = 0.98$. The failure rate is 1.0 at t_1 and 0.01 at t_N. A plot of Z versus cumulative time shows the relationship between failure intervals and clock time, see Figure 13-16.

Several extensions to the JM model have been proposed and studied[11]. For example, the Schick-Wolverton SW model assumes that the hazard function is proportional to the current number of errors.

The SW Model

The hazard function of the Schick-Wolverton model is linear in both the number of errors remaining and elapsed time t_i. The hazard function is equal to zero at the beginning of each interval and increases linearly to a maximum, which is determined by the error estimate given by the JM model. Thus,

$$Z(t_i) = C_{SW}[N - (i-1)] t_i$$

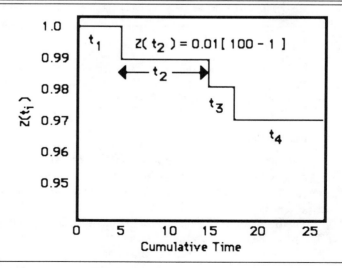

FIGURE 13-16. Hazard function JM

Schick and Wolverton[13] report a constant of proportionality of $C_{SW} = 3.3265 \times 10^{-4}$ based on empirical data provided by Wagoner of the Aerospace Corporation.

Using this model, Schick and Wolverton concluded the following:

- There exists a significant correlation between number of errors found and program size as measured by LOC.
- Both functional and path testing are needed, but evidence suggests that more errors can be found per unit of testing time by checking logic paths (complexity-based testing), than by functional (black box) testing.
- Application execution time (CPU clock) is more consistent in predicting and modeling software failures than calendar time.
- For Wagoner's data (based on 4,000 LOC of FORTRAN), a *Weibull distribution* is a better model of the error detection process than other models. A Weibull distribution is given by the *pdf* and *cdf* functions below:

$$\text{pdf}(t_i) = Z(t_i) \exp\{-Z(t_i)t_i/2\} \qquad \text{cdf}(t_i) = 1 - \exp\{-Z(t_i)t_i/2\}$$

  That is, the probability of an error in time interval t_i is given by $pdf(t_i)$.

Failure-Count Models

Shooman, Musa, Schneidewind, and Goel et al. have proposed a variety of execution time models that follow an exponential or Poisson distribution[11]. We will not survey all of them here, but instead describe one of the descendants of these early models as proposed by Goel and Okumoto (GO-NHPP model in the taxonomy presented earlier).

The GO-NHPP Model

Goel and Okumoto assume that software faults occur at random and that the process can be modeled by a nonhomogeneous Poisson equation with a time dependent failure rate, $m(t)$. The Poisson equation gives the probability that $N(t) = y$ faults will be detected at time t:

$$\text{pdf}(N(t) = y) = \{m(t)^y/y!\}\ e^{-m(t)}$$

where $m(t) = a(1 - e^{-bt})$ and a, b are determined by curve-fitting. The meaning of $m(t)$ is "total faults detected in time t."

This model was calibrated on Musa's data — 21,700 LOC of assembly language observed over a period of 25 hours of CPU time[10]. Values of a, b were obtained from this data yielding the equation,

$$m(t) = 142.32\ [1 - e^{-0.1246t}]$$

which is shown in the plot of Figure 13-17 along with the observed faults from Musa's data. This equation, along with the probability density function above, can be used to estimate number of remaining bugs and to perform risk analysis (probability of $N(t)$ bugs remaining after time t).

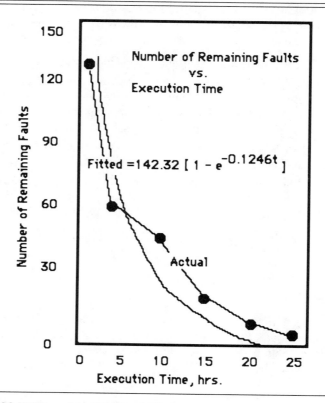

FIGURE 13-17. GO-NHPP model with Musa's data

Musa summarizes the assumptions underlying execution-time Failure-Count models:

- Errors are uniformly and randomly distributed throughout the program.
- Instruction types and execution time between failures are uniformly distributed.
- The program is used in the same manner as it is tested (testing covers use).
- Inputs are selected randomly, thus forcing the program to execute paths uniformly.
- All failures are observed.
- Single errors are fixed, and the program is put back into use after each error is fixed.

A comparison of these and other models is given by Troy and Moawad [14]. The execution time models appear to be the best for predictive work, but there is no consensus among practicing software engineers on which model should be used. More theoretical and empirical work is needed in this area.

MAINTENANCE TECHNOLOGY

Software quality is the sum total of the features of a software product that satisfy the needs of the user. Reliability is at the top of the list of these features. But how does a software development increase the quality and reliability of a software product? Which technique described in this book is best, and how is it successfully applied?

These and other pertinent questions are the topic of many research projects in software engineering. Preliminary findings by Card et al.[15] suggest some early answers:

- A major factor in reliability and productivity is people: use experienced and capable people to increase the quality, reliability, and productivity of a software development project.

- Intensive use of the development computer by the development team is associated with *low* productivity! Therefore, develop the application software as completely and thoroughly as possible before testing. This does not mean that careful planning and design should be skipped, rather these steps should be carried out completely before extensive testing or many computer runs are done.

- Reading code improves software reliability at little or no cost. Therefore, read all code developed.

- Documentation improves software reliability at little or no cost. Therefore, effectively document each phase of development.

- Walk-throughs and reviews improve software reliability at little or no cost. Therefore, conduct regular quality assurance reviews.

- Even limited use of software engineering technologies can produce up to 30% improvement in reliability. The technologies studied by Card et al. were:

  Design and code walk-throughs and reviews, independent verification and validation, configuration management and document reviews

  Software tools such as requirements and design languages, structured coding, static analysis aids, and on-line development (Programs were flight dynamics code written in FORTRAN and assembler languages.)

  Documentation that included design descriptions, test plans, user's guides, and progress reports

  Chief Programmer teams

This study was based on medium-sized projects: averages of 15 months duration, 8 person-years of effort, 62K LOC delivered per project, by people with an average of 8.5 years of experience. The study showed that software reliability and quality can be improved without added net cost.

Maintenance as Process

Most of this chapter has discussed software maintenance as artifact — the program documents and listings that are analyzed and modified to arrive at a new version of the software product. Maintenance is also a process. We end this chapter with a short description of this process.

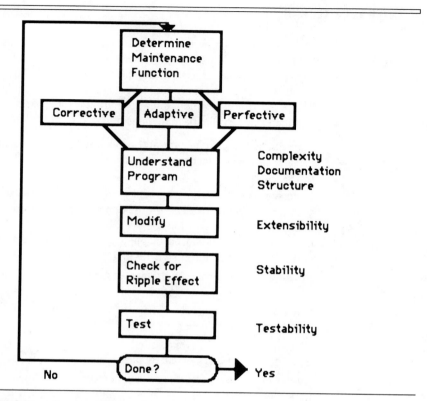

FIGURE 13-18. Safe software maintenance

Yau and Collofello[15] give an algorithm for "safe" software maintenance, see Figure 13-18. Along with this algorithm we list the attributes of concern to the maintenance programmer, such as complexity, extensibility, stability, and testability of the artifact.

Each pass through the algorithm corresponds to a refinement. These passes may occur several times for each version of the product, or they may occur after failures. In any case, the algorithm lists important considerations in achieving high quality and reliability.

Terms and Concepts

hazard function
maintainability
maintenance
  adaptive
  corrective
  perfective
reduce-to-fit
reliability

relations
  defined
  interface
  module map
  referenced
  uses
visibility
Weibull distribution

DISCUSSION QUESTIONS

1. What impact does reusability have on maintenance? Why do you think reusability holds such a great promise for reducing lifecycle costs?

2. Review the five laws of program evolution given in chapter one. How do these laws relate to software maintenance?

3. Make a list of software development and programming techniques that make maintenance easier or less costly to do.

4. Plot the hazard function for the JM models and the SW models on the same graph paper. How do these two models compare? Why do you think they are so different? What is a hazard function?

5. Use DD to analyze one of your programs. How does DD help to control the ripple effect of maintenance?

6. How does Pareto's law apply to maintenance? If Pareto's law were used to estimate the number of bugs in a program, how many bugs would be found in 20% of the code?

7. Suppose it is estimated that a maintenance operation will take 10 hours to do. Use Scott's method of revising this estimate when the worst-case situation is assumed for each factor.

8. Why is software reliability different from hardware reliability? Does software reliability always improve with time? Why?

9. The interface relation produced by DD is useful for tracing the flow of values through a system. Give one maintenance use for each of the five relations produced by DD.

10. What is the purpose of the graphical representation of a DD relation?

11. Assuming a program has 142 errors in it, use the JM, SW, and GO-NHPP models to compute the number of errors remaining after $i = 20$ time intervals (equivalent to 25 hours). Use the constants given in the text for each model. Can you explain why the values obtained from each model are different?

12. What are the most effective techniques for improving software reliability? What is the difference between reliability and quality?

13. Does software quality cost extra?

14. What is a documentation review?

15. Using the GO-NHPP model for $m(t)$, devise a mathematical model of testing. Your model must tell when to stop testing, given a certain desirable level of reliability.

16. How are reliability models used in software quality control?

REFERENCES AND FURTHER READING

1. Lientz, B., and E. Swanson. 1980. *Software Maintenance Management*: 151–157. Reading, MA: Addison-Wesley.

2. Boehm, B. W. 1987. "Industrial Software Metrics Top 10 List." *IEEE Software* 4, no. 5 (September): 84–85.

3. Gremillion, L. L. 1984. "Determinants of Program Repair Maintenance Requirements." *Communications of ACM* 27, no. 8 (August): 826–832.

4. Fagan, M. E. 1976. "Design and Code Inspections to Reduce Errors in Program Development." *IBM Systems Journal* 15, no. 3: 219–248.

5. Vessey, I., and R. Weber. 1983. "Some Factors Affecting Program Repair Maintenance: An Empirical Study." *Communications of ACM* 26, no. 2 (February): 128–134.

6. Scott, D. G. 1987. "Estimating Program Maintenance." *Software Maintenance News* 5, no. 7 (July): 14–15.

7. Martin, J., and C. McClure. 1983. *Software Maintenance: The Problem and Its Solution.* Englewood Cliffs, NJ: Prentice-Hall.

8. Schneidewind, N. F. 1987. "The State of Software Maintenance." *IEEE Transactions on Software Engineering* SE-13, no. 3 (March): 303–310.

9. Zvegintzov, N. *Software Maintenance News* 6, no. 3 (March): 24.

10. Musa, J. D. 1975. "A Theory of Software Reliability and Its Application." *IEEE Transactions on Software Engineering* SE-1, no. 3 (September): 312–327.

11. Goel, A. L. 1985. "Software Reliability Models: Assumptions, Limitations, and Applicability." *IEEE Transactions on Software Engineering* SE-11, no. 12 (December): 1411–1423.

12. Jelinski, Z., and P. Moranda. 1972. "Software Reliability Research." In *Statistical Computer Performance Evaluation*; ed. W. Freiberger: 465–484. New York: Academic Press.

13. Schick, G. J., and R. W. Wolverton. 1978. "An Analysis of Competing Software Reliability Models." *IEEE Transactions on Software Engineering* SE-4, no. 2 (March): 104–120.

14. Troy, R., and R. Moawad. 1985. "Assessment of Software Reliability Models." *IEEE Transactions on Software Engineering* SE-11, no. 9 (September): 849–856.

15. Card, D. N., F. E. McGarry, and G.T. Page. 1987. "Evaluating Software Engineering Technologies." *IEEE Transactions on Software Engineering* SE-13, no. 7 (July): 845–851.

14

Prototyping

PREVIEW

Prototyping as a software development process changes everything, leading to a new lifecycle model. In essence, prototyping replaces the design and implementation phases with a quick implementation. The quick implementation — called a rapid prototype — can be compared with the user's requirements for immediate review.

First, we develop a new lifecycle model based on the incremental building of software systems. The new lifecycle is called a step-wise spiral model, because it represents the lifecycle as a series of steps: each step moves the application closer to its final version. The step-wise spiral model is a special case of more general evolutionary models.

We examine a new approach to software development that makes step-wise development possible and practical. In this new approach, an application is developed by *showing* the computer what is desired rather than *telling* the computer through a programming language. Unfortunately, not all parts of an application can be developed with these CASE tools.

Finally, a discussion of the software tools of the next century is presented to illustrate the possible future of CASE.

THE SPIRAL LIFECYCLE MODEL

According to Boehm[1], the waterfall lifecycle model is inadequate for modern software development because of its extreme emphasis on full documentation of the requirement and design specification early in the lifecycle. Of course, the need for complete specification prior to implementation has come about because of the desire for early defect removal. Implementation of early defect removal, however, requires that specification and design documents be written in great detail. Therefore, the need for document-driven reviews pushes developers to write elaborate specifications of poorly understood requirements. These lengthy documents have two problems: 1) they are time-consuming for the designer to write and for the implementor to read, and 2) desirable features such as consistency, adequacy, correctness, and so forth, are nearly impossible to achieve.

Modern software systems are increasingly interactive, and their developers use 4GLs (4th Generation Languages) in place of traditional languages. In such systems, an evolutionary model is more suited for describing the process of development, because it quickly leads to a scaled-down early version of the operational application. This permits the end-user to evaluate the early application and give immediate feedback as to its correctness and usability. In effect, the end-user becomes an integral part of the development team.

Scaled-down, or partially completed applications produced in a relatively short time are called *prototypes*, mock-ups, or throw-away versions. A *rapid prototype* is an early version of an application that is functionally similar to the final version of the application, but lacks some features such as performance, error-recovery, and so forth. A broader definition of a rapid prototype includes simulations, analytical models, and executable specifications. We take a narrow view of a prototype and consider any operational version of the application under development to be a prototype. Accordingly, the final version is a prototype, even though it may not be obvious which version of an application is the "final one."

In this chapter, we introduce a new software lifecycle model to replace the traditional waterfall model. This new model is based on a radically different software engineering process with correspondingly different artifacts. In place of volumes of written documentation, the new methods produce running prototypes. In place of textual languages, the new paradigm uses direct manipulation of standard user interfaces as the programming language. In place of expensive maintenance and enhancement, the new technology advocates throw-away code!

These alternatives to traditional software development are based on *showing* rather than *telling*. In a *direct manipulation support environment*, the programmer shows the environment what is desired instead of telling through an editor and compiler. The showing is done by pointing, clicking, dragging, and reusing. The resulting "script" is automatically converted into a source code program by means of an expert system that generates source code from "show-me" scripts.

An Incremental Lifecycle Model

The lifecycle phases of the waterfall model are compressed, repeated, and often deleted when using direct manipulation support environments to develop rapid prototypes. This happens because of the high degree of automation inherent in showing versus telling. In addition, prototyping opens the door for immediate feedback from the end-user. Fast development plus user involvement encourages an incremental approach to development. Therefore, an incremental development lifecycle is needed to describe software development through prototypes.

A variety of models have been proposed to describe highly interactive, nontraditional, evolutionary development lifecycles in place of the traditional waterfall model[1,2]. These models all attempt to represent the high degree of interaction between requirements, design, and coding. The spiral model proposed by Boehm has been heavily simplified and recast as a *step-wise spiral* model as shown here.

Briefly, incremental development with prototypes contains these steps:

1. Obtain an initial understanding of the user's requirements through interviews and available documentation.

2. Build a rapid prototype based on what is known about the requirements.

3. Show the prototype to the user. Allow the user to use the system for a period of time.

4. Obtain feedback from the user, and use this feedback to modify the known requirements.

5. Build a next-generation prototype, incorporating the user's added requirements.

6. Repeat this process until the application is finished or retired.

To see how this relates to the waterfall model, consider the spiral model overlayed on the phases of the waterfall model shown in Figure 14-1. The project starts at the center of the pie chart and spirals around and toward the outer edge of the circle. The phases are only partially completed on each sweep of the spiral.

The pie chart represents the entire lifecycle of a "finished" application. One full circular sweep of the spiral represents that fraction of each phase which is completed by building a single version or prototype of the application. Thus, each 360° sweep defines a prototype, see the pie chart of Figure 14-2. Each 360° sweep also represents a single step in the step-wise spiral model.

The spiral model can contain one or more 360° sweeps, up to one sweep for each version. Think of the waterfall model as a special case of the step-wise spiral model — a single sweep spiral consisting of the circumference of the whole pie chart. This illustrates the inadequacy of the waterfall model: it attempts to do too much in the first (and only) version. Unlike traditional approaches, the spiral model proposes an iterative approach in which the application is constructed not just once, but many times before it is considered "finished."

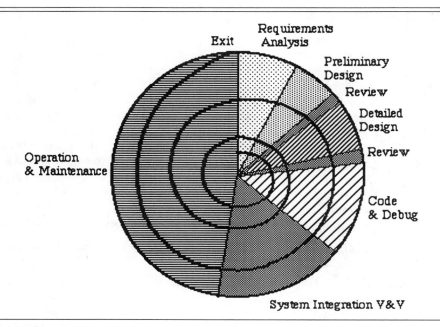

FIGURE 14-1. Spiral model compared to waterfall model

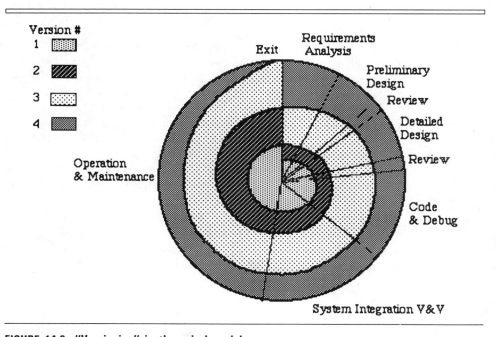

FIGURE 14-2. "Versioning" in the spiral model

CASE and Prototyping

Repetitious development might seem like a costly way to build software, and it is, unless automatic tools are used. There are two ways to accelerate incremental development and make the spiral model practical.

The time taken to develop and maintain a version of the application is proportional to the length of a 360° spiral, and the total development and maintenance time for the finished application is proportional to the length of the entire spiral from the center of the pie chart to the "Exit" point.

The development and maintenance lifecycle time can be reduced 1) by reducing the number of 360° sweeps, and 2) by reducing the time it takes to make a single sweep. Reducing both of these is the goal of 4GL and application development systems that support rapid prototyping. See the rapid prototype spiral model of Figure 14-3.

CASE tools for rapid prototyping incorporate user interface tools, program generation, and expert systems tools designed to automate as much of the work as possible, thereby reducing both the number of sweeps and the time required for each sweep around the spiral model. In the next section, we examine such a system for rapid prototyping.

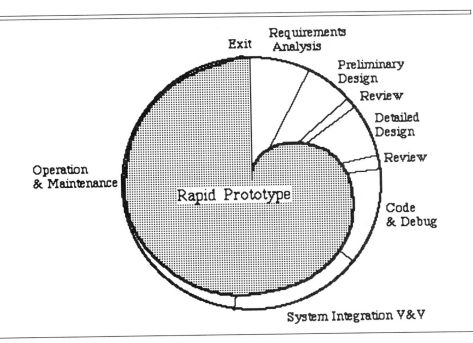

FIGURE 14-3. Rapid prototype model as a spiral model

MERGING CASE AND UIMS

Oregon Speedcode Universe (OSU) is a software development system employing on-screen editing of standard graphic user interface objects, prototyping, program generation, and automatic analysis tools which are typically used to accelerate the production of running applications. A programmer uses OSU to design and implement all user interface objects, including menus, windows, dialogs, and icons. These objects are then incorporated into an application-specific sequence which mimics the application during program development and performs the desired operations of the application during program execution. Experimental results suggest that the techniques employed by OSU can be used to develop 50–90% of an application without explicit programming, yielding productivity improvements of two- to tenfold.

Showing instead of Telling

Interest in visual programming, object-oriented design, and automated software design methods has been heightened by the rise of graphic workstations that support windows, icons, menus, and pointing devices[6]. The power of pictures over words has not been wasted on these workstations. Rather, graphics-based computing has been combined with idealized models of the world — paradigms — to reduce learning curves, increase productivity, and generally remove the burden of program operation from the user. At the same time, software developers have slowly come to realize that the user interface paradigm is itself a kind of programming language, a language that expresses the user's desires in pictures instead of words. This evolution toward pictures instead of words can be characterized as a shift from "telling" to "showing."

"Telling" involves manuals, programming languages, and other written documents, whose purpose is to convey "instructions" to user and machine alike. Telling requires two cognitive translations: from the idea to its textual representation, and then back again from text to idea. To a software developer, these translations take place when a user's requirements are converted into code, and then again when the code is executed. Unfortunately, this approach has been far from successful. The major problems of software engineering — getting correct specifications, design, and implementation — remain unsolved largely because of the imperfections of "telling."

"Showing" involves *doing* in the form of direct manipulation of "objects." No manuals, programming languages, or other written documents are needed to show a potential user how a computer might operate while solving a problem. Showing involves one level of cognitive translation: from the idea to its action. There is no linguistic ambiguity in showing because it is direct. Of course humans train other humans by showing every day. Most people learn to drive a car by doing rather than by reading a book, for instance. Showing is perhaps the most common form of learning in the animal world.

Showing a *computer* what to do, however, is difficult, and at present, less successful than traditional methods of giving instructions by "telling" via a programming language. Nonetheless, showing may potentially create major advances in programmer productivity, while telling has reached a 20-year plateau[4]. Even an imperfect software tool for programming by showing can have a dramatic impact on programmer productivity. Suppose, for example, that a certain application consists of 80% user interface code and 20% calculation code. Further suppose that the 80% user interface code can be automatically generated using a visual programming tool that captures what the user wants by "showing." The effort to produce 80% of the code can be ignored, leaving only 20% to be hand-crafted by "telling." This represents a fivefold increase in productivity. In general, programming can be accelerated by a factor of $S = 100/(100 - s)$, where s is the percentage of code produced by showing.

Standard graphical user interface management systems (UIMS) based on a paradigm like the metaphorical desktop provide a "platform" for showing versus telling. The desktop metaphor of the Apple Macintosh is used here as a platform, or prototyping language, for expressing sequences of user-machine interactions. The particular user interface platform is not as important as the concept of interface as language. In the remainder of this chapter, we show how the standards of a user interface, along with the consistency of a user interface paradigm, can be used to advantage in showing rather than telling.

Showing is the basis of the Oregon Speedcode Universe (OSU), a programming system for writing programs without programming languages. The heart of OSU is its user interface prototyping tools, which are described in this chapter. For additional information on other tools that make up the complete OSU system, see[5,6,7].

First, we provide a formal basis for prototyping, and distinguish between a *vacuous prototype*, which specifies full user interface sequences, and a full-fledged application prototype, which incorporates application functionality. We then show how OSU works and follow up with a brief discussion of how it is implemented. We compare OSU with related systems in the conclusion.

The Theory of Prototyping

A prototype Q is a collection of user interface objects U, a set of actions A, and a mapping function F:

$$Q = \{U, A, F\}$$

The user interface objects U are the alphabet of symbols defined by some paradigm. For example, the desktop paradigm of the Macintosh consists of user interface objects such as icons for trash cans, pull-down menus, scrollable windows, and user interaction dialogs.

The actions A are the behaviors defined on the objects of the application program. We say the application is implemented according to principles of object-oriented design when two conditions are met: 1) objects are encapsulated in clusters containing state and function — the state represents data in general, and the function represents the behaviors of the objects; and 2) the objects are manipulated exclusively by invocation of their functions. No state transitions are allowed as side effects of functions defined in any other encapsulation.

Our immediate concern is with user objects in U. These objects are manipulated by "calling" their functions. A menu, for example, is created and manipulated by its functions: GetNewMenu, for example. In a standard user interface management system, the behaviors for all user interface objects are defined and fixed. They constitute the "verbs" in the "language" of prototyping, while the state of each object constitutes the "nouns."

Manipulating a member of U changes the internal state of an object. An open window is closed by calling its CloseWindow function, and a menu is disabled by calling its DisableMenu function. At any point in time an interface is in a certain configuration — one window is open, another is closed, a menu is disabled, another is enabled, for example. The sum total of the states of U constitute the configuration of the user interface.

The mapping function F is a graph describing state transitions from one user interface configuration to another. State transitions in F are driven by user interactions and the behaviors of the objects in the application program. User interactions are captured by direct manipulation, and behaviors are integrated into the prototype by use of object-oriented programming techniques[8].

The state diagram for a simple modal dialog in Figure 14-4 illustrates the concept of state transition for a simple dialog consisting of three control buttons and two fields for entering and editing text. The dialog is defined by drawing its initial state on the screen. In this example, the initial state consists of two static text fields (NAME: and AGE:), two edit text fields (shown as rectangles), and three control buttons (shown as ovals).

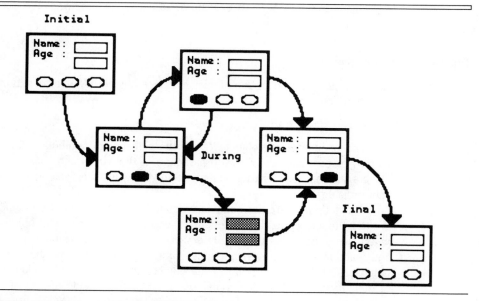

FIGURE 14-4. State machine for dialog processing

The programmer tells this dialog what to do by manipulating it — selecting a button for example, or entering data into an edit text field. "Doing" causes the dialog to enter a different state. Repetitious state transitions are permitted by entering a cluster of states designated as "during" states. These states are repeated for as long as the programmer manipulates the dialog during the period of time it is needed in the application. When the dialog is no longer needed, it is sent into its Final state, where the dialog is disposed of by the user. (Black or shaded items in the dialog indicate internal states of the dialog, such as Button Disabled and Edit Text Selected.)

We distinguish between a full-fledged application prototype and a *vacuous prototype* as described above. In a vacuous prototype, the application interface is completely simulated, but the application does nothing useful. That is, some of the processing functions of the application are missing, but the user interface works as it should.

A vacuous prototype is constructed for a standard user interface by following these steps:

1. Define all user interface objects in U; inherit the standard user interface object's behaviors as functions defined on each object.

2. Sequence the members of U by invoking the functions defined for objects in U. This gives rise to a set of configurations in F.

3. Generate code that implements U, A, and F per steps 1 and 2.

4. Compile, link, and run the code from step 3.

A full-fledged prototype is obtained in a similar fashion, but is considerably more detailed. Given a method of creating all objects in an application, and given a method of representing the actions on all objects (perhaps as a set of reusable components), a function F is constructed. A full-fledged prototype is then generated automatically from $Q = \{U, A, F\}$ defined in this way.

The central problem in prototyping research is to find methods of creating U, A, and F by showing rather than telling. In the terminology of object-oriented programming, the goal is to automatically produce objects and configurations of message-passing that implement a specific application. Prototyping goes even further than object-oriented programming or programming by reusing standard components, however, by attempting to automate program generation. This reduces the development time to one sweep through a 360° spiral in the spiral model.

Creating vacuous prototypes is relatively easy, but creating full-fledged prototypes for realistic applications is currently possible only when the domain of the application is severely restricted. Prototyping systems for general applications, which can currently be implemented by telling rather than showing, are beyond current technology.

OSU: A CASE Tool for Rapid Prototyping

OSU is a direct-manipulation support environment based on the notion of a wide-spectrum prototyper. OSU incorporates a number of domain-specific tools for automatically creating, manipulating, and "playing back" prototypes. Running applications are generated from OSU prototypes, currently in the form of compiled and linked Pascal programs.

First, we describe how to create a vacuous prototype based on the standard user interface and desktop paradigm of the Macintosh personal computer. Then we show how functionality can be added to the vacuous prototype using various domain-dependent software accelerators. A *software accelerator* is a tool for generating objects through telling. In OSU, an object is a Pascal unit that encapsulates both state and function.

The heart of OSU consists of three tools for graphically constructing $Q = \{U, A, F\}$: ResDez, The Graphical Sequencer, and The Program Generator.

RezDez: The Resource Designer

ResDez (Resource Designer) is used to graphically create and edit all user interface objects: menus, icons, dialogs, windows, alerts, error messages, prompts, and associated information[6]. These objects are "painted" on the screen exactly as they initially appear in the finished application.

For example, a dialog is "painted," dragged, resized, and annotated with control buttons by direct manipulation — see the illustration of Figure 14-5. The upper portion of the screen shows the dialog as it will appear when the application runs, and the lower portion shows a control panel for manipulating the user interface object. To place the two static texts NAME: and AGE: in the dialog, the programmer uses the mouse to drag a "static text" control item from the control panel onto the dialog.

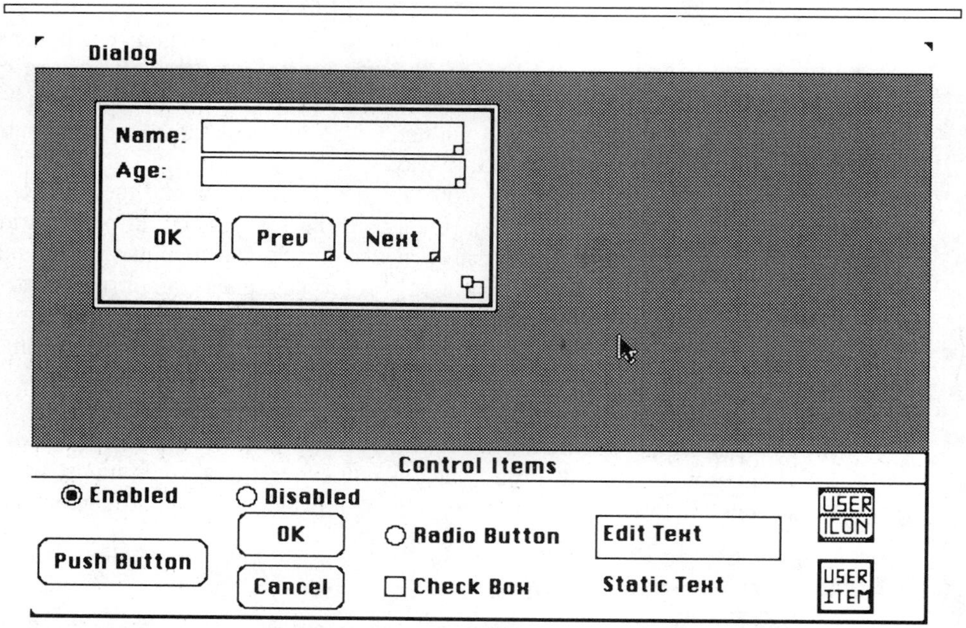

FIGURE 14-5. Building a dialog by direct manipulation

All items are editable. They can be resized, moved, deleted, and renamed by direct manipulation. (The small rectangles in the lower right-hand corner of each item are used to resize each item; placing the mouse arrow on the item, holding the mouse button down, and moving the mouse "drags" the item.)

The two edit text fields are shown as empty rectangles next to NAME: and AGE:. These rectangles will ultimately contain input values when the dialog is used by the application. Similarly, the control buttons PREVIOUS, NEXT, and ENTER become active during program execution.

ResDez not only creates each object, but also defines the initial internal state of the object. The description of the object, in its initial state, is stored as a separate resource, along with the application's executable code. The separation of user interface objects from the code that manipulates them is one of the most powerful features of the Macintosh. This separation permits rapid prototyping and the development of maintainable applications. The appearance of each user interface object can be altered independent of the code that manipulates it, even after the application is in the field. It is not necessary to compile and link an application after altering its appearance unless the type or number of items in an object change.

Graphical Sequencer

A second tool called a graphical sequencer is used to create A and F — the actions for transforming elements of U from one state to another, as well as all configurations of the user interface[5]. It is used by a programmer to "play out" the application by doing rather than writing instructions in the form of a script or textual language.

The actions of A are the behaviors of the desktop objects defined by the standard user interface (these "behaviors" are the 600 Macintosh Toolbox routines), and application objects defined by various software accelerators. The configurations of F are represented as a directed graph of "instances" of the user interface.

The desktop of OSU is shown in Figure 14-6. It contains the menus of the prototype in the menu bar, all dialogs and alerts of the prototype in miniature at the bottom of the screen, and control buttons on the right side of the screen. A sequence of user interactions is described by direct manipulation of the objects created by RezDez.

When the prototype is shown an action, such as pulling down a menu to make a menu selection, the graphical sequencer "calls" the appropriate behavior defined for the menu. The behavior carries out the operation, thus changing both the state of the object and the configuration of the user interface. These actions are chained together to form a sequence or "tree of sequences" as shown in Figures 14-7 and 14-8.

To illustrate, we show two simple sequences: one for an initial sequence (Figure 14-7) and another for a menu selection that leads to two dialogs (Figure 14-8). The dialogs labeled with the OSU icon are not part of the sequence, but rather part of the user interface of OSU itself. All dialogs that are used to obtain inputs from the programmer concerning the sequence itself are marked with this icon.

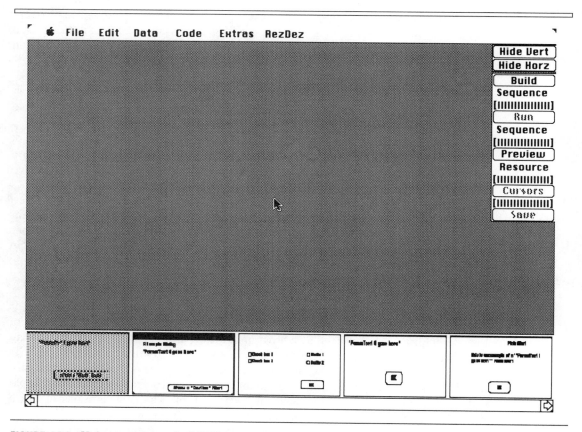

FIGURE 14-6. Main control panel of OSU

The menu selection sequence is started when the programmer selects the menu item "aDialog," see Figure 14-8. An OSU dialog appears with a list of resource options for the programmer to select — menu, dialog, alert, and so on, along with the order these objects are to be inserted into the sequence. In the example, the programmer chooses a dialog by pointing to it (all dialogs are displayed at the bottom of the screen, but this display is not shown).

Next, the programmer shows what is to be done with the selected dialog. Pushing one button causes the sequence to branch in one direction; pushing another button forces the sequence to go to a different configuration, as shown by branching in the example. For example, the left branch terminates the sequence, and the right branch causes a NoteAlert to appear on the desktop. The NoteAlert has only one button, which when pushed, also causes the sequence to be terminated.

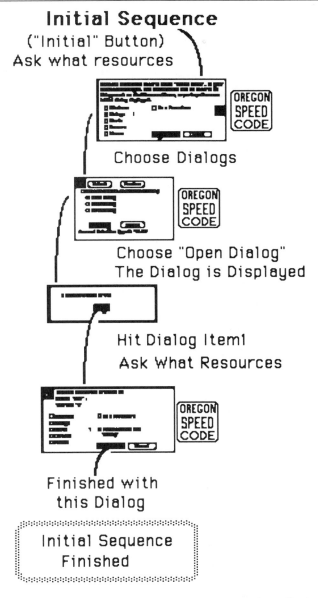

Initial Sequence
("Initial" Button)
Ask what resources

Choose Dialogs

Choose "Open Dialog"
The Dialog is Displayed

Hit Dialog Item1
Ask What Resources

Finished with
this Dialog

Initial Sequence
Finished

An initial sequence in OSU is a sequence of actions that must occur when the application initially starts. Thus, in this example, a simple dialog is initially displayed on the screen when the application is launched. The user discards the dialog by clicking on its button. The dialogs marked with the OSU icon are not part of the application, they are part of OSU. All "met-objects" are labeled with the OSU icon to distinguish them from the user interface of the application prototype.

FIGURE 14-7. An initial sequence in OSU

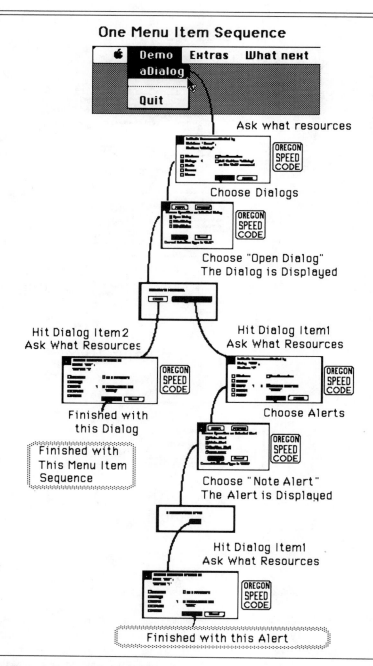

FIGURE 14-8. A typical sequence in OSU

Sequencing is "played out" for each menu item in all menus. The sum total of all traces through the prototype constitutes the transition map F. These configurations do not, however, include all possible states of all user interface objects since the prototype is still vacuous. Regardless, much of the state information can be captured in this way, including side effects on menus and dialogs that result from certain (restricted) actions by the end-user.

Program Generator

The third tool in OSU is a program generator that automatically writes compilable Pascal source code equivalent to the prototype defined by U and F. Several alternative methods of code generation might have been employed in OSU: direct compilation, translation into intermediate code, or direct interpretation. Source code generation is perhaps the best approach because it takes advantage of compiler code optimization and gives the programmer access to a maintainable version of the program. Furthermore, the resulting prototypes are easily combined with other program components taken from libraries and other languages.

A script of the recorded interactions between the hypothetical end-user and the prototype is produced as an intermediate representation of F, see Figure 14-9. The sequence script is automatically written in a sequence language specifically designed for OSU (this language is not intended for human comprehension). Translation into Pascal is done automatically; other translators can be used to produce C, Ada, or other languages.

SPECIFICATION OF A PROTOTYPE SEQUENCE

```
ITEMHIT = Data [4 = 0];
 ITEMHIT = Put [4 = 2];
   OPEN DIALOG [204];
     ITEMHIT = DITLITEM [1 = D204 = B];
       OPEN ALERT [302 = A3];
         INSERTSTR 1 [104];
         ITEMHIT = DITLITEM [1 = A302 = B];
         .;
       CLOSE DIALOG [204];
       .;
     ITEMHIT = DITLITEM [3 = D204 = B];
       DO [GetPrevious];
     .;
     ITEMHIT = DITLITEM [2 = D204 = B];
       DO [GetNext];
     .;
    .;
   .;
  .;
```

FIGURE 14-9. Specification of a prototype sequence

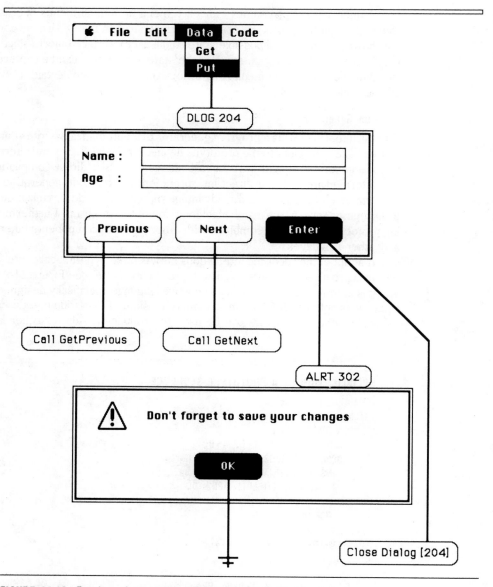

FIGURE 14-10. Portion of sequence defined in Figure 14-11

For example, the sequence language script shown in Figure 14-9 corresponds with the graphic sequence shown in Figure 14-10. The sequence describes what happens when menu item PUT is selected from menu DATA.

In the graphic sequence, menu selection leads to dialog 204 with three buttons: PREVIOUS, NEXT, and ENTER. The actions defined for the first two buttons are specified by active objects, "GetPrevious" and "GetNext." The third button, ENTER, is defined by a two-object sequence: display of Alert 302, followed by active object Close-Dialog.

In the sequence language script, the keywords ITEMHIT designate events; indentation designates nested actions; and verbs such as OPEN, INSERTSTR, CLOSE, and DO have obvious meanings.

In this example, the two events ITEMHIT = Data[4 = 0] and ITEMHIT = Put[4 = 2] specify menu selection. OPEN DIALOG[204] says to use dialog number 204 from the resource fork as the user interface object displayed following the menu selection. ITEMHIT = DITLITEM [1 = D204 = B] specifies the event corresponding to the user pressing dialog 204, item number 1, which is the button labeled ENTER. When this happens, OPEN ALERT [302 = A3] says to display alert number 302; INSERTSTR 1 [104] says to show "Don't forget to save your changes" in the alert; ITEMHIT = DITLITEM [1 = A302 = B] says to wait until the OK button is pressed in alert 302; and finally, CLOSE DIALOG[204] removes the dialog from the screen.

The other two possible events in the graphical sequence are represented by the sequence language scripts:

```
ITEMHIT = DITLITEM[3 = D204 = B]
```

and

```
ITEMHIT = DITLITEM[2 = D204 = B]
```

These events are "fielded" by behaviors GetPrevious and GetNext, respectively. Thus, the DO command provides an open-ended method for connecting vacuous sequences to application functions. These functions are generated automatically by various software accelerators, or alternately by hand.

OSU records these direct manipulations as they are done. The recorded sequence can be played back at any time and modified to suit changing requirements.

Software Accelerators

Software accelerators accept direct manipulation of various objects as inputs, and produce object-oriented source code modules as output. That is, data and the operations that can be performed on the data are encapsulated in the form of a module. This provides a homogeneous code interface to OSU and the standard user interface objects. The uniformity of code interfaces across all objects in the system enables OSU to import application functionality from domain-specific tools. In fact, the generality of OSU is directly related to the generality of these tools.

Meta-ECR is a software accelerator for designing and creating databases according to the Entity-Category-Relation model[7]. An ECR diagram is drawn on the screen to create entities, relations, and categories, see Figure 14-11. These database objects have attributes defined on them which are manipulated by various database routines such as INSERT, DELETE, SORT, LOOKUP, and so on.

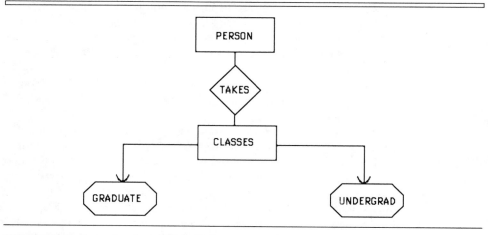

FIGURE 14-11. Example of an ECR model

Rectangles such as PERSON and CLASSES represent entities, files that contain information such as Names and Ages of people (PERSON). A diamond (TAKES) represents relationships between two entities. For example, a student from the PERSON file TAKES a class listed in the CLASSES file. Entities can be subdivided into categories as shown by the two octagons (GRADUATE and UNDERGRAD) — students take undergraduate and graduate classes.

The structure of a Meta-ECR file is defined by its attributes, for instance, Name and Age. The structure information is used to convert each Meta-ECR file into a relational file for processing by relational operations. The relational operations are functions defined on objects that are imported into an OSU prototype. Thus a rapid prototype can be created that performs relational database operations without writing a query!

To illustrate, suppose a dialog for capturing Name and Age is specified as part of a sequence by OSU's graphical sequencer (shown previously). The values entered into the dialog are inserted into file PERSON by connecting the INSERT file operator with the Name and Age fields of the dialog. To do this, the prototype is linked with the INSERT routine as if INSERT were an active object in the sequence. The resulting script contains ITEMHIT and DO [INSERT] commands corresponding to each of the fields Name and Age.

A Note on Implementation

Three design decisions had to be made before OSU was implemented: 1) how to create and edit user interface objects, 2) how to capture and represent "showing" by direct manipulation, and 3) how to generate a running program from the prototype. These decisions were heavily influenced by the software architecture of the Macintosh and its standard user interface.

How should we create and edit user interface objects? ResDez "decompiles" graphic user objects into resource fork parameters and stores these parameters in the resource fork of the target application's binary file. In addition, ResDez can extract parameters from other application's resource forks and add them to the target application's resources. User interface objects can thus be reused from application to application.

How should we capture and represent "showing" by direct manipulation? Showing by direct manipulation does not give enough information to fully specify the sequence of operations carried out by a rich user interface, because some "manipulations" trigger more than one operation, and others cause side effects. For example, one menu selection may trigger an open dialog, place a check mark next to the menu item, and initialize values in the application.

Multiple operations are triggered in a vacuous prototype by specifying miniature subsequences through intermediate OSU dialogs, which accompany direct manipulation of the user interface object. These subsequences consist of housekeeping chores such as placing check marks next to menu items and placing more than one event in each ITEMHIT clause corresponding to a major event. The examples shown here illustrate the placement of OSU dialogs in the sequence. (The OSU dialogs do not appear in the final prototype, but the "instructions" specified by them do.)

The side effects problem is solved by permitting user-defined procedures to be inserted into the sequence as if they were user interface objects. These active objects are produced by hand or by software accelerators. If produced by hand, OSU provides CASE-like tools for structured design. If produced by a software accelerator such as the Meta-ECR designer tool, the behaviors of the object produced by the accelerator are integrated into an OSU sequence as an active object. Details, such as matching actual parameters to formal parameters and selecting the appropriate collection of objects, are handled by a series of selections from lists. These lists are presented to the user by OSU, and depend on the source and type of active object being managed. This approach is admittedly akin to "telling" rather than "showing." As a consequence, OSU must be operated by knowledgeable programmers rather than novices.

How should we generate a running program from the prototype? Because Macintosh applications have a rather standard method of handling user interactions, OSU is able to use "macros" to generate much of the Pascal code. OSU contains a macro or *shell program* that takes events from the event queue, processes each event according to the sequences provided by the Graphical Sequencer, and continually repeats this cycle until a "quit" event is encountered. The shell program contains a generalized main event loop that is the same for all applications produced by OSU. Actually, most applications consist of the main event loop and many minor event loops that handle user interactions through window scrolls and modal dialogs.

In addition to the shell program, source code is generated by parsing and analyzing the script produced by the Graphical Sequencer.

Complete source code generation is done in two parts:

1. The parameterized shell program containing metavariables is copied and modified to produce a main event loop program. Modification consists of replacing all metavariables with actual values. For example, the metavariable which defines the number of menus in the application is replaced by a constant value, and the application's desktop icon is supplied from the resource fork.

2. Modules containing encapsulated objects are either generated from the sequence language or imported from libraries containing them. These modules are "used" by the main event loop program, and linked to the running application by the compile/link process required of all Pascal programs.

The parameterized macro used to produce the main event program contains many standard features of all applications that use the standard Macintosh user interface. For example, co-resident programs called DAs (Desk Accessories) are permitted activation from within any application. But DAs must be specifically managed by the application, so the shell program must include this code. Files can be printed from the desktop rather than from the application. This is done by special code which prints the application's documents, then returns immediately to the desktop.

The shell program can be replaced by other shell programs incorporating a vast array of features that are considered standard within certain domains of application. Telecommunications, networking, and laser printing are examples of this kind of shell customization.

External modules are connected to the shell program by inserting a *uses clause* into the shell. The uses clause is a mechanism for importing/exporting constants, types, variables, procedures, and functions that are visible from outside a unit. Thus modules are coupled via their interface parts and access procedure invocations. The Program Generator must know the unit name and procedure/function name of every operation used by the application. This information is included in the sequence of events passed to the Program Generator by the Graphical Sequencer.

This simplistic approach to program generation has its limits, however, because of the unhierarchical nature of events and the operations on these events. This can be easily demonstrated. Suppose two distinct portions of the prototype contain the following two sequences of events (the script has been simplified for illustration purposes):

```
    A:          B:
ItemHit = Menu      ItemHit = Menu
  ItemHit = Dialog      ItemHit = Alert
    ItemHit = Alert        ItemHit = Dialog
  ...         ...
```

Sequence *A* contains a nested sequence of events that accesses operations on Dialogs before operations on Alerts; conversely, sequence *B* contains a nested sequence of events that accesses operations on Alerts before operations on Dialogs. If the Program Generator blindly uses the modules in the order specified by sequence *A*, then when sequence *B* is encountered, the hierarchy of A:Menu – >Dialog – >Alert will not match the hierarchy of sequence B:Menu – >Alert – >Dialog. This deadlock between the two sequences shows up as a compiler error if not removed.

A purely object-oriented hierarchy among objects cannot be automatically produced by OSU, because A: uses B:, and B: uses A: cannot co-exist in the same application. It is tempting to move A and B to the same level and add a "supervisory module," but this fails because of illegal forward referencing in that module. Instead, node-splitting by code duplication is done, which results in inefficiency. This is a general problem for all rapid prototyping systems[9].

ILLUSTRATION: PROTOTYPING COCOPRO

OSU is a power tool for accelerating the process of programming. To illustrate this, a vacuous prototype of CoCoPro (the project used for illustration purposes in this book) is constructed.

CoCoPro took 6 students 4 months to build by hand, resulting in 6,400 LOC. When using OSU, 4,300 LOC were produced by one programmer in 2.5 hours! That is, 67% of the code was produced automatically, tripling productivity, using the formula: $100/(100 - s)$. However, if we compare these numbers with estimates given by CoCoMo with nominal cost drivers, the results are even more dramatic.

Actual: MM = 24, TDEV = 4 months, Avg. FSP = 6, Peak FSP = 6.

CoCoMo (6.4 KDSI Organic): MM = 22.47, TDEV = 8.16 months,
Avg. FSP = 2.75, Peak FSP = 3.34.

CoCoMo (2.1 KDSI Organic): MM = 6.97, TDEV = 5.23, Avg. FSP = 1.33,
Peak FSP = 1.62.

If it is true that the automatic production of CoCoPro leaves 2.1 KDSI of hand coding to do, then the savings in effort is (22.47 − 6.97 = 15.5) or 68%, a time savings of (8.16 − 5.23 = 2.93) or 36%, and a personnel savings of (2.75 − 1.33 = 1.42) or 52%, due to the need for fewer programmers. Managers will be interested in a 68% reduction in the cost to produce such software!

When using software accelerators to further automate programming, it is possible to realize tenfold or better improvements. This is the subject of vigorous research. Current technology can easily produce vacuous prototypes, but wide-spectrum prototyping must await future technology. We illustrate here only the vacuous prototype tools used to create CoCoPro.

Overview of Illustration

Due to space limitations, we will show only a small portion of the sequence carried out to prototype CoCoPro. This example has two major components: 1) initialization of CoCoPro, and 2) building sequences for the Project menu and for the CoCoMo menu. The outline of activities is

Initialize:
1. Show "About Dialog"
2. Disable menu items that are initially inactive

Build:
1. Project-New sequence is. . .
   Select Project-New item
   Show "New Project" Dialog
   Enable CoCoMo Menus

2. CoCoMo-Calculate Sequence. . .
   Calculate Component Button sequence. . .
      Show Calculate Component Dialog
   Delete Component Button sequence. . .
      Show external procedure for doing the calculation

3. . . .And so on. . .

These actions are carried out in the order listed above. Indentation is used to show the sub-actions that are carried out within each main action. The displays may become confusing because many dialogs are stacked on top of one another during the course of nested actions. Keep an eye out for the dialogs containing the OSU icon — these are metadialogs used to distinguish between the user interface and OSU itself.

OSU: The Movie

Figure 14-12 contains "snapshots" taken from OSU while running the steps listed in the outline above. We cannot show animation of the direct manipulation; instead, we annotate each snapshot, describing the programmer action in each snapshot.

The first snapshot (Figure 14-12a) shows the OSU desktop after all resources have been loaded and before any sequence is described. The resources are shown as a menu bar containing the actual menus of CoCoPro, and the windows, dialogs, and alerts of CoCoPro across the bottom of the screen. These resources are created by using the resource editor, RezDez, or by copying them from the resource fork of the hand-coded CoCoPro. Resource creation is not shown here.

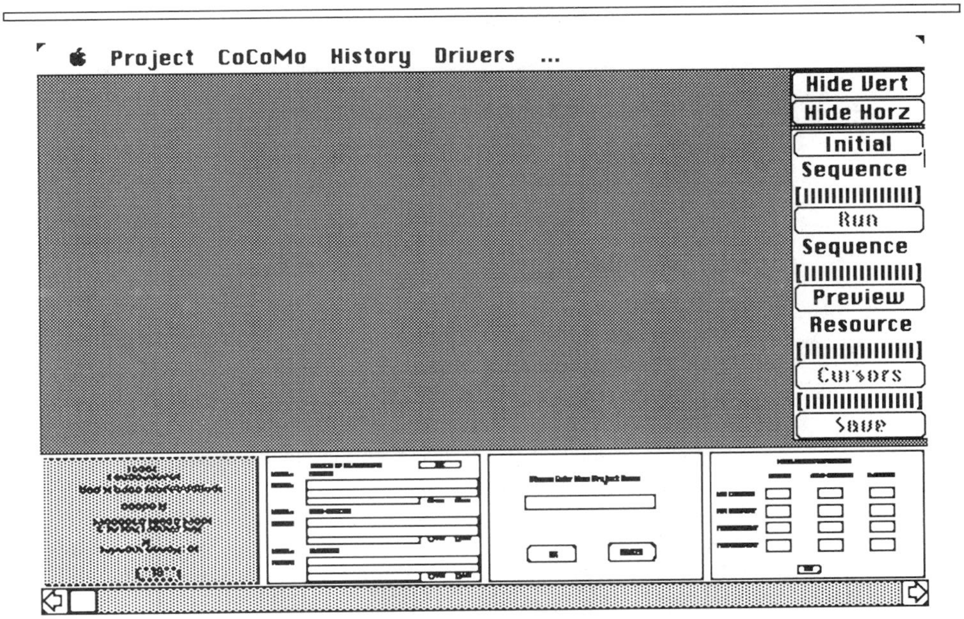

FIGURE 14-12a. OSU desktop after resources are loaded

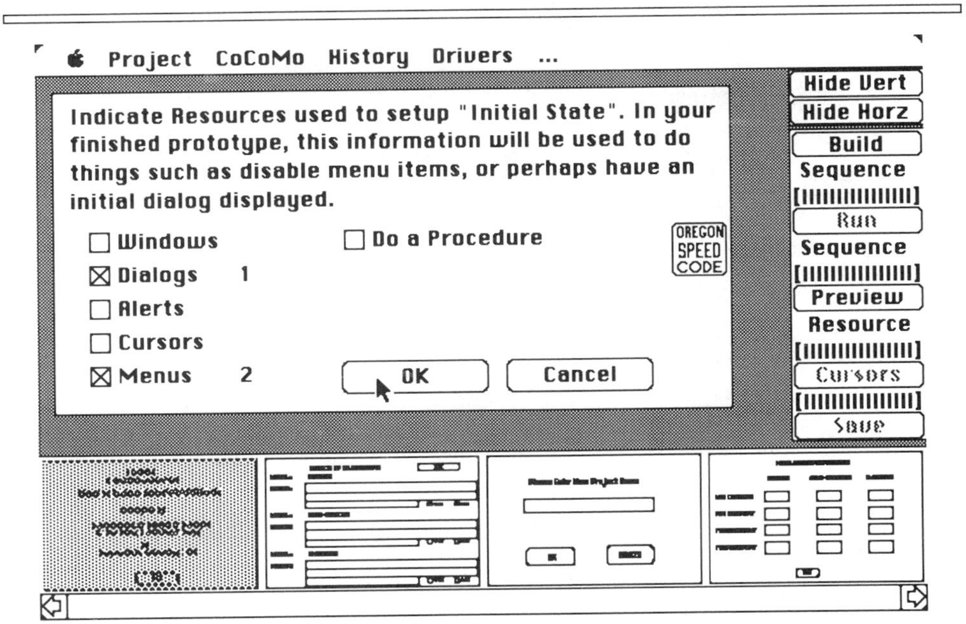

FIGURE 14-12b. Specifying an initial sequence

The second snapshot (Figure 14-12b) shows how to specify an initial sequence of actions to occur when the application is launched. The initialization step is selected by pressing the INITIAL button on the right-hand palette of OSU buttons — see Figure 14-12a. In the initialization step, we want to do two things:

Initialize:
1. Show "About Dialog"
2. Disable menu items that are initially inactive

These are selected from the list of check boxed items and numbered as shown — Dialogs 1, Menus 2. Any number of these items can be selected. The numbers give the order in which these actions will be done next. The idea is to show the "About Dialog" first, then disable the menu items.

The "About Dialog" — shown in the next snapshot (Figure 14-12c) — is directly manipulated as it will be in the actual application. There is only one button to push, so the programmer pushes it. A dialog appears with a list of things that can be done to dialogs. Selecting the right option (not shown) makes the dialog go away. This completes part 1 of the initialization step.

Part 2 of the initialization step disables certain menu items as shown in Figure 14-12d. Items in both PROJECT and COCOMO menus are disabled, but we show here only the COCOMO menu as disabled.

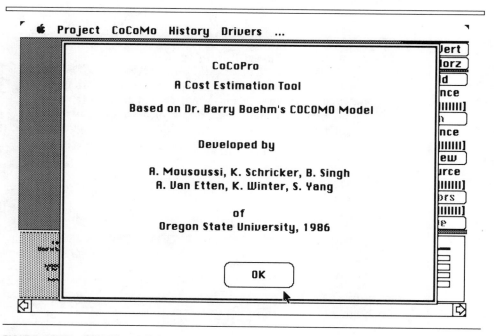

FIGURE 14-12c. The About dialog

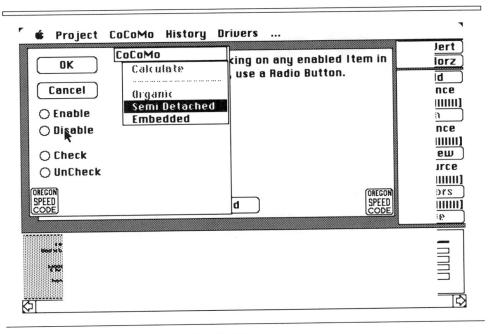

FIGURE 14-12d. CoCoMo menu with disabled items

This ends the initialization step. Next, the operational steps of the application are defined by pressing the BUILD button in the right-hand palette. We want to do many things in the operational phase, but space allows us to show only the following:

Build:

1. Project-New sequence is. . .
Select Project-New item
Show "New Project" Dialog
Enable CoCoMo Menus

2. CoCoMo-Calculate Sequence. . .
Calculate Component Button sequence. . .
   Show Calculate Component Dialog
Delete Component Button sequence. . .
   Show external procedure for doing the calculation

The PROJECT-NEW sequence is specified by selecting the order of resources to appear. We do this by direct manipulation. First, PROJECT-NEW is selected by pulling down the PROJECT menu. A list of resources that will appear next is then offered to the programmer. This is similar to the selection of Dialogs 1 and Menus 2 sequence as before, so we have skipped showing this detail. The programmer selects the type of dialog to be displayed as shown in Figure 14-13a. Selecting Open Dialog permits the

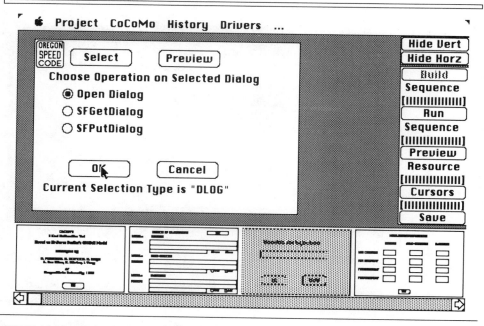

FIGURE 14-13a. Selecting type of dialog

programmer to choose one of the dialogs displayed at the bottom of the screen. Selecting SFGetDialog or SFPutDialog causes one of the standard file dialogs to appear. The SFGet/SFPut-dialogs are the familiar file list minifinders seen in every application that processes files.

Selecting Open Dialog and choosing a dialog from the row at the bottom of the screen causes that dialog to appear on the screen as shown in Figure 14-13b. Once again, the programmer directly manipulates the dialog to tell OSU what to do. In this case, two buttons, OK and CANCEL, must be defined. Pressing CANCEL must cause the dialog to go away and make the application return to a previous state. Pressing OK causes the dialog to go away and makes the application go to a new state. The new state is defined by a processing function that takes the name of the project from this dialog and stores it somewhere. We show how to describe a processing function in the CoCoMo menu sequence.

The next snapshot (Figure 14-13c) shows how to close a dialog and get rid of it when the sequence is done. This OSU dialog appears after pressing OK or CANCEL.

The menu items in menu COCOMO that were initially disabled must be enabled, now. This is done by selecting them from the menu dialog, and Enabling them, one at a time, see Figure 14-13d. This dialog also shows that menu items can also be check-marked for a special effect.

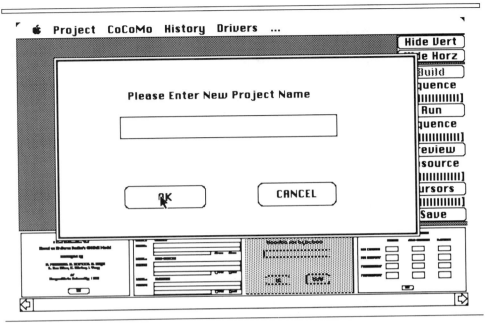

FIGURE 14-13b. Dialog appears after Open Dialog is selected

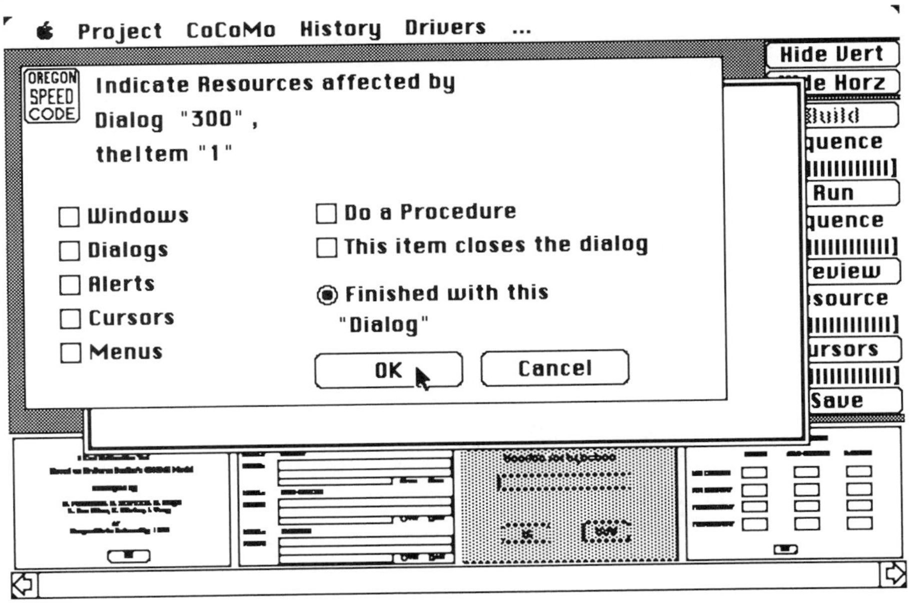

FIGURE 14-13c. Closing a dialog after sequencing

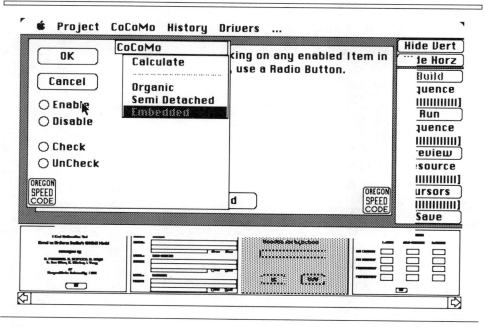

FIGURE 14-13d. Enabling menu items

The next sequence involves the COCOMO menu, so we pull it down to do the following sequence:

2. CoCoMo-Calculate Sequence. . .
   Calculate Component Button sequence. . .
   Show Calculate Component Dialog

The first snapshot (see Figure 14-14a) following the selection of COCOMO-CALCULATE repeats the OSU dialog for selecting what kind of dialog is desired. In this snapshot, the cursor is shown selecting one of the dialogs from the row of dialogs at the bottom of the screen. This row can be scrolled left/right to show all the dialogs, alerts, and windows defined for the application.

The next dialog (Figure 14-14b) shows the full-sized application dialog as it will appear in the application. Once again, this dialog is directly manipulated by pressing each of its buttons, radios, and so on. In the example, the CALC. COMPONENT button is selected.

The next two snapshots (Figures 14-14c and 14-14d) specify what happens when pressing the CALC. COMPONENT button. This leads to another dialog shown in Figure 14-14d. This dialog and its buttons are directly manipulated, thus showing what the prototype is supposed to do to calculate CoCoMo estimates for a single component.

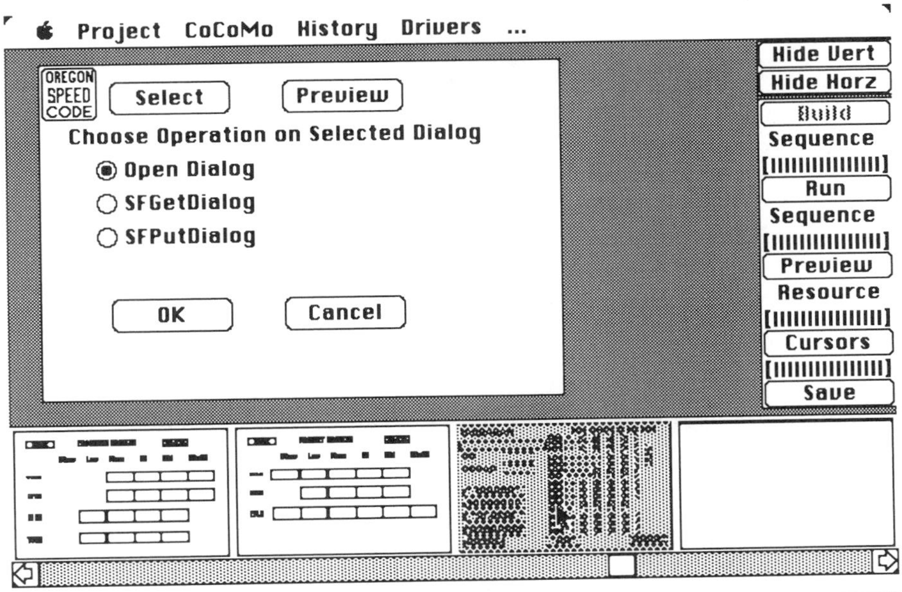

FIGURE 14-14a. After the selection of CoCoMo-Calculate

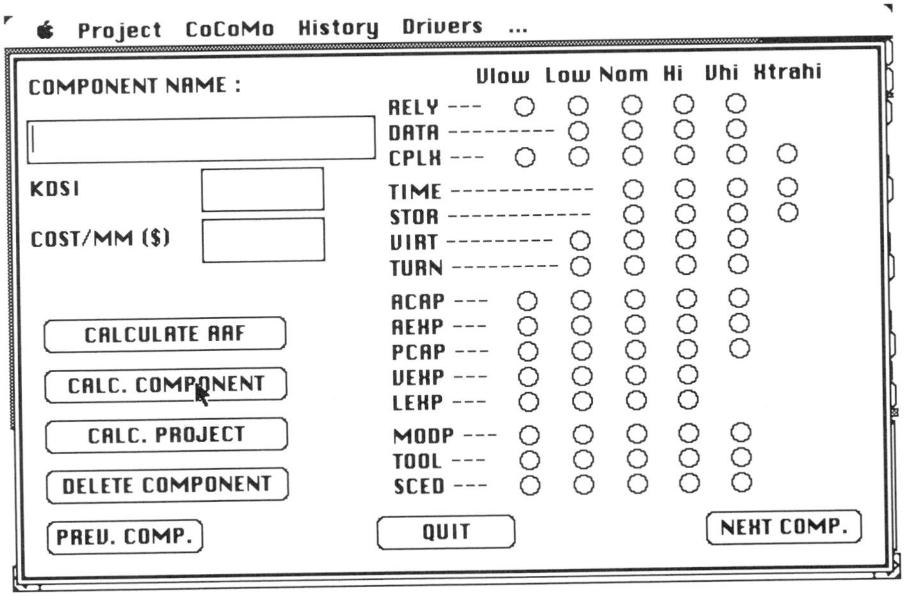

FIGURE 14-14b. Full-sized application dialog

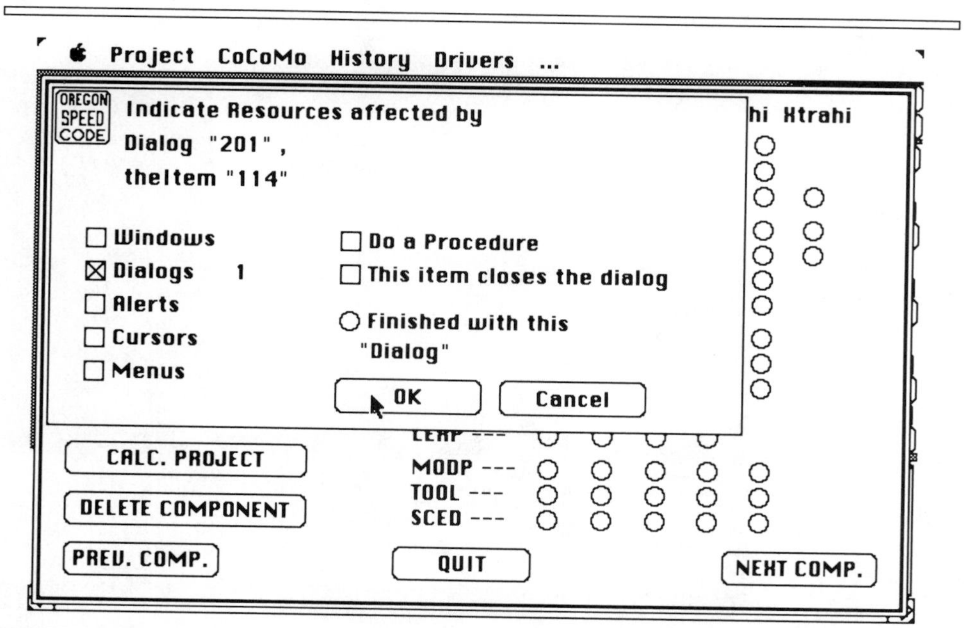

FIGURE 14-14c. After Calc. Component is selected

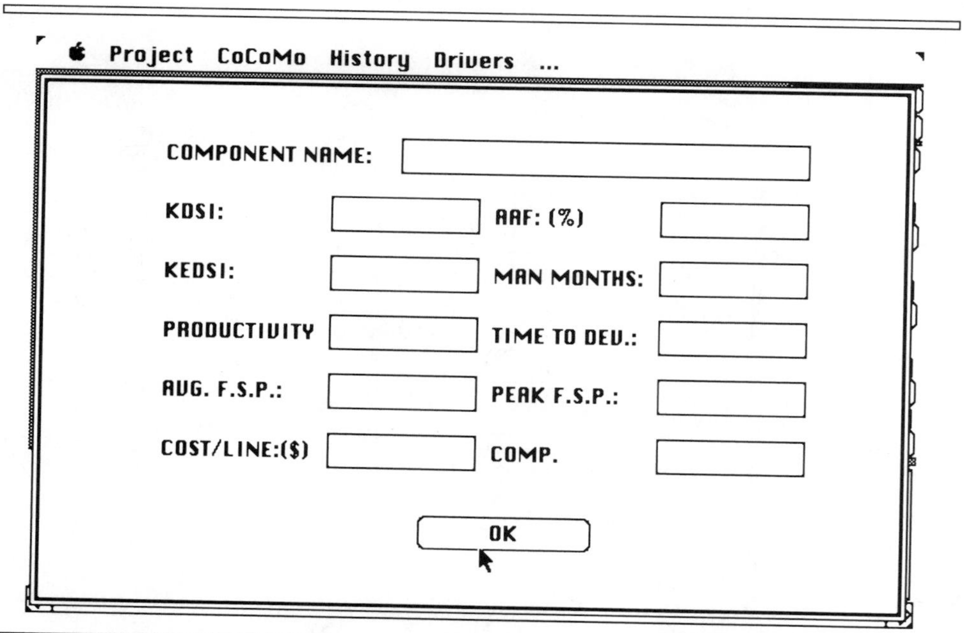

FIGURE 14-14d. Component dialog

We are down to the final sequence of this illustration:

Delete Component Button sequence. . .
   Show external procedure for doing the calculation

This sequence is very much like the others except for the inclusion of a processing function. This example shows how to add processing capabilities to a vacuous prototype by including a DO function in the sequence. The DO A PROCEDURE check box is checked, causing OSU to display a structure chart as shown in the snapshot of Figure 14-14e.

New functions can be added to the structure chart to include application-dependent functionality — the function is supplied by a library of reusable components, a software accelerator, or by hand coding. In this example, we load a function created by a software accelerator, Figure 14-14f. OSU displays the function in the picture language of Vigram so that the function can be understood and then modified, see Figure 14-14g.

This process of direct manipulation to *show* OSU what to do, rather than *telling* a high-level language compiler what to do, is very fast. Most of the operations are carried out by a single click of the mouse. The sequence can be played back by selecting the RUN button from the OSU palette before code generation. When the user interface and sequence is exactly the way the customer wants it, the sequence is written to a file in the form of the sequence language and code generated from it. It takes about 5 minutes of code generation time to produce the 4,300 lines of source code needed to fully specify a vacuous prototype for CoCoPro.

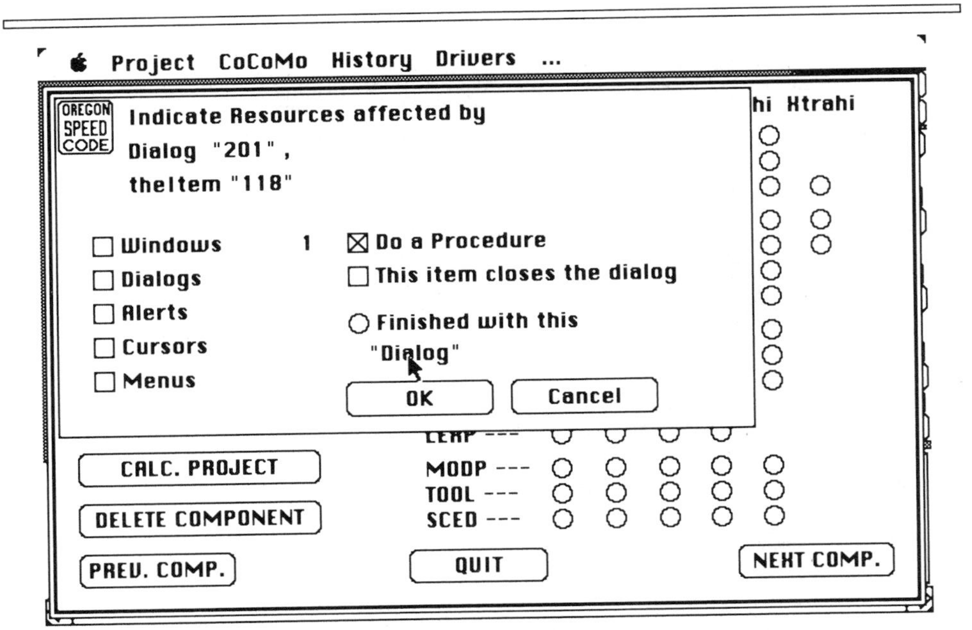

FIGURE 14-14e. Including a DO function in the sequence

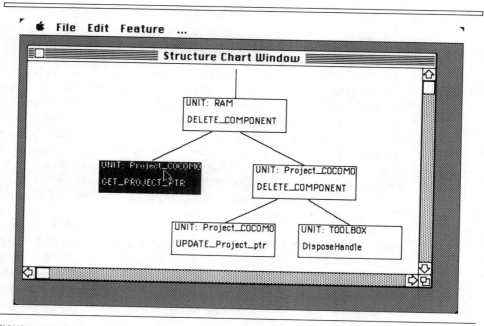

FIGURE 14-14f. Function created by a software accelerator

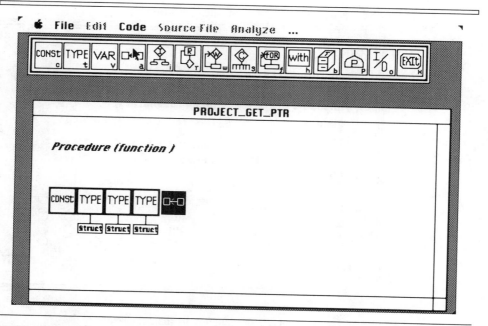

FIGURE 14-14g. Function described in Vigram terms

This illustration shows only a portion of the capability of OSU and what can be achieved with direct manipulation of standard user interface objects. Much remains to be done, however, before wide-spectrum prototyping is a daily reality.

BEYOND THE NEXT-EVENT HORIZON

Prototyping and the incremental lifecycle that it promotes is an alternative to the traditional waterfall model. As the power curves show, prototyping not only reduces the overall effort, but it moves most of the effort toward the front of the lifecycle. This shift makes it possible to involve the end-users sooner, leading to reductions in the number and thoroughness of specification documents. In addition, effort is reduced by reducing the number and duration of meetings typically needed to communicate among programmers and customers.

Boehm et al.[10] observed the advantages of prototyping in a classroom experiment where students compared the development of a CoCoMo estimation application by means of specifying versus prototyping. Four student teams used specification techniques, and three teams used a form of prototyping. The main results obtained from the 2 KDSI to 4 KDSI sized applications were:

1. Prototyping yielded applications with roughly equivalent performance, but with about 40% *less* code and 45% *less* effort.

2. The prototyped applications rated somewhat lower on functionality and robustness, but higher on ease of use and were more easily learned.

3. Specifying produced more coherent designs and software that was easier to integrate.

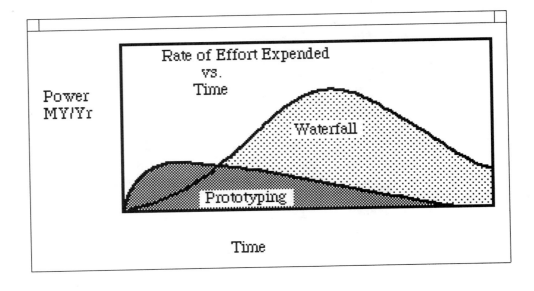

While enthusiastic about prototyping, Boehm et al. did not recommend abandonment of specifying. Instead, they recommended combining the best parts of both. Prototyping has advanced considerably, however, since this early experiment. When combined with program generation and user interface design, prototyping offers one of the few avenues for making great strides in software engineering.

The Promise of Rapid Prototyping

The approach described in this chapter is an advance over the earlier prototyping schemes, and so we should anticipate rapid improvements in software productivity and quality through CASE tools like OSU. OSU extends the capabilities of earlier prototyping systems by incorporating many desirable features of related systems and extending previous results into the more difficult realm of *showing* versus *telling*. For example, Panther[11] allows interaction to be specified in textual form. A similar system by Stelovsky and Sugaya[12] produces Modula-2 source code from textual commands. These systems support menus and dialogs similar to the dialogs of OSU, but specifications are created by typing numbers and commands in a special textual language.

Menulay is another prototyping system that allows a programmer to directly manipulate the user interface objects in much the same way as the RezDez portion of OSU. Each control is associated with a semantic routine which is also reminiscent of OSU's object-oriented approach. But, Menulay". . . has a rigid table-driven structure, so the interaction between the semantic level and the user interface is limited. This prevents all forms of semantic feedback"[9].

Trillium[13] is similar to Menulay with the added capability of immediate interpretation of the user interface prototype. Like OSU, Trillium interfaces can be "played back" upon demand. Unlike OSU, Trillium cannot link user interface configurations together to form a sequence that mimics the actual application.

Other systems such as RAPID[14], and RAPID/USE[15] perform various functions similar to OSU, but Peridot[16,17] comes closest to OSU in terms of functionality and versatility. Peridot (Programming by Example for Real-time Interface Design Obviating Typing) allows a programmer to design new interfaces by direct manipulation of rectangles, circles, text, and lines. Peridot is able to produce executable code from "showing" sequences, much like OSU. A programmer can create standard user interface objects in Peridot, but standard objects such as menus and windows are not assumed. Thus, a programmer must construct these from low-level graphical structures such as rectangles and lines. OSU, on the other hand, assumes the higher-level user interface objects of the Macintosh. A programmer need not reinvent these objects. However, nonstandard user interface objects cannot be created in OSU as they can in Peridot.

Myers[9] surveys current technology of prototyping using various user interface tools, and lists several problems with current systems:

1. Too difficult to use — most systems require the programmer to learn a new "prototyping language." Direct manipulation systems such as OSU largely overcome this problem, but even OSU requires knowledge of the Macintosh software architecture. OSU is for programmers, not end-users.

2. Too little functionality — most systems are limited to menus and simple dialogs. OSU is aimed at wide-spectrum prototyping, but in its current state it too is limited in functionality. To gain wide-spectrum prototyping functionality, many software accelerators must be designed and implemented. OSU cannot, for example, generate itself.

3. Not available/not portable — existing systems are very dependent on the host system. OSU is intimately connected to the Macintosh, and would require extensive rewriting to be ported to another system such as X-Windows. It is doubtful that portability is a desirable goal of such systems, but availability should be made a high priority.

4. Miscellaneous — Myers reports a number of other problems, including lack of concrete evidence of the worth of user interface prototyping systems; difficulty of understanding and editing specifications; belief that quality of user interface will suffer if developed by prototyping; programmer unwillingness to give up control; difficulty of building good tools; no support of evaluation of resulting prototypes; and difficulty of separating the user interface from the rest of the application. OSU overcomes many, but not all of these problems.

OSU demonstrates the power of standard user interfaces in prototyping. When a standard interface is assumed, the standard user interface objects become a kind of very-high-level language for showing rather than telling. What is the future of these "automatic programming" systems?

Future Software Development

Rich and Waters[18] surveyed the field of automatic programming and listed a number of myths about automatic programming which have influenced attempts to reduce the time and effort needed to develop software. In addition, they listed four general approaches to future software development by automatic means:

1. Database Query Systems. These systems combine near-natural language processing with a narrow domain focus to obtain huge gains in productivity through automation. However, the narrowness of their domain limits this approach to database processing applications.

2. 4GLs. Fourth-generation languages extend the range of application of database query systems by combining forms handling, very-high-level languages, and database functionality. However, they are relatively inefficient because they execute interpretively, leaving most of the difficult programming in the hands of Cobol programmers.

3. Program Generators. These systems are very similar to 4GLs, except they generate source code instead of running interpretively. The resulting code can be compiled, resulting in an efficient implementation. Most program generators are restricted to narrow domains of application.

MYTHS OF AUTOMATIC PROGRAMMING

End-user, general-purpose automatic programming is possible.
    Requirements can be complete.
    Programming is a serial process.
    There will be no more programming.
    There will be no more programming-in-the-large.
    End-user, automatic programming systems do not need domain-specific knowledge.

---

4. Very-high-level Prototyping Languages. Refine and Prolog are examples of very-high-level languages. Acceptance of this approach depends on progress in the quality of code produced by very-high-level languages and adoption of rapid prototyping as a viable methodology.

The future of software development may be summarized as follows:

1. Steadily increasing acceptance of CASE tools that automate programming and processes in software engineering.

2. Increased use of methods that support the spiral model of incremental development, because this approach brings together user and developer.

3. Gradual replacement of traditional programming languages by a variety of automatic systems for the production of applications.

Terms and Concepts

4GL	shell program
automatic programming	software accelerator
direct manipulation support environment	step-wise spiral model
DO Procedure	UIMS
graphical sequence	vacuous prototype
incremental lifecycle	wide-spectrum prototyper
rapid prototype	

DISCUSSION QUESTIONS

1. What is the spiral lifecycle model? How is it similar to the waterfall model? How is it different?

2. What are the steps in the step-wise spiral model?

3. What is a prototype? What is the difference between a prototype and a version?

4. Complete the vacuous prototype of CoCoPro.

5. What is a shell program?

6. The formula for the spiral of Archimedes is given in polar coordinates as $r = a \oslash$, where r is the radial distance from the origin, and $\oslash$ is the angular distance. The area under the spiral is equal to the total effort to construct a prototype in one 360° sweep. Compute this area and relate it to the area of a perfect circle encompassing the spiral model.

7. What is the role of reusable components in automatic programming?

8. How does rapid prototyping as illustrated in OSU relate to CASE tools for system design, such as Dataflow, OOD, and functional decomposition?

9. What is a wide-spectrum prototyper? What are the problems of building a wide-spectrum prototyper?

10. What is the impact on effort when $S\%$ of the LOC are done automatically? Justify your answer with a cost estimation formula such as the one in CoCoMo.

REFERENCES AND FURTHER READING

1. Boehm, B. W. 1988. "A Spiral Model of Software Development and Enhancement." *IEEE Computer* 21, no. 5 (May): 61–72.

2. Radice, R. A. et al. 1985. "A Programming Process Architecture." *IBM Systems Journal* 24, no. 2: 79–90.

3. Grafton, R. B., and T. Ichikawa. 1985. "Visual Programming." *IEEE Computer* 18, no. 8 (August).

4. Musa, J. D. 1985. "Software Engineering: The Future of a Profession." *IEEE Software* 2, no. 1 (January): 55–62.

5. Handloser III, F. T. 1988. "A Graphical Rapid Prototyper for the Macintosh." *Dept. Computer Science Technical Report 88-60-1.* Oregon State University, Corvallis, OR.

6. Bose, S. 1988. "RezDez: A Graphical Tool for Designing Resources in OSU." *Dept. Computer Science Technical Report 88-60-2.* Oregon State University, Corvallis, OR.

7. Maithel, N. 1988. "Implementation of Entity Category Relationship Data Model on Macintosh." *Dept. Computer Science Technical Report 88-60-3.* Oregon State University, Corvallis, OR.

8. Barth, P. S. 1986. "An Object-Oriented Approach to Graphical Interfaces." *ACM Transactions on Graphics* 5, no. 2 (April): 142–172.

9. Myers, B. A. 1989. "Tools for Creating User Interfaces: An Introduction and Survey." *IEEE Software* 6, no. 1 (January).

10. Boehm, B. W., T. E. Gray, and T. Seewaldt. 1984. "Prototyping Versus Specifying: A Multiproject Experiment." *IEEE Transactions on Software Engineering* SE-10, no. 3 (May): 290–302.

11. Helfman, J. 1987. "Panther: A Tabular User-Interface Specification System." *Proceedings of SIGCHI + GI'87: Human Factors in Computer Systems, Toronto, Ont., Canada. April 5–7, 1987*: 279–284.

12. Stelovsky, J., and H. Sugaya. 1988. "A System for Specification and Rapid Prototyping of Application Command Languages." *IEEE Transactions on Software Engineering* 14, no. 7 (July): 1023–1032.

13. Henderson, D. A. Jr. 1987. "The Trillium User Interface Design Environment." *Proceedings of SIGCH'86: Human Factors in Computer Systems, Toronto, Ont., Canada. April 5–7, 1987*: 279–284.

14. Freburger, K. 1987. "RAPID: Prototyping Control Panel Interfaces." *SIGPLAN Notices* 22, no. 12 (December): 416–422.

15. Wasserman, A. I., and D. T. Shewmake. "Rapid Prototyping of Interactive Information Systems." *ACM Software Engineering Notes* 7, no. 5: 171–180.

16. Myers, B. A. 1987. "Creating User Interaction Techniques by Demonstration." *IEEE Computer Graphics and Applications* 7, no. 9 (September): 51–60.

17. Myers, B. A. 1987. "Creating User Interfaces by Demonstration." PhD Dissertation, University of Toronto.

18. Rich, C., and R. C. Waters. 1988. "Automatic Programming: Myths and Prospects." *IEEE Computer* 21, no. 8 (August): 40–51.

A

ResEdit — A Resource Editor

ResEdit is a tool for opening resource files and displaying the resource objects such as windows, dialogs, icons, strings, and so forth, see Figure A-1. Recall that all Macintosh applications are stored as a two-part file: one part contains the actual binary code of the application; the second part contains the resource objects used by the application.

We will use ResEdit to explore the DeskTop and System files (Figure A-2). WARNING: changing these files can cause fatality! Use a copy of your system disk to experiment with ResEdit.

The DeskTop file contains *bundle* information on all applications on the disk. After launching ResEdit, select the DeskTop file (as shown) by single-clicking in the minifinder window, see Figure A-2.

FIGURE A-1.

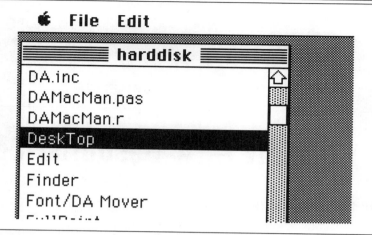

FIGURE A-2.

Pull down the File Menu and select Get Info, Figure A-3. This displays bundle information about the DeskTop file (Figure A-4). DeskTop contains information about all other files on the disk. This information is used by System and Finder to manage the desktop.

Think of the DeskTop file as a directory to the other files on the disk. It contains desktop icons that are used by Finder to display what is on the disk, for example. Note also that DeskTop is invisible — Finder does not display the DeskTop icon along with other (visible) files.

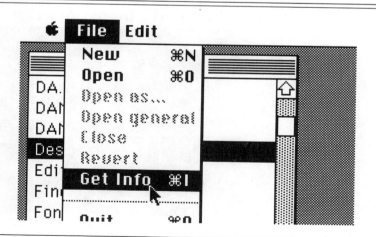

FIGURE A-3.

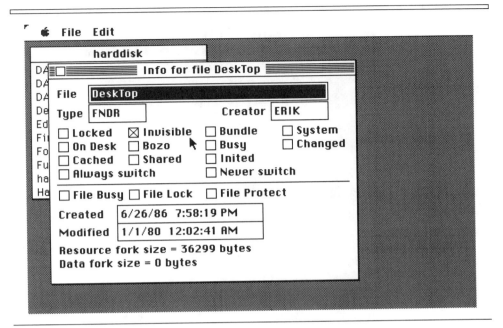

FIGURE A-4.

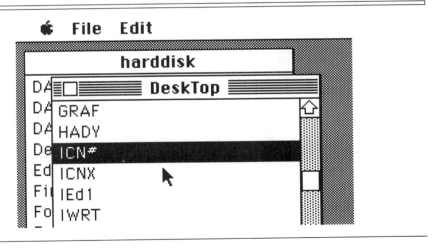

FIGURE A-5.

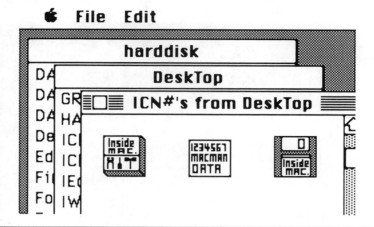

FIGURE A-6.

The Info Dialog contains the name, creator, type, and attribute list for DeskTop. The name corresponds to the name we selected — DeskTop. The creator of this file was ERIK, which is the name given to Finder by Apple Computer Corp. All resource files have both a creator and a type.

DeskTop is a file of type FNDR, which means it is a file that can be accessed by the Finder. A file can have any type. Type information is used by the File routine FSGetFile to filter out all files *not* of a certain type.

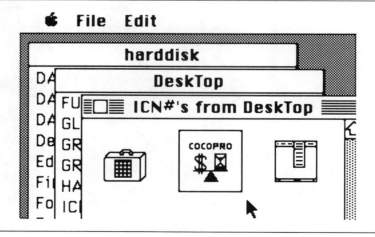

FIGURE A-7.

The attributes of DeskTop are its status bits. Invisible means it does not appear on the desktop. The date of creation and other details are also shown.

Close this dialog, and select the icon list as shown in Figure A-5. Resource type ICN# refers to the list of icons held in the resource file. For the DeskTop file, ICN# contains a list of all icons for all applications and data on the disk volume. Thus, we can observe, edit, change, and replace any and all desktop icons by selecting them one at a time as shown here.

Suppose we select the desktop icon for CoCoPro, since we are familiar with it in Figure A-6. Single-clicking the icon for CoCoPro causes it to be enclosed in a rectangle as shown in Figure A-7. Double-clicking it causes the icon and its mask to appear in "Fat Bits" format, in Figure A-8. You can edit this display to alter the icon and its mask. (Only the icon is shown here, but its mask appears on the right side of the display.)

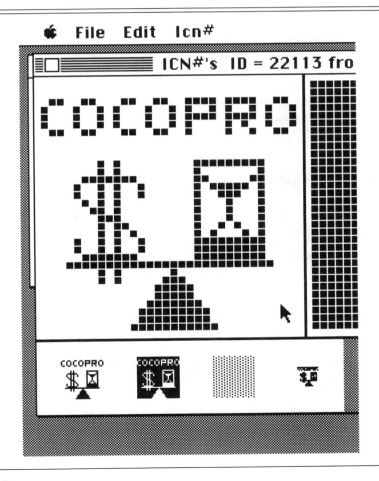

FIGURE A-8.

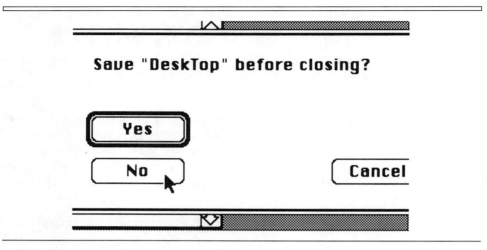

FIGURE A-9.

When closing the resource file, the dialog shown in Figure A-9 appears to ask if you want to save the changes made to the resource file. Answer NO unless you want to change an icon. Be warned that changes to the DeskTop can cause your entire system to crash. Be careful what you modify.

EXPLORING THE SYSTEM FILE

Return to the ResEdit dialog, and select the resource called System. This is the operating system file maintained by the Macintosh. It contains interesting resources such as patches to the ROM toolbox (code), fonts, DAs (Desk Accessories), error messages, icons for devices, the control panel resources, patterns, cursor images, and so forth.

We can learn something about how the Macintosh system operates by examining the System file. This file is invisible to the desktop, just like the DeskTop file.

The System file contains many resources of many different types: ALRT contains all the alerts in the system; bmap contains bitmaps; BNDL, CDEF, and so on are discussed in chapter eight, see Figure A-10.

Double-clicking the resource type opens a window containing details on each type. For example, double-clicking the ALRT resource type causes a list of alerts to appear in another window, see Figure A-11.

The list of alerts contains ID numbers, see Figure A-12. These numbers are forced to be unique by the system each time a new alert is added. This is why the numbers look unusual.

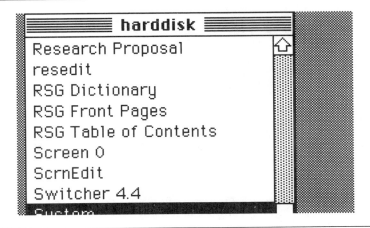

FIGURE A-10.

In an application written by a team of programmers, the IDs assigned by the team may not be unique when combined with other IDs in the system. For example, an application might number its desktop icon with ID = 128. When this icon is added to the DeskTop file, it will be changed to a unique ID, such as −13819.

The IDs assigned to resources that mingle with system resources are changed by the resource manager so that they are unique. Hence, the number you assign to a resource may not be its final designation.

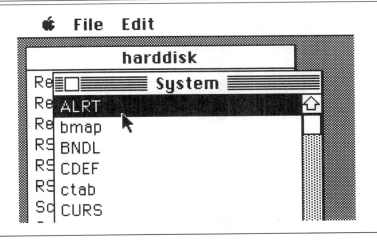

FIGURE A-11.

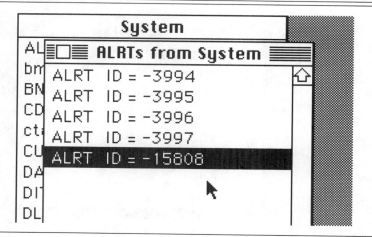

FIGURE A-12.

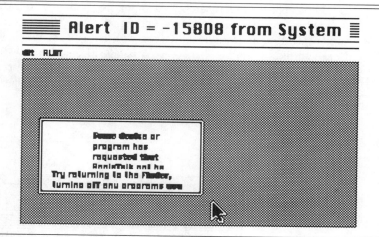

FIGURE A-13.

Double-clicking the alert ID from the ALRT list causes a miniature display to appear in another window; see Figure A-13. The text contents of the display cannot be edited from this window; instead, you can select another dialog from the ALRT menu that appears in the menu bar. Select the Display As Text item and see the alert information in a subsequent dialog, see Figures A-14 and A-15.

Note: the DITL resource contains alert items such as error messages, buttons, and so on. To see them, select the DITL resource corresponding to the desired alert.

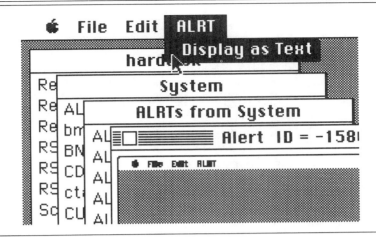

FIGURE A-14.

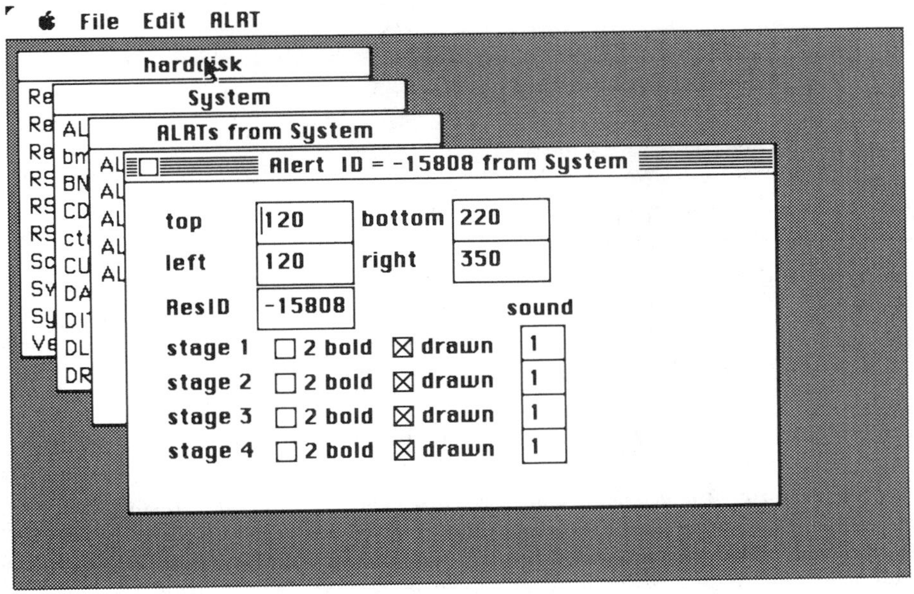

FIGURE A-15.

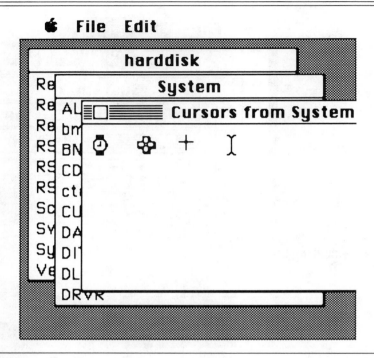

FIGURE A-16.

EXPLORING OTHER RESOURCES

Other resource types can be explored the same way — select the type by double-clicking, and then observe the contents of the window or dialog that appears.

For example, the system file contains the patterns used as cursors. Here we see the watch, cross, cross-hair, and edit cursors, see Figure A-16. These can be edited to tailor your system file to your own tastes.

One of the more interesting resource types is called DRVR — the system drivers, see Figure A-17. DAs belong to this type. A DA is a collection of code that is activated from the Apple Menu. DAs are restricted to 32K of executable code, but they are extremely useful because they can be accessed from within any application.

DAs have lost their appeal since the MultiFinder and multi-tasking versions of the Finder have appeared. It is still instructive to study DAs, however, because they give additional insight into the design of the Macintosh operating system. This system is a good example of software design, in terms of both its strengths and its weaknesses. Design is the art of making wise trade-offs, and the Macintosh operating system illustrates this art. When first introduced, the Macintosh had neither the power nor the memory for multi-tasking. DAs illustrate one of the many clever design trade-offs made by the Apple engineers.

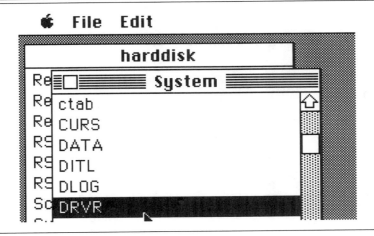

FIGURE A-17.

Here we show the selection of the MacMan DA and then the selection of a FONT resource, see Figures A-18 and A-19. These resources were inserted into the System file using a tool called Font/DA Mover, which is familiar to most users of the Macintosh. The System file can be enhanced in a number of ways, all similar to the examples shown here.

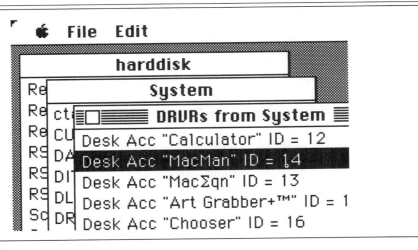

FIGURE A-18.

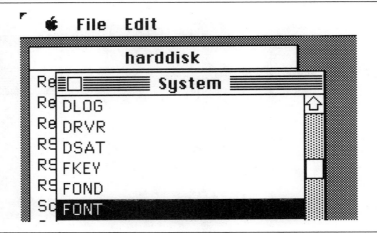

FIGURE A-19.

The Font/DA Mover copies code and data from one resource to another. For example, a font such as Avant Garde 24 is stored in a file as a bit map, see Figure A-20. This bit map is copied into the System file and assigned an ID (4248). Any application can access this font by simply reading it from the System file using the GetResource toolbox routine.

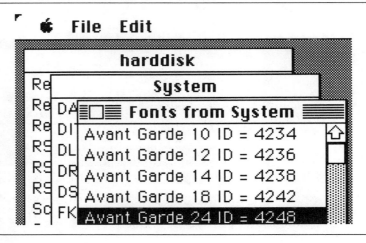

FIGURE A-20.

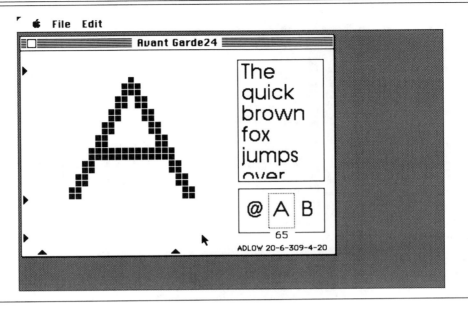

FIGURE A-21.

Double-clicking the font ID causes a "Fat Bits" version of the font to appear in an edit window, see Figure A-21. Clicking on the pixels turns them on or off with each click. The entire font can be changed in this way, but there are better tools for editing fonts that should be used instead.

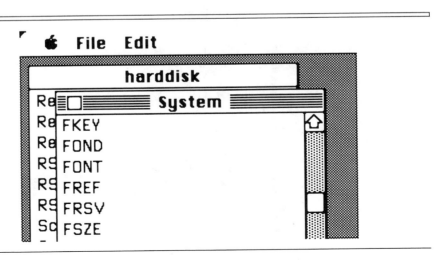

FIGURE A-22.

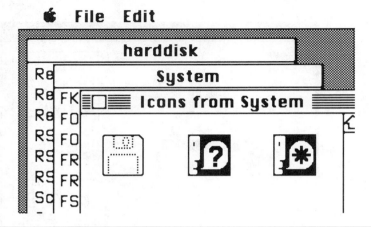

FIGURE A-23.

Similarly, the icons used by the system can be accessed, observed, and modified by selecting the resources of type ICON. For example, the alert icons shown here can be changed, see Figures A-22 and A-23.

There are special tools for editing icons, dialogs, windows, and patterns. These tools are more versatile and capable than the ResEdit tools. ResEdit should be used to explore the DeskTop and System, and in some cases to make small modifications in the system.

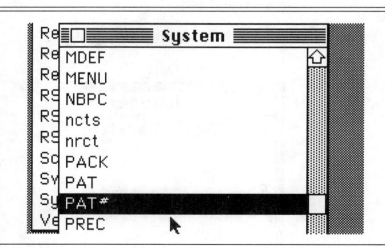

FIGURE A-24.

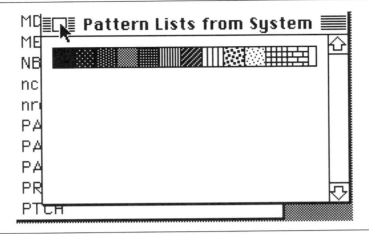

FIGURE A-25.

Resources were invented to reduce the complexity of an application, making maintenance much easier to do. For example, Patterns and Strings are often modified for cosmetic reasons, hence they should be placed in the resource fork of an application rather than in the code, see Figures A-24 and A-25.

The resource fork can be edited without recompiling the source code. In most cases, the source code is proprietary property of the developer, so it is not available for modification anyway. Thus, resource editing is the only alternative.

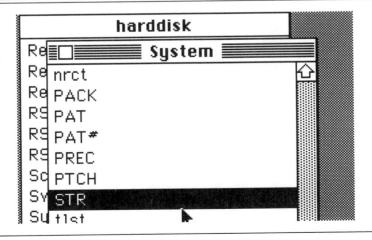

FIGURE A-26.

Strings are subject to modification when delivering application software to several countries where the natural languages differ. For example, the Macintosh is sold throughout the world: some users read Japanese, others French, and so forth. Editing the STR resource to accommodate different languages is much easier and more maintainable than searching through source code text to make changes, see Figures A-26 and A-27.

The idea of a separate resource fork for every application has intriguing consequences. Perhaps new programming languages will adopt this idea so that modularity can be global. Modules that separate interface part from implementation part already exist, but what about separating the user interface part from the rest? Might not this reduce the complexity for both developer and maintainer of future software systems?

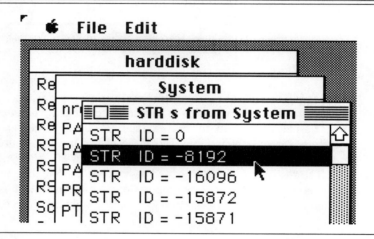

FIGURE A-27.

B

MacMan — A Toolbox Database

INSTALLING MACMAN — DA MOVER

One of the difficulties inherent in programming applications for Macintosh computers is the numerous and complex toolbox routines. There are over 500 toolbox routines to be mastered, and most are nontrivial. Yet, an application cannot be implemented without using at least thirty or forty of the most important toolbox routines, such as ShowDialog, InitGraf, and ModalDialog.

Each routine is fully described in *Inside Macintosh*. Thumbing through 1,000 pages of the many volumes of this tome is too tedious for most people, however, so MacMan (aka Macintosh Manual) was created.

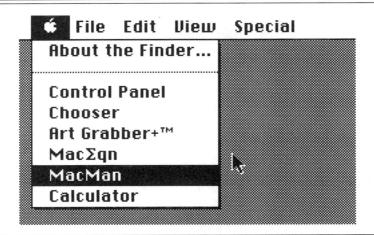

FIGURE B-1.

Font/DA Mover

Font/DA Mover is a tool for moving resources of type FONT and DRVR into and out of System files. It is used here to install the MacMan DA in the System resource file of your "boot" disk.

FIGURE B-2.

MacMan is both an application and a desk accessory (DA) for quickly retrieving the description of a toolbox routine, see Figure B-1. MacMan DA is installed in the Apple Menu using the Font/DA Mover, see Figure B-2. This process, while straightforward, is explained briefly. If your system disk already contains MacMan DA under the Apple Menu, the installation can be skipped.

After launching Font/DA Mover, select the Desk Accessory option shown at the top of the dialog, see Figure B-3. This causes the current DAs to be displayed in the scrollable window shown on the left side of the dialog. We want to add MacMan to this list.

Next, open the MacMan file, which should be provided on another disk containing the MacMan DA in either the second disk's System file or as a separate DA file, see Figure B-4.

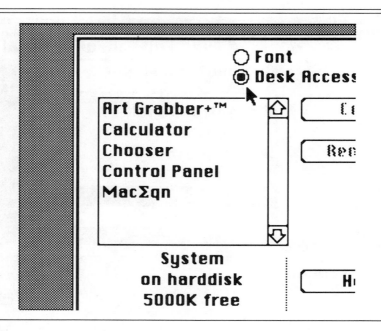

FIGURE B-3.

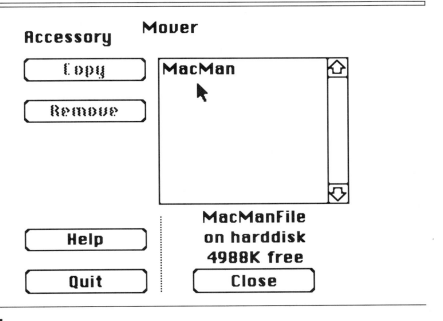

FIGURE B-4.

The opened MacMan file appears in the scrollable window on the right side of the dialog. Select it by single-clicking on it, and then click the < <Copy< < button to copy the file into the System resource, see Figure B-5.

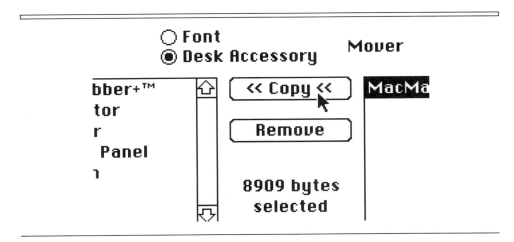

FIGURE B-5.

:w   Special   **Macman**

about Macman

Find By Name
View By Category

:r supported product, We encourage you to p
' you find   MACMAN   to be of use, suggestec
igly appreciated. With your support we can
il software tools.

FIGURE B-6.

Exit Font/DA Mover and begin using MacMan from the Apple Menu. When selected, MacMan adds a new menu to the menu bar and opens a window on top of whatever program is currently running. Closing the MacMan window causes the DA to terminate. Selecting an item from the MacMan menu causes MacMan to perform a database retrieval.

MacMan contains a database of over 500 toolbox routines and their descriptions. When MacMan is activated, it copies an index file into RAM. This index is used to quickly access the toolbox description each time you query the database. The index remains in memory until the MacMan window is closed. To avoid the time-consuming index load, keep the MacMan window open between queries. MacMan idles in between queries, but this does no harm. Reloading the index slows down retrieval time.

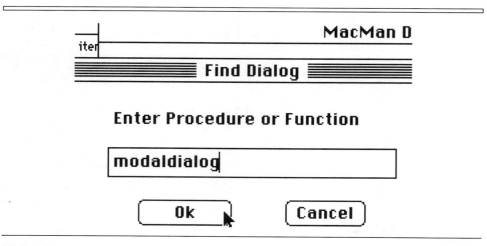

MacMan D

ite

Find Dialog

Enter Procedure or Function

modaldialog

Ok   **Cancel**

FIGURE B-7.

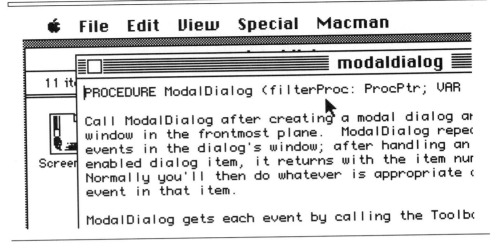

FIGURE B-8.

Toolbox queries can be made on two keys — the toolbox name, or the toolbox category. If you know the toolbox name, use it; if not, use the category corresponding to the tool manager.

For example, accessing the routine for displaying and controlling modal dialogs can be done quickly by selecting Find By Name from the MacMan menu, see Figure B-6.

Enter the name (modaldialog) and click the OK button, see Figure B-7. The description of the toolbox routine named ModalDialog appears in the MacMan window, see Figure B-8.

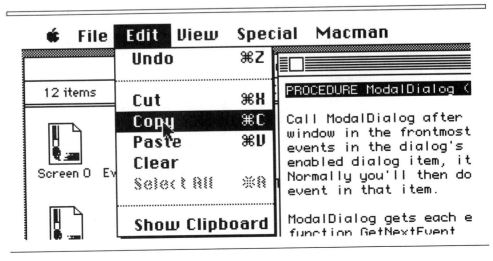

FIGURE B-9.

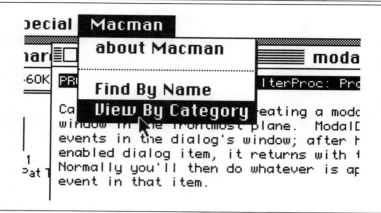

FIGURE B-10.

Text from this description can be copied into the Clipboard file using the Edit-Copy menu, see Figure B-9.

Similarly, queries can be made by selecting a toolbox manager — the View By Category option — and then browsing through the routine names in alphabetical order until encountering the desired routine, see Figure B-10.

Push the appropriate button to move forward and backward through the list of names. Click once on a radio to select a category, see Figures B-11 and B-12.

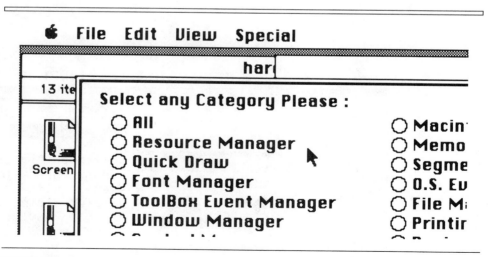

FIGURE B-11.

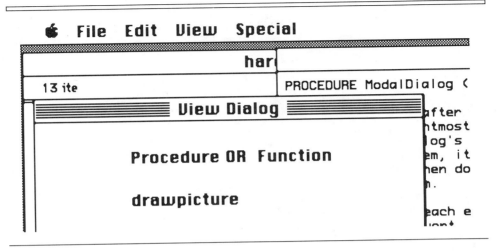

C

Screen Editing Tools

SCRNEDIT: THE PROGRAM

There are many software tools for constructing graphic resources for a Macintosh application: IEdit, Dialog Editor, Cursor Editor, and so forth. One of the earliest and most comprehensive is ScrnEdit.

ScrnEdit supports graphical construction of menu, window, dialog, alert, and icon resources, see Figure C-1. The specification of each resource object is done by drawing the object on the screen just as it is to appear in the application. The WYSIWYG graphic specification can be either saved as a compiled or text resource. If saved as a text resource, the resource compiler, RMaker, must be used to convert the text into a binary file. (RMaker is a "compiler" that converts text resource specifications into binary form. It is a tool provided to developers by Apple Computer. See chapters ten and eleven.)

In either case, the compiled resource must be linked together with the code portion of the application before the application can be executed. (When using the interactive Think compiler, the name of the compiled resource file must be given through the Project – View Project option. If the name is missing or not specified, an addressing error will result.)

FIGURE C-1.

The first illustration shows how to construct a menu, see Figure C-2. The "Menu-Make and Edit Menus" item is selected from the menu bar followed by clicking on the "Add or Edit Menu" button in the dialog that appears. The radio buttons indicate which menu to edit. All are shown as "Empty" here, but the "Empty" designation is replaced by the menu title after each menu is entered.

Menu items are simply typed into the text fields shown. Clicking the radio button next to each item selects the item. The check boxes are used to select options for the selected menu item. For example, the illustration shows menu item 5 selected: the check boxes show that the divider line in item 5 is disabled, see Figure C-3.

Once the menu is entered, press the button labelled "Use items entered." The dialog will disappear, and the entered menu title and items will appear in the menu bar. You can test the menu by "exercising" the menu bar containing the menus of your own design. The Project menu entered through the dialog box shown here is shown in action in the menu bar, see Figure C-4. Options such as Disable and Command Key (Quit/Z) were set by clicking the appropriate option check box.

Design Menus

Quit	New	● 1 empty	○ 6 empty
Add or Edit menu		○ 2 empty	○ 7 empty
Clear a menu list		○ 3 empty	○ 8 empty
Save in a text file		○ 4 empty	○ 9 empty
Save in a data file		○ 5 empty	○ 10 empty
Load from a data file		Swap 1	and 2
Load from a resource file			

FIGURE C-2.

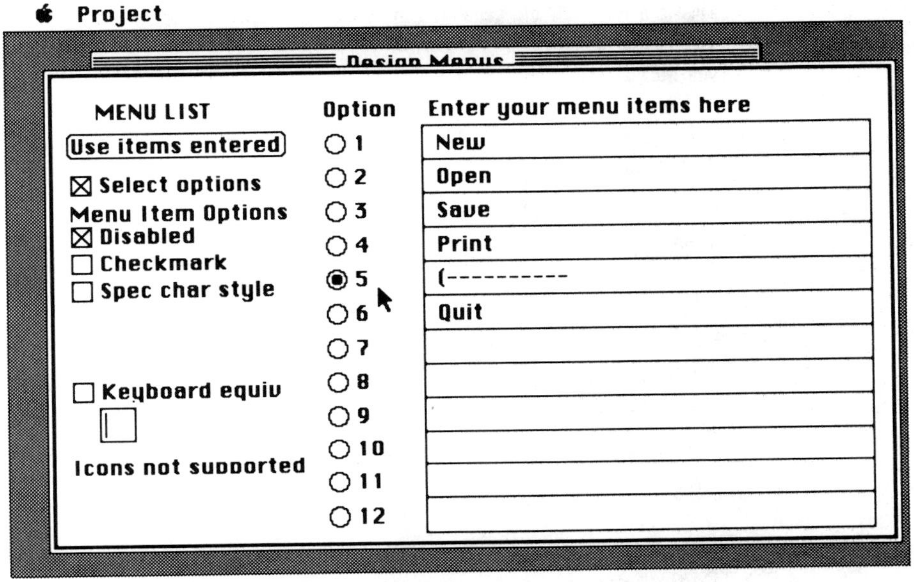

FIGURE C-3.

The resource can be saved as either a compiled binary resource or as a text file. The text file corresponding to the Apple and Project menus contain textual specifications for the WYSIWYG graphic specifications entered through ScrnEdit, see Figure C-5.

FIGURE C-4.

```
*This is a RMAKER file generated by the SCREEN EDITOR.
*This is the definition for the MENU.
Type MENU
,1
 \14
About CoCoPro...

,2
Project
New
Open
Save
Print
(-
Quit/Q
```

FIGURE C-5.

The textual representation of the two menu resources must follow a certain syntax. The type designator must be 4 characters, uppercase letters (MENU); the Apple symbol is hexadecimal fourteen — \14 is used as the title; the menus are numbered 1, 2, etc., see Figure C-5.

Icons, bold lettering, and other "special effects" are possible. Some of these are explained in the chapters. The (- designation means to place a dividing line in the menu; <B means to print the item in bold letters, and so on.

The text file is obtained by saving the resource as a text file. Compiled files are obtained by saving the resource as a data file.

FIGURE C-6.

WINDOWS

The other resources are entered and edited in a similar manner. To build window resources, for example, select the Make and Edit Windows menu item (see Figure C-6) from the Windows menu.

A window selection dialog appears at the top of the screen and a list of controls and items that can be placed inside the window appears at the bottom of the screen, see Figure C-7. Select the desired window kind — document, shadowed, rounded, or whatever — by clicking the appropriate radio. Then click the OK button to see the window you selected.

The "prototype" window can be dragged to any location on the screen, resized, and enhanced with buttons, icons, and controls. The example shown here has a single scroll control added to it, see Figure C-8.

Items are added by graphically "painting" them on the screen. For example, to place a scroll or button, simply point and drag the mouse with the mouse button pressed down. A rectangle will stretch to the desired size, see Figure C-9. Release the mouse button and the item is placed on the screen where you want it. The item can be resized, moved, and so forth by dragging it with the mouse.

The "Bubble Flow" window shown here was created by selecting a "Document" window, resizing it by dragging the lower right corner, and then placed in a certain position on the screen, see Figure C-8.

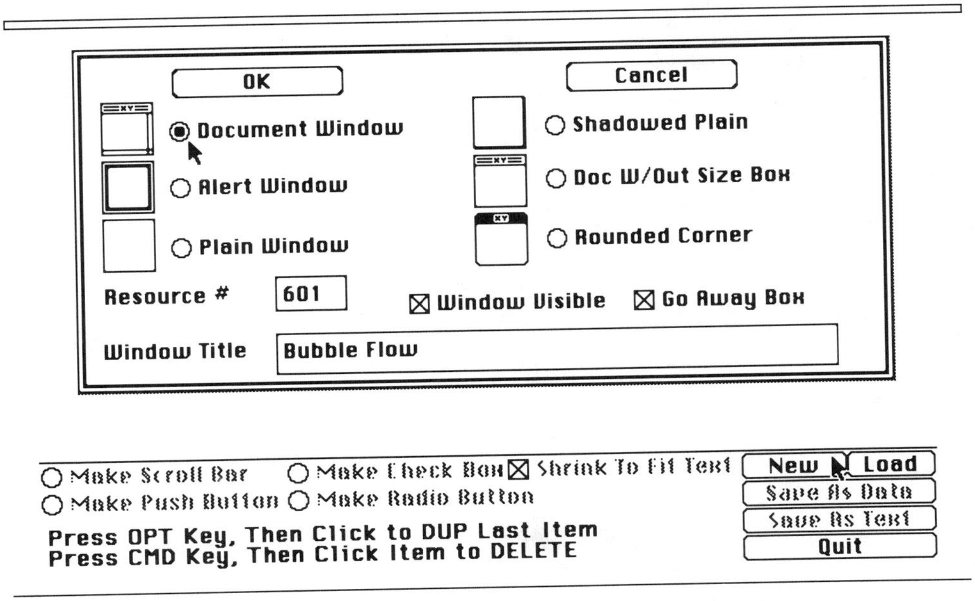

FIGURE C-7.

FIGURE C-8.

Next, the "Scroll Bar" option was selected from the list at the bottom of the screen, and the mouse dragged to define a vertical scroll bar, see Figure C-9. The result is shown after the mouse is released. The scroll bar appears where we want it, but of course it must be activated from within the running application.

The text resource file generated by ScrnEdit shows how both window and control (Scroll Bar) are specified, see Figure C-10. The three numbers at the end of the scroll bar specification define the minimum, maximum, and step increment to be used when adjusting the "thumb" of the scroll bar.

Windows are all of type WIND. They must be numbered or named — observe the leading comma before each number. If named, the name must appear before the comma. This is window number 601, titled "Bubble Flow," and is initially located at Top = 46, Left = 59, Bottom = 136, Right = 274. These are the coordinates of the rectangle

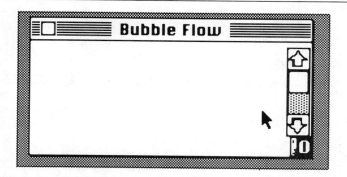

FIGURE C-9.

```
Type WIND
,601
Bubble Flow
46 59 136 274
Visible GoAway
0
0

Type CNTL
,0

4 197 74 215
Visible
16
0
0 0 1
```

FIGURE C-10.

containing the window. "Visible" means the window is visible to the user when it is initialized by the application. "Invisible" means the window does not appear on the screen until a ShowWindow routine displays it. "GoAway" means a Close Box is in the window control bar.

CNTL are control resources. In this case, the control is a scroll bar with a blank title, located at (4, 197), (74, 215) within the window, and initially visible. Its minimum is 0, maximum is 1, and increment step is 0. These values are usually recomputed by the running application.

These are *initial* specifications. They tell the initial values, but they may be changed by the running program. The window might be Invisible initially, but then made visible later on. The scrolls may or may not appear in the window until later in the program's execution.

ALERTS AND DIALOGS

Alerts and dialogs are special-purpose windows, and are specified in much the same way as windows, see Figure C-11. A dialog can be modal or modeless, it is numbered (or named), and it usually references a list of items, see Figure C-12. Therefore, you must enter the numbers shown — 200 as the dialog number, and 200 as the item list number. When compiled, these become DLOG and DITL resources.

The DITL resource can be numbered differently than the DLOG resource, but it is a good practice to use the same numbers to avoid confusion.

BtnItem, PicItem, CheckItem, and so forth, are specifications with obvious meanings. (RMaker only looks at the first letter of each code, see Figure C-13.)

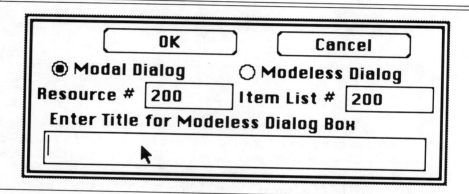

FIGURE C-11.

FIGURE C-12.

```
Type DLOG
,200
50 50 183 221
Visible NoGoAway
1
200

Type DITL
,200
1
BtnItem Enable
74 52 89 98
OK
```

FIGURE C-13.

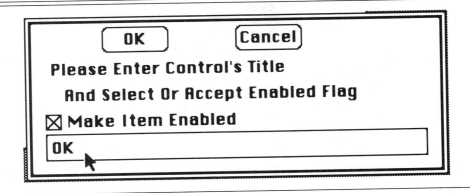

FIGURE C-14.

Controls, such as buttons, are entered by drawing them in the dialog. That is, the mouse is dragged to define a rectangular area on the screen that contains the control. When the mouse button is released, the title of the control is requested, and the state of that control indicated as either Enabled or Disabled, see Figure C-14.

The control can be resized and moved by dragging it, touching the lower right corner to stretch the control, or touching the center of the control to move it. When you are satisfied with the results, save either the data or text version, see Figure C-15.

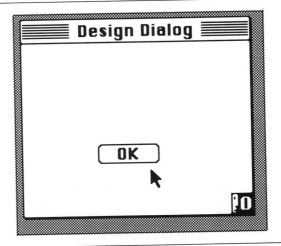

FIGURE C-15.

FIGURE C-16.

FIGURE C-17.

Alerts are very similar to dialogs except for two things: 1) they contain staging information, and 2) they contain an icon. The toolbox routine used to display the alert (NoteAlert, StopAlert, etc., see Figure C-16) defines which icon is defined.

The staging information is explained in chapter four. Four stages are available. Each stage is controlled by one of the four hexadecimal codes entered in the resource. The default button number and the number of beeps are defined by these hex digits, see Figure C-17.

FIGURE C-18.

ICONS

Every application has at least one resource of type ICN# and possibly other icon resources of type ICN, see Figure C-18. An ICN# list includes both the icon and its mask. The mask is exclusive-or'ed with the icon when the icon is selected — this is how the desktop icons are processed when Finder selects them.

An ICN resource is a single icon as defined by a 32 by 32 bit map. The bitmap can be entered into the resource file as an array of hex digits, but this is obviously tedious and prone to error. Instead, the "fat bits" editor provided by ScrnEdit (or a similar tool) should be used, see Figure C-19.

The hex equivalent of the bit map can be displayed, and of course the text version of the resource can be shown by saving the icon as a text file, and then reading the text file with an ordinary text editor. The resulting text file is compiled by RMaker to obtain the binary bit map, see Figure C-20.

Icon editing is done by clicking each pixel in the desired square. Pixels are toggled (clicking a white pixel turns it black, and clicking a black pixel turns it white). Any design can be drawn in this manner. Masks are drawn by exchanging the icon with its mask.

The example shows how a single pixel is converted to a hex digit. The rows of hex digits correspond with the rows of pixels. Turning a pixel "on" corresponds to changing a bit in the hex digit to a 1. The hex number represents 4 pixels, and there are 32 pixels per row, so 8 hex digits are needed to encode a row. The hex display shows 32 rows.

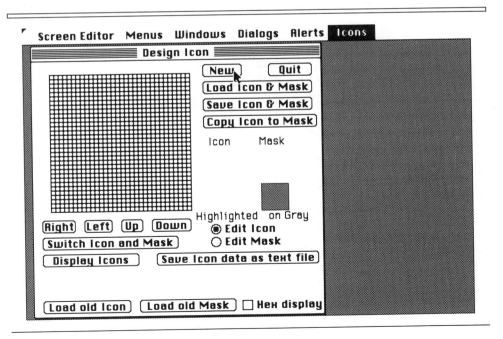

FIGURE C-19.

Icons are resized by the running application and are scaled to fit a rectangle defined by the running application. Thus, if a 32×32 bit icon is drawn inside of a $2'' \times 2''$ rectangle on the screen, the 32×32 bits are expanded to a greater number of bits to accommodate the larger area. Icons can appear almost anywhere in a program — in menus, windows, dialogs, alerts, and on the desktop.

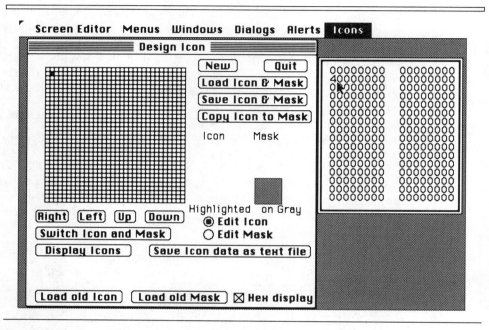

FIGURE C-20.

Index